Introduction to
Homeland Security
Third Edition

BUTTERWORTH-HEINEMANN HOMELAND SECURITY SERIES

Other titles in the Series

- *Emergency Management and Tactical Response Operations* (2008)
  ISBN: 978-0-7506-8712-6
  Thomas Phelan
- *Biosecurity and Bioterrorism* (2008)
  ISBN: 978-0-7506-8489-7
  Jeffrey R. Ryan and Jan F. Glarum
- *Maritime Security* (2008)
  ISBN: 978-0-12-370859-5
  Michael McNicholas
- *Introduction to Emergency Management, Third Edition* (2008)
  ISBN: 978-0-7506-8514-6
  George Haddow et al.
- *Terrorism and Homeland Security: An Introduction with Applications* (2007)
  ISBN: 978-0-7506-7843-8
  Philip P. Purpura
- *Emergency Response Planning for Corporate and Municipal Managers, Second Edition* (2006)
  ISBN: 978-0-12-370503-7
  Paul Erickson

Other related titles of interest:

- *Introduction to Security, Eighth Edition* (2008)
  ISBN: 978-0-7506-8432-3
  Robert J. Fischer, Edward P. Halibozek, and Gion Green
- *Background Screening and Investigations* (2008)
  ISBN: 978-0-7506-8256-5
  W. Barry Nixon and Kim M. Kerr
- *The Corporate Security Professional's Handbook on Terrorism* (2008)
  ISBN: 978-0-7506-8257-2
  Edward P. Halibozek et al.
- *Design and Evaluation of Physical Protection Systems, Second Edition* (2008)
  ISBN: 978-0-7506-8352-4
  Mary Lynn Garcia
- *Vulnerability Assessment of Physical Protection Systems* (2006)
  ISBN: 978-0-7506-7788-2
  Mary Lynn Garcia
- *Introduction to International Disaster Management* (2007)
  ISBN: 978-0-7506-7982-4
  Damon Coppola
- *Risk Analysis and the Security Survey, Third Edition* (2006)
  ISBN: 978-0-7506-7922-0
  James F. Broder
- *High-Rise Security and Fire Life Safety, Second Edition* (2003)
  ISBN: 978-0-7506-7455-3
  Geoff Craighead
- *Investigative Data Mining for Security and Criminal Detection* (2003)
  ISBN: 978-0-7506-7613-7
  Jesús Mena

Visit **http://elsevierdirect.com/security** for more information on these titles and other resources.

Introduction to Homeland Security
Principles of All-Hazards Response
Third Edition

Jane A. Bullock

George D. Haddow

Damon P. Coppola

Sarp Yeletaysi

With Contributions By:

Erdem Ergin

Lissa Westerman

AMSTERDAM • BOSTON • HEIDELBERG • LONDON
NEW YORK • OXFORD • PARIS • SAN DIEGO
SAN FRANCISCO • SINGAPORE • SYDNEY • TOKYO
Butterworth-Heinemann is an imprint of Elsevier

Butterworth-Heinemann is an imprint of Elsevier
30 Corporate Drive, Suite 400, Burlington, MA 01803, USA
Linacre House, Jordan Hill, Oxford OX2 8DP, UK

Library of Congress Cataloging-in-Publication Data
Application submitted

British Library Cataloguing-in-Publication Data
A catalogue record for this book is available from the British Library.

ISBN: 978-1-85617-509-8

For information on all Butterworth-Heinemann publications
visit our website at www.elsevierdirect.com

Typeset by Charon Tec Ltd., A Macmillan Company. (www.macmillansolutions.com)

Printed in Canada

11 12 13   10 9 8 7 6 5 4

Table of Contents

Acknowledgments

The authors of this book would like to express their appreciation for the continued support and encouragement we have received from Dr. Jack Harrald and Dr. Joseph Barbera, co-directors of the Institute for Crisis, Disaster and Risk Management at George Washington University. These two individuals provide outstanding leadership to institutions and governments in designing and implementing homeland security projects. Greg Shaw, also part of the institute, contributed a large dose of practical advice and humor. We would like to acknowledge the many individuals whose research, analysis, and opinions helped to shape the content of this volume.

We would also like to thank Pam Chester, Matthew Cater, and Monica Mendoza at Elsevier for their assistance in making the third edition of this text possible, and for their patience and faith in us.

Finally, we recognize the thousands of professionals and volunteers who, through their daily pursuits, are giving form and substance to creating a more secure and safe homeland.

Companion Website

All appendix materials are available online at:
www.elsevier.com/companions/9781856175098

Introduction

Since the events of September 11 and the subsequent anthrax mailings to the U.S. Congress, governments, organizations, and individuals have engaged in programs and activities to improve the security and safety of our nation. The most comprehensive reorganization of the federal government yet undertaken resulted in the creation of the Department of Homeland Security. Congress has continued to pass new laws to address all aspects of national security, including the Patriot Act, which provides the Attorney General of the United States with significant new authorities relative to civil liberties to fight the war on terrorism. Thousands of citizens have volunteered to participate in making our communities more secure.

Public safety officials, particularly emergency managers, are on the forefront of preparing for and responding to the potential threat of terrorism. The intent of this book is to provide a primer on homeland security for emergency managers and related disciplines.

New York, September 16, 2001 — Military and rescue workers stand amid the wreckage of the World Trade Center. (Photo by Andrea Booher/FEMA News Photo)

The federal government defines homeland security as follows:

Homeland security is a concerted national effort to prevent terrorist attacks within the United States, reduce America's vulnerability to terrorism, and minimize the damage and recover from attacks that do occur.

Starting with this definition, the early chapters provide a historical perspective on the threat of terrorism, before and after September 11, with detailed descriptions of the extraordinary legislative and organizational actions that were taken in reaction to September 11 and in support of preventing future attacks. The book continues with complete descriptions and fact sheets on the types of hazards and risks that make up the potential vulnerabilities in any future terrorist events. This section is followed by chapters that describe the programs and actions being undertaken by government agencies, organizations, and the private sector to reduce or minimize the threat. We have focused on the areas of security (intelligence, border and transportation, infrastructure and information/cyberspace); preparedness and mitigation (planning, initiatives, community and volunteers, private sector, best practices); communications (threat advisory system, public health strategies, public education); and new technologies (communications, information management, protective equipment).

Arlington, Virginia, September 17, 2001 — Work continues through the night at the site of the Pentagon terrorist attack. (Photo by Jocelyn Augustino/FEMA News Photo)

A significant section is devoted to response and recovery, as these responsibilities are a primary focus of emergency managers. In this chapter we describe the current state of the art in first responder applications and discuss the major changes that are under way within the national response system network. Case studies are included to demonstrate practical application to the materials being presented. In addition, we have included full texts of critical guidance documents for use and reference. Wherever possible, budget and resource charts show past allocations and future projections through 2009. The volume concludes with a chapter that examines future issues that public safety, emergency management, and other types of professionals may confront as we meet the challenges of establishing a secure homeland.

Homeland security is a relatively new, still-evolving discipline. This book was written at a particular point in time, and changes to programs, activities, and even organizations occur regularly. For that reason we have included online references wherever possible so the reader will have access to websites that can provide up-to-date information on program or organization changes, new initiatives, or simply more detail on specific issues.

Out of the tragic events of September 11 has arisen an enormous opportunity for improving the social and economic sustainability of our communities from all threats and disasters, not just terrorism. Public safety officials and emergency managers champion the concept of an all-hazards approach, and despite some unique characteristics, terrorism can be incorporated into that approach as well. With the increased funding being provided, we should have better-trained and better-equipped first responders; a stronger, less vulnerable national infrastructure; and an enhanced delivery system for public health and new technologies to improve and safeguard our information and communications networks.

These improvements will enhance our protection from everything from hurricanes, to energy and power outages, to tsunamis and earthquakes, to wildfires and mudslides. A new focus on research and development should lead to significant advances in the diverse fields included in the homeland security umbrella.

Since the second edition of this text was published, the United States experienced one of its most devastating disasters, in terms of both human and financial impacts. The consequences of Hurricane Katrina continue to affect residents of the Gulf Coast region. The problems experienced by emergency managers and responders, at all levels of government and in the private and nonprofit sectors, have served as the driving force behind an ongoing reassessment of homeland security's role in all-hazards disaster response in the United States. Katrina-related actions together represent the single greatest category of change included in this current third edition.

The authors' goal in writing this book was to provide as complete a source of practical information, programs, references, and best practices so that any emergency manager, public safety official, community leader, or individual could engage in actions to help make their communities safer and more secure. The homeland security function clearly has a ways to go before reaching any kind of stable footing. In the end, achieving homeland security will not be accomplished by the federal government but by each individual, each organization, each business, and each community working together to make a difference.

Historic Overview of the Terrorist Threat

What You Will Learn

- The process by which the emergency management function evolved within the United States, and the watershed events that drove these changes
- Measures taken to address the terrorism hazard within the United States, both prior to and following the September 11 terrorist attacks
- The influence exacted upon all-hazards emergency management in the United States by the series of post-event revisions to the nation's emergency management systems and structures
- The financial costs of disasters in the United States and around the world

Introduction

Harry Truman once said, "The only thing new is the history we don't know." For many Americans, the rush of activities by the government to pass new laws, reorganize government institutions, and allocate vast sums of money in the aftermath of the September 11, 2001, terrorist attacks may have seemed unprecedented. The reality is that similar actions in terms of both type and scope have happened in the past, and these historical experiences can provide insight into the prospect of the ultimate success or failure of the actions that have been taken since the September 11 attacks occurred.

The purpose of this chapter is to provide an historic perspective of the evolution of emergency management policies, statutes, and practices in the United States and to examine the chronology of events and actions leading up to and beyond September 11, 2001. This perspective will help frame the issues to be discussed in subsequent chapters of this book, which will detail the legislative, organizational, and operational underpinnings of America's homeland security structure.

This chapter provides summaries of the tragic events of September 11 including updated statistics, first responder anecdotes and perspectives, timelines, and review of after-action reports. Additional information is provided for three other major terrorist incidents: the 1993 World Trade Center (WTC) bombing, the 1995 Oklahoma City bombing of the Murrah Federal Office Building, and the 2001 anthrax incidents in Washington, DC.

Emergency Management in the United States

In this section, we explore the historical, organizational, and legislative history of modern emergency management in the United States. We review some of the significant events and people who have shaped the emergency management discipline over the years. Understanding this history and evolution is important because it can provide insight into why emergency management concepts have been applied differently at different times.

There is no single definition of emergency management, and those that have been applied tend to be extremely broad and all encompassing. Additionally, in the United States the discipline of emergency management has expanded and contracted in response to events, the desires of Congress, and leadership styles. Simply defined, emergency management is the discipline dealing with the identification and analysis of public hazards, the mitigation of and preparedness for public risk, and the coordination of resources in response to and recovery from associated emergency events. Risk represents a broad range of issues and includes an equally diverse set of players.

The range of situations that could possibly involve emergency management or various components of the emergency management system is extensive. Through time, as it has developed, the emergency management function has become integral to the security of our daily lives and has been integrated into our daily decisions. Emergency management professionals are no longer called upon only in times of disaster.

Emergency management has clearly become an essential role of government. The Constitution entrusted the states with responsibility for ensuring public health and safety — hence, responsibility for public risks — and assigned the federal government to a secondary, supportive role. The federal role was originally conceived such that it intervenes when the state, local, or individual entities are overwhelmed. This fundamental philosophy continues to guide the government function of emergency management.

The nation's strong foundation of emergency management was developed and has evolved over a period of many decades, and through all this the validity of the discipline has never come into question. Entities and organizations fulfilling the mission of this function, likewise, have existed at the state and local level for a considerable time, even before the federal government became involved. But as history-defining events occurred, political philosophies changed, and the nation developed, the federal role in emergency management steadily increased to the point where it stands today. The following section outlines the development of the emergency management function in the United States from the early 19th century to present day.

▪ ▪ Critical Thinking ▪

What are the benefits of a statutory authority that assigns the federal government a secondary, supportive role in the nation's emergency management system, while the local government maintains command and control authority? Are there any intrinsic problems with such a system? What is done to alleviate those problems?

Early History: 1800–1950

In 1803, a congressional act was passed to provide financial assistance to a New Hampshire town devastated by fire. This is the first example of the federal government becoming involved in a local disaster. Following this disaster it was not until the administration of Franklin Roosevelt began to use government as a tool to stimulate the economy that we saw a significant investment in emergency management functions in the federal government.

During the 1930s, the Reconstruction Finance Corporation and the Bureau of Public Roads were both granted the authority to make disaster loans available for repair and reconstruction of certain public facilities after disasters. The Tennessee Valley Authority (TVA) was created during this era to produce hydroelectric power and, as a secondary purpose, to reduce flooding in the region.

A significant piece of emergency management legislation, the Flood Control Act of 1934, was passed during this time. This act, which gave the U.S. Army Corps of Engineers increased authority to design and build flood control projects, ultimately made a significant and long-lasting impact on emergency management in this country. The Flood Control Act reflected the philosophy that humanity could control nature, thereby eliminating the risk of floods. The immediate-term success of this program promoted economic and population growth patterns along the nation's rivers, but history proved with a vengeance that such bold attempts at emergency management can be shortsighted and costly.

The Cold War and the Rise of Civil Defense: 1950s

The next notable period of emergency management evolution occurred during the 1950s. The Cold War era presented the potential for nuclear war and nuclear fallout as the principal disaster risk. Civil defense programs proliferated across communities during this time. Individuals and communities alike were encouraged to and did build bomb shelters to protect themselves and their families from a nuclear attack by the Soviet Union.

Almost every community appointed a civil defense director, and most states designed into their state government hierarchy a position whose incumbent managed civil defense activities in that state. These individuals tended to have military backgrounds, and their operations received little political or financial support from the state or local governments they served. Furthermore, the civil defense responsibilities they managed were often in addition to other duties.

Federal support for these activities was vested in the Federal Civil Defense Administration (FCDA), an organization with few staff and limited financial resources whose main role was to provide technical assistance. Despite these shortfalls, the local and state civil defense directors are the first recognized face of emergency management in the United States.

A companion office to the FCDA, the Office of Defense Mobilization, was established in the Department of Defense (DOD). The primary functions of this office were to allow for the quick mobilization of materials and the production and stockpiling of critical materials in the event of war. It included a function called *emergency preparedness*. In 1958, these two offices were merged into the Office of Civil and Defense Mobilization.

The 1950s were a quiet time for large-scale natural disasters, but not devoid of them. Hurricane Hazel, a Category 4 hurricane, inflicted significant damage in Virginia and North Carolina in 1954; Hurricane Diane hit several mid-Atlantic and northeastern states in 1955; and Hurricane Audrey, the most damaging of the three storms, struck Louisiana and north Texas in 1957. Congressional response to these disasters followed a familiar pattern of ad hoc legislation to provide increased disaster assistance funds to the affected areas.

Natural Disasters Bring Changes to Emergency Management: 1960s

As the 1960s began, three major natural disasters occurred. In a sparsely populated area of Montana in 1960, the Hebgen Lake earthquake struck, measuring 7.3 on the Richter scale, raising attention to the fact that the nation's earthquake risk extended far beyond California's borders. Later that year Hurricane Donna hit the west coast of Florida, and in 1961 Hurricane Carla blew across Texas. The incoming Kennedy administration decided to change the federal approach to disasters. In 1961, it created the Office of Emergency Preparedness inside the White House to deal with these large-scale events. It distinguished these activities from the civil defense responsibilities, which remained in the Office of Civil Defense within DOD.

During the remainder of the 1960s, the United States was struck by a series of major natural disasters. The 1962 Ash Wednesday storm devastated more than 620 miles of shoreline on the East Coast, inflicting more than $300 million in damages. In 1964, in Prince William Sound, Alaska, an earthquake measuring 9.2 on the Richter scale garnered front-page news throughout the nation and the world. This Easter quake killed 123 people and generated a tsunami that affected beaches as far south as the Pacific Coast of California. Hurricane Betsy struck in 1965, and Hurricane Camille in 1969, together killing and injuring hundreds and causing hundreds of millions of dollars in damage along the Gulf Coast.

The response to these events, as with previous disasters, was the passage of ad hoc legislation for funds. However, the financial losses resulting from Hurricane Betsy's path across Florida and Louisiana engendered a discussion of insurance as protection against future floods and a potential method to reduce continued government assistance after disasters. The unavailability of flood protection insurance on the standard homeowner policy, and the prohibitive cost of such insurance where it was available, prompted congressional interest. These discussions eventually led to the passage of the National Flood Insurance Act of 1968, which in turn created the National Flood Insurance Program (NFIP).

It is interesting to note how local and state governments have chosen to administer this flood risk program. At those levels, civil defense departments had usually been responsible for dealing with matters pertaining to risk and disasters. Although the NFIP pertained to these areas, responsibilities for the NFIP were given to local planning departments and state departments of natural resources. This is but one illustration of the fragmented and piecemeal approach to emergency management that began to evolve during the 1960s and continued during the following decade.

The Call for a National Focus on Emergency Management: 1970s

During the 1970s, responsibility for various emergency management tasks and functions was allotted to more than five separate federal departments and agencies, including the Department of Commerce (weather, warning, and fire protection), the General Services Administration (continuity of government, stockpiling, federal preparedness), the Treasury Department (import investigation), the Nuclear Regulatory Commission (power plants), and the Department of Housing and Urban Development (flood insurance and disaster relief).

With the passage of the Disaster Relief Act of 1974, prompted by the previously mentioned hurricanes and the San Fernando earthquake of 1971, the Department of Housing and Urban Development (HUD) possessed the most significant authority for natural disaster response and recovery through the NFIP, which it administered under the Federal Insurance Administration (FIA) and the Federal Disaster Assistance Administration (FDAA), which handled disaster response, temporary housing, and assistance. On the military side, there existed the Defense Civil Preparedness Agency (nuclear attack) and the U.S. Army Corps of Engineers (flood control). However, when one looked at the broad range of risks and potential disasters, more than 100 federal agencies were involved in some aspect of risk and disasters.

This pattern continued down to the state and, to a decreasing extent, local levels. Parallel organizations and programs added to confusion and turf wars, especially during disaster response efforts. The states and the governors grew increasingly frustrated over this fragmentation. In the absence of a single clear federal lead agency in emergency management, a group of state civil defense directors led by Lacy Suiter of Tennessee and Erie Jones of Illinois launched a drive, by means of the National Governors Association (NGA), to consolidate federal emergency management activities in one agency.

With the election of Jimmy Carter, a former governor from Georgia, the effort gained steam. President Carter arrived in Washington already committed to streamlining all government agencies and seeking more control over key administrative processes. The state directors lobbied the NGA and Congress for consolidation of federal emergency management functions. When the Carter administration finally proposed such an action, it was met with a receptive audience in the Senate. Congress had already expressed concerns about the lack of a coherent federal policy and the inability of states to know where to turn in the event of an emergency, so the state directors' concerns rang true for them.

In the midst of these discussions, an accident occurred at the Three Mile Island nuclear power plant in Pennsylvania, validating and further galvanizing the consolidation effort. This accident also brought national media attention to the lack of adequate off-site preparedness around commercial nuclear power plants and the role of the federal government in responding to such an event.

On June 19, 1978, President Carter transmitted to Congress the Reorganization Plan Number 3 (3 CFR 1978, 5 U.S. Code 903). The intent of this plan was to consolidate emergency preparedness, mitigation, and response activities into a single federal emergency management organization. The president stated that the plan would provide for the establishment of the Federal Emergency Management Agency (FEMA) and that the FEMA director would report directly to the president.

Reorganization Plan Number 3 transferred the following agencies or functions to FEMA: National Fire Prevention Control Administration (Department of Commerce), Federal Insurance Administration (HUD), Federal Broadcast System (Executive Office of the President), Defense Civil Preparedness Agency (DOD), Federal Disaster Assistance Administration (HUD), and the Federal Preparedness Agency (GSA).

Additional transfers of emergency preparedness and mitigation functions to FEMA were as follows: oversight of the Earthquake Hazards Reduction Program (Office of Science and Technology Policy), coordination of dam safety (Office of Science and Technology Policy), assistance to communities in the development of readiness plans for severe weather-related emergencies, coordination of natural and nuclear disaster warning systems, and coordination of preparedness and planning to reduce the consequences of major terrorist incidents.

The plan articulated several fundamental organizational principles.

First, to anticipate, prepare for, and respond to major civil emergencies, federal authorities should be supervised by one official responsible to the president and given attention by other officials at the highest levels. Second, an effective civil defense system requires the most efficient use of all available resources. Third, whenever possible, emergency responsibilities should be extensions of federal agencies. Fourth, federal hazard mitigation activities should be closely linked with emergency preparedness and response functions (Reorganization Plan Number 3, 3 CFR 1978; 5 U.S. code 903).

After congressional review and concurrence, the Federal Emergency Management Agency was officially established by Executive Order 12127 of March 31, 1979 (44 FR 19367, 3 CFR, Compilation, p. 376). A second executive order, Executive Order 12148, mandated reassignment of agencies, programs, and personnel into this new entity.

Creation of the new organization made sense. However, integrating the diverse programs, operations, policies, and people into a cohesive operation was a much bigger task than most people realized once the consolidation began, and its success required extraordinary leadership and a common vision. It also created immediate political problems. By consolidating these programs and the legislation that created them, the new agency would have to answer to 23 committees and subcommittees in Congress with oversight of its programs. Unlike most other federal agencies, it would have no organic legislation to support its operations and no clear champions to look to during the congressional appropriations process.

John Macy became the first director of FEMA, and his task was to unify an organization that was not only physically separated — parts of the agency were located in five different buildings around Washington — but also philosophically separate. Programs focused on nuclear war preparations were combined with programs focused on a new consciousness of the environment and flood-plain management.

Macy focused his efforts by emphasizing the similarities between natural hazards preparedness and civil defense by developing a new concept called the Integrated Emergency Management System (IEMS). This system was an all-hazards approach that included direction, control, and warning as functions common to all emergencies — from small isolated events to the ultimate emergency of nuclear attack.

For all of Macy's good efforts, FEMA's departments continued to operate as individual entities pursuing their own interests and answering to their different congressional bosses. It was a period of few major disasters, so virtually no one noticed this problem of disjointedness.

▪ ▪ Critical Thinking ▪

What are the primary benefits of having all of the nation's emergency management agencies under the umbrella of a single organization (the Department of Homeland Security)? What are the disadvantages, if any?

Civil Defense Reappears as Nuclear Attack Planning: 1980s

The early and middle 1980s saw FEMA facing many challenges, but no significant natural disasters. The absence of the need for a coherent federal response to disasters, as was called for by Congress when it approved the establishment of FEMA, allowed FEMA to continue to exist as an organization of many parts.

In 1982, President Ronald Reagan appointed Louis O. Guiffrida as director of FEMA. Guiffrida, a California friend of Ed Meese, one of the president's closest advisers, had a background in training and terrorism preparedness at the state government level. General Guiffrida proceeded to reorganize FEMA consistent with administration policies and his own background. Top priority was placed on government preparedness for a nuclear attack. Resources within the agency were realigned, and additional budget authority was sought to enhance and elevate the national security responsibilities of the agency. With no real role for the states in these national security activities, the state directors who had lobbied for the creation of FEMA saw their authority and federal funding declining.

Because of congressional questions about the agency's operations, the Department of Justice and a grand jury began investigations of senior political officials at FEMA. These inquiries led to the resignation of Guiffrida and top aides in response to a variety of charges, including misuse of government funds.

President Reagan then selected General Julius Becton to be director of FEMA. General Becton was a retired military general and had been director of the Office of Foreign Disaster Assistance in the State Department. From a policy standpoint, he continued to emphasize the programs of his predecessor, but in a less visible manner. Becton himself expanded the duties of FEMA when he was asked by DOD to take over the program dealing with the off-site cleanup of chemical stockpiles on DOD bases. This program was fraught with problems, and bad feelings existed between the communities and the bases over the funds available to the communities for the cleanup. FEMA had minimal technical expertise to administer this program and depended on the DOD and the army for the funding. This situation led to political problems for the agency and did not lead to significant advancements in local emergency management operations as promised by DOD.

An Agency in Trouble: 1989–1992

As Congress debated and finally passed major reform of federal disaster policy as part of the Stewart McKinney-Robert Stafford Act, the promise of FEMA and its ability to support a national emergency management system remained in doubt.

As the 1980s came to a close, FEMA was an agency in trouble. It suffered from severe morale problems, disparate leadership, and conflicts with its partners at the state and local levels over agency spending and priorities. In 1989 two devastating natural disasters called into question the continued existence of FEMA. In September, Hurricane Hugo slammed into North and South Carolina after first hitting Puerto Rico and the Virgin Islands. It was the worst hurricane in a decade, with more than $15 billion in damages and 85 deaths. FEMA was slow to respond, waiting for the process to work and for the governors to decide what to do. Senator Ernest Hollings (D-SC) personally called the FEMA director and asked for help, but the agency moved slowly. Hollings went on national television to berate FEMA in some of the most colorful language ever, calling the agency the "sorriest bunch of bureaucratic jackasses."

Less than a month later, the Bay Area of California was rocked by the Loma Prieta earthquake as the 1989 World Series got under way in Oakland Stadium. FEMA was not prepared to respond. While FEMA had spent the last decade focused on nuclear attack planning, FEMA's state partners in emergency management, especially in California, had been preparing for a more realistic risk, an earthquake. Although damages were great, few lives were lost. This was a testament to good mitigation practices in building codes and construction that were adopted in California and some good luck relative to the time the earthquake hit.

FIGURE 1-1 Hurricane Andrew, Florida, August 24, 1992 — Many houses, businesses, and personal effects suffered extensive damage from one of the most destructive hurricanes ever recorded in America. One million people were evacuated, and 54 died in this hurricane. (FEMA News Photo)

In 1992, FEMA was not so lucky. In August of that year, Hurricane Andrew struck Florida and Louisiana and Hurricane Iniki struck Hawaii within months of each other (Figure 1–1). FEMA wasn't ready, and neither were FEMA's partners at the state level. The agency's failure to respond was witnessed by Americans all across the country as major news organizations followed the crisis. The efficacy of FEMA as the national emergency response agency was in doubt. After dispatching then-Secretary of Transportation Andrew Card to take over the response operation, President George H.W. Bush sent in the military.

It was not just FEMA that failed during Hurricane Andrew; it was the whole federal emergency management process and system. In Hurricane Andrew, FEMA recognized the need to apply all of its resources to the response and began to use its national security assets for the first time in a natural disaster response. But these efforts came too late. Starting with Hurricane Hugo, public concern over natural disasters was high. People wanted and expected the government to be there to help in their time of need. FEMA seemed incapable of carrying out this essential government emergency management function.

In the aftermath of Hurricanes Andrew and Iniki, there came calls to abolish FEMA. Investigations by the General Accounting Office (GAO) and other governmental and nongovernmental watchdog groups called for major reforms. None of this was lost on the incoming Clinton administration.

The Witt Revolution: 1993–2001

When President William Jefferson Clinton appointed James Lee Witt as FEMA director, he breathed life back into the troubled agency and introduced a whole new style of leadership. Witt was the first director with emergency management experience. He was from a constituency that had played a major role in creating FEMA but had been forgotten — the state directors. With Witt, President Clinton had a politician with skill and credibility and, more important, an understanding of the importance of building partnerships and serving the customer.

Witt came in with a mandate to restore the trust of the American people that their government would be there for them during times of crisis. He initiated sweeping reforms both within and outside the agency. Inside FEMA, he reached out to all employees, implemented customer service training, and reorganized the agency to break down stovepipes. He supported the application of new technologies to the delivery of disaster services and emphasized mitigation and risk avoidance. Outside of the agency, he strengthened the relationships with state and local emergency managers and built new relationships with Congress, within the administration, and with the media. A hallmark of the Witt years at FEMA was open communication, both internally and externally.

Throughout the next several years, FEMA and its state and local partners would face almost every possible natural hazard, including killer tornadoes, ice storms, hurricanes, floods, wildfires, and drought.

When President Clinton elevated Witt to the position of director of FEMA and he became a member of Clinton's cabinet, the value and importance of emergency management were recognized. Witt used this newfound respect as an opportunity to lobby the nation's governors to include state emergency management directors in their cabinets.

The Oklahoma City bombing in April 1995 represented a new phase in the evolution of emergency management. This event, which followed the first bombing of the World Trade Center in New York City in 1993, raised the issue of our nation's preparedness for terrorism events (Figure 1–2). Because emergency management responsibilities are defined by risks and the consequences of those risks, responding to terrorist threats was included. The Oklahoma City bombing tested this thesis and set the stage for interagency disagreements over which agency would be in charge of terrorism.

The Nunn-Lugar legislation of 1995 left open the question as to who would be the lead agency in terrorism. Many fault FEMA leadership for not quickly claiming that role, and the late 1990s were marked by several different agencies and departments assuming various roles in terrorism planning. The question of who should respond first to a terrorism incident — fire or police department, emergency management, or emergency medical personnel — was closely examined, but no clear answers emerged. The state directors looked to FEMA to claim the leadership role. In an uncharacteristic way, the leadership of FEMA vacillated on this issue. Terrorism was certainly part of the all-hazards

FIGURE 1–2 Oklahoma City, Oklahoma, April 26, 1995 — A scene of the devastated Murrah Federal Office Building after the Oklahoma City bombing. (FEMA News Photo)

approach to emergency management championed by FEMA, but the resources and technologies needed to address specific issues, such as weapons of mass destruction and the consequences of a chemical/biological attack, seemed well beyond the reach of the current emergency management structure.

While this debate continued, FEMA took an important step in its commitment to disaster mitigation by launching a national initiative to promote a new community-based approach called Project Impact: Building Disaster Resistant Communities. This program was designed to mainstream emergency management and mitigation practices into every community in America. Project Impact's goal was to incorporate decisions about risk and risk avoidance into the community's everyday decision-making processes. By building a disaster-resistant community, it was believed, Project Impact's members would promote sustainable economic development, protect and enhance their natural resources, and ensure a better quality of life for all citizens.

As the decade and century ended, with a noticeable lack of major technological glitches from Y2K (when the nation was unsure about what would happen to computer programs when the year changed from 1999 to 2000), FEMA was recognized as the preeminent emergency management system in the world. Other countries began to emulate the agency within their own governments, and Witt became an ambassador for emergency management overseas. State and local emergency management programs had grown, and their value was recognized and supported by society. Private-sector and business continuity programs were flourishing. And with Hurricane Mitch, a vast international disaster, the world had even seen a change in American foreign policy toward promoting and supporting community-based mitigation projects.

The role and responsibility of emergency management had significantly increased, as had the partnerships supporting it. Its budget and stature had grown. Good emergency management became a way to get economic and environmental issues onto the table; it became a staple of discussion relative to a community's quality of life.

The profession of emergency management was attracting a different type of public servant. Political and management skills were critical, and candidates for state, local, and private emergency management positions were now being judged on the basis of their training and experience rather than their political connections. Undergraduate and advanced degree programs in emergency management were flourishing at more than 65 national colleges and universities. It was now a respected, challenging, and sought-after profession.

▪ ▪ Critical Thinking ▪

Why was open internal and external communication so important in terms of improving the emergency management function in the United States?

Terrorism Becomes Major Focus: 2001

Prior to the attacks of September 11, 2001, the Nunn-Lugar-Domenici legislation (Defense against Weapons of Mass Destruction Act of 1996) provided the primary authority and focus for domestic federal preparedness activities for terrorism. Several agencies, including FEMA, the Department of Justice (DOJ), the Department of Health and Human Services (HHS), DOD, and the National Guard, were involved, and all jockeyed for leadership on the issue. Some attempts at establishing coordination systems were launched, but in general, these individual agencies pursued their own agendas. The obvious lack of direction caused significant confusion for state and local governments, who as a result were largely unprepared for terrorist acts. These state and municipal governments complained to the federal government of the need to address what they recognized as an excessive vulnerability to the will of terrorists. The TOPOFF exercise, held in 1999, involving federal, state, and local emergency officials in a first ever weapons of mass destruction exercise, reinforced these concerns and vividly demonstrated the problems that could arise in a real event.

With the election of George W. Bush, Joe Allbaugh was nominated and approved by Congress to lead FEMA. As a former chief of staff to Governor Bush in Texas and President Bush's campaign manager in the 2000 presidential race, Allbaugh and Bush had a close personal relationship. As demonstrated by the relationship between Director Witt and President Clinton, such close rapport was clearly a positive aspect for the agency. Despite the fact that Allbaugh had an obviously weak emergency management background, the matter did not arise during his confirmation hearings.

As part of a major reorganization of the agency, Allbaugh recreated the Office of National Preparedness (ONP). This office was first established in the 1980s during the Guiffrida reign for planning for World War III and eliminated by Witt in 1992. The new director's actions raised some concerns among FEMA's constituents and FEMA staff, but their concerns fell on deaf ears in light of the fact that the office's mission was already moving toward an overall focus on terrorism adopted by the administration as a whole.

In a September 10, 2001, speech, Director Allbaugh spoke about his priorities as being firefighters, disaster mitigation, and catastrophic preparedness. These words seem prophetic in light of the events of September 11. As the events of that tragic day unfolded, FEMA activated the Federal Response Plan and response operations proceeded as expected in New York and in Virginia. Most of the agency's senior leaders, including the director, were in Montana, attending the annual meeting of the National Emergency Management Association (NEMA), an organization that represents state emergency management directors. The strength of the U.S. emergency management system was proven, however, as hundreds of response personnel initiated their operations within just minutes of the onset of events.

The Creation of the Department of Homeland Security: 2001–2004

Almost immediately following the terrorist attacks, President Bush created by executive order the Office of Homeland Security within the White House. The same day that announcement was made, Pennsylvania Governor Tom Ridge was sworn in to lead the office with the rank of "assistant to the president." The office, having only 120 employees and what was derided as a prohibitively small budget in light of the gravity of the events the nation had just witnessed, began to be seen as just another government bureaucracy.

In March 2002, President Bush signed Homeland Security Presidential Directive 3 (HSPD-3), which stated that:

> *The Nation requires a Homeland Security Advisory System to provide a comprehensive and effective means to disseminate information regarding the risk of terrorist acts to Federal, State, and local authorities and to the American people. Such a system would provide warnings in the form of a set of graduated "Threat Conditions" that would increase as the risk of the threat increases. At each Threat Condition, Federal departments and agencies would implement a corresponding set of "Protective Measures" to further reduce vulnerability or increase response capability during a period of heightened alert.*

This system is intended to create a common vocabulary, context, and structure for an ongoing national discussion about the nature of the threats that confront the homeland and the appropriate measures that should be taken in response. It seeks to inform and facilitate decisions appropriate to different levels of government and to private citizens at home and at work.

The product outcome of this directive was the widely recognizable color-coded Homeland Security Advisory System (HSAS). The HSAS has been called on repeatedly since its inception to raise and lower the nation's alert levels between elevated (yellow) and high (orange), although the frequency of these movements has decreased over time as standards for such movements have been developed.

On November 25, 2002, President Bush signed into law the Homeland Security Act of 2002 (HS Act) (Public Law 107-296), and announced that former Pennsylvania Governor Tom Ridge would become secretary of a new Department of Homeland Security (DHS) to be created through this legislation. This act, which authorized the greatest federal government reorganization since President Harry Truman joined the various branches of the armed forces under the Department of Defense, was charged with a threefold mission of protecting the United States from further terrorist attacks, reducing the nation's vulnerability to terrorism, and minimizing the damage from potential terrorist attacks and natural disasters.

The sweeping reorganization into the new department, which officially opened its doors on January 24, 2003, joined more than 179,000 federal employees from 22 existing federal agencies under a single, cabinet-level organization. Since that time, there have been many additions, movements, and changes to both the organizational makeup of the department and its leadership. The Department of Homeland Security, its importance within the framework of the U.S. government and society, and the changes that have taken place since its inception are discussed in much greater detail in Chapter 3.

▪ ▪ Critical Thinking ▪

Were members of Congress justified in making such a sweeping reform of the federal government as they did in the aftermath of the September 11 attacks? What could have, or should have, been done differently now that the benefit of hindsight exists?

Hurricane Katrina and Its Aftermath: 2005–2006

In the first few years following the creation of the Department of Homeland Security, the nation worked through many of the growing pains associated with such a drastic bureaucratic overhaul. Of all the criticisms associated with the new department, and of the many new and changing policies related to both national security and emergency management, that which sparked the greatest concern was that the focus of emergency management at all levels of government was being led away from the all-hazards philosophy to that of the single terrorism hazard. Several members of Congress even proposed legislation to remove the Federal Emergency Management Agency from DHS, although their efforts were ultimately rebuffed.

In late August 2005, Hurricane Katrina veered into the Gulf Coast states of Louisiana, Mississippi, and Alabama, dealing a blow considered by many emergency planners to be a worst case scenario. At the last minute, the category 5 storm weakened to a category 3, and its track turned just slightly askew, thus preventing a direct hit on the City of New Orleans, but the damage that followed this glancing blow was still enough to completely overwhelm all mitigation and preparative measures that had been taken to protect the city and its residents. The storm's impact covered a broad geographic area stretching from Alabama, across coastal Mississippi and southeast Louisiana, spanning an estimated 90,000 square miles. As of January 2007, the official death toll attributable to the storm stood at 1,836 with another 705 individuals listed as missing.

By any account, Hurricane Katrina was a massive storm, both deadly and destructive. But it was the failed response that followed which exposed severe cracks that had developed in the nation's emergency management system and its ability to respond to a catastrophic event. Both government and independent after-action reports, and several media accounts, judged the overall response an outright failure — with the ongoing recovery phase receiving the same poor evaluation. Many of the problems of the immediate response exposed the impacts of a priority focus on terrorism and homeland security that had developed in preceding years, which had likely been a major contributing factor in the decrease in local, state, and national capacities and capabilities.

In the actual response, elected officials at all levels of government stumbled badly as they tried to provide leadership in the face of this disaster. The business community, voluntary agencies, and nongovernmental organizations (NGOs) stepped up to provide the extraordinary services to storm victims of which many continue today. The general public, corporations, unions, and foundations donated billions of dollars for disaster relief. The storm impacted over 1.5 million people and displaced more than 800,000 citizens. Almost two and a half years later, in early 2008, over 200,000 individuals remained displaced from their homes and communities. Forty-four states and the District of Columbia received emergency declarations to cover their expenses for sheltering victims evacuated from the impacted Gulf Coast states.

Congress immediately tackled the apparent emergency management shortfalls, drawing up legislation aimed at patching many of the holes that had been exposed, and developing new systems that it was hoped would reduce overall risk for the future. For the moment, at least, it seemed as if the nation's emergency management focus was willing to regain its all-hazards approach. The resulting legislation, the Post Katrina Emergency Reform Act, was signed into law by the president on October 4, 2006. This law served to reconfigure the leadership hierarchy of the Department of Homeland Security, and to return many functions that were stripped from FEMA back into the agency. Additionally, FEMA was returned to its independent agency status, although it remained within the Department of Homeland Security as had been done with the U.S. Coast Guard and the U.S. Secret Service. The changes mandated according to this law, as described in greater detail in Chapters 2 and 3, became effective in early 2007.

The Future: 2008 and Beyond

In the aftermath of the terrorist attacks on September 11, FEMA and the newly formed Department of Homeland Security, together with partners in emergency management, fire, police, and public health at the state and local government levels, were charged with expanding and enhancing our nation's emergency management system. In the years following the creation of the Department of Homeland Security, billions of dollars were — and continue to be — allocated from the federal government to state and local governments in order to expand existing programs and establish new ones designed to meet the new terrorism threat.

Most notably within the United States, but also in many other countries around the world (several of which were themselves affected by major terrorist attacks, including the United Kingdom and Spain), a budgetary focus on the preparedness for and prevention of terrorist attacks that has emerged has steadily increased at the expense of other social and governmental programs. In the seven years after the September 11 attacks, there have been advancements in transportation security and commerce security, large increases in budgetary allowances for first responder terrorism training and related equipment acquisitions, the emergence of homeland security management structures at the state and local levels, a widespread public recognition of and preparedness for the terrorism threat, and many other positive changes. Whether as a result of these changes or in the absence of any realistic or significant attempts, there have been no major terrorist attacks within the borders of the United States since the attacks in 2001.

The response to Hurricane Katrina proved that the focus on terrorism has, as expected, altered much of the focus that once existed on the mitigation of and preparedness for natural and technological hazards, which by their very nature are much more likely to occur. In fact, during this same time period after the events of September 11, the nation experienced severe flooding, several seasons of extensive wildfires, record-breaking hurricanes, tornadoes, earthquakes, volcanic activity, drought, avalanches, ice storms, severe winter storms, and many more major and minor disaster events. One has to wonder whether the reversal in the country's accomplishment of reducing hurricane deaths is directly attributable to this shift in priorities (see Figure 1–3). The recognized failure of the federal response to Hurricane Katrina was a clear example of how an exclusive focus on terrorism prevention marginalized the federal government's and FEMA's capacity and capability to respond to a catastrophic natural disaster. One can only hope that the sweeping changes that occurred in this event's aftermath are sufficient to reverse such a disastrous course of policy decisions.

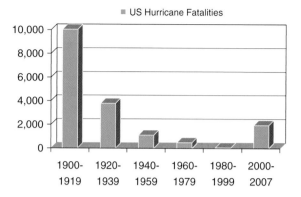

FIGURE 1–3 Number of fatalities attributable to hurricanes in the United States, 1900–2007. (Source: Atlantic Oceanographic and Meteorological Laboratory, 2007. http://www.aoml.noaa.gov/hrd/tcfaq/E12.html)

FIGURE 1–4 New York City, New York, October 13, 2001 — New York firefighters at the site of the World Trade Center. (Photo by Andrea Booher/FEMA News Photo)

The professional and operational environment of emergency management has continued to grow, and the quality, skill base, technical demands, and caliber of its practitioners have only increased (see Figure 1–4). The hyper-attention that is given to the terrorist threat has provided an unexpected opportunity to expand that base. The goal of this textbook is to provide the background and working knowledge of the disciplines, players, and organizations that are part of this nation's homeland security efforts.

As has often occurred following previous defining events, the environment for emergency management will continue to absorb major events and evolve to reflect their impacts. History has certainly shown itself capable of repeating itself in the case of Katrina, but still the focal shift to a more national approach to the problem has progressed. Likewise, there has been an increased emphasis on preparedness through training and equipment. Thankfully, the resilience of the system allows for midstream corrections. Ultimately, the long-term viability and measure of the influence of emergency management will continue to depend on its value to all citizens in all communities, every day, not just during times of crisis.

A summary of the 1993 World Trade Center bombing, the 1995 Murrah Federal Building bombing, and the September 11 attacks on the World Trade Center and the Pentagon follow.

World Trade Center Bombing

On February 23, 1993, a massive explosion occurred in the basement parking lot of the World Trade Center in New York City. The explosive device, which weighed more than 1,000 pounds, caused extensive damage to seven of the building's floors, six of which were below grade. A blast crater that resulted from the explosion measured 130 feet in width by 150 feet in length. More than 50,000 people were evacuated, 25,000 of whom were in the twin towers of the Trade Center. The entire evacuation process required approximately 11 hours to complete (Fusco, 1993).

At the time, the response to the bombing was described as being the largest incident that the City of New York Fire Department (FDNY) had ever managed in its 128-year history. In terms of the number of fire units that responded, the event was described as being "the equivalent of a 16-alarm fire" (Fusco, 1993). The following list provides a summary of relevant data from the bombing event:

- Deaths: 6
- Injuries: 1,042
- Firefighter injuries: 85 (one requiring hospitalization)
- Police officers injured: 35
- EMS workers injured: 1
- Firefighter, police, and EMS deaths: 0
- Number of people evacuated from WTC complex: approximately 50,000
- FDNY engine companies responding: 84
- FDNY truck companies responding: 60
- FDNY special units responding: 26
- FDNY personnel responding: 28 battalion chiefs, 9 deputy chiefs
- Percentage of FDNY on duty staff responding: 45% (Fusco, 1993)

Murrah Federal Building Bombing

On April 19, 1995, a massive truck bomb exploded outside of the Alfred P. Murrah Federal Building in downtown Oklahoma City. All told, 168 people died, including 19 children attending a day care program in the building. A total of 674 people were injured. The Murrah building was destroyed, 25 additional buildings in the downtown area were severely damaged or destroyed, and another 300 buildings were damaged by the blast. The ensuing rescue and recovery effort during the next 16 days involved, among many other resources, the dispatch of 11 FEMA urban search-and-rescue teams (see sidebar, "FEMA Urban Search . . .") from across the country to assist local and state officials

FIGURE 1–5 Oklahoma City, Oklahoma, April 26, 1995 — Search-and-rescue crews work to save those trapped beneath the debris after the Oklahoma City bombing. (FEMA News Photo)

search first for survivors and, ultimately, to recover victims' bodies (Figure 1–5) (City of Oklahoma City, 1996).

■ ■ ■ ▬▬▬▬▬▬▬▬▬▬▬▬▬▬▬▬▬▬▬▬▬▬▬▬▬▬▬

FEMA Urban Search and Rescue at Murrah Building Bombing in Oklahoma City, 1995

At 9:02 AM on the morning of April 19, 1995, a bomb exploded from inside a Ryder truck under the Alfred P. Murrah Federal Building in Oklahoma City. The blast caused a partial collapse of all nine floors of the 20-year-old building, and 168 people died.

Rescuers from the Oklahoma City Fire Department entered the building unsure of whether the building would continue to support its own weight. Most of the steel support system had been blown out.

Within five hours of the blast the first FEMA urban search-and-rescue task force was deployed. By 6 PM the task force was in the building, searching for victims. One of the first assignments was to search the second floor nursery for victims.

Teams with search-and-rescue dogs began the search in the nursery. The dogs are trained to bark when they find live victims. No dogs barked that night.

Eleven of FEMA's 27 USAR [U.S. Army Reserve] task forces worked in the building, with representation from virtually every task force in the country. The FEMA teams coordinated with local fire departments, police departments, and military and Federal agencies during the search-and-rescue effort.

The rescue effort involved extensive stabilization of the fragmented building, rescuing of people trapped within tight spaces, rescues from high angles, breaking through concrete, and hazardous materials analysis and removal.

An innovative plan was developed to help rescuers deal with the psychological and emotional trauma of such a grisly scene. The plan allowed workers to be briefed in advance and prepared for what they were to experience; extensive debriefing sessions were also included.

Source: FEMA, www.fema.gov.

■ ■ ■

September 11 Attacks on the World Trade Center and the Pentagon

On September 11, 2001, terrorists hijacked four planes and crashed them into the twin towers of the World Trade Center in New York City, the Pentagon in Washington, DC, and a field in Pennsylvania (see sidebar September 11, 2001, Terrorist Attacks Timeline . . .). These actions resulted in the collapse of both twin towers as well as a section of the Pentagon, and unprecedented deaths and injuries:

- Total deaths for all 9/11 attacks: 2,974 (not counting the 19 terrorists)
- Total injured for all 9/11 attacks: 2,337
- Total deaths in the World Trade Center towers: 2,603
- Total injured at World Trade Center: 2,261
- Total firefighter deaths at World Trade Center: 343
- Total police deaths at World Trade Center: 75
- Total deaths at Pentagon: 125
- Total injured at Pentagon: 76
- Total deaths, American Flight 77, Pentagon: 59
- Total deaths, United Airlines Flight 93, Pennsylvania: 40
- Total deaths, American Airlines Flight 11, WTC North Tower: 88
- Total deaths, United Airlines Flight 175, WTC South Tower: 59 (Sources: www.september11news.com/911Art.htm; http://en.wikipedia.org/wiki/September_11,_2001_Terrorist_Attack)

■ ■ ■

September 11, 2001, Terrorist Attacks Timeline for the Day of the Attacks

Note: All times in New York time (EDT). This is four hours before GMT.

Tuesday, September 11, 2001

7:58 AM: American Airlines Flight 11, a fully fueled Boeing 767 carrying 81 passengers and 11 crew members, departs from Boston Logan airport, bound for Los Angeles, California.

8:00 AM: United Airlines Flight 175, another fully fueled Boeing 767 carrying 56 passengers and 9 crew members, departs from Boston's Logan airport, bound for Los Angeles, California.

8:10 AM: American Airlines Flight 77, a Boeing 757 with 58 passengers and 6 crew members, departs from Washington's Dulles airport for Los Angeles, California.

8:40 AM: The Federal Aviation Administration (FAA) notifies North American Aerospace Defense Command (NORAD) about the suspected hijacking of American Airlines Flight 11.

8:42 AM: United Airlines Flight 93, a Boeing 757, takes off with 37 passengers and 7 crew members from Newark airport bound for San Francisco, following a 40-minute delay caused by congested runways. Its flight path initially takes it close to the World Trade Center.

8:43 AM: The FAA notifies NORAD about the suspected hijacking of United Airlines Flight 175.

8:46:26 AM: American Airlines Flight 11 crashes with a speed of roughly 490 miles per hour into the north side of the north tower of the World Trade Center, between floors 94 and 98. (Many accounts have given times that range between 8:45 AM and 8:50 AM) The building's structural type, pioneered in the late 1960s to maximize rentable floor space and featuring lightweight tubular design with no masonry elements in the facade, allows the jetliner to literally enter the tower, mostly intact. It plows to the building core, severing all three gypsum-encased stairwells and dragging combustibles with it. A massive shock wave travels down to the ground and up again. The combustibles, as well as the remnants of the aircraft, are ignited by the burning fuel. Because the building lacks a traditional full-cage frame and depends almost entirely on the strength of a narrow structural core running up the center, the fire at the center of the impact zone is in a position to compromise the integrity of all internal columns. People below the severed stairwells in the north tower start to evacuate. Officials in the south tower tell people shortly afterward by megaphone and office announcements that they are safe and can return to their offices. Some don't hear it; some ignore it and evacuate anyway; others congregate in common areas such as the 78th-floor sky lobby to discuss their options.

9:02:54 AM: United Airlines Flight 175 crashes with a speed of about 590 miles per hour into the south side of the south tower, banked between floors 78 and 84 in full view of media cameras. Parts of the plane leave the building at its east and north sides, falling to the ground six blocks away. A passenger on the plane, Peter Hanson, had called his father earlier from the plane reporting that hijackers were stabbing flight attendants in order to force the crew to open the cockpit doors.

8:46 AM to 10:29 AM: At least 20 people, primarily in the north tower, trapped by fire and smoke in the upper floors, jump to their deaths. There is some evidence that large central portions of the floor near the impact zone in the north tower collapsed soon after the plane hit, perhaps convincing some people that total collapse was imminent. One person at street level, firefighter Daniel Thomas Suhr, is hit by a jumper and dies. No form of airborne evacuation is attempted because the smoke is too dense for a successful landing on the roof of either tower, and New York City lacks helicopters specialized for horizontal rescue.

9:04 AM (approximately): The FAA's air route traffic control center in Boston stops all departures from airports in its jurisdiction (New England and eastern New York State).

9:06 AM: The FAA bans takeoffs of all flights bound to or through the airspace of New York center from airports in that center and the three adjacent centers — Boston, Cleveland, and Washington. This is referred to as a first-tier groundstop and covers the Northeast from North Carolina north and as far west as eastern Michigan.

9:08 AM: The FAA bans all takeoffs nationwide for flights going to or through New York center airspace.

9:24 AM: President George W. Bush is interrupted with the news of the second crash as he participates in a class filled with Florida schoolchildren. He waits out the lesson then rushes into another classroom commandeered by the Secret Service. Within minutes he makes a short statement, calling the developments "a national tragedy," and is hurried aboard Air Force One.

9:24 AM: The FAA notifies NORAD's Northeast Air Defense Sector about the suspected hijacking of American Airlines Flight 77. The FAA and NORAD establish an open line to discuss American Airlines Flight 77 and United Airlines Flight 93.

9:26 AM: The FAA bans takeoffs of all civilian aircraft regardless of destination — a national groundstop.

9:37 AM: American Airlines Flight 77 crashes into the western side of the Pentagon and starts a violent fire. The section of the Pentagon hit consists mainly of newly renovated, unoccupied offices. Passenger Barbara K. Olson had called her husband, Solicitor General Theodore Olson, at the Justice Department twice from the plane to tell him about the hijacking and to report that the passengers and pilots were held in the back of the plane. As bright flames and dark smoke envelop the west side of America's military nerve center, all doubts about the terrorist nature of the attacks are gone.

9:45 AM: United States airspace is shut down. No civilian aircraft are allowed to lift off, and all aircraft in flight are ordered to land at the nearest airport as soon as practical. All air traffic headed for the United States is redirected to Canada. Later, the FAA announces that civilian flights are suspended until at least noon, September 12. The groundings last until September 14, but there are exemptions for Saudi families who fear retribution if they stay in the United States. Military and medical flights continue. This is the fourth time all commercial flights in the United States have been stopped, and the first time a suspension was unplanned. All previous suspensions were military related (Sky Shield I–III) and took place from 1960 to 1962.

9:45 AM: The White House and the Capitol are closed.

9:50 AM (approximately): The Associated Press reports that American Airlines Flight 11 was apparently hijacked after departure from Boston's Logan Airport. Within an hour, this report is confirmed for both Flight 11 and United Airlines Flight 175.

9:57 AM: President Bush is moved from Florida.

9:59:04 AM: The south tower of the World Trade Center collapses. A vast TV and radio audience reacts primarily with horrified astonishment. It is later widely reported that the collapse was not directly caused by the jetliner's impact but that the intense sustained heat of the fuel fire was mostly or wholly responsible for the loss of structural integrity. Later, a growing number of structural engineers assert that the fire alone would not have caused the collapse. Both towers made use of external load-bearing mini columns, and on one face of each building approximately 40 of these were severed by the jetliners. Had they been intact to efficiently distribute the increasing gravity load as the bunched core columns and joist trusses weakened in the fires, the towers might have stood far longer or perhaps indefinitely. Concrete in the towers' facades might have prevented most of the debris and fuel from reaching the building core. Investigations that may radically change skyscraper design (or result in a radical retreat to full-cage construction with high concrete-to-steel ratios as in pre-1960s skyscrapers) are ongoing.

10:03 AM: United Airlines Flight 93 crashes southeast of Pittsburgh in Somerset County, Pennsylvania. Other reports say 10:06 or 10:10. According to seismographic data readings, the time of impact was 10:06:05. The first reports from the police indicate that none on board survived. Later reports indicate that passengers speaking on cell phones had learned about the World Trade Center and Pentagon crashes and at least three were planning on resisting the hijackers. It is likely that the resistance led to the plane crashing before it reached its intended target. Reports stated that an eyewitness saw a white plane resembling a fighter jet circling the site minutes after the crash. These reports have limited credibility, although fighter jets had been scrambled to defend the Washington, DC, region earlier. These jets, however, stayed within the immediate DC area.

10:10 AM: Part of the Pentagon collapses.

10:13 AM: Thousands are involved in an evacuation of the United Nations complex in New York.

10:15 AM (approximately): The Democratic Front for the Liberation of Palestine is reported to have taken responsibility for the crashes, but this is denied by a senior officer of the group soon after.

10:28:31 AM: The north tower of the World Trade Center collapses from the top down, as if being peeled apart. Probably as a result of the destruction of the gypsum-encased stairwells on the impact floors (most skyscraper stairwells are encased in reinforced concrete), no one above the impact zone in the north tower survives. The fact that the north tower stood much longer than the south one is later attributed to three facts: The region of impact was higher (which meant that the gravity load on the most damaged area was lighter), the speed of the airplane was lower, and the fireproofing in the affected floors had been partially upgraded. Also, the hottest part of the fire in the south tower burned in a corner of the structure, perhaps leading to a more concentrated failure of columns or joist trusses or both. The Marriott Hotel, located at the base of the two towers, is also destroyed.

10:35 AM (approximately): Police are reportedly alerted about a bomb in a car outside the State Department in Washington, DC. Later reports claim that nothing happened at the State Department.

10:39 AM: Another hijacked jumbo jet is claimed to be headed for Washington, DC. F-15s are scrambled and patrol the airspace above Washington, DC, while other fighter jets sweep the airspace above New York City. They have orders, first issued by Vice President Cheney and later confirmed by President Bush, to shoot down any potentially dangerous planes that do not comply with orders given to them via radio.

10:45 AM: CNN reports that a mass evacuation of Washington, DC, and New York has been initiated. The UN headquarters are already empty. A few minutes later, New York's mayor orders an evacuation of lower Manhattan.

10:50 AM: Five stories of part of the Pentagon collapse as a result of the fire.

10:53 AM: New York's primary elections are canceled.

11:15 AM (approximately): Reports surfaced that the F-15s over Washington had shot something down. There was no later confirmation of these reports.

11:16 AM: American Airlines confirms the loss of its two airplanes.

11:17 AM: United Airlines confirms the loss of Flight 93 and states that it is "deeply concerned" about Flight 175.

11:53 AM: United Airlines confirms the loss of its two airplanes.

11:55 AM: The border between the United States and Mexico is on highest alert, but has not been closed.

12:00 PM (approximately): President Bush arrives at Barksdale Air Force Base in Louisiana. He was on a trip in Sarasota, Florida, to speak about education but is now presumed to be returning to the capital. He makes a brief and informal initial statement to the effect that terrorism on U.S. soil will not be tolerated, stating that "freedom itself has been attacked and freedom will be protected."

12:02 PM: The Taliban government of Afghanistan denounces the attacks.

12:04 PM: Los Angeles International Airport, the intended destination of Flight 11, Flight 77, and Flight 175 is shut down.

12:15 PM: San Francisco International Airport, the intended destination of United Airlines Flight 93, is shut down.

12:15 PM (approximately): The airspace over the 48 contiguous United States is clear of all commercial and private flights.

1:00 PM (approximately): At the Pentagon, fire crews are still fighting fires. The early response to the attack had been coordinated from the National Military Command Center, but that location had to be evacuated when it began to fill with smoke.

1:04 PM: President Bush puts the U.S. military on high alert worldwide. He speaks from Barksdale Air Force Base and leaves for the Strategic Air Command bunker in Nebraska.

1:27 PM: Mayor Anthony A. Williams of Washington, DC, declares a state of emergency; the DC National Guard arrives on site.

2:30 PM: Senator John McCain characterizes the attack as an "act of war."

2:49 PM: At a press conference in New York, Mayor Rudy Giuliani is asked to estimate the number of casualties at the World Trade Center. He replies, "More than any of us can bear."

4:00 PM: National news outlets report that high officials in the federal intelligence community are stating that Osama bin Laden is the primary suspect in the attacks.

4:25 PM: The New York Stock Exchange, NASDAQ, and the American Stock Exchange report that they will remain closed on Wednesday, September 12.

5:20 PM: Salomon Brothers 7, commonly referred to as "7 World Trade Center," a 47-story building that had sustained what was originally thought to be light damage in the fall of the twin towers and was earlier reported on fire, collapses. Structural engineers are puzzled, and the investigation continues. The building was not designed by the same team responsible for the twin towers. The building contained New York's special emergency center, which may well have been intended for such a disaster as September 11.

6:00 PM: Explosions and tracer fire are reported in Kabul, the capital of Afghanistan, by CNN and the BBC. The Northern Alliance, involved in a civil war with the Taliban government, is later reported to have attacked Kabul's airport with helicopter gunships.

6:00 PM: Iraq announces that the attacks are the fruit of "U.S. crimes against humanity" in an official announcement on state television.

6:54 PM: President Bush finally arrives at the White House. Executive authority through much of the day had rested with Vice President Cheney.

7:00 PM: Frantic efforts to locate survivors in the rubble that had been the twin towers continue. Fleets of ambulances have been lined up to transport the injured to nearby hospitals. They stand empty. "Ground Zero" is the exclusive domain of the FDNY and NYPD, despite volunteer steel and construction workers who stand ready to move large quantities of debris quickly. Relatives and friends displaying enlarged photographs of the missing printed on home computer printers are flooding downtown. The New York Armory, at Lexington Avenue and 26th Street, and Union Square Park, at 14th Street, become vigil centers of vigil.

7:30 PM: The U.S. government denies any responsibility for reported explosions in Kabul.

8:30 PM: President Bush addresses the nation from the White House. Among his remarks: "Terrorist attacks can shake the foundations of our biggest buildings, but they cannot touch the foundation of America. These acts shatter steel, but they cannot dent the steel of American resolve."

9:00 PM: President Bush meets with his full National Security Council, followed roughly half an hour later by a meeting with a smaller group of key advisers. Bush and his advisers have evidence that Osama bin Laden is behind the attacks.

11:00 PM: There are reports of survivors buried in the rubble in New York making cell phone calls. These rumors were later proved to be wrong.

Source: www.wikipedia.com.

The response to these attacks by fire, police, and emergency medical teams was immediate, and their combined efforts saved hundreds if not thousands of lives, especially at the World Trade Center (Figure 1–6). The following facts provide additional insight into the situation faced by the responders that day:

- Year the World Trade Center was built: 1970
- Number of companies housed in the World Trade Center: 430
- Number working in World Trade Center on average working day before September 11: 50,000
- Average number of daily visitors: 140,000
- Maximum heat of fires, in degrees Fahrenheit, at World Trade Center site: 2,300
- Number of days underground fires at World Trade Center continued to burn: 69
- Number of days that workers dug up debris at Ground Zero, searching for body parts: 230
- Number of body parts collected: 19,500
- Number of bodies discovered intact: 291
- Number of victims identified by New York medical examiner: 1,102
- Number of death certificates issued without a body at request of victims' families: 1,616
- Number of people still classified as missing from the World Trade Center that day: 105
- Number of people who survived the collapse of the towers: 16 (Sources: http://observer.guardian.co.uk/waronterrorism/story/0,1373,776451,00.html and www.snopes.com/rumors/survivor.htm)

The addition of another stairway in each tower, the widening of existing stairways, and regular evacuation drills — actions implemented in the aftermath of the 1993 World Trade Center

FIGURE 1–6 New York City, New York, October 5, 2001 — Rescue workers continue their efforts at the World Trade Center. (Photo by Andrea Booher/FEMA News Photo)

bombing — are all credited with facilitating the evacuation of thousands of office workers in the towers before they collapsed. Federal, state, and nongovernmental groups (e.g., Red Cross, Salvation Army) also responded quickly, establishing relief centers and dispensing critical services to victims and first responders. The following list illustrates the relief efforts that ensued:

- Cases opened: 55,494
- Mental health contacts made: 240,417
- Health services contacts made: 133,035
- Service delivery sites opened: 101
- Shelters opened: 60
- Shelter population: 3,554
- Meals/snacks served: 14,113,185
- Response vehicles assigned: 292
- Disaster workers assigned: 57,434 (Source: www.redcrossalbq.org/04a_911statistics.html)

In addition to the stunning loss of life and the physical destruction caused by the attacks, two other losses are significant for their size and impact. First, 343 New York City firefighters and 75 New York City police officers were lost in the World Trade Center when the towers collapsed, setting a record for the highest number lost in a single disaster event in the United States. Their untimely deaths brought extraordinary attention to America's courageous and professional firefighters, police officers, and emergency medical technicians. They became the heroes of September 11, and this increased attention has resulted in increased funding for government programs that provide equipment and training for first responders. It has also resulted in a reexamination of protocols and procedures in light of the new terrorist threat. The examination of the after-action reports from the World Trade Center and the Pentagon in the next section of this chapter provides insight into the issues currently being addressed by the first responder community.

The second significant aspect of the September 11 attacks is the magnitude and the scope of the losses resulting from the attacks. The total economic impact on New York City alone is estimated to be between $82.8 and $94.8 billion. This estimate includes $21.8 billion in lost buildings, infrastructure, and tenant assets; $8.7 billion in the future earnings of those who died; and $52.3 to $64.3 billion gross city product (Curci, 2004). The economic impact of the attacks was felt throughout the United States and the world, causing jobs to be lost and businesses to fail in communities hundreds and thousands of miles from Ground Zero:

- Value of U.S. economy: $11 trillion
- Estimated cost of attacks to United States based solely on property losses and insurance costs: $21 billion
- Amount of office space lost, in square feet: 13.5 million
- Estimated number of jobs lost in lower Manhattan area following September 11: 100,000
- Estimated number of jobs lost in the United States as a result of the attacks, by the end of 2002: 1.8 million
- Number of jobs lost in U.S. travel industry in the final 5 months of 2001: 237,000
- Amount allocated by Congress for emergency assistance to airline industry in September 2001: $15 billion (Source: http://observer.guardian.co.uk/waronterrorism/story/0,1373,776451,00.html)

The federal government costs were extraordinary, and spending by FEMA on these events easily exceeded its spending on past natural disasters and disasters that have happened since (see also Table 1–1).

- Direct emergency assistance from FEMA: $297 million
- Aid to individuals and families: $255 million
- Direct housing: 8,957 applications processed; 5,287 applications approved (59%)
- Mortgage and rental assistance: 11,818 applications processed; 6,187 applications approved (52%)
- Individual and family grant program: 43,660 applications processed; 6,139 applications approved (14%)
- Disaster unemployment: 6,657 claims processed; 3,210 claims approved (48%)
- Crisis counseling: $166 million
- Aid to government and nonprofits: $4.49 billion
- Debris removal: $437 million
- Overtime for New York Police Department (NYPD): $295.4 million
- Overtime for Fire Department New York: $105.6 million (Source: Federal Emergency Management Agency, "A Nation Remembers, A Nation Recovers," Washington, DC: FEMA, September, 2003)

The insurance losses resulting from the September 11 events were also extraordinary, especially when considered in light of the relatively small amount of physical property that was directly affected by the events themselves. Despite that many natural hazards affect hundreds, if not thousands and even tens of thousands of square miles of inhabited and developed land, thereby affecting thousands of structures and infrastructure components, these terrorist attacks that were isolated to one neighborhood in

Table 1–1 Top Ten Natural Disasters (Ranked by FEMA Relief Costs)

Event	Year	FEMA Funding
World Trade Center attack (NY)	2001	$16.2 billion[a]
Hurricane Katrina (AL, LA, MS)	2005	$7.2 billion[b]
Northridge earthquake (CA)	1994	$6.999 billion
Hurricane George (AL, FL, LA, MS, PR, VI)	1998	$2.254 billion
Hurricane Ivan (AL, FL, GA, LA, MS, NC, NJ, NY, PA, TN, WV)	2004	$1.947 billion
Hurricane Andrew (FL, LA)	1992	$1.848 billion
Hurricane Charley (FL, SC)	2004	$1.559 billion
Hurricane Frances (FL, GA, NC, NY, OH, PA, SC)	2004	$1.425 billion
Hurricane Jeanne (DE, FL, PR, VI, VA)	2004	$1.407 billion
Tropical Storm Allison (FL, LA, MS, PA, TX)	2001	$1.387 billion
Hurricane Hugo (NC, SC, PR, VI)	1989	$1.307 billion

[a]Taken from the Congressional Budget Office report, "Federal Disaster Assistance after the September 11th Attacks," Appendix C, http://www.cbo.gov/ftpdoc.cfm?index=6049&type=0&sequence=5. Amount obligated from the President's Disaster Relief Fund for FEMA's assistance programs, hazard mitigation grants, federal mission assignments, contractual services, and administrative costs as of May 31, 2005. Figures do not include funding provided by other participating federal agencies, such as the disaster loan programs of the Small Business Administration and the Agriculture Department's Farm Service Agency. Note that funding amounts are stated in nominal dollars, unadjusted for inflation.
[b]Amount obligated from the President's Disaster Relief Fund for FEMA's assistance programs, hazard mitigation grants, federal mission assignments, contractual services, and administrative costs as of March 31, 2006. Figures do not include funding provided by other participating federal agencies, such as the disaster loan programs of the Small Business Administration and the Agriculture Department's Farm Service Agency.
Source: Federal Emergency Management Agency (FEMA), "Top Ten Natural Disasters: Ranked by FEMA Relief Costs," 2007.

New York City and one building in Arlington Virginia exceeded all but two events worldwide in terms of their insurance-related disaster losses (Tables 1–2 and 1–3). This comprehensive terrorist attack illustrates the far-reaching indirect, intangible consequences of terrorism, and their potential for damaging a nation's economy.

- Amount of federal aid New York received within 2 months of the September 11 events: $9.5 billion
- Amount collected by the 11 September Fund: $501 million
- Percentage of fund used for cash assistance and services such as grief counseling for families of victims and survivors: 89
- Quantity, in pounds, of food and supplies supplied by 11 September Fund at Ground Zero: 4.3 million
- Number of hot meals served to rescue workers by 11 September Fund: 343,000
- Number of displaced workers receiving job referrals: 5,000
- Amount of compensation sought by the families of civilian casualties of U.S. bombing in Afghanistan from the U.S. government: $10,000
- Amount of compensation sought for reckless misconduct and negligence from American Airlines by husband of September 11 victim: $50 million (Source: http://observer.guardian.co.uk/waronterrorism/story/0,1373,776451,00.html)

Table 1–2   Ten Most Costly World Insurance Losses, 1970–2006[a]

Date	Country	Event	Insured Loss ($ millions)[b]
August 25, 2005	United States, Bahamas, Gulf of Mexico, North Atlantic	Hurricane Katrina	$66,311
August 23, 1992	United States, Bahamas	Hurricane Andrew	$22,987
September 11, 2001	United States	Terrorist attack on WTC, Pentagon, and other buildings	$21,379
January 17, 1994	United States	Earthquake	$19,040
September 2, 2004	United States	Hurricane Ivan	$13,651
October 19, 2005	United States, Mexico, Haiti, Jamaica	Hurricane Wilma	$12,953
September 20, 2005	United States, Gulf of Mexico, Cuba	Hurricane Rita	$10,382
August 11, 2004	United States, Cuba, Jamaica	Hurricane Charley	$8,590
September 27, 1991	Japan	Typhoon Mireille	$8,357
September 15, 1989	Puerto Rico, United States, et al.	Hurricane Hugo	$7,434

[a] Property and business interruption losses, excluding life and liability losses. Includes flood losses in the United States insured via the National Flood Insurance Program.
[b] Adjusted to 2006 dollars by Swiss Re.
Source: International Insurance Institute, International Insurance Factbook, "World Rankings," 2007. http://www.iii.org/international/rankings/.

Table 1–3   Ten Most Costly Catastrophes, United States[a]

Date	Peril	Insured Loss When Event Occurred ($ millions)	In 2006 Dollars[b]
August 2005	Hurricane Katrina	$41,100	$42,426
August 1992	Hurricane Andrew	$15,500	$22,272
September 2001	World Trade Center	$18,800	$21,401
January 1994	Northridge Earthquake	$12,500	$17,004
Oct. 2005	Hurricane Wilma	$10,300	$10,632
August 2004	Hurricane Charley	$7,475	$7,978
September 2004	Hurricane Ivan	$7,110	$7,588
September 1989	Hurricane Hugo	$4,195	$6,820
September 2005	Hurricane Rita	$5,627	$5,809
September 2004	Hurricane Frances	$4,595	$4,904

[a] Property coverage only.
[b] Adjusted to 2007 dollars by the Insurance Information Institute.
Source: Insurance Services Office, Inc., Insurance Information Institute, http://www.iii.org/media/facts/statsbyissue/catastrophes/.

Additional information concerning these attacks and their impact is provided in subsequent chapters of the book.

First Responder Issues

In July and August 2002, two September 11–related after-action reports were released: "Improving NYPD Emergency Preparedness and Response," prepared by McKinsey & Company for the New York City Police Department, and "Arlington County After-Action Report on the Response to the

September 11 Terrorist Attack on the Pentagon," prepared for Arlington County, Virginia, by Titan Systems Corporation. Both reports are based on hundreds of interviews with event participants and reviews of organizational plans. These reports provide lessons learned and present hundreds of recommendations.

The NYPD report did not pass judgment on the success or failure of the NYPD on September 11 but rather assessed the NYPD's response objectives and instruments in order to identify 20 "improvement opportunities" for the NYPD, of which six merited immediate action:

- Clearer delineation of the roles and responsibilities of NYPD leaders
- Better clarity in the chain of command
- Radicommunications protocols and procedures that optimize information flow
- More effective mobilization of members of the service
- More efficient provisioning and distribution of emergency and donated equipment
- A comprehensive disaster response plan, with a significant counterterrorism component (Source: McKinsey & Company, 2002)

The Arlington County after-action report declared the response by the county and others to the Pentagon terrorist attack a success that "can be attributed to the efforts of ordinary men and women performing in extraordinary fashion" (Titan Systems Corporation, 2002). The terrorist attack on the Pentagon sorely tested the plans and skills of responders from Arlington County, Virginia; other jurisdictions; and the federal government.

The Arlington County report contains 235 recommendations and lessons learned. Of these many recommendations, the report highlights examples of lessons learned in two categories: things that worked well and contributed to the overall success of the response and challenges encountered and overcome by responders that could serve as examples for other jurisdictions in the future.

The events at the World Trade Center and the Pentagon vary significantly in size and impact, but from a responder's perspective, they are similar in terms of surprises and challenges. There are striking similarities between the "improvement opportunities" listed in the NYPD report and the "lessons learned" in the Arlington County report (Figure 1–7). While the specifics vary, both responses identified issues in five key areas:

- Command
- Communications
- Coordination
- Planning
- Dispatching personnel

Many of the actions taken after September 11 by government officials and emergency managers at the federal, state, and local levels reflect the need for changes in order to prepare for the next terrorist event.

Conclusion

The terrorist attacks of September 11 have forever changed America and, in many ways, the world. This event has been termed the most significant disaster since the attack on Pearl Harbor, and the first disaster that affected the United States on a national scale. It seemed that every American knew someone or knew of someone who perished in the attacks, and surely every citizen felt the economic impact in the form of lost jobs, lost business, and an immediate reduction in the value of college savings and retirement accounts. Moreover, the perception that nobody was immune from the risk of becoming the next victim of terrorism spread quickly across the nation in the days and weeks that

FIGURE 1–7 Arlington, Virginia, March 7, 2002 — A view of the Pentagon building shows the progress made in the reconstruction of the area damaged by the terrorist attack on the Pentagon on September 11, 2001. (Photo by Jocelyn Augustino/FEMA News Photo)

followed the attacks. The feelings of vulnerability were only strengthened in the wake of the October 2001 anthrax incidents and the sniper attacks in the Washington, DC, metropolitan area on October 2002. In 2008, seven years after the events transpired, their aftermath continues to shape decisions on everything from immigration to civil liberties. Including such measures as the global war on terrorism that is a direct result of the attacks themselves, the total cost of government spending on the issue has reached far beyond $1 trillion.

The threat portfolio under the area of terrorism has only expanded, thereby presenting the nation with a whole new set of hazards about which to worry (e.g., biological, chemical, radiological, and nuclear weapons), and which must now be studied and understood in much greater detail in order to best prepare both our first responders and our citizens (see Chapter 4) for their prevention and response. New laws and executive orders that have been established and which still await their certain passage, each addressing the terrorism threat, must seek to strike a balance between our sense of security and our civil rights (see Chapter 2). A new and very large federal government agency, the Department of Homeland Security, has been formed from the parts of 22 other agencies and programs to coordinate and guide our nation's efforts in fighting terrorism on the domestic front (see Chapter 3). And many new funding programs have been established, further guiding the operational focus for the nation's first responders.

These significant changes are reflected not only in the daily lives of the American people but also in the way in which the country's emergency management system operates. The emergency management community will continue to speculate whether or not this new focus on terrorism can be sustained, and whether the actual threat from terrorism merits the sacrifices the nation has made in terms of spending, prevention for and mitigation of other pressing hazards, and overall capacity of the function.

It is important to recall that FEMA, as noted earlier in this chapter, has traversed this path before, when its focus was shifted from all-hazards to nuclear attack planning in the 1980s — with disastrous results for the agency and the victims of Hurricane Hugo, the Loma Prieta earthquake, and Hurricane Andrew. Although it can be argued that FEMA, in its new location within the Department of Homeland Security, is avoiding this fate, only time and experience will be effective judges. FEMA required a full

14 years to become an effective agency. DHS has a long way to go before reaching that distinction. Nobody, however, can predict what challenges the future will bring. Even Hurricane Katrina, when measured against the full potential of nature's fury, was nowhere near the largest disaster event that must be planned for. As America's emergency management system continues to adapt to its ever-changing terrorism risk, these will be the critical issues that must be addressed to ensure that it can effectively reduce the impact of all future disasters and mount a timely response when these events occur.

Key Terms

Department of Homeland Security: A federal agency whose primary mission is to help prevent, protect against, and respond to acts of terrorism on United States soil.

Emergency Management: The discipline dealing with the identification and analysis of public hazards, the mitigation of and preparedness for public risk, and the coordination of resources in response to and recovery from associated emergency events.

Cold War: A struggle for power waged between the United States and the Soviet Union, which lasted from the end of World War II until the Soviet Union ultimately collapsed. This war was defined as being "cold" because the aggression was ideological, economic, and diplomatic rather than a direct military conflict.

National Flood Insurance Program (NFIP): A program that provides the availability of flood insurance in exchange for the adoption and enforcement of a minimum local floodplain management ordinance. The ordinance regulates new and substantially damaged or improved development in identified flood hazard areas.

TOPOFF (Top Officials): A national-level, multiagency, multijurisdictional, "real-time," limited-notice WMD response exercise, designed to better prepare senior government officials to effectively respond to an actual terrorist attack involving WMD. In addition, TOPOFF involves law enforcement, emergency management first responders, and other nongovernmental officials. Short of an actual attack, such exercises are the best possible way to train responders, gauge preparedness, and identify areas for improvement.

Homeland Security Presidential Directive (HSPD): Policy decisions, issued by the president, on matters that pertain to Homeland Security. As of January 2008, there have been 21 HSPDs issued by the president.

Review Questions

1. Identify the role the U.S. Constitution defines for federal, state, and local governments in the area of emergency management and public safety.
2. Which president established the Federal Emergency Management Agency (FEMA) and on what date? Which president established the Department of Homeland Security (DHS) and on what date?
3. Why did the National Governors Association and its members push the federal government to create FEMA? Why was DHS established?
4. After reviewing the difficulties that FEMA encountered in becoming a functioning emergency management agency, what issues do you anticipate DHS will encounter in its evolution into a functioning government agency? Identify some lessons learned in the FEMA experience that could guide DHS actions in the future. Will history repeat itself as DHS matures as a government agency?
5. Throughout the history of emergency management in the United States, the priorities set for government emergency management agencies have been driven by the most widely perceived threat or hazard. How do you think the new threat of terrorism and the hazards associated with terrorism will impact the practice of emergency management in the United States at all levels of government (federal, state, and local) and in the business sector?

References

City of Oklahoma City Document Management. "Final Report: Alfred P. Murrah Federal Building Bombing April 19, 1995." Stillwater: Department of Central Services Central Printing Division.

Curci, Lt. Col. Michael A. 2004. "Transnational Terrorism's Affect on the U.S. Economy." United States Army War College Strategy Research Project. PA: United States Army.

International Fire Service Training Association. "Essentials of Fire Fighting." Fire Protection Publications. Stillwater: Oklahoma State University.

Federal Emergency Management Agency (FEMA). 2003. "A Nation Remembers, A Nation Recovers." Washington, DC: FEMA.

Fusco, A.L. 1993. "The World Trade Center Bombing: Report and Analysis." Emmitsburg, MD: U.S. Fire Administration.

McKinsey & Company. 2002. "Improving NYPD Emergency Preparedness and Response." New York: New York City Police Department.

Titan Systems Inc. 2002. "Arlington County After-Action Report on the Response to the September 11 Terrorist Attack on the Pentagon." Washington, DC: Titan System Inc.

Statutory Authority

What You Will Learn

- Actions taken by the Federal Government to respond to and limit the threat of terrorism prior to the attacks of September 11, 2001
- The chronological legislative treatment of terrorism in the United States
- Legislation that was created in the immediate aftermath of the September 11, 2001, terrorist attacks, and the short- and long-term ramification of those actions
- Actions taken by President George W. Bush to address the terrorist threat, including presidential directives and executive orders
- The far-reaching powers of the USA PATRIOT Act, its criticisms, and changes that have occurred to this legislation in the years since its creation
- The broad scope of security-based legislation that has been considered but has not been enacted since 2001
- How and why the 9/11 Commission was created to assess the government's and Congress's ability to address the threats exposed in 2001, and how both reacted to the Commission's findings
- The funding of Homeland Security in the United States, and what drives that funding

Introduction

The Department of Homeland Security, and the function of homeland security as we know it today, is primarily the result of ongoing legislative actions that have continued since the September 11, 2001, terrorist attacks. However, the movement to establish such broad-sweeping measures was initiated long before those attacks took place. Domestic and international terrorists have been striking Americans, American facilities, and American interests, both within and outside the nation's borders, for decades — though only fleeting interest was garnered in the aftermath of these events. Support for counterterrorism focused legislation was, therefore, rather weak, and measures that did pass rarely warranted front-page status. Furthermore, the institutional cultures that characterized many of the agencies affected by this early legislation served as a resilient barrier to the fulfillment of goals. Only the spectacular nature of the September 11 terrorist attacks was sufficient to boost the issue of terrorism to primary standing on all three social agendas: the public, the political, and the media.

The purpose of this chapter is to trace the series of statutes, presidential directives, and executive orders that have been issued and implemented to establish the authorities and the infrastructure within which the federal government must now address the terrorism hazard. Terrorism authorities were vague and poorly established prior to September 11, and, as the 9/11 Commission discovered, not effective in coordinating terrorism prevention. Legislation that has continued to emerge in the years since the September 11 attacks has attempted, with mixed results, to solve many of the recognized shortfalls and inefficiencies that exist at the federal level. And in line with these statutory improvements and additions, massive changes have occurred in the organizational makeup of the federal government that have dramatically altered how terrorist attacks are managed.

Seven years after the September 11 attacks, these changes continue. In the initial days, weeks, and months that followed the attacks, much of the policy enacted was made in a manner later both criticized as being knee-jerk in nature but also heralded as being symbolic of a nation uniting to address a common problem. As time has passed, and the luxury of hindsight is applied, it has become obvious that changes must be continued to ensure that the laws enacted are done in a manner that their resulting ramifications serve the common good of the American people, with respect to their constitutional and human rights, while at the same time ensuring their safety from this emerging global threat. Additionally, the prospect of increasing risk from natural hazards — the direct consequence of changing climate — has mandated that all hazards' risks be considered in the justification of time, resources, and people committed to the management of the nation's hazard portfolio. The unwavering pace at which changes have progressed over the past seven years serves as testament that this process will continue for many more years to come.

A legislative timeline is presented in this chapter to provide a reference for the progression of terrorism-related legislation, presidential directives, and executive orders that have occurred. For several of the more significant legislative efforts, including the USA PATRIOT Act of 2001 and the Homeland Security Act of 2002, detailed description and analysis are provided. The PATRIOT Act, which is notorious for its quick passage, placed widely expanded investigative authority in the hands of the U.S. Justice Department to assist agents in their efforts to identify and detain suspected terrorists operating within the United States. The Homeland Security Act ultimately resulted in the largest government reorganization since 1947, thereby establishing the ever-expanding Department of Homeland Security.

Also included in this chapter are reviews of Homeland Security Presidential Directive No. 5, the fiscal year (FY) 2008 budget for the Department of Homeland Security, and an analysis of the ongoing struggle by public officials to balance the need for increased security in the domestic war on terrorism and the need to protect the civil liberties of all Americans.

Nunn-Lugar-Domenici Act

The contemporary roots of the Homeland Security Act of 2002 date back to the first term of the Clinton administration. Several major terror-related events occurred during Clinton's first three years in office, prompting the drafting and passage of the Nunn-Lugar-Domenici Weapons of Mass Destruction (WMD) Act (Public Law 104-201, September 23, 1996). These events included:

- 1993 bombing of the World Trade Center
- 1995 Oklahoma City bombing
- 1995 Tokyo subway sarin gas attacks

The primary result of the WMD Act was the provision of greater funding for training and equipment for the nation's first responders. This act addressed what could be done in the aftermath of a terrorist attack, but very little was done to change the way in which the federal government prevented terrorist acts from occurring in the first place. Always in the background, however, was a growing bipartisan movement calling for a less fragmented and more coordinated approach to combating terrorism.

Terrorism Annex to the Federal Response Plan

In 1996, during the Olympic competitions in Atlanta, Georgia, a bomb was detonated in a crowd, injuring dozens of people and killing one. The source of the attack was determined to have been domestic, apparently the act of a delusional individual, thereby negating any greater recognition by Americans of the need for better systems of terrorism prevention. This was, however, the third large terrorist attack on American soil in a period of three years, and as such it helped to build the steam behind the development of a terrorism annex to the Federal Response Plan (FRP). The criminal element of a terrorist attack, which had confounded previous responses to terrorism where the FRP had been invoked, was recognized as a component that needed special consideration (because it had not been addressed in the original FRP). This annex appended the original response document by dictating the coordination of the various federal agencies likely to respond to future terrorist events, including the events of September 11.

The Three Commissions

In 1998, President Clinton and House Speaker Newt Gingrich petitioned Congress to form a 14-member panel called the United States Commission on National Security/21st Century (USCNS/21), also known as the Hart-Rudman Commission, to make strategic recommendations on how the U.S. government could ensure the nation's security in the coming years. The independent panel, created by Congress, was tasked with conducting a comprehensive review of American security with the goal of designing a national security strategy.

The commission's report, titled "Road Map for National Security: Imperative for Change," dated January 31, 2001, recommended the creation of a new independent National Homeland Security Agency (NHSA) with responsibility for planning, coordinating, and integrating various U.S. government activities involved in homeland security. This agency would be built on the Federal Emergency Management Agency (FEMA), with the Coast Guard, the Customs Service, and the U.S. Border Patrol (now part of U.S. Customs and Border Protection [CBP] within the Department of Homeland Security) transferred into it. NHSA would assume responsibility for the safety of the American people as well as oversee the protection of critical infrastructure, including information technology. Obviously, the commission's recommendations were not heeded before 2001, but many of its findings would later be integrated into the justification and legislation behind the creation of the Department of Homeland Security (DHS).

Two other commissions were established to study the terrorist threat during these years: the Gilmore Commission and the Bremer Commission, as discussed next.

The Gilmore Commission, also known as the Advisory Panel to Assess Domestic Response Capabilities for Terrorism Involving Weapons of Mass Destruction, produced a series of annual reports beginning in 1999 (with the final report released in 2003). Each of these reports presented a growing base of knowledge concerning the WMD risk faced by the United States, and a recommended course of action required to counter that risk.

The Bremer Commission, also known as the National Commission on Terrorism, addressed the issue of the international terrorist threat. The commission was mandated by Congress to evaluate the nation's laws, policies, and practices for preventing terrorism, and for punishing those responsible for terrorist events. Its members drafted a report titled "Countering the Changing Threat of International Terrorism." This report, issued in the year 2000, arrived at the following conclusions:

- International terrorism poses an increasingly dangerous and difficult threat to America.
- Countering the growing danger of the terrorist threat requires significantly stepping up U.S. efforts.
- Priority one is to prevent terrorist attacks. U.S. intelligence and law enforcement communities must use the full scope of their authority to collect intelligence regarding terrorist plans and methods.
- U.S. policies must firmly target all states that support terrorists.
- Private sources of financial and logistical support for terrorists must be subjected to the full force and sweep of U.S. and international laws.
- A terrorist attack involving a biological agent, deadly chemicals, or nuclear or radiological material, even if it succeeds only partially, could profoundly affect the entire nation. The government must do more to prepare for such an event.

- The president and Congress should reform the system for reviewing and funding departmental counterterrorism programs to ensure that the activities and programs of various agencies are part of a comprehensive plan.

Each of these conclusions and recommendations would take on new meaning in the aftermath of the September 11 attacks, and would guide many of the changes incorporated into the Homeland Security Act of 2002. However, in the absence of a greater recognition of a terrorist threat within the borders of the United States, no major programs were initiated to combat the growing risk.

▦ ▦ Critical Thinking ▦

President Clinton and Congress were concerned enough about terrorism in the late 1990s that they chose to form and fund the three terrorism commissions. Do you feel that the United States public was adequately concerned or aware of the threat of terrorism during this time, and leading up to the September 11 terrorist attacks. Do you believe that the U.S. government was adequately concerned during this same time period? Explain your answer.

Presidential Decision Directives 62 and 63

As these commissions were conducting their research, President Clinton was addressing other recognized and immediate needs through the passage of several presidential decision directives (PDDs). Terrorist attacks continued to occur throughout the world, aimed at U.S. government, military, and private interests. In 1996, terrorists carried out a suicide bombing at U.S. military barracks (Khobar Towers) in Saudi Arabia, and in 1998, simultaneous bombings were carried out at the U.S. diplomatic missions in Kenya and Tanzania.

In May 1998, President Clinton issued Presidential Decision Directive 62 (PDD-62), "Combating Terrorism," which called for the establishment of the Office of the National Coordinator for Security, Infrastructure Protection and Counterterrorism. The directive's primary goal was to create a new and more systematic approach to fighting the terrorist threat. PDD-62 reinforced the mission of many U.S. agencies involved in a wide array of counterterrorism activities. The new national coordinator was tasked with overseeing a broad variety of relevant policies and programs including counterterrorism, critical infrastructure protection, WMD preparedness, and consequence management.

Soon after this directive, President Clinton issued Presidential Decision Directive 63 (PDD-63), "Protecting America's Critical Infrastructure." This directive tasked all of the departments of the federal government with assessing the vulnerabilities of their cyber and physical infrastructures and with working to reduce their exposure to new and existing threats.

Attorney General's Five-Year Interagency Counterterrorism and Technology Crime Plan

In December 1998, as mandated by Congress, the Department of Justice (DOJ), through the Federal Bureau of Investigation (FBI), began a coordinated project with other agencies to develop the Attorney General's Five-Year Interagency Counterterrorism and Technology Crime Plan. The FBI emerged as the federal government's principal agency for responding to and investigating terrorism. Congress had intended the plan to serve as a baseline for the coordination of a national strategy and operational capabilities to combat terrorism. This plan represented a substantial interagency effort, including goals, objectives, performance indicators, and recommended specific agency actions to help resolve interagency problems. It clearly did not, however, tear down the walls that prevented interagency sharing of information, as evidenced by the failures that resulted in the success of the 9/11 terrorists.

General Accounting Office Findings

The Department of Justice asserted that the Attorney General's Five-Year Interagency Counterterrorism and Technology Crime Plan, considered together with related PDDs as described earlier, represented a comprehensive national strategy to address the terrorist threat. However, after a thorough review, the General Accounting Office (GAO), Congress's investigative arm, concluded that additional work remained that would build on the progress that the plan represented. The GAO contended that a comprehensive national security strategy was lacking.

The GAO report "Combating Terrorism: Comments on Counterterrorism Leadership and National Strategy" (GAO-01-55T), released March 27, 2001, stated that the DOJ plan did not have measurable outcomes and suggested, for example, that it should include goals that improve state and local response capabilities. The report argued that without a clearly defined national strategy, the nation would continue to miss opportunities to focus and shape counterterrorism programs to meet the impending threat. It also made the criticism that the DOJ plan lacked a coherent framework to develop and evaluate budget requirements for combating terrorism since there was no single focal point. The report claimed that no single entity was acting as the federal government's top official accountable to both the president and Congress for the terrorism hazard, and that fragmentation existed in both coordination of domestic preparedness programs and in efforts to develop a national strategy.

The GAO released another report in early September 2001 entitled "Combating Terrorism: Selected Challenges and Related Recommendations" (GAO-01-822), which it finalized in the last days before the terrorist attacks occurred in Washington and New York. The report stated that the federal government was ill equipped and unprepared to counter a major terrorist attack, claiming also that — from sharing intelligence to coordinating a response — the government had failed to put in place an effective critical infrastructure system. It further stated that

> *Federal efforts to develop a national strategy to combat terrorism . . . have progressed, but key challenges remain. The initial step toward developing a national strategy is to conduct a national threat and risk assessment . . . at the national level (agencies) have not completed assessments of the most likely weapon-of-mass destruction agents and other terrorist threats . . .*

To prevent terrorist attacks, the GAO recommended:

- A national strategy to combat terrorism and computer-based attacks
- Better protection for the nation's infrastructure
- A single focal point to oversee coordination of federal programs
- Completion of a threat assessment on likely WMD and other weapons that might be used by terrorists
- Revision of the Attorney General's Five-Year Interagency Counterterrorism and Technology Crime Plan to better serve as a national strategy
- Coordination of research and development to combat terrorism

In a later report regarding Homeland Security, "Key Elements to Unify Efforts Are Underway But Uncertainty Remains" (GAO-02-610), the GAO called for more of the same in terms of needing central leadership and an overarching strategy that identifies goals and objectives, priorities, measurable outcomes, and state and local government roles in combating terrorism since the efforts of more than 40 federal entities and numerous state and local governments were still fragmented. It also called for the term *homeland security* to be defined properly since to date it had not.

September 11, 2001

The attacks on the World Trade Center in New York City and the Pentagon in Arlington, Virginia, on September 11, 2001, could arguably be considered the first truly national disaster event, outside of wartime, in the history of the United States. It is the first disaster in this country that impacted all Americans, leaving all citizens and communities with an unrelenting sense of vulnerability. The economic consequences of these attacks, felt in all parts of our country and, in fact, around the world, make this disaster event truly global in scope.

The attacks involved the hijacking of four commercial airliners by 19 trained terrorists. Three of the four planes were flown into major American landmarks: the two World Trade Center Twin Towers, and the headquarters of the U.S. military. The fourth, whose target may never be conclusively known, was prevented from reaching its target by passengers on the plane who overpowered its four terrorist hijackers. Almost 3,000 people were killed, and billions of dollars in property damage resulted. The full economic impacts, which include everything from lost revenues to increased spending on terrorism preparedness, may never be known.

This was not a simple act, but one that required years of surveillance, funding, training, intelligence gathering, practice, and breaching of U.S. immigration law. There were many instances during this time, as evidenced in the report of the National Commission on Terrorist Attacks Upon the United States (9/11 Commission), which was created to investigate the causes of the 9/11 attacks and means to prevent similar attacks from occurring the future, where individual agencies involved in counterterrorist activities recognized one or more of these activities. However, insufficient coordination between the agencies prevented the federal government system from piecing together the larger picture of what exactly was occurring and, as such, the terrorists were ultimately successful in their mission.

Immediate Response to the 9/11 Terrorist Attacks

In the immediate aftermath of the September 11 attacks, as search-and-rescue teams were still sifting through the debris and wreckage for survivors in New York, Pennsylvania, and Virginia, the federal government was analyzing what had just happened and what it could quickly do to begin the process of ensuring such attacks could not be repeated. It was recognized that nothing too substantial could take place without longer-term study and congressional review, but the circumstances mandated that real changes begin without delay.

On September 20, 2001, just nine days after the attacks, President George W. Bush announced that an Office of Homeland Security would be established within the White House by executive order. Directing this office would be Pennsylvania Governor Tom Ridge. Ridge was given no real staff to manage, and the funding he would have at his disposal was minimal. The actual order, cataloged as Executive Order 13228, was given on October 8, 2001. In addition to creating the Office of Homeland Security, this order created the Homeland Security Council, "to develop and coordinate the implementation of a comprehensive national strategy to secure the United States from terrorist threats or attacks."

Four days later, on September 24, 2001, President Bush announced that he would be seeking passage of an act entitled "Uniting and Strengthening America by Providing Appropriate Tools Required to Intercept and Obstruct Terrorism," which would become better known as the PATRIOT Act of 2001. This act, which introduced a large number of controversial legislative changes in order to significantly increase the surveillance and investigative powers of law enforcement agencies in the United States (as it states) to ". . . deter and punish terrorist acts in the United States and around the world," was signed into law by the president on October 26 after very little deliberation in Congress.

On October 29, 2001, President Bush issued the first of many homeland security presidential directives (HSPDs), which were specifically designed to "record and communicate presidential decisions about the homeland security policies of the United States" (HSPD-1, 2001). The sidebar titled "Select Homeland Security Presidential Directives" lists several of the HSPDs, their stated purposes, and their dates of issuance.

On March 21, 2002, President Bush signed Executive Order 13260 establishing the President's Homeland Security Advisory Council (PHSAC) and Senior Advisory Committees for Homeland Security.

Select Homeland Security Presidential Directives

HSPD-1: Organization and Operation of the Homeland Security Council — October 29, 2001

HSPD-2: Combating Terrorism through Immigration Policies — October 29, 2001

HSPD-3: Creation of the Homeland Security Advisory System — March 11, 2002

HSPD-4: National Strategy to Combat WMDs — December 11, 2002

HSPD-5: Management of Domestic Incidents (Creation of a National Incident Management System [NIMS]) — February 28, 2003

HSPD-6: Integration and Use of Screening Information (Creation of the Terrorist Threat Integration Center [TTIC]) — September 16, 2003

HSPD-7: Critical Infrastructure Identification, Prioritization, and Protection — December 17, 2003

HSPD-8: Strengthen National Preparedness ("Establish policies to strengthen the preparedness of the United States to prevent and respond to threatened or actual domestic terrorist attacks, major disasters, and other emergencies by requiring a national domestic all-hazards preparedness goal, establishing mechanisms for improved delivery of Federal preparedness assistance to State and local governments, and outlining actions to strengthen preparedness capabilities of Federal, State, and local entities.") — December 17, 2003

HSPD-9: Defense of United States Agriculture and Food — January 30, 2004

HSPD-10: Defense from Biological Weapons — April 28, 2004

HSPD-11: Comprehensive Terrorist-Related Screening Procedures — August 27, 2004

HSPD-12: Policy for a Common Identification Standard for Federal Employees and Contractors — August 27, 2004

HSPD-13: Maritime Security — December 21, 2004

HSPD-14: Domestic Nuclear Detection — April 15, 2005

HSPD-15: "On the War on Terrorism" (Classified) — March 2006

HSPD-16: "On Aviation Security and Threats to Commercial Aircraft" (Classified) — June 2006

HSPD-17: National Strategy to Combat Weapons of Mass Destruction (Classified) — January 2007

HSPD-18: Medical Countermeasures against Weapons of Mass Destruction — January 31, 2007

HSPD-19: Combating Terrorist Use of Explosives in the United States — February 12, 2007

HSPD-20: National Continuity Policy — April 4, 2007

HSPD-21: Public Health and Medical Preparedness — October 18, 2007

Legislative, Presidential Directive, and Executive Order Timeline

November 18, 1988 — Executive Order (EO) 12656 — Assignment of Emergency Preparedness Responsibilities. This executive order defines a national security emergency as any occurrence that seriously degrades or threatens the national security of the United States. Terrorist incidents were not specifically mentioned except for DOJ responsibilities. The National Security Council is assigned responsibility for developing and administering this policy. The director of the Federal Emergency Management Agency (FEMA) shall assist in the implementation of and management of national security emergency management preparedness policy by coordinating with other federal departments. FEMA is responsible for coordinating, supporting, developing, and implementing the following: civil national security emergency preparedness and response programs, continuity of government functions, and civil-military support. This EO was in draft and coordination for five years.

November 18, 1988 — EO 12657 — FEMA Assistance in Emergency Preparedness Planning at Commercial Nuclear Power Plants Responsibilities. This EO allows FEMA to initially respond in coordinating federal response activities when advance state and local commitments (e.g., response planning) are absent or inadequate off-site at commercial nuclear power plants. FEMA is authorized to assume any necessary command and control function, or delegate such function to another federal agency, in the event that no competent state and local authority is available to perform such function.

November 23, 1988 — President Reagan signs into law the Robert T. Stafford Disaster Relief and Emergency Assistance Act (Public Law [P.L.] 100-707) amending the Federal Disaster Relief Act of 1974.

March 23, 1989 — EO 12673 delegates Stafford Act authority with some exceptions (principally declarations) to the director of FEMA.

April 1992 — Federal Response Plan (FRP) is issued. This plan "established a process and structure for the systematic, coordinated, and effective delivery of Federal assistance to address the consequences of any major disaster or emergency declared under the Robert T. Stafford Disaster Relief and Emergency Assistance Act, as amended." Under the "Scope" section, the FRP states "[I]n some instances, a disaster or emergency may result in a situation [that] affects the national security of the United States. For those instances, appropriate national security authorities and procedures will be utilized to address the national security requirements of the situation." Law enforcement emergencies are defined under "Policies," and procedures are referenced under which DOJ and Department of Defense (DOD) personnel respond to law enforcement emergencies under 28 CFR Part 65 and 10 USC 331–333.

November 30, 1993 — P.L. 103-160 §1704. Joint Resolution of Congress on FEMA terrorism-preparedness planning provides that "[I]t is the sense of Congress that the president should strengthen Federal interagency emergency planning by the Federal emergency management agency and other appropriate Federal, state, and local agencies for development of a capability for early detection and warning of and response to (1) potential terrorist use of chemical or biological agents or weapons; and (2) emergencies or natural disasters involving industrial chemicals or the widespread outbreak of disease."

June 3, 1994 — EO 12919 — National Defense Industrial Resources Preparedness. This EO delegates authorities and addresses national defense industrial resource policies and programs under the Defense Production Act of 1950, as amended, except for the amendments to Title III of the act in the Energy Security Act of 1980 and excludes telecommunication authorities under EO 12472. Under this order the FEMA director (1) serves as an adviser to the National Security Council on issues of national security resource preparedness and on the use of the authorities and functions delegated by this order; (2) provides for the central coordination of the plans and programs incident to authorities and functions delegated under this order, and provides guidance and procedures approved by the assistant to the president for National Security Affairs to the federal departments and agencies under this order; (3) establishes procedures, in consultation with federal departments and agencies assigned functions under this order, to resolve in a timely and effective manner conflicts and issues that may arise in implementing the authorities and functions delegated under this order; and (4) reports to the president periodically concerning all program activities conducted pursuant to this order.

November 1994 — P.L. 103-337. This law repeals the Federal Civil Defense Act. In new Title VI of the Stafford Act, the policy of the federal government is for FEMA to provide necessary direction, coordination and guidance, and necessary assistance, as authorized in the title so that a comprehensive emergency preparedness system exists for all hazards in the United States. FEMA is directed to (1) prepare federal response plans and programs for the emergency preparedness of the United States, and (2) sponsor and direct such plans and programs to coordinate such plans and programs with state efforts. The FEMA director may request such reports on state plans and operations for emergency preparedness as may be necessary to keep the president, Congress, and the states advised of the status of emergency preparedness in the United States. Interstate emergency preparedness compacts are authorized to (1) assist and encourage the states to negotiate and enter into interstate emergency preparedness compacts; (2) facilitate uniformity between state compacts and consistency with federal emergency response plans and programs; (3) assist and coordinate the activities under state compacts; and (4) aid and assist reciprocal state emergency preparedness legislation that will permit mutual aid in the event of a hazard that cannot be adequately met or controlled by a state or political subdivision thereof. Public Law 103-337 amended P.L. 93-288 as previously amended by P.L. 100-707.

January 22, 1995 — Director of FEMA establishes the Office of National Security Coordination, which reports directly to him.

March 19, 1995 — Sarin gas attack on a subway in Tokyo, Japan.

April 19, 1995 — The Murrah Federal Office Building in Oklahoma City is bombed. Within 7 hours of the explosion, President Clinton signs an emergency declaration. This is the first use of the president's authority under the Stafford Act to "self-initiate" an emergency declaration for emergencies with federal involvement.

June 21, 1995 — Presidential Decision Directive 39. This directive states that it is the policy of the United States to use all appropriate means to deter, defeat, and respond to all terrorist attacks on our territory and resources, both people and facilities, wherever they occur. Established that DOJ personnel have lead responsibility for crisis management, and FEMA personnel have lead responsibility for consequence management. FEMA chairs the Senior Interagency Group for Training and Preparedness.

April 24, 1996 — Anti-Terrorism and Effective Death Penalty Act of 1996, P.L. 104-132 (110 stat. 1255). Congress funds first responder and firefighter training by grants. United States Fire Administration receives funds from DOJ to conduct first responder training.

May 1, 1996 — Federal Radiological Emergency Response Plan (FRERP) signed by FEMA Director James L. Witt. The FRERP addresses radiological sabotage and terrorism and states that a coordinated response to contain or mitigate a threatened or actual release of radioactive material would be essentially the same whether it resulted from an accidental or deliberate act. Therefore, sabotage and terrorism are not treated as separate types of emergencies; rather they are considered a complicating dimension of (radiological emergencies).

July 15, 1996 — EO 13010 — Critical Infrastructure Protection. This EO established the President's Commission on Critical Infrastructure Protection (PCCIP) and the Critical Infrastructure Protection Working Group (CIPWG). Certain national infrastructures are so vital that their incapacity or destruction would have a debilitating impact on the defense or economic security of the United States. It is essential that the government and private sector work together to develop a strategy for protecting them and ensuring their continued operation. These infrastructures include telecommunications, transportation, water supply systems, emergency services (including medical, police, fire, and rescue), and continuity of government.

1996 — Anti-Terrorism and Effective Death Penalty Act (P.L. 104-132). The president signs a law authorizing FEMA and the DOJ's Office of Justice Programs to fund and develop an emergency response to terrorism training program for fire, emergency medical service, and public safety personnel. Annual appropriation to DOJ is shared with FEMA through FY 2002. DOJ administers grants through its State and Local Domestic Preparedness Office (SLDo PO) in its Office of Justice Assistance (not in the FBI).

September 23, 1996 — Defense Against Weapons of Mass Destruction Act (P.L. 104-201), also called the Nunn-Lugar legislation. The president signs a law directing the DOD to lead, for three years, domestic preparedness for responding to and managing the consequences of a terrorist attack using WMD. The law authorizes transfer of this responsibility to another agency after three years with presidential concurrence.

February 7, 1997 — FEMA director adopts the Terrorism Incident Annex (TIA) to the Federal Response Plan. This annex provides federal emergency planners with information and a framework within which to address the consequences of terrorist attacks.

May 22, 1998 — Presidential Decision Directives (PDDs) 62, "Combating Terrorism," and 63, "Protecting America's Critical Infrastructure" are signed by President Clinton. The president designates a national coordinator for security, infrastructure protection, and counterterrorism (Richard Clarke of National Security Council staff) who is not to direct agencies' activities but is to integrate the government's policies and programs on unconventional threats to the homeland and Americans abroad, including terrorism. The national coordinator oversees the broad variety of relevant polices and programs including counterterrorism, protection of critical infrastructure, preparedness, and consequence management for WMD. The national coordinator works within the National Security Council process and reports to the president through the assistant to the president for National Security Affairs and produces an annual security preparedness report. The national coordinator will also provide advice regarding budgets for counterterrorism programs and lead in the development of guidelines that might be needed for crisis management.

August 7, 1998 — Bombings of the U.S. embassies in Nairobi, Kenya, and Dar es Salaam, Tanzania.

April 1999 — The Federal Response Plan is revised after full interagency coordination to incorporate the 11 changes published to the plan since 1992. The FRP was also revised to ensure consistency with current policy guidance; integrate recovery and mitigation functions into the response structure; and describe relationships to other emergency operations plans. The revised FRP as adopted includes four new support annexes (community relations, donations management, logistics management, and occupational safety and health), the terrorism incident annex, and two new appendices (FRP changes and revision, and an overview of a disaster operation).

May 2000 — Congressionally mandated No-Notice Operation TOPOFF Exercise, simulating terrorist attacks in both Denver, Colorado, and Portsmouth, New Hampshire. Communication difficulties and the lack of a lead agency severely hinder operations in both locations. The DOJ is assigned executive responsibility for after-action reports.

July 25, 2000 — House of Representatives passes HR 4210, which would have established a President's Council on Domestic Terrorism Preparedness composed of the president, directors of FEMA and Office of Management and Budget (OMB), the attorney general, the secretary of defense, the assistant to the president for national security affairs, and additional members appointed by the president. Purposes were to (1) improve federal assistance to state and local emergency preparedness and response for domestic terrorist attacks, (2) designate the President's Council to coordinate federal efforts, and (3) update federal authorities to reflect increased risk of terrorist attacks. Because the Senate did not act, this legislation died in the 106th Congress.

February 8, 2001 — Introduction of HR 525, the Preparedness against Domestic Terrorism Act of 2001. This resolution amends the Stafford Act to include acts of terrorism or other catastrophic events within its definition of "major disaster" for purposes of authorized disaster relief. It requires the president (then-current law authorized the director of FEMA) to be responsible for carrying out federal emergency preparedness plans and programs. It includes into the definition of hazards as covered under the Stafford Act a domestic terrorist attack involving a weapon of mass destruction. It also establishes the President's Council on Domestic Preparedness to eliminate duplication within federal terrorism-preparedness programs. It requires the council to (1) publish a domestic terrorism-preparedness plan and an annual implementation strategy; (2) designate an entity to assess the risk of terrorist attacks against transportation, energy, and other infrastructure facilities; and (3) establish voluntary minimum guidelines for preparedness programs. Finally, it authorizes the council to attend meetings of the National Security Council pertaining to domestic terrorist-attack preparedness matters, subject to the direction of the president.

March 21 and 29, 2001 — The introduction of HR 1158, which establishes a National Homeland Security Agency, and HR 1292, requiring the president to develop and implement a strategy for homeland security. It is anticipated that these bills will be combined with HR 525 addressing preparedness against acts of domestic terrorism.

September 11, 2001 — Terrorist attacks on the World Trade Center and the Pentagon. President George W. Bush issues a disaster declaration for New York City within 6 hours after Governor Pataki's state disaster declaration (approximately 6 hours after the initial attack at 8:43 AM EDT).

September 14, 2001 — President Bush signs a declaration of national emergency as a result of the terrorist attacks at the World Trade Center, the Pentagon, and the continuing and immediate threat of further attacks on the United States.

September 15, 2001 — Congress approves a $40 billion expenditure on disaster relief and anti- and counterterrorism (HR 2888).

September 23, 2001 — President Bush signs an EO that served to block property and prohibit transactions with persons who commit, threaten to commit, or who support terrorism (EO 13224).

October 8, 2001 — President Bush signs an EO establishing the Office of Homeland Security and the Homeland Security Council, to be headed by the assistant to the president for homeland security. Former Pennsylvania Governor Tom Ridge was sworn in as the first director of Homeland Security. (EO 13228 published at 66 Federal Register 51812–51817.)

October 26, 2001 — President Bush signs H.R. 3162: Uniting and Strengthening America by Providing Appropriate Tools Required to Intercept and Obstruct Terrorism (USA PATRIOT Act).

November 9, 2001 — President Bush signs an EO to establish a Presidential Task Force on Citizen Preparedness in the War on Terrorism (EO 13234).

January 29, 2002 — President Bush signs EO establishing the USA Freedom Corps (EO 13254).

March 19, 2002 — President Bush signs EO establishing the President's Homeland Security Advisory Council and Senior Advisory Committees on Homeland Security (EO 13260).

June 20, 2002 — President Bush signs EO establishing a Transition Planning Office for the Department of Homeland Security within the Office of Management and Budget (EO 13267).

November 25, 2002 — President Bush signs P.L. 107–296, establishing Department of Homeland Security, effective January 24, 2003.

November 25, 2002 — President Bush signs S. 1214: Maritime Transportation Security Act of 2002.

November 26, 2002 — President Bush signs H.R. 3210: Terrorism Risk Insurance Act of 2002.

January 24, 2003 — The Department of Homeland Security is activated.

April 29, 2003 — President Bush signs H.R. 1770: Smallpox Emergency Personnel Protection Act of 2003.

July 29, 2003 — President Bush signs EO to improve the sharing of Homeland Security information between the various intelligence agencies (EO 13311).

December 6, 2003 — President Bush signs S. 1152, Firefighting Research and Coordination Act.

July 21, 2004 — President Bush signs S. 15, Project BioShield Act of 2004.

August 8, 2004 — President Bush signs H.R. 2443, Coast Guard and Maritime Transportation Act of 2004.

August 27, 2004 — President Bush signs EO establishing a National Counterterrorism Center (EO 13354).

August 27, 2005 — President Bush signs EO strengthening the management of the various intelligence agencies (EO 13355).

August 27, 2004 — President Bush signs EO to strengthen the sharing of terrorism information (EO 13356).

October 24, 2004 — President Bush signs H.R. 2828, Water Supply, Reliability, and Environmental Improvement Act.

December 17, 2004 — President Bush signs S. 2845, National Intelligence Reform Act of 2004.

March 9, 2006 — President Bush signs H.R. 3199, USA PATRIOT Improvement and Reauthorization Act of 2005.

June 26, 2006 — President Bush signs EO to improve the national systems of public alert and warning (EO 13407).

October 4, 2006 — President Bush signs into law the Post-Katrina Emergency Reform Act.

October 13, 2006 — President Bush signs H.R. 4954, Safe Port Act.

August 3, 2007 — President Bush signs H.R. 1, Implementing Recommendations of the 9/11 Commission Act of 2007.

The PATRIOT Act of 2001

The PATRIOT Act of 2001 (P.L. 107-56), officially titled "Uniting and Strengthening America by Providing Appropriate Tools Required to Intercept and Obstruct Terrorism (USA PATRIOT Act) Act of 2001," was signed into law by President Bush on October 26, 2001. This legislation was introduced in the U.S. House of Representatives by Representative F. James Sensenbrenner, Jr. (R-WI) on October 23, 2001, "to deter and punish terrorist acts in the United States and around the world, to enhance law enforcement investigatory tools, and for other purposes" (www.congress. gov, 2003).

Under normal circumstances, legislation, especially that which has broad-sweeping reach and which brings into question constitutional rights, requires years and even decades of deliberation before it is finally passed — if that day ever comes. Considering the PATRIOT Act was passed less than a month after the event that inspired it, with almost no significant deliberation, it can be considered an anomalous case, and one that, considering its comprehensive nature and its impact on civil liberties, deserves more detailed description.

The principal focus of the PATRIOT Act is to provide law enforcement agencies with the proper legal authority to support their efforts to collect information on suspected terrorists, to detain people suspected of being or aiding terrorists and terrorist organizations, to deter terrorists from entering and operating within the borders of the United States, and to further limit the ability of terrorists to engage in money-laundering activities that support terrorist actions. The major provisions of the PATRIOT Act are as follows:

- Relaxes restrictions on information sharing between U.S. law enforcement and intelligence officers on the subject of suspected terrorists.
- Makes it illegal to knowingly harbor a terrorist.
- Authorizes "roving wiretaps," which allows law enforcement officials to get court orders to wiretap any phone a suspected terrorist would use. The provision was needed, advocates said, with the advent of cellular and disposable phones.
- Allows the federal government to detain non-U.S. citizens suspected of terrorism for up to 7 days without specific charges (original versions of the legislation allowed for the holding of suspects indefinitely).
- Allows law enforcement officials greater subpoena power for e-mail records of terrorist suspects.
- Triples the number of border patrol personnel, customs service inspectors, and Immigration and Naturalization Service inspectors at the northern border of the United States, and provides $100 million to improve technology and equipment on the U.S. border with Canada.
- Expands measures against money laundering by requiring additional record keeping and reports for certain transactions and requiring identification of account holders.
- Eliminates the statute of limitations for prosecuting the most egregious terrorist acts but maintains the statute of limitation on most crimes at five to eight years.

The PATRIOT Act immediately sparked concern among citizens and organizations involved in protecting the civil rights and liberties of all Americans, although this concern only became more vocal as the time between the attacks increased due to the emotional sensitivities associated with what had transpired. The critics that have emerged, and which continue to emerge in growing numbers as the act is repeatedly renewed, have questioned the constitutionality of several of the act's provisions, and have expressed grave concerns regarding the methods by which some of those new authorities will be used by law enforcement agencies in their pursuit of terrorists.

The U.S. attorney general at the time, John Ashcroft, and the Department of Justice that operated under his direction, countered that these authorities are necessary if the U.S. government is to more effectively track and detain terrorists. Regardless, the act very quickly began generating lawsuits, resistance from community officials, and concern about the way its provisions were being used and abused outside of their intended scope in a way that affected everyday Americans with no association with terrorist activities. The sidebars titled "Patriotic Act Perspective" present two perspectives on the PATRIOT Act, one in opposition and the other in support.

Patriot Act Perspective — There Is Nothing Patriotic about the Patriot Act By Faith Purnell, *Daily Utah Chronicle* (published July 7, 2004)

The right to life, liberty, property and the overall pursuit of happiness are all luxuries to which Americans have become accustomed. For Americans, these familiar words represent pride in our nation, democracy and freedom.

However, thanks to the Patriot Act, these rights and freedoms are being challenged. The Patriot Act is basically a culmination of new powers given to law enforcement and intelligence agencies to help prevent future acts of terror and to increase the overall safety of this country.

In turn, this act has given the government virtually unlimited control as it now has access to the personal records of all Americans, including both medical and financial documents. The act allows telephones to be tapped and even grants entrance into private homes and offices.

Due to clever government tactics, many Americans are still unaware of this act and all that it includes. Governmental leaders disguise the act to make it appear as though it only affects the "bad guys." This is a total fallacy because it affects many unsuspecting Americans on a daily basis. The full title of the act is the USA PATRIOT Act: Uniting and Strengthening America by Providing Appropriate Tools Required to Intercept and Obstruct Terrorism Act.

But it has segregated, enraged and insulted Americans.

The ongoing debate as to whether or not the act crosses any moral lines proves to be extremely relevant in 2004 as further provisions are being made to create Patriot Act II. But perhaps more importantly, this issue could be used as a crucial piece of criteria to influence votes in the upcoming presidential election.

The most criticized and controversial aspect of the act is the manner in which it blatantly violates the privacy of individuals as a result of heightened surveillance procedures.

This one act alone completely contradicts and disregards several amendments, which include (but are perhaps not limited to) the First, Fourth, Fifth, Sixth and Eighth Amendments.

The Patriot Act has the power to deny any American citizen the freedom of speech, religion and assembly. Similarly, it can waive protection against unreasonable searches and seizures without probable cause or even deprive a citizen the right to life, liberty or property.

Restrictions like these are not only a complete invasion of privacy and freedom of choice, but also a direct insult to the American public, as it implies that we are criminals who need to be monitored.

In essence, the act strips us of our basic freedoms guaranteed by the Constitution and rejects the principles this great nation is built upon.

In opposing the Patriot Act, I am in no way being insensitive to the terrorist attacks of Sept. 11, nor toward the good intentions of this act; rather, I am calling for a more reasonable and thoughtful solution to the problem.

I fully appreciate this act for its efforts in fighting terrorism. However, I strongly believe that the individual rights of American citizens outweigh the need for such an act. Furthermore, I find it irresponsible of our government to react so quickly and irrationally without exploring less intrusive solutions. The Department of Justice suggests that the Patriot Act is necessary and vital in "preserving the life and liberty" of American citizens, but ironically the act is invading the life and liberty of American citizens.

It is important to note that the act is self defeating as it takes away precisely what it is trying to restore and preserve.

While I recognize the need to change with the times, I find it idiotic to suddenly change the values and morals this country has maintained for hundreds of years merely to satisfy the personal agendas of our governmental leaders.

In my estimation, by provoking this issue and taking a stand, we can ignite change and hope that the government reforms this act into one that maintains the freedoms and standards of all Americans.

Source: *Daily Utah Chronicle*, July 7, 2004, www.dailyutahchronicle.com.

Patriot Act Perspective: No Rights Have Been Violated By F. James Sensenbrenner, Jr., R-Wisconsin, *USA Today*, March 1, 2006.

Zero. That's the number of substantiated USA PATRIOT Act civil liberties violations. Extensive congressional oversight found no violations. Six reports by the Justice Department's independent inspector general, who is required to solicit and investigate any allegations of abuse, found no violations.

Intense public scrutiny has yet to find a single civil liberty abuse. Despite many challenges, no federal court has declared unconstitutional any of the Patriot Act provisions Congress is renewing.

Building upon this stellar record, congressional negotiators added more than 30 civil liberty safeguards not included in current law to ensure that the Patriot Act's authorities would not be abused in the future. Remarkably, that's still not enough for some.

So what has the Patriot Act done? It has been a tremendous asset in helping thwart other terrorist attacks. The Justice Department and other agencies have properly utilized these new tools to detect, disrupt and dismantle terrorist cells in New York, Virginia and Oregon before they strike. Since 9/11, the Justice Department has charged hundreds of defendants, of whom more than half have been convicted or pleaded guilty, as a result of terrorism-related investigations.

Most important, this renewal would permanently tear down the pre-9/11 "wall" that prevented the FBI and CIA from communicating. This law recognizes the vital importance of sharing information to "connect the dots." The Patriot Act has made it much more difficult for America's enemies to live openly among us as they plot to murder innocent Americans.

Regrettably, some criticizing the government for weak port security tried to block the Patriot Act renewal, which helps law enforcement strengthen port security. The law also combats terrorism financing networks and enhances penalties for attacks against railroads and mass transit. In short, the Patriot Act is an essential tool in the war on terror.

We must never forget we are a nation at war with an enemy determined to extinguish our nation, our values and our civil liberties. The Patriot Act has kept us safer and has not violated anyone's civil rights. It deserves to be renewed.

Source: USA Today, March 1, 2006, http://www.usatoday.com/news/opinion/editorials/2006-03-01-opposing-view_x.htm.

▨ ▨ Critical Thinking ▨

Do you feel that the USA PATRIOT Act counters the basic freedoms bestowed upon Americans by the drafters of the Constitution? Why or why not? Would you be willing to give up some of your freedom for increased security from terrorism?

In the seven years since the act's passage, numerous communities across the country have passed resolutions opposing parts or all of the act's contents. These resolutions began appearing as early as January 2002, when the city of Ann Arbor, Michigan voiced their opposition to what they saw as an attack on the basic freedoms and rights that Americans considered sacred. As of December 2007, these resolutions continue to appear, with the latest passed in the city of Wichita Falls, Texas on December 4. The American Civil Liberties Union (ACLU), which monitors these actions, registered 414 local, county, and state resolutions that had been passed as of January 1, 2008, with another 275 efforts currently under debate (to see a complete list of resolutions passed, see http://www.bordc. org/list.phpfisortoAlpha=1 or http://www.aclu.org/resolutions). Similar resolutions have been passed in the cities of Dallas, Denver, Detroit, Honolulu, Minneapolis, and Seattle, and at the state level in Vermont, Montana, Maine, Hawaii, and Alaska (Bill of Rights Defense Committee, 2007). One of these resolutions, from Eureka Springs, AR, passed on May 14, 2007, is presented in the sidebar titled "A Resolution in Support . . ."

▨ ▨ ▨ ▬▬

A Resolution in Support of the Constitutions of the United States and the State of Arkansas and in Opposition to the Loss of Any of Our Constitutional Freedoms
Passed May 14, 2007.

WHEREAS, the City Council of Eureka Springs, Arkansas, has been requested to oppose any lessening of our constitutionally granted freedoms; and

WHEREAS issues have recently arisen regarding the constitutionality of certain recent acts of the Federal government; and

WHEREAS, attacks against the United States such as those that occurred on September 11, 2001, have necessitated the crafting of laws to protect the public from terrorist attacks but, at the same time, those laws must not infringe on the civil liberties and rights of innocent people as guaranteed in the Constitution and Bill of Rights; and

WHEREAS, the USA PATRIOT Act was enacted by Congress on October 26, 2001 and reauthorized in March 2006; and

WHEREAS, within the USA PATRIOT Act are provisions expanding the scope of national security letters ("NSL"), an administrative subpoena primarily issued by the FBI compelling third parties to turn over certain information without court approval, and the scope of warrants for the production of "tangible things," issued by a secret court created by the Foreign Intelligence Surveillance Act ("215 orders"); and

WHEREAS, provisions of the USA PATRIOT Act prohibited indefinitely the recipients of NSLs and 215 orders from disclosing the contents of the notices and the very fact that they had received the notices; and

WHEREAS, following much criticism and two adverse court decisions, Congress on March 2006, amended the provisions pertaining to NSLs and 215 orders to allow the recipient of an NSL or a 215 order to challenge the validity of the NSL or the 215 order in court and to allow the recipient to challenge the gag in court; and

WHEREAS, questions persist about the constitutionality of the provisions pertaining to NSLs and 215 orders, as amended, because to prevail in a challenge a recipient must meet a high burden of proof and no exchanges of information, even those between attorney and client and physician and patient are deemed confidential; and

WHEREAS, the City of Eureka Springs, AR, collects and retains many sensitive and non public records which the federal government could seek by the means of NSL or 215 order, and desires to ensure that the constitutional rights of City residents, employees and other persons using City facilities and services are safeguarded.

Be it resolved by the City Council of the City of Eureka Springs, Arkansas,

Section 1. That we wholeheartedly support the Constitutions of the United States of America and the State of Arkansas and the Freedoms therein guaranteed and abide by the oaths we swore upon entering the offices to which we were elected;

Section 2. Be it further resolved that we support all efforts by legal means to maintain the freedoms promised to the citizens of Eureka Springs, AR, by these two great Documents.

Section 3. That the City Council of Eureka Springs, AR supports the government of the United States of America in its campaign against terrorism and affirms its commitment that the campaign not be waged at the expense of civil liberties of the people of this country and community.

Section 4. The Mayor shall critically examine any NSL that he or she may receive to determine if compliance would be unlawful and if so, the Mayor shall consider a challenge to the validity of the NSL in court.

Section 5. If the City receives an NSL which contains a statement prohibiting it from disclosing to any person, other than the attorney for the City and the Mayor, that the issuer of the NSL is seeking certain information, the Mayor shall consider challenging the prohibition in court. The Mayor may decide to challenge the prohibition even though he or she decides not to challenge the validity of the NSL.

Section 6. The Mayor shall examine any 215 order that the City may receive to determine if it was lawfully issued, and if it was not, the Mayor shall consider a challenge to the validity of the 215 order in court.

Section 7. If the Mayor receives a 215 order, the Mayor shall consider challenging the prohibition on disclosure in court, after one year has elapsed if such delay mandated under the reenacted Act is determined to be constitutional. The Mayor may decide to challenge the prohibition even though he or she decides not to challenge the validity of the 215 order.

Section 8. The City Council of Eureka Springs, AR, urges its Congressional representatives to address concerns about these provisions in the USA PATRIOT Act, as amended, and other statutes that infringe on civil liberties and to oppose pending and future legislation to the extent that it unconstitutionally infringes on the rights and liberties of the people of the United States.

Read and adopted this 14th day of May, 2007

Source: American Civil Liberties Union, http://www.bordc.org/detail.php?id=753.

The lawmakers who enacted the PATRIOT Act were aware that controversy would accompany most of its provisions for a long time to come. Many of these lawmakers, if not all of them, are in fact concerned about the welfare and civil liberties of citizens, so they set within the legislation various "sunset" clauses that stipulate dates of expiration for many of the legal authorities granted to law enforcement agencies. The first major round of expirations came on December 31, 2005. Debate about the various components of the act was heated, unlike in the weeks following the September 11 attacks. However, the salience of the counterterrorism movement was still very strong, and many of these sunset provisions were merely extended under the Act's reauthorization that resulted, the PATRIOT Act Improvement and Reauthorization Act of 2005, signed into law on March 6, 2006.

With the luxury of time, politics and constituent concerns become a factor in many lawmakers' decisions, and extended analysis and provisional arrangements are possible without the belief that such delays will cause harm or prevent any major breakthroughs in the war on terror. It is likely that the back-and-forth volley with civil liberties will continue for years to come, and it is certain that the direction these debates take will ultimately be a factor of whether or not future terrorist attacks occur — thereby either negating or reinforcing the perceived need for citizens to weaken their own civil liberties in the name of security. The PATRIOT Act sidebar describes the reauthorization legislation that became law on March 6, 2006.

The PATRIOT Act

The following "temporary" provisions of the PATRIOT Act were set according to the original 2001 legislation to expire on December 31, 2005:

201 — wiretapping in terrorism cases
202 — wiretapping in computer fraud and abuse felony cases
203(b) — sharing wiretap information
203(d) — sharing foreign intelligence information
204 — Foreign Intelligence Surveillance Act (FISA) pen register/trap and trace exceptions
206 — roving FISA wiretaps
207 — duration of FISA surveillance of non-U.S. persons who are agents of a foreign power
209 — seizure of voicemail messages pursuant to warrants
212 — emergency disclosure of electronic surveillance
214 — FISA pen register/trap and trace authority
215 — FISA access to tangible items
217 — interception of computer trespasser communications
218 — purpose for FISA orders
220 — nationwide service of search warrants for electronic evidence
223 — civil liability and discipline for privacy violations
225 — provider immunity for FISA wiretap assistance

Source: Congressional Research Service, www.au.af.mil/au/awc/awcgate/crs/rs21704.pdf.

The bill that ultimately passed in 2006, however, made permanent 14 of the provisions set to sunset, and put a new four-year sunset date on three of the provisions:

1. Section 215 (known as the "library records" provision, but which actually applies to "any tangible thing"), which does not require any individualized suspicion to get a court order for any record wanted in intelligence investigations;
2. Section 206 (known as "John Doe" roving wiretaps in intelligence investigations, which allow multiple phones to be tapped), which does not require law enforcement to ascertain that a suspected foreign terrorist is using the phones being listened to by government agents;
3. The lone wolf provision (added by the 2004 intelligence bill), which applies the Foreign Intelligence Surveillance Act's secret surveillance powers to non-U.S. citizens in this country but without requiring that they be acting for a foreign power and without sufficient safeguards

The reauthorization bill that became law made a number of other changes, including:

- It explicitly stated that any business receiving an order for records of employees or customers has a right to consult with a lawyer.
- It allows lawyers to be consulted about whether to challenge the demand for records (and literally "any tangible thing"), including financial or Internet transactions, they possess.
- It stated that businesses do not have to get permission to consult an attorney or tell the federal government they have sought legal advice.
- It stated that customers or employees whose sensitive personal records are demanded can never be told their records were turned over to the government, unless the gag order that accompanies the demands is discontinued.
- It made it so that gag orders are not automatic and need not be permanent restrictions on the free speech rights of businesses.
- It allows businesses to challenge gag orders they receive, noting that recipients will not be allowed to challenge any restriction on their free speech for a year, and it imposed what has been called by some an unconstitutional standard for those challenges. It states that, if a high-level political appointee certifies that national security or diplomatic relations will be harmed, the court must consider that assertion "conclusive" unless the recipient proves that assertion was made in "bad faith" — meaning the gag order will stand.
- Businesses now have an express right to challenge records orders under Section 215 of the PATRIOT Act. However, the president refused to include a standard expressly allowing doctors, lawyers, and priests to challenge any effort by government agents to get privileged communications from clients, patients, or penitents.
- According to the law, NSLs, which are issued by the FBI for financial records and Internet or phone logs without a court order, will be made more coercive and more punitive. They will become National Security Subpoenas (NSSs) and businesses that do not comply can be held in contempt by courts. Any employee — from the mail clerk to the CEO of a company — who intentionally discloses a demand for these records can go to jail for five years under the new law.
- The law includes an initial 7-day period of delay on sneak and peek search warrants, subject to exceptions and extensions. However, these secret search warrants can be issued by the court to search any home or business without any link to terrorism whatsoever or even an emergency.
- Under the new law, the PATRIOT Act's broad definition of domestic terrorism, previously defined to reach any state or federal misdemeanor or felony dangerous to life committed to change government policy, is now limited to specific federal terrorism crimes.
- The new law expands the power of the Secret Service to limit access to so-called "national security events," whether or not security is needed to protect the president. Anyone who uses false credentials or violates a Secret Service perimeter at one of these events, which include such things as the Super Bowl, for instance, can now be charged with a federal crime.

The new law adds additional death penalties to federal crimes linked to terrorism, and allows the attorney general to certify that a state's system of providing counsel to criminal defendants is adequate, despite the incompetent actions of untrained or negligent counsel in any individual case. (Sources: ACLU, "The Patriot Act: Where It Stands," 2007, http://action.aclu.org/reformthepatriot act/whereitstands.html; U.S. Department of Justice, "Fact Sheet: USA PATRIOT Act Improvement and Reauthorization Act of 2005," 2006, http://www.usdoj.gov/opa/pr/2006/March/06_opa_113.html.)

Of interesting note is that a handful of legislators, at the beckoning of the Bush administration, proposed legislation entitled the "Domestic Security Enhancement Act," which was nicknamed in the press "Patriot Act II." This draft legislation, however, never made it to debate following heavy opposition from groups such as the ACLU and the Bill of Rights Defense Committee, among others. Provisions of the February 7, 2003 draft version included:

- Removal of court-ordered prohibitions against police agencies spying on domestic groups
- The FBI would be granted powers to conduct searches and surveillance based on intelligence gathered in foreign countries without first obtaining a court order
- Creation of a DNA database of suspected terrorists
- Prohibition of any public disclosure of the names of alleged terrorists including those who have been arrested
- Exemptions from civil liability for people and businesses who voluntarily turn private information over to the government
- Criminalization of the use of encryption to conceal incriminating communications
- Automatic denial of bail for persons accused of terrorism-related crimes, reversing the ordinary common law burden-of-proof principle. All alleged terrorists would be required to demonstrate why they should be released on bail rather than the government being required to demonstrate why they should be held.
- Expansion of the list of crimes eligible for the death penalty
- The U.S. Environmental Protection Agency would be prevented from releasing "worst case scenario" information to the public about chemical plants.
- United States citizens whom the government finds to be either members of, or providing material support to, terrorist groups could have their U.S. citizenship revoked and be deported to foreign countries.

The sidebar, titled "Department of Justice Fact Sheet," is an excerpt in support of the PATRIOT Act. This fact sheet is interesting in terms of its contrast with individuals and groups voicing concern over the loss of civil liberties imposed by the passage of the act, such as that displayed in the "Patriot Act Perspective" sidebar.

Department of Justice Fact Sheet "The USA PATRIOT Act: Preserving Life and Liberty"

The following is the original text of the Department of Justice fact sheet:

The Department of Justice's first priority is to prevent future terrorist attacks. Since its passage following the September 11, 2001 attacks, the Patriot Act has played a key part — and often the leading role — in a number of successful operations to protect innocent Americans from the deadly plans of terrorists dedicated to destroying America and our way of life. While the results have been important, in passing the Patriot Act, Congress provided for only modest, incremental changes in the law. Congress simply took existing legal principles and retrofitted them to preserve the lives and liberty of the American people from the challenges posed by a global terrorist network.

Congress enacted the Patriot Act by overwhelming, bipartisan margins, arming law enforcement with new tools to detect and prevent terrorism: The USA PATRIOT Act was passed nearly unanimously by the Senate 98–1, and 357–66 in the House, with the support of members from across the political spectrum.

The Act Improves Our Counterterrorism Efforts in Several Significant Ways

1. The Patriot Act allows investigators to use the tools that were already available to investigate organized crime and drug trafficking. Many of the tools the Act provides to law enforcement to fight terrorism have been used for decades to fight organized crime and drug dealers, and have been reviewed and approved by the courts. As Sen. Joe Biden (D-DE) explained during the floor debate about the Act, "the FBI could get a wiretap to investigate the mafia, but they could not get one to investigate terrorists. To put it bluntly, that was crazy! What's good for the mob should be good for terrorists" (Cong. Rec., 10/25/01).

   - Allows law enforcement to use surveillance against more crimes of terror. Before the Patriot Act, courts could permit law enforcement to conduct electronic surveillance to investigate many ordinary, nonterrorism crimes, such as drug crimes, mail fraud, and passport fraud. Agents also could obtain wiretaps to investigate some, but not all, of the crimes that terrorists often commit. The Act enabled investigators to gather information when looking into the full range of terrorism-related crimes, including: chemical-weapons offenses, the use of weapons of mass destruction, killing Americans abroad, and terrorism financing.

   - Allows federal agents to follow sophisticated terrorists trained to evade detection. For years, law enforcement has been able to use "roving wiretaps" to investigate ordinary crimes, including drug offenses and racketeering. A roving wiretap can be authorized by a federal judge to apply to a particular suspect, rather than a particular phone or communications device. Because international terrorists are sophisticated and trained to thwart surveillance by rapidly changing locations and communication devices such as cell phones, the Act authorized agents to seek court permission to use the same techniques in national security investigations to track terrorists.

   - Allows law enforcement to conduct investigations without tipping off terrorists. In some cases if criminals are tipped off too early to an investigation, they might flee, destroy evidence, intimidate or kill witnesses, cut off contact with associates, or take other action to evade arrest. Therefore, federal courts in narrow circumstances long have allowed law enforcement to delay for a limited time when the subject is told that a judicially-approved search warrant has been executed. Notice is always provided, but the reasonable delay gives law enforcement time to identify the criminal's associates, eliminate immediate threats to our communities, and coordinate the arrests of multiple individuals without tipping them off beforehand. These delayed notification search warrants have been used for decades, have proven crucial in drug and organized crime cases, and have been upheld by courts as fully constitutional.

   - Allows federal agents to ask a court for an order to obtain business records in national security terrorism cases. Examining business records often provides the key that investigators are looking for to solve a wide range of crimes. Investigators might seek select records from hardware stores or chemical plants, for example, to find out who bought materials to make a bomb, or bank records to see who's sending money to terrorists. Law enforcement authorities have always been able to obtain business records in criminal cases through grand jury subpoenas, and continue to do so in national security cases where appropriate. These records were sought in criminal cases such as the investigation of the Zodiac gunman, where police suspected the gunman was inspired by a Scottish occult poet, and wanted to learn who had checked the poet's books out of the library. In national security cases where use of the grand jury process was not appropriate, investigators previously had limited tools at their disposal to obtain certain business records. Under the Patriot Act, the government can now ask a federal court (the Foreign Intelligence Surveillance Court), if needed to aid an investigation, to order production of the same type of records available through grand jury subpoenas. This federal court, however, can issue these orders only after the government demonstrates that the records concerned are sought for an authorized investigation to obtain foreign intelligence information not concerning a U.S. person or to protect against international terrorism or clandestine intelligence activities, provided that such investigation of a U.S. person is not conducted solely on the basis of activities protected by the First Amendment.

2. The Patriot Act facilitated information sharing and cooperation among government agencies so that they can better "connect the dots." The Act removed the major legal barriers that prevented the law enforcement, intelligence, and national defense communities from talking and coordinating their work to protect the American people and our national security. The government's prevention efforts should not be restricted by boxes on an organizational chart. Now police officers, FBI agents, federal prosecutors, and intelligence officials can protect our communities by "connecting the dots" to uncover terrorist plots before they are completed. As Sen. John Edwards (D-N.C.) said about the Patriot Act, "we simply cannot prevail in the battle against terrorism if the right hand of our government has no idea what the left hand is doing" (Press release, 10/26/01).

   • Prosecutors and investigators used information shared pursuant to section 218 in investigating the defendants in the so-called "Virginia Jihad" case. This prosecution involved members of the Dar al-Arqam Islamic Center, who trained for jihad in Northern Virginia by participating in paintball and paramilitary training, including eight individuals who traveled to terrorist training camps in Pakistan or Afghanistan between 1999 and 2001. These individuals are associates of a violent Islamic extremist group known as Lashkar-e-Taiba (LET), which operates in Pakistan and Kashmir, and that has ties to the al Qaeda terrorist network. As the result of an investigation that included the use of information obtained through FISA, prosecutors were able to bring charges against these individuals. Six of the defendants have pleaded guilty, and three were convicted in March 2004 of charges including conspiracy to levy war against the United States and conspiracy to provide material support to the Taliban. These nine defendants received sentences ranging from a prison term of four years to life imprisonment.

3. The Patriot Act updated the law to reflect new technologies and new threats. The Act brought the law up to date with current technology, so we no longer have to fight a digital-age battle with antique weapons — legal authorities leftover from the era of rotary telephones. When investigating the murder of *Wall Street Journal* reporter Daniel Pearl, for example, law enforcement used one of the Act's new authorities to use high-tech means to identify and locate some of the killers.

   • Allows law enforcement officials to obtain a search warrant anywhere a terrorist-related activity occurred. Before the Patriot Act, law enforcement personnel were required to obtain a search warrant in the district where they intended to conduct a search. However, modern terrorism investigations often span a number of districts, and officers therefore had to obtain multiple warrants in multiple jurisdictions, creating unnecessary delays. The Act provides that warrants can be obtained in any district in which terrorism-related activities occurred, regardless of where they will be executed. This provision does not change the standards governing the availability of a search warrant, but streamlines the search-warrant process.
   • Allows victims of computer hacking to request law enforcement assistance in monitoring the "trespassers" on their computers. This change made the law technology-neutral; it placed electronic trespassers on the same footing as physical

trespassers. Now, hacking victims can seek law enforcement assistance to combat hackers, just as burglary victims have been able to invite officers into their homes to catch burglars.

4. The Patriot Act increased the penalties for those who commit terrorist crimes. Americans are threatened as much by the terrorist who pays for a bomb as by the one who pushes the button. That's why the Patriot Act imposed tough new penalties on those who commit and support terrorist operations, both at home and abroad. In particular, the Act:

- Prohibits the harboring of terrorists. The Act created a new offense that prohibits knowingly harboring persons who have committed or are about to commit a variety of terrorist offenses, such as: destruction of aircraft; use of nuclear, chemical, or biological weapons; use of weapons of mass destruction; bombing of government property; sabotage of nuclear facilities; and aircraft piracy.

- Enhanced the inadequate maximum penalties for various crimes likely to be committed by terrorists: including arson, destruction of energy facilities, material support to terrorists and terrorist organizations, and destruction of national-defense materials.

- Enhanced a number of conspiracy penalties, including for arson, killings in federal facilities, attacking communications systems, material support to terrorists, sabotage of nuclear facilities, and interference with flight crew members. Under previous law, many terrorism statutes did not specifically prohibit engaging in conspiracies to commit the underlying offenses. In such cases, the government could only bring prosecutions under the general federal conspiracy provision, which carries a maximum penalty of only five years in prison.

- Punishes terrorist attacks on mass transit systems.

- Punishes bioterrorists.

- Eliminates the statutes of limitations for certain terrorism crimes and lengthens them for other terrorist crimes.

The government's success in preventing another catastrophic attack on the American homeland since September 11, 2001, would have been much more difficult, if not impossible, without the USA PATRIOT Act. The authorities Congress provided have substantially enhanced our ability to prevent, investigate, and prosecute acts of terror.

Source: U.S. Department of Justice, http://www.lifeandliberty.gov/highlights.htm.

Homeland Security Act of 2002

The legislation to establish a Department of Homeland Security was first introduced in the U.S. House of Representatives by Texas Representative Richard K. Armey on June 24, 2003. Similar legislation was introduced into the Senate soon after. After differences between the two bills were quickly ironed out, the Homeland Security Act of 2002 (P.L. 107-296) was passed by both houses and signed into law by President Bush on November 25, 2002.

The Homeland Security Act provided authorization for a full range of federal government changes that came in response to not only the events of September 11, but the perceived inefficiencies in the government organization and operation that directly resulted in the vulnerabilities that allowed for such an event, and by logic, possible future attacks by similar terrorist organizations, to occur.

The act established the Department of Homeland Security within the executive branch, with the DHS secretary reporting directly to the president.

The act, which is outlined in Chapter 3 with regard to its organizational changes and makeup, outlined the DHS management structure, identified those agencies and programs to be migrated to the DHS, and detailed the roles and responsibilities of the five directorates that make up the DHS: Information Analysis and Infrastructure Protection, Science and Technology, Border and Transportation Security, Emergency Preparedness, and Response and Management. The act called for the migration of the Secret Service and the Coast Guard to the DHS and transfers the Bureau of Alcohol, Tobacco, Firearms, and Explosives from the Treasury Department to the DOJ. The act also established within the executive office of the president the Homeland Security Council to advise the president on homeland security matters and the Office for State and Local Coordination and Preparedness reporting to the DHS secretary.

Homeland Security Presidential Directive No. 5

On February 28, 2003, the White House released Homeland Security Presidential Directive No. 5 (HSPD-5) to enhance the ability of the United States to manage domestic incidents. The directive proclaimed that this would be done through the establishment of a single, comprehensive National Incident Management System (NIMS).

HSPD-5 tasked the DHS secretary to develop and administer NIMS, and subsequently a National Response Plan (NRP), which would replace the oft-applied and highly acclaimed Federal Response Plan. HSPD-5 set a timeframe for the development of initial versions of these documents, consultation with other federal agencies, and adoption by state and local departments and agencies. As of January 2005, all of these actions had taken place. Excerpts from the text of HSPD-5 are presented in the sidebar titled "Excerpts from Homeland Security Presidential Directive No. 5."

Excerpts from Homeland Security Presidential Directive No. 5: Management of Domestic Incidents

Purpose

To enhance the ability of the United States to manage domestic incidents by establishing a single, comprehensive national incident management system.

Policy

- To prevent, prepare for, respond to, and recover from terrorist attacks, major disasters, and other emergencies, the U.S. government (USG) shall establish a single, comprehensive approach to domestic incident management. The objective of the USG is to ensure that all levels of government across the nation have the capability to work efficiently and effectively together, using a national approach to domestic incident management. In these efforts, with regard to domestic incidents, the USG treats crisis management and consequence management as a single, integrated function, rather than as two separate functions.

- The secretary of Homeland Security is the principal Federal official for domestic incident management. Pursuant to the Homeland Security Act of 2002, the secretary is responsible for coordinating Federal operations within the United States to prepare for, respond to, and recover from terrorist attacks, major disasters, and other emergencies. The secretary shall coordinate the Federal government's resources utilized in response to or recovery from terrorist attacks, major disasters, or other emergencies if and when any one of the following four conditions applies: (1) a Federal department or agency acting under its own authority has requested the assistance of the secretary; (2) the resources of state and local authorities are overwhelmed and Federal assistance has been requested by the appropriate state and local authorities; (3) more than one Federal department or agency has become substantially involved in responding to the incident; or (4) the secretary has been directed to assume responsibility for managing the domestic incident by the president.

- Nothing in this directive alters, or impedes the ability to carry out, the authorities of Federal departments and agencies to perform their responsibilities under law. All Federal departments and agencies shall cooperate with the secretary in the secretary's domestic incident management role.

- The Federal government recognizes the roles and responsibilities of state and local authorities in domestic incident management. Initial responsibility for managing domestic incidents generally falls on state and local authorities. The Federal government will assist state and local authorities when their resources are overwhelmed, or when Federal interests are involved. The secretary will coordinate with state and local governments to ensure adequate planning, equipment, training, and exercise activities. The secretary will also provide assistance to state and local governments to develop all-hazards plans and capabilities, including those of greatest importance to the security of the United States, and will ensure that state, local, and Federal plans are compatible.

- The Federal government recognizes the role that the private and nongovernmental sectors play in preventing, preparing for, responding to, and recovering from terrorist attacks, major disasters, and other emergencies. The secretary will coordinate with the private and nongovernmental sectors to ensure adequate planning, equipment, training, and exercise activities and to promote partnerships to address incident management capabilities.

- The attorney general has lead responsibility for criminal investigations of terrorist acts or terrorist threats by individuals or groups inside the United States, or directed at United States citizens or institutions abroad, where such acts are within the Federal criminal jurisdiction of the United States, as well as for related intelligence collection activities within the United States, subject to the National Security Act of 1947 and other applicable law, EO 12333, and attorney general–approved procedures pursuant to that executive order. Generally acting through the Federal Bureau of Investigation, the attorney general, in cooperation with other Federal departments and agencies engaged in activities to protect our national security, shall also coordinate the activities of the other members of the law enforcement community to detect, prevent, preempt, and disrupt terrorist attacks against the United States. Following a terrorist threat or an actual incident that falls within the criminal jurisdiction of the United States, the full capabilities of the United States shall be dedicated, consistent with United States law and with activities of other Federal departments and agencies to protect our national security, to assisting the attorney general to identify the perpetrators and bring them to justice. The attorney general and the secretary shall establish appropriate relationships and mechanisms for cooperation and coordination between their two departments.

- Nothing in this directive impairs or otherwise affects the authority of the secretary of defense over the Department of Defense, including the chain of command for military forces from the president as commander in chief, to the secretary of defense, to the commander of military forces, or military command and control procedures. The secretary of defense shall provide military support to civil authorities for domestic incidents as directed by the president or when consistent with military readiness and appropriate under the circumstances and the law. The secretary of defense shall retain command of military forces providing civil support. The secretary of defense and the secretary shall establish appropriate relationships and mechanisms for cooperation and coordination between their two departments.

- The secretary of state has the responsibility, consistent with other United States government activities to protect our national security, to coordinate international activities related to the prevention, preparation, response, and recovery from a domestic incident, and for the protection of United States citizens and United States interests overseas. The secretary of state and the secretary shall establish appropriate relationships and mechanisms for cooperation and coordination between their two departments.

- The assistant to the president for Homeland Security and the assistant to the president for National Security Affairs shall be responsible for interagency policy coordination on domestic and international incident management, respectively, as directed by the president. The assistant to the president for Homeland Security and the assistant to the president for National Security Affairs shall work together to ensure that the United States' domestic and international incident management efforts are seamlessly united.

- The secretary shall ensure that, as appropriate, information related to domestic incidents is gathered and provided to the public, the private sector, state and local authorities, Federal departments and agencies, and, generally through the assistant to the president for Homeland Security, to the president. The secretary shall provide standardized, quantitative reports to the assistant to the president for Homeland Security on the readiness and preparedness of the nation — at all levels of government — to prevent, prepare for, respond to, and recover from domestic incidents.

- Nothing in this directive shall be construed to grant to any assistant to the president any authority to issue orders to Federal departments and agencies, their officers, or their employees.

Tasking

- The heads of all Federal departments and agencies are directed to provide their full and prompt cooperation, resources, and support, as appropriate and consistent with their own responsibilities for protecting our national security, to the secretary, the attorney general, the secretary of defense, and the secretary of state in the exercise of the individual leadership responsibilities and missions assigned above.

- The secretary shall develop, submit for review to the Homeland Security Council, and administer a National Incident Management System (NIMS). This system will provide a consistent nationwide approach for Federal, State, and local governments to work effectively and efficiently together to prepare for, respond to, and recover from domestic incidents, regardless of cause, size, or complexity. To provide for interoperability and compatibility among Federal, State, and local capabilities, the NIMS will include a core set of concepts, principles, terminology, and technologies covering the incident command system; multi-agency coordination systems; unified command; training; identification and management of resources (including systems for classifying types of resources); qualifications and certification; and the collection, tracking, and reporting of incident information and incident resources.

- The secretary shall develop, submit for review to the Homeland Security Council, and administer a National Response Plan (NRP). The secretary shall consult with appropriate assistants to the president (including the assistant to the president for Economic Policy) and the director of the office of Science and Technology Policy, and other such Federal officials as may be appropriate, in developing and implementing the NRP. This plan shall integrate Federal government domestic prevention, preparedness, response, and recovery plans into one all-discipline, all-hazards plan. The NRP shall be unclassified. If certain operational aspects require classification, they shall be included in classified annexes to the NRP.

- The NRP, using the NIMS, shall, with regard to response to domestic incidents, provide the structure and mechanisms for national level policy and operational direction for Federal support to state and local incident managers and for exercising direct Federal authorities and responsibilities, as appropriate.
- The NRP will include protocols for operating under different threats or threat levels; incorporation of existing Federal emergency and incident management plans (with appropriate modifications and revisions) as either integrated components of the NRP or as supporting operational plans; and additional operational plans or annexes, as appropriate, including public affairs and intergovernmental communications.
- The NRP will include a consistent approach to reporting incidents, providing assessments, and making recommendations to the president, the secretary, and the Homeland Security Council.
- The NRP will include rigorous requirements for continuous improvements from testing, exercising, experience with incidents, and new information and technologies.

Source: Office of the Press Secretary, the White House.

NIMS was designed to integrate emergency management practices, including mitigation, preparedness, response, and recovery, at all government levels, including federal, state, and local, into a comprehensive national framework. NIMS's central mission is tenable responders at all levels to work together more effectively to manage domestic incidents regardless of the cause, size, or complexity. The benefits of the NIMS, as stated by FEMA, include the following:

- Standardized organizational structures, processes, and procedures
- Standards for planning, training and exercising, and personnel qualification standards
- Equipment acquisition and certification standards
- Interoperable communications processes, procedures, and systems
- Information management systems
- Supporting technologies — voice and data communications systems, information systems, data display systems, and specialized technologies

The NRP, which was replaced in early 2008 with the new National Response Framework (NRF), was considered a single, comprehensive framework for the management of domestic incidents (which almost always involve many participants from all levels of government). The plan, like the framework that replaced it, directly addressed the prevention of terrorist attacks and the reduction in vulnerability to all natural and human-made hazards. Finally, it offered guidance on minimizing the damage and assisting in the recovery from any type of incident that occurred.

The NIMS, the NRP, and the NRF are each explained in much greater detail in Chapter 7.

The Post-Katrina Emergency Management Reform Act

Hurricane Katrina, which struck on August 29 of 2005 and resulted in the death of over 1,800 people (and the destruction of billions of dollars in housing stock and other infrastructure), exposed significant problems with the United States' emergency management framework. Clearly, the terrorism focus had been maintained at the expense of preparedness and response capacity for other hazards, namely the natural disasters that have proven to be much more likely to occur. FEMA, and likewise DHS, were highly criticized by the public and by Congress in the months following the 2005 hurricane season. In response, Congress passed the Post-Katrina Emergency Management Reform Act (H.R. 5441, Public Law 109-295), signed into law by the president on October 4, 2006.

This law established several new leadership positions within the Department of Homeland Security, moved additional functions into (several were simply returned) the Federal Emergency Management Agency (FEMA), created and reallocated functions to other components within DHS, and amended the Homeland Security Act in ways that directly and indirectly affected the organization and functions of various entities within DHS. The changes were required to have gone into effect by March 31, 2007. Transfers that were mandated by the Post-Katrina Emergency Management Reform Act included (with the exception of certain offices as listed in the Act):

- United States Fire Administration (USFA)
- Office of Grants and Training (G&T)
- Chemical Stockpile Emergency Preparedness Division (CSEP)
- Radiological Emergency Preparedness Program (REPP)
- Office of National Capital Region Coordination (NCRC)

The law determined that the head of FEMA, at the time R. David Paulison, would take on the new title of administrator. This official would now be supported by two deputy administrators. One is the deputy administrator and chief operating officer, who serves as the principal deputy and maintains overall operational responsibilities at FEMA. The other is the deputy administrator for National Preparedness, a new division created within FEMA.

The National Preparedness Division under FEMA included several existing FEMA programs, and several programs that were moved into the former Preparedness Directorate. This division focuses on emergency preparedness policy, contingency planning, exercise coordination and evaluation, emergency management training, and hazard mitigation (with respect to the Chemical Stockpile Emergency Preparedness (CSEP), and Radiological Emergency Preparedness Program (REPP) programs). The National Preparedness Division oversees two new divisions: Readiness, Prevention and Planning (RPP), and the National Integration Center (NIC). Readiness, Prevention and Planning is now the central office within FEMA handling preparedness policy and planning functions. The National Integration Center maintains the National Incident Management System (NIMS), the National Response Plan (NRP), and coordinates activities with the U.S. Fire Administration.

The existing Office of Grants and Training was moved into the newly expanded FEMA and was renamed the "Office of Grant Programs." The Training and Systems Support Divisions of the Office of Grants and Training was transferred into the National Integration Center (NIC). The Office of the Citizen Corps was transferred into the FEMA Office of Readiness, Prevention and Planning.

Additional headquarters positions created at FEMA by the new law included a Disability Coordinator (located in the FEMA Office of Equal Rights), a Small State and Rural Advocate, a Law Enforcement Advisor to the Administrator, and a National Advisory Council.

This act specifically excluded certain elements of the former DHS Preparedness Directorate from transfer into FEMA. The Preparedness Directorate was renamed the National Protection and Programs Directorate (NPPD), and it remained under the direction of DHS Under Secretary George Foresman. This Directorate includes the following offices:

- Office of the Under Secretary
- Office of Infrastructure Protection: This office identifies risks, threats, and vulnerabilities to critical infrastructure, and develops methods to mitigate them.
- Office of Cybersecurity and Communications (CS&C): CS&C was a combination of the Office of Cybersecurity and Telecommunications, the Office of the Manager of the National Communications System, and a new Office of Emergency Communications. CS&C focuses both on cybersecurity and on emergency and interoperable communications, identifying cyber

vulnerabilities and threats, and helps protect against and respond to cyberbased attacks, including performing analysis on the potential consequences of a successful attack.

- Office of Risk Management and Analysis: This office, formerly located within the Office of Infrastructure Protection, now reports directly to the under secretary and has expanded its focus from physical critical infrastructure to cybersecurity and other risk analysis areas.

- Office of Intergovernmental Programs: This office provides a department-level focal point for "coordinating communications and policies with departmental leadership, and ensuring consistent and coordinated component level interactions" (DHS, 2007).

- US-VISIT: This immigration-related office maintained its former role, but was administratively relocated to the National Protection and Programs Directorate.

And finally, the law created the Office of Health Affairs (OHA). OHA is led by the Chief Medical Officer, who was given the title of Assistant Secretary for Health Affairs and Chief Medical Officer. The Office of Health Affairs has three main divisions:

- Weapons of Mass Destruction (WMD) and Biodefense: This division is led by a deputy assistant secretary and it leads the department's biodefense activities, including the Bioshield and BioWatch programs (which were transferred from S&T) and the National Biosurveillance Integration System (which was transferred to OHA from Infrastructure Protection).

- Medical Readiness: This division oversees contingency planning, readiness of medical first responders, WMD incident management support, and medical preparedness grant coordination.

- Component Services: This division provides policy, standards, requirements, and metrics for DHS's occupational health and safety programs, and provides protective and operational medical services within DHS.

▨▨ Critical Thinking ▨

Several legislators and key emergency management officials proclaimed that, in order to truly reform emergency management in the United States, FEMA would have to be removed from the Department of Homeland Security and returned to its cabinet-level status. Do you agree or disagree with their sentiments, and why?

Future Legislation

Numerous possibilities exist for future legislation and executive action concerning homeland security in the United States. The range of topical areas covered under the umbrella of this function is expansive, ranging from immigration to weapons of mass destruction. These numerous bills are met with varying degrees of success, with little consistency in what kinds of issues result in the passage of laws and what types of bills eventually flounder in debate. One particular area that came under discussion, in 2003, is how communities, families, and individuals could become better prepared to respond to terrorist attacks. In September 2003, congressional members of the House Select Committee on Homeland Security proposed the Preparing America to Respond Effectively (PREPARE) Act of 2003 (full title, "To amend the Homeland Security Act of 2002 to establish a task force to determine essential capabilities for State and local jurisdictions to prevent, prepare for, and respond to acts of terrorism, to authorize the Secretary of Homeland Security to make grants to State and local governments to achieve such capability, and for other purposes"), which was billed as a comprehensive approach to prepare the nation to respond to acts of terrorism. The major elements of the PREPARE Act were as follows:

- Meeting the needs of first responders
- Making sense of threat alerts

- Improving information sharing
- Providing interoperable communications and equipment
- Encouraging participation of "second responders"
- Educating schoolchildren to be prepared

On October 5, 2003, this bill was referred to the Subcommittee on Telecommunications and the Internet, but never moved further. When the 108th congressional session ended, the bill was cleared from the books unresolved. However, several other bills have survived the legislative process and have led to new laws. While few have been as broad in nature as the USA PATRIOT Act and the Homeland Security Act of 2002, each of these has addressed some recognized or perceived shortfall in the nation's homeland security system. The furious pace with which homeland security–related bills are introduced has yet to subside, even seven full years following the terrorist events that spurred them. The sidebar titled "Select Legislation . . ." illustrates the range of homeland security and terrorism legislation introduced, under debate, and enacted by the U.S. Congress.

Select Legislation Relating to Homeland Security and Terrorism under Consideration

2007

H.R. 2290 — Cyber-Security Enhancement Act of 2007 (Introduced May 14, 2007)

H.R. 2761 — Terrorism Risk Insurance Revision and Extension Act of 2007 (Passed House, Passed Senate; November 16, 2007)

H.R. 3469 — America's Border Security Act of 2007 (Introduced August 4, 2007)

S. 735 — Terrorism Hoax Improvements Act of 2007 (Placed on Senate Legislative Calendar under General Orders, May 7, 2007)

S. 385 — Interoperable Emergency Communications Act (Placed on Senate Legislative Calendar under General Orders, March 5, 2007)

H.R. 1401 — Rail and Public Transportation Security Act of 2007 (Passed House, March 27, 2007)

S. 4 — Improving America's Security Act of 2007 (Passed Senate, March 13, 2007)

H.R. 599 — To Direct the Secretary of Homeland Security to Streamline the SAFETY Act and Antiterrorism Technology Procurement Processes (Passed House, January 23, 2007)

H.R. 1 — Implementing Recommendations of the 9/11 Commission Act of 2007 (Enacted, August 3, 2007)

H.R. 1717 — To Amend the Homeland Security Act of 2002 to Establish a National Bio- and Agro-defense Facility (Ordered to be Amended by Voice Vote, August 1, 2007)

S. 1294 — Homeland Security Education Act (Introduced May 3, 2007)

S. 807 — Agricultural Protection and Prosperity Act of 2007 (Introduced March 8, 2007)

H.R. 1398 — Agricultural Protection and Prosperity Act of 2007 (Introduced March 8, 2007)

H.R. 1392 — Homeland Security Transparency Act of 2007 (Introduced March 7, 2007)

H.R. 1796 — National Emergency Centers Establishment Act of 2007 (Introduced March 29, 2007)

S. 1018 — Global Climate Change Security Oversight Act (Introduced March 28, 2007)

S. 547 — Effective Homeland Security Management Act of 2007 (Introduced February 12, 2007)

S. 509 — Aviation Security Improvement Act (Placed on Senate Legislative Calendar under General Orders, March 5, 2007)

H.R. 1715 — Domestic Preparedness Act of 2007 (Introduced March 27, 2007)

H.R. 1695 — Preventing Radicalism by Exploiting and Vetting Its Emergence as a National Threat (PREVENT) Act (Introduced March 26, 2007)

H.R. 1686 — Department of Homeland Security Secure American Federal Equipment Procurement Act (DHS SAFE Procurement Act) (Introduced March 26, 2007)

H.R. 1685 — Data Security Act of 2007 (Introduced March 26, 2007)

H.R. 1640 — Protecting Americans Fighting Terrorism Act of 2007 (Introduced March 22, 2007)

H.R. 1633 — To Amend the Homeland Security Act of 2002 to prohibit the Secretary of Homeland Security from prescribing regulations that preempt more stringent State regulations governing chemical facility security (Introduced March 21, 2007)

H.R. 1574 — Safe Facilities Act (Introduced March 19, 2007)

H.R. 1530 — Chemical Facility Security Improvement Act of 2007 (Introduced March 15, 2007)

H.R. 1493 — Public Transportation and Rail Security Assistance Act of 2007 (Introduced March 13, 2007)

H.R. 1290 — Biosurveillance Enhancements Act of 2007 (Introduced March 1, 2007)

H.R. 296 — Urban Areas Security Initiative Improvement Act of 2007 (Introduced January 5, 2007)

H.R. 143 — To Provide for the Security of Critical Energy Infrastructure (Introduced January 4, 2007)

S. 83 — Rail Security Act of 2007 (Introduced January 4, 2007)

H.R. 534 — Rail Transit Security and Safety Act of 2007 (Introduced January 17, 2007)

S. 328 — Ensuring Implementation of the 9/11 Commission Report Act (Introduced January 17, 2007)

S. 184 — Surface Transportation and Rail Security Act of 2007 (Amendments Proposed by Senator Inouye from Committee on Commerce, Science, and Transportation, March 1, 2007)

S. 608 — Risk-Based Homeland Security Grants Act of 2007 (Introduced February 15, 2007)

2006*

S. 3678 — Pandemic and All-Hazards Preparedness Act (Enacted December 19, 2006)

S. 2271 — USA PATRIOT Act Additional Reauthorizing Amendments Act of 2006 (Enacted March 9, 2006)

S. 3875 — Real Security Act of 2006

H.R. 4981 — Dam Safety Act of 2006

H.R. 4942 — Promoting Antiterrorism Capabilities through International Cooperation Act

H.R. 6094 — Community Protection Act of 2006

H.R. 6061 — Secure Fence Act of 2006 (Enacted October 26, 2006)

H.R. 4954 — SAFE Port Act (Enacted October 13, 2007)

H.R. 5318 — Cyber-Security Enhancement and Consumer Data Protection Act of 2006

H.R. 5351 — National Emergency Management Reform and Enhancement Act of 2006

S. 2791 — Maritime Security Improvement Act of 2006

H.R. 3199 — USA PATRIOT Improvement and Reauthorization Act of 2005 (Enacted March 9, 2006)

S. 2454 — Securing America's Borders Act

S. 2145 — Chemical Facility Anti-Terrorism Act of 2006

H.R. 4941 — Homeland Security Science and Technology Enhancement Act of 2006

H.R. 5695 — Chemical Facility Anti-Terrorism Act of 2006

S. 1052 — Transportation Security Improvements Act of 2005

S. 3721 — Post-Katrina Emergency Management Reform Act of 2006

H.R. 6286 — DHS Stabilization and Security Enhancement Act of 2006

H.R. 6306 — Immigration and Border Security Act

H.R. 5441 — Post-Katrina Emergency Management Reform Act (Enacted October 4, 2006)

2005*

H.R. 4312 — Border Security and Terrorism Prevention Act of 2005

S. 2032 — Public Transportation Terrorism Prevention Act of 2005

S. 1266 — An original bill to permanently authorize certain provisions of the USA PATRIOT Act of 2001, to reauthorize a provision of the Intelligence Reform and Terrorism Prevention Act of 2004, to clarify certain definitions in the Foreign Intelligence Surveillance Act of 1978, to provide additional investigative tools necessary to protect the national security, and for other purposes

S. 21 — Homeland Security Grant Enhancement Act of 2005

H.R. 2237 — To help protect the public against the threat of chemical attacks

H.R. 2101 — To amend the Homeland Security Act of 2002 to direct the Secretary of Homeland Security to develop and implement the READICall emergency alert system

S. 1052 — A bill to improve transportation security, and for other purposes

H.R. 2351 — To provide for the safety and security of United States railroads, passengers, workers, and communities, and to establish an assistance program for families of passengers involved in rail accidents

H.R. 1794 — To direct the Secretary of Homeland Security to procure the development and provision of improved and up-to-date communications equipment for the New York City Fire Department, including radios

H.R. 1544 — Faster and Smarter Funding for First Responders Act of 2005

S. 1013 — A bill to improve the allocation of grants through the Department of Homeland Security, and for other purposes

S. 1032 — A bill to improve seaport security

H.R. 1763 — To increase criminal penalties relating to terrorist murders, deny Federal benefits to terrorists, and for other purposes

S. 975 — Project Bioshield II Act of 2005 (A bill to provide incentives to increase research by private sector entities to develop medical countermeasures to prevent, detect, identify, contain, and treat illnesses, including those associated with biological, chemical, nuclear, or radiological weapons attack or an infectious disease outbreak, and for other purposes)

H.R. 1731 — To improve the security of the Nation's ports by providing Federal grants to support Area Maritime Transportation Security Plans and to address vulnerabilities in port areas identified in approved vulnerability assessments or by the Secretary of Homeland Security

S. 969 — A bill to amend the Public Health Service Act with respect to preparation for an influenza pandemic, including an avian influenza pandemic, and for other purposes

H.R. 1805 — To establish the position of Northern Border Coordinator in the Department of Homeland Security

S. 629 — Railroad Carriers and Mass Transportation Protection Act of 2005

H.R. 1562 — To protect human health and the environment from the release of hazardous substances by acts of terrorism

H.R. 1795 — To amend the Robert T. Stafford Disaster Relief and Emergency Assistance Act to modify the terms of the community disaster loan program, to authorize assistance under that program for losses related to the terrorist attacks of September 11, 2001, and for other purposes

S. 378 — Reducing Crime and Terrorism at America's Seaports Act of 2005

H.R. 285 — To amend the Homeland Security Act of 2002 to enhance cybersecurity, and for other purposes

S. 855 — A bill to improve the security of the Nation's ports by providing Federal grants to support Area Maritime Transportation Security Plans and to address vulnerabilities in port areas identified in approved vulnerability assessments or by the Secretary of Homeland Security

S. 773 — A bill to ensure the safe and secure transportation by rail of extremely hazardous materials

S. 3 — A bill to strengthen and protect America in the war on terror

S. 729 — A bill to establish the Food Safety Administration to protect the public health by preventing food-borne illness, ensuring the safety of food, improving research on contaminants leading to food-borne illness, and improving security of food from intentional contamination, and for other purposes

S. 737 — A bill to amend the USA PATRIOT Act to place reasonable limitations on the use of surveillance and the issuance of search warrants, and for other purposes

H.R. 1320 — To secure the borders of the United States, and for other purposes

H.R. 1419 — To require that Homeland Security grants related to terrorism preparedness and prevention be awarded based strictly on an assessment of risk, threat, and vulnerabilities

H.R. 796 — To authorize the Secretary of Homeland Security to make grants to address homeland security preparedness shortcomings of units of municipal and county government

H.R. 895 — To provide for interagency planning for preparing for, defending against, and responding to the consequences of terrorist attacks against the Yucca Mountain Project, and for other purposes

S. 573 — A bill to improve the response of the federal government to agroterrorism and agricultural diseases

S. 572 — A bill to amend the Homeland Security Act of 2002 to give additional biosecurity responsibilities to the Department of Homeland Security

H.R. 1116 — To direct the Secretary of Homeland Security to carry out activities to assess and reduce the vulnerabilities of public transportation systems

S. 12 — A bill to combat international terrorism, and for other purposes

H.R. 228 — To establish a realistic, threat-based allocation of grant funds for first responders

H.R. 173 — To prevent and respond to terrorism and crime at or through ports

H.R. 418 — REAL ID Act of 2005

S. 376 — A bill to improve intermodal shipping container transportation security

H.R. 665 — To prevent access by terrorists to nuclear material, technology, and expertise, to establish an Office of Nonproliferation Programs in the Executive Office of the President, and for other purposes

S. 317 — A bill to protect privacy by limiting the access of the government to library, bookseller, and other personal records for foreign intelligence and counterintelligence purposes

H.R. 3704 — Protecting America Together Act of 2005

H.R. 3656 — National Emergency Management Restoration and Improvement Act

H.R. 3686 — Federal Disaster Response Improvement Act of 2005

H.R. 3659 — FEMA Reorganization Bill

H.R. 3816 — FEMA Reorganization Bill

H.R. 3805 — To Establish within the Office of the DHS Inspector General the Special Office of the Inspector General for Natural Disaster Response and Reconstruction

S. 1866 — Homeland Security Policy Act of 2005

H.R. 4009 — Homeland Security Reform Act of 2005
S. 1916 — Strengthening America's Security Act of 2005

2004*

S. 15 — Project BioShield Act of 2004 (Enacted July 21, 2004)
S. 2845 — Intelligence Reform and Terrorism Prevention Act of 2004 (Enacted December 17, 2004)
S. 2635 — A bill to establish an intergovernmental grant program to identify and develop homeland security information, equipment, capabilities, technologies, and services to further the homeland security needs of the United States and to address the homeland security needs of Federal, State, and local governments
S. 2393 — Aviation Security Advancement Act
S. 3010 — Firefighters Special Operation Task Force Act
H.R. 5392 — Volunteer First Responder Fairness Act of 2004
S. 2980 — Nunn-Lugar Cooperative Threat Reduction Act of 2004
H.R. 5329 — Disaster Area Health and Environmental Monitoring Act of 2004
H.R. 5326 — To provide additional security for nuclear facilities under certain circumstances
H.R. 5259 — Safe Food Act of 2004, and S. 2910 — Safe Food Act of 2004
H.R. 5082 — Public Transportation Terrorism Prevention and Response Act of 2004
S. 666 — Biological, Chemical, and Radiological Weapons Countermeasures Research Act
H.R. 5217 — Railroad Security and Public Awareness Act of 2004
H.R. 5223 — National Intelligence Reform Act of 2004
S. 2884 — Public Transportation Terrorism Prevention Act of 2004
S. 2273 — Rail Security Act of 2004
H.R. 5130 — Secure Borders Act
H.R. 5159 — Community Security Act
S. 2840 — National Intelligence Reform Act of 2004
H.R. 5150 — National Intelligence Reform Act of 2004
H.R. 5132 — Rail and Public Transportation Security Act of 2004
H.R. 5121 — To further protect the United States aviation system from terrorist attacks
S. 2279 — Maritime Transportation Security Act of 2004
H.R. 5118 — Prevention of Terrorist Access to Destructive Weapons Act of 2004
S. 2811 — 9-11 Act
H.R. 5068 — Department of Homeland Security Cybersecurity Enhancement Act of 2004
H.R. 5054 — Hardened Containers for Air Cargo Security Act of 2004
H.R. 5050 — Director of National Intelligence Act of 2004
S. 430 — Agriculture Security Preparedness Act
H.R. 4056 — Commercial Aviation MANPADS Defense Act of 2004
H.R. 4810 — Direct Funding for First Responders Act of 2004
H.R. 4883 — Terrorism against Animal-Use Entities Prohibition Improvement Act of 2004
S. 779 — Wastewater Treatment Works Security and Safety Act
S. 2726 — Flight Attendant Security Training Act
S. 2679 — Tools to Fight Terrorism Act of 2004
S. 2665 — Weapons of Mass Destruction Prohibition Improvement Act of 2004
H.R. 4830 — Private Sector Preparedness Act of 2004
H.R. 4824 — Extremely Hazardous Materials Transportation Security Act of 2004
S. 2653 — Reducing Crime and Terrorism at America's Seaport Act of 2004
S. 2632 — First Responders Homeland Defense Act of 2004
H.R. 3712 — United States Seaport Multiyear Security Enhancement Act

H.R. 4454 — Ecoterrorism Prevention Act of 2004

H.R. 4355 — Secure COAST Act

H.R. 4108 — High Risk Nonprofit Security Enhancement Act of 2004

H.R. 4361 — Safe TRAINS Act

S. 994 — Chemical Facilities Security Act of 2004

H.R. 4126 — Cockpit Security Technical Corrections and Improvements Act of 2004

H.R. 4008 — Anti-Terrorism Protection of Mass Transportation and Railroad Carriers Act of 2004

H.R. 4104 — Intelligence Transformation Act of 2004

S. 2239 — First Responders Homeland Defense Act of 2004

S. 930 — Emergency Preparedness and Response Act of 2003

H.R. 3798 — Secure Existing Aviation Loopholes Act

2003*

S. 1152 — Firefighting Research and Coordination Act (Enacted December 6, 2003)

H.R. 3644 — Homeland Security Technology Improvement Act of 2003

H.R. 3562 — Prevent Act of 2003

H.R. 2512 — First Responders Funding Reform Act of 2003

S. 1882 — Terrorist Apprehension Act

S. 1866 — Security Enhancement Act of 2003

H.R. 3456 — Port Anti-Terrorism and Security Act of 2003

S. 1657 — A bill to amend Section 44921 of Title 49, United States Code, to provide for the arming of cargo pilots against terrorism

S. 1043 — Nuclear Infrastructure Security Act of 2003

H.R. 3040 — Pretrial Detention and Lifetime Supervision of Terrorists Act of 2003

H.R. 3307 — Stop Terrorism of Property Act of 2003

H.R. 3274 — Regional Comprehensive Emergency Preparedness, Response, and Coordination Act of 2003

H.R. 3227 — National Preparedness Standards Act

H.R. 3158 — PREPARE Act

H.R. 3016 — Combating Terrorism Financing Act of 2003

H.R. 3179 — Anti-Terrorism Intelligence Tools Improvement Act of 2003

H.R. 3173 — Nuclear Terrorist Threat Reduction Act

S. 1039 — Wastewater Treatment Works Security Act of 2003

S. 1606 — Pretrial Detention and Lifetime Supervision of Terrorists Act of 2003

S. 1604 — Terrorist Penalties Enhancement Act of 2003

S. 1587 — Reducing Crime and Terrorism at America's Seaport Act of 2003

H.R. 2570 — State Threat Alert Reimbursement (STAR) Act of 2003

H.R. 2708 — Nuclear Infrastructure Security Act of 2003

H.R. 2926 — Nuclear Waste Terrorist Threat Assessment and Protection Act

S. 929 — Max Cleland Over-the-Road Bus Security and Safety Act of 2003

H.R. 2901 — Chemical Facility Security Act of 2003

S. 1507 — Library, Bookseller, and Personal Records Privacy Act

S. 1552 — Protecting the Rights of Individuals Act

S. 1441 — Protection against Terrorist Hoaxes Act of 2003

H.R. 2726 — National Defense Rail Act

S. 746 — Anti-Terrorism and Port Security Act of 2003

H.R. 2537 — Emergency Warning Act of 2003

H.R. 1118 — Staffing for Adequate Fire and Emergency Response Firefighters Act of 2003

H.R. 2329 — Global Pathogen Surveillance Act of 2003

S. 165 — Air Cargo Security Improvement Act

H.R. 1449 — First Responder and Emergency Preparedness Block Grant Program for Local Governments

H.R. 1389 — Homeland Emergency Response Act of 2003

H.R. 1392 — To require inspection of all cargo on commercial trucks and vessels entering the United States

S. 609 — Restoration of Freedom of Information Act of 2003

H.R. 891 — Dirty Bomb Prevention Act

H.R. 703 — Law Enforcement Partnership to Combat Terrorism Act

H.R. 1049 — Arming Cargo Pilots against Terrorism Act

H.R. 1007 — Homeland Security Block Grant Act of 2003

S. 466 — First Responders Partnership Grant Act of 2003

H.R. 764 — First Responders Expedited Assistance Act of 2003

S. 329 — Neighborhood Security Act of 2003

S. 311 — Commercial Airline Missile Defense Act

S. 315 — First Responders Partnership Grant Act of 2003

S. 266 — Antiterrorism Intelligence Distribution Act of 2003

H.R. 356 — Terrorist Elimination Act of 2003

H.R. 105 — Homeland Emergency Responders Organization Act of 2002

S. 104 — National Defense Rail Act

2002*

H.R. 5005 — Homeland Security Act of 2002 (Enacted November 25, 2002)

H.R. 3609 — Pipeline Safety Improvement Act of 2002 (Enacted December 17, 2002)

H.R. 3394 — Cyber Security Research and Development Act (Enacted November 27, 2002)

S. 1456 — Critical Infrastructure Information Security Act of 2001

H.R. 5710 — Homeland Security Information Sharing Act

S. 3148 — Biological, Chemical, and Radiological Weapons Countermeasures Research Act of 2002

S. 3121 — Nuclear and Radiological Terrorism Threat Reduction Act of 2002

H.R. 5490 — Tribal Government Homeland Security Coordination and Integration Act

H.R. 5483 — Regional Comprehensive Emergency Preparedness, Coordination, and Recovery Act of 2002

H.R. 5441 — Homeland Emergency Responders Organization Act of 2002

H.R. 5420 — Port Protection Act of 2002

H.R. 4864 — Anti-Terrorism Explosives Act of 2002

S. 2846 — Security and Liberty Preservation Act

S. 2887 — Homeland Security Information Sharing Act

H.R. 3448 — Public Health Security and Bioterrorism Preparedness and Response Act of 2002

S. 2579 — Community Protection from Chemical Terrorism Act

2001*

H.R. 3285 — Federal–Local Information Sharing Partnership Act of 2001

H.R. 3209 — Anti-Hoax Terrorism Act of 2001

H.R. 3435 — Empowering Local First Responders to Fight Terrorism Act of 2001

S. 1661 — Deadly Biological Agent Control Act of 2001

H.R. 3153 — State Bioterrorism Preparedness Act

S. 1546 — Biological Chemical Attack Bill

S. 1551 — Protecting the Food Supply from Bioterrorism Act

H.R. 3110 — Transportation Security Enhancement Act of 2001

H.R. 3069 — Securing American Families Effectively (SAFE) Act
S. 1508 — Biological and Chemical Attack Preparedness Act
H.R. 2928 — Keeping America Safe Act of 2001
H.R. 2958 — Passenger Airline Safety and Security Act
S. 1453 — Preparedness against Terrorism Act of 2001
H.R. 2795 — Agroterrorism Prevention Act of 2001
H.R. 2583 — Environmental Terrorism Reduction Act
H.R. 1158 — National Homeland Security Agency Act
H.R. 1292 — Homeland Security Strategy Act of 2001
H.R. 19 — Terrorist Elimination Act of 2001

---

*Bills proposed prior to 2006 that were not enacted are considered "failed legislation," and have thus been cleared from the Congressional calendar (and are no longer under consideration).
Source: www.govtrack.us.

■ ■ Critical Thinking ■

Each year, a considerable amount of legislation focused on homeland security, terrorism, and emergency management is introduced. However, only a tiny number of bills are ever enacted. Why do you think so few of these bills become law? Do you feel that the pace of the process ensures our security or that it inhibits it? Explain you answer.

9/11 Commission

To allow for a full investigation into the terrorist attacks of September 11, 2001, and to make recommendations as to how such attacks could be prevented in the future, Congress created the National Commission on Terrorist Attacks Upon the United States, more commonly known as the "9/11 Commission." The 9/11 Commission was created by Public Law 107-306, and signed by President George W. Bush on November 27, 2002. In addition to other tasks, this law required the commission to investigate "facts and circumstances relating to the terrorist attacks of September 11, 2001," including those relating to intelligence agencies; law enforcement agencies; diplomacy; immigration, nonimmigrant visas, and border control; the flow of assets to terrorist organizations; commercial aviation; the role of congressional oversight and resource allocation; and other areas determined relevant by the commission for its inquiry.

The commission was provided with an initial $3 million to carry out its tasks. When the investigation became much more involved than originally expected, Congress appropriated an additional $12 million in two separate allocations, bringing the total cost of the investigation to $15 million. In fulfilling its mission, the members and staff of the commission interviewed more than 1,200 individuals in 10 countries, reviewed more than 2.5 million documents, and held 19 days of public hearings, during which it received testimony from more than 160 federal, state, and local officials, and experts from the private sector.

On July 22, 2004, after 20 months of research and investigation, the 9/11 Commission released its final report. In this report, the commission issued 37 recommendations to help prevent future terrorist attacks, divided into sections detailing a global strategy and a government reorganization necessary to implement such a strategy. The commission summarized its recommended global strategy in three subject areas:

1. Attacking terrorists and their organizations
2. Preventing the continued growth of Islamist terrorism
3. Protecting and preparing for terrorist attacks

To implement this strategy, the commission proposed a five-part plan to build a coherent, unified effort across the various U.S. government agencies that would be involved:

1. Closing the foreign–domestic divide by linking intelligence and operational planning in a new National Counterterrorism Center
2. Bringing the intelligence community together under a national intelligence director and national intelligence centers
3. Encouraging information sharing throughout government through decentralized networks
4. Centralizing and strengthening congressional oversight of intelligence and homeland security issues
5. Strengthening the national security workforce within the FBI and clarifying the missions of the Departments of Defense and Homeland Security.

The response of Congress to the findings of the 9/11 Commission report was the passage of the Intelligence Reform and Terrorism Prevention Act of 2004 (P.L. 108-458) on December 17, 2004. This act was considered to be "the most important intelligence legislation since the National Security Act of 1947" (Grimmett, 2006). This act established a Director of National Intelligence (DNI) who served in addition to the Director of the CIA, and provided the individual serving in this position with authorities that extended beyond those associated with the former Director of Central Intelligence (DCI) position (including the authority to prepare the national intelligence budget, establishing priorities for collection and analysis, and managing "intelligence centers" supported by analysts from various intelligence and law enforcement agencies). This act, and other congressional actions, addressed several other recommendations of the 9/11 Commission report, including the following:

- Provided additional oversight for the intelligence community (per Senate Resolution 445)
- Improved problems related to the transition between presidential administrations related to security
- Mandated the appointment of a U.S. Coordinator of Policy on Afghanistan
- Provided development assistance and other aid to Pakistan
- Improved counterterrorism cooperation between the United States and Saudi Arabia
- Corrected and improved upon actions made law under the USA PATRIOT Act to stem terrorist financing
- Took action to prevent terrorists from traveling to the United States through deployment of biometric border verification systems, and expanded the terrorist watch list
- Addressed ongoing problems with transportation security by requiring DHS to develop, prepare, implement, and update a National Strategy for Transportation Security, to increase the use of biometric and other advanced detection systems, and other actions including the development of MANPADS (Man-Portable Air Defense Systems) defenses and expansion of the Air Marshal Program
- Passed the Safe Ports Act of 2006, which increased overall port security related to the threat of terrorism
- Directed DHS to create a National Strategy for Transportation Security to better fund transportation security according to risk, across all forms of transportation (In June 2006 DHS issued the National Infrastructure Protection Plan (NIPP), which serves as the government's

guide in applying risk management principles for prioritizing security funding in the various infrastructure sectors, including transportation.)

- Directed DHS to better prepare critical infrastructure (also addressed by the NIPP)

- Guided the governments of the National Capital Region to create stronger mutual aid agreements

- Directed DHS to develop interoperable communications standards for first-response agencies, and required that public safety agencies be given suitable bandwidth access by February 2009

The greatest criticism of this congressional action was that it did little to centralize management of the intelligence community as the commission had recommended. The act also did very little to promote international antiterrorism cooperation, did little to address Islamic extremism, and did not adequately address the threat from weapons of mass destruction.

In December 2005, the 9/11 Commissioners released a "report card" that graded the Bush administration and Congress on their implementation of the 9/11 Commission's recommendations. The grades both received were very poor, and included 5 F's, 12 D's, 9 C's, and 2 Incompletes. By late 2006, these grades had not improved, according to the commission. The "Final Report . . ." sidebar lists the 9/11 Commission's final report card. The U.S. House of Representatives Commission on Homeland Security also releases an annual report on the achievements of DHS, entitled "The State of Homeland Security." The executive summary of this report, including the "grades" received in 17 subject areas, is included as Appendix 2-1.

Final Report on 9/11 Commission Recommendations, December 5, 2005

Homeland Security and Emergency Response

- Radio Spectrum for First Responders (F)
- Incident Command System (C)
- Risk-Based Homeland Security Funds (F)
- Critical Infrastructure Assessment (D)
- Private Sector Preparedness (C)
- National Strategy for Transportation Security (C–)
- Airline Passenger Pre-Screening (F)
- Airline Passenger Explosive Screening (C)
- Checked Bag and Cargo Screening (D)
- Terrorist Travel Strategy (I)
- Comprehensive Screening System (C)
- Biometric Entry–Exit Screening System (B)
- International Collaboration on Borders and Document Security (D)
- Standardize Secure Identifications (B–)

Intelligence and Congressional Reform

- Director of National Intelligence (B)
- National Counterterrorism Center (B)
- FBI National Security Workforce (C)
- New Missions for CIA Director (I)
- Incentives for Information Sharing (D)
- Government-Wide Information Sharing (D)
- Northern Command Planning for Homeland Defense (B–)
- Full Debate on the PATRIOT Act (B)

- Privacy and Civil Liberties Oversight Board (D)
- Guidelines for Government Sharing of Personal Information (D)
- Homeland Security Committees (B)
- Unclassify Top-Line Intelligence Budget (F)
- Security Clearance Reform (B)

Foreign Policy and Nonproliferation

- Maximum Effort to Prevent Terrorists from Acquiring WMD (D)
- Afghanistan (B)
- Pakistan (C+)
- Saudi Arabia (D)
- Terrorist Sanctuaries (B)
- Coalition Strategy Against Islamist Terrorism (C)
- Coalition Detention Standards (F)
- Economic Policies (B+)
- Terrorist Financing (A−)
- Clear U.S. Message Abroad (C)
- International Broadcasting (B)
- Scholarship, Exchange, and Library Programs (D)
- Secular Education in Muslim Countries (D)

Source: Public Discourse Project, 2005 (http://www.9-11pdp.org/).

In 2007, the first action of the new Democratic-controlled Congress was to pass H.R. 1, The Implementing Recommendations of the 9/11 Commission Act of 2007 on January 9, 2007. This law, which will see the outlay of approximately $21 billion between 2007 and 2012, sought to shore up the remaining shortfalls that remained according to the 9/11 Commission report. In sum, this act:

- Requires that the federal government screen the contents of all cargo transported aboard passenger aircraft
- Prohibits shipping containers from entering the United States unless they have been sealed and scanned with imaging and radiation-detection equipment
- Authorizes appropriations for international broadcasting activities and assistance to Arab and predominantly Muslim countries, including Afghanistan and Pakistan
- Attempts to stem the proliferation of weapons of mass destruction (WMD) by creating an office in the White House that coordinates a comprehensive strategy for preventing WMD proliferation, and an advisory commission to survey current nonproliferation efforts and recommend improvements. It also expands ongoing nonproliferation efforts within the Department of Defense and the Department of Energy.
- Authorizes grants to improve interoperable communications systems for first responders

Budget Appropriations

Each year, the budget appropriation for the Department of Homeland Security is established and proposed by the Executive Office, and then debated and enacted by Congress as part of the legislative

Table 2–1   DHS Budget, 2003–2009

Fiscal Year	Amount ($ billions)	Increase Over Previous Year (%)
2003	$31.2	N/A
2004	$36.5	17.0
2005	$40.9	12.1
2006	$40.4	−1.2
2007	$43.0	6.4
2008	$47.0	9.3
2009 (requested)	$50.5	7.5

budget-setting process. Homeland Security has been a budgetary priority of both the executive and legislative branches of government since 2001, and the DHS budget has steadily increased since the 2003 inception of the department (other than a slight decrease from 2005 to 2006) (Table 2–1).

It can easily be argued that the creation of, maintained status of, and continued funding of the Department of Homeland Security together demonstrate the salience of and high-priority status afforded national security by both the Bush administration and Congress. In the budgets of many years, in fact, the President requested from Congress a dollar amount far greater than the previous year's budget, only to have it raised again by Congress in the version that is ultimately enacted. However, considering the high and rising budgets required to maintain these efforts, one must question their long-term sustainability. Supporting such a large federal endeavor has required the commitment of both Congress and the citizens who elect its members. Considering that the memory of September 11 has been kept fresh in the minds of citizens, and major terror attacks have struck in the interim with similar consequences in Indonesia, Spain, and the United Kingdom, among other countries, a great many American citizens have been willing to support measures that require such a great amount of budgetary outlay. However, such enthusiastic support is likely to wane as more time passes without another domestic attack transpiring. In other words, success by DHS in thwarting all terrorist attacks is what is most likely to result in its undoing.

The problem with such a close association between the Department of Homeland Security and national security itself is that security functions are only one of many components represented by the various agencies absorbed by the department in 2002. By examining the stated responsibilities of many of the agencies absorbed, as will be discussed in Chapter 3, we get a better picture of what types of functions homeland security funding supports. For example, the Coast Guard, one of the largest agencies absorbed and the recipient of approximately 20% of the DHS budget, carries out many tasks wholly unrelated to terrorism which include, for example, search and rescue and environmental protection. The funding for these tasks, however, is often lumped together in governmental and other reports along with more general "counterterrorism appropriations," just by the nature of it being included in the DHS budget. It will be contingent on the abilities of the DHS leadership to educate the American public about this disconnect in understanding for people to better justify in their minds what this large sum of money is supporting, outside of terrorism, for the DHS budget to remain sustainable. More often than not, arguments for the increased funding for "DHS activities" have hinged on the need for increased protection against the rising terrorist threat.

The DHS budget is explored in much greater detail, with regard to each departmental component, in Chapter 3. The sidebar titled "Fact Sheet . . ." explores the DHS FY 2009 budget request, and the five major themes to be addressed in that fiscal year.

FACT SHEET: U.S. DEPARTMENT OF HOMELAND SECURITY FY 2009 BUDGET REQUEST

President Bush's fiscal year 2009 budget request for the Department of Homeland Security (DHS) represents $50.5 billion in funding, which is an increase of 6.8 percent over the 2008 fiscal year level — excluding funds provided in emergency supplemental funding. The request targets five areas that are essential to preserving freedom and privacy, meeting future challenges, and fulfilling our mission of securing America.

Continue to Protect Our Nation from Dangerous People
The Department of Homeland Security's main priority is to prevent terrorist attacks against the nation and to protect our nation from dangerous people. DHS will continue to prevent the entry of terrorists while facilitating the legitimate flow of people by strengthening border security efforts and continuing to gain effective control of America's borders. Requested funding for the following initiatives will support this significant goal.

- An increase of $442.4 million is requested in the President's Budget to hire, train, and equip 2,200 new Border Patrol Agents. The additional agents represent the fiscal 2009 increment of the president's goal of adding 6,000 new Border Patrol Agents by the end of the first quarter of fiscal year 2009.
- Total funding of $140 million to support U.S. Customs and Border Protection's Western Hemisphere Travel Initiative (WHTI) to implement the rollout of WHTI to land and sea ports of entry after June 1, 2009. WHTI is mandated by law and requires that all travelers present acceptable documents for entry into the United States. Standardized, secure, and reliable documentation will enable the Department of Homeland Security to quickly, reliably, and accurately identify travelers at air, land, and sea ports-of-entry.
- Total funding of $100 million is requested for E-Verify. This U.S. Citizenship and Immigration Services program allows employers to use an automated system to verify name, date of birth and Social Security Number, along with immigration information for noncitizens, against federal databases to confirm the employment eligibility of both citizen and noncitizen new hires. The program will deploy additional staff to include information status verifiers, and compliance and monitoring staff.
- An increase of $30 million will support the Transportation Security Administration's (TSA) vetting programs to stabilize and enhance the agency's multiple systems such as crew vetting, Secure Identification Display Area checks, and the Alien Flight Student program. This enhancement will enable TSA to efficiently and effectively conduct vetting operations on populations that access the most vulnerable areas of the transportation system.
- An increase of $32 million will accelerate implementation of the Secure Flight program by replacing the current airline-managed passenger vetting program with a government-operated program. In addition to using improved technology, the Secure Flight program will alleviate the variability in performance of the current system and reduce the risk of compromised watch list data.
- An increase of $46 million will help provide 1,000 additional beds, staffing, and associated removal costs required to meet current demand and demand generated by increased enforcement activities.
- Total funding of $57 million for Immigration and Customs Enforcement (ICE) automation and modernization of information technology systems to acquire secure and interoperable tactical communications equipment, a biometric detainee-location tracking module, and to develop and integrate an enhanced Investigative Case Management system. These

(Continued)

improvements promote officer safety, emergency response coordination, and case
management efficiencies.

- An increase of $10 million is requested for improved border security law enforcement
  training through the Federal Law Enforcement Training Center (FLETC).
- An increase of $4.2 million to support National Protection and Programs Directorate's
  US-VISIT identity management and screening services program. This program provides
  biometric identity services to law enforcement, intelligence and civilian stakeholders with
  timely, accurate, and actionable information. Additional funding will complete the biometric
  interoperability between the US-VISIT IDENT system and the FBI's Integrated Automated
  Fingerprint Identification system.
- Total funding of $7.3 million to support continued development of Command 21, and
  additional watchstanders at U.S. Coast Guard command centers to meet increasing
  operational demands and support additional vessel monitoring, information collection, and
  interagency coordination. These initiatives will provide information sharing and situational
  awareness tools required to close the gap between current port and coastal surveillance
  capabilities and the need for greater maritime domain awareness in an all-hazards, all-
  threats operating environment.

Continue to Protect Our Nation from Dangerous Goods

As a part of its risk-based approach, the Department is expanding its programs to identify, track,
and intercept nuclear and radiological components and systems at ports of entry and in transportation systems within U.S. borders. The Department is also intensifying efforts to strengthen
capabilities that reduce the risk of a biological attack in the United States. The following initiatives
support the Department's mission to protect the nation from dangerous goods:

- Total funding of $334.2 million to support Domestic Nuclear Detection Office (DNDO)
  research, development and operations programs, which provides resources for the
  development and evolution of the global nuclear detection architecture. Included in this
  research is the development of an Advanced Spectroscopic Portal that is suitable for
  examining cargo containers, trucks and privately-owned vehicles. Funding will also provide
  for the development of Human Portable Radiation Detection Systems to be used as primary
  detection tools by Customs officers, Border Patrol agents, and Coast Guard personnel.
- An increase of $34.5 million is requested for the Office of Health Affairs' Next Generation
  BioWatch. Funding will procure BioWatch automated detection sensors and initiate
  deployment activities of the automated sensor system to all existing BioWatch jurisdictions.
  Automated detection will enhance the capabilities of the BioWatch environmental
  monitoring system designed for early warning of bioterrorism incidents.

Protect Critical Infrastructure

The Department aims to protect critical infrastructure and key resources, essential government
operations, public health and welfare, and the nation's economic and national security interests. Efforts to bolster the resiliency and protection of our nation's critical infrastructure and key
resources help to mitigate potential vulnerabilities and to ensure terrorist plans are not successful.
The following are funding requests essential to guarding the nation's infrastructure:

- Total funding of $19 million for the U.S. Secret Service's protective terrorist countermeasures
  will provide state-of-the-art equipment for use in the event of an explosive, chemical,

biological, or radiological attack. It is critical for the Secret Service to have the means to address new threats that may evolve or are identified.

- An increase of $13 million for National Protection and Programs Directorate's (NPPD) chemical security compliance project. The Department has issued regulations establishing risk-based security standards for chemical facilities. Additional funding is requested to increase the staff of this regulatory program and to provide tools and systems to collect and analyze vulnerability information, review plans, support and manage inspections activity, issue decisions, address appeals, and support compliance enforcement.

- An increase of $55 million for deploying the Transportation Security Administration's Travel Document Checking program to airports nationwide. This additional layer of defense for aviation security will help ensure only passengers with authentic boarding passes have access to the sterile area of airports and aboard aircraft.

- Total funding of $1.3 billion for Department-wide efforts to counter IED threats. This request includes more than $1.1 billion in funding for TSA explosives detection technology at airports, $50 million for Science and Technology development, $30 million for training of Transportation Security Officers, and $9 million for our Office for Bombing Prevention. The Department has also made billions of dollars in grants available to states and communities for IED prevention and protection, and we continue to work with other federal agencies to address this threat.

- A total of $293.5 million for the National Cyber Security Division to further deploy our EINSTEIN system on Federal networks to protect against cyber threats and intrusions. This includes additional funding for enhancing the United States Computer Emergency Readiness Team's ability to analyze and reduce cyber threats and vulnerabilities, to disseminate warning information, and to coordinate incident response.

Build a Nimble and Effective Emergency Response System and Culture of Preparedness

Improving the nation's ability to respond to disasters, human-made or natural, is a top priority for the Department. The Department is improving its capabilities and preparing those who respond to acts of terror and other emergencies by incorporating lessons learned from Hurricane Katrina, other disasters, and the 9-11 Commission Recommendations. The President's Budget requests funding for the following initiatives that support strengthening the Department's ability to build an effective emergency response system and culture of preparedness:

- An increase of $64.5 million in funding to support the Federal Emergency Management Agency's (FEMA) "Shape the Workforce" program. Phase II of FEMA's transformation will strengthen FEMA's ability to marshal an effective national response, deliver service of value to the public, reduce vulnerability to life and property, and instill public confidence.

- Total funding of $2.2 billion will support FEMA's state and local assistance programs, which prepare state and local governments to prevent or respond to threats or incidents of terrorism and other catastrophic events. This funding will support existing Homeland Security grants, Port and Rail Security grants, and Emergency Management Performance grants, and also proposes a new discretionary grant program targeted toward high-priority security initiatives including REALID implementation.

- Total funding of $209 million will support FEMA's disaster workforce, which will transition four-year Cadre On-Call Response Employees from temporary to permanent full-time personnel. This transition will achieve the level of readiness and response capability required in response to major disasters and emergencies declared by the president. An additional $200 million is provided in a new Disaster Readiness and Support Activities account to

(Continued)

FACT SHEET: U.S. DEPARTMENT OF HOMELAND SECURITY FY 2009 BUDGET REQUEST–(CONTINUED)

assist FEMA in working with state and local partners in preparing for future disasters and institutionalizing logistical and other capabilities in support of state disaster readiness leadership.

- A funding increase of $43 million to support S&T laboratory facilities to include initial operations of the National Bio-defense Analysis and Countermeasures Center (NBACC). NBACC will provide the nation with essential bio-containment laboratory space for biological threat characterization and bioforensic research. The programs conducted at NBACC will provide knowledge of infectious properties of biological agents, effectiveness of countermeasures, decontamination procedures, and forensics analyses to support policy makers and responders' development of policies, programs, and technologies.

Strengthen and Unify DHS Operations and Management

A cohesive and operationally efficient organization is essential to the rapid implementation of homeland security priorities, policies, and objectives. As such, the Department has aligned its resources into areas that will most effectively accomplish its mission. Successful mission performance is driven by human capital development, executing efficient procurement operations, and possessing state-of-the-art information technology resources. The following critical investments will ensure that DHS is managed and operated in an efficient and unified manner:

- A total of $1.65 million for the first Quadrennial Homeland Security Review (QHSR) will fund the research, organization, analysis, and development of the QHSR. This document will recommend long-term strategy and priorities of the nation for homeland security and comprehensively examine programs, assets, budget, policies, and authorities required to provide the United States with strong, sound and effective future homeland security capabilities.
- An increase of $15.5 million for the Office of the Chief Financial Officer (CFO) will continue implementation of the Transformation and Systems Consolidation (TASC) project. One of the main objectives of DHS at its formation was to consolidate the support systems of the component agencies to realize cost savings and operational efficiencies. The CFO aims to reduce the number of DHS financial systems, and ensure the manual processes for internal controls are integrated with these financial systems.
- An increase of $3.1 million for the Office of the Chief Procurement Officer's (CPO) DHS-wide acquisition workforce intern program will enhance the way the Department recruits, trains, certifies, and retains an appropriate workforce of acquisition professionals. In fiscal year 2009, the intern complement will be raised to 100 people.
- An increase of $6.4 million for the Office of the Inspector General (OIG) to expand staff oversight of DHS preparedness programs, through audits of preparedness grant programs, S&T programs, and Department-wide programs that establish baseline preparedness efforts; and to strengthen OIG oversight of DHS border security and enforcement programs through a proactive program of audits and on-going oversight of the policies, and initiatives and funds to secure the nation's borders.
- A total of $23.8 million will continue consolidation of the Department's 17 legacy data centers into two enterprise-wide data centers. This consolidation will result in improved cybersecurity, information sharing and configuration management.

Source: Department of Homeland Security, 2008. http://www.dhs.gov/xnews/releases/pr_1202151112290.shtm

▦ ▦ Critical Thinking ▦

Do you feel that the non–security-related functions housed within the Department of Homeland Security benefit or suffer, in terms of their annual funding, as a result of their inclusion?

Conclusion

The terrorism hazard, and the methods by which the federal government should prepare for and respond to terrorist threats, did not appear suddenly after the devastating events of September 11 transpired. As explained in this chapter, concerns about the threat of terrorism in the United States have existed since the early 1980s, and many actions were taken to address it since that time. Several precipitating events that had less spectacular yet similarly destructive results (including the 1993 bombing of the World Trade Center and the attacks on U.S. embassies and installations abroad) caught the attention not only of the investigative and intelligence agencies, but of Congress and the White House as well.

The domestic terrorist bombing of the Murrah Federal Office Building in Oklahoma City vividly demonstrated that there existed conflicts regarding incident command and control at the federal level. Although members of Congress passed legislation they believed would adequately address these conflicts, competition within the intelligence and law enforcement communities, and a general lack of counterterrorism resources, they failed to address the concerns and needs of first responders at the state and local levels. Despite such drastic shortfalls, the federal response worked surprisingly well on September 11. However, the enormous loss of lives among civilians and the first responder community demanded (and likewise resulted in) a flurry of legislative activity that sought to ensure that this measure of tragedy would never be repeated. Two of the most far-reaching pieces of legislation, the USA PATRIOT Act and the Homeland Security Act of 2002, dramatically changed the power, organization, and functions of the federal government. The USA PATRIOT Act gave the attorney general and the DOJ unsurpassed authority over the civil rights and liberties of individuals. Combining 22 federal entities with a mandate to establish a safe and secure homeland, the Homeland Security Act represented the largest single reorganization of the federal government since World War II.

Whether these actions have created a safer, more secure homeland will require many more years to determine. As the federal government further reorganizes, more and more of the funding authorized for the states and local communities has reached its intended target. Loopholes and gaps in security are constantly emerging, and legislation to address them follow at an equal rate. Many of the problems that were associated with the original, "fast-action" legislation have been exposed and addressed, even though many citizens feel there is still a long way to go. Judging by the continued pace with which security-based legislation is introduced in both the House and Senate, much more is likely to occur in the ongoing legislative recalibration. Nonetheless, the foundation of statutory authority is established. Historians will surely assess the effectiveness of the U.S. response to the threat of terror based on the success of these acts, and whether their implementation has accomplished the goals of a safe and secure homeland.

Key Terms

Statutory Authority: The legally granted authority, bestowed on the named recipient by a legislature, that provides a government agency, board, or commission the power to perform the various functions, expenditures, and actions as described in the law.

Executive Order: A declaration issued by the president or by a governor that has the force of law. Executive orders are usually based on existing statutory authority and require no action by Congress or the state legislature to become effective.

Presidential Directive: A form of executive order issued by the president that establishes an action or change in the structure or function of the government (generally within the

Executive Office). Under President Bush, directives have been termed Homeland Security Presidential Directives (HSPDs) and National Security Presidential Directives (NSPDs). Under President Clinton, they were termed Presidential Decision Directives (PDDs) and Presidential Review Directives (PRDs).

Federal Response Plan: The FRP was developed to establish a standard process and structure for the systematic, coordinated, and effective delivery of federal assistance to address the consequences of any major disaster or emergency declared under the Robert T. Stafford Disaster Relief and Emergency Assistance Act, as amended. This plan was later replaced by the National Response Plan.

National Response Plan: The NRP is a formal document that describes how the federal government will work in concert with state, local, and tribal governments and the private sector to respond to disasters. Using the template established by the National Incident Management System (NIMS), the NRP provides the structure and mechanisms to coordinate and integrate incident management activities and emergency support functions across federal, state, local, and tribal government entities; the private sector; and nongovernmental organizations. The NRP can be found by accessing the following DHS website: http://www.dhs.gov/nrp.

Interoperable Communications: One of the greatest first response shortfalls identified in the aftermath of the September 11 attacks was the ability of first and other responders to communicate with each other during large-scale disasters. The concept of interoperable communications focuses on the ability of these different agencies to increase their ability to effectively communicate with each other when they are required to work in concert in the same disaster response.

National Incident Management System: This is a system mandated by Homeland Security Presidential Directive (HSPD) 5 that provides a consistent nationwide approach for governments, the private sector, and nongovernmental organizations to work effectively and efficiently together to prepare for, respond to, and recover from domestic incidents, regardless of cause, size, or complexity.

Critical Infrastructure: Critical infrastructure includes any system or asset that, if disabled or disrupted in any significant way, would result in catastrophic loss of life or catastrophic economic loss. Some examples of critical infrastructure include the following:
Public water systems
Primary roadways, bridges, and highways
Key data storage and processing facilities, stock exchanges, or major banking centers
Chemical facilities located in close proximity to large population centers
Major power generation facilities
Hydroelectric facilities and dams
Nuclear power plants

Review Questions

1. What are the two principal purposes for establishing legislation to support government homeland security activities and programs?
2. What are the principal functions of the PATRIOT Act, the Homeland Security Act, and Homeland Security Presidential Directive No. 5?
3. What issues have been raised concerning some of the authorities granted government agencies in the PATRIOT Act? How have those issues been addressed?
4. If you were a member of Congress, what types of standards would you propose to measure the effectiveness of the spending that is occurring for homeland security? How would you propose to determine if the spending has raised individual, community, and private sector preparedness

for the new terrorist threat? How would these measurements be enforced and by what government agency(s) at what level of government (federal, state, and/or local)?

5. What additional statutory authorities and resources do you think emergency managers require in order to function effectively in homeland security? Should certain preparedness and mitigation actions and activities be made mandatory like building codes and seat belt use? Should greater emphasis be placed on enforcement of current and future restrictions and requirements? Should additional resources become part of a regular annual appropriation at all levels of government? How would the impact of the new authorities and resources be measured to ensure that they are successfully applied?

References

American Civil Liberties Union, San Jose, CA Resolution. 2003. www.aclu.org/SafeandFree/SafeandFree. cfm?ID=13900&c=207.

Baldwin, T.E. 2002. "Historical Chronology of FEMA Consequence Management, Preparedness and Response to Terrorism." Argonne National Laboratory, Argonne, IL.

Bohn, K. 2003. "ACLU Files against Patriot Act." CNN (July 30). www.cnn.com.

Doyle, C. 2004. "CRS Report for Congress: USA PATRIOT Act Sunset: A Sketch" (January 7). www.au.af.mil/au/awc/awcgate/crs/rs21704.pdf.

Gay, L. 2001. "How the New Antiterrorism Bill Could Affect You." Scripps Howard News Service (October 26). www.startribune.com.

Grimmett, R.F. 2006. 9/11 Commission Recommendations: Implementation Status. CRS Report for Congress, Report RL33742. http://www.fas.org/sgp/crs/homesec/RL33742.pdf.

Library of Congress. July 21, 2003. www.congress.gov.

Paul, R. 2005. "Reconsidering the Patriot Act, Texas Straight Talk: A Weekly Column" (May 2). www.house.gov/paul/tst/tst2005/tst050205.htm.

Rubin, C.B., Cummings, W.R., and Renda-Tanali, I. 2003. "Terrorism Time Line: Major Focusing Events and U.S. Outcomes (1993–2002)" <http://www.disaster-timeline.com>.

Shotwell, B. 2003. "Memorandum to Honorable Mayor and City Council, USA PATRIOT Act and Patriot Act II." September 19. www.sanjoseca.gov/cty_clk/9_23_03docs/09_23_03_3.4.pdf.

Taylor, A. 2005. "House Votes to Limit Patriot Act Rules." The Associated Press, June 16. www.washingtonpost.com/wp-dyn/content/article/2005/06/15/AR2005061502674.html.

U.S. Department of Justice. 2005. "USA PATRIOT Act Overview: What Is the Patriot Act?"www.nunes.house.gov/documents/PatriotActOverview.pdf.

The Washington Post. 2005. "Patriot Second Act." June 13. www.washingtonpost.com/wp-dyn/content/article/2005/06/12/AR2005061201436.html.

The White House. 2004. "Fact Sheet: President Bush Calls for Renewing the USA PATRIOT Act." April 18. www.whitehouse.gov/news/releases/2004/04/20040419-4.html.

3

Organizational Actions

What You Will Learn

- How the structural organization of the Department of Homeland Security has developed and changed, from its creation in 2002 until its third major reorganization in 2008
- The individual components that compose the Department of Homeland Security, the function of each component, and other interesting facts and figures about each
- What federal agencies other than the Department of Homeland Security provide funding at the community level, and what kinds of programs they support
- The various homeland security–related activities that the nation's state and local organizations participate in, and what types of assistance they provide their constituent members

Introduction

Prior to the September 11, 2001, terrorist attacks, the Nunn-Lugar-Domenici legislation provided the primary authority and focus for domestic federal preparedness activities for terrorism. Several agencies — including the Federal Emergency Management Agency (FEMA), Department of Justice (DOJ), Department of Health and Human Resources (DHHS), Department of Defense (DOD), and the National Guard — were involved in the terrorism issue, and all were jockeying for the leadership position. Several attempts at coordination among these various agencies were launched, but in general, each agency pursued their own agenda. The single factor that provided the greatest distinction between these agencies related to the levels of funding they received, with DOD and DOJ controlling the majority of what was allocated. State and local governments generally found themselves confused by the federal government's approach, and likewise felt unprepared as a result. While many of these state and local agencies appealed to the federal government to recognize local vulnerabilities and to establish stronger systems to accommodate anticipated needs, the majority rarely considered the possibility of an attack at all. The 1999 TOPOFF (short for "Top Officials") terrorism exercise was successful only in that it highlighted many of the concerns of state and local agencies, and vividly demonstrated to all participants the problems that would ultimately arise during a real event.

The events of September 11 were a real-world validation of the fact that the American emergency management system was unprepared to manage an emergency situation resulting from catastrophic terrorism, including prevention, preparedness, and response needs. Understandably, these events precipitated a major shift in the way the terrorism hazard was handled by all levels of government, beginning with the federal government.

There are five groups that must be fully engaged to be successful in the nation's war on terrorism: the diplomatic community, the intelligence community, the military, law enforcement (including investigations), and emergency management. The principal goal of the first four members of this group — the diplomatic community, intelligence community, the military, and law enforcement agencies — is to reduce, if not eliminate, the risk of future terrorist attacks on American citizens both within the nation's borders and abroad. Each of these performs a separate but critical function in the overall effort.

The goal of emergency management, however, is unique in that it addresses not the terrorists themselves but the consequences of their actions. The emergency management community attempts to both eliminate the ability of these actions to find success, through mitigation and preparedness activities like hardening targets and educating the public, and to respond to them effectively when they do occur and result in negative consequences. The emergency management community's main goal is not to stop the terrorists, but to reduce future loss of life, injuries, property damage, and economic disruption.

As President George W. Bush and many of his advisers have repeatedly recognized in both speeches and briefings, the question of the next terrorist attack is not one of if, but rather of when it will occur. It has therefore become incumbent for emergency managers to apply the same diligence to preparing for the next bombing or bioterror event as they have for the next hurricane or flood or tornado. The focus of emergency management in the war on terrorism has been and will remain on reducing the effects of future terrorist attacks on first responders, the general public, the business community, the economy, and the American way of life. Clearly, this is no small undertaking.

The establishment of a Department of Homeland Security (DHS) in 2002 represented a landmark change within the federal community, most notably for emergency management. This consolidation of federal agencies required to fight the war on terrorism followed similar logic to that which resulted in the creation of FEMA in 1979. At that time, President Jimmy Carter, at the request of the nation's governors, consolidated all of the federal agencies and programs involved in disaster relief, preparedness, and mitigation into one single federal agency, FEMA. It took 15 years and several reorganizations for FEMA to become a functioning agency. The question now is how long it will take the DHS to become fully functional.

The FEMA director reported directly to the president and, in 1996, President Bill Clinton elevated the director of FEMA to cabinet status. However, when FEMA was absorbed into the DHS, the secretary of homeland security joined the president's cabinet and the FEMA director no longer reported directly to the president. These adjustments in FEMA's organizational status have resulted in the terrorism-oriented mission of the DHS being imposed heavily on FEMA's all-hazards mission and regular programming priorities.

Prior to September 11, at the request of President Bush, FEMA established the Office of National Preparedness (in May 2001) to focus attention on the (then) largely undefined terrorist threat and other national security issues. This was the first step in refocusing the attention of FEMA's public safety mission from the all-hazards emergency management approach embraced by the Clinton administration to one of public security. The shift in focus was greatly accelerated by the events of September 11 and has since been embraced by state and local emergency management operations across the country. What impact the failure of the Hurricane Katrina response will have on this current focus on terrorism prevention at all levels of government has yet to be determined.

A similar shift of focus in FEMA occurred in 1981 at the beginning of the Reagan administration when all-hazards disaster management planning was replaced by a program that focused primarily on nuclear response planning. Until the end of President George H.W. Bush's administration, FEMA resources and personnel therefore focused their attention of ensuring continuity of government operations in the event of a nuclear attack, with little attention paid to natural hazard management. Ultimately, FEMA found itself unprepared to deal with a series of catastrophic natural disasters that started with Hurricane Hugo in 1989 and culminated with Hurricane Andrew in 1992.

Nobody can predict if the U.S. government is in the process of repeating history, but one must question whether the current change in focus away from the all-hazard approach of the 1990s could result in a weakening of FEMA's future natural disaster management capabilities. Certainly, the ineffective response to Hurricane Katrina in 2005 raises many of the same issues and concerns that were raised in the aftermath of Hurricane Andrew in 1992.

What is unique about the changes that are occurring today is that they are not isolated to one, or a few government agencies, but to virtually all of them. By nature of the terrorist threat itself, every government agency, as an extension of the U.S. government itself, is certainly a plausible terrorist target. Every government agency, by nature of its actions, has some specialty to offer in the fight against terrorism, be it financial, environmental, transportation related, health related, and so on. This chapter will examine how the legislative changes discussed in Chapter 2, and the organizational actions both within and in spite of these laws, have redefined the emergency management mechanisms at all levels of government. The Department of Homeland Security, in particular, will be explained in detail.

The Department of Homeland Security

On November 25, 2002, President Bush signed into law the Homeland Security Act of 2002 (HS Act) (Public Law 107-296), and announced that former Pennsylvania Governor Tom Ridge would become secretary of a new Department of Homeland Security (DHS) to be created through this legislation. This act, which authorized the greatest federal government reorganization since President Harry Truman joined the various branches of the armed forces under the Department of Defense, was charged with a threefold mission of protecting the United States from further terrorist attacks, reducing the nation's vulnerability to terrorism, and minimizing the damage from potential terrorist attacks and natural disasters.

The sweeping reorganization into the new department, which officially opened its doors on January 24, 2003, joined more than 179,000 federal employees from 22 existing federal agencies under a single, cabinet-level organization. The legislation, which was not restricted to the newly created department, also transformed several other federal agencies that at first glance may have appeared only remotely affiliated with the homeland security mission. To the affected government employees, millions of concerned American citizens, the entire world media, and even the terrorists themselves, it was clear that the U.S. government was entering a new era.

The creation of the DHS was the culmination of an evolutionary legislative process that began largely in response to criticism that increased interagency cooperation between federal intelligence organizations could have prevented the September 11 terrorist attacks. Based on the findings of several pre–September 11 commissions, it appeared that the country needed a centralized federal government agency whose primary reason for existence would be to coordinate the security of the "homeland" (a term that predated the attacks). The White House and Congress were both well aware that any homeland security czar position they conceived would require both an adequate staff and a large budget to succeed. Thus, in early 2002 deliberations began to create a new cabinet-level department that would fuse many of the security-related agencies dispersed throughout the federal government.

For several months during the second half of 2002, Congress jockeyed between differing versions of the homeland security bill in an effort to establish legislation that was passable yet effective. Lawmakers were particularly mired on the issue of the rights of the 179,000 affected employees — an issue that prolonged the legislative process considerably. Furthermore, efforts to incorporate many of the intelligence-gathering and investigative law enforcement agencies, namely, the National Security Agency (NSA), the Federal Bureau of Investigation (FBI), and the Central Intelligence Agency (CIA), into the legislation failed.

Despite these delays and setbacks, after the 2002 midterm elections, the Republican seats that were gained in both the House and Senate gave the president the leverage he needed to pass the bill without further deliberation (House of Representatives, 299–121 on November 13, 2002; Senate, 90–9 on November 19, 2002). While the passage of this act represented a significant milestone, the implementation phase to come presented a tremendous challenge; a concern that was echoed by several leaders from the agencies that were to be absorbed. On November 25, 2002, President Bush submitted his reorganization plan (as required by the legislation), which mapped out the schedule, methodology, and budget for the monumental task at hand.

Secretary Ridge was given exactly one year to develop a comprehensive structural framework for the DHS, and to name new leadership for all five directorates and other offices created under the legislation. Beginning on March 1, 2003, almost all of the federal agencies named in the act began their move, whether literally or symbolically, into the new department. Those remaining followed on June 1, 2003, with all incidental transfers completed by September 1, 2003. Although a handful of these agencies remained intact after the move, most were fully incorporated into one of four new directorates: Border and Transportation Security (BTS), Information Analysis and Infrastructure Protection (IAIP), Emergency Preparedness and Response (EP&R), and Science and Technology (S&T). A fifth directorate, Management, incorporated parts of the existing administrative and support offices within the merged agencies.

■ ■ Critical Thinking ■

Do you believe that the architects of the original structure of the Department of Homeland Security were wise in their choice to create "directorates" under which many of the incorporated agencies were placed, or should they have all remained independent agencies reporting directly to the Secretary of Homeland Security? Explain your answer.

In addition to the creation of the Department of Homeland Security (see Figure 3–1 and "DHS Establishment Timeline" sidebar), which is described in detail later in this chapter, the HS Act made

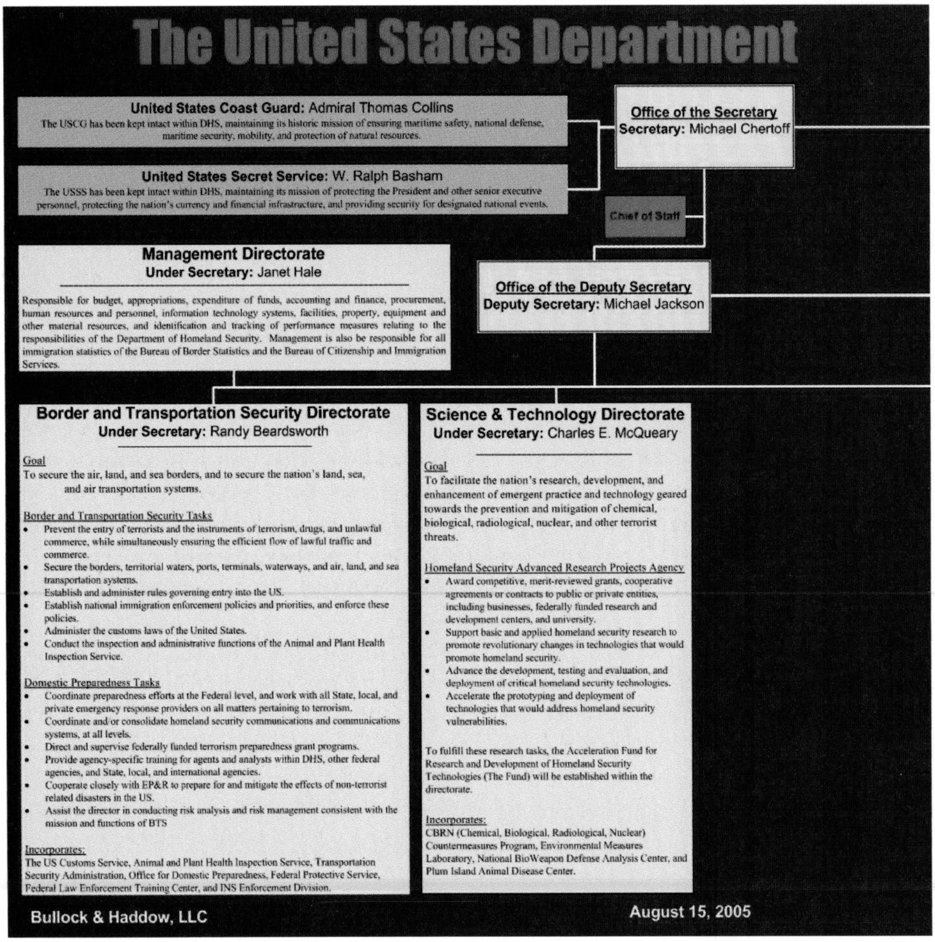

FIGURE 3–1 Original DHS organizational chart, with leadership figures holding office in July of 2005. (Designed by Damon Coppola for Bullock & Haddow, funding provided by the Annie E. Casey Foundation).

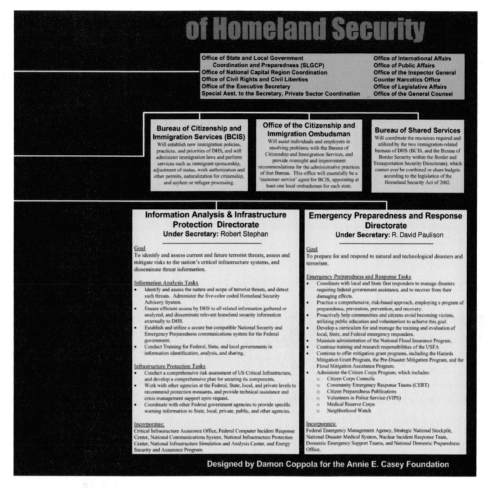

FIGURE 3–1 Continued

several changes to other federal agencies and their constituent partners, and created several new programs. A list of the most significant is presented below:

- Established a National Homeland Security Council within the Executive Office of the President, which assesses U.S. objectives, commitments, and risks in the interest of homeland security, oversees and reviews federal homeland security policies, and makes recommendations to the president

- Transferred the Bureau of Alcohol, Tobacco and Firearms (ATF) from the Department of the Treasury to the Department of Justice (DOJ)

- Explicitly prohibited both the creation of a national ID card and the proposed Citizen Corps "Terrorism Information and Prevention System" (Operation TIPS, which encouraged transportation workers, postal workers, and public utility employees to identify and report suspicious activities linked to terrorism and crime). The act also reaffirmed the Posse Comitatus Act, which prohibits the U.S. military from being used as a domestic police force except under constitutional or congressional authority (the Coast Guard is exempt from this act).

- The Arming Pilots against Terrorism Act, incorporated into the HS Act, allows pilots to defend aircraft cockpits with firearms or other "less-than-lethal weapons" against acts of criminal violence or air piracy, and provides antiterrorism training to flight crews.

- The Critical Infrastructure Information Act (2002), incorporated in the HS Act, exempts certain components of critical infrastructure from Freedom of Information Act (FOIA) regulations.

- The Johnny Michael Spann Patriot Trusts were created to provide support for surviving spouses, children, or dependent parents, grandparents, or siblings of various federal employees who die in the line of duty as a result of terrorist attacks, military operations, intelligence operations, or law enforcement operations.

On November 30, 2004, following the presidential election, DHS Secretary Ridge announced his resignation. After an initial nomination of NYPD commissioner Bernard Kerik for the position, which was withdrawn due to the immigration status of an employee in his home, Federal Judge Michael Chertoff was named to lead the agency.

Department of Homeland Security Establishment Timeline

September 11, 2001 — Terrorists attacks occur in Washington, DC, New York, and Pennsylvania.

September 20, 2001 — In an address to Congress, President Bush announces the creation of the Office of Homeland Security (OHS) and the appointment of Tom Ridge as director.

October 8, 2001 — President swears in Tom Ridge as assistant to the president for homeland security and issues an executive order creating the OHS.

October 9, 2001 — President swears in General Wayne Downing as director of the Office of Combating Terrorism (OCT) and issues an executive order creating the OCT.

October 16, 2001 — President Bush issues an executive order establishing the president's Critical Infrastructure Protection Board to coordinate and have cognizance of federal efforts and programs that relate to protection of information systems.

October 26, 2001 — President Bush signs the USA PATRIOT Act.

October 29, 2001 — President Bush chairs the first meeting of the Homeland Security Council (HSC) and issues Homeland Security Presidential Directive No. 1 (HSPD-1), establishing the organization and operation of the HSC, and HSPD-2, establishing the Foreign Terrorist Tracking Task Force and increasing immigration vigilance.

November 8, 2001 — President Bush announces that the Corporation for National and Community Service (CNCS) will support homeland security, "mobilizing more than 20,000 Senior Corps and AmeriCorps participants."

November 8, 2001 — President Bush creates the Presidential Task Force on Citizen Preparedness in the War against Terrorism to "help prepare Americans in their homes, neighborhoods, schools, workplaces, places of worship and public places from the potential consequences of terrorist attacks."

November 15, 2001 — FEMA announces Individual and Family Grant program for disaster assistance.

January 30, 2002 — President Bush issues an executive order establishing the U.S.A. Freedom Corps, encouraging all Americans to serve their country for the equivalent of at least two years (4,000 hours) over their lifetimes.

February 4, 2002 — President Bush submits the president's budget for FY 2003 to Congress, directing $37.7 billion to homeland security (up from $19.5 billion in FY 2002).

March 12, 2002 — President Bush establishes the Homeland Security Advisory System (HSPD-3).

March 19, 2002 — President Bush issues an executive order establishing the President's Homeland Security Advisory Council.

September 17, 2002 — President declares the National Strategy to Combat Weapons of Mass Destruction (HSPD-4).

November 25, 2002 — President Bush signs the Homeland Security Act of 2002 (HR 5005) as Public Law 107-296. Tom Ridge is announced as secretary, Navy Secretary Gordon England is nominated as deputy secretary of the DHS, and Drug Enforcement Agency (DEA) Administrator Asa Hutchinson is nominated as the undersecretary of border and transportation security.

January 24, 2003 — Sixty days after it was signed, the Homeland Security Act becomes effective.

February 28, 2003 — President Bush calls for the creation of the National Incident Management System (NIMS) through HSPD-5.

March 1, 2003 — Most affected federal agencies are incorporated into the DHS.

June 1, 2003 — All remaining affected federal agencies are incorporated into the DHS.

Source: Compiled from multiple sources by Damon Coppola, January 2003.

Homeland Security Department Subcomponents and Agencies

The Department of Homeland Security is a massive agency, juggling numerous responsibilities between a staggeringly wide range of program areas, employing approximately 180,000 people, and managing a massive multi–billion-dollar budget and an ambitious list of tasks and goals. The department leverages resources within federal, state, and local governments, coordinating the ongoing transition of multiple agencies and programs into a single, integrated agency focused on protecting the American people and their homeland. In total, more than 87,000 different governmental jurisdictions at the federal, state, and local level have homeland security responsibilities.

At the federal level, the DHS organizational composition still remains in a state of flux. Scattered readjustments have occurred throughout its first years of existence, with multiple offices being passed between the department's components. Though it seemed by the end of DHS Secretary Tom Ridge's years of service that the basic organizational makeup had been established, incoming DHS Secretary Chertoff proposed several fundamental changes to the department's organization, which were implemented under Secretary Chertoff's Reorganization Plan. Again, the department was reorganized following the 2005 hurricane season according to the requirements of the Post-Katrina Emergency Management Reform Act of 2006 (Figure 3–2).

The following sections describe the major components that constitute the Department of Homeland Security, explain their current organizational positioning, and detail the proposed changes to this organizational structure as stipulated by Secretary Chertoff and Congress. These components are grouped according to three subsections — Office of the Secretary, Pre-Existing Offices, and the Three Directorates — and other offices within the Department of Security that fall under the direction of the DHS Secretary.

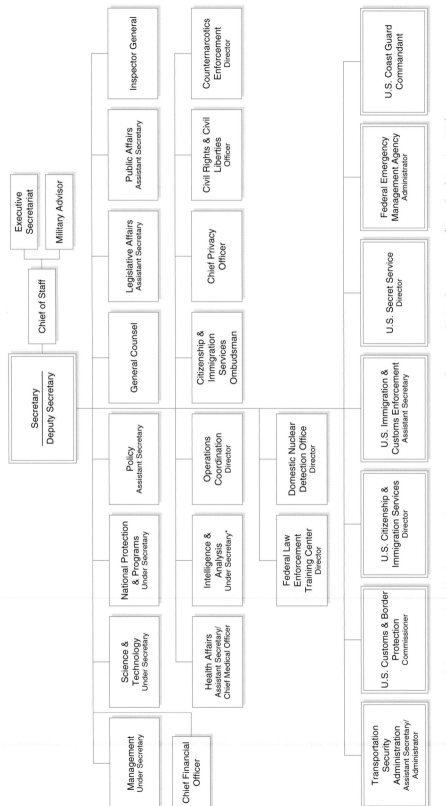

FIGURE 3-2 DHS organizational chart as stipulated by the Post-Katrina Emergency Management Reform Act of 2006. (Department of Homeland Security, 2007)

Office of the Secretary

The Secretary of Homeland Security is a cabinet-level official, within the executive branch, who leads the department. The first DHS secretary, who served from the department's opening day in March 2003 until February 2005, was former Pennsylvania Governor Tom Ridge. The current DHS secretary is Michael Chertoff, who formerly served as United States Circuit Judge for the Third Circuit Court of Appeals.

The secretary and his or her staff are responsible for managing the overall direction of the department. This office oversees the activities of the department. In conjunction with other federal, state, local, and private entities, as part of a collaborative effort to strengthen the nation's borders, the Office of the Secretary sets the direction for intelligence analysis and infrastructure protection, improved use of science and technology to counter weapons of mass destruction, and the creation of comprehensive response and recovery initiatives. Within the Office of the Secretary are multiple program and issues-related offices that contribute to the overall homeland security mission. These offices and their purposes include:

- The Privacy Office: Works to minimize the impact that the DHS mission has on the privacy of individuals, particularly with respect for their personal information and dignity

- Office of Civil Rights and Civil Liberties: Provides legal and policy advice to DHS leadership on civil rights and civil liberties issues; investigates and resolves complaints; and provides leadership to Equal Employment Opportunity Programs

- Office of the Inspector General: Responsible for conducting and supervising audits, investigations, and inspections relating to DHS programs and operations, and for recommending ways for DHS to carry out its responsibilities in the most effective, efficient, and economical manner possible

- Citizenship and Immigration Ombudsman: Provides recommendations for resolving individual and employer problems with the United States Citizenship and Immigration Services (USCIS) in order to ensure that both national security and the integrity of the legal immigration system are maintained, increases efficiencies in administering citizenship and immigration services, and improves overall customer service in these areas

- Office of Legislative Affairs: Serves as primary liaison to members of Congress and their staffs, the White House and Executive Branch, and to other federal agencies and governmental entities that have national security roles and concerns

- Office of Counternarcotics Enforcement: Serves as the primary policy adviser to the DHS Secretary for department-wide counternarcotics issues, develops policies that unify DHS counternarcotics activities, and coordinates efforts to monitor and combat connections between illegal drug trafficking and terrorism

- Office of General Counsel: Integrates approximately 1,700 lawyers from throughout DHS into an "effective, client-oriented, full-service legal team" (DHS, 2007)

- Office of Public Affairs: Responsible for making sure that the public and the press are informed of the department's activities and priorities

- Executive Secretariat: Ensures that all DHS officials are included in the correspondence drafting and policymaking process through a managed clearance and control system

- Military Advisor's Office: Provides sound military advice to the Secretary and other executive staff

Pre-Existing Offices Moved into DHS in 2002

Several agencies that existed elsewhere in the federal government prior to September 11 were transferred into the Department of Homeland Security intact and also report directly to the Office of the Secretary. Most notable of these agencies are the U.S. Coast Guard and the U.S. Secret Service. The Federal Emergency Management Agency (FEMA) was originally integrated into one of four original directorates, but after the bungled response to Hurricane Katrina, FEMA was reinstated as a stand alone agency reporting directly to the DHS Secretary. The Federal Law Enforcement Training Center (FLETC) was similarly incorporated into a DHS entity in 2002, but restored to its independent status under the DHS Secretary as part of this 2007 reorganization. These intact agencies are described individually in the following subsections.

The U.S. Coast Guard

The U.S. Coast Guard (USCG), under the direction of Commandant Thad W. Allen, was transferred to the DHS as an intact agency on March 1, 2003. The primary function of the Coast Guard within the DHS remains consistent with its historic mission, as identified in the following five functional areas:

- Maritime safety
- National defense
- Maritime security
- Mobility
- Protection of natural resources

As lead federal agency for maritime safety and security, the USCG protects several of the nation's vital interests; the personal safety and security of the American population; the natural and economic resources of the United States; and the territorial integrity of the country from both internal and external threats, natural and human-made. As a military, maritime service, the USCG is responsible for a blend of humanitarian, law enforcement, regulatory, diplomatic, and military duties — all for which it is entirely qualified — to provide maritime security, maritime safety, protection of natural resources, maritime mobility, and national defense services (Figure 3–3).

The USCG was recognized after September 11 as being a well-equipped military force with established jurisdiction within U.S. territory. Immediately following September 11, the importance of this fact was not lost on federal government officials who witnessed how, as naval ships were quickly leaving the nation's ports to protect themselves, the Coast Guard's ships were moving into position inside those same ports.

Since entering DHS, the U.S. Coast Guard has received a significant boost in its budget allocation, which has been used primarily to update a fleet of ships and aircraft that was considered outdated in relation to the other armed services (as part of the ongoing Integrated Deepwater System project). Additionally, many more employees have been added to the agency's payroll. As of 2008, the Coast Guard employed 41,873 active duty military members and 7,057 civilian employees, for a total of 48,930 people. In addition to these, the USCG maintains 8,100 selected reserve and 34,885 auxiliary employees. Between FY 2004 and FY 2007, the USCG saw its budget rise first from $6.994 billion to $7.559 billion in FY 2005, $8.675 billion in FY 2006, and $8.776 billion in 2007. However, the FY 2008 budget saw a decrease for USCG to $8.741 billion. The FY 2009 DHS budget request would increase USCG funding considerably to $9.346 billion, representing 19% of the total DHS budget in FY 2009 (see Figure 3–4).

U.S. Secret Service

The U.S. Secret Service (USSS), under the leadership of Mark J. Sullivan, was transferred to the DHS as an intact agency on March 1, 2003. The Secret Service was able to continue its historic mission of protecting the president and senior executive personnel, in addition to protecting the country's currency and financial infrastructure and providing security for designated national events (e.g., the Super Bowl and the Olympics). The USSS is also responsible for the protection of the vice president, immediate family members of these senior officials, the president-elect, and vice president-elect, or other officers next in the order of succession to the Office of the President and members of their

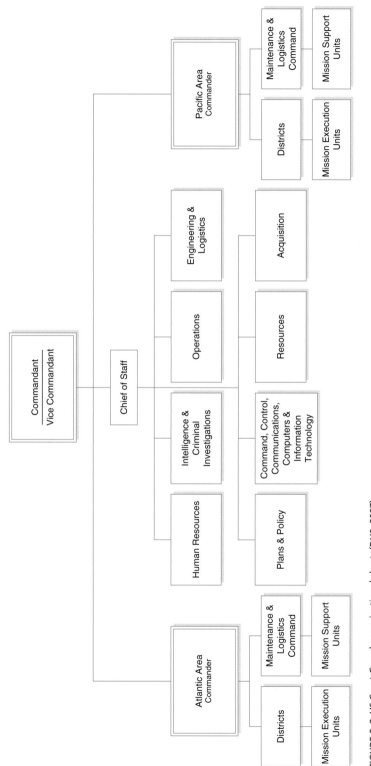

FIGURE 3–3 US Coast Guard organizational chart. (DHS, 2007)

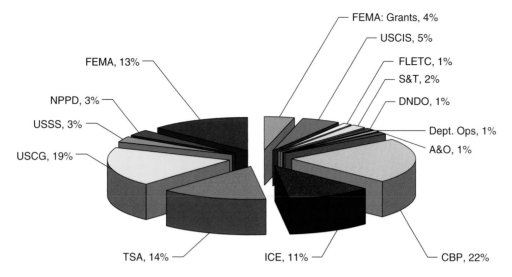

FIGURE 3–4 DHS budget allocation by agency, FY 2009. (DHS Budget Brief, 2008)

immediate families, presidential candidates, visiting heads of state and their accompanying spouses, and, at the direction of the president, other distinguished foreign visitors to the United States and official representatives of the United States performing special missions abroad. Former presidents, their spouses, and minor children are also offered USSS protection for life.

The USSS also protects the executive residence and grounds in the District of Columbia, buildings in which White House offices are located, the official residence and grounds of the vice president in the District of Columbia, foreign diplomatic missions located in the Washington metropolitan area, the headquarters buildings and grounds of the DHS and Treasury Department, and such other areas as directed by the president. The USSS is also responsible for telecommunications fraud, computer and telemarketing fraud, fraud relative to federally insured financial institutions, and other criminal and noncriminal cases. The Service is organized into two major components, one focused on protection and the other focused on investigation.

All people, places, and events that are protected represent key components of the nation's government and heritage. They are all, in addition to their intended roles, symbols of the country, and therefore prime terrorist targets. The loss of any of these, whether due to terrorist or other means, would threaten the security of the nation, and therefore their protection is integral to the homeland security of the nation. In 2008, the USSS employed 6,732 people. The Service budget allocation has gained slightly each year, rising from $1.334 billion in FY 2004 to $1.595 billion in FY 2008. The president's 2009 budget requests an increase for the Secret Service to $1.639 billion. This would account for about 3% of that year's total DHS budget.

Federal Emergency Management Agency
The Federal Emergency Management Agency (FEMA) is the government agency responsible for ensuring that the United States mitigates and is prepared for all types of disasters, whether they are natural, technological, or terrorism related (Figure 3–5), and manages the federal response and recovery efforts that follow disaster incidents declared by the president. FEMA also administers the National Flood Insurance Program.

FEMA hopes to maintain a full-time staff of 2,600 employees in 2008, who will continue to work at FEMA headquarters in Washington, DC, at regional and area offices across the country (including 10 regional offices, 2 area offices, and 5 recovery offices), at the Mount Weather Emergency Operations Center, and at the National Emergency Training Center in Emmitsburg,

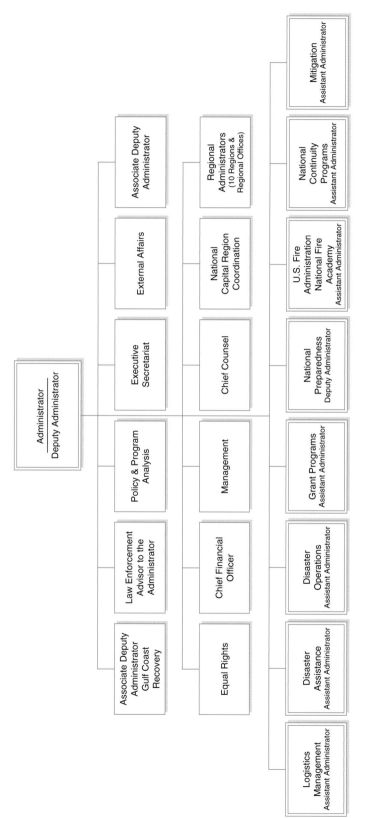

FIGURE 3–5 FEMA organizational chart. (DHS, 2007)

Maryland. FEMA also maintains a cadre of nearly 4,000 standby disaster assistance employees who are available for deployment after disasters.

While FEMA's central mission has remained the same since it was incorporated into DHS, its various functions have been transferred into and out of the agency during various organizational iterations that have occurred in the intervening years. One of its primary missions, as stated by DHS, is to "further the evolution of the emergency management culture from one that reacts to disasters to one that proactively helps communities and citizens avoid becoming victims." In addition, the directorate develops and manages a national training and evaluation system, designs curriculums, sets standards, and rewards performance in local, state, and federal training efforts.

Through the Disaster Relief Fund, FEMA provides individual and public assistance to help families and communities impacted by disasters rebuild and recover. FEMA also administers hazard mitigation programs to prevent or to reduce the risk to life and property from floods and other hazards. In addition to administering the National Incident Management System (NIMS), in FY 2007, FEMA's role as the lead federal agency for incident management, preparedness, and response was expanded to include the administration of DHS's grant programs and the United States Fire Administration. The inclusion of these programs was intended to reinforce FEMA's ability to provide the United States with a "unified, coordinated, and robust all-hazards preparedness and response capability at all levels of government including federal, state, tribal, and local government personnel, agencies, and regional authorities."

FEMA has been granted the leadership role, through the National Response Framework (NRF) and the Robert T. Stafford Disaster Relief and Emergency Assistance Act, to manage the DHS response to any sort of natural, technological, or terrorist attack disaster. This directorate is also in charge of coordinating the involvement of other federal response teams, such as the National Guard, in the event of a major incident. In accordance with the new National Response Plan, FEMA also leads federal government relief and recovery efforts that follow major declared disasters. These response and recovery processes are illustrated in much greater detail in Chapter 7.

FEMA currently offers five mitigation grant programs:

- Hazards Mitigation Grant Program
- Pre-Disaster Mitigation Program
- Flood Mitigation Assistance Program
- Repetitive Flood Claims Program
- Severe Repetitive Loss Program

In addition, FEMA offers the U.S. Fire Administration's Fire Management Assistance Grant Program, the Assistance to Firefighters Grant Program ("Fire Grants"), the Staffing for Adequate Fire and Emergency Response (SAFER) grants, and the Fire Prevention and Safety (FP&S) grants. Under the State Preparedness Grant Program, FEMA offers the Public Safety Interoperable Communications (PSIC) grants in partnership with the Department of Commerce.

FEMA also funds and administers the Citizen Corps Program. Citizen Corps funding supports the formation and training of local Citizen Corps Councils, which increase local involvement (in Citizen Corps Councils), develop community action plans, help in the performance of threat assessments and the identification of local resources for homeland security, and locally coordinate the Citizen Corps programs. The existing programs, administered by several federal agencies both internal and external to homeland security, involve leaders from law enforcement, fire, and emergency medical services, businesses, community-based institutions, schools, places of worship, health care facilities, public works, and other key community sectors. Current Citizen Corps programs include the following (Citizen Corps activities are documented in greater detail in Chapter 6 of this book):

- Community Emergency Response Teams (CERT), administered by DHS
- Volunteers in Police Service (VIPS) program, administered by DOJ

- Medical Reserve Corps, administered by HHS
- Neighborhood Watch (USA On Watch) programs, administered by DOJ
- Fire Corps Program, administered by the USA Freedom Corps and several nongovernmental partners
- Citizen-preparedness publications, which are public education guides that seek to increase individual knowledge and preparedness for crime, terrorism, and disasters at home, in neighborhoods, at places of work, and in public spaces

FEMA maintained a staff of 6,917 in FY 2008, of which 2,917 were full-time personnel and 4,000 were on call to be activated in times of disaster. FEMA saw its budget (as a component of the former Emergency Preparedness and Response Directorate until 2006) rise from $5.554 billion in FY 2004 to $7.541 billion in FY 2005, mostly because of biodefense funding. However, biodefense funding was cut from the FEMA budget in FY 2006, dropping the amount the agency received to $5.365 billion. In 2007, the FEMA budget jumped to $6.053 billion, but with the introduction of the FEMA Grants Program in 2008, this amount as requested stood at $9.639 billion. The FY 2009 budget requests a decrease in overall FEMA funding, mostly due to a drop in the amount of first responder grants being offered. The $8.766 billion will account for 17% of the total DHS budget. The FEMA budget can be increased by Congress through emergency appropriations to cover the costs of catastrophic disasters — as was the case following the September 11 attacks and the Hurricane Katrina response.

▪▪ Critical Thinking ▪

Do you believe that FEMA is appropriately placed within the DHS bureaucracy in its current position under the Secretary of Homeland Security, or should it have been placed somewhere else within the federal structure outside of DHS? Explain your answer.

Federal Law Enforcement Training Center

The Federal Law Enforcement Training Center (FLETC) serves as the federal government's principal provider of federal law enforcement personnel training. FLETC provides for the training needs of more than 80 federal agencies that carry out law enforcement responsibilities. The center also provides training and technical assistance to state and local law enforcement entities, and plans, develops, and presents formal training courses and practical exercise applications related to international law enforcement training. The center offers numerous basic law enforcement training programs of varying lengths, designed specifically for the duties and responsibilities of the personnel to be trained, and conducts numerous advanced and specialized training programs found nowhere else in the country.

FLETC currently operates four training sites throughout the United States. Its headquarters and primary training site is located in Glynco, Georgia. Two other field locations, both of which provide both basic and advanced training, are located in Artesia, New Mexico, and Charleston, South Carolina. The fourth training site, in Cheltenham, Maryland, provides in-service and requalification training for officers and agents in the Washington, DC, area. In cooperation with the State Department, FLETC also operates International Law Enforcement Academies in Gabarone, Botswana; San Salvador, El Salvador; Budapest, Hungary; Bangkok, Thailand; and Lima, Peru. FLETC maintained a staff of 1,106 in FY 2008, and saw budget allocations rise from $192 million in FY 2004 to $288 million in FY 2008. The president's FY 2009 budget request includes a decrease in funding for FLETC to $274 million, representing 1% of the DHS budget.

Transportation Security Administration (TSA)

The Transportation Security Administration (TSA) was created just two months after the September 11 terrorist attacks (on November 19, 2001), through the Aviation and Transportation Security Act

(ATSA — Public Law 107-071). TSA protects the nation's transportation systems in order to ensure the freedom of movement for both people and commercial goods and services. ATSA was created in recognition of failures in private security systems, and placed overall aviation transportation security under the direction and responsibility of the federal government. TSA's focus is on identifying risks to the transportation sector, prioritizing them, and managing them to acceptable levels through a variety of means, while working to mitigate the impact of incidents that may occur (Figure 3–6).

TSA began as an agency focused on airline security, which was understandable considering that the September 11 terrorists capitalized on lax aviation security measures to attack the nation. The agency's focus has steadily expanded to address other transportation modes such as intercity buses, rail travel, and ferry travel, but in terms of both dollars and people, its primary focus clearly remains on aviation security. TSA's specific responsibilities include ensuring thorough and efficient screening of all airline passengers and baggage through an appropriate mix of federalized and privatized screeners and technology. This screener workforce consists primarily of 43,000 passenger and baggage screeners located at 453 commercial and privatized airports throughout the country.

U.S. air carriers transport approximately 12.5 million tons of cargo, of which 2.8 million tons fly on board commercial passenger planes and 9.7 million tons are shipped in cargo planes (which, still today, are not inspected to the same degree as cargo that is shipped on the passenger carriers). TSA has been given the responsibility to devise and implement a system to screen, inspect, or otherwise ensure the security of all cargo that is to be transported aboard aircraft — a task that will likely require many years and significant financial investment.

TSA is also tasked with managing the security risk to the U.S. surface transportation systems. They are confronted with the paradox of trying to ensure the freedom of movement of people and commerce while preventing the same for terrorists. These transportation systems include approximately 775 million passengers traveling on buses each year, and over 9 billion passenger trips on mass transit per year; over 140,000 miles of railroad (of which 120,000 miles are privately owned); 3.8 million miles of roads (46,717 miles of Interstate highway and 114,700 miles of National Highway System roads), 582 bridges over 20 feet of span, 54 tunnels over 500 meters in length, and nearly 2.2 million miles of pipeline; and nearly 800,000 shipments of hazardous materials transported every day (95% by truck).

As part of Secretary Chertoff's reorganization plan, the Federal Air Marshals program was transferred from the U.S. Immigration and Customs Enforcement office to TSA, where it was originally located before being removed in 2003 under the original framework of DHS.

Edward Kip Hawley is the current assistant secretary for homeland security and administrator of TSA. The TSA maintained an employee base of 51,448 in FY 2008 (primarily federal airport security screeners), and saw its budget rise steadily from $4.578 billion in FY 2004 to $6.820 billion in FY 2008 (of which $4.809 billion was dedicated to aviation security). The president's FY 2009 budget request for the TSA is $7.102 billion, or 14% of the total DHS budget.

The Three Directorates

The Department of Homeland Security currently maintains three major multifunctional divisions, which have been termed directorates. Each of these divisions is led by an undersecretary. These divisions, which are described below, include:

- Directorate for National Protection and Programs
- Directorate for Science and Technology
- Directorate for Management

Directorate for National Protection and Programs

The Directorate for National Protection and Programs serves to accomplish the risk-reduction mission that is central to DHS. This Directorate was newly created for FY 2008 as a result of the

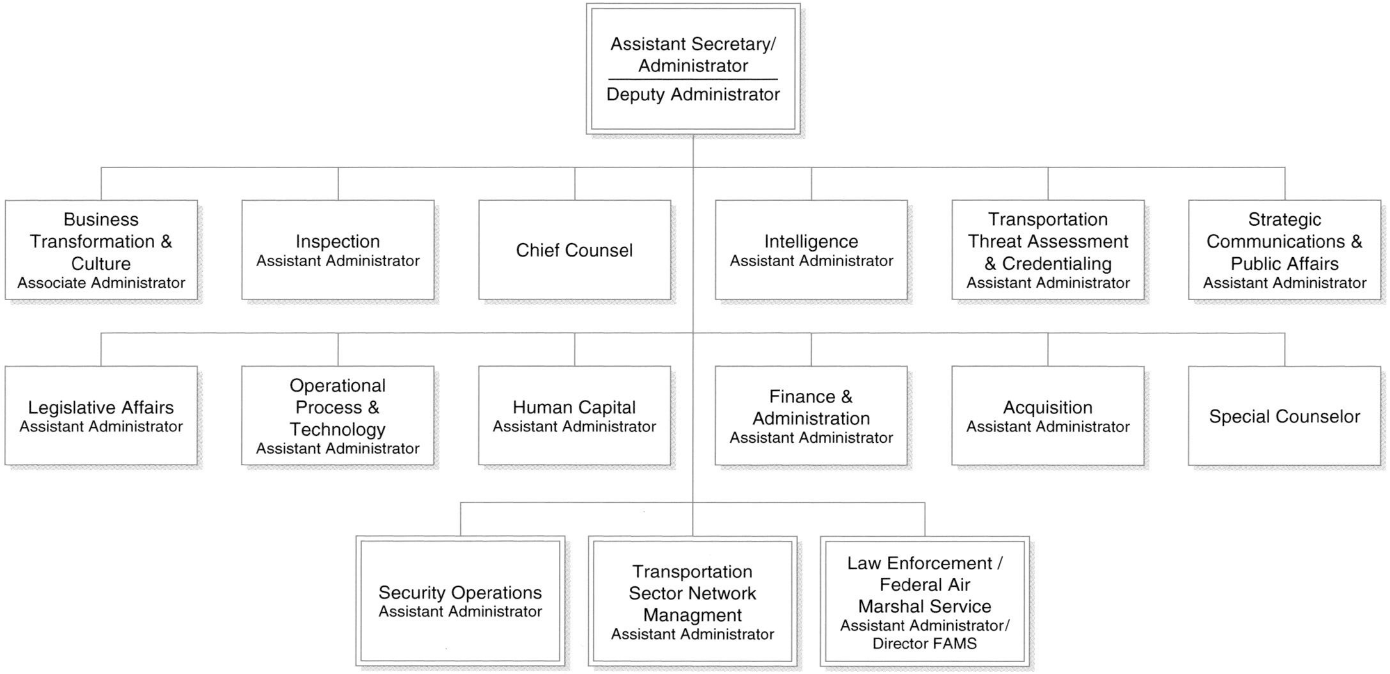

FIGURE 3–6 Transportation Security Administration organizational chart. (Department of Homeland Security, 2007)

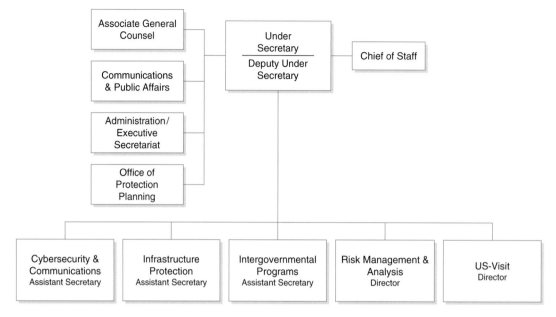

FIGURE 3–7 Directorate of National Protection and Programs organizational chart. (Department of Homeland Security, 2007)

Post-Katrina Emergency Management Reform Act, thereby assuming several functions that had existed previously in other areas spread throughout DHS. This office is led by DHS Undersecretary George Foresman, and maintains a full-time staff of 849 employees. The president's FY 2009 budget request includes $1.286 billion, representing 3% of the DHS budget request and an increase of $109 million over FY 2008 (Figure 3–7).

Prior to NPPD, the DHS Preparedness Directorate fulfilled three critical department-wide needs, namely:

1. To strengthen national risk management efforts for critical infrastructure
2. To define and synchronize DHS-level doctrine for homeland security protection initiatives that entail aggressive coordination internally within DHS, in planning and integration work across the federal government, and with state, communities, and the private sector
3. To deliver grants and related preparedness program and training activities

Of these three functions, the third was transferred to FEMA, while NPPD assumed the status as a "Department-level focal point" for the ongoing management of the first two. In addition, NPPD provides management support and direction for US-VISIT, an immigration tracking and technology program. NPPD is also the lead office for federal efforts to protect and prevent attacks on critical infrastructure, and as such, it works to improve cybersecurity and communications system resilience. NPPD is the office that interacts with the private sector and with state and local government leaders to ensure the full range of department-wide programs and policies are effectively integrated. This office is also working to standardize DHS risk management efforts. The NPPD responsibilities include:

- Promoting an integrated national approach to homeland security protection activities and verifying the approach and strategy via program metrics to assess performance and outcomes against mission goals
- Protecting the nation's critical infrastructure, both physical and virtual
- Ensuring operable and interoperable systems and networks to support emergency communications through a full spectrum of conditions

- Standardizing risk management approaches applied across the department ensuring polices, programs, and resources are driven by a consistent methodology
- Enhancing the security of citizens and people traveling to the United States through the use of biometric capabilities

The five components of NPPD include:

- The Office of Cybersecurity and Communications (CS&C): Works to ensure the security, resiliency, and reliability of the nation's cyber and communications infrastructure in collaboration with the public and private sectors, including international partners. Specifically, CS&C is focused on preparing for and responding to catastrophic incidents that could degrade or overwhelm the networks, systems, and assets that operate our nation's information technology and communications infrastructure. Programs contained within this office include:

  The National Communications System
  The National Cybersecurity Division
  The Office of Emergency Communications

- The Office of Infrastructure Protection (OIP): This office leads the coordinated national effort to reduce risk to critical infrastructures and key resources posed by terrorism. OIP facilitates the identification, prioritization, coordination, and protection of these resources in support of federal, state, local, territorial, and tribal governments, as well as the private sector and international entities. OIP shares this information with "partners" at the state, local, and private levels, communicating threats, vulnerabilities, incidents, potential protective measures, and best practices that enhance protection, response, mitigation, and restoration activities across the nation and the international community. OIP functions are guided by the National Infrastructure Protection Plan (which can be found by accessing http://www.dhs.gov/xprevprot/ programs/editorial_0827.shtm).

- The Office of Intergovernmental Programs (IGP): This office promotes an integrated national approach to homeland security by ensuring, coordinating, and advancing federal interaction with state, local, tribal, and territorial governments. OIG's purpose is to facilitate communication between the DHS's expert resources and the expert resources of the nation's autonomous governments; to act as an advocate for state, local, tribal, and territorial governments within DHS; and to coordinate and maintain constant awareness of the various communications occurring regularly throughout DHS.

- The Office of Risk Management and Analysis (RMA): This office leads DHS's efforts to establish a common framework to address the overall management and national risk. To do this, the following strategic objectives have been established for the office:

  Serve as DHS's executive agent for national-level risk management analysis standards and metrics
  Develop and embed a consistent, standardized approach to risk
  Develop a coordinated, collaborative approach to risk management that will allow the department to leverage and integrate risk expertise across components and external stakeholders
  Assess department-level risk performance to ensure programs are measurably reducing risk across the country
  Communicate the department's "risk story" in a manner that reinforces the value of the risk-informed approach

- United States Visitor and Immigrant Status Indicator Technology (US-VISIT): US-VISIT was established in order to accurately record the entry and exit of travelers to the United States by collecting biographic information and biometric information (such as digital fingerprints and photographs, for example). US-VISIT is part of an ongoing and growing system of security measures that begins overseas and continues through a foreign traveler's arrival in and departure from the United States.

Directorate for Science and Technology

The Science and Technology (S&T) Directorate provides leadership for directing, funding, and conducting research, development, test, and evaluation (RDT&E), and procurement of technologies and systems that can prevent the importation of chemical, biological, radiological, nuclear, and related weapons and material, and will help the nation protect against and respond to terrorist threats. The S&T Directorate partners and coordinates with federal, state, and local government and private-sector entities in conducting its activities, and is working to establish a system to transfer the fruits of these homeland security developments and technologies into DHS's operational elements. Through S&T research and development activities, DHS hopes to enhance its ability to execute all of its stated missions, now and in the future, and to help the nation meet its homeland security RDT&E needs (Figure 3–8).

The HS Act of 2002 effectively abolished the Office of Science and Technology that existed within the National Institute of Justice (which still exists within the DOJ) and transferred all applicable functions to S&T. Within the directorate, several programs were created to carry out the S&T mission, including:

- The Homeland Security Advanced Research Projects Agency (HSARPA), which focuses on homeland security research and development that could lead to significant technological breakthroughs
- The Homeland Security Centers of Excellence, which are institutes at academic and other institutions that bring together leading experts and researchers to conduct research on various homeland security–related topics
- The Homeland Security Institute, which is essentially a federally funded homeland security think tank
- The Office of National Laboratories, which provides coordination for the various national laboratory facilities working on homeland security issues
- SAFECOM, which is a communications program that provides research, development, testing and evaluation, guidance, tools, and templates on interoperable communications development
- The SAFETY Act, which is a DHS administered program providing liability protections to private sector developers of homeland security technologies and other applications
- Tech Solutions, which is a program that provides information resources and technology solutions addressing gaps in capabilities identified by local and state first response and emergency management agencies
- The Test and Evaluation Standards Program, which provides technical support and coordination to assist emergency responders in the acquisition of equipment, procedures, and mitigation measures and processes
- University Programs, which engages the academic community to create learning and research environments in areas critical to national security

The S&T Directorate maintained a staff of 381 full-time employees in FY 2007. The S&T budget allocation rose steadily from to $913 million in FY 2004 to $1.368 billion in FY 2006. In 2007, this amount fell to $968 million, and fell again in FY 2008 to $830 million. In FY 2009, the president requested a slight increase to $869 million, accounting for 2% of the total DHS FY 2009 budget. The S&T Directorate is expanded on in much greater detail in Chapter 9.

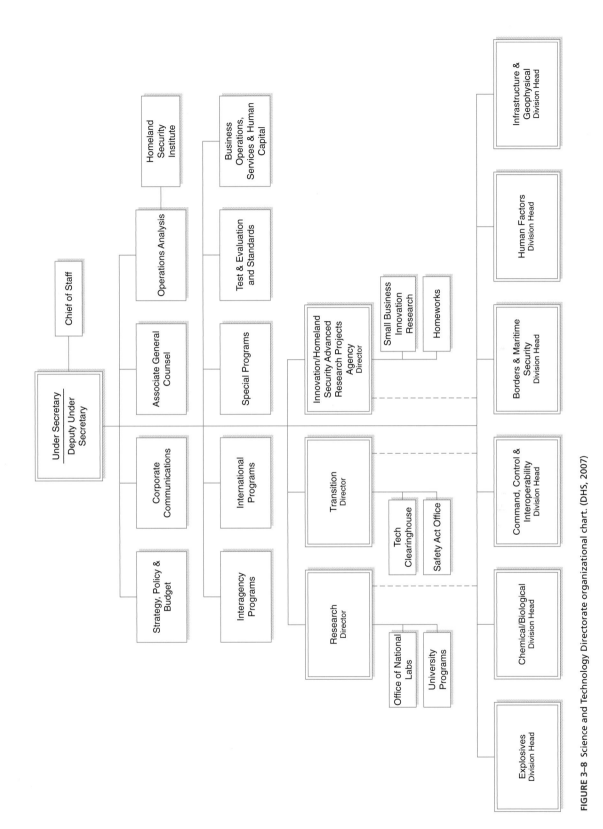

FIGURE 3–8 Science and Technology Directorate organizational chart. (DHS, 2007)

Directorate for Management

The Undersecretary for Management is responsible for budget, appropriations, expenditure of funds, accounting, and finance; procurement; human resources and personnel; information technology systems; facilities, property, equipment, and other material resources; and identification and tracking of performance measurements relating to the responsibilities of the DHS. The FY 2007 DHS budget included $604 million to carry out this mission. The president's FY 2008 budget decreased this amount to $572 million, but the FY 2009 request sought to increase this again to $753 million, representing 1% of the DHS budget that year. There were 1,307 employees involved in management activities in DHS, both within and outside of the Management Directorate, in FY 2008.

DHS goals from its strategic plan are summarized in the sidebar, "Select Strategic Goals . . ."

Select Strategic Goals for Protection and Response from the U.S. Department of Homeland Security Strategic Plan

In February 2004, in order to better organize the new department and to provide guidance to the 180,000 DHS employees transferred to the new agency, DHS released its own strategic plan. The plan contains vision and mission statements, strategic goals, and objectives that are intended to provide the framework guiding the actions that make up the department's daily operations. The strategic goals follow:

Strategic Goal 1: Awareness

Identify and understand threats, assess vulnerabilities, determine potential impacts and disseminate timely information to our homeland security partners and the American public.

- Objective 1.1 — Gather and fuse all terrorism-related intelligence; analyze and coordinate access to information related to potential terrorist or other threats.
- Objective 1.2 — Identify and assess the vulnerability of critical infrastructure and key assets.
- Objective 1.3 — Develop timely, actionable and valuable information based on intelligence analysis and vulnerability assessments.
- Objective 1.4 — Ensure quick and accurate dissemination of relevant intelligence information to homeland security partners, including the public.

Strategic Goal 2: Prevention

Detect, deter and mitigate threats to our homeland.

- Objective 2.1 — Secure our borders against terrorists, means of terrorism, illegal drugs and other illegal activity.
- Objective 2.2 — Enforce trade and immigration laws.
- Objective 2.3 — Provide operational end users with the technology and capabilities to detect and prevent terrorist attacks, means of terrorism and other illegal activities.
- Objective 2.4 — Ensure national and international policy, law enforcement and other actions to prepare for and prevent terrorism are coordinated.
- Objective 2.5 — Strengthen the security of the Nation's transportation systems.
- Objective 2.6 — Ensure the security and integrity of the immigration system.

Strategic Goal 3: Protection

Safeguard our people and their freedoms, critical infrastructure, property and the economy of our nation from acts of terrorism, natural disasters, or other emergencies.

- Objective 3.1 — Protect the public from acts of terrorism and other illegal activities.
- Objective 3.2 — Reduce infrastructure vulnerability from acts of terrorism.
- Objective 3.3 — Protect against financial and electronic crimes, counterfeit currency, illegal bulk currency movement and identity theft.
- Objective 3.4 — Secure the physical safety of the President, Vice President, visiting world leaders, and other protectees.
- Objective 3.5 — Ensure the continuity of government operations and essential functions in the event of crisis or disaster.
- Objective 3.6 — Protect the marine environment and living marine resources.
- Objective 3.7 — Strengthen nationwide preparedness and mitigation against acts of terrorism, natural disasters, or other emergencies.

Strategic Goal 4: Response

Lead, manage and coordinate the national response to acts of terrorism, natural disasters, or other emergencies.

- Objective 4.1 — Reduce the loss of life and property by strengthening nationwide response readiness.
- Objective 4.2 — Provide scalable and robust all-hazard response capability.
- Objective 4.3 — Provide search and rescue services to people and property in distress.

Strategic Goal 5: Recovery

Lead national, state, local and private sector efforts to restore services and rebuild communities after acts of terrorism, natural disasters, or other emergencies.

- Objective 5.1 — Strengthen nationwide recovery plans and capabilities.
- Objective 5.2 — Provide scalable and robust all-hazard recovery assistance.

Source: U.S. Department of Homeland Security Strategic Plan, www.dhs.gov.

Office of the Inspector General

The DHS Office of the Inspector General (OIG) was established by the Homeland Security Act of 2002, by amendment to the Inspector General Act of 1978. Inspector General Clark Kent Ervin was the first to hold the post. The inspector general has a dual reporting responsibility, both to the DHS secretary and to Congress. The OIG serves as an independent and objective inspection, audit, and investigative body that safeguards public tax dollars by promoting effectiveness, efficiency, and economy in DHS programs and operations, and by preventing and detecting fraud, abuse, mismanagement, and waste in such programs and operations.

Considering the massive changes that have resulted from the creation of DHS, and the billions of dollars that have been dedicated to the department's mission, an office such as this is critical. In 2008, OIG maintained a staff of 577 people. The OIG budget has remained relatively constant during the period of FY 2004 to FY 2006, with an allocation of approximately $83 million. In FY 2007 this jumped by nearly 25% to $103 million, as the perceived need for greater oversight was confirmed. This amount rose again in FY 2008 to $109 million. The president requested to $101 million for OIG in his FY 2009 budget. Clark Kent Ervin left the post of inspector general on December 8, 2004, and was replaced by Assistant Inspector General Richard L. Skinner who has held the office ever since.

United States Citizenship and Immigration Services

The U.S. Citizenship and Immigration Services (USCIS) is the component of the DHS that facilitates legal immigration for people seeking to enter, reside, or work in the United States. The office, led by Director Emilio T. Gonzalez, is responsible for "ensuring the delivery of the right immigration benefit to the right person at the right time, and no benefit to the wrong person." USCIS has established three priorities to accomplish this task:

1. Eliminating the immigration benefit application backlog
2. Improving customer service
3. Enhancing national security

Before September 11, all immigration issues were handled by the U.S. State Department through their consular services section, and through the Immigration and Naturalization Service (INS) of the Department of Justice. The State Department, which handled the granting of permission to apply for entry into the United States from overseas posts, has maintained its role since the government reorganization has taken place. The INS, however, which handled the creation of and enforcement of immigration policy within the United States, was absorbed into the DHS and broken into three distinct offices. USCIS was given responsibility for the immigration services (applications for residence, for instance), Immigration and Customs Enforcement (ICE) is responsible for enforcing immigration law within the United States, and Customs and Border Protection (CBP) enforces those same laws at the U.S. ports of entry and the borders (Figure 3–9).

USCIS processes more than 7 million applications each year. The office maintained a staff of 10,620 in FY 2008, and saw their budget rise from $1.550 billion in FY 2004 to $2.539 billion in FY 2008. The president's FY 2009 budget request includes $2.690 billion for USCIS, representing 5% of the department's budget.

United States Customs and Border Protection

U.S. Customs and Border Protection (CBP) is responsible for protecting the nation's borders, at and between official ports of entry. CBP is responsible for ensuring that all persons and cargo entering the United States do so both legally and safely. CBP inspectors are responsible for preventing cross-border smuggling of such contraband as controlled substances, WMDs, and illegal plants and animals. They also ensure that travelers and immigrants have appropriate documentation necessary to enter the country legally. Other tasks include preventing the illegal export of U.S. currency or other negotiable instruments, the export of stolen goods such as vehicles, and the export of strategically sensitive technologies that could be used overseas to compromise both the security and the strategic and economic position of the United States. The Border Patrol, which operates under the direction of CBP, is responsible for controlling all of America's 7,500 miles of land borders between ports of entry, and 95,000 miles of maritime border in partnership with the USCG.

CBP officials are also deployed overseas at major international seaports, through application of the Container Security Initiative (CSI). This project was established to allow agents to prescreen shipping containers in order to detect and interdict WMDs and other illicit material before they arrive in the United States. To date, there are 50 CSI ports throughout the world, covering almost 82% of inbound maritime containers. CBP's entry specialists and trade compliance personnel enforce U.S. trade and tariff laws and regulations in order to ensure that a fair and competitive trade environment exists for the United States. CBP's Air and Marine Operations Division patrols the nation's borders to interdict illegal drugs and terrorists before entry into the United States, and provides surveillance and operational support to special national security events.

CBP makes direct contact with more than 500 million people crossing the borders through ports each year, and with tens of thousands of shippers, drivers, pilots, and importers associated with more than 25 million officially declared trade entries. In FY 2008, CBP maintained a staff of 54,868, and

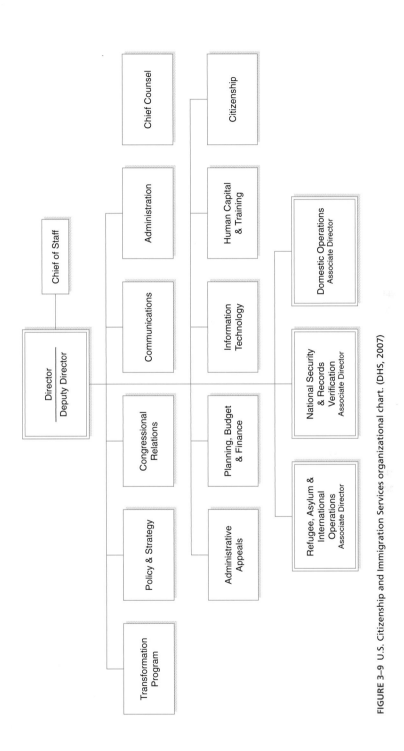

FIGURE 3-9 U.S. Citizenship and Immigration Services organizational chart. (DHS, 2007)

saw budgets rise steadily from $5.997 billion in FY 2004 to $10.812 billion in FY 2008. The president's FY 2009 budget request increases this even further to $10.941 billion for CBP, the single greatest item on this budget, accounting for 22% of the total (Figure 3–10).

Immigration and Customs Enforcement

As the largest investigative arm of the DHS, U.S. Immigration and Customs Enforcement (ICE) enforces federal immigration and customs laws. Through the Federal Protective Service, ICE also facilities security on federal property. The primary mission of ICE is to detect vulnerabilities and prevent violations that threaten national security. The various components of this directorate are as follows:

- Investigations is responsible for investigating a range of domestic and international activities arising from the movement of people and goods that violate immigration and customs laws and threaten national security such as visa security, illegal arms exports, financial and smuggling violations, immigration and customs fraud, human trafficking, identity and benefit fraud, child pornography, and sex tourism.

- Detention and Removal is responsible for ensuring that every alien who has been ordered removed departs the United States through fair enforcement of the nation's immigration laws and coordination with foreign governments to ensure countries will accept removable aliens.

- Federal Protective Service is responsible for ensuring a safe environment in which federal agencies can conduct business by reducing threats posed against approximately 9,000 federal government facilities nationwide.

- Intelligence is responsible for the collection, analysis, and dissemination of strategic and tactical intelligence data in support of ICE and DHS.

- Principal Legal Advisor is the legal representative for the U.S. government at immigration court hearings, and provides the legal advice, training, and services required to support the ICE mission while defending the immigration laws of the United States.

ICE works to protect and serve the United States and its people by deterring, interdicting, and investigating threats arising from the movement of people and goods into and out of the United States, and by policing and securing federal government facilities across the nation. In FY 2008, ICE employed 18,965 employees, and saw allocations rise steadily from $3.616 billion in FY2004 to $5.576 billion in FY 2008. The president's FY 2009 budget request included $5.676 billion for ICE, representing 11% of the department's budget (Figure 3–11).

Office of Policy

The Office of Policy, led by Assistant Secretary for Policy Stewart A. Baker, formulates and coordinates homeland security policy and procedures for the Department of Homeland Security. This office helps the enormous, widespread department to maintain a centralized, coordinated focus. Through their actions, the Office of Policy coordinates the department's prevention, protection, response, and recovery missions. The Office of Policy:

- Leads coordination of department-wide policies, programs, and planning, which will ensure consistency and integration of missions throughout the entire department

- Provides a central office to develop and communicate policies across multiple components of the homeland security network and strengthens the department's ability to maintain policy and operational readiness needed to protect the homeland

- Provides the foundation and direction for department-wide strategic planning and budget priorities

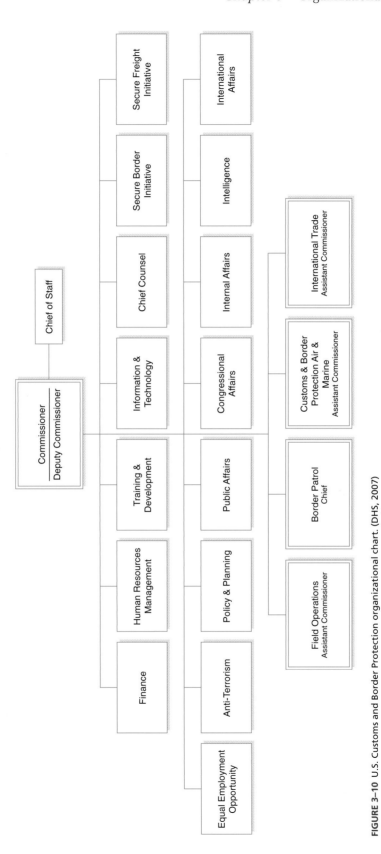

FIGURE 3–10 U.S. Customs and Border Protection organizational chart. (DHS, 2007)

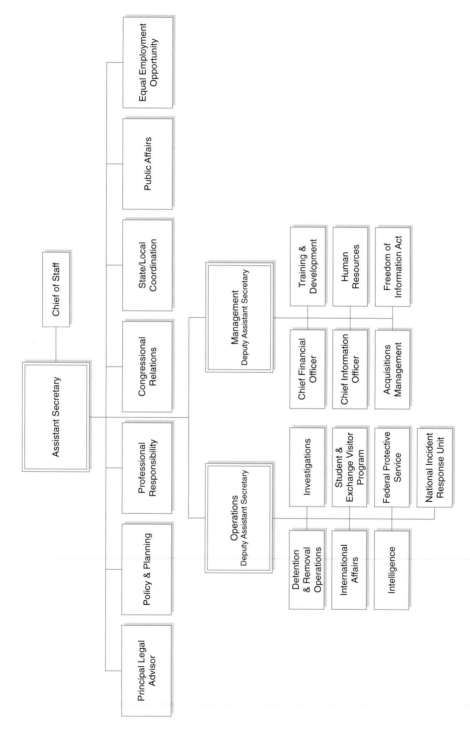

FIGURE 3-11 Immigration and Customs Enforcement organizational chart. (DHS, 2007)

- Bridges multiple headquarters' components and operating agencies to improve communication among departmental entities, eliminate duplication of effort, and translate policies into timely action
- Creates a single point of contact for internal and external stakeholders that will allow for streamlined policy management across the department

The Office of Policy operates through the actions of the following offices:

- Office of Policy Development: Ensures that a coordinated approach to DHS policy is adopted and advocated within its components, and ensures that DHS interests are effectively portrayed in national and international efforts
- Office of Strategic Plans: Maintains what is considered the "long-term view" for DHS, ensures that the DHS Secretary's strategic priorities are incorporated into all planning efforts (especially with regards to integration, component priorities, and resource allocation)
- Office of International Affairs: Develops DHS's strategy for promoting the department's mission overseas, and actively engages foreign allies to improve international cooperation for immigration policy, visa security, aviation security, border security and training, law enforcement, and cargo security
- Office of Immigration Statistics: Leads the development of statistical information useful to make decisions and analyze the effects of immigration in the United States
- Private Sector Office: Provides the nation's private sector with a direct line of communication (to DHS), utilizes information received from the private sector, and promotes DHS policies to the private sector
- Homeland Security Advisory Council: Leverages the experience, expertise, and national and global connections of its members to provide the DHS Secretary with real-time, real-world, sensing, and independent advice to support decision making for homeland security operations

The budget of this new office, created in 2007, falls under the Directorate for Management.

Office of Health Affairs

The Office of Health Affairs (OHA) coordinates all DHS medical activities to ensure appropriate preparation for and response to incidents having "medical significance." OHA serves as the principal medical adviser for the DHS Secretary and FEMA Administrator by providing timely incident-specific management guidance for the medical consequences of disasters. Additionally, OHA leads the department's biodefense activities; works with partner agencies to ensure medical readiness for catastrophic incidents; and supports the DHS mission through department-wide standards and best practices for the occupational health and safety of employees. This new office, created in 2007, is led by the Chief Medical Officer, who now has the title of Assistant Secretary for Health Affairs and Chief Medical Officer. The first person to assume this role was Dr. Jeffrey W. Runge.

The Office of Health Affairs will have three main divisions:

- Weapons of Mass Destruction (WMD) and Biodefense: This office is led by a deputy assistant secretary who leads the department's biodefense activities, including the Bioshield and BioWatch programs (which transferred to OHA from S&T) and the National Biosurveillance Integration System (which transferred to OHA from Infrastructure Protection).
- Medical Readiness: This office will coordinate contingency planning, medical readiness of first responders, WMD incident management support, and medical preparedness grant coordination.
- Component Services: This office will provide policy, standards, requirements, and metrics for the department's occupational health and safety programs and provide protective and operational medical services within DHS.

The president's FY 2009 budget request for this new office, which maintained a full-time staff of 80 employees in FY 2008, is $161 million (an increase of $45 million over FY 2008). This office has also been placed in charge of the department's Biodefense Countermeasures program, which itself carries a budget request of $2.175 billion.

Offices of Intelligence and Analysis and Operations Coordination

The Office of Intelligence and Analysis (I&A), created in 2007 in response to the changes brought about by the Post-Katrina Emergency Management Reform Act, is responsible for using the information and intelligence gleaned from the myriad sources throughout the federal government to identify and assess current and future threats to the United States. The Assistant Secretary for Intelligence and Analysis (ASIS), currently Charles E. Allen, leads this office, and serves as the DHS Chief Intelligence Officer (CINT). I&A ensures that information is gathered from all relevant DHS field operations and is fused with information from throughout the intelligence community to produce intelligence reports (and other products) for officials who require them inside and outside of DHS.

The Office of Operations Coordination is responsible for monitoring U.S. security on a daily basis and coordinating activities within DHS and with governors, Homeland Security Advisors, law enforcement partners, and critical infrastructure operators in all 50 states and more than 50 major urban areas nationwide. The Office of Operations Coordination is responsible for monitoring the security of the United States on a daily basis and coordinating activities within the department and with governors, Homeland Security Advisors, law enforcement partners, and critical infrastructure operators in all 50 States and more than 50 major urban areas nationwide. Information is shared daily by the two halves of the office, referred to as the "Intelligence Side" and the "Law Enforcement Side." Each half is identical and functions in tandem with the other but operates under different security clearance standards for information access purposes. The Intelligence Side focuses on pieces of highly classified intelligence and how the information contributes to the current threat picture for any given area. The Law Enforcement Side is dedicated to tracking the different enforcement activities across the country that may have terrorist significance. The two pieces fuse together to create a real-time picture of the nation's threat environment.

Operations Coordination oversees the National Operations Center (NOC), which collects and collates information from more than 35 federal, state, territorial, tribal, local, and private sector agencies. Through the NOC, the office provides real-time situational awareness and monitoring of the nation, coordinates incidents and response activities, and, in conjunction with the Office of Intelligence and Analysis, issues advisories and bulletins concerning threats to homeland security, as well as specific protective measures. The NOC — which is always operational — coordinates information sharing to help deter, detect, and prevent terrorist acts and to manage domestic incidents. Information on domestic incident management is shared with Emergency Operations Centers at all levels through the Homeland Security Information Network (HSIN). This office, also created in 2007 in response to the changes brought about by the Post-Katrina Emergency Management Reform Act, is led by Director for Operations Coordination Roger T. Rufe, Jr.

These two offices operate under a joined budget, termed Analysis and Operations, for which $306 million was appropriated in 2008. The president's FY 2009 budget requests $334 million for these offices, which together employed 594 people in FY 2008.

Domestic Nuclear Detection Office

The Domestic Nuclear Detection Office (DNDO) works to enhance the nuclear detection efforts of federal, state, territorial, tribal, and local governments, and the private sector and to ensure a coordinated response to such threats. DNDO was established April 15, 2005, to improve the capability of the U.S. government to detect and report unauthorized attempts to import, possess, store, develop, or transport nuclear or radiological material for use against the nation, and to further enhance this capability over time. The objectives of the office are to:

- Develop the global nuclear detection and reporting architecture.
- Develop, acquire, and support the domestic nuclear detection and reporting system.
- Fully characterize detector system performance before deployment.
- Establish situational awareness through information sharing and analysis.
- Establish operation protocols to ensure detection leads to effective response.
- Conduct a transformational research and development program.
- Establish the National Technical Nuclear Forensics Center to provide planning, integration, and improvements to USG nuclear forensics capabilities.

The DNDO is led by Director Vayl Oxford, and employed 137 people in FY 2008. The DNDO budget has risen from $317 million in FY 2006 to $484 million in FY 2008. The president's FY 2009 budget request for DNDO is $564 million.

▣ ▣ Critical Thinking ▣

Do you believe that it is possible to effectively lead a single federal department like the Department of Homeland Security, with over 170,000 employees, or does its existence combine too many unrelated functions under a single organizational mission? Explain your answer.

Secretary Chertoff's DHS Reorganization Plan

On July 13, 2005, DHS Secretary Michael Chertoff released a six-point agenda that was used to guide the first of two major reorganizations that have occurred within DHS, in this case aimed at streamlining what were considered inefficient and cumbersome efforts and operations. The agenda followed an initial comprehensive review of operations that Chertoff initiated immediately after assuming his leadership position. The review closely examined the department in search of ways in which leadership could better manage risk in terms of threat, vulnerability, and consequence; prioritize policies and operational missions according to this risk-based approach; and establish a series of preventive and protective steps that would increase security at multiple levels. According to the six-point agenda, changes were focused on the following:

- Increasing overall preparedness, particularly for catastrophic events
- Creating better transportation security systems to move people and cargo more securely and efficiently
- Strengthening border security and interior enforcement and reforming immigration processes
- Enhancing information sharing (with partners)
- Improving financial management, human resource development, procurement, and information technology within the department
- Realigning the department's organization to maximize mission performance

Secretary Chertoff initiated several new policy initiatives that were included in the overhaul of the department, including:

- New border security approaches, accomplished through additional personnel, new technologies, infrastructure investments, and more comprehensive enforcement — coupled with efforts to reduce the demand for illegal border migration by channeling migrants seeking work into regulated legal channels

- Restructuring the current immigration process to enhance security and improve customer service
- Reaching out to the state homeland security officials in order to improve information exchange protocols, refine the Homeland Security Advisory System, and support state and regional data fusion centers
- Investing in DHS personnel by providing professional career training and other development efforts

One of the most significant changes that occurred as result of the six-point agenda was an organizational restructuring of the department (Figure 3–12). Chertoff asserted that these changes were made "to increase [the department's] ability to prepare, prevent, and respond to terrorist attacks and other emergencies." Changes include the following:

- A new Directorate of Policy was created "to centralize and improve policy development and coordination." This directorate was led by an undersecretary, and served as the primary department-wide coordinator for policies, regulations, and other initiatives. This directorate was created to ensure the consistency of policy and regulatory development across various parts of the department as well as to perform long-range strategic policy planning. This new directorate, which later became the Office for Policy in 2007, included the following offices:

  Office of International Affairs
  Office of Private Sector Liaison
  Homeland Security Advisory Council
  Office of Immigration Statistics
  Senior Asylum Officer

- A new Office of Intelligence and Analysis was created to "strengthen intelligence functions and information sharing." This office still exists in the current structure of DHS as previously described.

- A Director of Operations Coordination position was created, with a corresponding Operations Coordination office, which also remains in the current structure of DHS.

- The Information Analysis and Infrastructure Protection Directorate was renamed the Directorate for Preparedness, which consolidated preparedness assets from across the department. The Directorate for Preparedness was created to facilitate grants and oversee nationwide preparedness efforts supporting first responder training, citizen awareness, public health, infrastructure security, and cybersecurity and ensure proper steps are taken to protect high-risk targets. Many of this directorate's functions, several of which were removed from FEMA according to Secretary Chertoff's Reorganization Plan, were returned to that and other agencies and offices spread across the department in 2007 according to the Post-Katrina Emergency Management Reform Act.

- FEMA was removed from the Emergency Preparedness & Response Directorate that was created in the original organization of DHS, and was given a direct reporting responsibility to the Secretary of Homeland Security. This change, which remains in place today, was first made in order to "improve national response and recovery efforts by focusing FEMA on its core functions," and involved drawing many of the preparedness functions from the agency. However, all of these original functions of FEMA were returned to the agency as stipulated by the Post-Katrina Emergency Management Reform Act.

- The Federal Air Marshal Service was moved from the Immigration and Customs Enforcement bureau to the Transportation Security Administration (where it was originally housed prior to the creation of DHS in 2002).

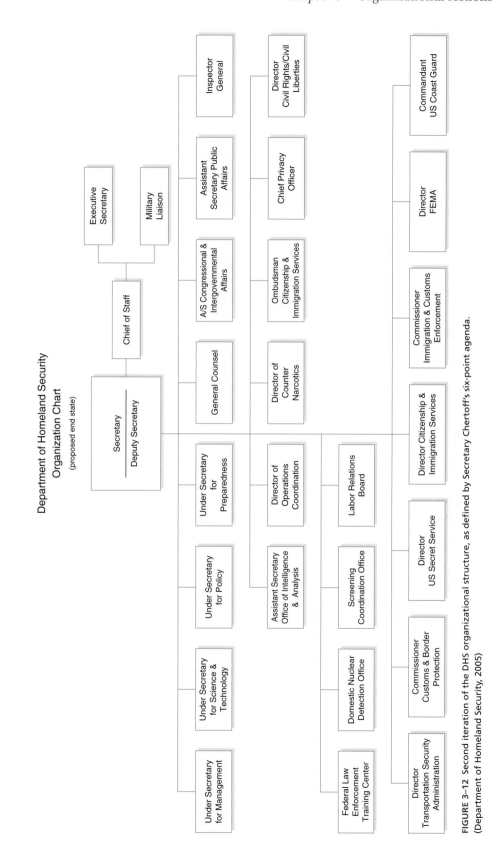

Department of Homeland Security
Organization Chart
(proposed end state)

FIGURE 3–12 Second iteration of the DHS organizational structure, as defined by Secretary Chertoff's six-point agenda. (Department of Homeland Security, 2005)

- A new Office of Legislative and Intergovernmental Affairs was created, which merged the functions of the original Offices of Legislative Affairs and of State and Local Government Coordination, in an effort to "streamline intergovernmental relations efforts and better share homeland security information with members of Congress as well as state and local officials." This office remains in the new organization of the department.

- The Office of Security, which develops, implements, and oversees the security policies, programs, and standards within DHS, was moved into the Directorate for Management "in order to better manage information systems, contractual activities, security accreditation, training and resources." This office, led by the Chief Security Officer, remains there today.

Of the changes that were made according to Secretary Chertoff's Reorganization Plan, there was one change that stood out above the rest as being particularly troubling — the disassembly of the Directorate of Emergency Preparedness and Response (EP&R). Although it made perfect sense that FEMA should exist as a standalone agency within the department — especially considering the fact that the functions of FEMA fully dominated this original directorate — it was somewhat inexplicable as to why FEMA would be stripped of its preparedness and mitigation functions. This action was clearly a complete reversal in the 30-year trend toward the comprehensive approach to emergency management's four functions: mitigation, preparedness, response, and recovery.

United Press International reported that critics both within FEMA and outside of DHS, especially from within the first responder community, felt that the change was a sure sign that DHS was making a significant departure from the traditional "all-hazards" approach to emergency management, which would see terrorism as but one of many hazards encompassing each community's hazard profile. Following the poor response to Katrina, members of Congress redressed this apparent mistake by reinstating all of the functions withdrawn from FEMA back under the direction of its administrator.

▨ ▨ Critical Thinking ▨

Do you believe that the problems attributed to FEMA in the response to Hurricane Katrina would have happened regardless of Secretary Chertoff's reorganization plan, or that it was something about this structure that caused the inefficiencies and shortfalls that were observed? Or were the problems entirely unrelated to the DHS structure? Explain your answer.

Other Agencies Participating in Community-Level Funding

As mentioned in the introduction to this chapter, the Department of Homeland Security may be the most recognized embodiment of federal homeland security action and have the most central role in its implementation, but it is not alone in the federal government by any means in this mission. Several other federal agencies outside of the new department have both maintained existing programs, and created entirely new programs, each addressing some aspect of homeland security. Many of these also fund or support homeland security efforts at the state and local levels as well. Several of these programs, as discussed next, are either in the transitional or developmental phase but have already begun active participation within the greater homeland security context.

U.S.A. Freedom Corps

The U.S.A. Freedom Corps is an umbrella organization within the Executive Office of the President that includes the Peace Corps, the Corporation for National and Community Service (CNCS), and Citizen Corps. CNCS and Citizen Corps, which operate domestically, are discussed here.

Corporation for National and Community Service

The CNCS administers several individual volunteer-based but grant-funded programs, including AmeriCorps, Senior Corps, and Learn and Serve America:

- AmeriCorps is a network of national service programs that "engage more than 70,000 Americans each year in intensive service to meet critical needs in education, public safety, health, and the environment." AmeriCorps members serve through more than 3,000 nonprofit and nongovernmental agencies, public agencies, and faith-based organizations, tutoring and mentoring youth, building affordable housing, teaching computer skills, cleaning parks and streams, running after-school programs, and helping communities respond to disasters. These programs engage more than 2 million Americans of all ages and backgrounds in service each year.

- Senior Corps is a network of programs that "tap the experience, skills, and talents of older citizens to meet community challenges." It includes three programs: Foster Grandparents, Senior Companions, and the Retired and Senior Volunteer Program. More than a half-million Americans ages 55 and older assist local nonprofits, public agencies, and faith-based organizations in carrying out their missions, together having provided over one billion volunteer hours nationwide.

- Learn and Serve America is a program that "supports service-learning programs in schools and community organizations that help nearly one million students from kindergarten through college meet community needs, while improving their academic skills and learning the habits of good citizenship." Service learning is defined as an educational method by which participants learn and develop through active participation in service that is conducted in and meets the needs of a community.

In July 2002, the Corporation for National and Community Service announced an initiative aimed at increasing citizen participation in homeland security. That year, CNCS awarded 43 grants totaling $10.3 million to communities, government agencies, and voluntary organizations to fund volunteer programs whose activities focused on the homeland security needs of communities. Since that time CNCS has continued to support community-level homeland security projects, including several of the following, which illustrate their accomplishments:

- AmeriCorps members serving in a program sponsored by the Florida Department of Elder Affairs recruited more than 600 disaster services volunteers who contributed more than 12,000 hours of service, distributed more than 200,000 disaster services publications, and reached nearly 2,500 residents with presentations on safety.

- AmeriCorps members serving with the Green River Area Development District in rural Kentucky utilized data from a Global Positioning System to map out information about fire stations, emergency shelters, hazardous materials (HAZMAT) storage facilities, medical facilities, and nursing homes.

- Just blocks from the World Trade Center site, Pace University AmeriCorps members trained 250 people in English, Chinese, and Spanish in emergency preparedness techniques, created a resource list that consolidates all important emergency numbers, and built a "Downtown Needs" website that serves as a volunteer clearinghouse for 2,000 organizations in the downtown area.

- AmeriCorps members in the California Safe Corps taught disaster preparedness classes to more than 1,000 community members, recruited more than 100 new volunteers who have provided more than 250 hours of service, and assisted more than 200 victims of disasters.

- In Iowa, AmeriCorps members made presentations on disaster preparedness at 400 schools across the state.

In the response to and recovery from the 2005 Gulf Coast hurricanes, CNCS became highly involved in the cleanup and rebuilding of the affected communities through volunteer participation. CNCS grantee programs from throughout the country sent volunteer participants. CNCS volunteers provided millions of hours of service in relief and recovery areas such as "mucking out" flooded houses, demolition, construction, tarping of damaged roofs, victim case management, counseling, and much more. The post-disaster assistance provided by the various CNCS programs is described in the sidebar, "National Service Responds to the Gulf Coast Hurricanes."

National Service Responds to the Gulf Coast Hurricanes

Since August 2005, the Corporation for National and Community Service has provided more than $130 million worth of resources to Gulf Coast states recovering from the devastating series of hurricanes. Working in cooperation with the Red Cross, FEMA, and local and state authorities, nearly 92,000 national service volunteers have contributed more than 3.5 million hours to the relief, recovery, and rebuilding effort. They also have coordinated an additional 260,000 community volunteers. Activities have included supporting shelter operations and housing placement; establishing call centers and warehousing sites; assisting with case work and benefits coordination; setting up school and youth programs; blue roofing, debris removal, mucking out homes, and construction of new homes for low-income families. As a result of its experience with hurricane relief and recovery, the Corporation has established a number of new procedures to provide more effective and timely response to disasters under authority of FEMA mission assignments. As of August 2007, trained AmeriCorps teams have been deployed under mission assignments to declared major disasters to respond to winter ice storms, tornados, and flooding and to assist in the recovery effort, including running the volunteer base camp in the tornado-struck Kansas town of Greensburg. The Corporation continues to shift its resources where possible to support a variety of disaster preparedness and response activities.

Senior Corps: More than 17,000 Senior Corps volunteers have served in disaster relief efforts, providing food and shelter, coordinating distribution of donated goods, managing community volunteers, and more.

AmeriCorps State and National: More than 85 grantee programs of AmeriCorps State and National, collectively representing more than 6,400 AmeriCorps members have provided nearly 1 million hours in hurricane relief and recovery assistance in the Gulf region, many through FEMA mission assignments. The Corporation also provided more than $66.6 million in additional funds to bring thousands of additional AmeriCorps members to the Gulf region through fiscal year 2009.

AmeriCorps NCCC: More than 2,900 AmeriCorps NCCC members have served on more than 500 separate disaster services projects in the Gulf Coast region since September 2005, in coordination with such groups as the Red Cross, the Salvation Army, the Army Corps of Engineers, and the various state service commissions. In all, NCCC members have contributed more than 1.4 million hours of service, valued at $26.4 million. They have assisted 2.9 million people, and trained and supervised more than 185,000 community volunteers, completed nearly 13,000 damage assessments, refurbished more than 6,500 homes, put tarps on thousands of homes, served 1.3 million meals, and distributed more than 2,200 tons of food.

AmeriCorps VISTA: More than 420 full-time AmeriCorps VISTA members have served in the Gulf Coast, building the capacity of nonprofit organizations and helping low income people out of poverty. In addition, through its Summer Associate Program, VISTA sent 125 members to the New Orleans area to staff free or low-cost summer camps for thousands of children that are operated by community organizations still recovering from Hurricane Katrina.

Learn and Serve America: Tens of thousands of students supported by Learn and Serve America raised funds and items needed for hurricane relief, assembled and distributed disaster relief kits, and traveled to the Gulf region to help in the recovery effort.

Challenge Grant Program: The Corporation revised its 2005 Challenge Grant competition to focus on disaster relief, resulting in the approval of $4 million to six multistate projects to recruit nearly 72,000 volunteers, with an emphasis on baby boomers.

"Skilled Service in the Gulf" Grants: In June 2007, the Corporation announced that Habitat for Humanity International, Xavier University of Louisiana, and Rebuilding Together were selected to receive awards totaling $900,000 to engage skilled volunteers in providing disaster recovery assistance to the Gulf states. The skilled construction volunteers will lead lesser-skilled volunteers and handle the most challenging aspects of rebuilding.

National Response Plan: The Corporation continues to work with the Department of Homeland Security and FEMA on their redrafting of the National Response Plan, noting how national service programs can provide additional value in the areas of volunteer management, mass care, and infrastructure support.

Ties to Disaster Organizations: In late January 2007, the Corporation signed a Memorandum of Understanding with the National Voluntary Organizations Active in Disaster to enable smarter, faster cooperation between the Corporation and the group's members, including Catholic Charities, American Red Cross, Volunteers of America and the Salvation Army.

Disaster Institute: In May 2007, the Corporation hosted a national Disaster Institute to help state service commissions and AmeriCorps grantees become more active in state preparedness and response.

Source: CNCS, August 2007, http://www.nationalservice.gov/pdf/07_0820_factsheet_katrina.pdf.

Citizen Corps Program

Citizen Corps is the arm of U.S.A. Freedom Corps that provides opportunities for citizens who want to help make their communities more secure. Since its January 2002 establishment, at which time President George W. Bush called for two years of volunteer service from every American citizen, tens of thousands of people from all 50 states and U.S. territories have volunteered to work with one or more of the Citizen Corps programs. These include the following:

- Citizen Corps Councils (CCC) are established at the state and local level to promote, organize, and run the various programs that fall under the Citizen Corps umbrella. Funding for these councils is provided by the federal government through grant awards. As of May 2008, there were Citizen Corps Councils in 55 states and U.S. territories and, 2,339 local communities, all of which serve 78% of the total population of the United States.

- Community Emergency Response Teams (CERTs) began in 1983 in Los Angeles, California. City administrators there recognized that in most emergency situations, average citizens — neighbors, coworkers, and bystanders, for example — were often on scene during the critical moments before professional help arrives. These officials acted on the belief that, by training average citizens to perform basic search and rescue, first aid, and other critical emergency response skills, they would increase the overall resilience of the community. Additionally, should a large scale disaster like an earthquake occur, where first response units would be stretched very thin, these trained citizens would be able to augment official services and provide an important service to the community.

Beginning in 1993, FEMA began to offer CERT training on a national level, providing funding to cover start-up and tuition costs for programs. Since that time, CERT programs have been established in more than 2,915 communities in all 50 states, the District of Columbia, and several U.S. territories. CERT teams remain active in the community before a disaster strikes, sponsoring events such as drills, neighborhood cleanup, and disaster-education fairs. Trainers offer periodic refresher sessions to CERT members to reinforce the basic training and to keep participants involved and practiced in their skills. CERT members also offer other nonemergency assistance to the community with the goal of improving the overall safety of the community.

- Volunteers in Police Service (VIPS) was created in the aftermath of September 11, 2001, to address the increased demands on state and local law enforcement. The basis of the program is that civilian volunteers are able to support police officers by doing much of the behind-the-scenes work that does not require formal law enforcement training, thereby allowing officers to spend more of their already strained schedules on the street. Although the concept is not new, the federal support for such programs is.

VIPS draws on the time and recognized talents of civilian volunteers. Volunteer roles may include performing clerical tasks, serving as an extra set of "eyes and ears," assisting with search-and-rescue activities, and writing citations for accessible parking violations, just to name a few. As of January 2008, there were 1,640 official VIPS programs registered throughout the United States.

- The Medical Reserve Corps (MRC) was founded after the 2002 State of the Union Address to establish teams of local volunteer medical and public health professionals who can contribute their skills and experience when called on in times of need. The program relies on volunteers who are practicing and retired physicians, nurses, dentists, veterinarians, epidemiologists, and other health professionals, as well as other citizens untrained in public health but who can contribute to the community's normal and disaster public health needs in other ways (which may include interpreters, chaplains, legal advisers, etc.).

Local community leaders develop their own MRC units and recruit local volunteers that address the specific community needs. For example, MRC volunteers may deliver necessary public health services during a crisis, assist emergency response teams with patients, and provide care directly to those with less serious injuries and other health-related issues. MRC volunteers may also serve a vital role by assisting their communities with ongoing public health needs (e.g., immunizations, screenings, health and nutrition education, and volunteering in community health centers and local hospitals). The MRC unit decides, in concert with local officials (including the local Citizen Corps Council), on when the community Medical Reserve Corps is activated during a local emergency. As of May 2008, there were 736 MRC programs established throughout the United States.

- The Neighborhood Watch Program has been in existence for more than 30 years in cities and counties throughout the United States. The program is based on the concept that neighbors who join together to fight crime will be able to increase security in their surrounding areas and, as a result, provide an overall better quality of life for residents. Understandably, after September 11, when terrorism became a major focus of the U.S. government, the recognized importance of programs like Neighborhood Watch took on much greater significance.

The Neighborhood Watch program is not maintained by the National Sheriff's Association, which founded the program initially. At the local level, the Citizen Corps Councils help neighborhood groups that have banded together to start a program to carry out their mission. Many printed materials and other guidance are available for free to help them carry out their goals.

Neighborhood watch programs have successfully decreased crime in many of the neighborhoods where they have been implemented. In total, as of January 2008, there were 14,791 programs spread out throughout the United States and the U.S. territories. In addition to serving a crime prevention role, Neighborhood Watch has also been used as the basis for bringing neighborhood residents together to focus on disaster preparedness and terrorism awareness; to focus on evacuation drills and exercises; and even to organize group training, such as the CERT training.

- Fire Corps was created in 2004 under the umbrella of U.S.A. Freedom Corps and Citizen Corps. The purpose of the program, like the VIPS program with the police, was to enhance the ability of fire departments to utilize citizen advocates and provide individuals with opportunities to support their local fire departments with both time and talent.

Fire Corps was created as a partnership between the International Association of Fire Chiefs' Volunteer Combination Officers Section (VCOS), the International Association of Fire Fighters (IAFF), and the National Volunteer Fire Council (NVFC). By participating in the program, concerned and interested citizens can assist in their local fire department's activities through tasks such as administrative assistance, public education, fund-raising, data entry, accounting, public relations, and equipment and facility maintenance, just to name a few examples.

Any fire department that allows citizens to volunteer support service is considered a Fire Corps program, but programs can become official through registering with a local, county, or state CCC, if one exists. Official Fire Corps programs will be provided with assistance on how to implement a nonoperational citizen advocates program, or improve existing programs. A Fire Corps National Advisory Committee has been established under the program in order to provide strategic direction and collect feedback from the field. As of January 2008, there were 687 established Fire Corps programs throughout the United States and the U.S. territories.

While some of these programs are relatively new, some, such as Neighborhood Watch, have been in place for more than a decade. More information on these programs is provided in Chapter 7.

U.S. Department of Agriculture

Considering the varied and wide-reaching impacts that both terrorism and other natural disasters (such as plant and animal diseases) could have on the both the U.S. food supply and on the U.S. economy, agriculture has assumed a very important role in the overall homeland security approach of the United States. Shortly after September 11, the U.S. Department of Agriculture (USDA) formed a Homeland Security Council (within USDA) to develop a department-wide plan and coordinate efforts among all USDA agencies and offices. Their efforts have since focused on three key areas of concern:

- Safety and security of the food supply and agricultural production
- Protection of USDA facilities
- USDA staff and emergency preparedness

The following section describes how USDA has fulfilled its homeland security mission to date.

Protecting U.S. Borders from Invasive Pests and Diseases

The USDA is contributing to the ongoing DHS effort to keep foreign agricultural pests and diseases from entering the country. In this effort, there has been a drastic increase in the number of veterinarians and food import surveillance officers that have been posted at borders and ports of entry. Although approximately 2,600 members of the USDA border inspection force were transferred to

DHS as stipulated in the Homeland Security Act of 2002, USDA has continued to train inspectors and set policy for plants, animals, and commodities entering the United States.

In March 2004, the former DHS Bureau of Customs and Border Protection's Border Patrol (BP) announced the 2004 Arizona Border Control Initiative. This initiative was aimed at securing the border with Mexico. The initiative required increased cooperation between DHS and the USDA Forest Service in allowing more access to public lands on the border. Forest Service resource managers continue to help DHS enhance border security in such a way as to avoid disturbing the environment, and Forest Service law enforcement personnel have assisted DHS in deterring illegal activities on National Forest System lands.

Protecting the Health and Safety of Farm Animals, Crops, and Natural Resources

The USDA created a National Surveillance Unit within its Animal and Plant Health Inspection Service's (APHIS) Veterinary Services program. The unit provides a focal point for the collection, processing, and delivery of surveillance information used to make risk analyses and to take further action when needed. The unit designs surveillance strategies and coordinates and integrates surveillance activities in order to protect the health of and enhance the marketability of livestock and poultry.

USDA appointed a National Surveillance System Coordinator whose purpose is to more efficiently lead the agency's animal health surveillance efforts. USDA also works with universities and state veterinary diagnostic laboratories to create plant and animal health laboratory networks that help to increase the nation's capability to respond in an emergency. USDA developed guidance documents to help remind farmers and ranchers of steps that they can take to secure their operations.

The Office of Food Defense and Emergency Response (OFDER) was created in 2002 to develop and coordinate all activities of the USDA Food Safety and Inspection Service (FSIS) to prevent, prepare for, respond to, and recover from nonroutine emergencies resulting from intentional and nonintentional contamination affecting meat, poultry, and egg products. OFDER serves as the agency's central office for homeland security issues and ensures coordination of its activities with the USDA Homeland Security Office, the Department of Homeland Security (DHS), the Food and Drug Administration (FDA) and other federal and state government agencies with food-related responsibilities, and industry.

USDA has provided tens of millions of dollars to states, universities, and tribal lands to increase homeland security prevention, detection, and response efforts. USDA also developed the National Animal Health Reserve Corps, which has resulted in the registration of almost 300 private veterinarians who will assist local communities during times of emergency.

USDA has also continued to perform research on rapid identification tests for biological agents considered to pose the most serious threats to our agricultural system, including foot and mouth disease, rinderpest, and soybean and wheat rust.

Ensuring a Safe Food Supply

The USDA has enhanced security at all food safety laboratories around the country, and expanded its abilities to test for "nontraditional" biological, chemical, and radiological agents. USDA established an Office of Food Security and Emergency Preparedness, which now serves as the lead coordinating body in the development of the infrastructure and capacity to prevent, prepare for, and respond to terrorism aimed at U.S. food supply. USDA also drafted and distributed guidance for field and laboratory personnel about what to do when the HSAS is raised to either orange or red levels.

New import surveillance liaison inspectors have been hired by the department, who are stationed around the United States to enhance surveillance of imported products. Using a food security plan they developed, USDA has conducted training for employees, veterinarians, and inspectors on threat prevention and preparedness activities. USDA food safety labs have maintained a lead role in creating a network to integrate the U.S. laboratory infrastructure and surge capacity at the local, state, and federal levels.

Protecting Research and Laboratory Facilities

The USDA has provided millions of dollars in grants aimed at security assessments, background investigations, physical security upgrades, and additional security personnel at research and laboratory facilities. Security countermeasures have been implemented based on the findings of these assessments. Furthermore, all USDA laboratories where dangerous agents and toxins are used are held to the requirements of the Agricultural Bioterrorism Protection Act of 2002.

Emergency Preparedness and Response

A department-wide National Interagency Incident Management System (NIIMS), based on the successful system utilized by USDA's Forest Service, has being implemented. This system includes incident command and control systems, coordination systems, training and qualification systems, and publication management systems. USDA's NIIMS uses the same systems within USDA for incident management as those standardized for the nation under the National Incident Management System (NIMS), which is described in Chapter 7.

The construction of an APHIS Emergency Operations Center (AEOC), which is used to coordinate and support emergency response within APHIS, has been completed. The AEOC, which enhances APHIS's ability to provide leadership during national emergencies, has already been utilized on several occasions, including the exotic Newcastle disease outbreak, the monkey pox outbreak, and the confirmations of bovine spongiform encephalopathy (BSE) in both Canada and the United States.

Protecting Other Infrastructure

The USDA Forest Service's law enforcement officers continue to conduct security assessments of research facilities and air tanker bases nationwide. USDA's Forest Service continues to enhance efforts to protect National Forest System lands and facilities, including dams, reservoirs, pipelines, water treatment plants, power lines, and energy production facilities on government property.

Securing Information Technology

The USDA has conducted tests of its network systems to assess threat levels. USDA upgraded the security status of key information technology personnel and conducted training and planning sessions to strengthen the department's continuity of operations plans.

Department of Commerce

The Department of Commerce promotes homeland security through actions conducted in three of its many offices and agencies. These include:

- Bureau of Industry and Security
- National Institute for Standards and Technology
- National Oceanographic and Atmospheric Administration

Bureau of Industry and Security

The mission of the Bureau of Industry and Security (BIS) is to advance U.S. national security, foreign policy, and economic interests. BIS's activities include regulating the export of sensitive goods and technologies and enforcing export control and public safety laws; cooperating with and assisting foreign countries on export control; helping U.S. industry to comply with international arms control agreements; and monitoring the U.S. defense industrial base to ensure that it is capable of handling national and homeland security needs. This agency gained more notoriety after September 11, when concerns about certain technologies and arms that could be used by terrorists abroad were raised. The bureau has enjoyed an increase in funding as a result of these changes.

National Institute for Standards and Technology

The National Institute for Standards and Technology (NIST) has provided significant contributions to the homeland security of the nation by assisting in the measurement infrastructure used to establish safety and security standards. NIST labs, which are detailed in Chapter 9, have enjoyed an increase in funding levels since September 11, and have developed technologies that are used for such actions as establishing standards for and measuring the safety and security of buildings, for the development of biometric identification systems, and for various radiation detection systems utilized at U.S. and foreign ports, among many others. NIST laboratories involved, at least partially, in homeland security include these:

- The Building and Fire Research Laboratory
- Chemical Science and Technology Laboratory
- Materials Science and Engineering Laboratory
- Physics Laboratory
- Technology Services

National Oceanographic and Atmospheric Administration

The National Oceanographic and Atmospheric Administration (NOAA) has been involved in disaster management since long before the creation of the DHS. NOAA monitors meteorological conditions, makes forecasts about storm risks, and recommends preparedness measures to FEMA and other federal, state, and local government agencies. The NOAA National Weather Service (NWS), under which the All-Hazards Radio Warning Network is managed, is another vital component to the overall homeland security needs of the nation. Although not focused on terrorism, the weather radio system is capable of being activated in the event of any type of disaster, regardless of its origin, to provide timely warning to people who may be in danger.

Department of Education

The Department of Education is responsible, among other things, for taking a leadership position in establishing standards and technical assistance for school safety. Schools are not only vulnerable to the effects of natural and technological disasters, but have been identified by many terrorism experts to be a primary target for terrorist activities due to the emotional factor involved with the injury or death of children. Both before and since September 11, there have been many terrorist or other attacks in schools throughout the world, including in Beslan, Russia, and in Cambodia — both of which resulted in fatalities — and elsewhere. Attacks on schools, exemplified by the 1999 Columbine attacks, provide further justification of the required homeland security role that is filled by the Department of Education.

The office of Safe and Drug Free Schools was created in September 2002 to manage all Department of Education activities related to safe schools, crisis response, alcohol and drug prevention, and health and well-being of students. Today, this office is responsible for leading the homeland security efforts of the department. Millions of dollars in funding have been made available to schools by the Department of Education through this office, including $30 million in both FY 2003 and FY 2004, to help them to better address emergency planning issues.

Emergency planning guidance and technical assistance are major concerns of the Department of Education, and this area of expertise is also handled through the Office of Safe and Drug Free Schools. Through the development and maintenance of a website (www.ed.gov/emergencyplan), the Department of Education has created what they call a "one-stop-shop" for schools to locate information to plan for all types of disasters, whether they are natural, terrorist, or other.

Environmental Protection Agency

The Environmental Protection Agency (EPA) has played a very important role in emergency management and homeland security for decades. The EPA was one of the signatory agencies of the Federal

Response Plan (FRP), and today plays a major role in the National Response Framework (NRF) (this response-related role is detailed in Chapter 7). The EPA is concerned primarily with emergencies involving the release, or threatened release, of oil, radioactive materials, or hazardous chemicals that have the potential to affect communities and the surrounding environment. These releases may be accidental, deliberate, or the result of a natural disaster. EPA works with a variety of private and public entities to prevent, prepare for, and respond to spills and other environmental emergencies. EPA's website provides information for these entities to be able to better prevent spills and releases and to better respond to them when they occur.

The EPA has a responsibility for preparing for and responding to terrorist threats involving WMDs. Because of its inherent role in protecting human health and the environment from possible harmful effects of certain chemical, biological, and nuclear materials, the EPA is actively involved in counterterrorism planning and response efforts. The EPA supports federal counterterrorism programs through the following four mechanisms:

1. Helping state and local responders to plan for emergencies
2. Coordinating with key federal partners
3. Training first responders
4. Providing resources in the event of a terrorist incident

Several offices within the agency are involved in these efforts, including these three:

- Chemical Emergency Preparedness and Prevention Office

- Office of Superfund Remediation Technology Innovation

- Office of Air and Radiation

Chemical Emergency Preparedness and Prevention Office

In 1985, one year after the Bhopal, India, chemical accident that killed thousands of people, the EPA established the Chemical Emergency Preparedness and Prevention Office (CEPPO). Through this office, EPA has taken a leading role within the federal government in building programs to respond to and prevent chemical accidents. CEPPO works with numerous federal, state, local, and tribal governments; industry groups; environmental groups; labor organizations; and community groups to help them better understand the risks posed by chemicals in their communities, to manage and reduce those risks, and to deal with emergencies.

CEPPO works with its state and local partners to develop new approaches to deal with emergency preparedness and accident prevention. They assist local emergency planning committees (LEPCs) and state emergency response commissions (SERCs) by providing leadership, issuing regulations, developing technical guidance, and enabling these committees to develop their own unique emergency planning systems appropriate to their individual needs.

CEPPO also works closely with the National Response Team (NRT) to help states and localities better prepare for, respond to, and prevent accidents. The NRT consists of 16 federal agencies with interests and expertise in various aspects of emergency response specifically to pollution incidents.

CEPPO's website links to general information and subject-specific data about the Emergency Planning and Community Right-to-Know Act (EPCRA), the risk management planning requirements of the Clean Air Act, up-to-date information on chemical accidents, as well as publications, regulations, conference listings, and links to other databases to help regulators, SERCs, LEPCs, industry, and the public find out more about chemical emergency preparedness and accident prevention.

Programs developed by CEPPO include the following:

- Risk Management Plans (RMPs) — RMPs, submitted from industry in June 1999, require certain facilities to tell the public and CEPPO what they are doing to prevent accidents and how they plan to operate safely and manage their chemicals in a responsible way.

- RMP*Info™ — Summaries of facility risk management programs are available to the public via the Internet. The data are useful to environmental groups, state and local agencies, community organizations, and the public in understanding the chemical risks in their communities.
- Counterterrorism — CEPPO is working with communities on how local emergency plans can address deliberate chemical releases and provide suggestions for rapid response.

Office of Superfund Remediation Technology Innovation

The Office of Superfund Remediation Technology Innovation (OSRTI), called the Office of Emergency and Remedial Response (OERR) until 2003, manages the Superfund program. The Superfund program was created to protect citizens from the dangers posed by abandoned or uncontrolled hazardous waste sites. Congress established Superfund in 1980 by passing the Comprehensive Environmental Response, Compensation, and Liability Act (CERCLA). CERCLA gives the federal government the authority to respond to hazardous substance emergencies, and to develop long-term solutions for the nation's most serious hazardous waste problems.

Office of Air and Radiation

The Office of Air and Radiation (OAR) develops national programs, technical policies, and regulations for controlling air pollution and radiation exposure. OAR is concerned with energy conservation and pollution prevention, indoor and outdoor air quality, industrial air pollution, pollution from vehicles and engines, radon, acid rain, stratospheric ozone depletion, and radiation protection. With regard to homeland security, this office is responsible for emergency response to radiation disasters, helping to design and implement air protection measures, monitoring ambient air (including project BioWatch and monitoring the air around the World Trade Center disaster), and maintaining a national air monitoring system.

In March 2004, the EPA Homeland Security Collaborative Network (HSCN) was established to facilitate the agency's collective approach to analyzing homeland security issues while formulating policy recommendations and actions cooperatively. The following is a list of EPA program offices that are members of the HSCN and a brief description of their homeland security tasks (where appropriate):

- Office of Air and Radiation (OAR)
  See earlier description
- Office of Administration and Resource Management (OARM)
  EPA facilities and employee security
  Physical critical infrastructure protection
  Design buildout of sensitive, classified information facilities/secured access facilities (SCIFs/SAFs)
  Monitoring of Homeland Security Advisory System (HSAD) threat conditions
- Office of the Chief Financial Officer (OCFO)
- Office of Enforcement and Compliance Assurance (OECA)
  Civil and criminal enforcement
  Incident response
  Counterterrorism support
  Forensics
- Office of Environmental Information (OEI)
  Information protection and access policy
  Information infrastructure and cyber protection
  Information technology
  Data management

- Office of Prevention, Pesticides, and Toxic Substances (OPPTS)

  Food and agriculture security support
  Emergency exemption requests
  Acute Exposure Guideline Limits (AEGLs)
  Chemical data/expertise on pesticides and industrial chemicals
  Licensing authority for antimicrobials to inactivate pathogens and pesticides
  Establishment of rules for storage/disposal of pesticides and pesticide applicator certification
    program

- Office of Research and Development (ORD)

  Water security research
  Building decontamination
  Rapid risk assessment

- Office of Solid Waste and Emergency Response (OSWER)

  Chemical industry infrastructure support
  Building and critical infrastructure decontamination
  Emergency response
  Lab capacity
  Continuity of operations plan/continuity of government (COOP/COG)
  Superfund

- Office of Water (OW)

  Drinking water and wastewater infrastructure protection
  Training, simulations, exercises
  Best water security practices
  Vulnerability assessments and emergency response plans
  Tools for preparedness and emergency response
  Framework for monitoring/surveillance network
  Financial assistance to states and tribes
  Information sharing with sector and partners

- Region 6
  Lead EPA region for homeland security responsibilities

NRF Participant Agencies

Many other federal agencies other than those just listed are involved in homeland security efforts, although most of these actions occur as a result of their contractual obligations set out in National Response Framework (NRF). Although these actions will be described in greater detail in Chapter 7, the following is a list of the federal agencies that participate in the response to disasters within the United States:

- Corporation for National and Community Service
- Department of Agriculture
- Department of Commerce
- Department of Defense
- Department of Education
- Department of Energy
- Department of Health and Human Services
- Department of Homeland Security
- Department of Housing and Urban Development
- Department of the Interior

- Department of Justice
- Department of Labor
- Department of State
- Department of Transportation
- Department of the Treasury
- Department of Veterans Affairs
- Central Intelligence Agency
- Environmental Protection Agency
- Federal Bureau of Investigation
- Federal Communications Commission
- General Services Administration
- National Aeronautics and Space Administration
- National Transportation Safety Board
- Nuclear Regulatory Commission
- Office of Personnel Management
- Small Business Administration
- Social Security Administration
- Tennessee Valley Authority
- United States Agency for International Development
- U.S. Postal Service

■ ■ Critical Thinking ■

Why do you think certain Homeland Security–related functions are still performed by other federal agencies that were not incorporated into DHS? Should they have been? Why or why not?

Activities by State and Local Organizations

State and local governments have expended considerable human and financial resources to secure their jurisdictions from the perceived threat of terrorism. Although considerable amounts of federal funding have gone to helping state and local agencies to better prepare for the terrorist threat, much of these efforts have been performed without any federal compensation. Also, each time the DHS Homeland Security Advisory System (HSAS) threat level has been raised, or when a major event that is identified as being a potential terrorist target is held within a jurisdiction, local leaders must divert sparse financial and human resources from other areas of need to adequately address those threats. These collective strains have prompted the many organizations representative of state and local governments to become actively engaged in the homeland security debate, from the passage of the Homeland Security Act of 2002 until today.

As early as September 2002, the municipal organizations, which include the U.S. Conference of Mayors (USCM), the National League of Cities (NLC), the National Association of Counties (NACo), and the National Governors Association (NGA), and the emergency management organizations, which include the National Emergency Management Association (NEMA) and the International Association of Emergency Managers (IAEM), began fighting for first responder funding for state and local governments and about the way the money was allocated — whether it would be to the states or directly to the local municipalities. Clearly, these organizations were and continue to be involved in informing the federal government's approach to funding state and local homeland security efforts. Each of these organizations is discussed next.

United States Conference of Mayors

The U.S. Conference of Mayors (USCM) is the official nonpartisan organization of the nation's 1,139 U.S. cities with populations of 30,000 or more. Each city is represented in the conference by its chief elected official, the mayor. The primary roles of the USCM are to:

- Promote the development of effective national urban/suburban policy.
- Strengthen federal–city relationships.
- Ensure that federal policy meets urban needs.
- Provide mayors with leadership and management tools.
- Create a forum in which mayors can share ideas and information.

The conference has historically assumed a national leadership role, calling early attention to serious urban problems and pressing successfully for solutions.

In December 2001, three months after the 9/11 attacks, the USCM released "A National Action Plan for Safety and Security in America's Cities." The document was prepared as part of the Mayors Emergency Safety and Security Summit held in Washington, DC, on October 23–25, 2001. It contained recommendations in four priority areas: transportation security, emergency preparedness, federal–local law enforcement, and economic security. In this document, the mayors made the following critical point:

It is important to understand that while the fourth area, economic security, is viewed as the ultimate goal of a nation, it cannot be achieved in the absence of the first three. That is, securing our transportation system, maximizing our emergency response capability, and coordinating our law enforcement response to threats and incidents at all levels are viewed as prerequisites to eliminating the anxiety that has accelerated the nation's economic downturn, and to achieving economic security for the nation.

The principal areas of concern in federal–local law enforcement for the mayors are communications, coordination, and border-city security. In the transportation security section, the mayors' paper presents recommendations concerning security issues in each of the major transportation modes: airport, transit, highway, rail, and port.

The USCM leadership has repeatedly expressed concern that a significant amount of funding from the federal government has not reached the cities for combating terrorism. The mayors expressed that they have been working on initiatives related to homeland security, largely without any federal assistance. Select initiatives, related to communities, that they mentioned include the following: (1) conducting exercises to help prepare for emergencies and improve response capabilities, (2) expanding public information and education efforts, and (3) conducting vulnerability assessments of potential key targets.

Funding for cities remains the principal focus of the USCM in the area of homeland security. In September 2003, the USCM released a report entitled, "First Mayors' Report to the Nation: Tracking Homeland Security Funds Sent to the 50 State Governments" (U.S. Conference of Mayors, 2003). Through release of the report, the USCM website announced that 90% of cities had not received funds from the largest federal homeland security program designed to assist first responders by the federally set deadline of August 1, 2003. The report also found that more than half of the cities had either not been consulted or had no opportunity to influence state decision making about how to use and distribute funding.

The USCM established a Homeland Security Monitoring Center to monitor the flow of homeland security funds from the federal government to states and localities. This focus on funding was at the heart of a March 12, 2004, message from Tom Cochran, executive director of the USCM, in a website column that stated, "Our goal is to do one thing: get the money down to our first responders on the front line in cities throughout America" (U.S. Conference of Mayors, 2004a). In June 2004, the USCM released a report of a survey that was conducted to assess the flow of federal homeland security funds through the states to the cities. Their study found that 52% of the 231 cities surveyed had not received any money at all, nor had they been notified that they will receive money from the state-block grant program, which is the largest homeland security program designed to assist first responders.

In 2006, the U.S. Conference of Mayors conducted a survey to determine levels of emergency and disaster readiness at the city level in the United States. The results of this survey were issued in a report titled "Five Years Post 9/11 and One Year Post Hurricane Katrina: The State of America's Readiness." Results announced in a press release (see "U.S. Conference of Mayors Press Release" sidebar) showed that cities still have a long way to go. The U.S. Conference of Mayors has continued to fight for municipal homeland security issues in the years since. In January 2007, the mayors released a 10-point legislative agenda that included a section on homeland security. This plan identified three areas of concern for the cities, including:

- Interoperable Communications — The mayors called for a well-funded, standalone, federal emergency communications grant program designed to improve interoperable communications, including flexible direct grants to cities and first responders.

- Transit Security — The mayors called for a flexible federal transit security initiative to improve security in the areas of communications, surveillance, detection systems, personnel, and training. Because of the negative experiences cities had previously encountered trying to find money locally to cover these kinds of expenses, and in trying to receive the actual funds once granted by the federal government, the mayors requested that there be no local or state match, and that security funds would go directly to the operator of the system or the jurisdiction providing the security.

- Funding Mechanism — The mayors contend that improvements must be made in the application process and delivery mechanism for federal homeland security grant resources to make sure that the process is more user-friendly, the funding reaches cities quickly, and that the funding is flexible enough to meet local needs.

U.S. Conference of Mayors Press Release, July 26, 2006

Five Years Post 9/11 and One Year Post Hurricane Katrina: The State of America's Readiness — The U.S. Conference of Mayors Releases 183-City Emergency Preparedness/Homeland Security Survey at National Press Club

As the nation approaches the five-year anniversary of the terrorist attacks of September 11 and the one-year anniversary of Hurricane Katrina, the U.S. Conference of Mayors, led by Conference President and Dearborn Mayor Michael A. Guido, held a media forum at the National Press Club today discussing the state of disaster preparedness in America's cities.

"The nation's mayors continue to focus on the need to strengthen emergency preparedness and homeland security," said Conference of Mayors President, Dearborn Mayor Michael Guido. "The devastation of Hurricane Katrina in New Orleans and the Gulf Coast area, and the terrorist attacks of 9–11 are like nothing this country has ever seen before. As mayors, we saw ourselves in our own unnamed disaster that could easily strike any one of our cities."

For the last five years, the Conference and the nation's mayors have dedicated themselves to making America's cities safer by both preventing possible acts of terrorism, and being ready to respond if a disaster — either terrorist or natural — should strike, including the new threat of avian flu.

One month after September 11, the leadership of the Conference of Mayors called an emergency homeland security summit in Washington, DC with mayors, police, fire and emergency management officials. At the summit they drafted a sweeping National Action Plan for Safety and Security in America's Cities. The National Action Plan was updated in October of 2005 following the hurricanes and then presented directly to Homeland Security Secretary Michael Chertoff and Congress.

Mayors acknowledge that more must be done at every level of government to make sure that cities, and the nation, are able to respond to the growing challenges of homeland security and emergency response. "This new survey shows that we must further strengthen our partnership with the federal government to make sure that our domestic 'first preventers' and 'first responders' have the resources and training they need to succeed, and that all necessary federal support is ready in the event of a major disaster," Guido said.

Survey Results

Survey responses were received from 183 cities representing 38 states in the nation, and the District of Columbia and Puerto Rico. Cities with populations up to 100,000 comprise the largest group of respondents (104); cities in the 100,001 to 300,000 population range comprise the next largest group (49). Twenty-nine (30) respondents are in the 300,001 and up range. Some of the key findings of the survey include:

1. When asked if cities have received sufficient federal resources to achieve full communications interoperability — so that first responders can talk to each other and key assets, 80 percent said no. This figure was fairly consistent for all population ranges.
2. When then asked how far away cities are from having full communications interoperability, the average response was four years.
3. When asked how much each city's level of disaster preparedness has improved since 9/11 — with 1 being the lowest and 10 being the highest amount of improvement, the average response was 6.3.
4. When asked if cities have recently created or updated an evacuation plan, the average response was 56 percent yes. This number climbed to 73 percent yes for the largest cities.
5. When asked about the level of confidence that FEMA will respond quickly in the event of a major disaster, the average response on a scale of 1 to 10 was 5.2.
6. As to the level of confidence that each city is prepared to survive on its own for up to 72 hours following a disaster, the average response was 6.9 on the same scale.
7. When asked if the federal government, or the city, has established a plan with a nearby military base to provide personnel and equipment to help stabilize a city in an emergency, the average response was 72 percent no.
8. As to whether or not cities have been notified that a Principal Federal Official has been preassigned to work with them in the event of a disaster, 72 percent said no. However, this number jumped to 60 percent yes for the larger cities.
9. When asked if cities are prepared to handle a bird flu pandemic on their own — for days and possibly weeks — as we have been warned might be required, 70 percent said no. This response was almost exactly the same for all population groupings.
10. Finally, when asked whether the federal government or the state has contacted each city to discuss a possible pandemic flu outbreak, the average response was 69 percent yes, climbing to 87 percent yes for the larger cities.

This entire survey, as well as six previous homeland security surveys released by the U.S. Conference of Mayors since 9/11, can be viewed online at The Conference of Mayors website at www.usmayors.org.

Mayors have been working with the federal government on many key homeland security issues. Mayors also have been working with each other to share best practices, develop innovative response systems, and implement city-to-city mutual aid agreements.

Source: U.S. Conference of Mayors, http://usmayors.org/uscm/news/press_releases/documents/disasterpreparedness_072606.pdf.

The mayor's influence was felt by Congress, and many of their 10-Point Plan requests were honored in the 9/11 Bill that was passed on August 3, 2007. For instance, the Urban Area Security Initiative (UASI), which is designed to assist high risk urban areas in preventing, preparing for, protecting against, and responding to terrorism, was altered to meet the mayors' preferences. For FY 2008, $850 million was authorized, with an additional $150 million every year thereafter. Eligible city governments were given the opportunity to present what they feel is relevant information about their city's threat, vulnerability, and likely consequences of a terrorist attack, and details about the intended allocation of funds within the local government. If approved, awards are still distributed to the state (a point of contention for the mayors), but the state is required to pass at least 80% of the funds to the appropriate urban area within 45 days. Any remaining amounts retained by the states must be put toward "items, services, or activities that benefit the high risk urban area." Under the law, the 100 most populous metropolitan areas in the United States are eligible for UASI grants. If a region is not ranked within the 100 most populous metropolitan areas, DHS can still determine it to be a high-risk urban area based on a risk formula, and DHS can designate regions consisting of more than one metropolitan area into several high-risk urban areas. Finally, a high-risk urban area can, with DHS permission, expand its jurisdiction to include additional regions.

The law also changed the Homeland Security Grant Program (HSGP), which seeks to enhance statewide homeland security management, personnel, training, and equipment. The new bill reduced the minimum amount of total funding each state would receive from 0.75% to 0.375% in FY 2008, 0.365% in FY 2009, and 0.360% for FY 2010 on. Like UASI, the state is responsible for allocating at least 80% of the funds to local governments within 45 days of receiving the grant. The factors that will ultimately determine the sums awarded to the states are risk level and the quality of the anticipated effectiveness of the proposal. The most important change to this grant that affects the mayors is the absence of a local match requirement, which had been included in earlier versions of the legislation and was opposed by the Conference of Mayors.

The new 9/11 Bill also increases the authorization for the Emergency Management Performance Grant program to $400 million for FY 2008, $535 million in FY 2009, $680 million in FY 2010, $815 million in FY 2011, and $950 million in FY 2012.

One of the most important changes brought about by the new legislation, in terms of the needs of cities, is the Interoperable Emergency Communications Grant Program. This grant program seeks to improve local, tribal, statewide, regional, and national interoperable communications as is needed in collective response to disasters and emergencies. The bill did not authorize a specific amount for FY 2008, but authorized $400 million each fiscal year between 2009 and 2012. States must submit an Interoperable Communication Plan to be approved by the Director of Emergency Communications on the basis of:

1. Risk, including likelihood of a state responding to a nearby jurisdiction, population size, and proximity to international borders
2. Anticipated effectiveness

States that receive the grant must distribute at least 80% of the awarded funds directly to local governments.

The USCM also saw its transit security recommendation in the 10-Point Plan integrated in the final version of the 9/11 Bill. Through a partnership between DHS and the Department of Transportation, the bill created the National Strategy for Public Transportation and Security that seeks to minimize security threats to the public transportation system and maximize recovery ability. To receive funding, the Administrator of the Federal Transit Administration of the Department of Transportation submits all public transportation security assessments to the DHS Secretary, who in turn considers the vulnerability of critical infrastructure, assets, and any other weaknesses. Furthermore, the DHS Secretary requires public transportation agencies deemed at high risk to develop comprehensive security plans. The Public Transportation Security Assistance Program also makes grants available for security improvements to transportation agencies that have performed a security assessment or have drawn up a security plan. For FY 2008, $650 million was authorized, increasing to $750 million for FY 2009, $900 million for 2010, and $1.1 billion for FY 2011. Grant funds from this program can be put toward physical improvements of transit systems, communication and emergency response equipment, and training as well as public awareness campaigns.

National League of Cities

The National League of Cities (NLC) is the oldest and largest national organization representing municipal governments throughout the United States. The NLC serves as a resource to and is an advocate for the more than 18,000 cities, villages, and towns it represents. More than 1,600 municipalities of all sizes pay dues to NLC and actively participate as leaders and voting members in the organization. The National League of Cities provides numerous benefits to its network of members, including:

- Advocates for cities and towns in Washington, DC, through full-time lobbying and grassroots campaigns
- Promotes cities and towns through an aggressive media and communications program that draws attention to city issues and enhances the national image of local government
- Provides programs and services that give local leaders the tools and knowledge to better serve their communities
- Keeps leaders informed of critical issues that affect municipalities and warrant action by local officials
- Strengthens leadership skills by offering numerous training and education programs
- Recognizes municipal achievements by gathering and promoting examples of best practices and honoring cities and towns with awards for model programs and initiatives
- Partners with state leagues to supplement resources and strengthen the voice of local government in the nation's capital and all state capitals
- Provides opportunities for involvement and networking to help city officials seek ideas, share solutions, and find common ground for the future.

Like the USCM, the NLC has also focused on the first-responder funding issue. It conducted a letter-writing campaign to the White House and Congress to build support for the original allocation of first responder funds. In 2002, NLC proposed a $75.5-billion stimulus package that would include $10 billion for unmet homeland security needs.

In January 2003, then-NLC President Karen Anderson appointed the special Working Group on Homeland Security to serve as NLC's front line resource on the subject. That group worked to prepare resources to help city officials in carrying out their new roles as the "front line of hometown defense."

The NLC has continued to lobby Congress and the Executive Office to increase or maintain funding support to strengthen "hometown" and homeland security, and develop extensive policy on these issues. The NLC reports the results of surveys on municipal responses to terrorism regarding vulnerable targets and the need for federal guidance and support. A variety of publications that NLC generates offer practical guidance to local officials to assist in their ongoing efforts to develop and refine local and regional homeland security plans.

In 2005, homeland security remained a top priority for the NLC. The two primary NLC issues were first responder funding and public safety communications. Presented in the "2005 Advocacy Priority" sidebar is text from an NLC document detailing advocacy policy regarding funding for first responders.

2005 Advocacy Priority — The Issue: Funding for First Responders

The nation's cities and towns need a well-funded, improved grant program to respond to terrorism threats in highly populated and high-threat areas. Local governments seek funding that allows jurisdictions to prepare for possible terrorist threats, with flexibility to use the funds for a range of risks based on their state homeland security plans.

Message to Congress

- Preserve direct funding. Preserve direct funding to local governments and regions based on the congressionally mandated 80-percent pass-through requirement from states to local governments.
- Improve homeland and hometown security. Improve security by increasing funding for Urban Area Security Grants and the State Homeland Security Grant program.
- Preserve funding. Preserve funding for both homeland security programs such as Law Enforcement Terrorism Prevention grants, the Urban Search and Rescue program and the Metropolitan Medical Response System, and traditional first responder and emergency management programs that existed before September 11, 2001.
- Provide flexibility. Provide flexibility for local governments to use homeland security funds to offset overtime expenditures during national high alerts, counterterrorism activities, and training exercises.
- Create a Federal clearinghouse. Create a web-based Federal clearinghouse of best practices and updated voluntary national consensus standards.
- Waive cost-sharing requirements. Waive matching or cost-sharing requirements for local governments.

Request to Congress

- Enact an authorization bill that provides funding for first responders to target terrorism threats in highly populated and high-threat areas, with maximum flexibility to use the funds for a range of risks based on their state homeland security plans.
- Fully fund the State Homeland Security Grant program, Urban Area Security Grants, and other critical homeland security programs.

Source: National League of Cities, www.nlc.org/content/Files/PFRHomeland%20Security1.pdf.

In 2005, the NLC developed a policy statement on homeland security that was included in its "National Municipal Policy." The policy statement addresses the following topics:

- Prevention, planning, and mitigation
- Disaster response and recovery

- Training and technical assistance
- Disaster insurance
- Domestic terrorism
- Border security
- Immigration enforcement
- Profiling

In support of these policies, NLC developed a publication "Protecting Hometown America: Lessons Learned from and for Small Cities and Towns," as presented in the "NLC Publication" sidebar.

NLC Publication "Protecting Hometown America: Lessons Learned from and for Small Cities and Towns"

The following lessons were developed for the National League of Cities Working Group on Homeland Security by the National League of Cities Small Cities Council based on experience by small communities since the September 11, 2001 terrorist attacks on the World Trade Center and the Pentagon. These points offer practical guidance to local officials in cities and towns of all sizes as they develop and refine local and regional homeland security plans.

1. Build and nurture partnerships and relationships based on trust and good communication. Strong working relationships are essential to effective response in any kind of emergency. Those partnerships are particularly important in a small community which will have to rely on good neighbors to provide support in an emergency. Creating and sustaining those relationships before a crisis event is a work in progress which demands constant attention. While technology is an important component of effective communication, people talking to people is the bottom line.

2. Know your community, its assets and vulnerabilities. Building a picture of every segment of your community, better known as "sectoring," will facilitate rapid response in case of emergency. That means developing a profile of every nook and cranny of the community which is easily understood, easily communicated, and easily shared with others who arrive to help out. Federal tools are available to help build this capacity.

3. Know your citizens — their special needs and concerns. Be sure to think about special groups — such as senior citizens, people with physical limitations, people living alone who may need extra help — when preparing evacuation and shelter plans. People with pets also will want to know what the options are for caring for animals in the event of an emergency. While city leaders can't plan for every contingency and every special need, clear instructions, advice, and guidance in advance will help individuals be well prepared and ready to make informed decisions about what to do, where to go, and what to expect in case of emergency.

4. Establish a secure and well-equipped emergency operations center. Even the smallest community needs a central place from which to manage emergency response. That place should be secure, known to all emergency responders, and equipped with the tools needed in case of an emergency. Basics like copies of the emergency plan, mutual aid agreements, telephone numbers of key responders, and fundamental tools like flashlights should be stored in a secure cabinet with specific guidelines for who responds to the center and who opens the cabinet.

5. Leverage local tools and resources to maximize readiness. Take advantage of existing resources — people and places within the community — to enhance response capability.

Business leaders, civic associations, and neighborhood groups should be included in local planning. And, local business facilities can be used to supplement government facilities in your response plan.

6. Invest in employees to broaden local capacity. Encourage your front line responders to reach out to learn from responders in other communities. That means supporting travel and professional development for police and fire chiefs and emergency personnel — even during tight budget times — to ensure that they are sharing ideas and learning from colleagues in other communities. No one needs to reinvent the wheel!

7. Develop a clear media action plan and be prepared for a potential media onslaught. An emergency in a small community can draw lots of national media which can be a hindrance to response if local leaders aren't prepared to handle the deluge. Establish clear roles and responsibilities for dealing with the media including who the primary spokesperson is, how often media briefings will be provided, and primary locations for media briefings and staging.

8. Prepare all the necessary paperwork in advance including proclamations, signed mutual aid agreements, and boilerplate citizen alerts. Take the time to prepare whatever paperwork is needed in the event of an emergency so that you don't have to be writing it all when an emergency occurs. Store copies of all the signed agreements in the emergency operations center so everything is available on the spot.

9. Plan for continuity of government during and after an emergency. Continuity plans should consider both physical government facilities (what to do if city hall or the emergency operations center are affected by the emergency) and leadership lines of succession.

10. Be creative and aggressive in finding federal resources to support local efforts. While new homeland security funds that are being distributed through the states are an important resource for local efforts, there are a variety of other sources of federal funding that can help support local efforts. Federal support can come in the form of small grants for special purposes and training programs for police, fire, and emergency personnel. Regional collaboration is particularly desirable for most federal grant programs.

11. Practice, practice, practice. Drills, simulations, and conversations about how to implement the emergency response plan are essential in communities of all sizes. Regular drills and reviews will ensure that the plan is both up to date and responders know how to implement it. Regular drills also build confidence and strengthen working relationships.

Source: National League of Cities, www.nlc.org/content/Files/2005%20NMP%20PSCP%20Chapter%20w%20toc.pdf.

The NLC has developed several other publications to assist local governments in participating in homeland security, including:

- "Homeland Security: Federal Resources for Local Governments" (http://www.missouriwestern.edu/RCPI/CD/Data/C2.pdf)

- "Homeland Security: Practical Tools for Local Governments" (http://www.nesc.wvu.edu/ndwc/pdf/terrorism.pdf)

- "Why Can't We Talk?" Emergency Communications Interoperability Guide (http://www.safecomprogram.gov/NR/rdonlyres/322B4367-265C-45FB-8EEA-BD0FEBDA95A8/0/Why_cant_we_talk_NTFI_Guide.pdf)

- "SARS: Lessons Learned for America's Cities and Towns" (http://www.nlc.org/ASSETS/386602175CEC41258CF159266DE26889/lessonslearnedsars.pdf)

In July 2007, NLC representatives met with Department of Homeland Security officials to exchange views and perspectives on homeland security in towns and cities. At this meeting, the NLC reiterated that all emergency situations are local events, and that local elected officials involved in the day-to-day operations of local government shoulder the burden ensuring that public safety resources are available to citizens in times of emergency or disaster. At this meeting, NLC highlighted the following seven topics as priorities for local elected officials:

1. Emergency communications
2. Emergency Management Assistance Compacts (EMACs)/Mutual Aid
3. All-hazards planning
4. Federalization of the National Guard
5. Intragovernmental collaboration and communication
6. Full funding of federal mandates, and
7. Immigration/border security

National Association of Counties

The National Association of Counties (NACo) was created in 1935, and remains the only national organization that represents county governments in the United States. NAC maintains a membership of more than 2,000 counties (over 80% of the U.S. population), but represents all of the nation's 3,066 counties to the White House and to Congress.

NAC is a full-service organization that provides many services to its members, including legislative, research, technical, and public affairs assistance. The association acts as a liaison with other levels of government, works to improve public understanding of counties, serves as a national advocate for counties, and provides them with resources to help them find innovative methods to meet the challenges they face. NAC is involved in a number of special projects that deal with such issues as the environment, sustainable communities, volunteerism, and intergenerational studies.

In 2001, NAC created the "Policy Agenda to Secure the People of America's Counties." This policy paper stated that "[c]ounties are the first responders to terrorist attacks, natural disasters and major emergencies" (National Association of Counties, 2002). NAC established a 43-member NAC Homeland Security Task Force that, on October 23, 2001, prepared a set of 20 recommendations in four general categories concerning homeland security issues: public health, local law enforcement and intelligence, infrastructure security, and emergency planning and public safety. Since that time, NAC has continued to release policy recommendations, with the 2007–2008 Policy Resolutions displayed in the sidebar titled "NAC Homeland Security Policy Resolutions . . ."

NAC Homeland Security Policy Resolutions for 2007–2008

Resolution Supporting Strengthening the Nation's Emergency Management System

NAC supports the following principles to strengthen national emergency management functions:

1. Preparedness functions must be linked both statutorily and operationally with response and recovery functions within federal emergency management.
2. Regardless of where located in the federal government, the federal emergency management Director must have a direct reporting relationship to the President during

periods of Presidential disaster and emergency declarations, similar to the Joint Chiefs of Staff relationship in military engagement.

3. Congress should require that criteria be developed for the federal emergency management Director position to ensure competent leadership and provide for a direct reporting relationship with the President. Congress should allow stakeholders to have input in the vetting process for nominees. Reductions should be made to the number of political appointments within federal emergency management functions and fill positions of authority with individuals who have requisite experience.

4. Federal emergency management leadership should be the lead for the National Response Plan (NRP) as outlined in the Homeland Security Act of 2002.

5. The role of the military should continue to be in support of civilian authorities. Procedures should be refined for requesting assistance from the Department of Defense (DoD) in those rare and catastrophic events when assets are needed that only DoD can provide.

6. Regional offices should be strengthened through adequate staffing and resources.

7. The federal emergency management organization must be fully staffed and have the capability to establish and maintain stockpiles and pre-position resources and equipment, as well as establish trained cadres of personnel to provide surge capacity in large disasters.

8. Integrated planning, training and exercise are a requirement for effective disaster response. Preparedness cannot be a separate function from disaster readiness, response and recovery.

9. Unity of effort is a prerequisite for effective disaster response. Relationships must be established and communications networks in place prior to events. The Department of Homeland Security should establish a field presence that interacts with state and local partners on a day-to-day basis.

10. Federal emergency management must provide additional focus on its ability to effectively implement recovery programs for local governments, individuals, families, and businesses.

11. Governors must remain the lead in disaster response within their states in support of and in consultations with local officials.

12. State and local governments should be consulted in policy decisions and initiatives related to preparedness, response, recovery and mitigation early in the process and rationale should be given when suggestions are not included. Process should support state and local advisory councils, task forces, and other relevant groups.

13. Incentives and educational programs should be implemented that focus local and state governments and insurance on public policy choices which better protect individuals and property during emergencies. Such incentives and educational programs should include land use planning and preparedness, building code requirements, and enforcement.

14. A federal/state/local working group of experienced professionals should be convened to review the National Response Plan (NRP) and make adjustments based on lessons learned from Hurricane Katrina response. A review of the NRP is necessary to include state and local stakeholders. Specifically, the "Incident of National Significance" is confusing and should be clarified in the NRP. The Principal Federal Official (PFO) position is not needed and repetitive, as the Stafford Act gives the Federal Coordinating Officers those responsibilities. Federal Coordinating Officers (FCOs) should be given decision-making authority and access to all Department of Homeland Security assets to respond to and recover from disasters.

15. Emergency management functions should be fire-walled and protected in legislation similar to the Secret Service and Coast Guard treatment in the Homeland Security Act of 2002. A firewall will prevent funding, personnel and resources from being used for other functions.

16. The Emergency Management Performance Grant's intended uses, formula, and distribution to state emergency management agencies should not be changed. The

program should remain all-hazards focused. Adequate and predictable funding is necessary to administer this program as the only source of all-hazards preparedness funding for state and local emergency management.

17. Major changes are not needed to refine the Stafford Act. The law served Congress well with flexibility in response to Hurricane Katrina and a separate system should not be developed for catastrophic disasters, as Congress has the ability to consider each disaster's need on a case by case basis. Any changes to the Stafford Act must fix some issues related to the last overhaul in 2000, and must be fully vetted with state and local governments.

18. The Catastrophic Disaster Preparedness Program should be authorized and appropriately funded to include planning, training, exercise, and action plans to implement lessons learned. State and local governments must be a partner in catastrophic disaster planning.

Resolution to Support DHS's Homeland Security Grant Programs

NAC urges Congress to restore funding to DHS's key state and local assistance programs. These programs are vital components for protecting our communities from terrorist threats and other hazards.

Resolution on Enhancing Homeland Security Grant Programs

NAC supports federal legislation or requirements that would improve homeland security grant programs by streamlining application and planning requirements, promote flexibility and provide first responders and county governments with additional resources in an expedited fashion. Priority funding decisions should be based on a regional and/or a multijurisdictional planning and collaborative effort between state and all levels of local governments.

Resolution Support for Increased Mutual Aid Agreements

NAC urges counties to become familiar with the Emergency Management Assistance Compact (EMAC). In addition, we urge Congress and the Administration to work with States to improve and strengthen EMAC as the primary vehicle for delivering interstate mutual aid. Furthermore, we urge States to establish formal and effective mechanisms for identifying and deploying local assets as an integral part of the EMAC process; and urge Congress to adopt an annual $4 million authorization of the program for the administrator of the EMAC compact.

Resolution in Support for Accelerating Qualifications and Credentialing

NAC urges the federal government to speed up the existing qualifications and credentialing project. The recent catastrophic events in the fall of 2005 demonstrated that qualified and credentialed field, supervisory, and management personnel would have ensured greater competence in responding to and recovering from these events. There must be qualified people in field, supervisory, and management positions that are qualified and competent to order, use, and manage resources. Further, NAC urges the federal government to adopt national consensus standards to the extent possible.

Resolution on Need for a Robust National Weather Service (NWS) in Support of Local Communities

NAC urges Congress and the Administration to ensure that funds budgeted for NWS operations in support of local communities are protected from reallocation and that the operating hours of local NWS forecast offices that warn and advise county emergency managers regarding severe weather threats are maintained at current hours of operation.

Resolution in Support of Federal Funding to Local Governments to Meet Federal Security Mandates at U.S. Ports

NAC urges Congress to pass legislation that assures that the federal government provides adequate funds for local governments to meet federal seaport security mandates, without impacting traditional seaport funding sources for capacity and other critical projects, including eligibility to use Homeland Security funds for operational costs.

Resolution on Changes to the National Flood Insurance Program

The Federal Emergency Management Agency should extend the grant performance period issued under the National Flood Insurance Program's Increased Cost of Compliance coverage from two years to five years so that policyholders may have an adequate period of time in which to bring their homes and real properties up to local zoning laws and codes associated with damage from federally recognized floods and other natural disasters. The grant performance period shall commence with the settlement of disaster-related litigation or mediation with a policyholder's primary property insurance carrier.

Resolution Supporting Task Force to Study the Need for Functional and Medical Registries Nationwide

NAC urges Congress to pass legislation that creates regional task forces that would study and provide recommendations for funding the development of functional and medical registries nationwide.

Resolution on Maintaining the Emergency Management Performance Grant Program as a Separate All-Hazards Program

NAC urges Congress and the Administration to address the current $287 million shortfall in EMPG funding, and: to maintain the current 50–50 match structure of the EMPG formula for all-hazards preparedness, and; ensure that the EMPG formula not be linked to any other homeland security grant reform package, but that EMPG funds shall be all-hazards focused and based on the currently recognized formulas and permitted use polices, maintaining the current flexibility of the program, and; that voluntary performance metrics based systems (such as the Emergency Management Accreditation Program [EMAP]) should be used to measure the capacity being built by EMPG, rather than Homeland Security–specific measurables.

Resolution in Support for the Provisions Included in the Improved Hurricane Tracking and Forecasting Act of 2007 (H.R. 2531/S. 1509)

NAC urges Congress to pass the Improved Hurricane Tracking and Forecasting Act of 2007 H.R. 2531 and S. 1509 to better protect property, lives, and the environment.

Resolution Supporting County Preparedness for Pandemic Influenza

The National Association of Counties urges the Administration and Congress to recognize that pandemic influenza response is primarily local in nature, and to provide adequate funding, sound guidance, and support that will enable counties to prepare effectively for pandemic influenza in a manner that is consistent with local emergency management plans and that permits optimally efficient use of local resources. Eighty percent of federal funds granted to states for pandemic influenza preparedness should be designated for use at the local level.

Resolution on Establishing Qualifications for State Homeland Security Advisors

The Department of Homeland Security should research, develop, and publish a set of criteria that any State Homeland Security Advisor must meet in order to serve in that capacity at the state level.

Resolution on Alignment of Communication to Homeland Security Advisors, State Emergency Management Agencies and State Administrative Agencies

The U.S. Department of Homeland Security must align its communications so that information originating from the Department reaches the Homeland Security Advisors, State Emergency Management Agencies, State Administrative Agencies, appropriate local agencies, and all entities consistently.

Source: National Association of Counties.

Like the other municipal organizations listed earlier, NAC is vitally interested in homeland security funding issues, and works to help its member counties to locally address the complex issues. In addition to advocacy, NAC develops toolkits and other publications that counties can use to decipher the flood of information that exists. Examples of these resources are listed in the sidebar titled "NAC Homeland Security Toolkits . . ."

NAC Homeland Security Toolkits and Other Relevant Publications

Decisionmaking in Times of Emergency: PowerPoint slide presentations on First Responder Interoperability (http://www.naco.org/Template.cfm?Section=New_Technical_Assistance&template=/ContentoManagement/ContentoDisplay.cfm&ContentID=24591)

Disaster and Terrorism Toolkit: A toolkit created to assist counties in locating information about disasters and terrorism (http://www.naco.org/Template.cfm?Section=New_Technical_Assistance&template=/ContentoManagement/ContentoDisplay.cfm&ContentID=23429

Best Practices: County Adoption of the National Incident Management System (NIMS): A collection of actual samples of county NIMS adoption resolutions from various NAC member counties (http://www.naco.org/Template.cfm?Section=New_Technical_Assistance&template=/ContentoManagement/ContentoDisplay.cfm&ContentID=22497)

NIMS Guide for County Officials: A guide to help county officials understand what NIMS is and the role counties play in planning to prepare for and respond to emergencies of any type and of any scale (http://www.naco.org/Template.cfm?Section=New_Technical_Assistance&template=/ContentoManagement/ContentoDisplay.cfm&ContentID=21694)

Source: National Association of Counties, www.naco.org.

In February 2004, NAC surveyed several of the nation's "core counties," which are those counties that are most representative of each of the nation's high-threat urban areas included in the DHS Urban Areas Security Initiative (UASI) (see Chapter 7). The survey solicited information about each county's involvement in the UASI and how well the process worked from their perspective. The results of the survey are presented in the sidebar titled "Excerpts from NAC UASI Survey Report."

■ ■ ■

Excerpts from NAC UASI Survey Report

During FY 2003, the DHS Office of Domestic Preparedness (ODP) created the Urban Areas Security Initiative (UASI). This initiative is designed to combat terrorism in the United States by targeting Federal funding to high threat urban areas. These areas have been determined to be high threats because they house significant national, state or business infrastructure, governmental systems and population centers and are considered most vulnerable to terrorist attacks. Each urban area is made up of a core city and county and includes jurisdictions that are contiguous and have established formal mutual aid agreements.

A core county is where the core city of the urban area is located. The funds were to address the unique equipment, training, planning, exercise and operation needs of these large urban areas. After the designation of the 30 urban high threat areas, each state worked with ODP to complete the process to determine the allocation for each urban area. The funds were then awarded to the states, each of which was responsible, through its State Administrative Agency, for managing the submission of assessments and strategies from each urban area that was eligible to receive funds.

In mid-February 2004, the National Association of Counties sent a survey to the core county in each of these high threat urban areas. This survey was designed to find out whether these targeted areas were receiving these much needed funds. In addition, the survey asked each responding county to comment on how the funding distribution process has worked in their states. Fifteen core counties completed the survey, representing 12 of the 20 states that had been awarded at that time.

Findings

Core counties were asked if their states had kept them well informed about the process it followed to submit a plan to the ODP to make their urban area eligible for UASI funds.

- One hundred percent of responding core counties, except Washington, DC, responded yes to that question.
- When asked if the core county participated in discussions with their states about the distribution of these funds, 80 percent of responding core counties report discussions with their states.
- Of the three core counties that indicated that they did not participate, all were in states where another core county responded that they had participated in such discussions. The states are California, Ohio, and Texas.

Core counties were next asked it they had participated in discussions with the other participating local governments in their high-threat area. All 15 responding counties (100%) report having these discussions.

Core counties were asked what percentage of the funds was asked for each of the four major expenditure areas.

- Of the four — training, exercises, equipment, and planning — in 80 percent of the core counties the largest percentage of the funds was requested for equipment. These requests ranged from a low of 30 percent to a high of 100 percent.
- Only Miami-Dade County and Multnomah County requested that the largest percentage of their funds be in the area of training.

Core counties were asked if they had received any of their UASI funds as of the date of their response to this survey.

- Forty-seven percent of responding counties responded yes.
- Fifty-three percent responded that they have not.
- These amounts ranged from a high of $18.5 million down to $40,000.
- When asked what percentage of the anticipated funds they had received, 81 percent report receiving from 0 to 25 percent.
- Only San Francisco County reports receiving 100 percent of its funds, which amount to more than $18.5 million.
- Only 47 percent of the core counties, representing six states, say that the state has appropriated its own funds to assist with homeland security efforts.
- Thirty-three percent of core counties did not know whether their states had appropriated these funds.

Among the core counties, 73 percent report that they have used their own general operating funds to enhance homeland security efforts. One hundred percent of the core counties report that the planning and funding process for the UASI grant program has better prepared their counties for responding to a terrorist threat.

Source: National Association of Counties, www.naco.org/ContentManagement/ContentDisplay. cfm?ContentID = 16077.

National Governors Association

The National Governors Association (NGA) — the bipartisan organization of the nation's governors — promotes visionary state leadership, shares best practices, and speaks with a unified voice on national policy. Its members are the governors of the 50 states and five territories. The NGA bills itself as the collective voice of the nation's governors and one of Washington, DC's most respected public policy organizations. NGA provides governors and their senior staff members with services that range from representing states on Capitol Hill and before the administration on key federal issues to developing policy reports on innovative state programs and hosting networking seminars for state government executive branch officials. The NGA Center for Best Practices focuses on state innovations and best practices on issues that range from education and health to technology, welfare reform, and the environment. NGA also provides management and technical assistance to both new and incumbent governors.

In August 2002, the Center for Best Practices of the NGA released "States' Homeland Security Priorities." A list of 10 major priorities and issues was identified by the NGA center through a survey of states' and territories' homeland security offices (NGA Center for Best Practices, 2002). These priorities clearly illustrated the main concerns of the state leadership in light of the massive changes that were occurring at the federal level, and included the following:

- Coordination must involve all levels of government.
- The federal government must disseminate timely intelligence information to the states.
- The states must work with local governments to develop interoperable communications between first responders, and adequate wireless spectrum must be set aside to do the job.
- State and local governments need help and technical assistance to identify and protect critical infrastructure.
- Both the states and federal government must focus on enhancing bioterrorism preparedness and rebuilding the nation's public health system to address 21st-century threats.

- The federal government should provide adequate federal funding and support to ensure that homeland security needs are met.

- The federal government should work with states to protect sensitive security information, including restricting access to information available through "freedom of information" requests.

- An effective system must be developed that secures points of entry at borders, airports, and seaports without placing an undue burden on commerce.

- The National Guard has proven itself to be an effective force during emergencies and crises. The mission of the National Guard should remain flexible, and Guard units should primarily remain under the control of the governor during times of crises.

- Federal agencies should integrate their command systems into existing state and local incident command systems (ICS) rather than requiring state and local agencies to adapt to federal command systems.

Source: NGA Center for Best Practices, Issue Brief, August 19, 2002.

The NGA Center for Best Practices (NGAC) provides support to the governors in their management of new homeland security challenges as they arise and the overall homeland security domain that exists as a result of September 11. NGAC provides these officials with technical assistance and policy research and facilitates their participation in national discussions and initiatives. Center activities focus on states' efforts to protect critical infrastructure, develop interoperable communications capabilities, and prepare for and respond to bioterrorism, agroterrorism, nuclear and radiological terrorism, and cyberterrorism (as it impacts the government's ability to obtain, disseminate, and store essential information). The NGA does recognize that, while terrorism must be a priority, natural and human-made disasters will continue to demand timely and coordinated responses from local, state, and federal government agencies.

The Association's position on homeland security is presented in the sidebar titled "NGA Position . . ."

NGA Position on Homeland Security

Although the Constitution delegates to Congress the power and responsibility to provide for the common defense, most of the responsibility for providing homeland defense rests with state and local governments. Governors, with the support of the Federal government and local jurisdictions, are responsible for ensuring the ability of state, territorial, and local authorities to deal with natural disasters and other types of major emergencies, including a terrorist incident. State homeland security efforts (infrastructure assets, people resources, and coordination) are critical components of the National Strategy for Homeland Security.

NGA policy and positions with regard to Homeland Security issues are guided by the following principles:

- There should be a base capacity in every state, which means that every state should receive some funds.
- The Department of Homeland Security should provide guidance to states for developing equipment and training standards for adequate levels of protection and preparedness.
- There should be flexibility in the allowable uses of grant funds.
- Governors and other high-ranking state and territorial officials need to receive timely and critical intelligence information related to terrorist threats.
- The traditional first responder programs that existed prior to September 11, 2001 should continue to be funded.

- There should be predictable and sustainable long-term funding of homeland security programs.
- All Federal funding, resources, programs and activities involving state and local governments must be coordinated through the nation's Governors for maximum effectiveness and efficiency.
- The role of the business community and the impact on the economic viability of a community when faced with recovery from a terrorist attack must be considered.

Source: National Governors Association, www.nga.org/nga/lobbyIssues/1,1169,D_4898,00.html.

Since 2004, the National Governors Association Center for Best Practices (NGA Center) has tracked the states' progress in developing homeland security structures and programs through an annual survey of state homeland security officials. The results of the 2007 survey are listed in the "NGA Survey Results" sidebar.

NGA Survey Results

For the 2007 survey, the NGA Center polled the 56 state and territorial homeland security advisors who, collectively, comprise the Governors Homeland Security Advisors Council. The survey results reflect the participation of roughly 80 percent of those officials; that is, 44 state homeland security officials completed the survey either in whole or in part, although the response rate for some questions was less than the full 80 percent. This year's survey shows that the top five priorities for states in 2007 were, in order:

- Developing interoperable communications
- Coordinating state and local efforts
- Protecting critical infrastructure
- Developing state fusion centers
- Strengthening citizen preparedness

These priorities have remained stable for several survey years. The survey also revealed that:

- States continue to report unsatisfactory progress in their relationship with the federal government, specifically with the Department of Homeland Security (DHS).
- In the view of the states, federal homeland security grant programs are not adequately funded and do not strike an adequate balance among preparedness, prevention, response, and recovery.
- The majority of states said DHS should coordinate policies with the states prior to the release or implementation of those policies.
- States need federal funding to support personnel to implement and sustain initiatives that are national in scope but that are carried out locally.
- Federal agencies should coordinate their security clearances to ensure that a clearance issued by one agency is recognized by other agencies.
- Only about one-third of states have at least 75 percent of their National Guard forces available to respond to a natural or manmade disaster.

- More than half the states have "significantly" involved local governments in the development of strategic plans, including grant funding allocation plans.

Full survey results can be found at: http://www.nga.org/Files/pdf/0712HOMELAND SURVEY.PDF.

Source: National Governors Association.

National Emergency Management Association

The National Emergency Management Association (NEMA) is a nonpartisan, nonprofit association that works to enhance public safety. NEMA is focused on the all-hazards approach to emergency management. NEMA began in 1974 when state directors of emergency services first united in order to exchange information on common emergency management issues in their constituencies. State emergency management directors form the core membership, but members also include key state staff, homeland security advisers, federal agencies, nonprofit organizations, private-sector companies, and concerned individuals.

NEMA's mission is to:

- Provide national leadership and expertise in comprehensive emergency management.
- Serve as a vital emergency management information and assistance resource.
- Advance continuous improvement in emergency management through strategic partnerships, innovative programs, and collaborative policy positions.

Following September 11, NEMA created the National Homeland Security Consortium, which includes key state and local organizations, elected officials, the private sector, and others with roles and responsibilities for homeland security prevention, preparedness, response, and recovery activities. Participating organizations began meeting in 2002. The consortium is an outgrowth of those initial discussions regarding the need for enhanced communication and coordination between disciplines and levels of government. The consortium is now recognized by DHS and works in partnership with other federal agencies such as the Centers for Disease Control and Prevention. The mission of the consortium is to provide a forum wherein key ideas on homeland security can be shared among and between various levels of government.

Terrorism-Related Activity among State Emergency Managers

A good indicator of the manner in which each of the state governments approaches the terrorism issue is the priorities set by their emergency managers. A survey of state homeland security structures by NEMA conducted in June 2002 found that all 50 states maintain primary point of contact for antiterrorism/homeland security efforts. At that time, these contacts were located in the following state government offices:

- Governor/Lieutenant Governor's office — 14 states
- Military/adjutant general — 12 states
- Public safety/law enforcement — 12 states
- Office of Homeland Security/Emergency Management — 10 states
- Attorney general — 2 states
- Land commissioner — 1 state (Source: National Conference of State Legislatures, 2005)

As of January 2008, these numbers had changed, reflecting a more thought-out approach to placement of these officials in the overall context of state government affairs. Many states had even created dedicated homeland security offices. These figures are as follows:

- Office of Homeland Security/Emergency Management — 34 states
- Military/adjutant general — 8 states
- Public safety/law enforcement — 7 states
- Governor's office — 2 states

On October 1, 2001, NEMA released a "White Paper on Domestic Preparedness" that was supported by the Adjutants Generals Association of the United States, the International Association of Emergency Managers (which represents local emergency management officials), and the National Guard Association of America. The document states that "NEMA thinks it critical that the following enhancements be incorporated into a nationwide strategy for catastrophic disaster preparedness" (National Emergency Management Association, 2001). A total of 22 enhancements were presented in the white paper in three general categories: emergency preparedness and response, health and medical, and additional WMD recommendations. A partial list of these enhancements is presented in the sidebar titled "Partial List of Enhancements . . ."

Partial List of Enhancements Presented in the NEMA Paper on Domestic Preparedness

Emergency Preparedness and Response

- Congress should provide to the states immediate Federal funding for full-time catastrophic disaster coordinators in moderate and high-risk local jurisdictions of the United States. (*Did happen*)
- States need financial assistance to improve catastrophic response and Continuity of Operations Plans (COOP) and Continuity of Government (COG) for states. (*Did happen*)
- Interstate and intrastate mutual assistance must be recognized and supported by the Federal government as an expedient, cost-effective approach to disaster response and recovery. (*Recognized in the NRP*)
- FEMA, state, and local emergency managers must implement renewed emphasis on family and community preparedness to ensure Americans have the skills necessary to survive a catastrophic disaster. (*Did happen*)
- A standardized national donations management protocol is needed to address the outpouring of food, clothing, supplies, and other items that are commonly sent to impacted states localities following a disaster. (*Addressed in the NRP*)

Health and Medical

- The medical surge capacity must be strengthened. The emergency management, medical, and public health professions must work with lawmakers to ensure each region of our nation has a certain minimum surge capacity to deal with mass casualty events. (*In process*)
- State–local disaster medical assistance teams should be developed across the country, with standardized equipment, personnel, and training. (*In process*)

Additional WMD Recommendations

- The Department of Justice should immediately release the FY00 and FY01 equipment funds in order to begin implementation of these recommendations and then require a basic statewide strategy in order to receive FY02 funds; and further, provide funding to states to administer the equipment program. (*Equipment funds now handled by DHS*)

- Congress and the Department of Defense should authorize homeland defense as a key Federal defense mission tasking for the National Guard. State and local Urban Search and Rescue capabilities should be developed across the country, with the standardized equipment, personnel, and training. (*Did happen*)
- National interagency and intergovernmental information management protocols are needed to support information sharing (i.e., damage/situation reports, warning/ intelligence reports, resource coordination). (*In process*)
- Better Federal interagency coordination is needed to assist states in identifying and accessing the full range of Federal resources and assistance available to them. (*Has happened through the DHS Office of State and Local Coordination and Preparedness*)
- FEMA's fire grant program should be expanded and modified to strengthen regional and national, not just local, fire protection capabilities to respond to catastrophic disasters. (*Has not happened*)
- There is a need for technology transfer from the Federal government and technology contractors to state and local governments to support an automated decision support system. (*Has not happened*)

Source: National Emergency Management Association, "White Paper of Domestic Preparedness," October 1, 2001.

The NEMA white paper presented "enhancements" that address coordination, communications, command, information sharing, funding, technology, and public health system and preparedness issues. Also included were the use of National Guard assets, increasing the capabilities of state–local urban search and rescue, expanding the FEMA Fire Grant program, and establishment of a standardized national donations protocol. Many states have taken significant action to address homeland security and counterterrorism planning. A report compiled by the White House Office of Homeland Security in 2002 showed what the earliest concerns were for states, cities, and counties, when the topic was still new. Their actions could be grouped into four general areas:

- Developing plans
- Information sharing
- Responding to biological threats
- Protecting critical infrastructure

International Association of Emergency Managers

The International Association of Emergency Managers (IAEM) is a nonprofit organization dedicated to promoting the goals of saving lives and protecting property during emergencies and disasters. Founded in 1952 as the U.S. Civil Defense Council, it became the National Coordinating Council on Emergency Management in 1985, and changed its name to the International Association of Emergency Managers in 1998.

The association brings together emergency managers and disaster response professionals from all levels of government, as well as the military, the private sector, and volunteer organizations in the United States and around the world. The purpose of IAEM is to serve the emergency management community by:

- Encouraging the development of disaster-resistant communities to reduce the effect of disasters on life and property
- Acting as a clearinghouse for information on comprehensive management issues
- Providing a forum for creative and innovative problem solving on emergency management issues
- Maintaining and expanding standards for emergency management programs and professionals
- Fostering informed decision making on public policy in the emergency management arena

The IAEM often issues policy briefs that relay the position of the nation's and the world's emergency managers, about salient issues being debated or considered in Congress. An example of one of these position papers, issued in 2007, is provided in the sidebar titled "IAEM Position Paper . . ."

IAEM Position Paper on Emergency Management Performance Grants, 2007

The IAEM Board of Directors on February 12 approved a position statement asserting that the Emergency Management Performance Grant Program (EMPG) should be maintained as a separate all-hazard program focused on capacity building for all-hazards preparedness, response, recovery and mitigation at the state and local levels.

Background

EMPG is the single federal all-hazards emergency preparedness grant program in support of capacity building at the state and local level. EMPG funds support the state and local foundation upon which the U.S. emergency response system is built. The program supports state and local initiatives for planning, training, exercise, public education, command and control, and emergency operations personnel. Emergency management is the governmental function that coordinates and integrates all activities necessary to build, sustain and improve the capability to prepare for, protect against, respond to, recover from or mitigate against threatened or actual natural disasters, acts of terrorism or other manmade disasters.

The EMGP program is authorized by the Stafford Act and has been in existence since the 1950s. It was created to be a 50/50 cost share to ensure participation by state and local governments to build strong emergency management capability. Administration proposals have attempted in the past to reduce the percentage of funds that could be used for personnel and to combine the funds with the homeland security grant programs. Congress has rejected the request to limit the percentage for personnel and has kept the EMPG program as a separate account.

EMPG is a program that works. During homeland security grant reform discussions with the House and Senate in 2004, IAEM (partnering with NEMA) successfully urged Congress to hold EMPG harmless and not link it with the homeland security grants. The International Association of Emergency Managers recommends the following regarding the Emergency Management Performance Grant Program (EMPG):

- EMPG should be funded at $375 million, the amount authorized in P.L.109–295, the Post-Katrina Emergency Management Reform Act of 2006.

- The EMPG match should be maintained at 50–50 to continue to reflect the state and local commitment to the emergency management program in partnership with the federal government.
- The formula and any authorization for EMPG should not be linked with any homeland security grant reform package.
- EMPG is authorized in the Stafford Disaster Relief Act and is a program that works. It should be held harmless in any homeland security grant reform package as are the other traditional pre-9/11 FEMA grants.
- EMPG allocation and uses should be based on emergency management plans and all-hazard capacity, rather than terrorism-based capabilities.
- Performance metrics-based systems, like the Emergency Management Accreditation Program (EMAP) standards, should be used to measure the capacity being built by EMPG, rather than homeland security specific measurables.

Source: National Emergency Management Association, IAEM Bulletin, Volume 24, Number 3, March 2007.

Local Government Terrorism Activities

Emergency preparedness, mitigation, response, and recovery all occur at the local community level. It is at the local level that the critical planning, communications, technology, coordination, command, and spending decisions matter the most. The priorities of groups such as the National Conference of Mayors and the National Association of Counties are to represent these very concerns shared by local communities about what is necessary for them to become resilient from the threat of terrorism. The drive toward a reduction in vulnerability from terrorism has spawned a series of new requirements in preparedness and mitigation planning for most local-level officials that, prior to September 11, rarely considered such issues.

Both NAC and the USCM policy papers identified issues in the areas of command, coordination, communications, funding and equipment, training, and mutual aid. These two organizations recognized and proclaimed the local concerns about protecting critical community infrastructure, including the public health system, most of which is maintained and secured at the local level by local government law enforcement, fire, and health officials.

The events of September 11 brought to the surface the notion that the security of community infrastructure, which was suddenly recognized as a potential target for terrorist attacks, was vital to the security of the nation as a whole. Community infrastructure has always been vulnerable to natural and other technological disaster events — so much so that FEMA's largest disaster assistance program, Public Assistance, is designed to fund the rebuilding of community infrastructure damaged by a disaster event. However, local government officials and local emergency managers were suddenly finding themselves dedicating a greatly increased amount of funding and personnel to protecting and securing community infrastructure from the increased threat of terrorist attack. They have also had to boost the abilities of the local public health system, which has been recognized by the federal government as the most likely area where an outbreak caused by a bioterrorism agent will be identified.

To illustrate several of the new issues that local governments, most notably the smaller, rural governments, have had to consider in light of the new terrorist threat, the following checklist designed for the City of Boone, North Carolina, is provided. This checklist is excerpted from that municipality's technological annex developed for the town's All-Hazards Planning and Operations Manual in March 2002:

- Identify the types of terrorist events that might occur in the community.
- Plan emergency activities in advance to ensure a coordinated response to terrorist attacks.

- Build capabilities necessary to respond effectively to the consequences of terrorism.
- Identify the type or nature of a terrorist attack when it does happen.
- Implement the planned response quickly and efficiently.
- Recover from the incident.

The response to terrorism is similar in many ways to that of other natural or human-made disasters for which Boone has already prepared. Through additions and modifications, the development of a completely separate system could be avoided. Training and public education have been vital to enhancing preparedness, and understanding the process by which available federal financial assistance is acquired has drastically increased local capacity. The general types of activities that Boone has needed to take to meet the abovementioned objectives follow:

- Strengthen information and communications technology.
- Establish a well-defined incident command structure that includes the FBI.
- Strengthen local working relationships and communications.
- Educate health-care and emergency response communities about identification of bioterrorist attacks and agents.
- Educate health-care and emergency response community about medical treatment and prophylaxis for possible biological agents.
- Educate local health department about state and federal requirements and assistance.
- Maintain locally accessible supply of medications, vaccines, and supplies.
- Address health-care–worker safety issues.
- Designate a spokesperson to maintain contact with the public.
- Develop comprehensive evacuation plans.
- Become familiar with state and local laws relating to isolation/quarantine.
- Develop or enhance local capability to prosecute crimes involving WMD or the planning of terrorism events.
- Develop, maintain, and practice an infectious diseases emergency response plan.
- Practice with surrounding jurisdictions to strengthen mutual agreement plans.
- Outline the roles of federal agency assistance in planning and response.
- Educate the public in recognizing events and ways to respond as individuals.
- Stay current.

Source: Town of Boone, All-Hazards Planning and Operations Manual, Technological Hazards Annex. Boone, NC: Town of Boone, March 2007.

▓ ▓ Critical Thinking ▓

Terrorism prevention and preparedness has added significant strain to already stretched local budgets. Do you feel that the local governments should determine their risk and act accordingly, or should they be expected to prescribe to a minimum level of preparedness regardless of the effect it has on other local programs that may suffer as a result of budget reallocations?

Conclusion

Emergency management in the United States was forever changed by the events of September 11, 2001, and many would say for the better. This opinion is in wide dispute, however, for a variety of reasons that are unique to each successive level of government, primarily in terms of a loss of dedication to more traditional, nonterrorism hazards. Regardless, it is undeniable that emergency management, and now homeland security, have been thrust to the forefront of the public and the policy agendas, and are one of many primary concerns of federal, state, and local administrators.

For local governments, terrorism is a new threat that greatly expands their already strained safety and security requirements, and adds to a long list of needs and priorities. But the threat of terrorism is one that cannot be ignored, and state and local governments have not done so. At these local levels, the drastic increase in funding that has provided training and equipment to local first responders has been greeted with mixed emotion. Many recipients feel it has remained singular in focus, addressing mainly the terrorism threat. Historically, and including the 2001 terrorist attacks, natural disasters have taken many more lives and have caused much more financial harm. These natural and technological hazards will continue to pose a threat and will continue to result in disaster. It is undeniable that a more comprehensive approach to building the capacity of the local government to respond would provide more long-term benefits. Whether or not these local government agencies will be better prepared overall remains to be seen.

At the state level, governors and state emergency management directors have resisted the push toward local control, and have been accused on many occasions of holding out federal homeland security funding from the local governments for which it was intended. In many circumstances it was determined that these accusations were correct. But state officials feel the same concerns about the terrorist threat as do to the locals, and have called for better coordination, new communications technologies, and, as always, more and more funding.

At the federal government level, the changes that have resulted with regard to emergency management have been the most visible — and the most dramatic. The creation in 2002 of the Department of Homeland Security, which absorbed FEMA and most of the former federal government disaster management programs, has resulted in DHS taking the lead in addressing these new issues. This new agency has been tested on several occasions, as will be displayed throughout this text, and has enjoyed relatively mixed but primarily positive success. Under the leadership of DHS, many federal disaster response, recovery, and mitigation programs have so far fared well, although their priorities have seen a drastic shift to accommodate the new terrorist concern. In general, the United States has taken the typical response to a new problem in that it reorganized and committed huge amounts of funding to reducing the newly recognized problem.

The "Select Websites for Additional Information" sidebar lists websites about the organizations discussed in this chapter.

Select Websites for Additional Information

AmeriCorps: www.americorps.org

Animal and Plant Health Inspection Service: www.aphis.usda.gov

Citizen Corps: www.citizencorps.gov

Corporation for National and Community Service: www.nationalservice.org

Department of Homeland Security: www.dhs.gov

Federal Emergency Management Agency: www.fema.gov

Medical Reserve Corps: www.medicalreservecorps.gov

Office for Domestic Preparedness: www.ojp.usdoj.gov/odp

National Association of Counties: www.naco.org

National Governors Association: www.nga.org

National League of Cities: www.nlc.org

Neighborhood Watch: www.usaonwatch.org
Senior Corps: www.seniorcorps.org
Transportation Security Administration: www.tsa.dot.gov
United States Coast Guard: www.uscg.mil
United States Conference of Mayors: www.usmayors.org
United States Customs Service: www.cbp.gov
United States Secret Service: www.secretservice.gov
U.S.A. Freedom Corps: www.usafreedomcorps.gov
Volunteers in Police Service: www.policevolunteers.org

Key Terms

Adjutant General: The chief administrative officer of a major military unit (the National Guard, in the case of the state government).

Civil Rights: The rights belonging to an individual by virtue of citizenship.

Cybersecurity: The protection of data and systems in networks that are connected to the Internet.

Directorate (DHS): A major division within the Department of Homeland Security that oversees several offices addressing a similar broad-reaching topic (like Science and Technology, for instance).

Ombudsman: A person or office that investigates complaints and mediates fair settlements.

Superfund: Another name for the Comprehensive Environmental Response, Compensation, and Liability Act of 1980 (CERCLA), which sought to define liability for individual toxic waste sites and then clean up those sites from a fund built from taxes and fines.

Review Questions

1. What is the principal role of emergency management in homeland security? Identify the other major players and their roles in homeland security.

2. Identify the three directorates of the Department of Homeland Security and discuss their respective missions.

3. Discuss the homeland security role of federal agencies other than DHS.

4. Make the case for retaining an all-hazards approach to emergency management that includes terrorism and its associated hazards as one of many hazards. Discuss the pros and cons of such an approach as it relates to all four phases of emergency management: mitigation, preparedness, response, and recovery.

5. If you had been in charge of establishing the Department of Homeland Security (DHS), would you have included the Federal Emergency Management Agency in DHS or would you have retained it as an independent Executive Branch agency reporting directly to the president? Discuss the possible ramifications of moving FEMA into DHS in terms of FEMA's mission, programs, and reporting structure. The director of FEMA no longer reports directly to the president; will this be a problem in future natural and terrorist related disasters? What will the impact of FEMA's inclusion in DHS be on the nation's emergency management system?

References

Department of Homeland Security. 2007. "Department Subcomponents and Agencies." www.dhs.gov/xabout/structure.

National Association of Counties (NACo). 2002. "Counties and Homeland Security: Policy Agenda to Secure the People of America's Counties." Washington, DC: NACo, August. http://www.naco.org/programs/homesecurity?policyplan.cfm.

National Association of Counties. 2004. "Homeland Security Funding—The Urban Areas Security Initiative: A Survey Report." www.naco.org/ContentManagement/ContentDisplay.cfm?ContentID=16077.

National Association of Counties. 2005. "Resolution in Support of HHS's State and Local Bioterrorism Grant Program." March 7. www.naco.org/Template.cfm?Section=homeland_security&template=/ContentManagement/ContentDisplay.cfm&ContentID=15321.

National Conference of State Legislatures. 2005. "State Offices of Homeland Security." www.ncsl.org/programs/legman/nlssa/sthomelandoffcs.htm.

National Emergency Management Association. 2001. "White Paper on Domestic Preparedness." October 1. www.nemaweb.org.

National Emergency Management Association. 2002. "NEMA Reports on State Homeland Security Structures." June. www.nemaweb.org/ShowExtendedNewscfm?ID=171.

National Governors Association. 2003. "EC-5. Homeland Security Comprehensive Policy." www.nga.org/nga/legislativeUpdate/1,1169,C_POLICY_POSITION^D_5102,00.html.

National Governors Association. 2005. "Homeland Security: NGA Position." www.nga.org/nga/lobbyIssues/1,1169,D_4898,00.html.

National Governors Association. 2005. "Issue Brief: Homeland Security in the States: Much Progress, More Work." January 24. www.nga.org/cda/files/0502homesec.pdf.

National Governors Association. 2005. "Survey: States Make Strides in Homeland Security, Challenges Remain." www.nga.org/center/divisions/1,1188,C_ISSUE_BRIEF^D_7987,00.html.

National Governors Association Center for Best Practices (NGAC). 2002. "Issue Brief: States' Homeland Security Priorities." Washington, DC: NGAC, August 19.

National League of Cities. 2005. "2005 Advocacy Priority—The Issue: Funding for First Responders." www.nlc.org/content/Files/PFRHomeland%20Security1.pdf.

National League of Cities. 2005. "2005 National Municipal Policy." www.nlc.org/content/Files/2005%20NMP%20PSCP%20Chapter%20w%20toc.pdf.

U.S. Conference of Mayors. 2001. "A National Action Plan for Safety and Security in America's Cities." December. www.usmayors.org/uscm/home.asp.

U.S. Conference of Mayors. 2003. "Homeland Security Report: 90 Percent of Cities Left Without Funds from Largest Federal Homeland Security Program." September 29. www.usmayors.org/uscm/us_mayor_newspaper/documents/09_29_03/homeland_report.asp.

U.S. Conference of Mayors. 2004a. "Executive Director's Column." March 12. www.usmayors.org/uscm/us_mayor_newspaper/documents/03_15_04/cochran.asp.

U.S. Conference of Mayors. 2004b. "2004 Adopted Resolutions 72nd Annual Meeting Boston." www.usmayors.org/uscm/resolutions/72nd_conference/csj_01.asp.

4

Terrorist-Related Hazards

What You Will Learn

- The various hazards associated with terrorism, including chemical, biological, radiological, nuclear, and explosive weapons, and the dangers that are posed by each
- Why it is so difficult to assess and evaluate the likelihood of terrorist attacks, both within the United States and throughout the world
- The growing threat of cyberterrorism, and what the Department of Homeland Security is doing to counter it
- The roles of the Centers for Disease Control and Prevention in emergency preparedness and response for terrorist attacks involving chemical, biological, and radiological weapons

Introduction

For most of the nation's municipalities, urban and rural alike, the threat or risk posed by terrorism has introduced an expanded set of hazards. These new hazards fall into four principal categories often referred to by the acronym CBRNE: chemical, biological, radiological/nuclear, and explosive. These CBRNE hazards must now be considered in concert with the myriad traditional natural and technological hazards such as hurricanes, tornadoes, floods, earthquakes, fires, hazardous materials transportation and storage accidents, power outages, and releases at nuclear power plants.

There are two significant differences between these new hazards and the more traditional ones. First, much is known about the traditional hazards as a result of years of research, actual occurrence, and response and recovery from these hazards. We can now predict with a fair amount of accuracy the track of a hurricane. We know enough about the destructive force of a tornado to design and build safe rooms. We have spent the better part of a century trying, with increasing success, to control flooding. We have developed building codes and standards that protect structures from earthquakes, fires, and wind damage. We have enough experience in responding to disaster events caused by these hazards to ensure that our first responders have effective protective gear and are trained and exercised in the best response protocols and practices.

While research is ongoing and new practices continue to emerge, the emergency management community in this country is well trained and experienced in dealing with the long list of traditional hazard events. This is not the case with the new hazards presented by the terrorist threat. Knowledge of the properties and the destructive qualities of the various chemical and biological threats is limited at best, even in the agencies charged with knowing the most about these hazards. The first responder community, the state and local emergency managers, and the general public remain almost completely uninformed about these hazards, and have little or no experience in facing their consequences. The same is largely true with community and national leaders, and the news media.

It took decades of research and practice for all parties to attain a level of fluency in the traditional mix of natural and technological disasters. Understandably, it will take considerable time before we have reached an adequate level of comfort with regard to our knowledge of the new hazards.

The second notable difference between the traditional hazards and the new hazards of terrorism is the manner in which we encounter each. Traditional hazards occur because of natural processes, whether geological, meteorological, or hydrological, or because of some human accident, oversight, or negligence. Hurricanes, tornadoes, and earthquakes are inherently natural hazards that have existed for eons, regardless of the presence of humans. Technological hazards, including HAZMAT spills, unintentional releases at nuclear power plants, and transportation accidents, for example, have traditionally been just that — accidents. The new terrorism hazards differ from these natural and technological hazards in that their genesis is intentional, and their primary purpose is maximized death and destruction. These hazards are weapons in every sense of the word, unique in that they primarily target civilian populations instead of military assets, and they are used specifically to advance political, ideological, or religious agendas. No hurricane or earthquake has ever advanced a human agenda.

Difficulty of Predicting Terror Attacks in the United States

A risk index published on August 18, 2003, by the World Markets Research Center (WMRC), a business intelligence firm based in London, ranked the United States fourth among the top five countries most likely to be targeted for a terrorist attack within the 12-month period that followed (www.wmrc. com). The index also predicted that "another September 11-style terrorist attack in the United States is highly likely." Colombia, Israel, and Pakistan ranked in the top three positions, respectively. After the United States, the Philippines, Afghanistan, Indonesia, Iraq, India, and Britain, which tied with Sri Lanka, rounded out the top 10. North Korea ranked as the least likely country to experience a terrorist attack within that next year. The index, which assessed the risk of terrorism to some 186 countries and their interests, was based on five criteria: "motivation of terrorists; the presence of terror groups; the scale and frequency of past attacks; efficacy of the groups in carrying out attacks; and how many attacks were thwarted by the country." Explaining the U.S. ranking, the index stated that while the presence of militant Islamic networks within the United States is less extensive than in Western Europe, "U.S.-led military action in Afghanistan and Iraq has exacerbated anti-U.S. sentiment" (Source: Homeland Security Monitor, August 19, 2003).

This rank designation made issues such as detection, containment, control, quarantine, and vaccination — to name just a few — significant factors in developing new response and recovery practices for first responders. Political affairs and events across the globe have factored heavily in efforts to prepare populations and to mitigate the impacts of these new hazards on those populations and on critical infrastructure, communities, economies, and the normality of daily life.

During the months that followed the WMRC risk prediction, the actual incidence of terrorism followed drastically different patterns than expected. Who, for instance, could have foreseen that the Maoist insurgency in Nepal would have heated up so quickly, with such deadly consequences? Or who could have guessed that Islamic separatists in the southern provinces of Thailand would have resorted to such brutal measures as to place that country near the top of the terrorism target list for many years to come? The situation in Iraq, by far the ongoing leader in both number of attacks and associated fatalities, spiraled out of control much faster than anyone could have imagined, thanks to the presence of third-country terrorists who imported their deadly methods and materials. The differences in what was predicted and what transpired highlight the difficulty of analyzing and evaluating intentional hazards such as terrorism that are dynamic and that respond to unforeseeable social, political, economic, and other anthropologically generated factors. Table 4–1 presents a list of terrorism-related deaths that occurred in 2005 and 2006, adapted from a National Counterterrorism Center (NCTC) study. This table illustrates how great uncertainty factors into any terrorism risk prediction from one year to the next.

A general lack of experience with and knowledge about these new hazards, and the realization that they will be deliberately used to harm or kill U.S. citizens, has resulted in a perception by nearly all Americans that they are potential terrorist targets. (See sidebar titled "Where Will Terrorists Strike?") And unlike hurricanes or tornadoes, which tend to have geographical boundaries, the general terrorist

Table 4–1   Top 17 Countries Ranked by Number of Terrorism-Related Fatalities in 2005 and 2006

Country	Rank 2005	Number of Fatalities	Rank 2006 (Change +/−)	Number of Fatalities (Change +/−)
Iraq	1	8,262	1 (0)	13,340 (+5,078)
India	2	1,361	2 (0)	1,256 (−105)
Colombia	3	813	6 (−3)	533 (−280)
Afghanistan	4	684	3 (+1)	1,042 (+358)
Thailand	5	498	7 (−2)	520 (+22)
Nepal	6	485	12 (−6)	261 (−224)
Pakistan	7	338	9 (−2)	387 (+49)
Russia	8	238	13 (−5)	115 (−123)
Sudan	9	157	4 (+5)	716 (+559)
DPR Congo	10	154	N/A	N/A
Philippines	11	144	10 (+1)	291 (+147)
Algeria	12	132	13 (−1)	115 (−17)
Sri Lanka	13	130	5 (+8)	627 (+497)
Chad	14	109	8 (+6)	518 (+409)
Uganda	15	109	N/A	N/A
Nigeria	N/A	N/A	14	97
Israel	N/A	N/A	15	83

threat and each of the new hazards must be considered national risks. People in Montana do not worry about hurricanes, and it rarely floods in the desert of Nevada. There have been few if any tornadoes reported in Maine. But residents of all states may consider themselves, however remotely, the next possible victims of terrorism, thereby reinforcing what has become a skewed perception of risk. The open nature of our governance system and our society has resulted in widespread press coverage of weapons of mass destruction (WMD) risk analyses at the federal level, especially in relation to belief among various government officials that terrorists will not only acquire WMD technologies in the near future, but that the heartland of America (i.e., small towns, shopping malls, restaurants, and other locations away from major, obvious, and hardened targets) is the most likely next target. The appearance of such weapons in literature, in the cinema, and in the media, as actual events occur around the world (a list of selected chemical, biological, radiological, and nuclear incidents compiled by the Central Intelligence Agency [CIA] is presented in the sidebar, "Selected Examples of Chemical, Biological, Radiological, and Nuclear Incidents"), buttresses the exaggerated perception of individual risk.

■ ▨ ▨ ▬▬▬▬▬▬▬▬▬▬▬▬▬▬▬▬▬▬▬▬▬▬▬▬▬▬▬▬▬▬▬▬▬▬▬▬▬▬▬

Where Will Terrorists Strike? Different Theories . . .

One of the greatest problems facing the Department of Homeland Security is trying to determine where terrorists will strike next. Major U.S. cities are considered the most likely targets for terrorist attacks, as evidenced by risk-based funding for terrorism that has clearly targeted urban centers with the greatest amount of counterterrorism related funding. There are, however, opinions that conflict with this majority assessment.

In 2003, Deputy Secretary of Health and Human Services Claude Allen stated that rural America should be considered among the most likely sites for the next terror attack in the United States, especially a bioterrorism attack. Deputy Secretary Allen stated that "[s]ome rural communities are among the most vulnerable to attack, simply because of their proximity to a missile silo or to a chemical stockpile. Other rural communities are vulnerable simply because they mistakenly believe that terrorism is an urban problem and they are safe from attack." While Allen said the federal government has increased funding for bioterrorism preparedness, he also noted that rural areas are vulnerable given their "limited infrastructure for public health as well as fewer health care providers and volunteer systems."

In March 2004, *CSO Online*, an industry journal for security executives, conducted a survey that asked where in the United States terrorists would likely strike next. The results of the poll indicated that these industry experts felt the next target would be the airline industry (3%), a seaport (7%), a large public event (23%), an urban mass transit system (27%), or a "different and unexpected target" (41%). Considering the efforts that are under way to block an attack on known or expected targets, it would follow in this line of thinking that terrorists would seek to exploit an unknown target that would likely be "soft," or more vulnerable to attack. Citing another major area of vulnerability, a Princeton University research group found that most Internet experts feel that a devastating cyber-attack will occur within the next 10 years, possibly affecting business, utilities, banking, communications, and other Internet-dependent components of society.

On June 23, 2005, the U.S. Senate Foreign Relations Committee released a report stating that there was a 50% chance of a major, WMD-based attack, between 2005 and 2010, somewhere in the world. The report was based on a poll of 85 national security and nonproliferation experts. The reports found that the risks of biological or chemical attacks were comparable to or slightly higher than the risk of a nuclear attack, but that there is a "significantly higher" risk of a radiological attack.

Sources: Homeland Security Monitor, August 28, 2003; ClickZ Network, January 9, 2005; CSO Online, March 25, 2004; Associated Press, June 23, 2005.

Selected Examples of Chemical, Biological, Radiological, and Nuclear Incidents

February 2008: Ricin was discovered in a hotel room occupied by a man who suddenly fell into a coma. The man had produced the toxin years earlier and had been storing it since, but claimed to have never used it for purposes of terrorism.

June 2007: A car bomb rigged with canisters of chlorine gas was detonated outside a U.S. military base located in Diyala, Iraq, sickening 62 soldiers but causing no fatalities.

May 2007: Bombs rigged with chlorine were detonated in two separate incidents in Iraq; one in an open-air market in the Diyala Province killing 32 and injuring 50 people, and the other at a police checkpoint in the Zangora District killing as many as 11 people (though most if not all fatalities in both incidents were attributed to the effects of the explosives, not the chemicals).

April 2007: Three separate incidents involving truck bombs rigged with chlorine occurred in Iraq; one incident at a Ramadi police checkpoint, killing 27 and injuring 30, another at a checkpoint outside Baghdad killing 1 and injuring 2, and a third near a restaurant in Ramadi, killing 6 and wounding 10 (though most if not all fatalities in all three incidents were attributed to the effects of the explosives, not the chemicals).

March 2007: Four attacks involving the detonation of tankers or other trucks containing chlorine occurred in Iraq; an attack at a Ramadi checkpoint wounded 2 people, an attack in Falluja killed 2 and injured hundreds, an attack in Falluja killed 6 and injured 250, and a fourth injured 71.

February 2007: Three attacks involving the detonation of explosives and the release of chlorine occurred in Iraq; a suicide bomber in Ramadi killed 2 and injured 16, the detonation of a tanker truck near Baghdad killed 9 and injured 148, and a truck bomb in Baghdad killed 5 and hospitalized over 50.

January 2007: A truck bomb in Iraq rigged with chlorine gas canisters was detonated in Ramadi, killing 16.

November 2006: Alexander Litvinenko, a former Russian Federal Security Service official was poisoned in a suspected assassination in London with radioactive polonium-210.

October 2006: A car bomb rigged with mortar shells and chlorine gas canisters was detonated in Ramadi, wounding 4 people.

February 2004: U.S. Senate Majority Leader Bill Frist received a letter containing ricin powder. Several staff members needed decontamination, but no injuries or fatalities occurred as a result of the attack.

October 2003: A metallic container was discovered at a Greenville, South Carolina, postal facility with ricin in it. The small container was in an envelope along with a threatening note. Authorities did not believe this was a terrorism-related incident. The note expressed anger against regulations overseeing the trucking industry.

August 2002: Ansar al-Islam, a Sunni militant group, was reported to have tested ricin powder as an aerosol on animals such as donkeys and chickens and perhaps even an unwitting human subject. Additional specific details have not been released.

February 2002: Italian authorities arrested as many as nine Moroccan nationals who may have been plotting to poison the water supply of the U.S. embassy in Rome. Authorities confiscated a detailed map of Rome's underground water system, highlighting the location of the U.S. embassy's pipes. The suspects also had 4 kilograms of potassium ferrocyanide in their possession.

December 2001: According to press reports, the military wing of HAMAS (Palestinian Islamic Resistance Movement) claimed that the bolts and nails packed into explosives detonated by a suicide bomber had been dipped into rat poison.

October 2001: U.S. and international law enforcement authorities stepped up investigations in the United States and abroad to determine the sources of confirmed cases of anthrax exposures in Florida, New York, and Washington, DC. In the past several years, there have been hundreds of hoaxes involving anthrax in the United States. In the aftermath of the September 11 terrorist attacks against the United States, these anthrax scares have spread across the globe and have exacerbated international concerns. The confirmed anthrax cases involved letters sent through the mail to the U.S. Congress and several media organizations. More than 50 individuals were exposed to *B. anthracis* spores, including 18 who became infected, and 5 people died from inhalation anthrax — the first reported cases in the United States in 25 years. U.S. and international health organizations have treated thousands of individuals associated with these incidents.

September 2001: Colombian police accused the Revolutionary Armed Forces of Colombia (FARC) of using improvised grenades filled with poisonous gas during an attack on the city of San Adolfin, Huila Department. According to media accounts, 4 policemen died and another 6 suffered respiratory problems from the attack.

January 2000: According to press reports, a Russian general accused Chechen rebels of delivering poisoned wine and canned fruit to Russian soldiers in Chechnya.

November 1999: Raw materials for making ricin were seized by law-enforcement authorities during the arrest of a U.S. citizen who threatened to poison 2 Colorado judges.

June 1998: U.S. law enforcement authorities arrested 2 members of the violent secessionist group called the Republic of Texas for planning to construct a device with toxins to kill selected government officials. A U.S. federal court convicted them in October 1998 for threatening to use a weapon of mass destruction.

December 1996: Sri Lankan press noted that government authorities warned the military in the northern region not to purchase food or stamps from local vendors, because some stamps had been found laced with cyanide.

August 1995: An MIT Center for Cancer Research employee ingested radioactive phosphorous-32, in what was believed to be a deliberate attempt to poison him.

July 1995: Four improvised chemical devices (ICDs) were found in restrooms at the Kayaba-cho, Tokyo, and Ginza subway stations and the Japanese railway's Shinjuku station. Each device was slightly different but contained the same chemicals.

May 1995: An ICD was left in Shinjuku station in Tokyo. The device consisted of two plastic bags, one containing sodium cyanide and the other sulfuric acid. If the device had not been neutralized, the chemicals would have combined to produce a cyanide gas.

May 1995: A U.S. citizen, and member of the neo-Nazi Aryan Nations, acquired three vials of *Yersinia pestis*, the bacteria that causes plague, from a Maryland lab. Law enforcement officials recovered the unopened material and arrested the individual. No delivery system was recovered, and no information indicated the subject's purpose in obtaining the bacteria.

March 20, 1995: Members of the Japanese cult Aum Shinrikyo used ICDs to release sarin nerve gas in the Tokyo subway station. Twelve people died, and thousands of others were hospitalized or required medical treatment.

March 15, 1995: Three briefcases were left at locations in the Kasumigaseki train station in Tokyo. No injuries resulted, but an Aum Shinrikyo member later confessed that this was a failed biological attack with Botulinum toxin.

January 1995: Tajik opposition members laced champagne with cyanide at a New Year's celebration, killing 6 Russian soldiers and the wife of another soldier, and sickening other revelers.

June 27, 1994: A substance identified as sarin was dispersed using a modified van in a residential area near Matsumoto; 7 people died, and more than 200 people were injured. Reportedly, an Aum Shinrikyo member confessed that the cult targeted 3 judges who lived there to prevent them from returning an adverse decision against the cult.

1993: A U.S. citizen was detained by the Canadian Customs Service as he attempted to enter Canada from Alaska. A white powdery substance was confiscated and later identified through laboratory analysis as ricin. The individual, traveling with a large sum of cash, told officials that he was carrying the poison to protect his money.

1992: Four individuals were convicted by a U.S. federal court for producing ricin and advocating the violent overthrow of the government. The subjects, who had espoused extremist, antigovernment, antitax ideals, specifically had targeted a deputy U.S. marshal who previously had served papers on one of them for tax violations.

1984: An outbreak of salmonella poisoning that occurred in Oregon during a two-week period was linked to the salad bars of eight restaurants. More than 700 people were affected, but no fatalities occurred. Investigators of the outbreak determined that 2 members of the Rajneesh religious sect produced and dispensed salmonella bacteria in the restaurants, in order to influence a local election by incapacitating opposition voters.

Sources: CIA, "Terrorism: Guide to Chemical, Biological, Radiological, and Nuclear Weapons Indicators," 2002; CNN, February 4, 2004; CNS Reports, February 3, 2004; BBC News, "Timeline: Iraq," 2007.

The greatest achievements in public fear reduction have grown out of attaining better understanding of these new hazards, and how individuals, communities, and countries can deal with them. The purpose of this chapter is to present basic information concerning the relatively new CBRNE hazards. Much of this information is supported by and expanded upon by websites maintained and reports prepared by the Centers for Disease Control and Prevention (CDC) and the Federal Emergency Management Agency (FEMA). In certain instances, as noted, the authors have adapted or reprinted the information provided by these sources and others in order to present the most accurate background on the particular hazard.

▪ ▪ Critical Thinking ▪

Will it ever be possible to accurately predict terrorist attacks in the United States? Why or why not? What tools, skills, and other options may be used to increase the accuracy of predictions?

Conventional Explosives and Secondary Devices

Conventional explosives have existed for centuries, since explosive gunpowder invented by the Chinese (for use in firecrackers) was modified for use in weaponry. Traditional (manufactured) and improvised explosive devices (IEDs) are generally the easiest weapons to both obtain and use. In fact, instruction for their assembly and deployment are widely available in print and on the Internet, as well as through the transfer of institutional knowledge within informal criminal networks. These widely available weapons, when skillfully used, can inflict massive amounts of destruction to property and can cause significant injuries and fatalities to humans. Conventional explosives are most troubling as WMDs in light of their ability to effectively disperse chemical, biological, or radiological agents.

Conventional explosives and IEDs can be either explosive or incendiary in nature. Explosives use the physical destruction caused by the expansion of gases that result from the ignition of "high- or low-filler" explosive materials to inflict damage or harm. Examples of explosive devices include simple pipe bombs, made from common plumbing materials; satchel charges, which are encased in a common looking bag such as a backpack, and left behind for later detonation; letter or package bombs, delivered through the mail; or a car bomb, which can be used to deliver a large amount of explosives. Incendiary devices, also referred to as firebombs, rely on the ignition of fires to cause damage or harm. Examples include Molotov cocktails (gas-filled bottles capped with a burning rag), napalm bombs, and fuel-air explosives (thermobaric weapons).

Explosions and conflagrations can be delivered via a missile, or projectile device, such as a rocket, rocket-propelled grenade (RPG), mortar, or air-dropped bomb. Nontraditional explosive delivery methods are regularly discovered, and include the use of fuel-filled commercial airliners flown into buildings as occurred on September 11, 2001. Because these weapons rely on such low technology and are relatively easy to transport and deliver, they are the most common choice of terrorists. Although suicide bombings, in which bombers manually deliver and detonate the device on or near their person, are becoming more common, most devices are detonated through the use of timed, remote (radio, cell phone), or other methods of transmission (light sensitivity, air pressure, movement, electrical impulse, etc.).

Although almost 50% of terrorist attacks involve the use of conventional explosives, less than 5% of actual and attempted bombings are preceded by any kind of threat or warning. These devices can be difficult to detect because most easily attainable explosive materials are untraceable. Commercial explosives in the United States are now required to contain a chemical signature that can be used to trace their source should they be used for criminal means, but this accounts for only a fraction of materials available to terrorists. What is particularly troubling about these devices is that it is easy to detonate multiple explosives in single or multiple municipalities, and secondary explosives can be used to target bystanders and officials who are responding to the initial, often smaller, explosion. Because of the graphic nature of the carnage resulting from explosives, and the widespread fear associated with their historic use, these weapons are very effective as terror-spreading devices (FEMA, 2002).

▪ ▪ Critical Thinking ▪

Conventional explosives can be manufactured using ingredients commonly found in hardware stores, pharmacies, and other sources available to the general public. What can planners do to prevent terrorists from using these much-needed materials for sinister purposes short of banning them entirely?

Chemical Agents

Like explosives, chemical weapons have existed for centuries and have been used repeatedly throughout history. The first organized application and most significant modern use of chemical weapons occurred during World War I. In Belgium, during a German attack against allied forces in World War I (WWI), German troops released 160 tons of chlorine gas into the air, killing more than 10,000 soldiers and injuring another 15,000. In total, 113,000 tons of chemical weapons were used in WWI, resulting in the deaths of more than 90,000 people and the injury to over 1.3 million.

Chemical weapons are created for the sole purpose of killing, injuring, or incapacitating people. They can enter the body through inhalation, ingestion, or through the skin or eyes. Many different kinds of chemicals have been developed as weapons, falling under six general categories that are distinguished according to physiological effects on victims:

1. Nerve agents (Sarin, VX)
2. Blister agents (mustard gas, lewisite)
3. Blood agents (hydrogen cyanide)
4. Choking/pulmonary agents (phosgene)
5. Irritants (tear gas, capsicum [pepper] spray)
6. Incapacitating agents (BZ, Agent 15)

Terrorists can deliver chemical weapons by means of several different mechanisms. Aerosol devices spread chemicals in liquid, solid (generally powdered), or gas form by causing tiny particulates of the chemical to be suspended into the air. Explosives can also be used to disperse the chemicals through the air in this manner. Devices that contain chemicals, either for warfare or everyday use (such as a truck or train tanker), can be breached, thereby exposing the chemical to the air. Chemicals can also be mixed with water or placed into food supplies. Chemicals that are easily absorbed through the skin can be placed directly onto a victim to cause harm or death.

Chemical attacks, in general, are recognized immediately (some indicators of the possible use of chemical agents are listed in the sidebar titled "General Indicators of Possible Chemical Agent Use"), although it may be unclear to victims and responders until further testing has taken place that an attack has occurred, and whether the attack was chemical or biological in nature. Chemical weapons may be persistent (remaining in the affected area for long after the attack) or nonpersistent (evaporating quickly, due to their lighter-than-air qualities, resulting in a loss of ability to harm or kill after approximately 10 or 15 minutes in open areas). In unventilated rooms, however, any chemical can linger for a considerable time.

General Indicators of Possible Chemical Agent Use

- Stated threat to release a chemical agent
- Unusual occurrence of dead or dying animals
  - For example, lack of insects, dead birds
- Unexplained casualties
- Multiple victims
- Surge of similar 911 calls
- Serious illnesses
- Nausea, disorientation, difficulty breathing, or convulsions
- Definite casualty patterns
- Unusual liquid, spray, vapor, or powder

- Droplets, oily film
- Unexplained odor
- Low-lying clouds/fog unrelated to weather
- Suspicious devices, packages, or letters
- Unusual metal debris
- Abandoned spray devices
- Unexplained munitions

Source: Federal Emergency Management Agency, Interim Planning Guide for State and Local Government: Managing the Emergency Consequences of Terrorist Incidents, Washington, DC: FEMA, July 2002.

The effect of chemical weapons on victims is usually fast and severe. Identifying what chemical has been used presents special difficulties, and responding officials (police, fire, EMS, HAZMAT) and hospital staff treating the injured are at risk from their effects. Without proper training and equipment, there is little these first response officials can do in the immediate aftermath of a chemical terrorist attack to identify or treat the consequences (FEMA, 2002).

A simple list of agents compiled by the CDC is presented in the sidebar, "List of Chemical Agents." Fact sheets about cyanide, sulfur mustard (mustard gas), sarin, ricin, and chlorine, which have been compiled from the CDC website, are presented in five sidebars bearing these chemical names in respective titles. The sidebar titled, "Additional Information on Cyanide, Sulfur Mustard, Sarin, Ricin, and Chlorine," provides sources for further information about these chemical agents.

List of Chemical Agents

Compiled by the Centers for Disease Control and Prevention.
  Abrin
  Adamsite (DM)
  Agent 15
  Ammonia
  Arsenic
  Arsine (SA)
  Benzene
  Bromobenzylcyanide (CA)
  BZ
  Cannabinoids
  Chlorine (CL)
  Chloroacetophenone (CN)
  Chlorobenzylidenemalononitrile (CS)
  Chloropicrin (PS)
  Cyanide
  Cyanogen chloride (CK)
  Cyclohexyl sarin (GF)
  Dibenzoxazepine (CR)
  Diphenylchlorarsine (DA)

Diphenylcyanoarsine (DC)
Diphosgene (Do P)
Distilled mustard (HD)
Ethyldichloroarsine (ED)
Ethylene glycol
Fentanyls and other opioids
Hydrofluoric acid
Hydrogen chloride
Hydrogen cyanide (AC)
Lewisite (L, L-1, L-2, L-3)
LSD
Mercury
Methyldichloroarsine (MD)
Mustard gas (H) (sulfur mustard)
Mustard/lewisite (HL)
Mustard/T
Nitrogen mustard (HN-1, HN-2, HN-3)
Nitrogen oxide (NO)
Paraquat
Perflurorisobutylene (PHIB)
Phenodichlorarsine (PD)
Phenothiazines
Phosgene (CG)
Phosgene oxime (CX)
Phosphine
Potassium cyanide (KCN)
Red phosphorus (RP)
Ricin (considered to be both a chemical and biological weapon)
Sarin (GB)
Sesqui mustard
Sodium azide
Sodium cyanide (NaCN)
Soman (GD)
Stibine
Strychnine
Sulfur mustard (H) (mustard gas)
Sulfur trioxide-chlorosulfonic acid (FS)
Super warfarin
Tabun (GA)
Teflon and perflurorisobutylene (PHIB)
Thallium
Titanium tetrachloride (FM)
VX
White phosphorus
Zinc oxide (HC)

Source: Centers for Disease Control and Prevention, www.bt.cdc.gov/agent/agentlistchem.asp.

Facts about Cyanide

What Is Cyanide?

- Cyanide is a rapidly acting, potentially deadly chemical that can exist in various forms.
- Cyanide can be a colorless gas, such as hydrogen cyanide (HCN) or cyanogen chloride (CNCl), or a crystal form such as sodium cyanide (NaCN) or potassium cyanide (KCN).
- Cyanide sometimes is described as having a "bitter almond" smell, but it does not always give off an odor, and not everyone can detect the odor when it does exist.
- Cyanide is also known by the military designations AN (for hydrogen cyanide) and CK (for cyanogen chloride).

Where Cyanide Is Found and How It Is Used

- Hydrogen cyanide, under the name Zyklon B, was used as a genocidal agent by the Germans in World War II.
- Reports have indicated that during the Iran-Iraq War in the 1980s, hydrogen cyanide gas may have been used along with other chemical agents against the inhabitants of the Kurdish city of Halabja in northern Iraq.
- Cyanide is naturally present in some foods and in certain plants such as cassava. Cyanide is contained in cigarette smoke and the combustion products of synthetic materials such as plastics. Combustion products are substances given off when things burn.
- In manufacturing, cyanide is used to make paper, textiles, and plastics. It is present in the chemicals used to develop photographs. Cyanide salts are used in metallurgy for electroplating, metal cleaning, and removing gold from its ore. Cyanide gas is used to exterminate pests and vermin in ships and buildings.
- If accidentally ingested (swallowed), chemicals found in acetonitrile-based products that are used to remove artificial nails can produce cyanide.

How People Can Be Exposed to Cyanide

- People may be exposed to cyanide by breathing air, drinking water, eating food, or touching soil that contains cyanide.
- Cyanide enters water, soil, or air as a result of both natural processes and industrial activities. In air, cyanide is present mainly as gaseous hydrogen cyanide.
- Smoking cigarettes is probably one of the major sources of cyanide exposure for people who do not work in cyanide-related industries.

How Cyanide Works

- Poisoning caused by cyanide depends on the amount of cyanide a person is exposed to, the route of exposure, and the length of time that a person is exposed.
- Breathing cyanide gas causes the most harm, but ingesting cyanide can be toxic as well.
- Cyanide gas is most dangerous in enclosed places where the gas will be trapped.
- Cyanide gas evaporates and disperses quickly in open spaces, making it less harmful outdoors.
- Because cyanide gas is less dense than air, it will rise.
- Cyanide prevents the cells of the body from getting oxygen. When this happens, the cells die.
- Cyanide is more harmful to the heart and brain than to other organs because the heart and brain use a lot of oxygen.

Immediate Signs and Symptoms of Cyanide Exposure

People exposed to a small amount of cyanide by breathing it, absorbing it through their skin, or eating foods that contain it may have some or all of the following symptoms within minutes:

- Rapid breathing
- Restlessness
- Dizziness
- Weakness
- Headache
- Nausea and vomiting
- Rapid heart rate

Exposure to a large amount of cyanide by any route may cause the following health effects as well:

- Convulsions
- Low blood pressure
- Slow heart rate
- Loss of consciousness
- Lung injury
- Respiratory failure leading to death

Showing these signs and symptoms does not necessarily mean that a person has been exposed to cyanide.

What the Long-Term Health Effects May Be

Survivors of serious cyanide poisoning may develop heart and brain damage.

How People Can Protect Themselves and What They Should Do If They Are Exposed to Cyanide

- First, get fresh air by leaving the area where the cyanide was released. Moving to an area with fresh air is a good way to reduce the possibility of death from exposure to cyanide gas.
- If the cyanide release was outside, move away from the area where the cyanide was released.
- If the cyanide release was indoors, get out of the building.
- If leaving the area that was exposed to cyanide is not an option, stay as low to the ground as possible.
- If you are near a release of cyanide gas, emergency coordinators may tell you to either evacuate the area or "shelter in place" (stay put and take cover) inside a building to avoid being exposed to the chemical.
- Remove any clothing that has liquid cyanide on it. If possible, seal the clothing in a plastic bag, and then seal that bag inside a second plastic bag. Removing and sealing the clothing in this way will help protect people from chemicals that might be on their clothes.
- If clothes were placed in plastic bags, inform either the local or state health department or emergency coordinators upon their arrival. Do not handle the plastic bags.
- Rinse the eyes with plain water for 10 to 15 minutes if they are burning or if vision is blurred.
- Wash any liquid cyanide from the skin thoroughly with soap and water.

- If cyanide is known to be ingested (swallowed), do *not* induce vomiting or give fluids to drink.
- Seek medical attention right away. Dial 911 and explain what has happened.

How Cyanide Poisoning Is Treated

Cyanide poisoning is treated with specific antidotes and supportive medical care in a hospital setting. The most important thing is for victims to seek medical treatment as soon as possible.

Source: Centers for Disease Control and Prevention, www.cdc.gov.

Facts about Sulfur Mustard

What Is Sulfur Mustard?

- Sulfur mustard is a type of chemical warfare agent. These kinds of agents are called vesicants, or blistering agents, because they cause blistering of the skin and mucous membranes on contact.
- Sulfur mustard is also known as "mustard gas or mustard agent" or by the military designations H, HD, and HT.
- Sulfur mustard sometimes smells like garlic, onions, or mustard, and sometimes has no odor. It can be a vapor (the gaseous form of a liquid), an oily textured liquid, or a solid.
- Sulfur mustard can be clear to yellow or brown when it is in liquid or solid form.

Where Sulfur Mustard Is Found and How It Is Used

- Sulfur mustard is not found naturally in the environment.
- Sulfur mustard was introduced in World War I as a chemical warfare agent. Until recently, it was available for use in the treatment of a skin condition called psoriasis. Currently, it has no medical use.

How People Can Be Exposed to Sulfur Mustard

- If sulfur mustard is released into the air as a vapor, people can be exposed through skin contact, eye contact, or breathing. Sulfur mustard vapor can be carried long distances by wind.
- If sulfur mustard is released into water, people can be exposed by drinking the contaminated water or getting it on their skin.
- People can be exposed by coming in contact with liquid sulfur mustard.
- Sulfur mustard can last from 1 to 2 days in the environment under average weather conditions and from weeks to months under very cold conditions.
- Sulfur mustard breaks down slowly in the body, so repeated exposure may have a cumulative effect (i.e., it can build up in the body).

How Sulfur Mustard Works

- Adverse health effects caused by sulfur mustard depend on the amount to which people are exposed, the route of exposure, and the length of exposure time.
- Sulfur mustard is a powerful irritant and blistering agent that damages the skin, eyes, and respiratory (breathing) tract.

- It damages DNA, a vital component of cells in the body.
- Sulfur mustard vapor is heavier than air. The vapor will settle in low-lying areas.

Immediate Signs and Symptoms of Sulfur Mustard Exposure

- Exposure to sulfur mustard is usually not fatal. When sulfur mustard was used during World War I, it killed fewer than 5% of people who were exposed and got medical care.
- People may not know right away that they have been exposed, because sulfur mustard often has no odor or the odor might not cause alarm.
- Typically, signs and symptoms do not occur immediately. Depending on the severity of the exposure, symptoms may not occur for 2 to 24 hours. Some people are more sensitive to sulfur mustard than are other people and may have symptoms sooner.
- Sulfur mustard can have the following effects on specific parts of the body:
  Skin: Redness and itching of the skin may occur 2 to 48 hours after exposure and change eventually to yellow blistering of the skin.
  Eyes: Irritation, pain, swelling, and tearing may occur within 3 to 12 hours of a mild to moderate exposure. A severe exposure may cause symptoms within 1 to 2 hours and may include the symptoms of a mild or moderate exposure plus light sensitivity, severe pain, or blindness (lasting up to 10 days).
  Respiratory tract: Runny nose, sneezing, hoarseness, bloody nose, sinus pain, shortness of breath, and cough may occur within 12 to 24 hours of a mild exposure and within 2 to 4 hours of a severe exposure.
  Digestive tract: Abdominal pain, diarrhea, fever, nausea, and vomiting may occur.
- Showing these signs and symptoms does not necessarily mean that a person has been exposed to sulfur mustard.

What the Long-Term Health Effects May Be

- Exposure to sulfur mustard liquid is more likely to produce second- and third-degree burns and later scarring than is exposure to sulfur mustard vapor. Extensive skin burning can be fatal.
- Extensive breathing in of the vapors can cause chronic respiratory disease, repeated respiratory infections, or death.
- Extensive eye exposure can cause permanent blindness.
- Exposure to sulfur mustard may increase a person's risk for lung and respiratory cancer.

How People Can Protect Themselves and What They Should Do If They Are Exposed to Sulfur Mustard

- Because no antidote exists for sulfur mustard exposure, the best thing to do is to avoid it. Immediately leave the area where the sulfur mustard was released. Try to find higher ground, because sulfur mustard is heavier than air and will settle in low-lying areas.
- If avoiding sulfur mustard exposure is not possible, rapidly remove the sulfur mustard from the body. Getting the sulfur mustard off as soon as possible after exposure is the only effective way to prevent or decrease tissue damage to the body.
- Quickly remove any clothing that has liquid sulfur mustard on it. If possible, seal the clothing in a plastic bag, and then seal that bag inside a second plastic bag.
- Immediately wash any exposed part of the body (eyes, skin, etc.) thoroughly with plain, clean water. Eyes need to be flushed with water for 5 to 10 minutes. Do not cover eyes with bandages, but do protect them with dark glasses or goggles.
- If someone has ingested sulfur mustard, do not induce vomiting. Give the person milk to drink.
- Seek medical attention right away. Dial 911 and explain what has happened.

How Sulfur Mustard Exposure Is Treated

The most important factor is removing sulfur mustard from the body. Exposure to sulfur mustard is treated by giving the victim supportive medical care to minimize the effects of the exposure. Although no antidote exists for sulfur mustard, exposure is usually not fatal.

Source: Centers for Disease Control and Prevention, www.cdc.gov.

Facts about Sarin

What Is Sarin?

- Sarin is a human-made chemical warfare agent classified as a nerve agent. Nerve agents are the most toxic and rapid-acting of the known chemical warfare agents. They are similar to certain kinds of pesticides (insect killers) called organophosphates in terms of how they work and the type of harmful effects they cause. However, nerve agents are much more potent than organophosphate pesticides.
- Sarin originally was developed in 1938 in Germany as a pesticide.
- Sarin is a clear, colorless, and tasteless liquid that has no odor in its pure form. However, sarin can evaporate into a vapor (gas) and spread into the environment.
- Sarin is also known as GB.

Where Sarin Is Found and How It Is Used

- Sarin and other nerve agents may have been used in chemical warfare during the Iran–Iraq War in the 1980s.
- Sarin was used in two terrorist attacks in Japan in 1994 and 1995.
- Sarin is not found naturally in the environment.

How People Can Be Exposed to Sarin

- Following release of sarin into the air, people can be exposed through skin contact or eye contact. They can also be exposed by breathing air that contains sarin.
- Because sarin mixes easily with water, it could be used to poison water. Following release of sarin into water, people can be exposed by touching or drinking water that contains sarin.
- After contamination of food with sarin, people can be exposed by eating the contaminated food.
- A person's clothing can release sarin for about 30 minutes after it has come in contact with sarin vapor, which can lead to exposure of other people.
- Because sarin breaks down slowly in the body, people who are repeatedly exposed to sarin may suffer more harmful health effects.
- Because sarin vapor is heavier than air, it will sink to low-lying areas and create a greater exposure hazard there.

How Sarin Works

- The extent of poisoning caused by sarin depends on the amount of sarin to which a person was exposed, the way the person was exposed, and the length of time of the exposure.

- Symptoms will appear within a few seconds after exposure to the vapor form of sarin and within a few minutes up to 18 hours after exposure to the liquid form.
- All nerve agents cause their toxic effects by preventing the proper operation of the chemical that acts as the body's "off switch" for glands and muscles. Without an "off switch," the glands and muscles are constantly being stimulated. They may tire and no longer be able to sustain breathing function.
- Sarin is the most volatile of the nerve agents, which means that it can easily and quickly evaporate from a liquid into a vapor and spread into the environment. People can be exposed to the vapor even if they do not come in contact with the liquid form of sarin.
- Because it evaporates so quickly, sarin presents an immediate but short-lived threat.

Immediate Signs and Symptoms of Sarin Exposure

- People may not know that they were exposed because sarin has no odor.
- People exposed to a low or moderate dose of sarin by breathing contaminated air, eating contaminated food, drinking contaminated water, or touching contaminated surfaces may experience some or all of the following symptoms within seconds to hours of exposure:
Runny nose
Watery eyes
Small, pinpoint pupils
Eye pain
Blurred vision
Drooling and excessive sweating
Cough
Chest tightness
Rapid breathing
Diarrhea
Increased urination
Confusion
Drowsiness
Weakness
Headache
Nausea, vomiting, and/or abdominal pain
Slow or fast heart rate
Low or high blood pressure
- Even a small drop of sarin on the skin can cause sweating and muscle twitching where sarin touched the skin.
- Exposure to large doses of sarin by any route may result in the following harmful health effects:
Loss of consciousness
Convulsions
Paralysis
Respiratory failure possibly leading to death

Showing these signs and symptoms does not necessarily mean that a person has been exposed to sarin.

What the Long-Term Health Effects Are

Mild or moderately exposed people usually recover completely. Severely exposed people are not likely to survive. Unlike some organophosphate pesticides, nerve agents have not been associated with neurological problems lasting more than 1 to 2 weeks after the exposure.

How People Can Protect Themselves and What They Should Do If They Are Exposed to Sarin

Recovery from sarin exposure is possible with treatment, but the antidotes available must be used quickly to be effective. Therefore, the best thing to do is to avoid exposure:

- Leave the area where the sarin was released and get to fresh air. Quickly moving to an area where fresh air is available is highly effective in reducing the possibility of death from exposure to sarin vapor.
- If the sarin release was outdoors, move away from the area where the sarin was released. Go to the highest ground possible because sarin is heavier than air and will sink to low-lying areas.
- If the sarin release was indoors, get out of the building.
- If people think they may have been exposed, they should remove their clothing, rapidly wash their entire body with soap and water, and get medical care as quickly as possible.

Removal and disposal of clothing is recommended:

- Quickly take off clothing that has liquid sarin on it. Any clothing that has to be pulled over the head should be cut off the body instead of pulled over the head. If possible, seal the clothing in a plastic bag. Then seal the first plastic bag in a second plastic bag. Removing and sealing the clothing in this way will help protect people from any chemicals that might be on their clothes.
- If clothes were placed in plastic bags, inform either the local or state health department or emergency personnel upon their arrival. Do not handle the plastic bags.
- If helping other people remove their clothing, try to avoid touching any contaminated areas, and remove the clothing as quickly as possible.

Washing the body is also recommended:

- As quickly as possible, wash any liquid sarin from the skin with large amounts of soap and water. Washing with soap and water will help protect people from any chemicals on their bodies.
- Rinse the eyes with plain water for 10 to 15 minutes if they are burning or if vision is blurred.
- If sarin has been swallowed, do not induce vomiting or give fluids to drink.

Finally, seek medical attention immediately. Dial 911 and explain what has happened.

How Sarin Exposure Is Treated

Treatment consists of removing sarin from the body as soon as possible and providing supportive medical care in a hospital setting. Antidotes are available for sarin. They are most useful if given as soon as possible after exposure.

Source: Centers for Disease Control and Prevention, www.cdc.gov.

Facts about Ricin

What Is Ricin?

- Ricin is a poison that can be made from the waste left over from processing castor beans.
- It can be in the form of a powder, mist, or pellet, or it can be dissolved in water or weak acid.
- It is a stable substance. For example, it is not affected much by extreme conditions such as very hot or very cold temperatures.

Where Is Ricin Found and How Is It Used?

- Castor beans are processed throughout the world to make castor oil. Ricin is part of the waste "mash" produced when castor oil is made. Amateurs can make ricin from castor beans.
- Ricin has some potential medical uses, such as in bone marrow transplants and cancer treatment (to kill cancer cells).

How Can People Be Exposed to Ricin?

- It would take a deliberate act to make ricin and use it to poison people. Accidental exposure to ricin is highly unlikely.
- People can breathe in ricin mist or powder and be poisoned.
- Ricin can also get into water or food and then be swallowed.
- Pellets of ricin, or ricin dissolved in a liquid, can be injected into people's bodies.
- Depending on the route of exposure (such as injection), as little as 500 micrograms of ricin could be enough to kill an adult. A 500-microgram dose of ricin would be about the size of the head of a pin. A much greater amount would be needed to kill people if the ricin were inhaled (breathed in) or swallowed.
- Ricin poisoning is not contagious. It cannot be spread from person to person through casual contact.
- In 1978 Georgi Markov, a Bulgarian writer and journalist who was living in London, died after he was attacked by a man with an umbrella. The umbrella had been rigged to inject a poison ricin pellet under Markov's skin.
- Some reports have indicated that ricin may have been used in the Iran–Iraq war during the 1980s and that quantities of ricin were found in al Qaeda caves in Afghanistan.

How Does Ricin Work?

- Ricin works by getting inside the cells of a person's body and preventing the cells from making the proteins they need. Without the proteins, cells die, and eventually the whole body can shut down and die.
- Specific effects of ricin poisoning depend on whether ricin was inhaled, swallowed, or injected.

What Are the Signs and Symptoms of Ricin Exposure?

- Inhalation: Within a few hours of inhaling significant amounts of ricin, the likely symptoms would be coughing, tightness in the chest, difficulty breathing, nausea, and aching muscles. Within the next few hours, the body's airways (such as the lungs) would become severely inflamed (swollen and hot), excess fluid would build up in the lungs, breathing would become even more difficult, and the skin might turn blue. Excess fluid in the lungs would be diagnosed by x-rays or by listening to the chest with a stethoscope.
- Ingestion: If someone swallows a significant amount of ricin, he or she would have internal bleeding of the stomach and intestines that would lead to vomiting and bloody diarrhea. Eventually, the person's liver, spleen, and kidneys might stop working, and the person could die.
- Injection: Injection of a lethal amount of ricin at first would cause the muscles and lymph nodes near the injection site to die. Eventually, the liver, kidneys, and spleen would stop working, and the person would have massive bleeding from the stomach and intestines. The person would die from multiple organ failure.

Death from ricin poisoning could take place within 36 to 48 hours of exposure, whether by injection, ingestion, or inhalation. If the person lives longer than five days without complications, he or she will probably not die.

Showing these signs and symptoms does not necessarily mean that a person has been exposed to ricin.

How Is Ricin Poisoning Treated?

No antidote exists for ricin. Ricin poisoning is treated by giving the victim supportive medical care to minimize the effects of the poisoning. The types of supportive medical care would depend on several factors, such as the route by which the victim was poisoned (that is, by inhalation, ingestion, or injection). Care could include such measures as helping the victim breathe and giving him or her intravenous fluids and medications to treat swelling.

How Do We Know for Sure People Have Been Exposed to Ricin?

- If we suspect that people have inhaled ricin, a possible clue would be that a large number of people who had been close to each other suddenly developed fever, cough, and excess fluid in their lungs. These symptoms could be followed by severe breathing problems and possibly death.
- No widely available, reliable test exists to confirm that a person has been exposed to ricin.

What Can People Do If They Think They May Have Been Exposed to Ricin?

Unintentional ricin poisoning is highly unlikely. CDC has no reports of intentional ricin poisoning. If people think they might have been exposed to ricin, however, they should contact the regional poison control center at 1-800-222-1222.

Source: Centers for Disease Control and Prevention, www.cdc.gov.

Facts about Chlorine

What Is Chlorine?

- Chlorine is an element used in industry and found in some household products.
- Chlorine is sometimes in the form of a poisonous gas. Chlorine gas can be pressurized and cooled to change it into a liquid so that it can be shipped and stored. When liquid chlorine is released, it quickly turns into a gas that stays close to the ground and spreads rapidly.
- Chlorine gas can be recognized by its pungent, irritating odor, which is like the odor of bleach. The strong smell may provide an adequate warning to people that they have been exposed.
- Chlorine gas appears to be yellow-green in color.
- Chlorine itself is not flammable, but it can react explosively or form explosive compounds with other chemicals such as turpentine and ammonia.

Where Chlorine Is Found and How It Is Used

- Chlorine was used during World War I as a choking (pulmonary) agent.
- Chlorine is one of the most commonly manufactured chemicals in the United States. Its most important use is as a bleach in the manufacture of paper and cloth, but it is also used to make pesticides (insect killers), rubber, and solvents.
- Chlorine is used in drinking water and swimming pool water to kill harmful bacteria. It is also used as part of the sanitation process for industrial waste and sewage.
- Household chlorine bleach can release chlorine gas if it is mixed with other cleaning agents.

How People Can Be Exposed to Chlorine

- People's risk for exposure depends on how close they are to the place where the chlorine was released.
- If chlorine gas is released into the air, people may be exposed through skin contact or eye contact. They may also be exposed by breathing air that contains chlorine.
- If chlorine liquid is released into water, people may be exposed by touching or drinking water that contains chlorine.
- If chlorine liquid comes into contact with food, people may be exposed by eating the contaminated food.
- Chlorine gas is heavier than air, and thus would settle in low-lying areas.

How Chlorine Works

- The extent of poisoning caused by chlorine depends on the amount of chlorine a person is exposed to, how the person was exposed, and the length of time of the exposure.
- When chlorine gas comes into contact with moist tissues such as the eyes, throat, and lungs, an acid is produced that can damage these tissues.

Immediate Signs and Symptoms of Chlorine Exposure

During or immediately after exposure to dangerous concentrations of chlorine, the following signs and symptoms may develop:

- Coughing
- Chest tightness
- Burning sensation in the nose, throat, and eyes
- Watery eyes
- Blurred vision
- Nausea and vomiting
- Burning pain, redness, and blisters on the skin if exposed to gas; skin injury similar to frostbite if exposed to liquid chlorine
- Difficulty breathing or shortness of breath (may appear immediately if high concentrations of chlorine gas are inhaled, or may be delayed if low concentrations of chlorine gas are inhaled)
- Fluid in the lungs (pulmonary edema) within 2 to 4 hours

Showing these signs or symptoms does not necessarily mean that a person has been exposed to chlorine.

What the Long-Term Health Effects Are

Long-term complications from chlorine exposure are not found in people who survive a sudden exposure unless they suffer complications such as pneumonia during therapy. Chronic bronchitis may develop in people who develop pneumonia during therapy.

How People Can Protect Themselves and What They Should Do If They Are Exposed to Chlorine

- Leave the area where the chlorine was released and get to fresh air. Quickly moving to an area where fresh air is available is highly effective in reducing exposure to chlorine.
- If the chlorine release was outdoors, move away from the area where the chlorine was released. Go to the highest ground possible, because chlorine is heavier than air and will sink to low-lying areas.
- If the chlorine release was indoors, get out of the building.
- If you think you may have been exposed, remove your clothing, rapidly wash your entire body with soap and water, and get medical care as quickly as possible.
- Remove and dispose of clothing:
  Quickly take off clothing that has liquid chlorine on it. Any clothing that has to be pulled over the head should be cut off the body instead of pulled over the head. If possible, seal the clothing in a plastic bag. Then seal the first plastic bag in a second plastic bag. Removing and sealing the clothing in this way will help protect you and other people from any chemicals that might be on your clothes. If you placed your clothes in plastic bags, inform either the local or state health department or emergency personnel upon their arrival. Do not handle the plastic bags.
  If you are helping other people remove their clothing, try to avoid touching any contaminated areas, and remove the clothing as quickly as possible.
- Wash the body:
  As quickly as possible, wash your entire body with large amounts of soap and water. Washing with soap and water will help protect people from any chemicals on their bodies. If your eyes are burning or your vision is blurred, rinse your eyes with plain water for 10 to 15 minutes. If you wear contacts, remove them before rinsing your eyes, and place them in the bags with the contaminated clothing. Do not put the contacts back in your eyes. You should dispose of them even if you do not wear disposable contacts. If you wear eyeglasses, wash them with soap and water. You can put the eyeglasses back on after you wash them. If you have ingested (swallowed) chlorine, do not induce vomiting or drink fluids.

  Seek medical attention right away. Dial 911 and explain what has happened.

How Chlorine Exposure Is Treated

No antidote exists for chlorine exposure. Treatment consists of removing the chlorine from the body as soon as possible and providing supportive medical care in a hospital setting.

Source: Centers for Disease Control and Prevention, www.cdc.org.

Additional Information on Cyanide, Sulfur Mustard, Sarin, Ricin, and Chlorine

For more information on cyanide, sulfur mustard, sarin, ricin, and chlorine, contact one of the following:

- Regional poison control center: 1-800-222-1222
- Centers for Disease Control and Prevention
- Public response hotline (CDC)
- English: 1-888-246-2675

- Español: 1-888-246-2857
- TTY: 1-866-874-2646
- Emergency Preparedness and Response website at www.fema.gov
- E-mail inquiries: cdcresponse@ashastd.org
- Mail inquiries: Public Inquiry, Bioterrorism Preparedness and Response Planning, Centers for Disease Control and Prevention, Mailstop C-18, 1600 Clifton Road NE, Atlanta, GA 30333
- Agency for Toxic Substances and Disease Registry (ATSDR): 1-888-422-8737
- E-mail inquiries: atsdric@cdc.gov
- Mail inquiries: Agency for Toxic Substances and Disease Registry Division of Toxicology, Mailstop E-29, 1600 Clifton Road NE, Atlanta, GA 30333
- Centers for Disease Control and Prevention (CDC), National Institute for Occupational Safety and Health (NIOSH), Pocket Guide to Chemical Hazards

Source: Centers for Disease Control and Prevention, www.cdc.org.

Biological Agents

Biological or "germ" weapons are live organisms (either bacteria or viruses) or the toxic by-products generated by living organisms that are manipulated in order to cause illness, injury, or death in humans, livestock, or plants. Although awareness of the potential for use of bacteria, viruses, and toxins as weapons existed long before an unknown terrorist used anthrax spores to deliver multiple attacks through the U.S. mail system, this event certainly put them on the forefront of the public and political agendas. Evidence of biological warfare applications exists as early as the 14th century, when the Mongols used plague-infected corpses to spread disease among enemies. Thanks to advances in weapons technology that have allowed much more effective use of bioweapons reaching much greater geographic limits, biological weapons have elicited an increased concern from counterterrorism officials and emergency planners alike.

Bioweapons may be dispersed overtly or covertly by perpetrators. When covertly applied, bioweapons are extremely difficult to recognize because their negative consequences can take hours, days, or even weeks, to emerge. This is especially true with bacteria and viruses, although toxins (which are, in essence, poisons) generally elicit an immediate reaction. Attack recognition is made through a range of methods, including identification of a credible threat, the discovery of weapons materials (dispersion devices, raw biological material, or weapons laboratories), and correct diagnosis of affected humans, animals, or plants. Detection depends on a collaborative public health monitoring system, trained and aware physicians, patients who elect to seek medical care, and equipment suitable for confirming diagnoses. Bioweapons are unique in this regard, in that detection is likely to be made not by a first responder, but by members of the public health community.

The devastating potential of bioweapons is confounded by the fact that people normally have no idea that they have been exposed. During the incubation period, when they do not exhibit symptoms but are contagious to others, they can spread the disease by touch or through the air. Incubation periods can be as short as several hours but as long as several weeks, allowing for wide geographic spreading due to the efficiency of modern travel. The spread of the SARS virus (which was not a terrorist attack) throughout all continents of the world is evidence of this phenomenon.

Biological weapons are also effective at disrupting economic and industrial components of society, even when they only target animals or plants. Terrorists could potentially spread a biological agent over a large geographic area, undetected, causing significant destruction of crops. If the agent spread easily, as is often the case with natural diseases such as Dutch elm disease, the consequences could be devastating to an entire industry. Cattle diseases such as foot and mouth disease and mad cow disease, which occur naturally, could be used for sinister purposes with little planning, resources, or technical knowledge. In 1918, the German army did just this, spreading anthrax and other diseases through exported livestock and animal feed. With globalization, such actions would require much less effort to conduct.

The primary defense against the use of biological weapons is recognition, which is achieved through proper training of first responders and public health officials. Early detection, before the disease or illness has spread to critical limits, is key to preventing a major public health emergency.

Biological agents are grouped into three categories, designated A, B, and C. Category A agents are those that have great potential for causing a public health catastrophe, and that are capable of being disseminated over a large geographic area. Examples of Category A agents are anthrax, smallpox, plague, botulism, tularemia, and viral hemorrhagic fevers. Category B agents are those that have low mortality rates, but which may be disseminated over a large geographic area with relative ease. Category B agents include salmonella, ricin, Q fever, typhus, and glanders. Category C agents are common pathogens that have the potential for being engineered for terrorism or weapon purposes. Examples of Category C agents are hantavirus and tuberculosis (Sources: FEMA, 2002; Wikipedia, 2005, www.wikipedia.org).

▩ ▩ Critical Thinking ▩

Why do chemical and biological agents instill such fear into the minds of Americans? Do you think that most people overestimate or underestimate their actual risk? What can be done to correct misperceptions of risk? What is most likely causing these misperceptions?

Some Indicators of Biological Attack

- Stated threat to release a biological agent
- Unusual occurrence of dead or dying animals
- Unusual casualties
- Unusual illness for region/area
- Definite pattern inconsistent with natural disease
- Unusual liquid, spray, vapor, or powder
- Spraying, suspicious devices, packages, or letters

Source: Federal Emergency Management Agency, Interim Planning Guide for State and Local Anthrax Government: Managing the Emergency Consequences of Terrorist Incidents, Washington, DC: FEMA, July 2002.

For indicators of biological attack and a list of biological agents, see the sidebars of the same respective titles. Fact sheets compiled from the CDC website for the following selected biological agents are presented in sidebars with matching titles:

- Anthrax
- Smallpox
- Plague
- Botulism
- Tularemia

Next, for a discussion of using vaccines in an emergency-response scenario, see the sidebar titled, "The Difficulties of Preventing or Treating Biological Attacks with Vaccines."

List of Biological Agents

Compiled by the Centers for Disease Control and Prevention.

Anthrax (*Bacillus anthracis*)
Botulism (*Clostridium botulinum* toxin)
Brucellosis (*Brucella* species)
Cholera (*Vibricholerae*)
E. coli O157:H7 (*Escherichia coli*)
Epsilon toxin (*Clostridium perfringens*)
Emerging infectious diseases such as Nipah virus and hantavirus
Glanders (*Burkholderia mallei*)
Melioidosis (*Burkholderia pseudomallei*)
Typhoid fever (*Salmonella typhi*)
Typhus fever (*Rickettsia prowazekii*)
Plague (*Yersinia pestis*)
Psittacosis (*Chlamydia psittaci*)
Q fever (*Coxiella burnetii*)
Ricin (considered to be both a chemical and biological weapon)
Salmonellosis (*Salmonella* species)
Smallpox (*Variola major*)
Staphylococcal enterotoxin B
Tularemia (*Francisella tularensis*)
Viral encephalitis (alphaviruses [e.g., Venezuelan equine encephalitis, eastern equine encephalitis, western equine encephalitis])
Viral hemorrhagic fevers (filoviruses [e.g., Ebola, Marburg] and arenaviruses (e.g., Lassa, Machupo])
Water safety threats (e.g., Vibricholerae, Shigellosis [Shigella], *Cryptosporidium parvum*)

Source: Centers for Disease Control and Prevention, www.bt.cdc.gov/agent/agentlist.asp.

Facts about Anthrax

What Is Anthrax

Anthrax is a serious disease caused by *Bacillus anthracis*, a bacterium that forms spores. A bacterium is a very small organism made up of one cell. Many bacteria can cause disease. A spore is a cell that is dormant (asleep) but may come to life with the right conditions.

There are three types of anthrax:

- Skin (cutaneous)
- Lungs (inhalation)
- Digestive (gastrointestinal)

How Do You Get It?

Anthrax is not known to spread from one person to another. Humans can become infected with anthrax by handling products from infected animals or by breathing in anthrax spores from infected animal products, such as wool. People also can become infected with gastrointestinal anthrax by eating undercooked meat from infected animals. Anthrax also can be used as a weapon. This happened in the United States in 2001. Anthrax was deliberately spread through the postal system by sending letters with powder containing anthrax. This caused 22 cases of anthrax infection.

How Dangerous Is Anthrax?

The CDC classifies agents with recognized bioterrorism potential into three priority areas (A, B, and C). Anthrax is classified a Category A agent. Category A agents are those that do the following:

- Pose the greatest possible threat for a bad effect on public health
- May spread across a large area or need public awareness
- Need a great deal of planning to protect the public's health

In most cases, early treatment with antibiotics can cure cutaneous anthrax. Even if untreated, 80% of people who become infected with cutaneous anthrax do not die. Gastrointestinal anthrax is more serious because between one-fourth and more than half of cases lead to death. Inhalation anthrax is much more severe. In 2001, about half of the cases of inhalation anthrax ended in death.

What Are the Symptoms?

The symptoms of anthrax are different depending on the type of the disease:

- Cutaneous: The first symptom is a small sore that develops into a blister. The blister then develops into a skin ulcer with a black area in the center. The sore, blister, and ulcer do not hurt.
- Gastrointestinal: The first symptoms are nausea, loss of appetite, bloody diarrhea, and fever, followed by severe stomach pain.
- Inhalation: The first symptoms of inhalation anthrax are like those associated with cold or flu and can include a sore throat, mild fever, and muscle aches. Later symptoms include cough, chest discomfort, shortness of breath, tiredness, and muscle aches. (Caution: Do not assume that just because a person has cold or flu symptoms that they have inhalation anthrax.)

How Soon Do Infected People Get Sick?

Symptoms can appear within 7 days of coming in contact with the bacterium for all three types of anthrax. For inhalation anthrax, symptoms can appear within a week or can take up to 42 days to appear.

How Is Anthrax Treated?

Antibiotics are used to treat all three types of anthrax. Early identification and treatment are important. Treatment is different for a person who is exposed to anthrax but is not yet sick. Health-care providers will use antibiotics (such as ciprofloxacin, doxycycline, or penicillin) combined with the anthrax vaccine to prevent anthrax infection.

Treatment after infection usually calls for a 60-day course of antibiotics. Success depends on the type of anthrax and how soon treatment begins.

Can Anthrax Be Prevented?

There is a vaccine to prevent anthrax, but it is not yet available to the general public. Anyone who may be exposed to anthrax, including certain members of the U.S. armed forces, laboratory workers, and workers who may enter or reenter contaminated areas, may get the vaccine. Also, in the event of an attack using anthrax as a weapon, people exposed would get the vaccine.

What Should I Do If I Think I Have Been Exposed to Anthrax?

If you are showing symptoms of anthrax infection, call your health-care provider right away.

What Should I Do If I Think I Have Been Exposed to Anthrax?

Contact local law enforcement immediately if you think that you may have been exposed to anthrax. This includes being exposed to a suspicious package or envelope that contains powder.

What Is CDC Doing to Prepare for a Possible Anthrax Attack?

CDC is working with state and local health authorities to prepare for an anthrax attack. Activities include the following:

- Developing plans and procedures to respond to an anthrax attack
- Training and equipping emergency response teams to help state and local governments control infection, gather samples, and perform tests; educating health-care providers, media, and the general public about what to do in the event of an attack
- Working closely with health departments, veterinarians, and laboratories to watch for suspected cases of anthrax; developing a national electronic database to track potential cases of anthrax
- Ensuring that there are enough safe laboratories for quick testing of suspected anthrax cases
- Working with hospitals, laboratories, emergency response teams, and health care providers to make sure they have the supplies they need in case of an attack

Source: Centers for Disease Control and Prevention, www.cdc.gov.

Facts about Smallpox

What Smallpox Is

Smallpox is a serious, contagious, and sometimes fatal infectious disease. There is no specific treatment for smallpox disease, and the only prevention is vaccination. The name smallpox is derived from the Latin word for "spotted" and refers to the raised bumps that appear on the face and body of an infected person.

There are two clinical forms of smallpox. *Variola major* is the severe and most common form of smallpox, with a more extensive rash and higher fever. There are four types of *Variola major* smallpox: ordinary (the most frequent type, accounting for 90% or more of cases); modified (mild and occurring in previously vaccinated persons); flat; and hemorrhagic (both rare and very severe). Historically, *Variola major* has an overall fatality rate of about 30%; however, flat and hemorrhagic smallpox usually are fatal. *Variola minor* is a less common presentation of smallpox and a much less severe disease, with death rates historically of 1% or less.

Smallpox outbreaks have occurred from time to time for thousands of years, but the disease is now eradicated after a successful worldwide vaccination program. The last case of smallpox in the United States was in 1949. The last naturally occurring case in the world was in Somalia in 1977. After the disease was eliminated from the world, routine vaccination against smallpox among the general public was stopped because it was no longer necessary for prevention.

Smallpox Disease

- Incubation period: Duration is 7 to 17 days. Not contagious. Exposure to the virus is followed by an incubation period during which people do not have any symptoms and may feel fine. This incubation period averages about 12 to 14 days but can range from 7 to 17 days. During this time, people are not contagious.
- Initial symptoms (prodrome): Duration is 2 to 4 days. Sometimes contagious (smallpox may be contagious during the prodrome phase, but is most infectious during the first 7 to 10 days after onset of rash). The first symptoms of smallpox include fever, malaise, head and body aches, and sometimes vomiting. The fever is usually high, in the range of 101° to 104°F. At this time, people are usually too sick to carry on their normal activities.
- Early rash: Duration is about 4 days. Most contagious. A rash emerges first as small red spots on the tongue and in the mouth. These spots develop into sores that break open and spread large amounts of the virus into the mouth and throat. At this time, the person becomes most contagious.
- Rash distribution: Around the time the sores in the mouth break down, a rash appears on the skin, starting on the face and spreading to the arms and legs and then to the hands and feet. Usually the rash spreads to all parts of the body within 24 hours. As the rash appears, the fever usually falls and the person may start to feel better. The distribution of the rash in smallpox is distinguished from that of chickenpox in that it tends to concentrate more on the face and extremities rather than on the face and trunk (see Figure 4–1). By the third day of the rash, the rash becomes raised bumps. By the fourth day, the bumps fill with a thick, opaque fluid, and often have a depression in the center that looks like a belly button. (This is a major distinguishing characteristic of smallpox.) Fever often will rise again at this time and remain high until scabs form over the bumps.
- Pustular rash: Duration is about 5 days. Contagious. The bumps become pustules — sharply raised, usually round and firm to the touch as if there's a small round object under the skin. People often say the bumps feel like BB pellets embedded in the skin.

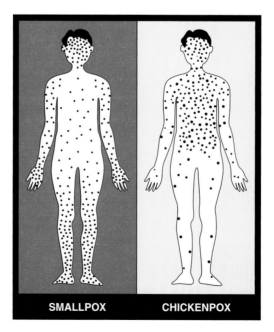

FIGURE 4–1 Rash distribution in (left) smallpox and (right) chickenpox.

- Pustules and scabs: Duration is about 5 days. Contagious. The pustules begin to form a crust and then scab. By the end of the second week after the rash appears, most of the sores have scabbed over.
- Resolving scabs: Duration is about 6 days. Contagious. The scabs begin to fall off, leaving marks on the skin that eventually become pitted scars. Most scabs will have fallen off 3 weeks after the rash appears. The person is contagious to others until all of the scabs have fallen off.
- Scabs resolved: Not contagious. Scabs have fallen off. Person is no longer contagious.

Where Smallpox Comes From

Smallpox is caused by the variola virus that emerged in human populations thousands of years ago. Except for laboratory stockpiles, the variola virus has been eliminated. However, in the aftermath of the events of September and October 2001, there is heightened concern that the variola virus might be used as an agent of bioterrorism. For this reason, the U.S. government is taking precautions for dealing with a smallpox outbreak.

Transmission

Generally, direct and fairly prolonged face-to-face contact is required to spread smallpox from one person to another. Smallpox also can be spread through direct contact with infected body fluids or contaminated objects such as bedding or clothing. Rarely, smallpox has been spread by virus carried in the air in enclosed settings such as buildings, buses, and trains. Humans are the only natural hosts of variola. Smallpox is not known to be transmitted by insects or animals.

A person with smallpox is sometimes contagious with onset of fever (prodrome phase), but the person becomes most contagious with the onset of rash. At this stage the infected person is usually very sick and not able to move around in the community. The infected person is contagious until the last smallpox scab falls off.

Source: Centers for Disease Control and Prevention, www.cdc.gov.

Facts about Plague

What Is Plague?

Plague is a disease caused by *Yersinia pestis* (*Y. pestis*), a bacterium found in rodents and their fleas in many areas around the world.

Why Are We Concerned about Pneumonic Plague as a Bioweapon?

Yersinia pestis used in an aerosol attack could cause cases of the pneumonic form of plague. One to 6 days after becoming infected with the bacteria, people would develop pneumonic plague. Once people have the disease, the bacteria can spread to others who have close contact with them. Because of the delay between being exposed to the bacteria and becoming sick, people could travel over a large area before becoming contagious and possibly infecting others. Controlling the disease would then be more difficult. A bioweapon carrying *Y. pestis* is possible because the bacterium occurs in nature and could be isolated and grown in quantity in a laboratory. Even so, manufacturing an effective weapon using *Y. pestis* would require advanced knowledge and technology.

Is Pneumonic Plague Different from Bubonic Plague?

Yes. Both are caused by *Y. pestis*, but they are transmitted differently and their symptoms differ. Pneumonic plague can be transmitted from person to person; bubonic plague cannot. Pneumonic plague affects the lungs and is transmitted when a person breathes in *Y. pestis* particles in the air. Bubonic plague is transmitted through the bite of an infected flea or exposure to infected material through a break in the skin. Symptoms include swollen, tender lymph glands called buboes. Buboes are not present in pneumonic plague. If bubonic plague is not treated, however, the bacteria can spread through the bloodstream and infect the lungs, causing a secondary case of pneumonic plague.

What Are the Signs and Symptoms of Pneumonic Plague?

Patients usually have fever, weakness, and rapidly developing pneumonia with shortness of breath, chest pain, cough, and sometimes bloody or watery sputum. Nausea, vomiting, and abdominal pain may also occur. Without early treatment, pneumonic plague usually leads to respiratory failure, shock, and rapid death.

How Do People Become Infected with Pneumonic Plague?

Pneumonic plague occurs when *Yersinia pestis* infects the lungs. Transmission can take place if someone breathes in *Y. pestis* particles, which could happen in an aerosol release during a bioterrorism attack. Pneumonic plague is also transmitted by breathing in *Y. pestis* suspended in respiratory droplets from a person (or animal) with pneumonic plague. Respiratory droplets are spread most readily by coughing or sneezing. Becoming infected in this way usually requires direct and close (within 6 feet) contact with the ill person or animal. Pneumonic plague may also occur if a person with bubonic or septicemic plague is untreated and the bacteria spread to the lungs.

Does Plague Occur Naturally?

Yes. The World Health Organization reports 1,000 to 3,000 cases of plague worldwide every year. An average of 5 to 15 cases occur each year in the western United States. These cases are usually scattered and occur in rural to semirural areas. Most cases are of the bubonic form of the disease. Naturally occurring pneumonic plague is uncommon, although small outbreaks do occur. Both types of plague are readily controlled by standard public health response measures.

Can a Person Exposed to Pneumonic Plague Avoid Becoming Sick?

Yes. People who have had close contact with an infected person can greatly reduce the chance of becoming sick if they begin treatment within 7 days of their exposure. Treatment consists of taking antibiotics for at least 7 days.

How Quickly Would Someone Get Sick If Exposed to Plague Bacteria through the Air?

Someone exposed to *Yersinia pestis* through the air — either from an intentional aerosol release or from close and direct exposure to someone with plague pneumonia — would become ill within 1 to 6 days.

Can Pneumonic Plague Be Treated?

Yes. To prevent a high risk of death, antibiotics should be given within 24 hours of the first symptoms. Several types of antibiotics are effective for curing the disease and for preventing it. Available oral medications are a tetracycline (such as doxycycline) or a fluoroquinolone (such as ciprofloxacin). For injection or intravenous use, streptomycin or gentamicin antibiotics are used. Early in the response to a bioterrorism attack, these drugs would be tested to determine which is most effective against the particular weapon that was used.

Would Enough Medication Be Available in the Event of a Bioterrorism Attack Involving Pneumonic Plague?

National and state public health officials have large supplies of drugs needed in the event of a bioterrorism attack. These supplies can be sent anywhere in the United States within 12 hours.

What Should People Do If They Suspect They or Others Have Been Exposed to Plague?

Get immediate medical attention. To prevent illness, a person who has been exposed to pneumonic plague must receive antibiotic treatment without delay. If an exposed person becomes ill, antibiotics must be administered within 24 hours of the first symptoms to reduce the risk of death. Immediately notify local or state health departments so they can begin to investigate and control the problem right away. If bioterrorism is suspected, the health departments will notify the CDC, FBI, and other appropriate authorities.

How Can Someone Reduce the Risk of Getting Pneumonic Plague from Another Person or Giving It to Someone Else?

People having direct and close contact with someone with pneumonic plague should wear tightly fitting disposable surgical masks. Patients with the disease should be isolated and medically supervised for at least the first 48 hours of antibiotic treatment. People who have been exposed to a contagious person can be protected from developing plague by receiving prompt antibiotic treatment.

How Is Plague Diagnosed?

The first step is evaluation by a health worker. If the health worker suspects pneumonic plague, samples of the patient's blood, sputum, or lymph node aspirate are sent to a laboratory for testing. Once the laboratory receives the sample, preliminary results can be ready in less than two hours. Confirmation will take longer, usually 24 to 48 hours.

How Long Can Plague Bacteria Exist in the Environment?

Yersinia pestis is easily destroyed by sunlight and drying. Even so, when released into air, the bacterium will survive for up to 1 hour, depending on conditions.

Is a Vaccine Available to Prevent Pneumonic Plague?

Currently, no plague vaccine is available in the United States. Research is in progress, but we are not likely to have vaccines for several years or more.

Source: Centers for Disease Control and Prevention, www.cdc.gov.

Facts about Botulism

What Is Botulism?

Botulism is a rare but serious paralytic illness caused by a nerve toxin that is produced by the bacterium *Clostridium botulinum*. There are three main kinds of botulism. Food-borne botulism is caused by eating foods that contain the botulism toxin. Wound botulism is caused by toxin produced from a wound infected with *Clostridium botulinum*. Infant botulism is caused by consuming the spores of the botulinum bacteria, which then grow in the intestines and release toxin. All forms of botulism can be fatal and are considered medical emergencies. Food-borne botulism can be especially dangerous because many people can be poisoned by eating a contaminated food.

What Kind of Germ Is *Clostridium botulinum*?

Clostridium botulinum is the name of a group of bacteria commonly found in soil. These rod-shaped organisms grow best in low oxygen conditions. The bacteria form spores that allow them to survive in a dormant state until exposed to conditions that can support their growth. There are seven types of botulism toxin designated by the letters A through G; only types A, B, E, and F cause illness in humans.

How Common Is Botulism?

In the United States an average of 110 cases of botulism are reported each year. Of these, approximately 25% are food-borne, 72% are infant botulism, and the rest are wound botulism. Outbreaks of food-borne botulism involving two or more persons occur most years and usually are caused by eating contaminated home-canned foods. The number of cases of food-borne and infant botulism has changed little in recent years, but wound botulism has increased because of the use of black-tar heroin, especially in California.

What Are the Symptoms of Botulism?

The classic symptoms of botulism include double vision, blurred vision, drooping eyelids, slurred speech, difficulty swallowing, dry mouth, and muscle weakness. Infants with botulism appear lethargic, feed poorly, are constipated, and have a weak cry and poor muscle tone. These are all symptoms of the muscle paralysis caused by the bacterial toxin. If untreated, these symptoms may progress to cause paralysis of the arms, legs, trunk, and respiratory muscles. In food-borne botulism, symptoms generally begin 18 to 36 hours after eating a contaminated food, but they can occur as early as 6 hours or as late as 10 days.

How Is Botulism Diagnosed?

Physicians may consider the diagnosis if the patient's history and physical examination suggest botulism. However, these clues are usually not enough to allow a diagnosis of botulism. Other diseases, such as Guillain-Barré syndrome, stroke, and myasthenia gravis, can appear similar to botulism, and special tests may be needed to exclude these other conditions. These tests may include a brain scan, spinal fluid examination, nerve conduction test (electromyography, or EMG), and a Tensilon test for myasthenia gravis. The most direct way to confirm the diagnosis is to demonstrate the Botulinum toxin in the patient's serum or stool by injecting serum or stool into mice and looking for signs of botulism. The bacteria can also be isolated from the stool of persons with food-borne and infant botulism. These tests can be performed at some state health department laboratories and at CDC.

How Can Botulism Be Treated?

The respiratory failure and paralysis that occur with severe botulism may require a patient to be on a breathing machine (ventilator) for weeks, plus intensive medical and nursing care. After several weeks, the paralysis slowly improves. If diagnosed early, food-borne and wound botulism can be treated with an antitoxin that blocks the action of toxin circulating in the blood. This can prevent patients from worsening, but recovery still takes many weeks. Physicians may try to remove contaminated food still in the gut by inducing vomiting or by using enemas. Wounds should be treated, usually surgically, to remove the source of the toxin-producing bacteria. Good supportive care in a hospital is the mainstay of therapy for all forms of botulism. Currently, antitoxin is not routinely given for treatment of infant botulism.

Are There Complications from Botulism?

Botulism can result in death due to respiratory failure. However, in the past 50 years the proportion of patients with botulism who die has fallen from about 50 to 8%. A patient with severe botulism may require a breathing machine as well as intensive medical and nursing care for several months. Patients who survive an episode of botulism poisoning may have fatigue and shortness of breath for years and long-term therapy may be needed to aid recovery.

How Can Botulism Be Prevented?

Botulism can be prevented. Food-borne botulism has often been from home-canned foods with low acid content, such as asparagus, green beans, beets, and corn. However, outbreaks of botulism have also been linked to more unusual sources, such as chopped garlic in oil, chili peppers, tomatoes, improperly handled baked potatoes wrapped in aluminum foil, and home-canned or fermented fish. Persons who do home canning should follow strict hygienic procedures to reduce contamination of foods. Oils infused with garlic or herbs should be refrigerated. Potatoes that have been baked while wrapped in aluminum foil should be kept hot until served or refrigerated. Because the botulism toxin is destroyed by high temperatures, people who eat home-canned foods should consider boiling the food for 10 minutes before eating it to ensure safety. Instructions on safe home canning can be obtained from county extension services or from the U.S. Department of Agriculture. Because honey can contain spores of *Clostridium botulinum*, and this has been a source of infection for infants, children younger than 12 months of age should not be fed honey. Honey is safe for people 1 year of age and older. Wound botulism can be prevented by promptly seeking medical care for infected wounds and by not using injectable street drugs.

What Are Public Health Agencies Doing to Prevent or Control Botulism?

Public education about botulism prevention is an ongoing activity. Information about safe canning is widely available for consumers. State health departments and CDC offices have persons knowledgeable about botulism available to consult with physicians 24 hours a day. If antitoxin is needed to treat a patient, it can be quickly delivered to a physician anywhere in the country. Suspected outbreaks of botulism are quickly investigated, and if they involve a commercial product, the appropriate control measures are coordinated among public health and regulatory agencies. Physicians should report suspected cases of botulism to a state health department.

Source: Centers for Disease Control and Prevention, www.cdc.gov.

Facts about Tularemia

What Is Tularemia?

Tularemia is an infectious disease caused by a hardy bacterium, *Francisella tularensis*, found in animals (especially rodents, rabbits, and hares).

How Do People Become Infected with the Tularemia Bacteria?

Typically, persons become infected through the bites of arthropods (most commonly, ticks and deerflies) that have fed on an infected animal, by handling infected animal carcasses, by eating or drinking contaminated food or water, or by inhaling infected aerosols.

Does Tularemia Occur Naturally in the United States?

Yes. It is a widespread disease of animals. Approximately 200 cases of tularemia in humans are reported annually in the United States, mostly in persons living in the south-central and western states. Nearly all cases occur in rural areas and are associated with the bites of infective ticks and biting flies or with the handling of infected rodents, rabbits, or hares. Occasional cases result from inhaling infectious aerosols and from laboratory accidents.

Why Are We Concerned about Tularemia as a Bioweapon?

Francisella tularensis is highly infectious: A small number of bacteria (10 to 50 organisms) can cause disease. If *F. tularensis* were used as a bioweapon, the bacteria would likely be made airborne for exposure by inhalation. Persons who inhale an infectious aerosol would generally experience severe respiratory illness, including life-threatening pneumonia and systemic infection, if they were not treated. The bacteria that cause tularemia occur widely in nature and could be isolated and grown in quantity in a laboratory, although manufacturing an effective aerosol weapon would require considerable sophistication.

Can Someone Become Infected with the Tularemia Bacteria from Another Person?

No. People have not been known to transmit the infection to others, so infected persons do not need to be isolated.

How Quickly Would Someone Become Sick If Exposed to the Tularemia Bacteria?

The incubation period for tularemia is typically 3 to 5 days, with a range of 1 to 14 days.

What Are the Signs and Symptoms of Tularemia?

Depending on the route of exposure, the tularemia bacteria may cause skin ulcers, swollen and painful lymph glands, inflamed eyes, sore throat, oral ulcers, or pneumonia. If the bacteria were inhaled, symptoms would include the abrupt onset of fever, chills, headache, muscle aches, joint pain, dry cough, and progressive weakness. Persons with pneumonia can develop chest pain, difficulty breathing, bloody sputum, and respiratory failure. Of people with the lung and systemic forms of the disease, 40% may die if they are not treated with appropriate antibiotics.

What Should Someone Do If They Suspect They or Others Have Been Exposed to the Tularemia Bacteria?

Seek prompt medical attention. If a person has been exposed to *Francisella tularensis*, treatment with tetracycline antibiotics for 14 days after exposure may be recommended. Local and state health departments should be immediately notified so an investigation and control activities can begin quickly. If the exposure is thought to be due to criminal activity (bioterrorism), local and state health departments will notify CDC, the FBI, and other appropriate authorities.

How Is Tularemia Diagnosed?

When tularemia is clinically suspected, the health care worker will collect specimens, such as blood or sputum, from the patient for testing in a diagnostic or reference laboratory. Laboratory test results for tularemia may be presumptive or confirmatory. Presumptive (preliminary) identification may take less than 2 hours, but confirmatory testing will take longer, usually 24 to 48 hours.

Can Tularemia Be Effectively Treated with Antibiotics?

Yes. After potential exposure or diagnosis, early treatment is recommended with an antibiotic from the tetracycline (such as doxycycline) or fluoroquinolone (such as ciprofloxacin) class, which is taken orally, or the antibiotics streptomycin or gentamicin, which are given intramuscularly or intravenously. Sensitivity testing of the tularemia bacterium can be done in the early stages of a response to determine which antibiotics would be most effective.

How Long Can *Francisella tularensis* Exist in the Environment?

Francisella tularensis can remain alive for weeks in water and soil.

Is There a Vaccine Available for Tularemia?

In the past, a vaccine for tularemia has been used to protect laboratory workers, but it is currently under review by the Food and Drug Administration.

Source: Centers for Disease Control and Prevention, www.cdc.gov.

The Difficulties of Preventing or Treating Biological Attacks with Vaccines

Unlike chemical, radiological, nuclear, or other WMDs, biological weapons may be prevented before an attack or treated during an attack with the use of vaccines. Vaccines work by helping the body to recognize and destroy a biological agent, thereby developing immunity to it. Vaccines have been used for centuries to prevent or eradicate common diseases, first appearing in 1796 when English physician Edward Jenner developed a vaccine to prevent smallpox. Since then, several diseases have been minimized or eradicated through widespread vaccination programs, including smallpox, polio, measles, rubella, and many other once-common diseases.

Vaccines, however, often come at a high cost. Vaccine development requires significant investments in research, testing, and public relations. For some diseases, including HIV and tuberculosis, expensive, drawn out campaigns to develop vaccines have thus far proven fruitless despite heavy investment in cash and human resources and decades of time. A second cost of vaccines is the risk associated with administering them. Almost without exception, vaccines carry associated health risks for recipients. For instance, it is estimated that 1 in every million people given the smallpox vaccine will die as a result of complications directly related to the vaccine itself. In addition to fatalities caused by the vaccine, 1 in 10,000 vaccine recipients experienced one or many other adverse affects directly related to the vaccine itself. These include corneal scarring (blindness), eczema, generalized smallpox-like reaction, and encephalitis.

For many of the biological weapons that are considered to be viable threats, including anthrax and smallpox, there already exist vaccines that could offer a much higher level of resistance in the human population. However, because of the aforementioned costs and risks associated with these vaccines, policymakers are faced with determining whether the vaccine-related injuries and deaths outweigh the potential deaths and injuries that would occur in the event that a terrorist was able to effectively use a biological weapon containing the agent in question. For instance, assuming that approximately 40 million people in the United States would need to be vaccinated (CDC, n.d.), and the administration of the vaccine causes one death for every million people, we should expect that 40 people would die as a result of the vaccine regardless of whether or not an actual smallpox attack ever occurred. Using this baseline, we can then determine whether or not a mass vaccination program is worth the expected vaccine-related fatalities only if we can safely say that the expected result of not vaccinating the population would be a fatality rate greater than 40. To calculate this number, we must first estimate the number of people that would likely be exposed in an attack, multiply this number by 30% (the fatality rate of smallpox), and multiply this again by the expected probability of an attack over the lifetime of the population. So, let's just say that 100,000 people are estimated to be infected in a scenario (a figure chosen for illustrative purposes only). This number would likely lead to 30,000 deaths given the fatality rate of the disease. But if it is determined, for instance, that there is only a 1 in 1,000 chance that an attack like that could happen, then the expected fatality rate based upon the scenario is only 30 deaths — 10 fewer deaths than would be guaranteed in a mass evacuation campaign. Under this scenario the risk associated with the vaccination program is more deadly than the risk associated with an attack.

Because of these and other costs associated with the vaccination of the entire population to certain biological warfare agents, policy has generally dictated that only those specific people who have an individual risk that places the benefit of vaccination greater than the risk of vaccination-related complications (such as active members of the military, public health officials, laboratory workers, and emergency responders), there has never been a single mass vaccination campaign for a biological weapon. Instead, the U.S. government, as well as governments of other countries, has chosen instead to stockpile large amounts of the vaccine to be administered only after an attack is imminent or has already occurred, for the purposes of limiting the spread of the resulting disease. This too has presented problems, however, because the expensive stockpiles quickly expire, and it is doubtful that vaccine programs can be effectively managed in the panic and uncertainty that would result in the aftermath of a biological attack. Further compounding this problem is the fact that weaponized forms of certain biological agents can render the protective benefits of vaccines useless, as is postulated in the case of weaponized anthrax.

For more information on U.S. efforts to stockpile vaccines against biological weapons, see the CDC article "Developing New Smallpox Vaccines" by Stephen Rosenthal, Michael Merchlinsky, Cynthia Kleppinger, and Karen Goldenthal (http://www.cdc.gov/ncidod/eid/vol7no6/rosenthal.htm).

Nuclear/Radiological

Nuclear and radiological weapons are those that involve the movement of energy through space and through material. There are three primary mechanisms by which terrorists can use radiation to carry out an attack: detonation of a nuclear bomb, dispersal of radiological material, or an attack on a facility housing nuclear material (power plant, research laboratory, storage site, etc.).

Nuclear weapons are the most devastating of the various attack forms listed earlier. They are also the most difficult to develop or acquire, and thus are considered the lowest threat of the three in terms of terrorist potential (likelihood). A nuclear weapon causes damage to property and harm to life through two separate processes. First, a blast is created by the detonation of the bomb. An incredibly large amount of energy is released in the explosion, which is the result of an uncontrolled chain reaction of atomic splitting. The initial shock wave, which destroys all built structures within a range of up to several miles, is followed by a heat wave reaching tens of millions of degrees close to the point of detonation. High winds accompany the shock and heat waves.

The second process by which nuclear weapons inflict harm is through harmful radiation. This radiation and radiological material is most dangerous close to the area of detonation, where high concentrations can cause rapid death, but particles reaching high into the atmosphere can pose a threat several hundreds of miles away under the right meteorological conditions. Radiation can also persist for years after the explosion occurs.

Radiological dispersion devices (RDDs) are simple explosive devices that spread harmful radioactive material upon detonation, without the involvement of a nuclear explosion. These devices are often called "dirty bombs." Radiological dispersion devices also exist that do not require explosives for dispersal. Although illnesses and fatalities very close to the point of dispersal are likely, these devices are more likely to be used to spread terror. Like many biological and chemical weapons, it may be difficult to initially detect that a radiological attack has occurred. Special detection equipment and the training to use it are a prerequisite. See the sidebar, "General Indicators of Possible Nuclear Weapon/Radiological Agent Use."

General Indicators of Possible Nuclear Weapon/Radiological Agent Use

- Stated threat to deploy a nuclear or radiological device
- Presence of nuclear or radiological equipment
- Spent fuel canisters or nuclear transport vehicles
- Nuclear placards/warning materials along with otherwise unexplained casualties.

Source: Federal Emergency Management Agency, "Interim Planning Guide for State and Local Government: Managing the Emergency Consequences of Terrorist Incidents," Washington, DC: FEMA, July 2002.

A third scenario involving nuclear/radiological material entails an attack on a nuclear facility. There are many facilities around the country where nuclear material is stored, including nuclear power plants, hazardous materials storage sites, medical facilities, military installations, and industrial facilities. An attack on any of these facilities could result in a release of radiological material into the atmosphere, which would pose a threat to life and certainly cause fear among those who live nearby.

If a radiological or nuclear attack were to occur, humans and animals would experience both internal and external consequences. External exposure results from any contact with radioactive material outside the body, while internal exposure requires ingestion, inhalation, or injection of radiological materials. Radiation sickness results from high doses of radiation, and can result in death if the dosage is high enough. Other effects of radiation exposure can include redness or burning of the skin and eyes, nausea, damage to the body's immune system, and a high life-time risk of developing cancer (Source: FEMA, 2002).

Information developed by the CDC on a radiation event is presented in the sidebar, "Facts about a Radiation Emergency."

Facts about a Radiation Emergency

What Is Radiation?

- Radiation is a form of energy that is present all around us.
- Various types of radiation exist, some of which have more energy than others.
- Amounts of radiation released into the environment are measured in units called curies. However, the dose of radiation that a person receives is measured in units called rem.

How Can Exposure Occur?

- People are exposed to small amounts of radiation every day, both from naturally occurring sources (such as elements in the soil or cosmic rays from the sun), and human-made sources. Human-made sources include some electronic equipment (such as microwave ovens and television sets), medical sources (such as x-rays, certain diagnostic tests and treatments), and from nuclear weapons testing.
- The amount of radiation from natural or human-made sources to which people are exposed is usually small; a radiation emergency (such as a nuclear power plant accident or a terrorist event) could expose people to small or large doses of radiation, depending on the situation.
- Scientists estimate that the average person in the United States receives a dose of about one-third of a rem per year. About 80% of human exposure comes from natural sources, and the remaining 20% comes from human-made radiation sources — mainly medical x-rays.
- Internal exposure refers to radioactive material that is taken into the body through breathing, eating, or drinking.
- External exposure refers to an exposure to a radioactive source outside of our bodies.
- Contamination refers to particles of radioactive material that are deposited anywhere that they are not supposed to be, such as on an object or on a person's skin.

What Happens When People Are Exposed to Radiation?

- Radiation can affect the body in a number of ways, and the adverse health effects of exposure may not be apparent for many years.
- These adverse health effects can range from mild effects, such as skin reddening, to serious effects such as cancer and death, depending on the amount of radiation absorbed by the body (the dose), the type of radiation, the route of exposure, and the length of time a person was exposed.
- Exposure to very large doses of radiation may cause death within a few days or months.
- Exposure to lower doses of radiation may lead to an increased risk of developing cancer or other adverse health effects later in life.

What Types of Terrorist Events Might Involve Radiation?

- Possible terrorist events could involve introducing radioactive material into the food or water supply, using explosives (such as dynamite) to scatter radioactive materials (called a "dirty bomb"), bombing or destroying a nuclear facility, or exploding a small nuclear device.
- Although introducing radioactive material into the food or water supply most likely would cause great concern or fear, it probably would not cause much contamination or increase the danger of adverse health effects.
- Although a dirty bomb could cause serious injuries from the explosion, it most likely would not have enough radioactive material in a form that would cause serious radiation sickness among large numbers of people. However, people who were exposed to radiation scattered by the bomb could have a greater risk of developing cancer later in life, depending on their dose.
- A meltdown or explosion at a nuclear facility could cause a large amount of radioactive material to be released. People at the facility would probably be contaminated with radioactive material and possibly be injured if there was an explosion. Those people who received a large dose might develop acute radiation syndrome. People in the surrounding area could be exposed or contaminated.

- Clearly, an exploded nuclear device could result in a lot of property damage. People would be killed or injured from the blast and might be contaminated by radioactive material. Many people could have symptoms of acute radiation syndrome. After a nuclear explosion, radioactive fallout would extend over a large region far from the point of impact, potentially increasing people's risk of developing cancer over time.

What Preparations Can I Make for a Radiation Emergency?

- Your community should have a plan in place in case of a radiation emergency. Check with community leaders to learn more about the plan and possible evacuation routes.
- Check with your child's school, the nursing home of a family member, and your employer to see what their plans are for dealing with a radiation emergency.
- Develop your own family emergency plan so that every family member knows what to do.
- At home, put together an emergency kit that would be appropriate for any emergency. The kit should include the following items:
- A flashlight with extra batteries
- A portable radio with extra batteries
- Bottled water
- Canned and packaged food
- A hand-operated can opener
- A first-aid kit and essential prescription medications
- Personal items such as paper towels, garbage bags, and toilet paper

How Can I Protect Myself During a Radiation Emergency?

- After a release of radioactive materials, local authorities will monitor the levels of radiation and determine what protective actions to take.
- The most appropriate action will depend on the situation. Tune to the local emergency response network or news station for information and instructions during any emergency.
- If a radiation emergency involves the release of large amounts of radioactive materials, you may be advised to "shelter in place," which means to stay in your home or office; or you may be advised to move to another location.

If you are advised to shelter in place, you should do the following:

- Close and lock all doors and windows.
- Turn off fans, air conditioners, and forced-air heating units that bring in fresh air from the outside. Only use units to recirculate air that is already in the building.
- Close fireplace dampers.
- If possible, bring pets inside.
- Move to an inner room or basement.
- Keep your radio tuned to the emergency response network or local news to find out what else you need to do.

If you are advised to evacuate, follow the directions that your local officials provide. Leave the area as quickly and orderly as possible. In addition:

- Take a flashlight, portable radio, batteries, first-aid kit, supply of sealed food and water, hand-operated can opener, essential medicines, and cash and credit cards.
- Take pets only if you are using your own vehicle and going to a place you know will accept animals. Emergency vehicles and shelters usually will not accept animals.

Should I Take Potassium Iodide During a Radiation Emergency?

- Potassium iodide (KI) should only be taken in a radiation emergency that involves the release of radioactive iodine, such as an accident at a nuclear power plant or the explosion of a nuclear bomb. A "dirty bomb" most likely will not contain radioactive iodine.
- A person who is internally exposed to radioactive iodine may experience thyroid disease later in life. The thyroid gland will absorb radioactive iodine and may develop cancer or abnormal growths later on. KI will saturate the thyroid gland with iodine, decreasing the amount of harmful radioactive iodine that can be absorbed.
- KI only protects the thyroid gland and does not provide protection from any other radiation exposure.
- Some people are allergic to iodine and should not take KI. Check with your doctor about any concerns you have about potassium iodide.

Source: Centers for Disease Control and Prevention, www.cdc.gov.

Preparedness and Sheltering in Place

There are many options for members of the general public who wish to prepare for the effects of terrorist attacks involving the use of chemical, biological, or radiological weapons. In general, these options involve various implements or methods to avoid contact with the agents themselves, or with infected or contaminated individuals. One of the most effective means of preventing exposure to these weapons is to remain indoors after an attack has occurred, termed "sheltering in place," thereby avoiding the likelihood of coming into contact with the pathogen, chemical, or radiation by traveling unprotected through an area of contamination. The federal government, through the Ad Council, has developed and published several options for those wishing to take preparative measures on the Ready. Gov website, as have several other agencies including the Centers for Disease Control and Prevention, the Department of Energy, and many state and local offices of emergency management and homeland security. Levels of actual application of these measures by the general public are assumed to be very low, however, due to a combination of risk perception factors that generate a sense of inability to mitigate WMD effects, and a prioritization of risk reduction measures by these individuals that places such actions lower in priority ranking.

The "Preparedness and Response for a Bioterror or Chemical Attack" sidebar discusses how the general population can prepare for a bioterror or chemical attack. Preparedness against dispersion of a chemical agent is further discussed in the sidebar, "Chemical Agents: Facts about Sheltering in Place."

Preparedness and Response for a Bioterror or Chemical Attack

Before a Biological Attack

- Check with your doctor to ensure all required or suggested immunizations are up to date. Children and older adults are particularly vulnerable to biological agents.
- Consider installing a High Efficiency Particulate Air (HEPA) filter in your furnace return duct. These filters remove particles in the 0.3 to 10 micron range and will filter out most biological agents that may enter your house. If you do not have a central heating or cooling system, a stand-alone portable HEPA filter can be used.

During a Biological Attack

In the event of a biological attack, public health officials may not immediately be able to provide information on what you should do. It will take time to determine what the illness is, how it should be treated, and who is in danger. Watch television, listen to radio, or check the Internet for official news and information including signs and symptoms of the disease, areas in danger, if medications or vaccinations are being distributed, and where you should seek medical attention if you become ill. The first evidence of an attack may be when you notice symptoms of the disease caused by exposure to an agent. Be suspicious of any symptoms you notice, but do not assume that any illness is a result of the attack. Use common sense and practice good hygiene.

If you become aware of an unusual and suspicious substance nearby:

- Move away quickly
- Wash with soap and water
- Contact authorities
- Listen to the media for official instructions
- Seek medical attention if you become sick

If you are exposed to a biological agent:

- Remove and bag your clothes and personal items. Follow official instructions for disposal of contaminated items
- Wash yourself with soap and water and put on clean clothes
- Seek medical assistance. You may be advised to stay away from others or even quarantined.

Using HEPA Filters

HEPA filters are useful in biological attacks. If you have a central heating and cooling system in your home with a HEPA filter, leave it on if it is running or turn the fan on if it is not running. Moving the air in the house through the filter will help remove the agents from the air. If you have a portable HEPA filter, take it with you to the internal room where you are seeking shelter and turn it on. If you are in an apartment or office building that has a modern, central heating and cooling system, the system's filtration should provide a relatively safe level of protection from outside biological contaminants. HEPA filters will not filter chemical agents.

After a Biological Attack

In some situations, such as the case of the anthrax letters sent in 2001, people may be alerted to potential exposure. If this is the case, pay close attention to all official warnings and instructions on how to proceed. The delivery of medical services for a biological event may be handled differently to respond to increased demand. The basic public health procedures and medical protocols for handling exposure to biological agents are the same as for any infectious disease. It is important for you to pay attention to official instructions via radio, television, and emergency alert systems.

Before a Chemical Attack

Check your disaster supplies kit to make sure it includes:

- A roll of duct tape and scissors
- Plastic for doors, windows, and vents for the room in which you will shelter in place. To save critical time during an emergency, pre-measure and cut the plastic sheeting for each opening
- Choose an internal room to shelter, preferably one without windows and on the highest level

During a Chemical Attack

If you are instructed to remain in your home or office building, you should:

- Close doors and windows and turn off all ventilation, including furnaces, air conditioners, vents, and fans
- Seek shelter in an internal room and take your disaster supplies kit
- Seal the room with duct tape and plastic sheeting
- Listen to your radio for instructions from authorities.

  If you are caught in or near a contaminated area, you should:

- Move away immediately in a direction upwind of the source
- Find shelter as quickly as possible

After a Chemical Attack

Decontamination is needed within minutes of exposure to minimize health consequences. Do not leave the safety of a shelter to go outdoors to help others until authorities announce it is safe to do so. A person affected by a chemical agent requires immediate medical attention from a professional. If medical help is not immediately available, decontaminate yourself and assist in decontaminating others. Decontamination guidelines are as follows:

- Use extreme caution when helping others who have been exposed to chemical agents
- Remove all clothing and other items in contact with the body. Contaminated clothing normally removed over the head should be cut off to avoid contact with the eyes, nose, and mouth. Put contaminated clothing and items into a plastic bag and seal it. Decontaminate hands using soap and water. Remove eyeglasses or contact lenses. Put glasses in a pan of household bleach to decontaminate them, and then rinse and dry.
- Flush eyes with water
- Gently wash face and hair with soap and water before thoroughly rinsing with water
- Decontaminate other body areas likely to have been contaminated. Blot (do not swab or scrape) with a cloth soaked in soapy water and rinse with clear water
- Change into uncontaminated clothes. Clothing stored in drawers or closets is likely to be uncontaminated
- Proceed to a medical facility for screening and professional treatment.

Source: FEMA. 2004. "Are You Ready?" <http://www.fema.gov/areyouready/>

Chemical Agents: Facts about Sheltering in Place

What "Sheltering in Place" Means

Some kinds of chemical accidents or attacks may make going outdoors dangerous. Leaving the area might take too long or put you in harm's way. In such a case it may be safer for you to stay indoors than to go outside. "Shelter in place" means to make a shelter out of the place you are in. It is a way for you to make the building as safe as possible to protect yourself until help arrives. You should not try to shelter in a vehicle unless you have no other choice. Vehicles are not airtight enough to give you adequate protection from chemicals.

How to Prepare to Shelter in Place

Choose a room in your house or apartment for your shelter. The best room to use for the shelter is a room with as few windows and doors as possible. A large room, preferably with a water supply, is desirable — something like a master bedroom that is connected to a bathroom. For chemical events, this room should be as high in the structure as possible to avoid vapors (gases) that sink. This guideline is different from the sheltering-in-place technique used in tornadoes and other severe weather, when the shelter should be low in the home. You might not be at home if the need to shelter in place ever arises, but if you are at home, the following items would be good to have on hand. (Ideally, all of these items would be stored in the shelter room to save time.)

- First-aid kit
- Food and bottled water. Store 1 gallon of water per person in plastic bottles as well as ready-to-eat foods that will keep without refrigeration at the shelter-in-place location. If you do not have bottled water, or if you run out, you can drink water from a toilet tank (not from a toilet bowl).
- Flashlight, battery-powered radio, and extra batteries for both
- Duct tape and scissors
- Towels and plastic sheeting
- A working telephone.

How to Know If You Need to Shelter in Place

- You will hear from the local police, emergency coordinators, or government officials on the radio and on television if you need to shelter in place.
- If there is a "code red" or "severe" terror alert, you should pay attention to radio and television broadcasts to know right away whether a shelter-in-place alert is announced for your area.
- If you are away from your shelter-in-place location when a chemical event occurs, follow the instructions of emergency coordinators to find the nearest shelter. If your children are at school, they will be sheltered there. Unless you are instructed to do so, do not try to get to the school to bring your children home.

What to Do

Act quickly and follow the instructions of your local emergency coordinators. Because every situation can be different, local emergency coordinators might have special instructions for you to follow. In general, do the following:

- Go inside as quickly as possible.
- If there is time, shut and lock all outside doors and windows. Locking them may provide a tighter seal against the chemical. Turn off the air conditioner or heater. Turn off all fans, too. Close the fireplace damper and any other place that air can come in from the outside.
- Go in the shelter-in-place room, and shut the door.
- Tape plastic over any windows in the room. Use duct tape around the windows and doors and make an unbroken seal. Use the tape over any vents into the room and seal any electrical outlets or other openings. Sink and toilet drain traps should have water in them (you can use the sink and toilet as you normally would). If it is necessary to drink water, drink the stored water, not water from the tap.
- Turn on the radio. Keep a telephone close at hand, but don't use it unless there is a serious emergency.

Sheltering in this way should keep you safer than if you are outdoors. Most likely, you will be in the shelter for no more than a few hours. Listen to the radio for an announcement indicating that it is safe to leave the shelter. After you come out of the shelter, emergency coordinators may have additional instructions on how to make the rest of the building safe again.

Source: Centers for Disease Control and Prevention, www.cdc.gov.

Combined Hazards

By combining two or more methods of attack, terrorists can achieve a synergistic effect. And in doing so, they often increase the efficacy of each agent in terms of its potential to destroy, harm, or kill, thereby creating a sum total consequence much more devastating than had each agent been used independently. The dirty bomb, in which radiological material is added to a conventional explosive, is a perfect illustration of this effect. Explosives function by causing physical damage resulting from the expansion of gases, while the radiological material works by inducing a range of adverse health effects. The combination of the two results in an attack that not only causes both physical damage and harmful radiation, but disperses the radiological material over a much larger area, contaminates both the crime scene and the surrounding structures and environment, and instills a sense of fear into the entire affected population (which can extend to include the entire nation as would likely be the case if a dirty bomb was used anywhere in the country). The sidebar, "Facts about Dirty Bombs," comprises a fact sheet compiled by the CDC describing dirty bombs and their effects.

Facts about Dirty Bombs

Because of recent terrorist events, people have expressed concern about the possibility of a terrorist attack involving radioactive materials, possibly through the use of a "dirty bomb" and the harmful effects of radiation from such an event. The CDC has prepared this fact sheet to help people understand what a dirty bomb is and how it may affect their health.

What Is a "Dirty Bomb"?

A dirty bomb, or radiological dispersion device, is a bomb that combines conventional explosives, such as dynamite, with radioactive materials in the form of powder or pellets. The idea behind a dirty bomb is to blast radioactive material into the area around the explosion. This could possibly cause buildings and people to be exposed to radioactive material. The main purpose of a dirty bomb is to frighten people and make buildings or land unusable for a long period of time.

Dirty Bomb versus Atomic Bombs in Hiroshima and Nagasaki

The atomic explosions that occurred in Hiroshima and Nagasaki were conventional nuclear weapons involving a fission reaction. A dirty bomb is designed to spread radioactive material and contaminate a small area. It does not include the fission products necessary to create a large blast like those seen in Hiroshima and Nagasaki.

Sources of the Radioactive Material

There has been a lot of speculation about where terrorists could get radioactive material to use in a dirty bomb. The most harmful radioactive materials are found in nuclear power plants and nuclear weapons sites. However, increased security at these facilities makes obtaining materials from them more difficult.

Because of the dangerous and difficult aspects of obtaining high-level radioactive materials from a nuclear facility, there is a greater chance that the radioactive materials used in a dirty bomb would come from low-level radioactive sources. Low-level radioactive sources are found in hospitals, on construction sites, and at food irradiation plants. The sources in these areas are used to diagnose and treat illnesses, sterilize equipment, inspect welding seams, and irradiate food to kill harmful microbes.

Dangers of a Dirty Bomb

If low-level radioactive sources were to be used, the primary danger from a dirty bomb would be the blast itself. Gauging how much radiation might be present is difficult when the source of the radiation is unknown. However, at the levels created by most probable sources, not enough radiation would be present in a dirty bomb to cause severe illness from exposure to radiation.

Past Use of Dirty Bombs

According to a United Nations report, Iraq tested a dirty bomb device in 1987 but found that the radiation levels were too low to cause significant damage. Thus, Iraq abandoned any further use of the device.

What People Should Do After an Explosion

Radiation cannot be seen, smelled, felt, or tasted by humans. Therefore, if people are present at the scene of an explosion, they will not know whether radioactive materials were involved at the time of the explosion. If people are not too severely injured by the initial blast, they should attempt the following:

- Leave the immediate area on foot. Do not panic. Do not take public or private transportation such as buses, subways, or cars because if radioactive materials were involved, they may contaminate cars or the public transportation system.
- Go inside the nearest building. Staying inside will reduce your exposure to any radioactive material that may be on dust at the scene.
- Remove your clothes as soon as possible, place them in a plastic bag, and seal it. Removing clothing will remove most of the contamination caused by external exposure to radioactive materials. Saving the contaminated clothing would allow testing for exposure without invasive sampling.
- Take a shower or wash yourself as best you can. Washing will reduce the amount of radioactive contamination on your body and will effectively reduce total exposure.
- Be on the lookout for information. Once emergency personnel can assess the scene and the damage, they will be able to tell people whether radiation was involved.

Even if people do not know whether radioactive materials were present, following these simple steps can help reduce injury from other chemicals that might have been present in the blast.

If Radioactive Materials Were Involved

Keep televisions or radios tuned to local news networks. If a radioactive material is released, people will be told where to report for radiation monitoring and blood tests to determine whether they were exposed to the radiation as well as what steps to take to protect their health.

Risk of Cancer from a Dirty Bomb

Some cancers can be caused by exposure to radiation. Being at the site where a dirty bomb exploded does not guarantee that people were exposed to the radioactive material. Until doctors are able to check people's skin with sensitive radiation detection devices, it will not be clear whether they were exposed. Just because people are near a radioactive source for a short time or get a small amount of radioactive material on them does not mean that they will get cancer. Doctors will be able to assess risks after the exposure level has been determined.

Source: Centers for Disease Control and Prevention, www.cdc.gov.

Explosives can also be used to deliver chemical or biological weapons in a similar manner. This presents a dangerous scenario in that the trauma resulting from the explosion will demand immediate attention from responders, who may enter a contaminated attack scene without first recognizing or taking the time to check if a biological or chemical agent is present. Victims who are rushed to hospitals can cause secondary infections or injuries to EMS and hospital staff. Additionally, contaminated debris can help to spread certain viruses that may not otherwise have so easily entered the body. There have even been cases of HIV-positive suicide bombers passing their infection to victims struck with bits of shrapnel and bone.

When multiple chemicals, biological agents, or a combination of the two are used in an attack, the consequences can confound even those considered experts. The combination of symptoms resulting from multiple injuries or infections will make diagnosis extremely difficult, because these diagnoses often depend on a defined set of effects. The multiple agents will cause physiological effects in humans, animals, or plants that do not fit any established models. The extra time required for identification of the agents used will undoubtedly cause an overall increase in the efficacy of the terrorist attack.

Other Armed Attacks Using Firearms or Other Tactics

In addition to the CBRNE weapons described above, terrorists may employ tactical methods to instill terror and cause death and destruction. In fact, of the 14,352 attacks that took place in 2006, only 33% of those involved the use of bombs, incendiary devices, or suicide bomb attacks (NCTC, 2007). The remaining 67% of attacks involved armed assault. Table 4–2 illustrates how the 2006 attacks were distributed by both method of attack and resulting deaths.

Terrorists generally use the weapons that best meet their budget, expertise, target, and the resources they have accessible. Based on these statistics, it is clear that terrorists favor weapons

Table 4–2   Worldwide Incidents of Terrorism in 2006 by Attack Type and Number of Fatalities

Method of Terrorist Attack	Percent of Total Attacks in 2006 (14,352 total attacks)	Percent of Total Fatalities in 2006 (20,753 fatalities)
Bomb, incendiary devices, or suicide bomb attack	33	44
Armed attack using firearms, knives, and other nonexplosive weapons	49	46
Kidnapping	11	4
Assault	3	2
Other	4	4

Source: National Counterterrorism Center. Report on Terrorist Incidents. Washington, DC, April 30, 2007.

Table 4–3 Selected Terrorism Hazards

Threat	Application Mode	Duration	Extent of Effects; Static/Dynamic	Mitigating and Exacerbating Conditions
Armed attack — Ballistics (small arms) — Stand-off weapons (rocket-propelled grenades, mortars)	Tactical assault or sniper attacks from a remote location.	Generally minutes to days.	Varies, based on the perpetrator's intent and capabilities.	Inadequate security can allow easy access to target, easy concealment of weapons, and undetected initiation of an attack.
Cyber attacks	Electronic attack using one computer system against another.	Minutes to days.	Generally no direct effects on built environment.	Inadequate security can facilitate access to critical computer systems, allowing them to be used to conduct attacks.
High-altitude electromagnetic pulse (HEMP)	An electromagnetic energy field produced in the atmosphere by the power and radiation of a nuclear explosion. It can overload computer circuitry with effects similar to, but causing damage much more swiftly than a lightning strike.	It can be induced hundreds to a few thousand kilometers from the detonation.	Affects electronic systems. There is no effect on people. It diminishes with distance, and electronic equipment that is turned off is less likely to be damaged.	To produce maximum effect, a nuclear device must explode very high in the atmosphere. Electronic equipment may be hardened by surrounding it with protective metallic shielding that routes damaging electromagnetic fields away from highly sensitive electrical components.
High-power microwave (HPM) EMP	A non-nuclear radio-frequency energy field. Radio frequency weapons can be hidden in an attaché case, suitcase, van, or aircraft. Energy can be focused using an antenna, or emitter, to produce effects similar to HEMP, but only within a very limited range.	An HPM weapon has a shorter possible range than HEMP, but it can induce currents large enough to melt circuitry, or it can cause equipment to fail minutes, days, or even weeks later. HPM weapons are smaller-scale, are delivered closer to the intended target, and can sometimes be emitted for a longer duration.	Vulnerable systems include electronic ignition systems, radars, communications, data processing, navigation, and electronic triggers of explosive devices. HPM capabilities can cause a painful burning sensation or other injury to a person directly in the path of the focused power beam, or can be fatal if a person is too close to the microwave emitter.	Very damaging to electronics within a small geographic area. A shockwave could disrupt many computers within a 1-mile range. Radio frequency weapons have ranges from tens of meters to tens of kilometers. Unlike HEMP, however, HPM radiation is composed of shorter wave forms at higher frequencies, which make it highly effective against electronic equipment and more difficult to harden against.

Source: FEMA 452: Risk Assessment: A How-To Guide to Mitigate Potential Terrorist Attacks. http://www.fema.gov/library/file;jsessionid=915FD2C15FC952A846936EC2686E7DBF?type=publishedFile&file=fema452_step1.pdf&fileid=3e18f9b0-0247-11dc-a1f1-000bdba87d5b.

other than CBRNE weapons, and of the CBRNE weapons that are used, the overwhelming majority are explosive or incendiary in nature. Judging by the number of fatalities caused by these explosive attacks, they are much more effective at causing the fatalities sought by the perpetrators. However, it is undeniable that terrorist attacks using more simple methods of attack can be devastatingly effective, together causing over 50% of all fatalities worldwide in 2006 (as well as in 2005). FEMA describes several of these other terrorism hazards in their guide "FEMA 452: Risk Assessment: A How-To Guide to Mitigate Potential Terrorist Attacks," displayed in Table 4–3.

▨ ▨ Critical Thinking ▨

What is the difference between a terrorist attack and an act of war? Do you think that the terrorist attacks that occur in Iraq are terrorism? Why or why not? Will it ever be possible to eradicate terrorism entirely? Why or why not?

Role of CDC in Preparedness and Response

The Centers for Disease Control Prevention is a full partner in the nation's emergency management system. With the advent of the new hazards, the CDC has assumed a significant role in defining the characteristics of these hazards and how they may be used as terrorist weapons. This information is critical in preparing first responders, community leaders, businesspeople, and individuals to deal with these hazards. These data are also useful in the design and development of protective gear and clothing, mitigation and prevention measures, and response and cleanup protocols and practices.

The CDC, and Department of Health and Human Services within which the agency is housed, helps the nation to prepare for and respond to terrorist attacks using CBRNE weapons in a number of ways. First, the CDC provides information and training to local offices of public health, physicians, clinics, and hospitals, who are likely to be the first to encounter the victims of these weapons if an attack were to take place. Second, the CDC conducts and supports research on the detection, prevention, and treatment of CBRNE weapons. Third, the CDC helps local agencies of public health to detect when a chemical, biological, or radiological attack has occurred, and to contain the spread of a biological attack when the agent in question is transmissible. It has often been said that the CDC, the state public health departments, and the local public health practitioners working throughout the country are likely to be the first responders in the event of a terrorist using a chemical, biological, or radiological weapon, and the action that has been required thus far to prepare for such an event only supports this statement. Their primary difficulty comes in the need to train and equip a cadre of tens of thousands of local responders and physicians with the knowledge and tools required to manage a threat they have no experience with, and to ensure they remain motivated to maintain a high level of preparedness despite that they will likely never see such an attack during the course of their careers. And finally, the CDC helps to educate the general public about actions they can take in advance of and following a terrorist attack involving CBRNE weapons.

The CDC has developed two fact sheets on preparedness and response and the CDC's responsibilities in the event of a radiological event that are presented in the sidebars titled "Preparedness and Response" and "The CDC's Roles in the Event of a Radiological Terrorist Event," respectively.

▨ ▨ ▨ ━━━

Preparedness and Response

What Should I Do to Be Prepared?

We continue to hear stories of the public buying gas masks and hoarding medicine in anticipation of a possible bioterrorism or chemical attack. We do not recommend either. As Secretary

Thompson said recently, people should not be scared into thinking they need a gas mask. In the event of a public health emergency, local and state health departments will inform the public about the actions individuals need to take.

Does Every City Have an Adequate Emergency Response System, Especially One Geared for a Bioterrorist Attack? How Quickly Can It Be Implemented?

The emergency response system varies from community to community on the basis of each community's investment in its public health infrastructure. Some components of these emergency systems can be implemented very quickly, while others may take longer.

Are Hospitals Prepared to Handle a Sudden Surge in Demand for Health Care?

The preparedness level in hospitals depends on the biological agent used in an attack. Because a sudden surge in demand could overwhelm an individual hospital's resources, hospitals collaborate with other hospitals in their area in order to respond to a bioterrorist attack on a citywide or regional basis. Hospitals are required to maintain disaster response plans and to practice applying them as part of their accreditation process. Many components of such plans are useful in responding to bioterrorism. Specific plans for bioterrorism have been added to the latest accreditation requirements of the Joint Commission on Accreditation of Healthcare Organizations. In an emergency, local medical care capacity will be supplemented with federal resources.

Are Health Department Labs Equipped/Capable of Doing Testing?

The CDC, the Association of Public Health Laboratories, and other officials are working together to ensure that all state health departments are capable of obtaining results of tests on suspected infectious agents. The nation's laboratories are generally classified as Level A, B, C, or D.

- Level A laboratories are those typically found in community hospitals and are designated to perform initial testing on all clinical specimens.
- Level B laboratories can confirm or refute preliminary test results and can usually perform antimicrobial susceptibility tests.
- Level C laboratories, which are reference facilities and can be public health laboratories, perform more rapid identification tests.
- Level D laboratories are designed to perform the most sophisticated tests and are located in federal facilities such as the CDC.

The CDC is currently working with public and private laboratory partners to develop a formal National Laboratory System linking all four levels.

Every state has a Laboratory Response Network (LRN) contact. The LRN links state and local public health laboratories with advanced-capacity laboratories, including clinical, military, veterinary, agricultural, water, and food-testing laboratories. Laboratory workers should contact their state public health laboratory to identify their local LRN representative.

With All This Talk about Possible Biochemical Agents, Just How Safe Is Our Water? Should I Be Disinfecting My Water Just in Case?

The U.S. public water supply system is one of the safest in the world. The general public should continue to drink and use water just as they would under normal conditions. Your local water treatment supplier and local governments are on the alert for any unusual activity and will notify you immediately in the event of any public health threat. At this point, we have no reason to believe that additional measures need to be taken.

The U.S. Environmental Protection Agency (EPA) is the lead federal agency that makes recommendations about water utility issues. The EPA is working closely with the CDC and the U.S. Departments of Defense and Energy to help water agencies assess their systems, determine actions that need to be taken to guard against possible attack, and develop emergency response plans. For more information, visit http://www.epa.gov/safewater.

Source: Centers for Disease Control and Prevention, www.cdc.gov.

The CDC's Roles in the Event of a Radiological Terrorist Event

Because of recent terrorist events, people may be concerned about the possibility of a terrorist attack involving radioactive materials. People may wonder what the Centers for Disease Control and Prevention (CDC) would do to protect people's health if such an event were to occur. CDC has prepared this fact sheet to help people understand the roles and responsibilities of CDC during such an incident.

Lead Federal Agencies

In the event of a radiological accident or terrorist attack, the agency that is responsible for the site of the incident also has responsibility for responding to the emergency and protecting the people, property, and environment around the area. For example, if the incident occurs on property owned by the federal government, such as a military base, research facility, or nuclear facility, then the federal government takes responsibility. In areas that are not controlled by the federal government, the state and local governments have the responsibility to respond to the emergency and protect people, property, and the environment (see figure).

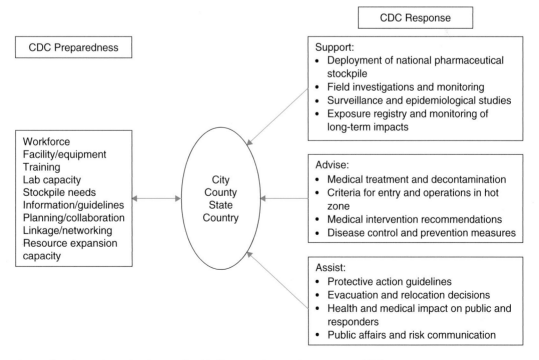

Centers for Disease Control and Prevention (CDC) preparedness and response capabilities.

Regardless of whether the state, local, or federal government is responsible for responding to the emergency, a federal agency would be sent to the terrorist incident site and would act as the lead federal agency (LFA). This agency would work with the state and local government and might be the Nuclear Regulatory Commission (NRC), the Federal Bureau of Investigation (FBI), or another agency, depending on what type of incident occurred (accidental or intentional release of radioactive materials) and where it occurred (nuclear power plant versus a spilled radioactive material in an urban or suburban area). The LFA would implement the Federal Radiological Emergency Response Plan (FRERP); within this plan, the Department of Health and Human Services (HHS) has the major role in protecting people's health through the following measures:

- Monitoring, assessing, and following up on people's health
- Ensuring the safety of workers involved in and responding to the incident
- Ensuring that the food supply is safe
- Providing medical and public health advice

The CDC's Roles

As part of HHS, CDC would be the chief public health entity to respond to a radiological incident, whether accidental or intentional. As the chief public health entity, CDC's specific roles and responsibilities would include the following:

- Assessing the health of people affected by the incident
- Assessing the medical effects of radiological exposures on people in the community, emergency responders and other workers, and high-risk populations (such as children, pregnant women, and those with immune deficiencies)
- Advising state and local health departments on how to protect people, animals, and food and water supplies from contamination by radioactive materials
- Providing technical assistance and consultation to state and local health departments on medical treatment, follow-up, and decontamination of victims exposed to radioactive materials
- Establishing and maintaining a registry of people exposed to or contaminated by radioactive materials

CDC's Partners

To carry out its roles, CDC would work with many other agencies to ensure that people's health is protected. These agencies may include the following:

- State and local health departments
- Department of Defense (DOD)
- Department of Energy (DOE)
- Department of Transportation (DOT)
- HHS
- Food and Drug Administration (FDA)
- Agency for Toxic Substances and Disease Registry (ATSDR)
- Office of Emergency Response (OER)
- Health Resources and Services Administration (HRSA)
- Substance Abuse and Mental Health Services Administration (SAMHSA)
- Environmental Protection Agency (EPA)

- FBI
- Federal Emergency Management Agency (FEMA)
- NRC
- Department of Agriculture (USDA)

CDC's Actions

In the hours and days following a radiological incident, CDC would assist and advise the LFA and the state and local health departments on recommendations that the community would need to accomplish the following:

- Protect people from radioactive fallout
- Protect people from radioactive contamination in the area
- Safely use food and water supplies from the area
- Assess and explain the dangers in the area of the incident

If necessary, CDC would also deploy the National Pharmaceutical Stockpile, a federal store of drugs and medical supplies set aside for emergency situations. In addition, CDC would give workers in the area information on the following:

- The amount of time they can safely work in an area contaminated with radioactive materials
- Equipment needed to protect themselves from radiation and radioactive materials
- Types of respiratory devices needed to work in the contaminated area
- How to use radiation-monitoring devices

Radiation Exposure Registry

After an incident involving radioactive materials, CDC would work with ATSDR to establish an exposure registry. The purpose of this registry would be to monitor people's exposure to radiation and perform dose reconstructions to determine the exact amount of radiation to which people were exposed. This registry would help CDC determine the necessary long-term medical follow-up for those who were affected by the incident.

Source: Centers for Disease Control and Prevention, www.cdc.gov.

Cyberterrorism

Cyberterrorism is the newest of all terrorist attack methods, and is defined as the use or destruction of computing or information technology resources aimed at harming, coercing, or intimidating others in order to achieve a greater political or ideological goal (thus differentiating cyberterrorism from cybercrime, which seeks only personal gain or notoriety). Cyberterrorism is a hazard that has only just recently become a major threat, but one which continues to increase in severity with each passing year as our nation's and the world's reliance on information technology, computers, and the Internet grows. This reliance has come to exist in virtually all sectors of society, beginning with our economic engines, spanning through almost every component of our critical and other infrastructure systems (including communication systems, power generation facilities, water treatment plants, dams, transportation, and many other areas), and even including the nation's military command and control mechanisms and facilities. While much action has already been taken to protect these systems from attack, either foreign or domestic, the reliance on technology of all of these systems that only increases from year to year greatly increases the potential consequences were these systems to be compromised, disrupted, or destroyed. Additionally, criminals and terrorists are constantly developing new and innovative ways to compromise the ever-more complex systems on which we rely.

Cybersecurity and cyberterrorism have been concerns of the private sector and government agencies including the military and the FBI since the 1980s. Following the September 11 terrorist attacks, cybersecurity as a terrorist risk was pushed closer into the limelight, and was referred to directly in the National Strategy for Homeland Security as a national concern, and again as a central component of the subsequent National Strategy to Secure Cyberspace. Additionally, it was addressed through the executive office by means of the issuance of Homeland Security Presidential Directive (HSPD) 7: Critical Infrastructure Identification, Prioritization, and Protection. Through these actions and plans, the Department of Homeland Security was tasked with managing the nation's cyberterrorism threat through its risk management division, the Directorate for National Protection and Programs. Within this broad overarching agency component, which includes the infrastructure protection program, the US-VISIT immigration program, and other offices, is the Office of Cybersecurity and Communications (CS&C). This office, described in Chapters 3 and 4, develops and maintains the systems by which the government is able to ensure the security and reliability of both the cyber and communications infrastructure, including that existing in both the public and private sectors (where most infrastructure is maintained). And within this office, cybersecurity in particular is managed by the National Cybersecurity Division (NCSD). The NCSD works to achieve two primary objectives, namely:

- Build and maintain an effective national cybersecurity response system.
- Implement a cyber-risk management program for protection of critical infrastructure.

The mission of the NCSD is a difficult one: "Protect the critical cyber infrastructure 24 hours a day, 7 days a week" (NCSD, 2008). The National Cyberspace Response System has been developed to coordinate the leadership, processes, and protocols that will ultimately determine what action(s) need to be taken and when as cyber incidents arise. Examples of current cyber preparedness and response programs include:

- Cybersecurity Preparedness and the National Cyber Alert System — This system allows both technical and non-technical computer users to stay informed of, and likewise prepared for the constantly changing cyber threats by signing up for the National Cyber Alert System. Under this system, they will receive security alerts and tips generated and disseminated by US-CERT (see below).

- US-CERT — US-CERT, the United States Computer Emergency Readiness Team, is responsible for analyzing and reducing cyber threats and vulnerabilities, disseminating cyber threat warning information, and coordinating incident response activities. US-CERT was formed through the partnership of DHS and public- and private-sector components in 2003. The primary function of US-CERT is to protect the internet infrastructure, but it also provides a forum for private citizens, businesses, and other institutions to communicate and coordinate directly with the United States government about cybersecurity.

- National Cyber Response Coordination Group — Made up of 13 federal agencies, this is the principal federal agency mechanism for cyber incident response. In the event of a significant cyber-related incident affecting the security of the nation, the NCRCG will help to coordinate the federal response, including US-CERT, law enforcement, and the intelligence community.

- Cyber Cop Portal — Coordination with law enforcement helps capture and convict those responsible for cyber attacks. The Cyber Cop Portal is an information sharing and collaboration tool accessed by over 5,300 investigators worldwide who are involved in electronic crimes cases.

- National Outreach Awareness Month — Every October the National Cybersecurity Division coordinates with multiple states, universities, and the private sector to produce National Cybersecurity Awareness month.

- Software Assurance Program — This program seeks to reduce software vulnerabilities, minimize exploitation, and address ways to improve the routine development and deployment of software products. These activities help to ensure that the software supporting critical infrastructure systems and operations are both secure and reliable.

In February 2006, DHS planned and conducted a national-level cyberterrorism exercise called "Cyber Storm." This exercise was held in order to assess the nation's preparedness capacity and response capabilities in regard to cyber incidents that have countrywide significance. Cyber Storm was the Department of Homeland Security's first cyber exercise to test response across the private sector as well as international, federal, and state governments. See the sidebar titled "Cyber Storm Exercise" for more information.

Cyber Storm Exercise

DHS's National Cybersecurity Division (NCSD) executed Cyber Storm, the first such government-led, full-scale national cybersecurity exercise of its kind, from February 6 through February 10, 2006.

Exercise Goals and Objectives

Cyber Storm was designed to test communications, policies, and procedures in response to various cyber attacks and to identify where further planning and process improvements are needed. Activities included:

- Exercising interagency coordination through the activation of the National Cyber Response Coordination Group (NCRCG) and the Interagency Incident Management Group (IIMG)
- Exercising intergovernmental and intragovernmental coordination and incident response
- Identifying policies and issues that either hinder or support cybersecurity requirements
- Identifying public and private information sharing mechanisms to address communications challenges
- Identifying the interdependence of cyber and physical infrastructures
- Raising awareness of the economic and national security impacts associated with a significant cyber incident
- Highlighting available tools and technologies for cyber incident response and recovery

Participants

More than 110 public, private, and international agencies, organizations, and companies were involved in the planning and implementation of Cyber Storm. Participants included federal and state agencies and private sector partners from the information technology (IT), telecommunications, energy, and transportation industries, as well as foreign governments. Participants also provided their own support staff to help plan and control the exercise, and to ensure that their organizations' objectives were met.

The Scenario

The exercise simulated a sophisticated cyber-attack campaign through a series of scenarios directed at several critical infrastructure sectors. The intent of these scenarios was to highlight the interconnectedness of cyber systems with physical infrastructure and to exercise coordination and communication between the public and private sectors. Each scenario was developed with the assistance of industry experts and was executed in a closed and secure environment. Cyber Storm scenarios had three major adversarial objectives:

- To disrupt specifically targeted critical infrastructure through cyber attacks
- To hinder the governments' ability to respond to the cyber attacks
- To undermine public confidence in the governments' ability to provide and protect services

The exercise was a simulated event with no real-world effects on, tampering with, or damage to any critical infrastructure. While the scenarios were based on hypothetical situations, they were not intended as a forecast of future terrorist-related events.

On September 13, 2006, DHS released their report assessing the exercise. The report listed eight principal lessons learned, including:

- Interagency coordination: Interagency and cross-sector information sharing enhanced overall coordination, communication, and response.
- Contingency planning, risk assessment and roles and responsibilities: Clearly defined processes and procedures increased overall ability to plan for and assess situations.
- Correlation of multiple incidents between public and private sectors: The cyber community was effective in addressing individual threats and attacks, but faced challenges in cross-sector situational awareness during a coordinated cyber-attack campaign.
- Exercise program: Ongoing exercises will strengthen awareness of cyber incident response, roles, policies, and procedures.
- Coordination between entities of cyber incidents: Establishing expectations, roles, processes and communications in advance will dramatically improve coordination and response.
- Common framework for response to information access: Early and ongoing information sharing across governments and sectors created a common framework for response and strengthened relationships between domestic and international response partners.
- Strategic communications and public relations: Public messaging is an important aspect of incident response and empowers individuals and industry to take appropriate action to protect themselves and the nation's critical infrastructure.
- Improvement of process, tools and technology: Improved processes, tools, and technology focused on the physical, economic and national security effects of a cyber incident will benefit the quality, speed, and coordination of a response.

Source: DHS, 2008.

Conclusion

Terrorism has presented the United States with a range of new hazards — many of which are just now emerging, and many others that have existed elsewhere in the world for centuries but are now legitimate threats to the nation. These hazards have required a significant investment in education of the general public, local officials, the media, and our first responders. This requirement is surpassed in cost by the need to invest in training, protective equipment and gear, specialized technical capabilities, and enhancements of our public health networks. The threat of terrorism in the United States has presented a unique opportunity to integrate many groups responsible for mitigating, preparing, responding to, and recovering from less traditional consequences of disasters, such as the public health service, that will likely assist not only with terrorist hazards but also in just about any devastating disaster event that might occur. It has given us the opportunity to include many of these public health concerns into general disaster planning efforts, and has increased cooperation with the private sector in emergency management systems and efforts (often because privately owned and maintained financial and communications infrastructures are primary terrorist targets). The research and development efforts associated with these new hazards, described in greater detail in Chapter 9, have already begun to result in advances spanning a broad spectrum of human activities from medicine to communications technology, and have led to the development of safer personal protective equipment (PPE), vaccines, and other defenses for the first responders that must manage attack consequences. Most importantly, these new hazards, and the financial resources connected with addressing them, can provide an opportunity to actually embrace and apply an all-hazards approach to achieving a homeland that is more secure from the threat of weapons of mass destruction, technological hazards, and natural hazards alike.

Key Terms

Aerosol Device: A tool, device, or machine that converts liquid or solid matter into a gas or otherwise airborne suspension.

Biological Weapon: A warfare or terrorist device capable of projecting, dispersing, or disseminating a biological warfare agent (bacteria, virus, or toxin).

Blister Agent: Also known as a vesicant, a blister agent is any chemical compound that, upon contact with exposed skin, eyes, or other tissue, causes severe pain and irritation.

Blood Agent: Any chemical compound that is inhaled, ingested, or absorbed, which prevents otherwise normal blood cells from carrying oxygen.

Category A Biological Weapon: Organisms that can be easily disseminated or transmitted from person to person; result in high mortality rates and have the potential for major public health impact; might cause public panic and social disruption; and require special action for public health preparedness.

Category B Biological Weapon: Second-highest-priority agents, including those that are moderately easy to disseminate; result in moderate morbidity rates and low mortality rates; and require specific enhancements of diagnostic capacity and enhanced disease surveillance.

Category C Biological Weapon: Third-highest-priority agents, including emerging pathogens that could be engineered for mass dissemination in the future because of availability; ease of production and dissemination; and potential for high morbidity and mortality rates and major health impact.

CBRNE: Weapons that are chemical, biological, radiological/nuclear, or explosive in nature, often referred to as "weapons of mass destruction" (WMDs).

Chemical Weapon: A warfare or terrorist device capable of projecting, dispersing, or disseminating a chemical warfare agent.

Choking/Pulmonary Agent: A chemical weapon affecting the lungs, designed to impede a victim's ability to breathe (ultimately resulting in their suffocation).

Containment: The prevention of spread of biological, chemical, or radiological materials.

Cyberterrorism: The use or destruction of computing or information technology resources aimed at harming, coercing, or intimidating others in order to achieve a greater political or ideological goal.

Detection: Recognition of the existence of a WMD agent, or the consequences of such an attack. Detection is often achieved through various public health service working together to recognize trends in disease symptoms and geographical coverage.

Explosive Weapon (Conventional Explosives): A device relying on the expansion of gases and/or the propelling of bits of metal, glass, and other materials, to achieve bodily harm, death, and destruction.

High-Filler Explosive: An explosive that combusts nearly instantaneously, thereby producing a violent, shattering effect. High-filler explosives, which are most often used by the military in shells and bombs, may be detonated by a spark, flame, or by impact, or may require the use of a detonator. Examples include TNT, RDX, and HBX.

Incapacitating Agent: A chemical warfare agent that produces a temporary disabling condition (physiological or psychological) that persists. Oftentimes, incapacitating agents result in death to those exposed due to unexpected physical reactions.

Incendiary Weapon: A weapon that disperses a chemical weapon that causes fire. Napalm bombs, used extensively in the Vietnam War to reduce forest coverage, are one example.

Irritant: A noncorrosive chemical that causes a reversible inflammatory effect on living tissue at the site of contact (skin, eyes, or respiratory tract).

Low-Filler Explosives: Also called "low explosives," a low-filler explosive is a mixture of a combustible substance and an oxidant that decomposes rapidly once ignited. Under normal conditions, low explosives undergo combustion rates that vary from a few centimeters per second to approximately 400 meters per second. It is possible, however, for low-filler explosives to combust so quickly as to produce an effect similar to detonation (see high-filler explosive) as often occurs when ignited in a confined space. Gun powder and pyrotechnics (including flares and fireworks) are generally low explosives.

Nerve Agent: A chemical weapon that is absorbed through the skin, eyes, or lungs, that disrupts the body's nervous system.

Nuclear Weapon: A weapon whose destructive force is derived from the energy produced and released during a fission or fusion reaction.

Persistent Chemical: A chemical agent or weapon that maintains its toxic properties for an extended period of time following release into the atmosphere (several hours or days).

Quarantine: The imposed isolation placed upon people, animals, or objects that are confirmed or suspected of being contaminated or infected with a chemical or biological agent, for the purpose of limiting the spread of exposure.

Radiological Dispersion Device: A bomb or other weapon used to spread radiological waste across a wide area for the purpose of causing contamination and bodily harm (often called a "dirty bomb").

Radiological Weapon: See Radiological dispersion device.

Satchel Charge: A powerful yet portable explosive device traditionally used by infantry forces, but which has become a terrorist weapon of choice in that they blend easily for effective concealment in public places.

Synergistic Effect: Simultaneous action of separate things that have a greater total effect than the sum of their individual effects.

Vaccination: The process of administering weakened or dead pathogens to a healthy person or animal, with the intent of conferring immunity against a targeted form of a related disease agent.

Review Questions

1. Discuss the two major differences between traditional hazards (i.e., hurricanes, floods, tornadoes, earthquakes, hazardous materials incidents) and the new hazards associated with terrorism.

2. What are five major categories of hazards associated with terrorism?

3. Discuss the appropriate responses to the new hazards associated with terrorism. For each hazard, when is it appropriate to shelter in place, evacuate, and/or quarantine?

4. Understanding the new hazards associated with terrorism will be critical to reducing the fear among the public of these hazards. This was done very successfully in the past in understanding and dispelling the fear surrounding traditional hazards. How would you design and implement a public education campaign concerning the new hazards? What information would you present and how?

5. If you were a member of Congress, what role would you foresee for the federal government in researching these new hazards, identifying appropriate response and preparedness measures, and educating the public? What role would you have if you were a governor? What role would you have if you were a mayor or county executive?

Reference

Federal Emergency Management Agency (FEMA). 2002. "Managing the Emergency Consequences of Terrorist Incidents—Interim Planning Guide for State and Local Governments." Washington, DC: FEMA.

5

Safety and Security

What You Will Learn

- Components of safety and security within the broader concept of homeland security
- Safety and security programs, funding, and initiatives
- Elements of intelligence community and restructuring of statutory authority based on recommendations of the 9/11 Commission
- Detailed overview of essential intelligence agencies such as the CIA, NSA, NRO, and NGA
- New coordination body of national intelligence: Office of the Director of National Intelligence
- Functional and budgetary overview of essential Homeland Security agencies
- Transportation security and Transportation Security Agency
- Critical infrastructure protection and security
- Homeland Security initiatives for public works
- Involvement of the private sector in homeland security
- Information Sharing and Analysis Centers (ISAC's)
- Crisis management and business continuity as essential elements of corporate disaster preparedness
- Best practices and success stories
- Opinions of emergency management practitioners

Introduction

The September 11 attack precipitated many changes in the American way of life, as well as in the political structure and organization of the U.S. government. Securing the safety of the American people inside the borders of their homeland became a critical priority. On September 20, 2001, only 9 days after the attacks, President George W. Bush began what would become a major governmental transformation when he announced the establishment of the Office of Homeland Security within the White House, and appointed Tom Ridge, then governor of Pennsylvania, as his homeland security chief. Some months later, after originally rejecting the idea, President Bush proposed the creation of a cabinet-level Department of Homeland Security whose primary purpose would be to unify those agencies responsible for homeland security missions and achieve greater accountability in the execution of those missions. On November 19, 2002, the U.S. Senate voted overwhelmingly to create a Department of Homeland Security (DHS), spurring the most extensive reorganization of the federal government since the 1940s. This chapter will focus on the key components of safety and security in the context of homeland security that already existed and that have arisen as a result of these changes. We will also identify many of the important stakeholders in charge of these components.

The next section will discuss how safety and security are maintained in the United States through an examination of the many agencies that make up the U.S. intelligence community under the umbrella of the newly created (2005) Office of the Director of National Intelligence, and the agencies and programs that serve to control the nation's borders, transportation systems, commerce, information systems, and infrastructure.

The Intelligence Community

Within the U.S. government, the intelligence community has developed such that its many components (agencies and offices) are spread out across the vast range of civilian and military departments (Figure 5–1). Like most national governments, the government of the United States has always performed some form of intelligence gathering and analysis activities. However, the extensive intelligence community as we know it today is largely the result of expansion during the Cold War era. The cadre of federal employees that form the intelligence function of government grew by the mid-1980s to include more than 100,000 people, who are disbursed throughout 25 individual organizations and specialize in the collection and analysis of information. More than $30 billion of the federal budget

Office of the Director of National Intelligence

Central Intelligence Agency   Defense Intelligence Agency   National Security Agency   National Reconnaissance Office

National Geospatial-Intelligence Agency   Air Force Intelligence   Army Intelligence   Navy Intelligence

Marine Corps Intelligence   Department of Homeland Security   Federal Bureau of Investigation   Department of State

U.S. Coast Guard (DHS)   Department of Energy Intelligence   Department of Treasury Intelligence   Drug Enforcement Administration (USDOJ)

FIGURE 5–1 Members of the intelligence community.

was dedicated to their collective activities. Considering the highly secretive and critical information needs of the government during this period of showdown between the world's great superpowers, such growth was not surprising.

After the Cold War ended, the number of agencies and employees was reduced by consolidation of activities and reduction of budgetary allocations. The military intelligence services saw the steepest cuts. Total reductions in the employee base were about 20%. Because intelligence capacity grew so large during the Cold War era, however, a vast intelligence capacity remains despite these cuts. Today, the government intelligence capacity involves a full range of activities and operations:

- Technical collection (TECHINT): The gathering of intelligence through the use of technical devices such as satellites, aircraft, and ship- and land-based antenna arrays
- Human source collection (HUMINT): The use of agents (recruited foreign nationals) and attaches, and interviews with individuals who have traveled to or reside in areas of interest. Various reports that looked at the U.S. intelligence community after the end of the Cold War underlined diminished human intelligence capabilities within various agencies. The 9/11 Commission identified lack of reliable human intelligence in the Mideast as one of the factors that prohibited the prevention of the September 11, 2001 terrorist attacks.
- Open-source collection: The collection of books, newspapers, and reports, recording of radio and television broadcasts, and the exploitation of computer databases
- Shared intelligence: Intelligence gathered through meetings conducted with foreign intelligence services and information exchanges
- Counterintelligence: The study and penetration of foreign intelligence and security services
- Covert action: Influence placed on foreign political events without the U.S. role being admitted
- Intelligence analysis, production, and dissemination: The evaluation of information, the display of that information in printed, electronic, or video form, and the transmission of that information to "customers"

These activities are performed primarily by four individual organizations within the federal government:

- Central Intelligence Agency (CIA)
- National Security Agency (NSA)
- National Reconnaissance Office (NRO)
- National Geospatial-Intelligence Agency (NGA)

Several other smaller agencies, which fall under the Department of Defense (DOD) or other civilian intelligence organizations, also perform these duties to a lesser degree (Richelson et al., 2003). The next sections provide a brief explanation of the background, duties, and organization of those agencies followed by an overview of the Office of the Director of National Intelligence, which is tasked by the president and the Intelligence Reform and Terrorism Prevention Act of 2004 to oversee the coordination of the national intelligence effort.

Central Intelligence Agency

The recognized intelligence needs of modern warfare that surfaced during World War II resulted in the creation of America's first central intelligence organization, the Office of Strategic Services (OSS). The OSS was created to perform a variety of functions, including traditional espionage, covert action (ranging from propaganda to sabotage), counterintelligence, and intelligence analysis. The OSS represented a revolution in U.S. intelligence, not only because of the varied functions performed by a single, national agency, but also because of the breadth of its intelligence interests and its use of scholars to produce finished intelligence.

In the aftermath of World War II, the OSS was disbanded, officially ceasing all operations on October 1, 1945 by executive order from President Truman. However, several of its branches were retained and were distributed among other governmental departments. For instance, the X-2 (Counterintelligence) and Secret Intelligence branches were transferred to the War Department to form the Strategic Services Unit, and the Research and Analysis Branch was transferred into the Department of State (Smith, 1983).

As Truman was ordering the termination of the OSS, he was also commissioning studies to determine the requirements of and changes to the U.S. intelligence structure in the post–World War II climate. Based on these studies, the National Intelligence Authority (NIA) and its operational element, the Central Intelligence Group (CIG), were created. The CIG was initially responsible for coordinating and synthesizing the reports produced by the military service intelligence agencies and the FBI, but it soon after assumed the task of secret intelligence collection.

National security needs and the intelligence reorganization were addressed by the National Security Act of 1947. The Central Intelligence Agency (CIA) was established as an independent agency within the executive office of the president to replace the CIG. According to the act, the CIA was to have five functions:

1. To advise the National Security Council in matters concerning such intelligence activities of the government departments and agencies related to national security
2. To make recommendations to the National Security Council for the coordination of such intelligence activities of the departments and agencies of the government as relate to national security
3. To correlate and evaluate the intelligence relating to national security, and to provide for the appropriate dissemination of such intelligence within the government using, where appropriate, existing agencies and facilities
4. To perform for the benefit of existing intelligence agencies such additional services of common concern as the National Security Council determines can be more effectively accomplished centrally
5. To perform other such functions and duties related to intelligence affecting the national security as the National Security Council may from time to time direct (U.S. Congress, 1983)

The organizational structure of the CIA as it exists today began to take shape in the early 1950s under Director Walter Bedell Smith. In 1952, the Office of Policy Coordination was transferred under CIA control and merged with the secret intelligence-gathering Office of Special Operations to form the Directorate of Plans. That same year, the offices involved in intelligence research and analysis were placed under a Directorate of Intelligence. A third unit, the Directorate of Administration, was established to perform administrative functions.

The principal functions of the Directorate of Plans were clandestine collection and covert action. A separate directorate was later formed to perform technical collection operations, but before that time the Directorate of Plans was heavily involved in the development and operation of overhead collection systems like the U-2 spy plane and CORONA reconnaissance satellite. In 1973, the Directorate of Plans became the Directorate of Operations. On October 13, 2005, the creation of the National Clandestine Service was announced by the Director of Central Intelligence and the Director of National Intelligence, which absorbed all functions of the Directorate of Operations (Figure 5–2). Today, its functions within the National Clandestine Service include clandestine collection, covert action, counternarcotics and counterterrorism activities, and counterintelligence. On the day of the establishment of this new function within the CIA, John Negroponte, the first Director of National Intelligence underlined that the National Clandestine Service will significantly improve the human intelligence (HUMINT) capability of the nation (Office of the Director of National Intelligence, 2005).

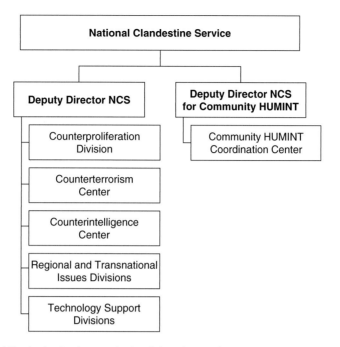

FIGURE 5–2 CIA, National Clandestine Service organizational chart. (Source: http://www.cia.gov)

A fourth directorate, the Directorate of Research, was established in 1962. This directorate consolidated into a single unit all agency components involved in technical collection activities. In 1963, it was renamed the Directorate of Science and Technology and assumed control of scientific intelligence analysis. Its present functions include the following:

- Developing technical collection systems
- Collecting intelligence from embassy sites (in cooperation with the National Security Agency)
- Recording foreign radio and television broadcasts (through its Foreign Broadcast Information Service)
- Developing and producing technical devices (such as bugging devices, hidden cameras, and weaponry) for agents and officers
- Providing research and development in support of intelligence collection and analysis

Until late 1996, the directorate also managed the National Photographic Interpretation Center (NPIC), which interpreted satellite and aerial reconnaissance imagery. NPIC was absorbed by the newly established National Imagery and Mapping Agency (Richelson et al., 2003).

Another vital directorate of the CIA is the Intelligence and Analysis Directorate (Figure 5–3). This directorate is primarily in charge of analyzing the intelligence data and information collected to make sense out of it for the development of more comprehensive intelligence products. The next section will briefly cover the specific duties of different offices within the Intelligence and Analysis Directorate.

Crime and Narcotics Center

The Crime and Narcotics Center (CNC) focuses on international narcotics trafficking and organized crime for policymakers and the law enforcement community. CNC's workforce is diverse, utilizing individuals with a variety of backgrounds, experience, and specialties. CNC strategic analysts research

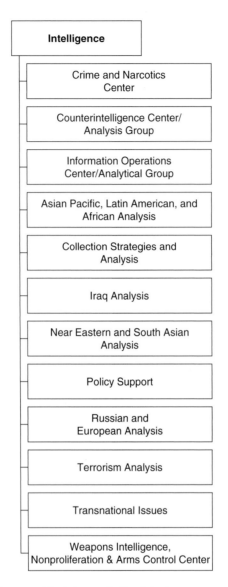

FIGURE 5–3 CIA, Directorate of Intelligence and Analysis organizational chart.

long-term trends and keep U.S. policymakers informed about new developments. They estimate the impact of the drug trade and of organized crime on U.S. national security, uncover trafficking trends and routes, and monitor relationships between organized crime groups, traffickers, and terrorists. Targeting analysts use technology to identify key people, organizations, trends, and components in criminal organizations. Operational support specialists and program managers provide fast-paced operational research, management, and support to colleagues overseas. They develop substantive expertise on organized crime and narcotics issues, and often travel to support operations or collect information. Analysts specializing in technologies such as remote sensing and geographic information systems capitalize on those tools to locate and estimate quantities of illegal crops in countries where those plants are known to be grown (Central Intelligence Agency, "The CIA Crime and Narcotics Center," 2008).

Counterintelligence Center/Analysis Group

The Counterintelligence Center/Analysis Group (CIC/AG) identifies, monitors, and analyzes the efforts of foreign intelligence entities against U.S. persons, activities, and interests. CIC/AG analysts focus on two specific types of counterintelligence threats to U.S. national security: transnational threats, such as the counterintelligence aspect of terrorism, or the threats posed by emerging or changing technologies to the U.S. government's intelligence operations and information systems. CIC/AG also tracks threats posed by foreign intelligence services and monitors their activities.

Information Operations Center/Analysis Group

The Information Operations Center/Analysis Group (IOC/AG) evaluates foreign threats to U.S. computer systems, particularly those that support critical infrastructures. The group provides its analysis to the president, his senior advisers, high-level officials on cyber issues in the Departments of Defense, State, and Treasury, and to senior private-sector officials responsible for operating critical infrastructures. IOC/AG analysts consider potential threats from state and nonstate actors and evaluate a wide array of information, including foreign intentions, plans, and capabilities.

Office of Asian Pacific, Latin American, and African Analysis

The Office of Asian Pacific, Latin American, and African Analysis (APLAA) studies the political, economic, leadership, societal, and military developments in Asia, Latin America, and Sub-Saharan Africa.

Office of Collection Strategies and Analysis

The Office of Collection Strategies and Analysis (CSAA) provides comprehensive intelligence collection expertise to the DCI, a wide range of senior agency and intelligence community officials, and key national policymakers. CSAA staff work with analysts in the CIA's National Clandestine Service and Directorate of Science and Technology, the DOD, the National Security Agency, the National Geospatial-Intelligence Agency, the National Reconnaissance Office, and other intelligence community agencies to craft new approaches to solving complex collection issues.

Office of Iraq Analysis

The Office of Iraq Analysis is the newest office within the Intelligence and Analysis Directorate. This office was created in November 2003 at a point in time when the collection and analysis of intelligence from Iraq became increasingly important in the aftermath of the war. Since its creation the analysis workforce of the Office has covered important events such as the captures of Saddam Hussein and many other top Iraqi officials, the rise of the Iraqi insurgency, the nation's first post-Saddam elections, and Iraqi economic development (Central Intelligence Agency, "History of the Intelligence and Analysis Directorate," 2008).

Office of Near Eastern and South Asian Analysis

The Office of Near Eastern and South Asian Analysis (NESA) provides policymakers with comprehensive analytic support on Middle Eastern and North African countries, as well as on the South Asian nations of India, Pakistan, and Afghanistan.

Office of Policy Support

The Office of Policy Support (OPS) customizes defense intelligence (DI) analysis and presents it to a wide variety of policy, law enforcement, military, and foreign liaison recipients.

Office of Russian and European Analysis

The Office of Russian and European Analysis (OREA) provides intelligence support on a large set of countries that have long been of crucial importance to the United States as allies or as adversaries and are likely to continue to occupy a key place in U.S. national security policy. OREA officers are a mix of generalists and specialists who concentrate on issues ranging from ethnic conflict in the Balkans to the U.S.–Russian relationship. Previous historical events covered by analysts include the Solidarity movement in Poland, the breakup of the former Soviet Union, the fall of the Berlin Wall, NATO expansion, and numerous wars in the Balkans. Some current focus areas are arms control negotiations and treaty-monitoring efforts, analysis of potential benefits and challenges of EU enlargement, and reporting on the political and economic landscape of Central Asia.

Office of Terrorism Analysis

The Office of Terrorism Analysis (OTA) is the analytic component of the DCI Counterterrorism Center. OTA analysts work to inform policymakers and support the intelligence, law enforcement, homeland security, and military communities by performing the following tasks:

- Tracking terrorists and the activities of states that sponsor them, and assessing terrorist vulnerabilities by analyzing their ideology and goals, capabilities, associates, and locations
- Analyzing worldwide terrorist threat information and patterns to provide warnings aimed at preventing terrorist attacks
- Monitoring worldwide terrorism trends and patterns, including emerging and nontraditional terrorist groups, evolving terrorist threats or operational methods, and possible collusion between terrorist groups
- Identifying, disrupting, and preventing international financial transactions that support terrorist networks and operations

Office of Transnational Issues

The Office of Transnational Issues (OTI) produces analytic assessments on critical intelligence-related issues that transcend regional and national boundaries. Drawing on a broad range of experts in engineering, science, and social science disciplines, OTI's analysis addresses energy and economic security, illicit financial activities, societal conflicts, humanitarian crises, and the long-term military and economic strategic environment.

Weapons Intelligence, Nonproliferation, and Arms Control Center

The Weapons Intelligence, Nonproliferation, and Arms Control Center (WINPAC) provides intelligence support aimed at protecting the United States and its interests from all foreign weapons threats. WINPAC officers are a diverse group with a variety of backgrounds and work experiences, and include mathematicians, engineers (nuclear, chemical/ biological, mechanical, and aerospace, among others), physicists, economists, political scientists, computer specialists, and physical scientists. On any given day, those analysts could be answering a question from the president, assessing information about a foreign missile test, or developing new computational models to determine blast effects. A key part of its mission includes studying the development of the entire spectrum of threats, from weapons of mass destruction (nuclear, radiological, chemical, and biological weapons) to advanced conventional weapons such as lasers, advanced explosives, and armor, as well as all types of missiles, including ballistic, cruise, and surface-to-air missiles. The center studies systems from their earliest development phase through production, deployment, and transfers to other countries, and monitors strategic arms control agreements. WINPAC also supports military and diplomatic operations.

The CIA is probably the most widely recognized of the various U.S. intelligence agencies, primarily because of its celebrated and cinematized involvement in covert action, and also because of the central role it plays in providing intelligence to the president. However, as noted earlier, there are several U.S. intelligence agencies, some of which rival the CIA in influence and exceed it in budget. The most important of these other agencies are the three "national" agencies: the National Security Agency, the National Reconnaissance Office, and the National Geospatial-Intelligence Agency. Each of these is described in detail next.

National Security Agency

On May 20, 1949, Secretary of Defense Louis Johnson established the Armed Forces Security Agency (AFSA) and placed it under the command of the Joint Chiefs of Staff. In theory, the AFSA was to direct the communications intelligence and electronic intelligence activities of the military service signals intelligence units (at the time, the Army Security Agency, Naval Security Group, and Air Force Security Service). In practice, however, the AFSA had little power, and its functions were characterized as activities not performed by the service units.

On October 24, 1952 — the same day that he sent a (now-declassified) top-secret eight-page memorandum entitled "Communications Intelligence Activities" to the Secretaries of State and Defense — President Truman abolished the AFSA and transferred its personnel to the newly created National Security Agency (NSA). As its name indicated, the new agency was to have national, not just military, responsibilities. In 1971, NSA became the National Security Agency/Central Security Service (NSA/CSS). The second half of NSA's title, which is rarely used, refers to its role in coordinating the signals intelligence activities of the military services (Richelson, 1999). Today the NSA has two primary responsibilities: information assurance and signals intelligence.

NSA's Information Assurance Directorate (IAD) is dedicated to providing information assurance solutions that serve to protect U.S. information systems from harm. This mission involves many activities, including the following:

- Detecting, reporting, and responding to cyber threats
- Making encryption codes to securely pass information between systems
- Embedding information assurance measures directly into the emerging global information grid
- Building secure audio and video communications equipment
- Making tamper-proof products
- Providing trusted microelectronics solutions
- Testing the security of its partners' and customers' systems
- Providing operational security assistance
- Evaluating commercial software and hardware against set standards

The NSA Signals Intelligence Directorate collects, processes, and disseminates foreign signals intelligence (SIGINT). It provides information in the form of SIGINT products and services that enables the U.S. government to make critical decisions. NSA's SIGINT mission provides military leaders and policymakers with intelligence to ensure national defense and to advance U.S. global interests. This information is specifically limited to that which focuses on foreign powers, organizations, or persons and international terrorists. NSA responds to requirements of its intelligence partners and customers, which include all departments and levels of the Executive Branch (NSA, 2005).

National Reconnaissance Office

The National Reconnaissance Office (NRO) was established on September 6, 1961, to coordinate CIA reconnaissance activities with those of the DOD. NRO's primary function has been to oversee the research and development, procurement, deployment, and operation of imaging, signals intelligence, and ocean surveillance satellites. It awards contracts, oversees the research and development efforts of contractors, supervises the launch of the payloads, and, in conjunction with the CIA and NSA, operates these spacecraft. It has also been involved in the research, development, and procurement of selected aerial reconnaissance systems, such as the SR-71. From its inception until September 18, 1992, when its existence was formally acknowledged, the NRO operated as a classified organization. A major restructuring of the NRO also began to be implemented in 1992, which turned the NRO into a functional organization instead of a stand-alone organization (Richelson et al., 2003).

In its current setting, the NRO designs, builds, and operates the nation's reconnaissance satellites. NRO products, provided to an expanding list of customers such as the CIA and the DOD, can warn of potential trouble spots around the world, help plan military operations, and monitor the environment. The NRO is a DOD agency and is staffed by DOD and CIA personnel. The NRO has historically been one of the most clandestine intelligence organizations in the United States, but many parts of its operations have now been declassified. For example, the location of its headquarters, in Chantilly, Virginia, was declassified in 1994. In February 1995, CORONA, a photoreconnaissance program in operation from 1960 to 1972, was declassified and 800,000 CORONA images were transferred to the National Archives and Records Administration.

National Geospatial-Intelligence Agency

By the mid-1990s, imagery was the basis for both imagery intelligence and map-based imagery products, and the intelligence community wished to centralize the management of both of these functions. The National Imagery and Mapping Agency (NIMA), formally proposed by the Secretary of Defense and Director of the CIA in November 1995, was established on October 1, 1996. Through this creation, NIMA joined five existing imagery interpretation and mapping organizations: the National Photographic Interpretation Center, the Defense Mapping Agency, the CIA's Office of Imagery Analysis, the DIA's Office of Imagery Analysis, and the Central Imagery Office. Other offices absorbed into the new agency included the Defense Dissemination Program Office and elements of the Defense Airborne Reconnaissance Office and National Reconnaissance.

Initially NIMA was organized into three main directorates: operations, systems and technology, and corporate affairs. Three key units within the Operations Directorate were Imagery Analysis, Geospatial Information and Services, and the Central Imagery Tasking Office. The latter was responsible for allocating targets to imagery collection systems and determining when the imagery was obtained. Formed from several defense and intelligence agencies, NIMA merged imagery, maps, charts, and environmental data to produce what has been coined geospatial intelligence. The Imagery Analysis Unit combined the activities of NPIC and the CIA and DIA imagery analysis organizations, while the Geospatial Information and Services Unit provided the mapping, charting, and geodesy products formerly provided by the DMA. The unit was responsible for producing strategic and tactical maps, charts, and databases, and specialized products to support current and advanced weapons and navigation systems (Richelson et al., 2003).

Between 1995 and 1998, NIMA products helped resolve many national and international issues, including long-standing border disputes between Peru and Ecuador and between Israel and Southern Lebanon. NIMA products also supported the Dayton Peace Accord efforts in the Balkans. In February 2000, the space shuttle Endeavor's shuttle radar topography mission (SRTM) provided the most detailed measurements of the planet's elevation ever gathered — data that will prove invaluable in supporting the National Geospatial-Intelligence Agency's geospatial-intelligence efforts.

NIMA played a critical role in homeland security following the attacks of September 11. In the response and recovery phases of the disaster in New York City, NIMA partnered with the U.S. Geological Survey (USGS) to survey the World Trade Center site and determine the extent of the destruction. Then, in 2002, NIMA partnered with federal organizations to provide geospatial assistance to the 2002 Winter Olympics in Utah.

On November 24, 2003, the president signed the 2004 Defense Authorization Bill, which included a provision to change NIMA's name to the National Geospatial-Intelligence Agency (NGA).

Office of the Director of National Intelligence

The National Commission on Terrorist Attacks upon the United States (the 9/11 Commission) recommended the following in its final report:

The current position of Director of Central Intelligence should be replaced by a National Intelligence Director with two main areas of responsibility: (1) to oversee national intelligence centers on specific subjects of interest across the U.S. government and (2) to manage the national intelligence program and oversee the agencies that contribute to it.

In efforts to move forward with the commission's recommendation, Senators Susan Collins and Joe Lieberman, and Speaker of the House of Representatives Dennis Hastert, separately introduced legislation to create the national intelligence director (NID) position. Both bills sought to establish a presidentially nominated, Senate-confirmed position of NID, who would serve as the head of the intelligence community's 15 distinct intelligence agencies, including the CIA. Both bills also sought to establish a separate Senate-confirmed director of central intelligence, who would manage the CIA, and would be prohibited from serving simultaneously as the NID.

The House of Representatives passed the Collins-Lieberman Intelligence Reform and Terrorism Prevention Act on December 7, 2004, by a vote of 336 to 75. On December 8, 2004, the bill was approved by an 89-to-2 vote in the U.S. Senate and was sent to the president for his signature. The president signed the bill and nominated John Negroponte, the former U.S. ambassador to the United Nations and recently U.S. ambassador to Iraq, for the position of national intelligence director on February 17, 2005. John Negroponte was confirmed by the Senate on April 21, 2005, and was officially sworn in on May 18, 2005.

The primary goal of this new position is to ensure coordination and cooperation between all intelligence communities in the United States. Unifying the national intelligence effort is another key responsibility of the Director of National Intelligence as he took over the duty of daily presidential intelligence briefing from the Director of Central Intelligence. Providing the president with the most comprehensive and reliable daily intelligence information derived from the intelligence products of all elements of the intelligence community is going to be a key challenge. The Director of National Intelligence has authority and responsibility over the following critical tasks and activities:

- Create national intelligence centers to incorporate capabilities from across the intelligence community in order to accomplish intelligence missions.
- Control the national intelligence budget in terms of dollar amounts and distribution among different intelligence agencies.
- Transfer personnel and funds to ensure that the intelligence community is flexible and can respond to emerging threats.
- Create a Privacy and Civil Liberties Board to protect privacy and civil liberties concerns potentially created by proposals to fight terrorism.
- Establish an information-sharing network to break down the stovepipes that currently impede the flow of information between federal, state, and local agencies and the private sector (Sources: Congressional Research Service, "RS21948 — The National Intelligence Director and Intelligence Analysis," 2004; Congressional Research Service, "RL32506 — The

Proposed Authorities of a National Intelligence Director: Issues for Congress and Side-by-Side Comparison of S.2845, H.R. 10, and Current Law," 2004).

In its first three years of existence, the new office accomplished some of the goals mentioned above, but more importantly this period has been one of transition in the intelligence community with the creation of new functions, reshaping of others, and some changes in key officials.

On October 13, 2005, approximately six months after taking the office, Director Negroponte together with the Director of Central Intelligence created the National Clandestine Service within the CIA to boost the nation's human intelligence capabilities. Within the same timeframe, the Directorate released the National Intelligence Strategy, a document that details the national intelligence framework and established goals, priorities, and measures of effectiveness in adapting to the changing intelligence needs of the United States in the aftermath of the 9/11 attacks. The implementation of the strategy kicked off with the creation of DNI Open Source Center in an attempt to better exploit openly available information (such as websites, reports, videos, radio, television, books, etc.) for intelligence gathering and analysis purposes. Shortly before the end of 2005, the DNI created the DNI National Counterproliferation Center (NCPC). The office is tasked with the unification of efforts to prevent the proliferation of weapons of mass destruction. (Office of the Director of National Intelligence, "ODNI Press Releases 2005," 2008).

On February 17, 2006, the Drug Enforcement administration became the 16th member of the intelligence community. On May 5, CIA Chief Porter Goss resigned and the media reported that the cause of the resignation was a combination of differences between Goss' and DNI Negroponte's management styles, and the changes made in the direction of the intelligence community that Goss did not agree with. Later in the same month, General Mike Hayden (U.S. Air Force) was sworn in as the new chief of CIA. General Hayden previously served as the first Principal Deputy Director of National Intelligence, which is the highest ranking intelligence post within the U.S. Armed Forces (Office of the Director of National Intelligence, "ODNI Press Releases 2006," 2008).

The year 2007 saw another change of key officials when President Bush announced that DNI John Negroponte would be moving to the State Department as the Deputy Secretary of State, and nominated Admiral Mike McConnell as his replacement. Although McConnell was holding a senior management position with a private consulting company focusing on intelligence and national security prior to his appointment as the DNI, he had previously served as the Director of the National Security Agency earlier. As his first major move in his new post, McConnell created the Information Sharing and Steering committee within the DNI to further improve coordination and collaboration between different members of the intelligence community. Within this new setting, every member of the intelligence community must appoint an Information Sharing Executive who works closely with the committee to share vital information processed by his or her agency. Just a few days after the announcement of the creation of the new committee, the DOD Chief Information Officer (CIO) and the ODNI CIO signed an agreement that created a Unified Cross Domain Management Office to enhance information sharing between the DOD and the intelligence community. On March 27, 2007, the DNI announced the release of the National Counterintelligence Strategy, which details the intelligence community's goals and priorities toward a reduction in intelligence threats aimed at the United States (Office of the Director of National Intelligence, "ODNI Press Releases 2007," 2008).

While the details of the National Intelligence Program's Budget, controlled by the Director of National Intelligence, are classified, the DNI office reported that the combined budget for the Program activities was $43.5 billion in fiscal year 2007.

Border Control

The borders of any country are strategically important because of the critical role they play in its economic vitality and commerce. Increasing globalization of economic systems and transportation networks has made it possible for every community in the United States to be connected to the outside world through a vast system of airports, seaports, pipelines, roadways, and waterways. Borders are gateways for imported and exported goods; therefore, their effectiveness and efficiency are important measures for the trade capacity and capability of the country. Borders also have an important role for the international tourism and travel capability of the country.

At the same time, borders provide access into the country, through both major and clandestine entry points, for illegal immigrants and goods. Therefore, the security and control of borders is of the utmost importance in the drive to mitigate the risk posed by the penetration of unwanted or dangerous people and goods into the country. Human traffickers, smugglers, drug dealers, criminals, terrorists, illegal drugs, conventional weapons, undeclared or counterfeit products, biological agents, and weapons of mass destruction (WMD) are but a small sample of the many possible individuals and items that together mandate strong national borders.

The United States shares 5,525 miles of border with Canada and 1,989 miles with Mexico. The maritime border includes 95,000 miles of shoreline and a 3.4-million square-mile exclusive economic zone. Each year, more than 500 million people cross these borders to enter the United States, and approximately 330 million of them are foreign nationals (White House, 2005, www.whitehouse.gov).

Each year, more than 500 million people cross these borders to enter the United States, and approximately 330 million of them are foreign nationals. In its initial organization, DHS consolidated the various agencies responsible for the safety, security, and control of the borders under the Directorate of Border and Transportation Security. These agencies include the Immigration and Customs Enforcement Agency (previously the Immigration and Naturalization Service), the U.S. Customs and Border Protection (previously the Customs Service), the U.S. Coast Guard (USCG), and the Transportation Security Agency (TSA). With the reorganization effort that was initiated in the later half of 2005, the Directorate of Border and Transportation Security was replaced with the Directorate of Policy, and its policy functions were transferred to the new directorate. In today's DHS the agencies mentioned above have direct reporting responsibility to the Secretary of Homeland Security.

The increasing urgency for better customs and border protection has forced government agencies to come up with new initiatives that aim to minimize breaches along the borders to minimize the entry of illegal immigrants and substances into the United States while preserving the efficient travel of legal people and goods into the country. The details of initiatives specific to agencies will be covered in subsequent sections; however, the following list provides descriptions of a sample of the types of programs that help to ensure the security of the nation's borders:

- Improving border control through installation of physical barriers: This type of program primarily consists of installing permanent or temporary barriers to make it more difficult for illegal immigrants to enter the United States through wide ranges of land borders such as the Mexican or Canadian borders. The most evident example of such a program is the Southwestern Border Fence mandated by the Secure Fence Act of 2006. According to the Act, a total 850 miles of double-fenced physical barriers will be installed on the southwestern border to prevent the entry of illegal immigrants into the United States. Currently there is an existing fence in San Diego along a 14-mile stretch of the Mexican border that is composed of double-fenced and triple-fenced barriers. Department of Homeland Security's goal is to complete the construction of 670 miles of fencing by December 2008.

- Improving border control through better surveillance: As part of the Arizona Border Control Initiative, U.S. Customs and Border Protection is increasing its number of border patrol personnel in high-risk sections of land borders, and installing better lighting, surveillance cameras, and thermal detectors as deterrent measures against illegal border crossings and to more efficiently detect and respond to illegal actions where they occur.

- Improving border control through better technology and information management: Advances in technology and information management find applications in border control and protection.

After 9/11, the U.S. State Department started scanning two fingers of every nonimmigrant visa applicant at the U.S. embassy, which is passed to a computer database to be cross-checked at the point of entry by a U.S. Customs and Border Protection official. In late 2007, this initiative was extended to a 10-finger scan setting to ensure more reliable detection of illegal entry attempts. The SEVIS (Student and Exchange Visitor Information System), an initiative of U.S. Immigration and Customs Enforcement provides for real-time information regarding immigration details of students and other temporary exchange visitors. SBInet, another program of the Secure Border Initiative requires the development of an advanced technological solution that integrates essential functions of DHS departments with border control responsibilities, such as U.S. Immigration and Customs Enforcement, U.S. Customs and Border Protection (CBP), United States Citizenship and Immigration Services, and the United States Coast Guard. Program goals and requirements include but are not limited to: (1) act as a deterrent against illegal border crossing, (2) predict illegal activities at the border before occurrence, (3) detect illegal crossing, (4) identify type of entry, (5) estimate threat level of the entry before interdiction, (6) track the movements of illegal entrants, (7) support decision making for response, and (8) bring interdictions to an appropriate resolution. The SBInet project is being implemented by Boeing on behalf of the Department of Homeland Security and will cover 6,000 miles of border when complete.

- Use of manned and unmanned airborne vehicles (UAVs): As part of the Arizona Border Control Initiative Phase 2 put into effect in April 2005, the U.S. Customs and Border Protection increased the number and types of aerial vehicles it is using the patrol the border from the air. The innovative thing about this development was the first use of UAVs for border control purposes. UAVs have been previously used by the U.S. military in Iraq and Afghanistan. The advantages of the UAVs over manned aircraft are their relatively low costs and great endurance, making them perfect for long patrol missions. On the other hand their biggest disadvantage is the very high accident rate, almost 100 times higher than the average manned aircraft (Sources: Congressional Research Service, "Border Security: Barriers along the U.S. International Border," 2006; Congressional Research Service, "Border Security and Unmanned Aerial Vehicles," 2004; DHS, "Fact Sheet: Arizona Border Control Initiative," 2004; DHS, "DHS Moves Forward on Border Fencing and Technology Improvement," 2007; U.S. Customs and Border Protection, "SBInet: Securing U.S. Borders," 2006; U.S. Customs and Border Protection,"FY 2007 Performance and Accountability Report," 2008; U.S. Immigration and Customs Enforcement, "ICE FY 2007 Accomplishments," 2008).

The following section summarizes the duties of agencies that have a direct role in border control and security.

DHS/U.S. Coast Guard

The Coast Guard is the lead federal agency for maritime drug interdiction and shares lead responsibility for air interdiction with the U.S. Customs Service. As such, it is a key player in combating the flow of illegal drugs into the United States. The Coast Guard's mission is to reduce the supply of drugs from its source by denying smugglers the use of air and maritime routes in the Transit Zone, a 6-million square-mile area that includes the Caribbean Sea, the Gulf of Mexico, and Eastern Pacific Ocean. In patrolling this vast area, the Coast Guard coordinates closely with other federal agencies and countries located within the region to disrupt and deter the flow of illegal drugs. Coast Guard drug interdiction accounts for a high number of drug seizures performed by the U.S. government, including more than 50% of all seizures of cocaine each year. In FY 2006, the USCG seized 93,209 pounds of drugs which is a significant increase over the 83,149 pounds of drugs seized in the fiscal years 2004 and 2005 *combined*. In FY 2007, the breadth of these seizures snowballed, with a 355,755 pounds of cocaine alone interdicted (with an approximate market value of more than $4.7 billion), further highlighting the important role the Coast Guard plays in securing the nation's borders. (U.S. Coast Guard, 2007).

As the primary maritime law enforcement agency, the Coast Guard is tasked with enforcing immigration law at sea. The Coast Guard conducts patrols and coordinates with other federal agencies and foreign countries to interdict undocumented migrants at sea, denying them entry via maritime routes to the United States, its territories, and possessions. By interdicting migrants at sea, the Coast Guard is able, by law, to quickly return them to their countries of origin without the costly processes required if they successfully enter the United States. Specifically, the Coast Guard's mission includes:

- Maritime safety: Eliminate loss of life, injuries, and physical damage associated with maritime transportation, fishing, and recreational boating.

- National defense: Defend the nation as one of the five U.S. armed services. Enhance regional stability in support of the National Security Strategy, utilizing the Coast Guard's unique and relevant maritime capabilities.

- Maritime security: Protect America's maritime borders from all intrusions by (1) halting the flow of illegal drugs, aliens, and contraband into the United States through maritime routes; (2) preventing illegal fishing; and (3) suppressing violations of federal law in the maritime arena.

- Mobility: Facilitate maritime commerce and eliminate interruptions and impediments to the efficient and economical movement of goods and people, while maximizing recreational access to and enjoyment of the water.

- Protection of natural resources: Eliminate environmental damage and the degradation of natural resources associated with maritime transportation, fishing, and recreational boating (Source: "Budget in Brief FY 2006". http//:www.dhs.gov/xlibrary/assets/budget_bib-fy2006.pdf).

Table 5–1 displays the USCG budget for FY 2007–2009, broken down by program, and the sidebar, "Accomplishments of U.S. Coast Guard in 2006 and 2007" lists some of the USCG's major tasks. An important responsibility of the Coast Guard is its role as one of the two primary federal agencies during federal responses to oil and hazardous material incidents — a responsibility the Coast Guard shares with the Environmental Protection Agency (EPA). The EPA or the USCG, depending on whether the incident affects inland or coastal zones, serves as the primary agency for emergency support Function 10 (ESF #10) actions under the National Response Framework. For incidents where DHS/USCG is the primary agency, the USCG Chief of the Office of Response serves as the lead for ESF #10. During these incidents, the USCG assumes the following responsibilities:

- Maintains close coordination between DHS/USCG headquarters and the affected area and district offices; the EPA, as appropriate; the Domestic Readiness Group (DRG); the National Response Coordination Center (NRCC); other ESFs; and the National Response Team (NRT)

- Provides damage reports, assessments, and situation reports to support ESF #5 (emergency management)

- Facilitates resolution of any conflicting demands for hazardous materials response resources and ensures coordination between NRT and Incident Management Planning Team (IMPT) activities, and Regional Response Team (RRT) and the Joint Field Office (JFO) activities, as appropriate. Coordinates (through headquarters) the provision of personnel and logistics support from other districts to the affected area

- Provides technical, coordination, and administrative support and personnel, facilities, and communications for ESF #10

- Coordinates, integrates, and manages the overall federal effort to detect, identify, contain, clean up, or dispose of or minimize releases of oil or hazardous materials, or prevent, mitigate, or minimize the threat of potential releases

- Provides Federal On-Scene Coordinators (OSCs) for incidents within its jurisdiction (including for the coastal zone response for incidents for which EPA is the primary agency, but the incident affects both the inland and coastal zone) (Source: DHS, "The National Response Framework ESF#10 Annex," 2007)

Table 5–1   U.S. Coast Guard Budget Allocation, FY 2007–2009

	FY 2007 Revised Enacted		FY 2008 Enacted		FY 2009 President's Budget		FY 2009 +/− FY 2008	
	FTE	$000	FTE	$000	FTE	$000	FTE	$000
Search and Rescue	5,004	928,782	4,893	889,849	4,826	923,680	−67	33,831
Marine Safety	4,109	755,280	3,814	749,186	3,809	753,546	−5	4,360
Aids to Navigation	8,550	1,321,449	7,330	1,265,595	7,269	1,189,133	−61	−76,462
Ice Operations	854	132,157	810	148,034	791	133,117	−19	−14,917
Marine Environmental Protection	1,222	298,329	1,174	371,668	1,138	359,283	−36	−12,385
Living Marine Resources	4,849	972,050	3,955	770,925	3,841	833,227	−114	62,302
Drug Interdiction	6,159	1,280,433	6,006	1,199,560	5,798	1,275,705	−208	76,145
Migrant Interdiction	4,350	873,692	2,460	506,822	2,375	514,620	−85	7,798
Other Law Enforcement	800	160,423	608	104,550	595	136,323	−13	31,773
Port Waterways and Coastal Security	7,710	1,362,220	13,578	1,974,028	15,066	2,593,223	1,498	619,195
Defense Readiness	4,039	691,435	3,644	760,836	3,422	634,165	−222	−126,671
Total	47,646	$8,776,250	48,272	$8,741,053	48,930	9,346,022	658	604,969
Adjustments	—	($429,308)	—	$27,264	—	—	—	($27,264)
Emergency Funding	—	—	286	$166,100		—	(286)	($166,100)
Adjusted Budget Authority	47,646	$8,346,942	48,558	$8,934,417	48,930	$9,346,022	372	$411,605

Source: USCG Budget Overview, FY 2009 DHS Budget in Brief Document, Washington, DC, 2008.

Accomplishments of U.S. Coast Guard in 2006 and 2007

- Marine Incident Response: In 2006–2007, the Coast Guard responded to more than 55,000 calls for assistance and saved the lives of more than 10,000 mariners.
- Counterdrug Mission: The Coast Guard successfully conducted its counterdrug mission. In 2006, counterdrug boardings from U.S. and Royal Navy vessels resulted in all-time records for seizures and arrests. The 93,209 pounds of drugs seized in FY 2006 was more than the 83,149 pounds of drugs seized in FY 2004 and FY 2005 combined. In 2007, the Coast Guard seized 355,000 pounds of cocaine, 12,000 pounds of marijuana, and 350 pounds of heroine. It also performed the largest cocaine seizure operation in its history where 33,359 pounds of cocaine were seized from a vessel.

- National Defense: In 2006, the Coast Guard took on an important new mission in defense of the National Capitol Region airspace as it implemented Rotary Wing Air Intercept capability on a 24/7 basis in support of the North American Aerospace Defense Command's Operation NOBLE EAGLE (ONE).

- Addition of Advanced Vessel Assets to the Fleet: The Coast Guard christened Cutter *Bertholf* (WMSL 750), its first new high-endurance cutter in more than 35 years and the first National Security Cutter of the Deepwater acquisition program. The cutter will meet the Coast Guard's multimission responsibilities in homeland security, national defense, marine safety, and environmental protection, and will play an important role in strengthening the Coast Guard's operational readiness, capacity and effectiveness. The Coast Guard also procured six 33-foot Special Purpose Craft to meet its needs for faster, more maneuverable boats. These unique assets provide the Coast Guard with the capability to intercept high-speed noncompliant vessels, as well as to stop illegal fishing, and migrant and drug smuggling especially along our southern maritime border. In 2006, the Coast Guard replaced 39 obsolete cutter boats in the entire high-endurance and medium-endurance cutter fleets with the significantly more capable cutter boat–over the horizon (CB-OTH), with speed nearly doubling that of the boat it replaced, along with increased secure communications capabilities.

- Participation in International Exercise: In 2006, the Coast Guard Cutter *Rush* (WHEC 723) completed an important multilateral/international exercise with coast guard vessels from China, Japan, Canada, India, and South Korea to enhance the ability to operate effectively with our international partners. The *Rush* was the first U.S. Coast Guard Cutter visit to mainland China since World War II.

- Protection of Marine Resources and Prohibition of Illegal Fishing: In support of the Coast Guard's vital mission to protect the nation's living marine resources, the Coast Guard cutter *Walnut* and a Coast Guard C-130 airplane observed a foreign fishing vessel fishing illegally inside the Howland/Baker Exclusive Economic Zone, about 1,700 miles south of Honolulu. The *Walnut* seized the vessel and escorted it to Guam. The vessel had approximately 500 metric tons of illegally caught skipjack tuna worth about $350,000.

- Law Enforcement and Counterdrug Mission: In an operation off the coast of San Diego in 2006, the Coast Guard, along with federal drug agents, arrested Mexican drug lord Francisco Javier Arellano-Felix, leader of a major violent gang, known as the "Tijuana Cartel," responsible for digging elaborate tunnels to smuggle drugs under the U.S. border.

- Emergency Response: In January 2006, shortly after commencing the U.S. Antarctic Program's resupply effort to open a channel through the ice into McMurdo Station, the chartered Russian icebreaker *Krasin* suffered a major casualty when a blade on one of its three propellers was sheared off by thick ice. The Coast Guard cutter *Polar Star* deployed on extremely short notice to Antarctica to assist the *Krasin* and completed the critical resupply effort.

- Transitioning of the Inland Rivers Vessel Movement Center: The Coast Guard successfully transitioned the Inland Rivers Vessel Movement Center (IRVMC) from a small start-up to a fully funded, permanently staffed component of the Coast Guard's Navigation Center. IRVMC strengthens homeland security by tracking barges and vessels transporting dangerous chemicals, and provides mission-critical maritime domain awareness to Coast Guard units on more than 10,000 miles of the western rivers.

- Analysis of Energy Facility Proposals for Environmental Impact and Maritime Security: The Coast Guard helped the nation meet its urgent and growing energy needs by extensively analyzing multiple energy facility site proposals in the Northeast for environmental impacts and maritime security. Working with Department of Energy, Federal Energy Regulatory Commission, Maritime Administration, and other federal, state, and local entities — and with much public input — the Coast Guard has provided thorough review of seven liquid natural gas and two wind-farm facility proposals.

- Illegal Immigration Mission: In FY 2006, there were 5,552 successful migrant arrivals out of an estimated threat of 51,134 migrants, yielding a deterrence and interdiction rate of 89.1%, just over the 89% performance target. In FY 2007, the Coast Guard interdicted 6,000 illegal aliens.
- Training of Iraqi Security Forces: Coast Guard Patrol Forces Southwest Asia fabricated a training facility in Umm Qasr, Iraq. The facility enables the training of Iraqi security forces in vessel boarding procedures, close-quarters battle techniques, and container inspections. The first group of Iraqi marines successfully completed the two-week course on October 21, 2006.
- Role of Coast Guard Reservists: The Coast Guard provided escorts in and out of key U.S. ports and naval vessel protection zones during the loading/unloading of ships involved in the transport of military equipment to Iraqi and Afghanistan theaters. Staffing for these operations was provided by reservists mobilized under Title 10 of the United States Code.
- Creation of Deployable Operations Group: To ensure rapid response and deployment of Coast Guard resources to global threats, the Deployable Operations Group was established in 2007 under a single unified command encompassing 3,000 Coast Guard personnel.
- National Response Framework: In 2007, the Coast Guard contributed to the development and advancement of the new National Response Framework.
- Environmental Stewardship: The Coast Guard in cooperation with the EPA conducted an exercise of a Spill of National Significance (SONS) where a multijurisdiction, multiagency response to a major oil spill was simulated and responded to.
- Assets Management, Maintenance, and Procurement: The Coast Guard continued in 2007 its program in recapitalizing on aging assets and their maintenance, and where feasible and necessary the replacement of old equipment. New systems, equipment, and capabilities were added into Coast Guard assets in 2007, including new vessels, helicopters, communications and command centers, and vessel tracking and notification systems (Sources: Department of Homeland Security, "Budget in Brief FY 2008," 2007; DHS, "Budget in Brief FY 2009," 2008).

U.S. Customs and Border Protection

U.S. Customs and Border Protection (CBP) is the only agency responsible for protecting the sovereign borders of the United States at and between the official ports of entry. CBP is considered the "front line" in protecting the nation against terrorist attacks. CBP also ensures national economic security by regulating and facilitating the lawful movement of goods and persons across U.S. borders.

The U.S. Border Patrol is the primary operational agency within the Bureau of Customs and Border Protection, which is responsible for protecting the borders. Therefore, it is the mobile uniformed border law enforcement arm of the Department of Homeland Security. The primary mission of the Border Patrol is the detection and apprehension of illegal aliens and smugglers of aliens at or near the land border. This is accomplished by maintaining surveillance, following up leads, responding to electronic sensor alarms and aircraft sightings, and interpreting and following tracks. Some of the major activities include maintaining traffic checkpoints along highways leading from border areas, conducting city patrols and transportation checks, and antismuggling investigations. Since 1994 the Border Patrol has made more than 15.6 million apprehensions nationwide. In FY 2005, Border Patrol agents apprehended almost 1.2 million persons for illegally entering the country. An increase in smuggling activities has pushed the Border Patrol to the front line of the U.S. war on drugs. Its role as the primary drug-interdiction organization along the southwest border continues to expand (see sidebar, "DHS Arizona Border Control Initiative"). In FY 2005, Border Patrol agents seized more than 12,300 pounds of cocaine and more than 1.2 million pounds of marijuana, with a total street value of more than $1.4 billion. In 2006, the Border Patrol officers processed 422.9 million individuals at the ports and about 400,000 of them were found to be inadmissible (U.S. Customs and Border Protection, "Border Patrol Overview," 2006).

CBP officials are also deployed overseas at major international seaports through the Container Security Initiative (CSI) to prescreen shipping containers to detect and interdict terrorists' weapons and other illicit material before arrival on U.S. shores. Through programs like CSI, CBP is partnering with foreign nations and private industry to expand the nation's zone of security and ensure that U.S. borders are not the last line of defense. As of 2008, the following international ports joined the Container Security Initiative:

Americas and Caribbean
Montreal, Vancouver, and Halifax, Canada
Santos, Brazil
Buenos Aires, Argentina
Puerto Cortes, Honduras
Caucedo, Dominican Republic
Kingston, Jamaica
Freeport, The Bahamas
Balboa, Colón, and Manzanillo, Panama
Cartagena, Colombia

Europe
Rotterdam, The Netherlands
Bremerhaven and Hamburg, Germany
Antwerp and Zeebrugge, Belgium
Le Havre and Marseille, France
Gothenburg, Sweden
La Spezia, Genoa, Naples, Gioia Tauro, and Livorno, Italy
Felixstowe, Liverpool, Thamesport, Tilbury, and Southampton, United Kingdom (UK)
Piraeus, Greece
Algeciras, Barcelona, and Valencia, Spain
Lisbon, Portugal

Asia and the East
Singapore
Yokohama, Tokyo, Nagoya, and Kobe, Japan
Hong Kong
Pusan, South Korea
Port Klang and Tanjung Pelepas, Malaysia
Laem Chabang, Thailand
Dubai, United Arab Emirates (UAE)
Shenzhen and Shanghai
Kaohsiung and Chi-Lung
Colombo, Sri Lanka
Port Salalah, Oman
Port Qasim, Pakistan
Port of Ashdod, Israel
Port in Haifa, Israel

Table 5–2   CBP Budget Allocation, FY 2007–2009

	FY 2007 Revised Enacted		FY 2008 Enacted		FY 2009 President's Budget		FY 2009 + / − FY 2008	
	FTE	$000	FTE	$000	FTE	$000	FTE	$000
Headquarters Management and Administration	3,588	$1,199,367	3,689	$1,221,341	3,767	$1,266,651	74	$45,310
Border Security Inspections and Trade Facilitation at POEs	15,850	$1,813,691	16,801	$2,008,247	18,043	$2,273,104	1,242	$264,857
Border Security and Control Between POEs	14,656	$2,276,010	18,384	$3,037,232	21,596	$3,515,320	3,212	$478,088
Air and Marine Operations, Salaries	1,226	$180,796	1,472	$212,740	1,674	$254,279	202	$41,539
Air and Marine Interdiction, Operations, Maintenance, and Procurement	—	$365,187	—	$476,047	—	$528,000	—	$51,953
Automation Modernization	62	$451,440	63	$476,609	63	$511,334	—	$34,725
Construction	—	$122,978	—	$287,363	—	$363,501	—	$76,138
Border Security Fencing, Infrastructure, and Technology	39	$28,365	160	$172,000	185	$775,000	25	$603,000
Subtotal	35,421	$6,437,834	40,569	$7,891,579	45,328	$9,487,189	4,755	$1,595,610
Small Airports	51	$7,180	54	$7,057	54	$7,057	—	—
Gross Discretionary	35,472	$6,445,014	40,623	$7,898,636	45,382	$9,494,246	4,755	$1,595,610
Customs Unclaimed Goods	—	$5,897	—	$5,897	—	$5,897	—	—
Mandatory Fees	8,285	$1,295,348	9,486	$1,402,192	9,486	$1,441,088	—	$38,896
Emergency/ Supplemental	—	$1,601,200	308	$1,531,000	—	—	(304)	($1,531,000)
Supplemental (P.L. 110-28)	301	$150,000	—	—	—	—	—	—
Less Prior Year Rescissions	—	—	—	($25,621)	—	—	—	$25,621
Total	44,058	$9,497,459	50,417	$10,812,104	54,868	$10,941,231	4,451	$129,127

POE, port of entry.

Source: CBP Budget Overview, Department of Homeland Security (DHS), "Budget in Brief FY 2009," Washington, DC, 2008.

Alexandria, Egypt

Africa

Durban, South Africa (Source: U.S. Customs and Border Protection, "Ports in CSI," 2008)

CBP's entry specialists and trade compliance personnel also enforce U.S. trade and tariff laws and regulations in order to ensure a fair and competitive trade environment as stipulated by existing international agreements and treaties. CBP's Air and Marine Operations Division patrols the nation's borders to interdict illegal drugs and terrorists before entry into the United States and provides surveillance and operational support to special national security events ("Budget in Brief FY 2006". http//: www.dhs.gov/xlibrary/assets/budget_bib-fy2006.pdf).

One component of border security (also included in the Arizona Border Control Initiative) that is gaining increased recognition for its abilities is the use of the Hermes 450 unmanned aerial vehicles (UAVs). These remote-guided airplanes have already begun monitoring the border regions in the hunt for illegal movements. By using the unmanned vehicles for border protection — their first nonmilitary use — DHS enjoys greater border coverage and is able to respond much faster to incidents in rugged areas of the country. Additionally, the recordings made by the UAVs provide evidence for convicting apprehended criminals in court. The high-tech airplanes are an indication of the technological advancements that will increasingly dictate both the direction and the success of homeland security in the United States. Table 5–2 illustrates U.S. Customs and Border Protection budget allocations for FY 2007–2009.

DHS Arizona Border Control Initiative

The Arizona Border Control (ABC) Initiative is a joint effort by several DHS agencies to improve border protection and reduce the number of trespassing aliens from the Mexican border into the United States. The goal of the initiative is to establish federal, state, and local coordinated efforts to achieve operational control of the Arizona border and support of the DHS priority mission of antiterrorism, detection, arrest, and deterrence of all cross-border illicit trafficking, to significantly impair the ability of the smuggling organizations to operate, to decrease the rate of violent crime, and to reduce the need for social services in southern Arizona.

The ABC Initiative is built on the combined assets within Homeland Security of Customs and Border Protection (CBP), Immigration and Customs Enforcement (ICE), the TSA, the Department of the Interior (DOI), and other federal agencies. Close liaison is maintained with the Tohono O'odham Nation and state and local law enforcement.

Phase I of the initiative announced by DHS in March 2004 added 60 additional U.S. Border Patrol agents who are specially trained in search, rescue, and remote tactical operations. Those agents were deployed temporarily to support the ABC Initiative, but some have been transformed in permanent positions due to the success of the program. Two hundred experienced Border Patrol agents were permanently assigned to Arizona in summer 2005, bringing the Tucson Sector to more than 2,000 agents.

In March 2005, DHS announced the Phase II of the Arizona Border Initiative, and the deployment of more resources including a 25% increase in permanent Border Patrol agents, an addition of 155 seasoned agents, and the deployment of 20 helicopters and three fixed-wing aircraft.

The ABC Initiative pioneered the use of nonconventional aviation resources for border surveillance of illegal activities. In this capacity, unmanned aerial vehicles (UAVs) have been used beginning in early June 2005 along the border.

Immigration and Customs Enforcement Air and Marine Operations fly additional hours patrolling the area with both helicopters and fixed-wing aircraft. CBP/Border Patrol has assigned four additional A-Star 350 helicopters to assist with these efforts. Air and Marine

Operations and the Border Patrol use aircraft to rapidly transport search, rescue, and enforcement assets to remote areas of the Arizona desert.

Meanwhile, hundreds of civilian volunteers (The Minuteman Program) began monitoring a 20-mile stretch of Arizona's border with Mexico in 2005. The use of volunteers for law enforcement purposes, which was tested during a one-month pilot program with success, was found highly controversial by civil liberties and human rights groups. "We think there's a real danger of something bad occurring," said Mark Potok, director of the Intelligence Project, which monitors hate groups. "People around the country, on white supremacist and neo-Nazi Web sites, are talking about going down there." The Minuteman Program continues to exist as of 2008 and is engaged in pockets of volunteer border watch activities (in some instances with use of advanced technology such as thermal cameras) and some voluntary border fence construction activities.

The Department of Homeland Security reports that the Arizona Border Initiative reduced border crossing–related deaths of illegal immigrants by 20%. The combined DHS budget to U.S. Customs and Border Protection for all secure border initiatives (including Border Patrol Staffing, SBInet, and Border Patrol Facilities) is approximately $1.75 billion for the fiscal year 2008.

Sources: DHS, 2005; *USA Today*, 2005; Minuteman Civil Defense Corps, 2008.

U.S. Immigration and Customs Enforcement

U.S. Immigration and Customs Enforcement (ICE) promotes public safety and national security by deterring illegal migration, preventing immigration-related crimes, and removing individuals, especially criminals, who are unlawfully present in the United States. This mandate is carried out by the Immigration Investigations, Detention and Removal, and Intelligence programs. (See sidebar titled, "FY 2008 ICE Initiatives in President's Budget.")

Traditionally, the primary mission of the customs enforcement component of ICE was to combat various forms of smuggling. Over time, however, this mission has been expanded to other violations of law involving terrorist financing, money laundering, arms trafficking (including WMD), technology exports, commercial fraud, and child pornography, to name a few. In total, ICE enforces more than 400 different laws and regulations, including those of 40 other agencies.

Within the new organization of the Department of Homeland Security, the primary mission of ICE is to detect vulnerabilities and prevent violations that threaten national security. There are several distinct offices that carry out separate tasks within this collective mission. The Office of Congressional Relations (OCR) maintains relationships between ICE and the Congress through federal liaison activities in an effort to promote the agency's mission and values at the highest levels of government decision making. The Office of Detention and Removal Operations (DRO) is tasked with the detention and deportation of undocumented, illegal, or out-of-status aliens and visitors. The Office of Federal Protective Service (FPS) is responsible for providing a safe and secure work environment at federal facilities, which it ensures through security investigations and physical presence when needed. The Office of Intelligence is responsible for collecting, analyzing, and sharing strategic and tactical intelligence data for use by other ICE offices and the DHS. Office of International Affairs (OIA) is the largest investigative unit within DHS and it coordinates ICE relationships with international entities such as foreign governments. The Office of Investigations is responsible for investigating a range of domestic and international activities arising from the movement of people and goods that violate immigration and customs laws and threaten national security. Table 5–3 illustrates U.S. Immigration and Customs Enforcement budget allocations for FY 2007–2009.

Table 5–3 ICE Budget Allocation, FY 2007–2009

	FY 2007 Revised Enacted		FY 2008 Enacted		FY 2009 President's Budget		FY 2009 +/− FY 2008	
	FTE	$000	FTE	$000	FTE	$000	FTE	$000
Salaries and Expenses	15,083	$3,887,000	16,065	$4,171,117	17,395	$4,690,905	1330	$519,788
Federal Protective Service	1,295	$516,011	950	$613,000	950	$616,000	0	$3,000
Automation Modernization	7	$15,000	7	$30,700	11	$57,000	4	$26,300
Construction	9	$26,281	9	$6,000	9	$0	0	($6,000)
Gross Discretionary	16,394	$4,444,292	17,031	$4,820,817	18,365	$5,363,905	1334	$543,088
Fee Accounts	460	$252,349	474	$233,500	600	$312,180	126	$78,680
Emergency Supplemental	—	$36,000	433	$526,900	—	—	(433)	($526,900)
Less Prior Year Rescissions	—	—	—	($5,137)	—	—	—	$5,137
Total	16,854	$4,732,641	17,938	$5,576,080	18,965	$5,676,085	1,027	$100,005

Source: ICE Budget Overview, DHS Budget in Brief FY 2009, Washington, DC, 2008.

FY 2008 ICE Initiatives in President's Budget

- Detention Bed Space ($31.0 million): Funding will provide 600 additional detention beds, contract services, and support personnel for the Detention Management Operation program. An additional 350 new beds are requested as part of the State and Local Law Enforcement Support Program.
- Criminal Alien Program (CAP) ($28.7 million): Through CAP, ICE identifies and removes criminal aliens encountered in federal, state, and local detention facilities. The increase provides for the deployment of 22 additional 10-person CAP teams. An estimated 600 interviews, resulting in 300 apprehensions, will be made by each CAP officer.
- State and Local Law Enforcement Support ($26.4 million): This funding will allow training of 250 state and local law enforcement officers, 350 detention beds and associated staffing, the installation of T-1 data transmission lines, computers with IDENT/ ENFORCE capabilities, and connectivity to ICE databases for the participating state and local agencies.
- Information Technology Investments ($15.7 million): This program increase will fund Detention and Removal Operations Information Technology modernization ($11.5 million, 4 positions, 2 FTE); mobile IDENT/ENFORCE devices ($2.2 million); and an Immigration Enforcement Systems upgrade ($2 million).
- Removal Management Operations ($10.8 million): The request funds Centralized Ticketing Operations and additional air transportation support, including the use of the Justice Prisoner and Alien Transportation System (JPATS) and leasing of aircraft for alien removals.
- Border Enforcement Security Task Forces (BEST) ($10.7 million): BEST Task Forces identify and prioritize emerging and existing threats to border security. The Task Forces

will coordinate a unified response that leverages federal, state, local, tribal, and foreign law enforcement and intelligence entities to disrupt and dismantle cross-border criminal organizations to improve border security. The request includes funding for the existing BEST Task Force in Laredo, Texas, and to establish six additional task forces (56 agents and 7 support personnel).

- Improved Integrity Oversight ($7.0 million): The request funds 32 special agents, 3 supervisory special agents, and 2 mission support staff within the Office of Professional Responsibility to conduct criminal and serious misconduct investigations involving the activities of ICE and CBP employees deployed domestically and overseas. Timely attention to allegations of misconduct is critical to workforce integrity.
- Gang Enforcement ($5.0 million): ICE will use the additional resources to enhance its anti-gang initiative and increase the number of transnational gang members that are identified, arrested, and removed from the United States. The request provides resources for 35 positions for assignment to field offices in critical high-threat gang areas.
- ICE Mutual Agreement between Government and Employers (IMAGE) ($5.0 million): Through IMAGE, ICE will work with private employers to improve worksite enforcement. IMAGE will result in the reduced hiring of unauthorized workers as companies develop strong business practices. The request funds 10 special agents, 10 forensic auditors, and 9 investigative assistants.
- Bulk Cash Smuggling Center (BCSC) ($2.1 million): The requested funding will support the hiring of 11 new personnel, equipment, and training for ICE investigators, state and local law enforcement officers, and Assistant U.S. Attorneys to support the BCSC.
- Trade Transparency Unit (TTU) ($1.8 million): These resources will expand the capacity and capabilities of the TTU program to build partnerships with foreign governments and undertake coordinated investigations with foreign law enforcement counterparts to combat trade-based money laundering.

Source: DHS, "FY 2008 Budget in Brief," 2007.

Transportation Safety and Security

Transportation is a general term that refers to the movement of things or people from one location to another. However, in today's modern world, where transportation systems are intertwined into a global network that moves millions of people and products throughout the world on a daily basis, such simple definitions do not give justice to the complexity that exists in this sector. Furthermore, the safety and security needs to address such a complex system are equally complex and interconnected. Historically, the United States has relied on the private sector for both the transportation network and the promise of domestic transportation safety and security. The events of September 11, 2001, however, illustrated the vulnerabilities of our systems and spurred a massive change in the existing approaches. Transportation security and the identification and reduction of vulnerabilities within the vast transportation networks have since experienced significant challenges and changes. Because of the complexity of these systems as a whole and the complexity of the subsystems included, this has not been an easy task.

In the United States, the Department of Transportation (DOT) and the DHS Transportation Security Agency are the main government bodies that address the system's security of the transportation infrastructure.

The US-VISIT Program

US-VISIT is a DHS program that enhances the nation's entry and exit system. It enables the United States to effectively verify the identity of incoming visitors and confirm compliance with visa and immigration policies. The program's goals are to enhance the security of U.S. citizens and visitors who travel in and out of the country, to expedite legitimate travel and trade, to ensure the integrity of the immigration system while safeguarding the personal privacy of visitors.

The changes that are associated with the implementation of the new system start at U.S. posts and embassies abroad when the prospective foreign visitor to the United States applies for a U.S. visa. The applicant gets all ten of his or her fingers digitally scanned and those images are saved in a database where other relevant information about the applicant is saved. The fingerprints are later used to verify the identity of the visitor when he or she enters or leaves the country.

On arrival in the United States, as part of the enhanced procedures, most visitors traveling on visas will have two fingerprints scanned by an ink-less device and a digital photograph taken. All of the data and information are then used to assist the border inspector in determining whether or not to admit the traveler. These enhanced procedures add only seconds to the visitor's overall processing time.

All data obtained from the visitor is securely stored as part of the visitor's travel record. This information is made available only to authorized officials and selected law enforcement agencies on a need-to-know basis in their efforts to help protect against those who intend to harm American citizens or visitors.

The most notable change for international visitors is the new exit procedure. Most visitors who require a visa will eventually need to verify their departure. This checkout process will be completed by use of automated self-service workstations in the international departure areas of airports and seaports. By scanning travel documents and capturing fingerprints on the same inkless device, the system validates the visitor's identity, verifies his or her departure, and confirms his or her compliance with U.S. immigration policy.

Source: DHS, 2004, www.dhs.gov. "US-VISIT programe." http://www.dhs.gov/xtrvlsec/programs/content_multi_image0006.htm

TSA's security focus is on identifying risks, prioritizing them, managing these risks to acceptable levels, and mitigating the impact of potential incidents that may arise as result of these risks. Sharing of information among agencies and stakeholders — including intelligence information — has become a cornerstone of its risk management model. Recognizing that differences exist between transportation modes, TSA has needed to adapt to the complex and unique needs of both passenger and cargo security, in an attempt to instill citizen confidence in the security of the transportation system. TSA's stated guiding principle is that it will focus on the leveraging of prevention services, new technologies, best practices, public education, stakeholder outreach, and regulation compliance across transportation modes. The Federal Air Marshal Service (FAMS) is responsible for promoting confidence in the nation's civil aviation system through the deployment of federal air marshals to detect, deter, and defeat hostile acts targeting U.S. air carriers, airports, passengers, and crews.

TSA provides security to the nation's transportation systems with a primary focus on aviation security. TSA's specific responsibilities include screening of all aviation passengers and baggage through a mix of federalized and privatized screeners and technology. This screener workforce consists primarily of the 45,000 passenger and baggage screeners located at 448 commercial airports. TSA screeners augment screening through the most modern technologies, including metal detectors, x-ray machines, explosives trace detection machines, and explosives detection systems.

U.S. air carriers annually transport approximately 12.5 million tons of cargo, 2.8 million tons of which is now secured on passenger planes. The remaining 9.7 million tons of freight, shipped in cargo planes, remains a unique threat to the nation. TSA is working on the development of a screening operation to ensure the security of this cargo as well, although no system is yet in place, nor is the funding for one available.

TSA is also tasked with managing the security risk to the U.S. surface transportation systems. These systems include 9 billion passenger trips per year on the nation's mass transit systems, more than 161,000 miles of interstate and national highways and their integrated bridges and tunnels, and nearly 800,000 shipments of hazardous materials (95% of which are made by truck). These systems have come under heightened security considerations since the repeat bombings of the London subway and bus systems in July 2005. For these systems, TSA addresses these security responsibilities in partnership with other components of the DHS as well as the Department of Transportation and other departments. Table 5–4 illustrates the budget allocation for the Transportation Security Agency for FY 2007–2009.

Air Transportation Safety and Security

The primary agency for aviation safety is the Office of System Safety of the Federal Aviation Administration (FAA) within the Department of Transportation (DOT). The principal function of the

Table 5–4   TSA Budget Allocation, FY 2007–2009

	FY 2007 Revised Enacted		FY 2008 Enacted		FY 2009 President's Budget		FY 2009 +/– FY 2009	
	FTE	$000	FTE	$000	FTE	$000	FTE	$000
Aviation Security	47,259	$5,117,844	48,897	$4,808,741	49,697	$5,289,810	800	$481,069
Surface Transportation Security	288	$37,200	326	$46,613	230	$37,000	(96)	($9,613)
Transportation Threat Assessment and Credentialing	166	$72,670	166	$168,490	183	$170,018	17	$1,528
Transportation Security Support	1,476	$525,283	1,476	$523,515	1,332	$926,000	(144)	$402,485
Federal Air Marshals	—	$719,294	—	$769,500	—	—	—	($769,500)
Gross Discretionary	49,189	$6,472,291	50,865	$6,316,859	51,442	$6,422,828	577	$105,969
Fee Accounts (Mandatory)	6	$252,000	6	$503,000	6	$679,000	—	$176,000
Gross Budgetary Resources	49,195	$6,724,291	50,871	$6,819,859	51,448	$7,101,828	577	$281,969
Less Prior Year Resources	—	($66,712)	—	($4,500)	—	—	—	$4,500
Total	49,195	$6,657,579	50,871	$6,815,359	51,448	$7,101,828	577	$286,469

Source: TSA Budget Overview, DHS, Budget in Brief 2009, Washington, DC, 2008.

office is to develop and implement improved tools and processes for hazard identification, risk assessment, and risk management. The office attempts to facilitate effective use of air safety data, both inside and outside the agency for the purpose of improving overall aviation safety. The office provides international leadership in monitoring airline safety, and identifies emerging aviation safety issues and concerns. It has become a focal point for aviation safety data and information worldwide as a result.

The agency has many goals:

- To create an environment that facilitates and encourages sharing aviation safety information
- To identify appropriate data and analysis techniques and make them readily available to the international aviation community
- To develop tools to help identify safety issues
- To promote system safety methodologies within and outside the FAA
- To maximize impact of safety resource investments
- To develop, market, and promote safety information (Source: FAA, 2005, www.faa.gov)

The Aviation and Transportation Security Act (P.L. 107-71), signed by President Bush on November 19, 2001, created the Transportation Security Administration (TSA) in the Department of Transportation. With the creation of the Department of Homeland Security, the agency was absorbed into the former Directorate for Border and Transportation Security. Currently, TSA exists as a stand-alone agency with the Department of Homeland Security.

The Aviation and Transportation Security Act made many fundamental changes in the way transportation security is performed and managed in the United States. For instance, for the first time this law made aviation security a direct federal responsibility. In addition, all transportation security activities are now managed by one agency. Because of the events of September 11, aviation security is one of the highest-priority responsibilities of TSA, and the agency commits significant budget and human resources for developing strategies and implementing necessary technologies to prevent any future terrorist events connected to the abuse of the aviation system and air transportation. Figure 5–4 displays the internal budget allocations of the TSA, illustrating its heavy emphasis toward aviation

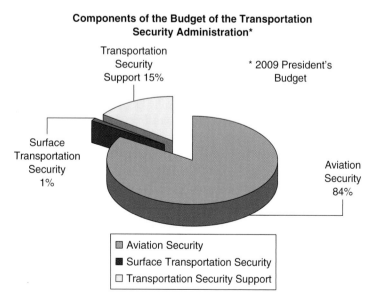

FIGURE 5–4 Components of the TSA budget. (Source: DHS, 2008)

security. It is expected that, in light of the continuing threat posed by terrorists to all public transportation systems, these trends will change and the spending gap between aviation security and other types of transportation security will diminish over time.

Since its initial full year of funding in 2003, TSA has accomplished several important projects that seek to improve air transportation security. The 2003 budget for TSA totaled $4.8 billion, an increase of more than $3.5 billion from 2002 funding levels. The 2003 budget included the costs of well over 30,000 airport security personnel, including screeners, law enforcement personnel, and screener supervisors. The budget also included funding for the purchase of explosive detection systems that had to be in place to screen all checked baggage, and the maintenance of that equipment. The 2003 budget was also the first year reflecting full funding of the greatly expanded federal air marshal program.

The president's budget request of $4.82 billion for TSA in FY 2004 was over $1 billion more than the previous year. The FY 2004 budget was spent primarily on four programs, among which the aviation security program was the largest at $4.22 billion (86%) of overall funds. The aviation security program consisted of a passenger screening program for which $1.80 billion was allocated, a baggage screening program with a budget of $944 million, and a security direction and enforcement program for which $1.47 billion was allocated (TSA, 2005, www.dhs.gov).

When TSA celebrated its fifth anniversary on November 19, 2006 it had accomplished several of its Congressionally-mandated goals and responsibilities. During that time period, TSA detected and removed more than 40 million items that are prohibited on board of airplanes. TSA installed advanced explosive detection systems in all major airports. TSA redesigned the Air Cargo Rules to ensure that air cargo transported within U.S. airspace on a daily basis is safe. TSA officials assisted the air evacuation of 25,000 hurricane victims in the aftermath of Hurricane Katrina. During that same five year period TSA grew its National Explosives Detection Canine Team Program to 425 teams at more than 80 airports and 11 public transportation systems in the nation (Transportation Security Administration, 2006).

As of 2008, TSA has grown its personnel to more than 51,000 and its budget $7.1 billion. The FY 2009 budget of the agency includes funding to complete projects that have been initiated in previous years, as well as some new projects that will further advance transportation security. Some of the FY 2009 initiatives of the TSA include:

- Behavioral Detection Officers (BDO) Program: The FY 2009 TSA budget includes $43 million for this relatively new program announced in 2006. The program includes the training of Transportation Security Officials for detecting involuntary physical and physiological reactions of passengers to identify potentially high-risk individuals. When the program is fully implemented, 90% of passengers that travel through the U.S. air transportation will be checked by a BDO.

- Aviation Direct Access Screening Program (ADASP): The $36 million allocated for this program will ensure that airport/aviation workers who have direct access to certain areas of the air transportation system are more thoroughly screened for proper identification, explosives, and other means of potential harm.

- Visible Intermodal Protection and Response (VIPR) Teams: The $30 million allocated for this program will be used to deploy physical security teams to different transportation modes that will act as deterring factors against potential terrorist plots.

- Canine Explosive Detection Program (K-9) Teams: The $14-million funding will be used to increase the number of teams to more than 750.

- Secure Flight Initiative: The goal of the Secure Flight Initiative is to replace the current passenger vetting process performed by individual airliners with a program managed by the Transportation Security Administration. The budget in FY 2009 allocated for this initiative is $32 million (Source: TSA Budget Overview; DHS, "Budget in Brief," 2009).

Trucking Security

Trucking security is an important component of transportation security because a significant portion of the nation's hazardous materials (HAZMATS) are transported by trucks on public highways and roads. TSA is tasked with managing the security risk to the U.S. surface transportation systems, while ensuring the freedom of movement of people and commerce. For these systems, TSA addresses these security responsibilities in partnership with other components of the DHS as well as DOT and other departments.

A serious HAZMAT incident is defined by DOT's Research and Special Programs Administration (RISPA) as an incident that involves a fatality or major injury caused by the release of a hazardous material, the evacuation of 25 or more persons as a result of release of a hazardous material or exposure to fire, a release or exposure to fire that results in the closure of a major transportation artery, the alteration of an aircraft flight plan or operation, the release of radioactive materials from Type B packaging, the release of over 11.9 gallons or 88.2 pounds of a severe marine pollutant, or the release of a bulk quantity (over 119 gallons or 882 pounds) of a hazardous material. Table 5–5 illustrates the number of these serious incidents that have occurred on U.S. highways between 1997 and 2006.

The Office of Hazardous Materials Safety of DOT/RISPA is responsible for coordinating a national safety program for the transportation of hazardous materials by air, rail, highway, and water in the United States. The Code of Federal Regulations (CFR) 49 Part 107 documents the steps being taken to enhance hazardous material transportation security. Subchapter C, Part 107, specifically discusses regulations for HAZMAT transportation on U.S. highways. The subparts of the document include information about regulations for loading and unloading of HAZMAT transportation vehicles, segregation and separation of HAZMAT vehicles and shipments in transit, accidents, and regulations applying to hazardous material on motor vehicles carrying passengers for hire. To supplement safety efforts, the DHS Office of Screening Coordination and Operations (SCO) within the (former) BTS Directorate initiated hazardous materials trucker background checks in 2005 in an effort to secure the highways and trucks. Since then the office's name has been changed to the "Screening Coordination Office" and it has been tasked with the coordination of all screening activities and systems administered and maintained by DHS.

In fiscal years 2005 and 2006, TSA provided grants totaling $4.8 million to trucking companies. This funding level increased to $11.6 million in fiscal year 2007, and again to $15.5 million for fiscal year 2008. The funding priorities for 2008 were the following:

1. Participant Identification and Recruitment: Identification and recruitment of highway professionals, such as truckers, school bus drivers, motor coach drivers, highway workers, and first responders to participate in highway security efforts; and development of a five-year strategic plan

Table 5–5   Classification of Serious HAZMAT Incidents in the United States by Mode of Transportation and Yearly Frequency

Mode	1997	1998	1999	2000	2001	2002	2003	2004	2005	2006	Total
Air	13	25	18	35	37	15	13	6	18	17	197
Highway	397	356	447	449	488	377	399	400	423	400	4,136
Railway	61	72	68	83	63	71	58	82	85	76	719
Water	1	4	0	2	1	3	2	4	2	1	20
Total	472	457	533	569	589	466	472	492	528	494	5,072

Source: U.S. Department of Transportation, Hazardous Materials Information System, Washington, DC, 2008.

2. Planning: Development of emergency response and contingency plans based on identified high-risk scenarios (e.g., truck hijacking, HAZMAT) and conducting hazard analysis and risk assessment in an effort to improve the plan

3. Training: Development of a Web-based security training system to train highway professionals, specialized HAZMAT drivers, and state and local law enforcement organizations. Design of an evaluation methodology for all training programs; and the development of a five-year strategic plan for training

4. Communications: Maintain a full-service (24/7) communications/call center staffed with well-trained responders who will provide nationwide first responder/enforcement contact numbers and electronic linkage to registered participants, and the development of a five-year strategic plan for communications

5. Information Analysis and Distribution: The applicant will provide management consulting services and oversight in cooperation with ODP leadership to maintain the Highway Information Sharing and Analysis Center (ISAC), located at the Transportation Security Operations Center (TSOC) in Herndon, Virginia. This center is dedicated exclusively to highway and highway transport–related security needs and issues. The applicant will provide recommendations, implementation strategies, and a completed plan for continued Highway ISAC operations. Responsibilities may include identifying the appropriate role of a highway-specific ISAC, identification of benefits of highway-specific ISAC separation from existing rail or other centers, optimal configuration and location of a new ISAC, and optimal staffing or implementation strategies (Sources: DHS, "FY 2006 Critical Infrastructure Protection Program DHS, 2005"; DHS, "FY 2007 Critical Infrastructure Protection Program DHS," 2006; "FY 2008 Critical Infrastructure Protection Program Transportation Security Administration," 2007; DHS, "FY 2008 Trucking Security Program Fact Sheet").

The Bureau of Customs and Border Protection in 2005 requested $125 million for a WMD Detection Technology Program. The need for this purchase of additional radiation portal monitors is considered critically important because the equipment will provide CBP with a passive, nonintrusive means of screening trucks and other vehicles for the presence of radiological materials, which will allow for much faster and effective processing of time-sensitive cargo. The first of the 200 such radiation detection trucks ordered by the DHS was deployed at the Port of New York/New Jersey in May 2006.

Ports and Shipping Security

The nation's ports are together a critical component of the U.S. transportation infrastructure, and are vital to the economic prosperity of the country. Seventy-seven U.S. ports are open to international trade, import, and export, 30 of which account for almost 99% of all international maritime trade activity. Securing maritime transportation is a critical task for DHS, because a successful terrorist attack on any major U.S. port could not only result in significant loss of life and tremendous physical damage, but also serious disruption to the economy and commerce of the United States and its trade partners. As mandated by the SAFE Port Act of October 2006, DHS is tasked with responsibility for assuring the security of the maritime transportation system and the ports through risk mitigation, vulnerability analysis and the establishment of preventive measures in those facilities. The SAFE Port Act also tasked DHS with the creation of a resumption plan to minimize the disruption to economic activity in the case of a major terrorist attack to the nation's seaports.

The USCG has its own maritime strategy for homeland security, where duties, responsibilities, and strategic missions of the agency are clearly defined. The homeland security mission of the Coast Guard is to protect the U.S. maritime domain and the U.S. marine transportation system and deny their use and exploitation by terrorists as a means for attacks on U.S. territory, population, and critical infrastructure and to prepare for and, in the event of attack, conduct emergency response operations. When directed by the supported or supporting commander, the USCG conducts military homeland defense operations. The Coast Guard is the lead federal agency for maritime homeland security. In accomplishing its homeland security mission, the strategic goals of the Coast Guard are as follows:

- Increase maritime domain awareness.
- Conduct enhanced maritime security operations.
- Close port security gaps.
- Build critical security capabilities.
- Leverage partnerships to mitigate security risks.
- Ensure readiness for homeland defense operations.

The DHS Transportation Security Agency's main role in maritime and port security has been to provide grants to support port security and related issues. From 2002 until 2007, the Department of Homeland Security awarded more than $1 billion in grants to many port owners, operators, and service providers as part of the Port Security Grant Program within its broader Infrastructure Protection Grant Program. In 2008 the Port Security Grant Program budget was increased to $388.6 million (DHS, "Overview: FY 2007 Infrastructure Protection Program Final Awards," 2007; DHS, "FY 2008 Port Security Grant Program," 2008).

Due to the importance of commerce through seaports, and the relatively complex supply chain operations involved, assuring the security of seaports is a unique challenge. The supply chain's complexity is due not only to the multistep process needed by each cargo item as it safely navigates its way to the recipient, but due to the nature of the various stakeholders involved including private companies and foreign governments. Figure 5–5 provides a simplified overview of the process for a typical container shipped to the U.S. from a foreign destination.

A careful examination at Figure 5–5 quickly reveals that nine out of the 16 cargo security steps occure outside the jurisdiction of U.S authorities. However, if prevention is key to security, all 16 of these steps are vital to the detection and mitigation of threats to containers in transit. For each step, DHS has implemented individual security measures based on risk assessments that have prioritized intervention measures at key ports and processes in the shipment process. To ensure the effectiveness of each prevention measure, the U.S. government works in cooperation with foreign governments and their

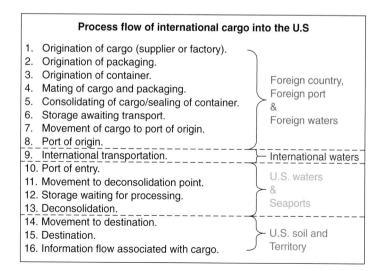

FIGURE 5–5 Process flow of international cargo into the United States. (Source: DHS, 2007)

corresponding port authorities. In many of these foreign ports, U.S. Customs and Border Protection officials perform daily audits and inspections of containers bound for the U.S., and work with foreign counterparts to ensure that chemicals, biological agents, nuclear materials, and explosives that may be hidden in containers are detected and interdicted before they pose a threat to life and commerce.

DHS is systematically addressing vulnerabilities that are specific to different stages of the seaborne supply chain. In that framework, the risk intervention measures and initiatives used by DHS can be categorized into three major groups: (1) overseas vulnerability reduction, (2) in-transit vulnerability reduction, and (3) vulnerability reduction in U.S. waters and on U.S. shores. An overview of various initiatives in each group follows.

Initiatives for overseas vulnerability reduction:

1. 24-Hour Advanced Manifest Rule — Awareness: All sea carriers with the exception of bulk carriers and approved break bulk cargo are required to provide proper cargo descriptions and valid consignee addresses 24 hours before cargo is loaded at the foreign port for shipment to the United States through the Sea Automated Manifest System. Failure to meet the 24-hour Advanced Manifest Rule results in a "do not load" message and other penalties. The information collected by the Customs and Border Protection (CBP) is analyzed and cargo deemed as high risk is inspected at the port of origin before it starts its journey into the United States.

2. Container Security Initiative (CSI) — Awareness and Prevention: Under the CSI program, the screening of containers that pose a risk for terrorism is accomplished by teams of CBP officials deployed to work in concert with their host nation counterparts. As of 2008, there are 56 international ports that take part in the CSI and those ports account for 90% of all trans-Atlantic and trans-Pacific cargo imported into the U.S. that is subject to prescreening prior to loading. A full list of all enrolled international ports has been provided in this chapter in the section on U.S. customs and border protection.

3. Customs–Trade Partnership against Terrorism (C-TPAT) — Awareness and Prevention: Through C-TPAT, thousands of importers, carriers, brokers, forwarders, ports and terminals, and foreign manufacturers, most of whom are private companies, have taken the necessary steps to secure their supply chains. Under the C-TPAT initiative, business participants providing verifiable security information are eligible for special benefits. The security enhancements put in place by C-TPAT participants allow DHS to devote more resources to high-risk shipments. As of last reported count (2005) more than 9,000 companies had enrolled in the program.

4. International Ship and Port Facility Security (ISPS) Code — Awareness and Prevention: The ISPS Code requires large vessels operating internationally and port facilities that serve them to conduct security assessments, to develop security plans, and to hire security officers. By establishing a standard for security, the world has increased its ability to prevent maritime related attacks by making ports around the world more aware of unusual or suspicious activity. In the United States, the code is followed by the enactment of provisions of the Marine Transportation Security Act of 2002, and by aligning domestic marine security regulations with the guidelines of ISPS.

5. International Port Security Program — Awareness and Prevention: Under this effort, the U.S. Coast Guard and the host nations work jointly to evaluate the countries' overall compliance with the ISPS Code. The Coast Guard uses the information gained from site visits to improve the United States' own security practices and to determine if additional security precautions are required for vessels arriving in the United States from other countries.

6. Operation Safe Commerce (OSC) — Awareness and Prevention: Operation Safe Commerce (OSC) was the name of the DHS pilot program dedicated to analyzing security in the commercial supply chain and testing solutions to close security gaps. The technologies tested through the program will enhance maritime cargo security, protect the global supply chain,

and facilitate the flow of commerce. DHS has awarded a total of more than $200 million in grants to participants of the program. The ports of Seattle and Tacoma, Los Angeles, and Long Beach and the Port Authority of New York/New Jersey as well as selected international ports participated in the program. Operation Safe Commerce was completed by year-end 2004. The findings, outcomes, and lessons learned in the pilot project have been largely incorporated into the DHS "Strategy to Enhance International Supply Chain Security" of 2007.

Initiatives for "in-transit" vulnerability reduction:

1. Smart Box Initiative — Prevention: One core element of Container Security Initiative is using smarter, tamper-evident containers that will better secure containerized shipping. Designed to be "tamper evident," the smart box couples an internationally approved mechanical seal affixed to an alternate location on the container door with an electronic container security device designed to deter and detect tampering of the container door. If someone attempts to open the cargo door after it has been sealed, the smart box device on the door would reflect that there had been an attempted intrusion into the container. As of 2008, the container security market was rapidly growing, and there are various smart box devices available on the market with different capabilities and relying on different technologies (radio frequency, cellular, satellite), although regular use of such devices in all containers has not yet occurred.

2. Ship Security Alert System (SSAS) — Response: Like a silent alarm in a bank, an SSAS allows a vessel operator to send a covert alert to shore for incidents involving acts of violence (such as piracy or terrorism), indicating the security of the ship is under threat or has been compromised. The International Maritime Organization requires all vessels of 500 gross tons or larger to have SSAS on board to ensure covert alerting of a designated authority ensuring a timely response during a threat.

3. Automated Targeting System (ATS) — Awareness: CBP's ATS serves as the premier tool for performing transactional risk assessments and evaluating potential national security risks posed by cargo and passengers arriving by sea, air, truck, and rail. Using prearrival information and input from the intelligence community, this rules-based system identifies high-risk targets before they arrive in the United States.

4. 96-Hour Advance Notice of Arrival — Awareness and Prevention: Ships must notify the Coast Guard 96 hours before arriving in a U.S. port and provide detailed information on the crew, passenger, cargo, and voyage history. This information is analyzed using databases and intelligence information, including reviewing previous security problems with the vessel or illegal activity on the part of the crew. Part of this analysis will also account for the security environment in previous ports of call. By obtaining this information well in advance of a vessel's arrival, the U.S. Coast Guard is able to make determinations about which vessels require additional attention, including security precautions such as an at-sea boarding or armed escort during transit to and from port.

Initiatives for vulnerability reduction "in U.S. waters and on U.S. shores":

1. National Targeting Center (NTC) — Prevention and Response: The priority mission of CBP's NTC is to provide tactical targeting and analytical research support for CBP antiterrorism efforts. Experts in passenger and cargo targeting at the NTC operate around the clock using tools like the Automated Targeting System (ATS) to identify tactical targets and support intradepartmental and interagency antiterrorist operations. The NTC also supports operations in the field, including the Container Security Initiative (CSI) personnel stationed at critical foreign ports throughout the world.

2. Maritime Intelligence Fusion Centers — Prevention: Located in Norfolk, Virginia, and Alameda, California, these units compile and synthesize intelligence products from the federal, state, and local level dealing with maritime security. These intelligence products are then disseminated to homeland security professionals across the country responsible for securing ports and waterways.

3. High-Interest Vessel Boardings — Prevention: Before they are allowed to enter port, all vessels are screened for the security risk they pose to the United States based on information about the vessel's cargo, size, voyage, security history, and any intelligence information. Those identified as higher risk are targeted for offshore boardings to ensure potential security issues are addressed prior to entry into port. In addition, the Coast Guard randomly selects vessels for security boardings to ensure an element of unpredictability and thus deterrence. Specially trained Coast Guard teams board the boats through traditional water-based methods or via fast roping from helicopters.

4. Automatic Identification System — Awareness: AIS is a type of vessel-tracking equipment that automatically sends detailed ship information to other ships and shore-based agencies, allowing for comprehensive, virtually instantaneous vessel tracking and monitoring, to increase security and safety in shipping channels. Currently, most vessels required to use this technology are large vessels on international voyages. The Coast Guard's goal is to complete the implementation of a Nationwide Automatic Identification System by 2014.

5. Area Maritime Security Committees — Awareness, Prevention, and Response: The Coast Guard has established committees in all the nation's ports to coordinate the activities of all port stakeholders, including other federal, local, and state agencies, industry, and the boating public. These groups are tasked with collaborating on plans to secure their ports so the resources of an area can be best used to deter, prevent, and respond to terror threats.

6. Port Security Assessment Program — Awareness: This program is aimed at increasing the information and best practices available to port officials across the country to help them make decisions about how to reduce the vulnerability of their ports. The Coast Guard prioritized the examination of key infrastructure in the nation's 55 most economically and strategically important ports for potential vulnerabilities. Some ports have also used DHS Port Security grant funds to perform risk assessments and vulnerability analysis of their facilities. In addition to these assessments, the Coast Guard is creating a geographic information systems (GIS) database that can be easily searched for national, regional, and local information. A Government Accountability Office study identified inadequate project planning and delayed implementation regarding the USCG GIS project.

7. Port Security Grants — Awareness, Prevention, and Response: The Port Security Grant, Program provides federal resources for projects to enhance facility and operational security for critical national seaports. Funds assist ports in analyzing vulnerabilities and then closing gaps in security through physical enhancements like access control gates, fencing, lighting, and advanced communication and surveillance systems. The program also funds the implementation of security strategies to prevent and respond to terror threats. From 2002 to until 2007, the Department of Homeland Security awarded more than $1 billion in grants to many port owners, operators, and service providers as part of the Port Security Grant Program within its broader Infrastructure Protection Grant Program.

8. Non-Intrusive Inspection Technology (NII) — Prevention: Nonintrusive inspection (NII) technologies allow U.S. Customs and Border Protection to screen a larger portion of the stream of commercial traffic in less time while facilitating legitimate trade. CBP officers use large-scale gamma ray and x-ray imaging systems to safely and efficiently screen conveyances for contraband, including weapons of mass destruction. These units can scan the interior of a full-size 40-foot container in under a minute. Inspectors also use personal radiation detectors to scan for signs of radioactive materials, as well as special high-tech tools such as density meters

and fiber-optic scopes to peer inside suspicious containers. Finally, if necessary, containers are opened and unloaded for a more intensive manual inspection.

9. Maritime Safety and Security Teams (MSSTs) — Prevention and Response: MSSTs are a Coast Guard rapid response force assigned to vital ports and capable of nationwide deployment via air, ground, or sea transportation to meet emerging threats. MSSTs were created in direct response to the terrorist attacks on September 11, 2001. They have unique capabilities, including explosive-detection dogs, personnel trained to conduct fast-roping deployments from a helicopter to a hostile vessel, and antiterrorism/force protection small boat handling training. As of 2006 there are 13 distinct MSSTs within the U.S. Coast Guard, each with approximately 75 personnel.

10. Guarding In-Between the Ports — Prevention: Coast Guard, U.S. CBP Border Patrol, and U.S. Immigration and Customs Enforcement's Air and Marine Operations units are responsible for patrolling and securing the nation's borders between the ports of entry.

11. Transportation Workers Identity Card (TWIC) — Awareness and Prevention: The goal of the TWIC program is to develop a secure uniform credential to prevent potential terrorist threats from entering sensitive areas of the transportation system. When implemented, the TWIC program will ensure that credentials contain a biometric identifier to positively authenticate identities of TWIC holders. By having one universally recognized credential, workers avoid paying for redundant cards and background investigations to enter secure areas at multiple facilities. Transportation Security Administration kicked off the first TWIC credentialing in October 2007 at Port of Wilmington, Delaware and since then laid out a schedule for other critical ports' credentialing dates. TSA is expecting to complete the TWIC process for more than 1 million transportation workers by end of 2008 (Sources: DHS, "Budget in Brief 2009," 2008; DHS, "Strategy to Enhance International Supply Chain Security," 2007; Government Accountability Office, "GAO-07-412 Port Risk Management," 2007; Government Accountability Office, "GAO-04-1062 Maritime Security," 2004; Transportation Security Administration, "DHS Agencies Announce Enrollment Dates for TWIC in 10 Ports," 2007; United States Coast Guard, "Secure Seas, Open Ports," 2004).

Bus Transportation Security

Bus transportation safety is an often-neglected link in the nation's transportation infrastructure, and represents a substantial homeland security vulnerability. In the first edition of this text, we described the issue of bus transportation security as follows: "The bus transportation system is likely to eventually become a target of terrorists because the system has comparatively less protection against terrorist attacks, which makes it 'soft' for terrorists searching for less risky but high-consequence attacks." On July 7, 2007, a terrorist detonated a bomb in a London double-decker bus in a coordinated attack on the bus and rail networks of that city, killing 13 people and injuring many more. The incident highlighted the vulnerability of the bus transportation system, despite that the majority of transportation security efforts focus on air and sea transport. Securing the bus system is an extremely challenging task as public ground transportation is much more dynamic and state-changing than other types of transport. With multiple stops and frequently changing passengers over short periods of time, securing the bus system becomes a very resource intensive and in some instances impractical process. However, there are ways to reduce our vulnerabilities even if we cannot totally eliminate the security risks of bus transportation.

To support the intercity bus transportation sector, DHS established the Intercity Bus Security Grant Program as part of its Infrastructure Protection Program. DHS uses this program to provide funding to intercity bus companies for the improvement of their transport security measures. Over the past five years it has provided more than $60 million in grants to eligible recipients (Table 5–6).

Table 5–6 Distribution of Department of Homeland Security Intercity Bus Security Grant Funding by Year and Recipient

Grantee	FY03	FY04	FY05	FY06	FY07	Total
Academy	$582,386	$370,431	$267,279	$136,476	$854,575	$2,211,147
Greyhound	$9,074,355	$1,603,084	$5,471,365	$5,105,000	$3,283,584	$24,537,388
Peter Pan	$1,173,875	$402,750	$142,500	$261,250	$174,234	$2,154,609
All Others	$8,969,391	$7,549,267	$3,775,994	$4,000,274	$7,327,607	$31,622,533
Total	$19,800,007	$9,925,532	$9,657,138	$9,503,000	$11,640,000	$60,525,677

Source: Department of Homeland Security, Overview: FY 2007 Infrastructure Protection Program Final Awards, Washington, DC, 2007.

In FY 2008 the Bus Security Grant Program was funded at $11.2 million, and the following funding priorities were announced by the Department of Homeland Security:

- Developing a vulnerability assessment and security plan
- Covering operating and capital costs associated with over-the-road bus security awareness, preparedness, and response training)
- Conducting live or simulated exercises
- Conducting public awareness campaigns
- Covering operational costs to hire, train, and employ police and security officers, including canine units
- Modifying over-the-road buses
- Installing cameras and video surveillance equipment on over-the-road buses and at terminals, garages, and bus facilities
- Constructing and modifying terminals, garages, and facilities
- Establishing and improving emergency communications systems
- Implementing and operating passenger screening programs for weapons and explosives
- Protecting or isolating drivers of over-the-road buses
- Conducting chemical, biological, radiological, or explosive detection initiatives
- Acquiring, upgrading, installing, or operating equipment, software, or services for the collection, storage, or exchange of passenger and driver information
- Covering overtime reimbursement for security personnel during periods of high threat levels (Source: Transportation Security Administration, "FY 2008 Intercity Bus Security Grant Program," 2008)

The president's 2009 budget for the Department of Homeland Security included $12 million funding for intercity bus security grants. Those grants will be provided to projects with respect to the revised funding priorities (Congressional Research Service, 2008).

Railway Transportation Security

The railroad system is another highly utilized and valuable component of the U.S. transportation infrastructure that must now be protected against potential terrorist and other vulnerabilities. DHS made its most noticeable references to the protection of the railway system in the National Strategy for the Physical Protection of Critical Infrastructure and Key Assets and in the announcement of Operation Liberty Shield.

The National Strategy for the Physical Protection of Critical Infrastructure and Key Assets document mentions potential vulnerabilities and talks about possible terrorist attack scenarios to the railroad system, and it identifies four priorities for improvement in the railroad security:

1. The need to develop improved decision-making criteria regarding the shipment of hazardous materials: DHS and DOT, coordinating with other federal agencies, state and local governments, and industry, will facilitate the development of an improved process to ensure informed decision making with respect to hazardous materials shipment.

2. The need to develop technologies and procedures to screen intermodal containers and passenger baggage: DHS and DOT will work with sector counterparts to identify and explore technologies and processes to enable efficient and expeditious screening of rail passengers and baggage, especially at intermodal stations.

3. The need to improve security of intermodal transportation: DHS and DOT will work with sector counterparts to identify and facilitate the development of technologies and procedures to secure intermodal containers and detect threatening content. DHS and DOT will work with the rail industry to devise or enable a hazardous materials identification system that supports the needs of first responders, yet avoids providing terrorists with easy identification of a potential weapon.

4. The need to clearly delineate roles and responsibilities regarding surge requirements: DHS and DOT will work with industry to delineate infrastructure protection roles and responsibilities to enable the rail industry to address surge requirements for resources in the case of catastrophic events. Costs and resource allocation remain a contentious issue for the rail sector. DHS and DOT will also convene a working group consisting of government and industry representatives to identify options for the implementation of surge capabilities, including access to federal facilities and capabilities in extreme emergencies.

The national physical protection strategy clearly identifies the transportation of HAZMAT within the railroad infrastructure as the greatest vulnerability of the system. This assessment was reiterated by Admiral James Loy, former TSA administrator, in a meeting with the North American Rail Shippers Association where he identified the following as the primary threats to the railway system: (1) hazardous material, (2) nuclear and radiological material, (3) food and livestock, and (4) intermodal containers.

In response to Admiral Loy's assessment, DOT and DHS released a document regarding the HAZMAT transportation vulnerability and measures to be taken to minimize the terrorist threat to the system. This document provides background information on the improvements accomplished in the railroad system since September 11. It discusses the security task force established by the Association of American Railroads (AAR) to assess vulnerabilities in several critical areas, such as physical assets, information technology, chemicals and hazardous materials, defense shipments, train operations, and passenger security. In March 2003, DHS announced Operation Liberty Shield, which details the following steps to enhance railway security:

1. To improve rail bridge security: State governors have been asked to provide additional police or National Guard forces at selected bridges.

2. To increase railroad infrastructure security: Railroad companies will be asked to increase security at major facilities and key rail hubs.

3. AMTRAK security measures: AMTRAK will implement security measures consistent with private rail companies.

4. To increase railroad hazardous material safety: At the request of the Department of Transportation, private railroad companies will monitor shipments of hazardous material and increase surveillance of trains carrying this material.

On April 8, 2004, the Senate's Commerce, Science, and Transportation Committee approved the Rail Security Act of 2004, which authorized an increase in rail security funding by $1.1 billion, over the initial funding of only $65 million. The Rail Security Act, as proposed, required DHS to conduct a vulnerability assessment of the nation's rail systems and report back to Congress with its findings. The vulnerability assessment requires a review of freight and passenger rail transportation, including the identification and evaluation of critical assets and infrastructures; threats to those assets and infrastructures; vulnerabilities that are specific to rail transportation of hazardous materials; and security weaknesses. Based on the assessment, DHS is expected to develop prioritized recommendations for improving the security of rail infrastructure and facilities, terminals, tunnels, bridges, and other at-risk areas; deploying weapons detection and surveillance equipment; training employees; and conducting public outreach campaigns. The results of the DHS freight and passenger rail transportation vulnerability assessment will also be used to distribute future funding for the Rail Security Grant Program.

The bill authorized $5 million for FY 2005 for the vulnerability assessment and development of recommendations. The bill also requires DHS to conduct a pilot program of random security screening of passengers and baggage at five passenger rail stations served by Amtrak. The program included testing a wide range of explosives-detection technologies, devices, and methods, and a requirement that intercity rail passengers produce government-issued photo identification prior to boarding.

In 2007, the Government Accountability Office (GAO) conducted an extensive study of passenger rail security. The study found that as of early 2007, the Transportation Security Administration was about to complete the risk and vulnerability assessment for the largest rail transit agencies, but the agency is not yet in a position to have complete information that can be used to prioritize the different rail infrastructures based on their security risks and vulnerabilities in a nationwide setting. The funding requirements for the FY 2008 Freight Rail Security Grant Program also support this claim in that it allows Class II and Class III freight rail companies (i.e., companies with annual revenues of less than $319.2 million) to use the funds for conducting risk and vulnerability assessments, whereas having those assessments in place is a precondition for Class I freight rail companies to apply for funding.

To comply with the Rail Security Act, TSA began the prototype phase of its Transportation Worker Identity Credential (TWIC) program on November 17, 2004, on five pilot sites that were initially port facilities. Each site uses biometric technology to provide authorized transportation workers access to controlled areas. Using fingerprint and iris scan technology, the TWIC ties the transportation worker to the credential and threat assessment and can be used in conjunction with access control to critical components of the nation's transportation infrastructure. The TWIC program is designed to enhance security at U.S. transportation facilities while boosting the efficiency of commercial activity. The prototype phase of the project concluded in 2005 and after careful review of requirements, data, and comments, DHS released the final notice of proposed rulemaking (NPRM) in late 2006. DHS used 2007 to obtain necessary equipment for the full deployment and initiation of the TWIC program and by late 2007 the rollout of the program had officially started in port facilities. As of early 2008 the rollout was still continuing on port facilities and rail infrastructure and facilities had not begun their credentialing process.

The Association of American Railroads coordinated and conducted a comprehensive risk analysis covering the entire railway industry. The scope of this risk assessment included the train operations, communication and cybersecurity aspects, identification and protection of critical assets, transportation of hazardous materials, and identification of a military liaison. The association worked closely with the federal intelligence community and security experts and identified and prioritized more than 1,300 critical assets. As a result of the vulnerability analysis, more than 50 permanent changes were made to procedures and operations, including restricted access to facilities, increased tracking of certain shipments, enhanced employee security training, and cybersecurity improvements. In addition to those measures, it was decided that one rail police officer should sit on the FBI's National Joint Terrorism Task Force, and two rail analysts should sit in the Department of Homeland Security intelligence offices to help evaluate data at the top-secret level. The association created a DOD-certified, full-time operations center, working at the secret level to monitor and evaluate intelligence on potential threats and communicate with railroads through the Railway Alert Network (RAN). A Surface Transportation Information Sharing and Analysis Center (ST-ISAC) — operating at the top secret level — was also created to collect, analyze, and disseminate information on physical and cybersecurity threats (Association of American Railroads, 2004).

The TSA provided the top 10 mass transit and passenger rail agencies with TSA-certified explosives detection canine teams to aid in the identification of explosives materials within the mass transit/rail transportation system. The pilot inspection program was named the Transit and Rail Inspection Pilot (TRIP), which is a first-time rail security technology study conducted by DHS in cooperation with several other entities. TRIP was conducted in three phases. TRIP Phase I occurred at the New Carrollton, Maryland, rail station and evaluated the use of technologies for screening rail passengers and their baggage prior to boarding a train. TRIP Phase II occurred at Union Station in Washington, DC, and tested the use of screening equipment for checked baggage and cargo prior to their loading onto an Amtrak passenger train, as well as screening of unclaimed baggage and temporarily stored items inside Union Station. TRIP Phase III occurred on board a Shoreline East commuter rail car. The goal of Phase III was to evaluate the use of existing technologies installed on a rail car to screen passengers and their baggage for explosives, while the rail car is in transit. By 2007, DHS increased its deployment and coverage of explosive detection and canine teams to 13 mass transit systems and a total of 53 canine teams.

In addition to the TRIP program, TSA hired and deployed 100 surface transportation (rail) inspectors to enhance the level of national transportation security by leveraging private and public partnerships through a consistent national program of compliance reviews, audits, and enforcement actions pertaining to required standards and directives.

The DHS FY 2005 Freight Rail Security Program was appropriated total funds of $5 million. The funding priorities for the program were as follows:

1. Development of a Rail Corridor Risk Management Tool: The focus of this priority is on the development of a web-based Rail Corridor Risk Management Tool (RCRMT) for use by the federal, state, and local governments and private industry. The RCRMT is expected to leverage existing technologies and accepted risk management practices already in use by DHS and DOT where feasible, and incorporate new technologies and elements where necessary. In addition, the RCRMT must complement and support the rail corridor assessments currently being conducted by TSA, IAIP, and FRA in eight locations nationwide. This project also has to include the development of a comprehensive training curriculum for use of the RCRMT by state and local governments and industry. The final stage of the program includes a field test of the RCRMT and associated training program in Chicago, Illinois. Total funding available for this project priority was $3 million.

2. Development of a Rail Corridor Hazmat Response and Recovery Tool: DOT is in the process of updating and revising regulatory requirements previously implemented under PHMSA docket HM-232 — Hazardous Materials: Security Requirements for Offerors and Transporters of Hazardous Materials, published on March 25, 2003 (68 FR 14509), as a result of responses to a request for comments published on August 16, 2004 (69 FR 50987) and experiences obtained through the joint DHS/DOT toxic inhalation hazard working group. One aspect the departments are considering is the requirement to conduct safety/security risk analyses of current and alternative Toxic Inhalation Hazard (TIH) routes. These requirements, if adopted, would mandate carriers to evaluate the safety and security risks present on each TIH route and at each railroad facility (yard, storage location, dispatching center) along the route, noting the specific measures the railroad has taken to ameliorate the noted risks. Among the factors to be considered in the analysis are:

   • Volume of material transported
   • Presence or absence of signals and train control systems along route (dark vs. signaled territory)

- Track conditions
- Proximity to iconic targets or environmentally sensitive areas
- Population density along route
- Venues along route (stations, events, places of congregation)
- Emergency response capabilities along route
- Trip length for route
- Areas of high vulnerability along route
- Presence of passenger traffic along route (shared track)
- Number and types of grade crossings and public access points
- Grade and grade curvature
- Hazard detection equipment installed along the right-of-way
- Single vs. double track
- Density and speed of train operations

To address these challenges, the Rail Corridor Hazmat Response and Recovery Tool (RCHRRT) project exists to focus on the development of a Web-based tool that would support assessment of routes based on risk, and assist federal, state, and local emergency response and recovery agencies in allocating appropriate resources in the most needed TIH rail corridors and rail segments. Specifically, the RCHRRT exists to provide:

- A protocol for performing route-specific risk reviews to identify and evaluate HAZMAT risk factors and to inform route selection decisions. The protocol will identify risk factors and alert levels of communities along specific routes, but it will not attempt to quantify associated risks.
- Route-specific risk indices for specific routes that measure relative route-level risks for HAZMAT shipments, and which can be implemented without an extensive, time-consuming effort to identify, manipulate, and compile data
- A rail HAZMAT transportation risk model to quantify the likelihood and consequences of HAZMAT releases due to railroad accidents that accounts for emergency response capabilities where applicable. The model should be able to meet key user requirements without requiring an excessively complex and time-consuming development effort.

The RCHRRT is also expected to complement and benefit from the activities proposed in the first project. Whereas the RCRMT is intended to advise and inform decisions about security and countermeasure enhancements, RCHRRT would provide state and local emergency managers with a tool that would significantly enhance their response planning and incident response and recovery capabilities related to rail operations. The RCHRRT must leverage existing commercial and government off-the-shelf solutions, which would in turn facilitate connectivity with a broader user community. The final stage of the project will include a field test of the tool in Chicago. As with the RCRMT, this project must leverage the work and existing structure of the CREATE partnership. This would also allow for side-by-side usage of the two tools to determine their compatibility and potential for integration.

3. Development and Demonstration of "Safe Haven" Concepts for In-Route TIH Shipments: The "safe haven" concept will provide an enhanced level of security for "lock-down" facilities that handle bulk TIH shipments. The strategy will also focus on expediting the movement of trains carrying bulk TIH from lock-down facilities to customers' secured facilities or other rail lock-down facilities. The first phase of this project must involve the evaluation of potential procedures

and technologies to reduce access to railcars carrying TIH materials. This evaluation would include consideration of the alert level security actions developed by the railroad and chemical industries (customer storage of hazardous materials on leased track, reducing inventory in yards and plants, protocols for handling and securing in-route shipments, and coordination with FBI WMD district offices). The second phase of the project must include field tests of the solution sets at several sights along the New Jersey Freight Rail Corridor. These field tests would be conducted in partnership with industry, as well as applicable state and local authorities.

The project plan established by the Railroad Research Foundation indicates an expected completion date of January 2008 by the chosen contractor (IIT EWA), but as of March 2008 there was no indication that the project was concluded.

The FY 2008 Freight Rail Security Grant Program provided $15 million to freight rail service providers that operate in at least one high population-density area and have completed the development of a vulnerability assessment and security plan. For Class I rail carriers, the requirement of having a complete vulnerability assessment and security plan is a very strict requirement as they cannot use any of the funding they receive for this purpose. For Class II and Class III rail carriers, the requirement is still valid but those carriers can use the funding to conduct further vulnerability analysis or for the expenses of improving their current security plan. The FY 2008 Freight Rail Security Program was designed to fund the following priorities:

- Vulnerability assessments and security plans: Freight railroad vulnerability assessments will provide a broader picture of the mode's preparedness, as well as security risks that need to be mitigated. In an effort to "buy down" these security risks, security plans will help target resources and mitigation strategies toward gaps in the mode's security identified by the vulnerability assessments. The information captured in the vulnerability assessments and security plans (including any all mitigation strategies) will form the basis of funding priorities for this grant program in future years, as appropriate. Freight railroad carriers without complete vulnerability assessments and security plans will not be considered for other projects in future grant years. Only Class II and Class III carriers are eligible for this type of funding.

- Security training for railroad frontline employees: Effective employee training programs address individual employee responsibilities and provide heightened security awareness. Training will cover adequately assessing and reporting incidents, appropriate employee response, crew communication and coordination, and incident evacuation procedures. For example, a well-trained railroad employee can help ensure that trespassers on railroad property are identified and reported. This type of funding is available for all eligible participants of the grant program (Sources: DHS, "Fiscal Year 2005 Freight Rail Security Program Application Kit," 2004; Government Accountability Office, "Passenger Rail Security — Federal Strategy and Enhanced Coordination Needed to Prioritize and Guide Security Efforts," 2007; Transportation Security Administration, "Fact Sheet: FY 2008 Freight Rail Security Grant Program," 2007; Transportation Security Administration, "FAQ: Transportation Worker Identification Credential (TWIC)," 2007; Transportation Security Administration, "FY 2008 Freight Rail Security Grant Program," 2007).

Information Security and National Network Infrastructure Security

Information security is defined as the techniques, technical measures, and administrative measures used to protect information assets from deliberate or inadvertent unauthorized acquisition, damage, disclosure, manipulation, modification, loss, or use (McDaniel, 1994). Network infrastructure security refers to the protection of the physical infrastructure of data networks and peripherals, such as fiber-optic cables, routers, switches, and servers that allow data in digital format to be transferred from one location to another one or process it to meet user demands.

These two systems are linked because most of the complex systems are digitally controlled, wherein data transfer and processing is done by large telecommunication networks and servers, with clients connected to them in a network fashion. The fact that complex systems are digitally controlled brings a potential vulnerability to those systems. The possible scenario that proposes terrorists can gain access to these controlling systems is not an unrealistic one. Once the terrorists have gained control of the system, they can abuse it in such a way as to cause major damage to human life and the government, thereby creating major social and economic disruption. To cause this harm, it is not even necessary for the terrorists to be physically co-located within the system facilities, or even within the United States. This type of terrorist behavior is called "cyberterrorism."

DHS acts as the coordinating body of the U.S. government to secure the cyberspace and the network infrastructure in the United States. The National Cybersecurity Division within the Office of Cybersecurity and Communications of the Directorate of National Protection and Programs and the Directorate of Science and Technology of the Department of Homeland Security are the main units within the department that identify and assess current and future terrorist threats, assess and mitigate risks to the nation's critical infrastructure systems, and disseminate threat information. The two most important responsibilities of the National Cybersecurity Division follow:

1. To build and maintain an effective national cyberspace response system
2. To implement a cyber risk-management program for protection of critical infrastructure.

When the National Protection and Programs Directorate (named as Directorate for Information Analysis and Infrastructure Protection or IAIP by then) was formed in 2003, by the Homeland Security Act of 2002, it incorporated the Critical Infrastructure Assurance Office, Federal Computer Incident Response Center, National Communications System, National Infrastructure Protection Center, National Infrastructure Simulation and Analysis Center, and Energy Security and Assurance Program, each of which previously managed some component of the overall infrastructure protection task (Coppola, 2003).

The National Protection and Programs Directorate is in charge of protecting the cyber infrastructure from terrorist attack by unifying and focusing the key cybersecurity activities performed by the Critical Infrastructure Assurance Office (formerly within the Department of Commerce) and the National Infrastructure Protection Center (formerly within the FBI). The directorate augments those capabilities with the response functions of the National Cybersecurity Division's (NCSD's) U.S. Computer Emergency Response Team (US-CERT). Because the information and telecommunications sectors are increasingly interconnected, DHS also assumes the functions and assets of the National Communications System (within DOD), which coordinates emergency preparedness for the telecommunications sector.

US-CERT is a partnership between DHS and the public and private sectors. The team was established in 2003 to protect the nation's Internet infrastructure. The team is charged with protecting the nation's Internet infrastructure by coordinating defense against and response to cyber attacks. It is responsible for analyzing and reducing cyber threats and vulnerabilities, disseminating cyber-threat warning information, and coordinating incident response activities. US-CERT interacts with federal agencies, industry, the research community, state and local governments, and others to disseminate reasoned and actionable cybersecurity information to the public. The National Cyber Response Coordination Group made up of 13 federal agencies' representatives acts as the principal federal agency mechanism for cyber, incident response. In the event of a nationally significant cyber-related incident, the NCRCG will help to coordinate the federal response, with representatives from US-CERT, law enforcement, and the intelligence community. One of the tools created and used by US-CERT to create public awareness and to disseminate information about known cyber threats is the Cyber Security Preparedness and the National Cyber Alert System where both technical and nontechnical computer users can stay prepared for these threats by receiving current information by signing up for receiving automatic notifications from the system. Another initiative of the National Cybersecurity Division is the "Cyber Cop Portal" which is an Internet portal where more than 5,300 cyber-crime investigators worldwide can share information and collaborate.

The Directorate of Science and Technology (S&T) is also involved in the protection of critical cyber infrastructure and information. Some strategic objectives of S&T, for example, are to develop methods and capabilities to test and assess threats and vulnerabilities, to prevent technological surprise, and to anticipate emerging threats. Such threats include cyber threats as well. S&T established the Cybersecurity Research and Development Center in March 2004. The center is the umbrella under which the DHS's cybersecurity research and development (R&D) activities are coordinated and performed. Charged with creating partnerships between government and private industry, the venture capital community, and the research community, the center develops and fortifies security technology to better protect the cyber infrastructure of the United States. The Homeland Security Advanced Research Projects Agency (HSARPA) is responsible for funding the center's research and development. As part of its cybersecurity mission, HSARPA uses the center to focus cybersecurity research, development, and test and evaluation activities and to involve expertise from academic, private industry, and federal and national laboratories. HSARPA invests in programs offering the potential for revolutionary changes in technologies that promote homeland security and accelerates the prototyping and deployment of technologies intended to reduce homeland vulnerabilities.

The center supports the DHS's responsibility to secure a substantial portion of the nation's critical infrastructure (including information and telecommunications, transportation, postal and shipping, emergency services, and government continuity). Because DHS does not own or control this infrastructure, it faces unique challenges related to technologies that must be developed and deployed in support of the DHS mission.

The National Plan for Research and Development in Support of Critical Infrastructure Protection of 2004 suggests that the critical infrastructure of the United States, including its cyberspace, should operate under a national "Common Operating Picture" (COP). COP is defined as the communication and computing system architecture around which the nation's critical infrastructures operate in a safe and secure fashion. The plan identifies nine critical areas that have to be prioritized in terms of research and development for the sake of critical infrastructure protection and the achievement of COP:

- Detection and sensor systems
- Protection and prevention
- Entry and access portals
- Insider threats
- Analysis and decision support systems
- Response, recovery, and reconstitution
- New and emerging threats and vulnerabilities
- Advanced infrastructure architectures and systems design
- Human and social issues

Detection and Sensor Systems

This CIP R&D scope includes developing sensors to detect intruders to cyber infrastructures, including sensors that monitor and report the status and condition of the infrastructure. In addition, there are detection and sensing R&D tasks that are not related to a particular device, but rather to ways of processing sensor data to extract anomalies and identify patterns that are part of the CIP R&D

scope. In cyber systems, the sensors may take the form of intelligent autonomous software agents that can travel throughout a computing or communications network. These networked systems of sensors must be smart, self-organizing, self-healing, and capable of analysis and reporting. Cyber intrusion detection considers surveillance in many forms, as well as the interpretation of that surveillance data in digital network space. For example, wireless technologies are increasingly crucial to automation, communication, and information technology systems pervasive throughout the critical infrastructure sectors. However, they are already vulnerable due to limited security, and face increased risks from mobile wireless nodes that can enter, traverse, and leave the network.

Protection and Prevention

The nations's cyber infrastructure is threatened by infiltration by foreign networks; exfiltration, disclosure, exposure, or corruption of stored data or rendering stored data inaccessible; interception, interruption, or redirection of data or communications transmission; viruses and other malicious software; compromised (infected) software applications or hardware components; local or widespread disruption of services; and compromised or hijacked machines. To achieve a secure communications network, CIP needs to ensure effective protection against cyber intruders. Protection from cyber intrusion is an extremely difficult challenge due to the rapidly evolving nature of computer systems, the increased application of computer-based technologies, and the ever-increasing sophistication of cyber criminals and terrorists. Within the vast array of legacy, current, and planned systems there are weaknesses that can be accessed by cyber intruders of all skill levels.

Another protection and prevention task is to prevent or minimize disruption and denial-of-service and access attacks. Fairly common in today's sophisticated network systems and the Internet, such attacks can be devastating. Overwhelming a process by forcibly inserting tasks, dramatically increasing demands on a system, or denying availability of needed resources such as communication systems can result in serious consequences. These actions can divert attention, consume resources, and displace capability making other portions of both physical and cyber critical infrastructure systems more vulnerable. To minimize the impacts of such attacks, protective identification, confirmation, and authorization access measures must be rigorous and well managed. Systems should be designed in a manner such that they provide redundancy, rerouting options, and self-healing or self-sustaining attributes to rapidly restore or at least provide a minimum level of service until recovery actions can be implemented for both cyber and physical systems.

Entry and Access Portals

Cyber portals for the exchange of critical data and information will require widely available and technologically advanced protections that are well beyond the basic password systems commonly used today. They also will require adaptation to attacks that are continuously changing and evolving. Emerging security issues will require that physical portals (entryways, checkpoints) and cyber portals (network access, secure transmissions) manage increasingly similar scopes of information, to include accurate identification, authentication, data protection, and information exchange regarding people, material, or information. Future needs of both physical portals and cyber portals can benefit from similar ongoing applied R&D approaches, communication standards development, and engineering requirements. Focus areas for entry and access portals are identification, authentication, authorization, access control, tracking, and dynamic situational control (which refers to the ability of a system to infer actions or intent and potentially control or direct the outcome of a given security situation).

Response, Recovery, and Reconstitution

Certain classes of attacks in cyberspace can be detected very quickly. In fact, in some cases it is even possible to detect indications of an attack prior to its actual onset. For such attacks, taking the correct action quickly enough makes it possible not only to reduce the effects of an attack, but also to possibly avert it altogether. On increasingly shortening time scales, closely coupled automated sensing of, and response to, malicious activity is viewed not simply as a damage mitigation approach, but as a key protective strategy. Important research areas in this context include analysis to automatically determine appropriate corrective actions, and effective coupling of both the analytical approaches and the technological interfaces associated with detection and response systems, which may be comprised of hardware, software, or both. Because some types of attacks (such as worms) are capable of propagating very quickly, the speed associated with detection, analysis, and response capability becomes critical. It is generally accepted that for some attacks, any response that requires human intervention, to help identify an attack, determine appropriate action, or take corrective action, is doomed to failure because the attack would propagate too quickly and would effectively outrun the response. The implication here is that in addition to improving the capabilities of automated detection, analysis, and response approaches, technological advances are also needed along a different dimension to increase their speed. For those responding, having access to a secure Internet will provide critical access to "experts at a distance" as they are conduits for experts in science, engineering, technology, decision making, alternative actions, and much more from other responder communities. COP provides awareness of events that might affect their actions and use or availability of resources that may be critical if there is a coordinated attack or multiple impacts from a natural disaster. It has been proposed that unattended devices, such as robotic platforms, must be developed to provide the information essential for effective decision support.

New and Emerging Threats and Vulnerabilities

New software virus architectures that arrive in pieces and self-assemble later and new, more damaging network infestations that appear, perform, and self-destruct leaving no forensic trail are considered as potential emerging cyber threats and vulnerabilities and the CIP R&D plan identifies the need to start the preparedness efforts to deal with such threats and vulnerabilities when they become real.

Advanced Infrastructure Architectures and Systems Design

Networking and systems research that produced the Internet has yielded radical change and a society globally focused on information. In addition to rapid communication, the Internet provides a cyber-computational grid by enabling high-performance and clustered, smaller computers, and massive data centers that are connected and shared. Internet-based sharing of computational facilities and data resources has created opportunities for collaborative virtual working environments, and virtual control of sensing and control systems for monitoring, operation, prediction, and control within the country's CI sector networks. However, the current architecture of the Internet and the tools within it are largely insecure. Protecting these systems against a knowledgeable community of adversaries requires massive overhaul to make them fully secure.

To develop the next generation of cyber infrastructure, research needs must address its architecture and design, by building the fundamental basis on new concepts for robust and secure networking, systems software for real-time sensing and control, and integrated data acquisition, information management, and simulation technology. The Internet of the future must be designed with its incorporation in the nation's critical infrastructure sectors in mind. Cyber systems must be capable of detecting and responding to a large number of threats that change frequently over the course of even a few hours or days. Next-generation cyber systems and control systems will be designed in the early planning stages to incorporate security-related standards, secure hardware designs, common secure communication protocols, and other requirements and guidelines. New cyber platforms need to leverage advances in grid-based computing concepts, increasingly powerful computer systems on-a-chip, and wireless communications technology. Advanced systems will include self-organizing networks that can spontaneously communicate and collaborate with other networks in a larger system. These "smart" networks can adjust their roles and deliver new levels of communication and computing capacity.

Codesign of physical and information systems needs improvement. Design and systems infrastructure approaches are needed that enable safe, reliable, automatic transition from failure to recovery modes. Current systems are generally static in their designs; new research is needed to enable safe dynamic composition and specialization of open, cooperating systems as they are deployed. Design capability is particularly lacking for reactive, reconfigurable, high-confidence systems.

The National Strategy to Secure Cyberspace of 2003 provides the national framework for ensuring information security and protecting the cyberspace. In this document the three strategic objectives to secure cyberspace are listed as follows:

1. Prevent cyber attacks against America's critical infrastructures.
2. Reduce national vulnerability to cyber attacks.
3. Minimize damage and recovery time from cyber attacks that do occur.

The National Strategy to Secure Cyberspace articulates five national priorities as discussed next.

Priority 1: A National Cyberspace Security Response System

Rapid identification, information exchange, and remediation can often mitigate the damage caused by malicious cyberspace activity. For those activities to be effective at a national level, the United States needs a partnership between government and industry to perform analyses, issue warnings, and coordinate response efforts. Privacy and civil liberties must be protected in the process. Because no cybersecurity plan can be impervious to concerted and intelligent attack, information systems must be able to operate while under attack and have the resilience to restore full operations quickly. The National Strategy to Secure Cyberspace identifies eight major actions and initiatives for cyberspace security response:

1. Establish a public–private architecture responding to national-level cyber incidents.
2. Provide for the development of tactical and strategic analysis of cyber attack vulnerability assessments.
3. Encourage the development of a private-sector capability to share a synoptic view of the health of cyberspace.
4. Expand the Cyber Warning and Information Network to support the DHS in coordinating crisis management for cyberspace security.
5. Improve national incident management.
6. Coordinate processes for voluntary participation in the development of national public–private continuity and contingency plans.
7. Exercise cybersecurity continuity plans for federal systems.
8. Improve and enhance public–private information sharing involving cyber attacks, threats, and vulnerabilities.

Priority 2: A National Cyberspace Security Threat and Vulnerability Reduction Program

By exploiting vulnerabilities in cyber systems, an organized attack may endanger the security of the United States' critical infrastructures. The vulnerabilities that most threaten cyberspace occur in the information assets of critical infrastructure enterprises themselves and their external supporting structures, such as the mechanisms of the Internet. Lesser secured sites on the interconnected network of networks also present potentially significant exposures to cyber attacks. Vulnerabilities result from weaknesses in technology and because of improper implementation and oversight of technological products. The National Strategy to Secure Cyberspace identifies eight major actions and initiatives to reduce threats and related vulnerabilities:

1. Enhance law enforcement's capabilities for preventing and prosecuting cyberspace attacks.
2. Create a process for national vulnerability assessments to better understand the potential consequences of threats and vulnerabilities.

3. Secure the mechanisms of the Internet, improving protocols and routing.
4. Foster the use of trusted digital control systems/supervisory control and data acquisition systems.
5. Reduce and remediate software vulnerabilities.
6. Understand infrastructure interdependencies and improve the physical security of cyber systems and telecommunications.
7. Prioritize federal cybersecurity research and development agendas.
8. Assess and secure emerging systems.

Priority 3: A National Cyberspace Security Awareness and Training Program

Many cyber vulnerabilities exist because of a lack of cybersecurity awareness on the part of computer users, systems administrators, technology developers, procurement officials, auditors, chief information officers (CIOs), chief executive officers, and corporate boards. Such awareness-based vulnerabilities present serious risks to critical infrastructures regardless of whether they exist within the infrastructure itself. A lack of trained personnel and the absence of widely accepted, multilevel certification programs for cybersecurity professionals complicate the task of addressing cyber vulnerabilities. The National Strategy to Secure Cyberspace identifies four major actions and initiatives for awareness, education, and training:

1. Promote a comprehensive national awareness program to empower all Americans, businesses, the general workforce, and the general population to secure their own parts of cyberspace.
2. Foster adequate training and education programs to support the nation's cybersecurity needs.
3. Increase the efficiency of existing federal cybersecurity training programs.
4. Promote private-sector support for well-coordinated, widely recognized professional cybersecurity certifications.

Priority 4: Securing Governments' Cyberspace

Although governments administer only a minority of the nation's critical infrastructure computer systems, governments at all levels perform essential services in the agriculture, food, water, public health, emergency services, defense, social welfare, information and telecommunications, energy, transportation, banking and finance, chemicals, and postal shipping sectors that depend on cyberspace for their delivery. Governments can lead by example in cyberspace security, including fostering a marketplace for more secure technologies through their procurement. The National Strategy to Secure Cyberspace identifies five major actions and initiatives for the securing of governments' cyberspace:

1. Continuously assess threats and vulnerabilities to federal cyber systems.
2. Authenticate and maintain authorized users of federal cyber systems.
3. Secure federal wireless local-area networks.
4. Improve security in government outsourcing and procurement.
5. Encourage state and local governments, consider establishing information technology security programs, and participate in information sharing and analysis centers with similar governments.

Priority 5: National Security and International Cyberspace Security Cooperation

America's cyberspace links the United States to the rest of the world. A network of networks spans the planet, allowing malicious actors on one continent to act on systems thousands of miles away. Cyber attacks cross borders at light speed, and discerning the source of malicious activity is difficult. America must be capable of safeguarding and defending its critical systems and networks. Enabling the ability to do so requires a system of international cooperation to facilitate information sharing, reduce vulnerabilities, and deter malicious actors. The National Strategy to Secure Cyberspace identifies six major actions and initiatives to strengthen U.S. national security and international cooperation:

1. Strengthen cyber-related counterintelligence efforts.
2. Improve capabilities for attack attribution and response.
3. Improve coordination for responding to cyber attacks within the U.S. national security community.
4. Work with industry and through international organizations to facilitate dialogue and partnerships among international public and private sectors focused on protecting information infrastructures and promoting a global "culture of security."
5. Foster the establishment of national and international watch-and-warning networks to detect and prevent cyber attacks as they emerge.
6. Encourage other nations to accede to Council of Europe Convention on Cyber Crime or to ensure that their laws and procedures are at least as comprehensive (Source: Department of Homeland Security (DHS), "National Strategy to Secure Cyberspace," February 2003, www. dhs.gov).

Exercising for Cybersecurity

No emergency preparedness or emergency response program is of much value unless the plans and procedures are tested, that is, exercised. This is also true to ensure proper response to cybersecurity incidents. While the TOPOFF (Top Official) Exercises mandated to the federal government by the Congress are useful for the overall emergency management and incident command capabilities of the federal government, due to the generic all-hazards nature of those exercises it is difficult to simulate in detail the steps that may need to be taken during a cybersecurity attack of national scope. The biennial "Cyber Storm" Exercise series mandated by the Congress and organized and moderated by the National Cybersecurity Division are just designed to close this gap.

The first government-led, full-scale cybersecurity exercise "Cyber Storm I" was conducted in February 2006 with the participation of over 115 organizations, mostly federal, state, and local governments. The four sectors covered in the exercise were information technology, communications, energy, and air transportation. The exercise scenario included various degradations of cybersecurity and the communications infrastructure and allowed participants to simulate a response to the situation at various levels including tactical, strategic, policy, and public affairs response. The publicly available version of the exercise after-action review and lessons learned document summarized the strengths and areas that need further improvement as follows:

- Interagency Coordination: Interagency and cross-sector information sharing enhanced overall coordination, communication, and response.
- Contingency Planning, Risk Assessment, and Roles and Responsibilities: Clearly defined processes and procedures increased overall ability to plan for and assess situations.
- Correlation of Multiple Incidents between Public and Private Sectors: The cyber community was effective in addressing individual threats and attacks, but faced challenges in cross-sector situational awareness during a coordinated cyber attack campaign.
- Exercise Program: Ongoing exercises will strengthen awareness of cyber incident response, roles, policies, and procedures.
- Coordination between Entities of Cyber Incidents: Establishing expectations, roles, processes, and communications in advance will dramatically improve coordination and response.
- Common Framework for Response to Information Access: Early and ongoing information sharing across governments and sectors created a common framework for response and strengthened relationships between domestic and international response partners.

- Strategic Communications and Public Relations: Public messaging is an important aspect of incident response and empowers individuals and industry to take appropriate action to protect themselves and the nation's critical infrastructure.

- Improvement of Process, Tools, and Technology: Improved processes, tools, and technology focused on the physical, economic, and national security effects of a cyber incident will benefit the quality, speed, and coordination of a response.

The second of the "Cyber Storm" exercise series was conducted in March 2008. This time, the exercise not only included participants from the federal, state, and local governments, but also international participants such as the governments of Australia, New Zealand, Canada, and the UK, and over 40 private-sector participants such as Microsoft, McAfee, Cisco, NeuStar, and Wachovia. The scenario impacted information technology, chemical, communications, and transportation (rail/pipe) sectors. The goal of the exercise was to test the processes, procedures, technology, and organizational response of participating entities during a simulated attack to the global cyber infrastructure. The objective was to incorporate lessons learned from Cyber Storm I and to identify other areas that require further improvement and attention (Department of Homeland Security, "National Cybersecurity Division," 2008; DHS, "Cyber Storm: Securing Cyber Space," 2008; DHS, "DHS Releases Cyber Storm Public Exercise Report," 2006).

ANOTHER VOICE: RISK COMMUNICATIONS

Trust the Public, Good News or Bad

Stephen Flynn argues in his book, *The Edge of Disaster: Rebuilding a Resilient Nation,* that the events of 9-11 might have been different had the government been more forthcoming with information it had. If the government had told the public about the increased level of "chatter" and suspected threats, would the passengers of the three planes that hit the Pentagon and the Twin Towers have acted differently and attempted to thwart the hijackers, as the passengers of Flight 93 did?

What was the difference between Flight 93 and the other three planes? It turns out that it left later than planned because of some delay, and in the air, passengers learned of the other plane crashes via telephones. Thus the argument goes — it was the information that the Flight 93 passengers possessed, coupled with their ability to predict their own fate, that led to their selfless and heroic acts, which saved many strangers' live at the cost of their own.

The 9/11 case is an example of the government withholding information that could have potentially led to alternate outcomes. This is an example of a risk communications failure. There are many reasons for this type of risk communications failure. A common one is that people in positions of power are often afraid of what the release of the information might cause. They further fear that the public cannot handle the information and that it will tarnish their own image, or believe that there is no benefit to its public release.

This was a problem identified in the Corps of Engineers in the post Katrina analysis and reforms. The agency released the risks to the public ineffectively. Poor communication skills can be common among engineers and other people in technical professions, but this cannot serve as an excuse. Steps have been taken to integrate better communications strategies in the future.

However, the culture of protecting information that may be negative is still pervasive throughout the government. The idea that the public cannot handle sensitive information is completely false. The public has a fundamental right to know consequential information, good or bad, complex or vague, particularly because negative information can catalyze change, serve as a warning, and form the basis for major decisions.

(Continued)

Utilities and Industrial Facilities

Utilities are the lifelines of American society. They include essential daily needs such as electricity, energy, water, sewerage, and telecommunications that are characterized as critical infrastructure. Today's complex terrorist attacks target people and economies, as well as important critical infrastructure such as these utilities, in order to cause destruction of property and disruption of society and commerce. For this reason, utilities are recognized as an important terrorist target, and their protection is seen as a critical national security priority.

Protection of U.S. utilities' infrastructures is, understandably, another of DHS's many security responsibilities. The Directorate of National Protection and Programs is the operational branch of DHS responsible for protecting the nation's utility infrastructure. However, this task is complex and extremely difficult. For one thing, almost 85% of the utility infrastructure of the United States is owned or operated by the private sector. Therefore, strong relationships and coordination between DHS and the private sector are essential to successfully protect these facilities. A separate section is dedicated for the role of the private sector in homeland security, discussed below. The following section will address federal initiatives dedicated to protecting the utility infrastructure of the United States.

The primary publication guiding the federal protection of utilities is, again, the National Strategy for the Physical Protection of Critical Infrastructures and Key Assets of 2003. The document covers utilities protection in its "Water," "Energy," and "Telecommunication" subtitles.

Water

The nation's water sector is critical from both a public health and an economic standpoint. The water sector consists of two basic, yet vital, components: freshwater supply and wastewater collection and treatment (wastewater treatment will be mentioned later). Sector infrastructures are diverse, complex, and distributed, ranging from systems that serve a few customers to those that serve millions. On the supply side, the primary focus of critical infrastructure protection efforts is the nation's 170,000 public water systems. These utilities depend on reservoirs, dams, wells, and aquifers, as well as treatment facilities, pumping stations, aqueducts, and transmission pipelines.

The water sector has taken great strides to protect its critical facilities and systems. For instance, government and industry have developed vulnerability assessment methodologies for both drinking water and wastewater facilities and trained thousands of utility operators to conduct them. In response to the Public Health Security and Bio-Terrorism Preparedness and Response Act of 2002, the Environmental Protection Agency (EPA) has developed baseline threat information to use in conjunction with vulnerability assessments. EPA has provided assistance to state and local governments for drinking water systems to enable them to undertake vulnerability assessments and develop emergency response plans. To improve the flow of information among water-sector organizations, the industry has begun development of its sector ISACs.

Water-ISAC is the first sectorwide information sharing and analysis center for the water sector. Since its creation in December 2002, the Water-ISAC has served as a secure forum for gathering, analyzing, and sharing water-related security information. The center is funded by the EPA, but also receives income from subscription fees for its online notification system. The Water-ISAC's notification system is an Internet-based, rapid notification system and information resource focused on threats to America's drinking water and wastewater systems, and is the only centralized, up-to-the-minute resource of its kind serving the water sector. The Water-ISAC functions as a subscription service that gathers and quickly disseminates alerts, expert analyses, and other information specific to the water community. The system provides services such as timely e-mail alerts about potential and actual physical or cyber attacks against drinking or wastewater systems; information on water security from the federal law enforcement, intelligence, public health, and environment agencies; access to an extensive database of information on chemical, biological, and radiological agents; notifications about cyber vulnerabilities and technical fixes, research, reports, and other water security–related information; a highly secure means for quickly reporting incidents; vulnerability assessment tools and resources; guidance about emergency preparedness and response; the ability to participate in and review secure electronic forums on water security topics; and helpful summaries of open-source security information (Water-ISAC, 2008, www.waterisac.org).

Several federal agencies are working together to improve the warehousing of information regarding contamination threats, such as the release of biological, chemical, and radiological substances into the water supply, and how to respond to their presence in drinking water. With respect to identifying new technologies, the EPA has an existing program that develops testing protocols and verifies the performance of innovative technologies. It has initiated a new program to verify monitoring technologies that may be useful in detecting or avoiding biological or chemical threats.

To support the water industry, the EPA has been providing grants for vulnerability assessments and related security improvements at large drinking water utilities since 2003. EPA's funding priority is to provide grant assistance to large (regularly serving 100,000 people or more), publicly owned, community drinking water systems, for up to $115,000 to teach the eligible utility to develop/revise a vulnerability assessment (V/A), emergency response/operating plan (EOP), security enhancement plans and designs, or a combination of these efforts. A total of 449 large water utilities received a total of $51 million in grants as part of this program, and conducted risk and vulnerability assessment of their water treatment facilities. As part of the program, EPA developed and made available vulnerability assessment methodology, guidelines, and software to water utility owners and operators.

Between 2003 and 2008, EPA awarded grants for counterterrorism coordination activities to the states and territories, at a total of $5 million per year. According to the distribution scheme of those funds, each state receives a minimum of $50,000, and each territory at least $16,700. The grant program was continued in the FY 2009 president's budget request.

In 2004 EPA allocated $1 million in funding for small wastewater system security training. The goal of the grant was to increase security among small- and medium-sized wastewater systems. Short-term objectives of the program included incorporating immediate basic security enhancements, improving the capacity for emergency response, and accomplishing vulnerability assessments. Another objective was to implement long-range security measures and institutionalize security-related issues into existing wastewater programs. The funding was to be used for the sole purpose of providing on-site training assistance or classroom wastewater security training activities to wastewater utilities on the use of the wastewater security vulnerability assessment tools, emergency response plan development and upgrades, and physical system security enhancements.

In FY 2006, EPA launched two new water security initiatives — The WaterSentinel Initiative (in 2007 the name was changed to "Water Security Initiative") and the Water Alliance for Threat Reduction. The overall goal of the WaterSentinel Initiative is to design and demonstrate an effective system for timely detection and appropriate response to drinking water contamination threats and incidents through a pilot program that would have broad application to the nation's drinking water utilities. WaterSentinel demonstrates the concept so that drinking water utilities of all sizes and characteristics can adopt and implement an effective contamination warning system. The WaterSentinel initiative is a three-phase program; as of 2008 EPA was expected to initiate contamination warning system pilots. The Water Alliance for Threat Reduction initiative is a program to train utility operators at the highest-risk systems. In response to a $42 million inaugural funding request in FY 2006, the Congress appropriated $8 million for those initiatives. In FY 2008, the president's budget included $22 million for those initiatives, but only $11.7 million were appropriated. The president's FY 2009 budget request includes $22.6 million for those programs.

The basic human need for water and the concern for maintaining a safe water supply are driving factors for water infrastructure protection. Public perception regarding the safety of the nation's water supply is also significant, as is the safety of people who reside or work near water facilities. To set priorities among the wide range of protective measures that should be taken, the water sector is focusing on the types of infrastructure attacks that could result in significant human casualties and property damage or widespread economic consequences. In general, there are four areas of primary concentration:

1. Physical damage or destruction of critical assets, including intentional release of toxic chemicals
2. Actual or threatened contamination of the water supply
3. Cyber attack on information management systems or other electronic systems
4. Interruption of services from another infrastructure

To address these potential threats, the sector requires additional focused threat information in order to direct investments toward enhancement of corresponding protective measures. The water sector also requires increased monitoring and analytic capabilities to enhance detection of biological, chemical, or radiological contaminants that could be intentionally introduced into the water supply. Some enterprises are already in the process of developing advanced monitoring and sampling technologies, but additional resources from the water sector will likely be needed.

Environmental monitoring techniques and technologies and appropriate laboratory capabilities require enhancement to provide adequate and timely analysis of water samples to ensure early warning capabilities and assess the effectiveness of cleanup activities should an incident occur. Specific innovations needed include new broad-spectrum analytical methods, monitoring strategies, sampling protocols, and training.

Currently, approaches to emergency response and the handling of security incidents at water facilities vary according to state and local policies and procedures. With regard to the public reaction associated with contamination or perceived contamination, it is essential that local, state, and federal departments and agencies coordinate their protection and response efforts. Maintaining the public's confidence regarding information provided and the timeliness of the message is critical. Suspected events concerning water systems to date have elicited strong responses that involved taking systems out of service until their integrity could be verified, announcing the incident to the public, and issuing "boil water" orders.

The operations of the water sector depend extensively on other sectors. The heaviest dependence is on the energy sector. For example, running pumps to move water and wastewater and operating drinking water and wastewater treatment plants require large amounts of electricity. Water infrastructure protection initiatives are guided both by the challenges that the water sector faces and by recent legislation. Additional protection initiatives include efforts to do the following:

1. Identify high-priority vulnerabilities and improve site security: EPA, in concert with DHS, state and local governments, and other water-sector leaders, will work to identify processes and technologies to better secure key points of storage and distribution, such as dams, pumping stations, chemical storage facilities, and treatment plants. EPA and DHS will also continue to provide tools, training, technical assistance, and limited financial assistance for research on Vulnerability Assessment VA methodologies and risk management strategies.

2. Improve sector monitoring and analytic capabilities: EPA will continue to work with sector representatives and other federal agencies to improve information on contaminants of concern and to develop appropriate monitoring and analytical technologies and capabilities.

3. Improve sectorwide information exchange and coordinate contingency planning: DHS and EPA will continue to work with the sector coordinator and the Water-ISAC to coordinate timely information on threats, incidents, and other topics of special interest to the water sector. DHS and EPA will also work with the sector and the states to standardize and coordinate emergency response efforts and communications protocols.

4. Work with other sectors to manage unique risks resulting from interdependencies: DHS and EPA will convene cross-sector working groups to develop models for integrating priorities and emergency response plans in the context of interdependencies between the water sector and other critical infrastructures.

In May 2007, EPA released the Water Sector Specific Infrastructure Protection Plan that will become part of the National Infrastructure Protection Plan. As suggested by the sector-specific plan development guidance provided by DHS, the Water Sector Specific Infrastructure Protection Plan covers the following areas:

1. Profile and goals of the water sector
2. Identification of assets, systems, networks, and functions
3. Assessment of water security risks (consequences, vulnerabilities, and threats)
4. Prioritization of water infrastructure
5. Development and implementation of protective programs
6. Procedures to measure progress
7. CI/KR protection research and development
8. Management and coordination of sector-specific agency (EPA) responsibilities (Sources: EPA, "Water Sector Specific Infrastructure Protection Plan," 2007; EPA, "EPA Budget in Brief FY 2007," 2006; EPA, "EPA Budget in Brief FY 2008," 2007; EPA, "EPA Budget in Brief FY 2009," 2008; EPA, "EPA Water Security Initiative (WaterSentinel)," 2006; Congressional Research Service, "Terrorism and Security Issues Facing the Water Infrastructure Sector," 2007)

Energy

Energy drives the foundation of many of the sophisticated processes at work in American society today. It is essential to the economy, national defense, and virtually all aspects of a modern quality of life. The energy sector is commonly divided into two segments in the context of critical infrastructure protection: electricity and oil and natural gas.

The electricity sector services almost 130 million households and institutions. The United States as a nation consumed nearly 3.82 trillion kilowatt-hours in 2006. Oil and natural gas facilities and assets are also widely distributed, consisting of more than 300,000 production sites, 4,000 off-shore platforms, more than 600 natural gas processing plants, 153 refineries, and more than 1,400 product terminals and 7,500 bulk stations.

Electricity

Almost every form of productive activity — whether in businesses, manufacturing plants, schools, hospitals, or homes — requires electricity. Electricity is also necessary to produce other forms of energy, such as refined oil. Were a widespread or long-term disruption of the power grid to occur, many of the activities critical to the economy and national defense — including those associated with response and recovery — would be impossible.

The North American electric system is an interconnected, multinodal distribution system that accounts for virtually all the electricity supplied to the United States, Canada, and a portion of Baja

California Norte, Mexico. The physical system consists of three major parts: generation, transmission and distribution, and control and communications.

Generation assets include fossil fuel plants, hydroelectric dams, and nuclear power plants. Transmission and distribution systems link areas of the national grid (see Figure 5–6). Distribution systems manage and control the distribution of electricity into homes and businesses. Control and communications systems operate and monitor critical infrastructure components.

The North American electric system is the world's most reliable, a fact that can be attributed to industry efforts to identify single points of failure and system interdependencies and to institute appropriate backup processes, systems, and facilities. The North American Electric Reliability Council (NERC), in charge of developing guidelines and procedures for ensuring electricity system reliability, is a nonprofit corporation made up of 10 regional reliability councils, whose voluntary membership represents all segments of the electricity industry, including public and private utilities from the United States and Canada. Through NERC, the electricity sector coordinates programs to enhance security for the electricity industry. The sidebar titled, "The August 14, 2003, Blackout in the United States and Canada," discusses an incident that affected about 50 million Americans and Canadians.

The electricity sector is highly regulated even as the industry is being restructured to increase competition. The Federal Energy Regulatory Commission (FERC) and state utility regulatory commissions regulate some of the activities and operations of certain electricity industry participants. The Nuclear Regulatory Commission (NRC) regulates nuclear power reactors and other civilian nuclear facilities, materials, and activities.

The electricity sector is highly complex, and its numerous component assets and systems span the North American continent. The stakeholders in the sector are diverse in size, capabilities, and focus. Currently, individual companies pay for levels of protection that are consistent with their resources and customer expectations. Typically, these companies seek to recover the costs of new security investments through proposed rate or price increases. Under current federal law, however, there is

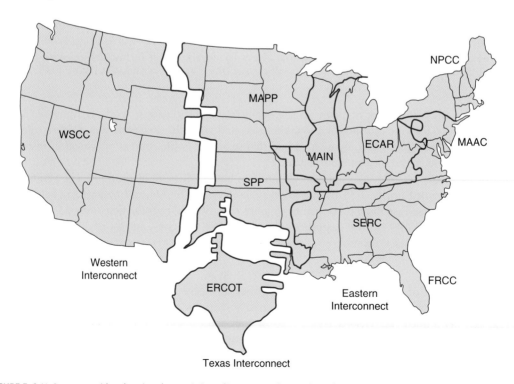

FIGURE 5–6 U. S. power grid and regional commissions. (Source: North American Electric Reliability Council)

no assurance that electricity industry participants would be allowed to recover the costs of federally mandated security measures through such rate or price increases.

Another challenge for the electricity industry is effective, sectorwide communications. The owners and operators of the electric system are a large and heterogeneous group. Industry associations serve as clearing houses for industry-related information, but not all industry owners and operators belong to such organizations.

Data needed to perform thorough analyses on the infrastructure's interdependencies is not readily available. A focused analysis of the time-phased effects of one infrastructure on another, including loss of operations metrics, would help identify dependencies and establish protection priorities and strategies.

For certain transmission and distribution facilities, providing redundancy and increasing generating capacity provide greater reliability of electricity service. However, this approach faces several challenges. Long lead times, possible denials of rights-of-way, state and local site selection requirements, "not-in-my-back-yard" (NIMBY) community perspectives, and uncertain rates of return when compared with competing investment needs are hurdles that may prevent owners and operators of electricity facilities from investing sufficiently in security and service assurance measures.

Building a less vulnerable electricity grid is a priority for protecting the national electricity infrastructure. Work is ongoing to develop a national R&D strategy for the electricity sector. Additionally, FERC has developed R&D guidelines, and the Department of Energy's (DOE) National Grid Study contains recommendations focused on enhancing physical and cybersecurity for the transmission system.

The electricity industry has a history of taking proactive measures to ensure the reliability and availability of the electricity system. Individual enterprises also work actively in their communities to address public safety issues related to their systems and facilities. Since September 11, 2001, the sector has reviewed its security guidelines and initiated a series of intra-industry working groups to address specific aspects of security. It has created a utility-sector security committee at the chief executive officer level to enhance planning, awareness, and resource allocation within the industry.

The sector as a whole, with NERC as the sector coordinator, has been working in collaboration with DOE since 1998 to assess its risk posture in light of the new threat environment, particularly with respect to the electric system's dependence on information technology and networks. In the process, the sector has created an awareness program that includes a "Business Case for Action" for industry senior executives, a strategic reference document titled "An Approach to Action for the Electric Power Sector," and security guidelines related to physical and cybersecurity.

The August 14, 2003, Blackout in the United States and Canada

On August 14, 2003, large portions of the Midwest and Northeast United States and Ontario, Canada, experienced an electric power blackout. The outage affected an area with an estimated 50 million people and 61,800 megawatts (MW) of electric load in the states of Ohio, Michigan, Pennsylvania, New York, Vermont, Massachusetts, Connecticut, New Jersey, and the Canadian province of Ontario. The blackout began a few minutes after 4:00 PM. Eastern Daylight Time (16:00 EDT), and power was not restored for 4 days in some parts of the United States. Parts of Ontario suffered rolling blackouts for more than a week before full power was restored. Estimates of total costs in the United States range between $4 billion and $10 billion (U.S. dollars). In Canada, gross domestic product was down 0.7% in August, there was a net loss of 18.9 million work-hours, and manufacturing shipments in Ontario were down $2.3 billion (Canadian dollars).

A joint commission from the United States and Canada was tasked to investigate why this blackout happened and what can be done to prevent it from happening again. The commission found out that a wide range of events, problems, or actions initiated or contributed to the initiation of the power outage.

Examples of such causes include but are not limited to human decisions by various organizations that affected conditions of the power grid that day, deficiencies in corporate policies, lack of adherence to industry policies, and inadequate technical decisions.

The commission provided its recommendations under four separate subtitles: (1) Institutional Issues Related to Reliability, (2) Support and Strengthen NERC's Actions of February 10, 2004, (3) Physical and Cybersecurity of North American Bulk Power Systems, and (4) Canadian Nuclear Power Sector.

For the sake of this chapter only the recommendations regarding the physical and cybersecurity of North American bulk power systems will be provided. Those recommendations are:

- Implement NERC IT standards.
- Develop and deploy IT management procedures.
- Develop corporate-level IT security governance and strategies.
- Implement controls to manage system health, network monitoring, and incident management.
- Initiate U.S.–Canada risk management study.
- Improve IT forensic and diagnostic capabilities.
- Assess IT risk and vulnerability at scheduled intervals.
- Develop capability to detect wireless and remote wireline intrusion and surveillance.
- Control access to operationally sensitive equipment.
- NERC should provide guidance on employee background checks.
- Confirm NERC ES-ISAC as the central point for sharing security information and analysis.
- Establish clear authority for physical and cybersecurity.
- Develop procedures to prevent or mitigate inappropriate disclosure of information.

Source: Adapted from U.S.–Canada Power System Outage Task Force, "Final Report on the August 14, 2003 Blackout in the United States and Canada: Causes and Recommendations, April 5, 2004."

With respect to managing security information, the sector has established an indication, analysis, and warning program that trains utilities on incident reporting and alert notification procedures. The sector has also developed threat alert levels for both physical and cyber events, which include action-response guidelines for each alert level.

The industry has also established an Electricity Sector Information Sharing and Analysis Center (ES-ISAC) to gather incident information, relay alert notices, and coordinate daily briefs between the federal government and electric grid operators around the country. ES-ISAC is operated by the North American Electric Reliability Council on behalf of the electricity sector. The most active program of the ES-ISAC is the Indications, Analysis, and Warnings (IAW) Program. The program consists of a set of guidelines for reporting operational and cyber incidents that adversely affect the electric power infrastructure. The IAW Standard Operating Procedure (SOP) defines the criteria and thresholds for event reporting. The program's primary objective is the development of a national-level system that will provide timely, reliable, and actionable warnings of threats and impending attacks on critical power infrastructures. Incident information submitted by government agencies and the private sector is being utilized to develop key indicators of threats and attacks. The objectives include maintaining the health and capabilities of critical customers served by the infrastructures.

Power management control rooms are probably the most protected aspect of the electrical network. NERC's guidelines require a backup system and/or manual workarounds to bypass damaged systems. FERC is also working with the sector to develop a common set of security requirements for all enterprises in the competitive electric supply market.

Additional electricity sector protection initiatives include efforts to do the following:

1. Identify equipment stockpile requirements: DHS and DOE will work with the electricity sector to inventory components and equipment critical to electric-system operations and to identify and assess other approaches to enhance restoration and recovery to include standardizing equipment and increasing component interchangeability.
2. Reevaluate and adjust nationwide protection planning, system restoration, and recovery in response to attacks: The electric power industry has an excellent process and record of reconstitution and recovery from disruptive events. Jointly, industry and government need to evaluate this system and its processes to support the evolution from a local and regional system to an integrated national response system. DHS and DOE will work with the electricity sector to ensure that existing coordination and mutual aid processes can effectively and efficiently support protection, response, and recovery activities as the structure of the electricity sector continues to evolve.
3. Develop strategies to reduce vulnerabilities: DHS and DOE will work with state and local governments and the electric power industry to identify the appropriate levels of redundancy of critical parts of the electric system, as well as requirements for designing and implementing redundancy in view of the industry's realignment and restructuring activities.
4. Develop standardized guidelines for physical security programs: DHS and DOE will work with the sector to define consistent criteria for criticality, standard approaches for vulnerability and risk assessments for critical facilities, and physical security training for electricity sector personnel (Source: DHS, "National Strategy for the Protection of Physical Infrastructure and Key Assets," 2003).

One unique challenge in ensuring the protection and reliability of the energy infrastructure is the extent of interdependencies between various infrastructures and sectors. This is especially true for the electricity grid as it is in the heart of every vital economic activity and does not only supply residential, commercial, and industrial facilities, but also the generation and logistics of other types of energy and commodities. It is known that during Hurricanes Katrina and Rita, which caused major electricity outages in the Gulf of Mexico, the oil and natural gas industry not only suffered physical damage due to the hurricane, but also business interruption losses due to the electricity outages. Many refineries, storage areas, marketing terminals, and ports were not operational for days due to the electricity outages and the limitations of emergency power generators. Plantation and Colonial pipelines which are two major pipelines that pump finished petroleum products from the Gulf Coast to the Eastern Coast could not operate for days due to the electricity outage that caused gasoline and other petroleum product shortages in Eastern states. Diminishing gasoline supply and inventories resulted in skyrocketing gasoline prices in some localities. This is just one example of how the interdependencies between different infrastructures cause ripple effects when something goes wrong with one, in this case the electricity grid. Figure 5–7 more formally identifies some of those interdependencies.

As required by the National Infrastructure Protection Plan, the energy sector in the leadership of the Department of Energy put together a sector specific plan in 2007. The plan identifies the following important principles for the electricity sector to ensure safe, secure, and reliable continuity of its services:

1. Balance power generation and demand continuously.
2. Balance reactive power supply and demand to maintain scheduled voltages.

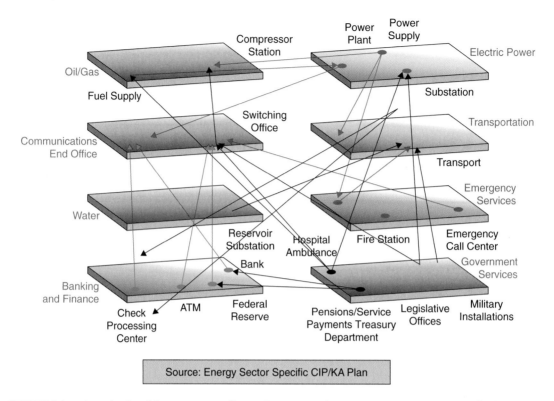

FIGURE 5–7 Interdependencies of the energy sector. (Source: Department of Energy, Energy CIP/KA Sector Specific Plan, 2007, p. 17)

3. Monitor flows over transmission lines and other facilities to ensure that thermal (heating) limits are not exceeded.
4. Keep the system in a stable condition.
5. Operate the system so that it remains in a reliable condition even if a contingency occurs, such as the loss of a key generator or transmission facility (the "N-1 criterion").
6. Plan, design, and maintain the system to operate reliably.
7. Prepare for and respond to emergencies. (Source: Department of Energy, "Energy Sector Specific Infrastructure Protection Plan," 2007).

Oil and Natural Gas

The oil and natural gas industries are closely integrated. The oil infrastructure consists of five general components: oil production, crude oil transport, refining, product transport and distribution, and control and other external support systems. Oil and natural gas production include exploration, field development, on- and off-shore production, field collection systems, and their supporting infrastructures. Crude oil transport includes pipelines (160,000 miles), storage terminals, ports, and ships. The refinement infrastructure consists of about 150 refineries that range in size and production capabilities from 5,000 to over 500,000 barrels per day. Transport and distribution of oil includes pipelines, trains, ships, ports, terminals and storage, trucks, and retail stations.

The natural gas industry consists of three major components: exploration and production, transmission, and local distribution. The United States produces roughly 20% of the world's natural gas supply. There are 278,000 miles of natural gas pipelines and 1,119,000 miles of natural gas distribution

FIGURE 5–8 Petroleum fire. (Source: U.S. Army)

lines in the United States. Distribution includes storage facilities, gas processing, liquid natural gas facilities, pipelines, city gates, and liquefied petroleum gas storage facilities.

The pipeline and distribution segments of the oil and natural gas industries are highly regulated. Oversight includes financial, safety, and site selection regulations. The exploration and production side of the industry is less regulated, but it is affected by safety regulations and restrictions concerning property access. The sidebar "Oil and Gas as Weapons" illustrates a unique side to the oil and gas industry (see Figure 5–8).

Protection of critical assets requires both heightened security awareness and investment in protective equipment and systems. One serious issue is the lack of metrics to determine and justify corporate security expenditures. In the case of natural disasters or accidents, there are well-established methods for determining risks and cost-effective levels of investments in protective equipment, systems, and methods for managing risk (e.g., insurance). It is not clear what levels of security and protection are appropriate and cost effective to meet the risks of terrorist attack.

The first government responders to a terrorist attack on most oil and natural gas sector facilities will be local police and fire departments. In general, these responders need to improve their capabilities and preparedness to confront well-planned, sophisticated attacks, particularly those involving chemical, biological, and radiological (CBR) weapons. Fortunately, because of public safety requirements related to their operations and facilities, the oil and natural gas industries have substantial protection programs already in place.

Quick action to repair damaged infrastructure in an emergency can be impeded by a number of hurdles, including the long lead time needed to obtain local, state, and federal construction permits or waivers; requirements for environmental reviews and impact statements; and lengthy processes for obtaining construction rights-of-way for the placement of pipelines on adjoining properties if a new path becomes necessary. The availability of necessary materials and equipment and the uniqueness of such equipment are also impediments to rapid reconstitution of damaged infrastructure.

The current system for locating and distributing replacement parts needs to be enhanced significantly. The components themselves range from state-of-the-art systems to mechanisms that are decades old. While newer systems are standardized, many of the older components are unique and must be custom manufactured. Moreover, there is extensive variation in size, ownership, and security across natural gas facilities. There are also a large number of natural gas facilities scattered over broad geographical areas — a fact that complicates protection.

■ ■ ■ ▬▬▬▬▬▬▬▬▬▬▬▬▬▬▬▬▬▬▬▬▬▬▬▬▬▬▬▬▬▬

Oil and Gas as Weapons

There is a unique risk associated with the oil and gas sector. Other kinds of critical infrastructure are deemed to be vulnerable to disasters primarily due to the adverse economical or human consequences should they be damaged or destroyed. This holds true for the oil and gas sectors as well, but there are additional, unique hazards associated with these two sectors. Both oil and gas are highly flammable materials, which are very hazardous if they are not adequately obtained, processed, stored, and transported. For these reasons, the two resources have become highly attractive to terrorists.

For terrorists targeting oil or gas, the target itself is a weapon that is designed for ignition. The involvement of oil or gas materials in a terrorist attack can drastically enlarge the scope of the incident and in some cases create secondary disasters that overshadow the primary ones. The September 11 attacks are an example of such a disaster. Initially the incident was perceived as an accident where an airliner crashed into a high-rise building. But since the airliners that crashed into the towers carried approximately 10,000 gallons of unused jet fuel each at the time of impact, the incident became not only a physical crash incident, but also a highly technical and very difficult high-rise fire incident. Were it not for the excess fuel, it is unlikely that the buildings would have collapsed, but the fire that started burning as a result of that fuel increased the temperature of the buildings' structures to temperatures as high as 1,500°F.

According to the FEMA report about the collapse of the towers, this heat was transferred over the huge steel blocks in the center of the building, which acted as the primary load carriers of the buildings. When steel gets as hot as 1,500°F, it quickly loses the physical properties that it typically has in its solid state. The steel softens and eventually melts, thereby reducing its strength significantly, making it impossible to carry the load it was designed to carry. September 11 was, therefore, an incident where jet fuel was used as a primary weapon against civilians.

The ignition of the oil fields and wells by Saddam Hussein during the first Gulf War (Operation Desert Storm) is also another example of oil being used as a weapon. Liquid fuel fires are also extremely difficult to fight especially when the amount of involved fuel is significant (see Figure 5–4). The best responders can usually do is control the fire (making sure that it does not spread to other locations) and then use adequate foam to insulate the fire from the air and to use water to cool down the surroundings at the fire's base.

▬▬▬▬▬▬▬▬▬▬▬▬▬▬▬▬▬▬▬▬▬▬▬▬▬▬▬▬▬▬ ■ ■ ■

Oil and natural gas sector protection initiatives include efforts to do the following:

1. Plan and invest in research and development for the oil and gas industry to enhance robustness and reliability: Utilizing the federal government's national scientific and research capabilities, DHS and DOE will work with oil and natural gas sector stakeholders to develop an appropriate strategy for research and development to support protection, response, and recovery requirements.
2. Develop strategies to reduce vulnerabilities: DHS and DOE will work with state and local governments and industry to identify the appropriate levels of redundancy of critical components and systems, as well as requirements for designing and enhancing reliability.

3. Develop standardized guidelines for physical security programs: DHS and DOE will work with the oil and natural gas industry representatives to define consistent criteria for criticality, standard approaches for vulnerability and risk assessments for various facilities, and physical security training for industry personnel.

4. Develop guidelines for measures to reconstitute capabilities of individual facilities and systems: DHS and DOE will convene an advisory task force of industry representatives from the sector, construction firms, equipment suppliers, oil engineering firms, state and local governments, and federal agencies to identify appropriate planning requirements and approaches.

5. Develop a national system for locating and distributing critical components in support of response and recovery activities: DHS and DOE will work with industry to develop regional and national programs for identifying parts, requirements, notifying parties of their availability, and distributing them in an emergency.

The first Information Sharing and Analysis Center for the oil and natural gas sector was established in 2001 with participation from the sector's stakeholders. As of 2007, the Energy-ISAC listed close to 50 member companies or organizations. The ISAC is providing the following services and benefits to its members:

- Continuous (24/7) information monitoring and dissemination with alerts and warning pages, e-mails, and faxes from the Energy-ISAC operations center

- Physical vulnerability alerts and advisories from the FBI's National Infrastructure Protection Center, Department of Transportation's Office of Pipeline Safety, U.S. Coast Guard, Office of Homeland Security, and other government entities

- Cyber vulnerability alerts involving enterprise software, major viruses, worms, and exploits from anti-virus vendors, research groups, Internet security firms, associations, and advisory groups

- Information sharing and analysis among Energy-ISAC participants via the Energy ISAC website (with an option to remain anonymous)

- Access to monthly intelligence audio-conferences (nominal cost per call) (Sources: Government Accountability Office, "Critical Infrastructure Protection: Progress Coordinating Government and Private Sector Efforts Varies by Sectors' Characteristics," 2006; American Petroleum Institute, "Energy Security: Help Reduce the Threat," 2008)

The Oil and Gas Sector Homeland Security Coordinating Council serves as a broad industry-wide network for coordinating ongoing industry initiatives, government partnerships, and responsibilities, but most importantly in communications with DHS on issues relating to sector coordination. This council represents more than 90% of the sector's owners and operators. The mission of the council is to foster and facilitate the coordination of oil and natural gas sectorwide voluntary activities and initiatives designed to improve critical infrastructure protection and homeland security. Objectives of the council include, but are not limited to, the following:

- Provide broad industry representation for critical infrastructure protection and homeland security and related matters for the oil and natural gas sector and for voluntary sectorwide partnership efforts.

- Provide a forum for policy discussion and coordination, with implementation of policy through the council members.

- Foster and promote coordination and cooperation among participating sector constituencies on critical infrastructure protection and homeland security–related activities and initiatives, including the Energy-ISAC.

- Establish and promote broad sector activities and initiatives that improve critical infrastructure protection and homeland security.

- Identify barriers to and recommend initiatives to improve sectorwide voluntary critical infrastructure protection and homeland security information and knowledge sharing and the timely dissemination processes for critical information sharing among all sector constituencies.

- Improve sector awareness of critical infrastructure protection and homeland security issues, available information, sector activities/initiatives, and opportunities for improved coordination (Source: Oil and Gas Sector Homeland Security Coordinating Council, "September 2004 Update," 2004).

Critical infrastructure protection in the oil and gas sector is an exceptionally challenging task for several reasons. First, as mentioned earlier, the flammable nature of those materials makes them natural targets for terrorists. Second, the overall operations of the oil and gas sectors are distributed over a very large geographical area with different types of infrastructures that need to be protected. Every single node within that infrastructure is vulnerable. Included in that vast infrastructure are drilling facilities, refineries, pipelines, highways, ports, and offshore facilities. Last but not least, an added challenge comes from the necessity to protect the different transportation modes used by the oil and gas sectors. Ground transportation and maritime transportation are the two most commonly used means by those sectors. Protecting each mode requires unique expertise, making such protection very costly and resource intensive.

Telecommunications

The telecommunications sector is constantly evolving because of the rapid rate by which technology in this sector advances, pressures from business and competition, and changes in the regulatory environment. Despite its dynamic nature, the sector has consistently provided robust and reliable communication services and processes designed to meet the needs of business and government. In the modern threat environment, the sector faces significant challenges to protect its vast and dispersed critical assets, both cyber based and physical. Because the government and critical infrastructure industries rely heavily on the public telecommunications infrastructure for vital communications services, the sector's vulnerabilities and protection initiatives are particularly important.

Every day the sector must contend with traditional natural and human-based threats to its physical infrastructure, such as weather events, unintentional cable cuts, and the technology threat (e.g., physical and cyber sabotage). The September 11 attacks revealed the threat that terrorism poses to the telecommunications sector's physical infrastructure. While it was not a direct target of the attacks, the telecommunications sector suffered significant collateral damage. In the future, certain concentrations of key sector assets themselves could become attractive direct targets for terrorists, particularly with the increased use of collocation facilities. The telecommunications infrastructure withstood the September 11 attacks in overall terms and demonstrated remarkable resiliency because damage to telecommunications assets at the attack sites was offset by diverse, redundant, and multifaceted communications capabilities. Priorities for telecommunications carriers are service reliability, cost balancing, security, and effective risk management postures. The government places high priority on the consistent application of security across the infrastructure. Although private- and public-sector stakeholders share similar objectives, they have different perspectives on what constitutes acceptable risk and how to achieve security and reliability. Therefore, an agreement on a sustainable security threshold and corresponding security requirements remains elusive.

Because of growing interdependencies among the various critical infrastructure components, a direct or indirect attack on any of them could result in cascading effects across the others. Such interdependencies increase the need to identify critical assets and secure them against both physical and cyber threats. Critical infrastructures rely on a secure and robust telecommunications infrastructure.

Redundancy within the infrastructure is critical to ensure that single points of failure in one infrastructure will not create an adverse impact in others. It is vital that government and industry work together to characterize the state of diversity in the telecommunications architecture. They must also collaborate to understand the topography of the physical components of the architecture to establish a foundation for defining a strategy to ensure physical and logical diversity.

Despite significant challenges, the telecommunications marketplace remains competitive, and customer demand for services is steady, if not increasing. An economic upturn within the industry could rapidly accelerate service demands. The interplay of market forces and FCC oversight will ensure the continuance of service delivery to sustain critical telecommunications functions. Nevertheless, recent economic distress has forced companies to spend their existing resources on basic network operations rather than recapitalizing, securing, and enhancing the infrastructure, which could amplify the financial impact of necessary infrastructure protection investments.

Given the reality of the physical and cyber threats to the telecommunications sector, government and industry must continue to work together to understand vulnerabilities, develop countermeasures, establish policies and procedures, and raise awareness necessary to mitigate risks. The telecommunications sector has a long, successful history of collaboration with government to address concerns over the reliability and security of the telecommunications infrastructure. The sector has undertaken a variety of new initiatives to further ensure both reliability and quick recovery and reconstitution. Within this environment of increasing emphasis on protection issues, public–private partnership can be further leveraged to address a number of key telecommunications initiatives, including efforts to do the following:

1. Define an appropriate threshold for security: DHS works with industry to define appropriate security thresholds for the sector and develops requirements derived from these definitions. DHS also works with industry to close the gap between respective security expectations and requirements. The reaching of agreements on methodologies for ensuring physical diversity is a key element of this effort.

2. Expand infrastructure diverse routing capability: DHS leverages and enhances the government's capabilities to define and map the overall telecommunications architecture. Through this effort, critical intersections among the various infrastructures are identified, which leads to strategies that better address security and reliability.

3. Understand the risks associated with vulnerabilities of the telecommunications infrastructure: The telecommunications infrastructure, including the PSTN, the Internet, and enterprise networks, provides essential communications for governments at all levels and other critical infrastructures. DHS works with the private sector to conduct studies to understand physical vulnerabilities within the telecommunications infrastructure and their associated risks. These studies focus on facilities where many different types of equipment and multiple carriers are concentrated.

4. Coordinate with key allies and trading partners: The nation relies on vital communications circuits and processes with key allies and trading partners. DHS works with other nations to consider innovative communications paths that provide priority communications processes to link governments, global industries, and networks in such a manner that vital communications are ensured (Source: DHS, "National Strategy for the Protection of Physical Infrastructure and Key Assets," 2003).

DHS is undertaking a major telecommunications security overhaul under the Homeland Secure Data Network (HSDN). The HSDN effort will streamline and modernize the classified data capabilities of DHS in order to facilitate high-quality and high-value classified data communication and collaboration within DHS and with other federal agencies and organizations, including DOD. Based on modern network and telecommunications designs, the HSDN will optimize both the classified data exchanges between DHS offices, and other networks of classified data such as the Anti-Drug Network, U.S. Customs and Border Protection (ADNET), Automatic Digital Network (AUTODIN), and Defense Message System (DMS). It will provide a scalable infrastructure, capable of supporting the growth and evolution of the DHS mission. The project has been awarded to Northrop Grumman and is expected to be completed by FY 2010. The project has been funded at $44 million, $32.7 million, and $33.1 million in fiscal years 2006, 2007, and 2008. The president's budget request for FY 2009 includes $47.7 million for the project. As of 2008, the project had completed some pilot phases including the deployment of a data center and at least 60 baseline HSDN sites. The expected total spending for the project is $337 million by time of completion.

The private and nonprofit stakeholders in the telecommunications sector are also actively working toward ensuring a higher level of protection and security of their critical infrastructures. One of such initiatives is the Telecommunications Infrastructure Information Sharing and Analysis Center (Telecom-ISAC). The Telecom-ISAC mission is to facilitate voluntary collaboration and information sharing among government, the telecommunications industry, and the national critical infrastructure protection goals; to gather information on vulnerabilities, threats, intrusions, and anomalies from multiple sources; and to perform analysis with the goal of averting or mitigating impact on the telecommunications infrastructure. The scope of the Telecom-ISAC's mission is all hazards, which include natural and human-made disasters and physical and cyber attacks.

Operational goals of Telecom-ISAC include, but are not limited to, facilitation of voluntary collaboration to support both government and industry information sharing requirements, fostering working liaisons with external sources and liaison partners, adding value and providing information not available elsewhere, filtering appropriately, performing high-quality analyses, and ensuring protection of information and the rights of data owners. The National Communication System operates the on-site and full-time Telecom-ISAC watch and analysis operation (WAO). The WAO consists of senior analysts closely integrated with the government NCC operations staff and industry representatives from Telecom-ISAC member companies. The Telecom-ISAC watch and analysis operation serves a dual function as the operational arm of the Telecom-ISAC and as one of DHS's Information Analysis and Infrastructure Protection watch and analysis centers. Information received by Telecom-ISAC is shared with participating entities only if the originator of information approves its release to anyone or any entity.

The Telecom Industry Association (TIA) is another important DHS partner in its efforts to protect the telecommunication critical infrastructure. TIA is active in both the standards and public policy arenas of homeland security and related critical infrastructure protection. The association supports interoperable communications for first responders and has worked with the public safety community for many years to create standards for such equipment. TIA currently has a large number of American National Standards supporting homeland security, emergency communications, and the needs of first responders. The association continues to work with the public safety community at the federal, state, and local levels through various activities to enhance and upgrade these standards and support emergency and security initiatives.

As a sector coordinator and neutral industry forum, TIA provided input to the National Response Plan Private Sector Support Annex working via Telecom-ISAC and the DHS Private Sector Office. TIA and its member companies have been actively engaged with communications network security/critical infrastructure protection and asset protection issues. Critical infrastructure protection responsibilities for the sector include raising awareness of vulnerabilities and risks to the sector and its infrastructure; assisting the sector to eliminate/mitigate its vulnerabilities; facilitating establishment and operation of sector ISACs; developing cooperative efforts with other countries and international organizations to achieve compatible security policies and strategies; and providing industry with information on results from complementary U.S. government research and development on critical infrastructure and assets protection. TIA is partnering with DHS to support the requirements of those responsibilities for the telecommunications sector.

Another vital coordination body of the communications sector is the Communications Sector Coordinating Council. The main purpose of the Communication Sector Coordinating Council (CSCC) is to facilitate the coordination of sectorwide activities and initiatives designed to improve physical and cybersecurity of the critical infrastructures and related information flow within the sector, cross-sector, and with DHS. Through the CSCC, private-sector owners, operators, and suppliers establish a platform to work together with DHS and other federal agencies, to contribute to the following critical infrastructure assurance goals:

- Identification, prioritization, and coordination of policy issues for the purposes of critical infrastructure and key resources protection

- To facilitate information sharing related to physical and cyber threats, vulnerabilities, incidents, potential protective measures, and best practices in the communications sector domain

- To tackle policy issues related to emergency response, recovery, and emergency communications following an incident or event

The CSCC was established in 2005, and it is a separate function from the Communications-ISAC run by the National Coordination Center for Telecommunications. The Communications ISAC is more operationally oriented whereas the CSCC is the body of coordination primarily for strategic and policy level directions. Separation is established from the existing NCC responsibilities through separate meetings, management processes, and supporting infrastructure. The CSCC has also taken the lead in developing the Communications Sector Specific Critical Infrastructure Plan as an input to the National Infrastructure Protection Plan. The plan identifies the following communication sector programs that are designed to ensure the protection and continuity of communications services before, during, and in the aftermath of disasters and incidents:

- Government Emergency Telecommunications Service (GETS): Provides emergency access and priority processing in the local and long distance segments of the Public Switched Telephone Network (PSTN). This service increases the likelihood that National Security and Emergency Preparedness (NS/EP) personnel can complete critical calls during periods of PSTN disruption and congestion resulting from natural or manmade disasters. GETS supports federal, state, and local government, industry, and nonprofit organization personnel in performing their NS/EP missions. GETS uses three major types of networks: major long-distance networks, local networks, and government-leased networks.

- Wireless Priority Service (WPS): Provides priority Commercial Mobile RadiService (CMRS) during and after emergencies for NS/EP personnel by ensuring WPS calls receive the next available radio channel during times of wireless congestion. In conjunction with GETS, it provides an end-to-end solution.

- Special Routing Arrangement Service (SRAS): Supports continuity of operations by providing survivable communications links to federal and defense end users over the public network.

- Next Generation Priority Service (NGPS): The NGPS Program develops technology to provide priority service capabilities over the Internet, standardizes the technology across industry through the commercial standards process, and migrates current priority service features to the technology.

- Hotline System: The NCS provides technical oversight of hotline systems to foreign countries for supporting national security and global security missions. The hotline supports the Secretary of State, Secretary of Defense, Nuclear Risk Reduction Center, and other DOD circuits, and establishes international connectivity for robust, secure crisis communications.

- Telecommunications Service Priority (TSP) Program: This program provides the regulatory, administrative, and operational framework for priority restoration and provisioning of NS/EP communication circuits in the event of an emergency. Eligibility in the TSP program extends to federal government, state government, local government, private industry, or foreign governments that have communications services supporting an NS/EP mission.

- Shared Resources (SHARES) High Frequency (HF) Radio Program: The program enhances information sharing during an incident. It provides a single, interagency emergency message handling system for the transmission of NS/EP information. The SHARES program brings together existing HF radio resources of federal, state, and industry organizations when normal communications are destroyed or unavailable (Sources: Communications Sector Coordinating Council, "Communications Sector Specific Infrastructure Protection Plan, 2007; DHS, "Budget in Brief FY 2009," 2008; Communications Sector Coordinating Council, "What Is the CSCC?," 2008; Northrop Grumman, "Press Release: HSDN," 2004; National Coordination Center for Telecommunications, "Program Information," 2008).

Pipelines

The United States has a vast pipeline infrastructure, consisting of many hundreds of thousands of miles of pipes, many of which are buried underground. These lines move a variety of substances, such as crude oil, refined petroleum products, and natural gas. Pipeline facilities already incorporate a variety of stringent safety standards that account for the potential effects a disaster could have on surrounding areas. Moreover, most elements of pipeline infrastructures are designed such that they can be quickly repaired or bypassed to mitigate localized disruptions. Destruction of one or even several of its key components could not disrupt the entire system. As a whole, the response and recovery capabilities of the pipeline industry are well proven, and most large control-center operators have established extensive contingency plans and backup protocols.

Pipelines are not independent entities but rather integral parts of industrial and public service networks. Loss of a pipeline could have an impact on a wide array of facilities and industrial factories that depend on reliable fuel delivery to operate.

Several hundred thousand miles of pipeline span the country, and it is unrealistic to expect total security for all facilities. As such, protection efforts focus on infrastructure components whose impairment would have significant effects on the energy markets and the economy as a whole. For the pipeline industry, determining what to protect and when to protect it is a factor in cost-effective infrastructure protection. During periods of high demand, such as the winter months, pipeline systems typically operate at peak capacity and are more important to the facilities and functions they serve.

The pipeline industry as a whole has an excellent safety record, as well as in-place crisis management protocols to manage disruptions as they occur. Nevertheless, many of the products that pipelines deliver are inherently volatile. Hence, their protection is a significant issue.

Pipelines cross numerous international, state, and local jurisdictional boundaries. The range of stakeholders creates a confusing — and sometimes conflicting — array of regulations and security programs for the industry to manage, especially with respect to the ability of pipeline facilities to recover, reconstitute, and reestablish service quickly after a disruption. The pipeline industry's increasing interdependencies with the energy and telecommunications sectors necessitate cooperation with other critical infrastructures during protection and response planning. Individually, companies have difficulty assessing the broader implications of an attack on their critical facilities. These interdependencies call for cross-sector coordination for them to be truly responsive to national concerns. Additionally, some issues concerning recovery or reconstitution will require at least regional planning within the industry, as well as the sharing of sensitive business information that may run into proprietary concerns.

Historically, individual enterprises within this sector have invested in the security of their facilities to protect their ability to deliver oil and gas products. Representatives from major entities within this sector have examined the new terrorist risk environment. As a result, they have developed a plan for action, including industry-wide information sharing. Within the federal sector, the DHS and DOT's Office of Pipeline Safety assists industry in enhancing pipeline security. DOT has developed a methodology for determining pipeline facility criticality and a system of recommended protective measures that are synchronized with the threat levels of the Homeland Security Advisory System.

However, operationally, several challenges still need to be met. As mentioned earlier, the DOT's Office of Pipeline Safety historically had the responsibility of ensuring the security of the U.S. pipeline infrastructure by developing standards and guidelines, arranging site visits, and organizing drills.

However, subsequent to the establishment of DHS, TSA and its associated Pipeline Security Program Office have become important players in securing the pipeline infrastructure. The Pipeline Security Program Office engages in the following activities:

1. Develops security standards for pipeline infrastructure and for hazardous materials movement
2. Implements protective and preventive measures to mitigate risk and avert terrorist activities and other threats
3. Builds and maintains strong stakeholder relations, coordination, education, and outreach for transportation industry security issues
4. Monitors adherence to and compliance with standards, requirements, and regulations

These activities partially overlap with the activities of the Office of Pipeline Safety. While one office's primary responsibility is the safety of the pipelines, and that of the other is the security of the pipelines, operationally the difference in activities is not great. While the agencies' offices are currently cooperating, there is no formal agreement between the TSA and the OPS that makes this cooperation official.

Additional pipeline mode protection initiatives include efforts to do the following:

1. Develop standard reconstitution protocols: DHS, in collaboration with DOE, DOT, and industry, will initiate a study to identify, clarify, and establish authorities and procedures as needed to reconstitute facilities as quickly as possible after a disruption.
2. Develop standard security assessment and threat deterrent guidelines: DHS, in collaboration with DOE and DOT, will work with state and local governments and the pipeline industry to develop consensus security guidance on assessing vulnerabilities, improving security plans, implementing specific deterrent and protective actions, and upgrading response and recovery plans for pipelines.
3. Work with other sectors to manage risks resulting from interdependencies: DHS, in collaboration with DOE and DOT, will convene cross-sector working groups to develop models for integrating protection priorities and emergency response plans (Source: DHS, 2003a).

Since September 11, industry and federal, state, and local governments have taken significant steps to secure the nation's critical energy infrastructure. Efforts have ranged from increasing surveillance of pipelines and conducting more thorough employee background checks to further restricting access to pipeline facilities and Internet mapping systems. Private companies have also formed task forces with federal, state, and local law enforcement officials to share security information and develop emergency notification and response plans.

Along with issuing new security measures in 2002, DOT developed criteria to evaluate an operator's implementation of those measures. Each operator was asked to submit a statement certifying that he or she had a security plan and had instituted the appropriate security procedures.

Today, 95% of oil pipeline operators have already implemented the measures and returned confirmation statements to DOT. The remaining 5% are primarily small operators that are in other businesses but run pipelines between plant facilities.

Some additional steps oil pipeline operators have taken include the following:

- Developing direct relationships with FBI regional field personnel
- Obtaining secret-level security clearances for selected operational personnel to ensure that threat information can be communicated directly from federal officials to the company
- Joining government–industry threat information dissemination services
- Installing additional surveillance cameras and physical barriers to entrances at certain facilities
- Conducting response drills using terrorist scenarios as a basis for training personnel and working with new federal law enforcement officials

- Using guard patrol at certain facilities during certain threat condition levels
- Limiting access to facilities and permitting entrance only after positive identification.

In addition to procedural improvements, the pipeline sector is also undergoing major improvements in its utilization of science and technology to make the infrastructure safer and more secure. Some of the more recent technologies being used by pipeline security organizations to secure their infrastructure are as follows:

- SCADA encryption: SCADA systems are commonly used software packages in the pipeline industry that remotely monitor and control system status and functions, such as valve openings and pipeline pressure, from a central control point, often called a master station. The commands that are sent over the existing network to control the infrastructure are normally not encrypted. However, in today's sophisticated networking environment with its increased number of cyber threats, those messages really need to be encrypted in order not to be accessed by hackers or terrorists. To ensure proper encryption of the messages, the American Gas Association (AGA) recently released recommendations for procedures that pipelines and other energy utilities can use to encrypt their SCADA transmissions between master stations and remote sites. The new design will provide robust 1,024-bit key encryption, the same level used by banks.
- GASNET: The Gasline Network Sensor System (GASNET™) is a distributed network of multipurpose sensors for communicating information on the real-time state of a natural gas distribution network to utility operators. The goal of GASNET is to help optimize the functioning of the nation's natural gas distribution infrastructure. When in use, GASNET will be an inexpensive way to monitor the status of pipelines over large areas, and it could later incorporate the ability to take further security-related measurements.
- Wide-range sensing: Sandia National Laboratories is studying shoulder-mounted devices that use backscatter absorption gas imaging (BAGI) technology. The devices would be used to detect chemical leaks that are not visible to the naked eye. While the technology has existed for years, in its newest incarnation it would be able to instantaneously survey a large area for gas leaks. The device could potentially be mounted on vans or on survey aircraft.
- Explorer robots: Robots that explore pipelines already exist, and they are improving. In conjunction with the Department of Energy and Carnegie Mellon University's National Robotics Engineering Consortium, the New York Gas Group has developed the so-called EXPLORER robot, essentially an untethered moving camera that monitors pipeline conditions in real time. The EXPLORER robot is equipped with a miniaturized fish-eye imager that sends pictures of the pipeline to a monitor above ground through a wireless connection. Because it provides pictures of a pipe's interior in real time, the system provides an accurate, complete view of a pipeline's health.
- Acoustic Detecting and Locating Gas Pipeline Infringement: West Virginia University has been assessing acoustic technology that "listens" for the unique sound wave generated when a pipeline break releases a large discharge of gas after being damaged. The objective of this project is to develop a centralized and automated acoustic monitoring system to detect leaks in, and infringements on, high-pressure natural gas pipelines. This system will detect the unique sound waves and vibrations that are generated when a pipeline break releases gas due to landslides, excavations, demolitions, or other sudden disturbances. The system will be designed to monitor background noise inside the pipe and identify any new frequencies that might signal a pipeline rupture or pipeline infringement (Sources: Security Management and U.S. Department of Energy).

The most significant test for the pipeline industry in the aftermath of 9/11 was the 2005 hurricane season with several strong hurricanes that damaged or disrupted parts of the pipeline network.

Pipeline systems in the Gulf of Mexico and the southeastern region were significantly impacted by these events. Due to the fact that most pipeline infrastructure is underground, physical damages have in most cases been limited. Some smaller aboveground or within-sea pipelines that connect smaller gathering systems have received physical damage, whereas larger pipeline systems have primarily been impacted by electricity outages that shut down compressors and pumps that generate the pressure to keep commodities within the pipe moving to their destination. Although very different in nature than a terrorist attack, those incidents have given the industry the opportunity to activate and implement their emergency response and contingency plans.

In April 2005, the American Petroleum Institute released the third edition of its "Security Guidelines for Petroleum Industry." The document covers in detail the process of comprehensive security management for the petroleum industry. There is a section dedicated to the development of a security plan with emphasis on specific sections such as security administration, personnel training, drills and exercises, record and documentation, response to changes in national alert levels, communications, security systems, security measures for access control, protected/controlled/restricted areas, monitoring, security incident procedures, audits, and security vulnerability analysis. The concept of security vulnerability analysis is explained in detail and in conjunction with risk control and risk mitigation. A chapter dedicated to cybersecurity covers cybersecurity policies, security awareness and education, accountability and ownership, data/information classification, access controls and identity management, network security, systems development, change control, viruses and other malicious code, intrusion detection and incident management, business continuity, business resumption, disaster recovery, regulatory compliance, and auditing.

Another key development in the pipeline security area is the release of the Transportation Sector Specific Infrastructure Protection Plan in May 2007. This plan includes a Pipeline Annex where the sector profile and specific pipeline security programs and tools are mentioned. Some of those programs, initiatives, and tools follow:

- Pipeline System Relative Risk Ranking and Prioritization Tool: This tool helps the TSA and involved industry partners prioritize pipeline infrastructures based on the standard data and analytics collected as part of the security vulnerability analysis. This statistical tool helps rank the relative risks of different pipeline facilities and infrastructures.

- Pipeline Corporate Security Review Program: The TSA uses this program to inspect individual pipeline owners or operators to ensure proper compliance with security guidelines and to verify the validity of security plans they submitted. Based on the inspections the security plans and procedures of pipeline operators are validated or feedback is provided for areas of improvement.

- Cyber Attack Awareness Program: The TSA and Gas Technology Institute run this program to educate pipeline owners and operators on potential vulnerabilities of the SCADA systems.

- Landscape Depiction and Analysis Tool: The TSA uses this tool to create a descriptive and graphic depiction of the pipeline domain including an overview of risk factors and components.

- Pipeline Cross Border Vulnerability Assessment Program: This joint program of TSA and Natural Resources Canada is designed to assess pipeline systems, control systems, interdependencies, and to support assault planning in critical cross-border pipelines.

- International Pipeline Security Forum: This is a forum for U.S. and Canadian pipeline officials to discuss pipeline issues, share knowledge, information, and best practices.

- Pipeline Policy and Planning: The joint program of TSA, DHS, DOT, and DOE coordinates the development, implementation, and monitoring of national pipeline planning.

- Regional Gas Pipeline Studies: The TSA, national labs, and industry collaborate in this program and conduct gas supplies studies in key national markets.

- Security Awareness Training Compact Discs: The TSA disseminates those informational CD's on pipeline security issues and improvised explosive devices to create awareness within the pipeline industry.

- TSA Pipeline Security Stakeholder Conference Calls: Those periodic conference calls connect TSA, industry, and other government stakeholders in pipeline security and discuss latest issues and developments.

- Pipeline Blast Mitigation Studies: The TSA, DOD, and Transportation Systems Sector Working Group conduct research and tests on various pipeline configurations to determine resiliency characteristics.

- Homeland Security Information Network (HSIN): This Internet-based communications system and information sharing tool provides security information, threat alerts, indications, and warnings to subscribed pipeline owners and other eligible users of security information.

- Homeland Security Advisory System (HSAS): The five-color–coded DHS alert system that provides real-time threat information when specific intelligence or knowledge is available during a real or before a potential incident.

- DOE Visualization and Modeling Working Group: The working group consists of government officials, national labs scientists, industry representatives, and other stakeholders in visualization and modeling of critical infrastructures. The group capitalizes on visualization and modeling methodologies such as GIS and systems simulation to understand behavior of critical infrastructure and their interdependencies. Homeland security is a vital application of the tools developed by the working group.

- DOT, DOE, DHS Incident Drill Programs: DOT, DOE, and DHS schedule exercises and drills to ensure written plans are tested and validated. Industry stakeholders such as pipeline operators are invited to the exercises if the scenario assumes impact on the pipeline infrastructure.

Before closing this section, one important fact to mention is that almost all of the TSA pipeline programs mentioned above are financed with funds from the general operating budget of the administration as there are no direct line items for pipeline security in its FY 2008 budget (DHS, "Budget in Brief FY 2009," 2008; Transportation Sector Government Coordinating Council, 2007; American Petroleum Institute, 2005).

Public Works

The phrase "public works," in its general definition, refers to all facilities and services provided by the government (usually state and local governments) to meet the basic sanitary needs and comfort of its citizens. Common responsibilities of public works departments include waste management, recycling, street lighting, trash removal, water management, and wastewater management.

Although these facilities are localized, they represent a collective high vulnerability because of the potentially high and widespread health consequences in the case of a successful terrorist attack on one or more of the facilities. Water treatment plants, wastewater plants, and landfills are three widely cited examples of these vulnerable facilities.

Water Treatment Plants

When a water supply facility takes untreated water from a river or reservoir, the water often contains dirt and tiny pieces of leaves and other organic matter, as well as trace amounts of certain contaminants. At their treatment plants, the facilities often add chemicals called coagulants to the water, which act on the water as it flows very slowly through tanks to remove these contaminants by forming clumps that settle to the bottom. The water usually follows this procedure by flowing through filters to remove even the smallest contaminants, such as harmful viruses and bacteria.

The most common drinking water treatment, considered by many to be one of the most important scientific advances of the 20th century, is disinfection. To perform this task, most water facilities add chlorine or another disinfectant to kill bacteria and other germs. Water supply facilities use other treatments as needed, according to the quality of their source water. For example, systems whose water is contaminated with organic chemicals can treat their water with activated carbon, which adsorbs or attracts the chemicals dissolved in the water.

The disinfection and purification of water is a rather complex process. It consists of several subprocesses such as prechlorination, coagulation, flocculation, sedimentation, filtration, fluoridation, post-chlorination, and corrosion control treatment. These steps are needed in order to produce water that will meet federal and state drinking water standards that is free of pathogens and suitable for public consumption.

As Figure 5–9 demonstrates, the water goes through several subprocesses until it is purified, and each of these subprocesses, especially the ones that involve chemical additives, are vulnerable to potential terrorist attacks. The terrorists can secretly change the additives with hazardous materials that they acquired beforehand and therefore change the contents of the city water into a potential chemical weapon against the served population. Water with extremely high or low pH can be very dangerous and even poisonous for the body. Extreme chemical changes with the water can usually be detected quickly; however, even so, the panic, stress, and potential psychological effects of such a terrorist attack can be devastating.

Terrorists can introduce biological agents that do not naturally exist inside the groundwater for which the water treatment systems do not have any countermeasures. Live, infectious bacteria can be transported to the city and housing with the water, and can infect people when they drink the water, thereby initiating a serious public health consequence. This risk has been determined to be very low, because of the amount of pathogen that would have to be introduced to cause high enough concentrations that would sicken the population, but it is still a very real risk. For this reason, the ability to detect biological attacks is considered an important issue that is still very much open for research and improvement. Drinking water utilities today find themselves facing these new responsibilities. While their mission has always been to deliver a dependable and safe supply of water to their customers, the challenges inherent in achieving that mission have expanded to include security and counterterrorism. In the Public Health Security and Bioterrorism Preparedness and Response Act of 2002, Congress recognized the need for drinking water systems to undertake a more comprehensive view of water safety and security. The act amended the Safe Drinking Water Act and specified actions community water systems and the EPA must take to improve the security of the nation's drinking water infrastructure. In its Strategic Plan for Homeland Security, EPA has six critical infrastructure protection goals. One of them states, "EPA will work with the states, tribes, drinking water and wastewater utilities (water utilities), and other partners to enhance the security of water and wastewater utilities." In accomplishing this goal, EPA is planning to use the following approaches:

1. EPA will work with the states, tribes, associations, and others to provide tools, training, and technical assistance to assist water utilities in conducting vulnerability assessments, implementing security improvements, and effectively responding to terrorist events. In 2002, while developing tools and providing training for all utilities, EPA provided direct grants to large drinking water utilities for vulnerability assessments, security enhancement designs, and/or emergency response plans. EPA will work with states, tribes, associations, and water utilities to identify needs and provide assistance for vulnerability assessments for medium and small utilities, and for high-priority security enhancements identified in the water utility vulnerability assessments for all systems. As plans are completed, emphasis on implementation of security enhancements will continue to increase. By the end of FY 2003, EPA expected all water utility managers to have access to basic information to understand potential water threats, and basic tools to identify security needs. By the end of FY 2003, all large community drinking water utilities were to have identified key vulnerabilities and be prepared to respond to any emergency.

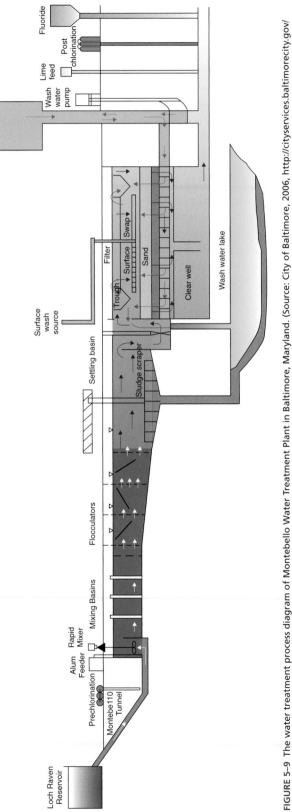

FIGURE 5–9 The water treatment process diagram of Montebello Water Treatment Plant in Baltimore, Maryland. (Source: City of Baltimore, 2006, http://cityservices.baltimorecity.gov/dpw/waterwastewater03/waterquality5a.html)

By the end of 2004, all medium community drinking water utilities were to be similarly positioned. By 2005, unacceptable security risks at water utilities across the country were to significantly reduced through completion of appropriate vulnerability assessments; design of security enhancement plans; development of emergency response plans; and implementation of security enhancements. The 2003 budget of EPA included $3.214 billion for safe water that was more than 41% of its total budget (Source: EPA, 2003). The 2004 budget of EPA included $2.95 billion and the 2005 budget included $2.94 billion for safe water. For fiscal year 2006, the EPA budget included $2.81 billion for clean and safe water, which accounted for 37.2% of its annual budget. The fiscal year 2007 budget of EPA included $2.73 billion and the fiscal year 2008 included $2.85 for safe and clean water. The president's budget request for FY 2009 includes $2.58 billion for EPA's clean water mission.

2. EPA will work with the DHS, other federal agencies, universities, and the private sector to solicit and review methods to prevent, detect, and respond to chemical, biological, and radiological contaminants that could be intentionally introduced in drinking water systems and wastewater utilities; review methods and means by which terrorists could disrupt the supply of safe drinking water or take other actions against water collection, pretreatment, treatment, storage, and distribution facilities; and review methods and means by which alternative supplies of drinking water could be provided in the event of a disruption.

3. EPA will work with states, tribes, and water utilities to implement water security practices in ongoing water utility operations. EPA will also work with states and tribes to build security concerns into ongoing review systems (e.g., sanitary survey, capacity development, operator certification, and treatment optimization program for drinking water systems and pretreatment program, environmental management systems, and operator certification programs for wastewater).

4. EPA will work with other government agencies, utility organizations, and water utilities to establish formal communication mechanisms to facilitate the timely and effective exchange of information on water utility security threats and incidents.

5. EPA and DHS will work together to foster coordination among federal, state, tribal, and local emergency responders, health agencies, environmental and health labs, the medical community, and the law enforcement community at all levels (federal, state, and local) concerning the response to potential terrorist actions against water utilities. This will be achieved through training and support of simulations and emergency response exercises.

6. EPA will work with other critical infrastructure sectors to further understand and reduce the impact on water utilities of terrorist attacks on related infrastructure as well as the impacts of attacks on water utilities on other critical infrastructure (Source: EPA, n.d.).

In March 2004, the EPA released its Water Security Research and Technical Support Action Plan. The plan details potential risks and vulnerabilities associated with the water systems and other possible waterborne threats. The plan identifies the following priorities that are related to the protection of water treatment plants:

- Protecting drinking water systems from physical and cyber threats
- Identifying drinking water threats, contaminants, and threat scenarios
- Improving analytical methodologies and monitoring systems for drinking water
- Containing, treating, decontaminating, and disposing of contaminated water and materials
- Planning for contingencies and addressing infrastructure interdependencies
- Targeting impacts on human health and informing the public about risks (Source: EPA, 2004)

As of 2008 many improvements have been achieved in the protection of clean water facilities. GAO and Congressional Research Service (CRS) reports confirm that most large- and medium-sized water utilities have completed their security and vulnerability assessments. Many of them have ceased using potentially dangerous chemicals such as chlorine, which can be exploited by terrorists to cause significant casualties to life, property and the environment. While the same CRS reports mention that there are no federal standards or industry best practices governing readiness, security, response, and recovery activities, a draft American National Standard entitled "Guidelines for the Physical Security of Water Utilities," (developed jointly by the American Society of Civil Engineers and the American Water Works Association) addresses these issues in detail. (Congressional Research Service, "Terrorism and Security Issues Facing the Water Infrastructure Sector," 2007; American Society of Civil Engineers/American Water Works Association, 2006; Government Accountability Office, "Securing Wastewater Facilities," 2006).

Wastewater Plants

Wastewater is the spent, or used, water originating in homes, businesses, farms, and industry that contains enough harmful material to negatively affect water quality. Wastewater includes both domestic sewage and industrial waste from manufacturing sources. Metals, organic pollutants, sediment, bacteria, and viruses all may be found in wastewater. As a result, untreated wastewater has the potential to cause serious harm to the environment and threaten human life.

EPA regulates the discharge and treatment of wastewater under the Clean Water Act. The National Pollutant Discharge Elimination System (NPDES) issues permits to all wastewater dischargers and treatment facilities. These permits establish specific discharge limits, monitoring and reporting requirements, and may also require these facilities to undertake special measures to protect the environment from harmful pollutants.

The basic function of wastewater treatment is to enable the processes by which water is purified. There are two basic stages in the treatment of wastes; primary and secondary. In the primary stage, solids are allowed to settle and are removed from the wastewater. The secondary stage uses biological processes to further purify wastewater. In some instances, these two stages are combined into a single operation.

The nation's wastewater infrastructure consists of approximately 16,000 publicly owned wastewater treatment plants, 100,000 major pumping stations, 600,000 miles of sanitary sewers, and another 200,000 miles of storm sewers, with a total value of more than $2 trillion. Taken together, the sanitary and storm sewers form an extensive network that runs near or beneath key buildings and roads, the heart of business and financial districts, and the downtown areas of major cities and is contiguous to many communication and transportation networks.

There are several vulnerabilities and risks associated with the wastewater treatment infrastructure. A potential scenario is the abuse of the wastewater collected in a wastewater treatment plant by terrorists and its use as a biological or chemical weapon. The terrorists can accomplish this by diverting the waste into the clean water and making it toxic. Another scenario would be a direct attack on one of the wastewater facilities where hazardous materials are filtered from the wastewater and stored for further processing. The blast on such a facility (assuming that it contains nuclear waste, such as waste from nuclear power plants) can have the effects of a dirty bomb, making the removal of the contaminated debris very difficult and risky for the first responders. The primary consequences, however, would be environmental and psychological.

Vulnerability assessments and risk reduction programs are necessary to minimize the potential impacts of terrorist attacks to these facilities. As mentioned in the previous section, EPA has programs to improve water security and wastewater security. EPA in cooperation with the Association of Metropolitan Sewerage Agencies (AMSA) released two new Vulnerability Self Assessment Tools (VSAT™). One of those tools is for joint water/wastewater utilities and another for small- and medium-sized water utilities. VSAT water/wastewater provides the valuable online vulnerability assessment capabilities to utilities providing both wastewater treatment and water supply services. Its new counterpart, VSAT™ water, will do the same for both public and private water utilities. These new software tools, developed by the AMSA for the EPA, provide an approach to evaluate, prioritize, and remediate vulnerabilities based upon five critical utility assets — physical plant, information technology, knowledge base, employees, and customers.

Another program by EPA to improve safety and security on wastewater plants is the Wastewater Treatment Plant Operator On-Site Assistance Training Program. The goal of the program is to provide direct on-site assistance to operators at small underserved community wastewater treatment facilities, in order to help the facility achieve and maintain consistent permit compliance, maximizing the community's investment in improved water quality. In a cooperative effort with EPA, states, state coordinators, municipalities, and operators focus on issues such as wastewater treatment plant capacity, operation training, maintenance, administrative management, financial management, troubleshooting, and laboratory operations. The program identifies any need to repair or build new facilities to meet existing or future permit limits, assists the town during the process of selecting consultants and design review, recommends ways to improve preventive maintenance of equipment and structures, and often reduces energy and chemical costs through more efficient operation techniques.

A significant contribution to EPA's wastewater treatment security efforts came from the Water Environment Research Foundation (WERF). In 2003, the WERF was awarded a cooperative research grant from the EPA's Office of Water to coordinate seven new projects to protect the nation's wastewater infrastructure and public health. The $2.1 million grant for the fiscal years form 2003 to 2007 funded seven projects to assist in addressing a broad spectrum of issues related to security and public health protection of water and wastewater infrastructure, as well as risk communications in the event of potential threats or terrorist attacks. Projects that were funded follow:

- Identify, screen, and treat contaminants in water/wastewater: The goal of the project is to identify methods to screen for common biological, chemical, and radiological compounds and then determine the removal efficacy of wastewater treatment processes. This project with a total multiyear budget of $450,000 was ongoing as of 2008.

- Security measures for computerized and automated systems at wastewater facilities: The project is providing guidance to utilities on how to secure and protect automated systems and will document currently available technology to detect and correct such security breaches. This project with a total multiyear budget of $294,748 was ongoing as of 2008.

- Contingency planning for wastewater treatment facilities: The project is helping water and wastewater treatment facilities and their communities nationwide develop individual contingency plans in the event of an emergency. This project with a total multiyear budget of $300,000 was completed as of late 2005. The outcome of the project is a final report that guides wastewater utilities in the creation of emergency response plans for all hazards, and identifies data that should be part of the emergency response plan. Additionally, the report focuses on vital emergency planning concepts for wastewater utilities, such as incident command, crisis communications and call trees, planning for personnel safety, plan invocation procedures, emergency operations centers, training, and exercising. The report is available at the WERF website.

- Communicating with your local government and community: The project is aimed at helping public agencies, such as water and wastewater utilities and elected officials, effectively communicate with the public. This project with a total multiyear budget of $150,000 was ongoing as of 2008.

- Software and guidance for assessing and inventorying wastewater treatment infrastructure: The project's goal is to provide a valuable tool for utilities to identify and categorize their underground and aboveground assets and then to better assess their system condition. This project was completed as of late 2005. The outcome of the project was a software tool that calculates new indices to assess security risk, another index for strategic asset information, and an index for combining those two independent measures of utility management. Users can use it to prioritize assets in several ways, and are provided with a compelling visual display of any existing overlaps.

- Feasibility testing/demonstration of support systems for use in wastewater treatment plants (WWTP): The project tests the feasibility of using computer models, decision trees, or other expert systems to ensure public and ecosystem health by learning from and preventing future WWTP system upsets. This project with a total multiyear budget of $175,000 was ongoing as of early 2008. The outcome of the project will be a software prototype designed to provide wastewater utility managers with Web-based, near real-time decision support to assist in detecting, mitigating, and recovering from treatment plant impacts as a result of cyber attacks (Sources: Association of Metropolitan Sewage Agencies, "Water Environment Research Foundation," 2004; Water Environment Research Foundation, "WERF Research Projects Online Database," 2008).

There are two important obstacles facing wastewater plant security. The first is that no federal law directly and comprehensively governs the security of wastewater facilities. Second, high capital investment is required to convert from the use of chlorine to less toxic materials. Despite these barriers wastewater utility owners and operators have taken several steps to significantly improve wastewater security since the 9/11 attacks (Government Accountability Office, "Securing Wastewater Facilities," 2006).

Landfills

Although conservation, reuse, recycling, and composting have reduced municipal waste, most of the waste that is generated still ends up in landfills. At present, there are more than 3,000 landfills in the United States. Many are modern, well-engineered facilities that are located, designed, operated, monitored, and financed to ensure compliance with federal regulations. These regulations include restrictions that require landfills to be located away from wetlands, floodplains, and other restricted areas; clay-reinforced liners; operating practices that reduce odor and control insects and rodents; groundwater monitoring; postclosure care; and corrective action to clean up landfill sites. In addition, the EPA encourages the use of landfill gas as a renewable fuel source through its Landfill Methane Outreach Program.

Location restrictions ensure that landfills are built in suitable geological areas away from faults, wetlands, floodplains, or other restricted areas. Liners are geo-membrane or plastic sheets reinforced with two feet of clay on the bottom and sides of landfills. Operating practices such as compacting and covering waste frequently with several inches of soil help reduce odor; control litter, insects, and rodents; and protect public health. Groundwater monitoring requires testing groundwater wells to determine whether waste materials have escaped from the landfill. Closure and postclosure care includes covering landfills and providing long-term care of closed landfills. Corrective action controls and cleans up landfill releases and achieves groundwater protection standards. Financial assurance provides funding for environmental protection during and after landfill closure (i.e., closure and post-closure care). However, there are still risks and vulnerabilities associated with landfills.

More than 40 million tons of hazardous waste are produced in the United States each year by large industrial facilities such as chemical manufacturers, electroplating companies, petroleum refineries, and by more common businesses including dry cleaners, auto repair shops, hospitals, exterminators, and photo-processing centers. The EPA has produced a list of more than 500 hazardous wastes and works closely with businesses and state and local authorities to make sure these wastes are properly treated and disposed of. The EPA conducts risk management studies to ascertain the potential health effects of exposure to these wastes and oversees Superfund and other programs that clean up contaminated waste sites.

Radioactive waste is produced by a number of activities, including nuclear power generation, mining, medicine, and industry. Some radioactive waste can remain hazardous for thousands of years. The EPA works with the Nuclear Regulatory Commission (NRC), DOT, DOE, and local authorities to regulate the storage and disposal of radioactive waste. The EPA is responsible for developing environmental standards that apply to radioactive waste disposal facilities. The EPA ensures that waste facilities comply with all federal environmental laws and regulations.

The physical security of landfill sites still poses a potential terrorist threat. Recognizing the amount of hazardous toxic waste every year in the United States and the existence of radiological waste, the physical security of landfill sites rises in importance. A scenario in which terrorists attack and blow up a landfill where radiological waste was stored could potentially cause a major disaster. Given that terrorists look for easy targets with the largest potential impact, this scenario is fairly realistic. If physical security of landfills cannot be ensured, they then become an easy, or soft, target of terrorist attacks.

Currently there are a few local and state initiatives to improve physical security of landfills, and federal support, while essential to providing greater physical security, has been limited. EPA, in cooperation with DHS, is the appropriate source for technical and financial assistance. However, because of other competing priorities, there has been limited attention paid to coordinate the initiatives and support state, local, and publicly held landfill sites for improved physical security.

A relatively recent study suggests that it would be generally safe to store debris from a building contaminated with a chemical weapon. A computer model of interactions of chemicals that can be typically found in landfills with potential chemical weapon agents has shown that most of the chemical agents would bind themselves to organic material in the landfill or transform themselves to less toxic molecules when they interact with water in the landfill. The model also allowed the inspection of further contamination in gaseous form and contamination of ground water and in both cases found the likelihood to be slim. The findings of the study are yet to be proven in the laboratory environment (Medical News Today, 2006).

■ ■ Critical Thinking ■

The Department of Homeland Security has been widely criticized for not implementing a proper federal response to Hurricane Katrina. The Director of FEMA and the Secretary of Homeland Security both received criticism for the botched response in this event, although the justification for this criticism differed in each case. While such criticism was constructive and sincere in most instances, a closer look at the unique challenges facing the secretary of Homeland Security quickly explains why DHS could yet be functioning at levels short of optimal effectiveness:

- Largest government reorganization: The establishment of the DHS was the largest government reorganization since the Second World War. The reorganization within the DHS is not yet completed. The Secretaries of Homeland Security in following years will spend significant time figuring out the most effective organizational and management structures for the department.

- Amalgamation of organizational cultures: For the department to be effective in its role it has to create its own organizational culture that amalgamates cultures of various agencies it absorbed. The classical example is the emergency management culture (i.e., FEMA) versus the law enforcement/security culture (i.e., FBI, TSA, U.S. Customs and Border Protection, etc.). This is a challenging and time-consuming process.

- Asymmetric threat environment: Since intelligence is an integral part of homeland security, and the terrorist threat dealt with is asymmetric, information sharing with the public is not as straightforward as in other functions of the government, which makes maintaining a constant connectivity with the public, an essential stakeholder, more difficult.

- Human psychology and behavior: There are two elements of this that make the secretary's job more difficult. First, as we get further away from 9/11, public sensitivity toward security and preparedness may be weakening. Second, as more security measures are implemented that interfere with the general public on a daily basis, inconveniences or inefficiencies of the security process can reduce public support for the necessity of those measure. This is especially true for periods where there are no major terrorist attacks. Long lines at airport security checkpoints and increased layers of security are examples.

- Difficulty of defining and communicating success: In keeping with the security implications of the asymmetric threat environment, it is also impossible for the Secretary of Homeland Security and other government officials to fully define homeland security successes. The secretary is only successful if she or he prevents all terrorist attacks, whereas it is enough for the terrorists to succeed only once to convert that success into failure. Not only is it a challenge to actually prevent all terrorist attempts, but in many instances it is even impossible to immediately share the success of prevented terrorist attacks with the public due to the investigations and intelligence operations that may be going on in the background.

Role of Private Sector in Homeland Security and Changes in Business Continuity and Contingency Planning

The terrorist attacks of September 11 affected thousands of private businesses, not just businesses in New York or near the Pentagon, but businesses that were as far away as Hawaii and Seattle. The attacks killed nearly 3,000 people, most of whom were employees of private corporations that had offices in or near the World Trade Center (WTC). Some companies lost hundreds of employees. In downtown Manhattan, almost 34.5 million square feet of office space was destroyed. Totaling $50 billion to $70 billion in insured losses, the WTC attack became one of the costliest disasters in U.S. history. Most of these direct economic losses were incurred by the private sector. In addition to the physical resources and systems lost by businesses in the WTC, changes in public behavior following the attacks had a severe impact on travel, tourism, and other businesses. Because the biggest portion of the impact was absorbed by the private sector, September 11 has been perceived as a sudden wake-up call for disaster preparedness, business continuity planning, and corporate crisis management in the private sector.

The changes in private-sector disaster preparedness after September 11 can be analyzed from two perspectives: (1) the direct involvement of the private sector in disaster preparedness and response in coordination with the Department of Homeland Security and as foreseen by the National Response Framework and the National Incident Management System, and (2) the self-reassessment of the private sector in terms of corporate crisis management and business continuity as a competitive requirement as opposed to cost of business. Our reference point in addressing the changing expectations of the federal government from the private sector will be several major federal documents and strategies, such as the National Strategy for Homeland Security and official press releases from relevant departments and agencies. While addressing the change of internal processes and procedures among the private sector, we will refer to publications and press releases that address changes in particular companies and try to find general trends between different approaches.

Expectations of DHS from the Private Sector

The National Strategy for Homeland Security defines the basic approach of DHS and briefly describes the characteristics of the partnership the department is planning to achieve with the private sector. Given the fact that almost 85% of the infrastructure of the United States is owned or managed by the private sector, there is no doubt that the private sector must be included as a major stakeholder in homeland security. Reducing the vulnerabilities and securing the private sector means the same as securing the vast portion of U.S. infrastructure and economic viability.

According to the National Strategy for Homeland Security, a close partnership between the government and private sector is essential in ensuring that existing vulnerabilities of critical infrastructures to terrorism are identified and eliminated as quickly as possible. The private sector is expected to conduct risk assessments on their holdings and invest in systems to protect key assets. The internalization of these costs is interpreted by the DHS as not only a matter of sound corporate governance and good corporate citizenship but also an essential safeguard of economic assets for shareholders, employees, and the nation.

The National Strategy for the Protection of Physical Infrastructure and Key Assets provides more direct clues about what the DHS expects from the private sector as a partner and stakeholder in homeland security. The strategy defines the private sector as the owner and operator of the bulk of U.S. critical infrastructures and key assets and mentions that private-sector firms prudently engage in risk management planning and invest in security as a necessary function of business operations and customer confidence. Moreover, since in the present threat environment the private-sector generally remains the first line of defense for its own facilities, the DHS expects private-sector owners and operators to reassess and adjust their planning, assurance, and investment programs to better accommodate the increased risk presented by deliberate acts of violence (Figure 5–10).

Since the events of September 11, many businesses have increased their threshold investments and undertaken enhancements in security in an effort to meet the demands of the new threat environment. For most enterprises, the level of investment in security reflects implicit risk-versus-consequence trade-offs, which are based on (1) what is known about the risk environment, (2) what is economically justifiable and sustainable in a competitive marketplace or in an environment of limited government resources, (3) potential consequences of disasters, and (4) priorities for the protection of human capital, processes, physical infrastructure, organizational reputation, stakeholder confidence, and vital records that require immediate attention. Given the dynamic nature of the terrorist threat and the severity of the consequences associated with many potential attack scenarios, the private sector naturally looks to the government for better information to help make its crucial security investment decisions. The private sector is continuing to look for better data, analysis, and assessment from DHS to use in the corporate decision-making process.

Similarly, the private sector looks to the government for assistance when the threat at hand exceeds an enterprise's capability to protect itself beyond a reasonable level of additional investment. In this light, the federal government promises to collaborate with the private sector (and state and local governments) to ensure the protection of nationally critical infrastructures and assets; provide timely warning and ensure the protection of infrastructures and assets that face a specific, imminent threat; and promote an environment in which the private sector can better carry out its specific protection responsibilities.

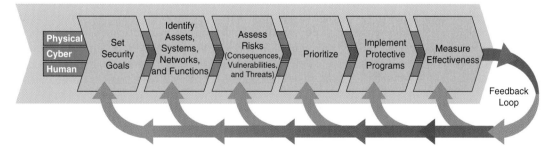

FIGURE 5–10 Operational framework for critical infrastructure and key assets protection. (Source: National Infrastructure Protection Plan)

Table 5–7   Operating Status of Sectoral ISACs as of 2008

Sector	ISAC	ISAC Established
Agriculture and food	Food	February 2002
Banking and finance	Financial Services	October 1999
Chemical	Chemical	April 2002
Commercial facilities	Real Estate	February 2003
Drinking water and water treatment systems	Water	December 2002
Emergency services	Emergency Management and Response	October 2000
Energy	Electric	October 2000
	Energy	November 2001
Government facilities	Multistate	January 2003
Information technology	Information Technology	December 2000
	Research and Education Network	February 2003
Telecommunications	National Coordinating Center for Telecommunications	January 2000
Transportation systems	Public Transit	January 2003
	Surface Transportation (rail)	May 2002
	Highway	March 2003
	Maritime	February 2003

ISAC, Information Sharing and Analysis Center.
Source: Government Accountability Office, GAO-07-39, Washington, DC, 2006.

A good example of partnership between the private sector and DHS are the sectoral ISACs. ISACs are established by the owners and operators of a national critical infrastructure to better protect their networks, systems, and facilities within the coordination of DHS. ISACs serve as central points to gather, analyze, sanitize, and disseminate private-sector information to both industry and DHS. These centers also analyze and distribute information received from DHS to the private sector. The objectives of this program are to seek participation from all sector segments/entities, representation of all segments on ISAC Advisory Board in order to establish a two-way, trusted information sharing program between ISAC entities and DHS, and to provide cleared industry expertise to assist DHS in evaluating threats and incidents. Currently, ISACs exist and are being created in a variety of critical infrastructure sectors. The DHS document that defines the relationships between the private sector and DHS is the National Infrastructure Protection Plan (NIPP) of January 2006 and the subsequent sector-specific annexes that have been developed in 2007. These plans define mechanisms that serve to build those relationships and create a system where the government and private entities can work in harmony to achieve a higher level of protection for critical infrastructures and key resources of the United States. Table 5–7 gives a list of operating ISACs and their dates of establishment.

As mentioned earlier, the primary building block of this relationship is the formation of sectoral ISACs, which promote the coordination, cooperation, best practices, lessons learned, information flow, and information sharing among sector-specific entities. The NIPP defines another coordination body for the achievement of the public–private integration. Those coordinating bodies are called Critical Infrastructure and Key Resources Sector Coordinating Councils. They are private-sector coordinating mechanisms that comprise private sector infrastructure owners and operators and supporting associations, as appropriate. Sector coordinating councils bring together the entire range of infrastructure protection activities and issues to a single entity.

One role of the sector coordinating councils is to identify, establish, support the information sharing mechanisms (ISMs) that are most effective for their sector, drawing on existing mechanisms (e.g., ISACs) or creating new ones as required. The NIPP also creates Critical Infrastructure and Key

Resources Government Coordinating Councils, which are government coordinating councils for each sector comprised of representatives from DHS, the sector specific agency (SSA), and the appropriate supporting federal departments and agencies. The government coordinating councils work with and support the efforts of the sector coordinating councils to plan, implement, and execute sufficient and necessary broad-based sector security, planning, and information sharing to support the nation's homeland security mission.

As indicated by the NIPP, the private sector will be engaged by DHS, in collaboration with the relevant SSAs, to promote awareness of and feedback on the NIPP framework and to solicit their involvement in the national CIP program. The private sector will also be working with the appropriate SSAs to begin implementation of the SSPs for their sectors. As the interim NIPP is implemented, the private sector will be provided with more coordinated data calls from government agencies, enhanced engagement through sector coordinating councils, and subsequent versions of the NIPP and SSPs will reflect discussions among DHS, the SSAs, and other stakeholders, including the private sector. The NIPP serves as a guide for the private sector to identify and implement the procedures to protect the critical infrastructure against specific threats and the general threat environment. There are five major goals identified in the plan, and objectives to meet those goals are also listed. Those goals and the respective objectives are as follows:

- Goal 1: Protect CI/KR against plausible and specific threats. Objectives to meet this goal include:

  Increase awareness of the threat environment across CI/KR sectors.
  Integrate threat and vulnerability information into specific vulnerability reduction prioritization decisions.
  Use vulnerability assessment information when responding to specific threats.
  Identify and implement protective measures against specific threats.

- Goal 2: Long-term reduction of CI/KR vulnerabilities in a comprehensive and integrated manner. Objectives to meet this goal include:

  Develop and maintain comprehensive national inventory of CI/KR assets and vulnerabilities that includes cyber, physical, and human aspects of each asset, including intangibles.
  Complete mapping of interdependencies among assets and across CI/KR sectors.
  Conduct vulnerability assessments for the nation's critical infrastructure and key resources for both specific and general threats.
  Integrate infrastructure protection activities with those called for in other national-level plans to avoid overlaps and gaps.
  Reduce general vulnerabilities within and across sectors where needed.

- Goal 3: Maximize efficient use of resources for infrastructure protection. Objectives to meet this goal include:

  Prioritize possible protective measures considering return on investment in light of inherent vulnerabilities, existing protective measures, and (when applicable) threat information.
  Encourage and support SSA responsibility for sectors to leverage sector-specific expertise.
  Identify market-based incentives for voluntary action by owners and operators.
  Ensure lessons learned and best practices are captured and shared for evolution into sector-accepted operational practices over time.

- Goal 4: Build partnerships among federal, state, local, tribal, international, and private-sector stakeholders to implement CIP programs. Objectives to meet this goal include:

  Delineate roles, responsibilities, and accountability for actions.
  Develop necessary organizations, staffing, and training to carry out responsibilities.
  Request appropriate authorities and funding to allow actions to be implemented.
  Establish mechanisms for coordination and information exchange among partners.
  Develop mechanisms for tracking involvement and progress.

- Goal 5: Continuously track and improve national protection. Objectives to meet this goal include:

  Develop mechanisms for tracking national- and sector-level vulnerabilities and progress in reducing those vulnerabilities.

  Make infrastructure protection activities and metrics part of the organization's overall operational metrics to reinforce the importance of CIP initiatives and activities.

  Develop a national risk profile (a high-level summary of the risk and protection for all sectors) to align threats with strategic decision making.

  Develop an information sharing system to support rapid dissemination of lessons learned.

These goals are to be achieved using the national risk management framework as defined by the NIPP. The framework is similar for specific and general threat environments (see Figure 5–6); therefore, we will not address both frameworks separately.

DHS has acknowledged that it is well aware that effective protection of the critical infrastructure in the United States is only achievable through direct involvement of and strong partnership with the private sector. The private sector is not only an integral part of the national infrastructure protection effort, but it lies in the center of all protection strategies designed by DHS. That said, DHS is responsible for creating the environment where public- and private-sector entities talk to each other and work together to achieve a well-established national goal. Understanding the needs of each sector, building trust among officials and decision makers, making plausible assumptions, and setting realistic milestones are all key success factors. The real challenge is addressing cross-sectoral vulnerabilities due to interdependencies where involvement of multiple sectors is necessary for sustainable protection of a critical infrastructure and creation of realistic recovery objectives and procedures. Creation of cross-sector vulnerability assessment teams and utilization of multiple-sector expertise is critical to successfully plan for contingencies that may simultaneously hit interdependent critical infrastructures.

Corporate Crisis Management, Business Continuity, and Contingency Planning: The New Cost of Doing Business

September 11 was the most devastating day in modern history for American corporations. The attack in New York City was a direct attack on not only the symbols of corporate America, but on the businesses themselves. The private sector lost human resources, expertise, buildings, office space, data, records, and revenue. Some of these losses were irreplaceable, such as people. The affected companies also suffered time-dependent and continuous losses such as business interruption, loss of customer trust, and employee loyalty. The property and human losses could not have been prevented because the private sector itself could not have stopped the hijacked planes from crashing into the towers. However, effective corporate crisis management and business continuity planning absolutely could have, and in many places did, minimize the continuous losses.

To put this discussion in perspective, the following statistics and charts are provided to illustrate the vulnerability of the private sector in terms of terrorist actions. The Department of State report Patterns of Global Terrorism reports on the total number of facilities struck by international terrorist attacks (see Figure 5–11). The statistics show attacks with respect to the year they occurred and the type of facility struck (e.g., private sector, government, diplomatic, military). These figures are important because they show changing trends in the type of facilities terrorists have chosen to attack. There is a common belief that terrorists are more likely to attack military and government facilities, because of the stated political ideologies of the terrorist groups. However, the facts prove this theory wrong. In actuality, it is the soft-target private-sector facilities that have most commonly been victimized by the scourge of terrorism.

Clearly, a reduction in the number of attacks on businesses worldwide occurred after 2001. This reduction may be attributable to several factors that have changed since that time. One of these factors is the increased global effort to reduce terrorist acts. This effort is primarily led by the United States and its allies, which are the most likely targets but which also have spent billions on preventing

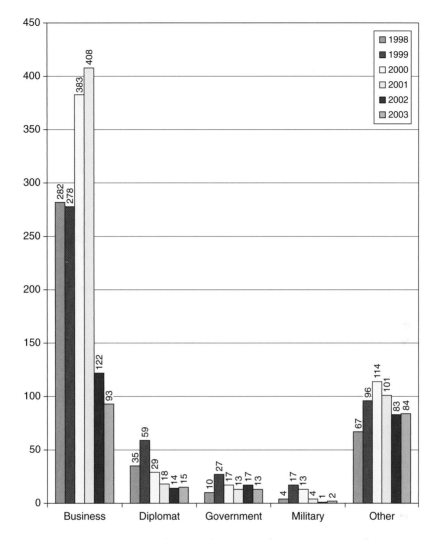

FIGURE 5–11 Total facilities attacked by terrorists (worldwide), 1998–2003. (Source: Department of State, "Patterns of Global Terrorism," 2003)

such attacks. As terror cells become more and more international and decentralized, international cooperation and intelligence sharing become critical to prevent acts of terrorism. Since 2001, significant amounts of resources have been allocated to achieve this goal, and this may serve as a contributing factor to the reduced number of terrorist attacks.

However, the preceding explanation does not account for why the reduction in the total number of attacks to businesses is steeper compared to other potential targets. As seen in Figure 5–11, the number of terrorist attacks aimed at businesses was reduced from 409 in 2001, to 122 in 2002 and 93 in 2003, whereas such reductions were not as significant for diplomatic facilities, government buildings, or military or other facilities.

Businesses have historically been targets of terrorists primarily because they have been perceived as soft targets that are easier to attack and minimally protected. After the 9/11 attacks, the vulnerability of businesses to disasters such as terrorism became obvious. Businesses learned through tragic experience that they constitute a potential target for terrorists. So they began to invest more into their security, risk management, crisis management, and business continuity programs. Research shows that all sophisticated terrorists carefully observe their prospective targets before deciding on their actual target.

ANOTHER VOICE: SAFETY AND SECURITY CONCERNS IN THE PRIVATE SECTOR

Security in Public vs. Private Sectors

The phone rang at 15 minutes before 3 AM. It was January 26, 2007. Sound asleep, I instinctively reached for my phone, wondering who could be calling at this hour. It was little surprise to me that it was my boss on the line. He was notifying me that an explosion had just occurred outside the entrance of one of our hotels in South Asia. An unidentified man attempted to penetrate hotel security. Strapped with a homemade explosive device, he was confronted by our guards who prevented access to the property. A scuffle ensued and the bomber detonated the device. The security guard was killed instantly alongside the bomber and seven bystanders were injured.

Through the system we had established years earlier, all of our crisis management team members were on a conference call within 15 minutes. We concluded the conference call an hour later with tasks assigned to each member. The team convened again a few hours later to report on their assignments. Since the damage to the hotel's building structure was minimal, the hotel was able to resume its normal operations later that day. Later, a relief fund was set up to help the deceased employee's family.

This is an example of one of those phone calls you do not wish to receive, regardless of the time of day. A phone call like this precipitates a crisis lasting anywhere from one day to several weeks. Everyone in the security department will be tested dealing with this on a 24-hour basis. It is our employee, our company, our reputation, after all.

There is little distinction between the security responsibilities of government agencies and private sector entities. Both protect people, facilities, assets, and reputation. However, the ramifications are far more complex for the private sector when it comes to dealing with the aftermath of a crisis. When working in the government sector, there is little concern about the stock performance, shareholders, a potential increase in insurance premiums, public relations disasters, or lawsuits by customers. These elements can be extremely challenging for someone who makes the decision to cross over into the private sector.

In a corporate crisis environment, pressure comes from many areas. It most often manifests itself from stockholders, legal advisors, consultants, rank-and-file employees, customers and, naturally, competitors. Everyone is a stakeholder.

If FEMA had been a privately owned company and its directors performed in much the same manner that they did during Hurricane Katrina, FEMA's stock would have plunged and no insurance company would have dared to insure them again. Senior executives in the parent company (which would be the Department of Homeland Security in this example) and its board of directors would have fired them all and, needless to say, the PR department would have their own crisis trying to mitigate the negative publicity.

The Hurricane Katrina story could have been very different if it had been handled in an effective and efficient manner. When such disasters occur, mass evacuations and major rescue operations require extensive efforts. In this case, government waste was rampant and communication between agencies broke down. Politics obfuscated good judgment. Conversely, a private company has to be self sufficient. Its contingency plans need to cover all aspects from start to finish. If a private company fails to manage a crisis effectively, profits will plunge, customers will not return, stock holders will sell, and the company will eventually go under.

Private companies have to have a strategic focus, think ahead, and prepare resources. They should assess the situation from the perspective of each stakeholder. Hurricane plans should include shelters both inside and outside of the facility, prenegotiated contracts with chartered airlines, and supplies such as food, beds, and toilets. Having these plans and provisions in place will boost customer confidence, increase business, please shareholders, and drive revenue. Everyone is happy.

Another aspect to consider is that many companies are global, thereby expanding the horizon and adding more elements to the crisis plan. Different parts of the world involve various kinds of threats that might not exist in corporate America. Wars, government instability, foreign languages, customs, laws, and restrictions need to be considered and evaluated in order to allow for fast and seamless reaction during a crisis.

A private company's plan needs to be all encompassing, including preventative methods as well as solutions. A comprehensive review of the business continuity plan is always needed after a crisis comes to an end.

Last but not least, cooperation from company executives is the key. Without it, no crisis plan can function as they always require top down support, money, time, and resources.

Jack Suwanlert
Director — International Loss Prevention
Marriott International Inc.

Corporate Security

Terrorists often select targets they consider to be soft — that is, those that are easy to hit. Therefore, it is not only the operational benefits gained by corporate security programs, but also their visibility, that serves as a deterrent for terrorists. For example, if a terrorist organization aims to damage a country's tourism sector, it may attempt to detonate a bomb in a hotel. As terrorists determine which hotel to attack, they will likely consider several alternatives and select that which has the least visible security. Overall, business sector preparedness is much greater today than it was in 2001, which is one obvious explanation for why attacks on business targets have decreased. This reduction can be attributed to businessess "hardening" themselves against their former "soft target" image.

Another factor that is changing private-sector perceptions is insurance and losses. The Insurance Information Institute has plotted the distribution of different types of insured damage from the September 11 attacks and it presents some interesting facts (see Figure 5–12). The most notable figure in this graph is the amount of damage from business interruption: $9.8 billion (31% of all estimated damage) of the total damage is caused by business interruption. This is a significant portion of the damage, one over which we have some degree of control if adequate business impact analysis and business continuity planning activities can be established before the crisis. One needs to remember that despite significant losses in the 2001 attack, due the 1993 WTC bombing and the potential Y2K threat, private-sector members located inside the WTC complex were among the more prepared stakeholders compared to private organizations in other parts of the nation.

Insurance companies are taking into account the existence of preparedness programs as they calculate the premiums and business interruption insurance coverage for private corporations. Due to the heavy losses they incurred after 9/11, insurance companies looked for ways to limit their exposure to potential future catastrophic losses caused by acts of terrorism. Since re-insurers were also hit hard with the costly claims of 9/11, one option was to exclude terrorism coverage completely from the portfolio of available insurance product. At this point, the U.S. government intervened and passed the Terrorism Risk Insurance Act of 2002 (TRIA), which essentially mandated enrolled insurance companies to offer terrorism insurance and in exchange the U.S. government would take the responsibility of paying a significant portion of claims for terrorism incidents that meet a certain criteria. The initial act was designed as a temporary provision to the insurance industry until it figures out a feasible way to offer terrorism insurance and was set to expire by end of 2005. However the act was

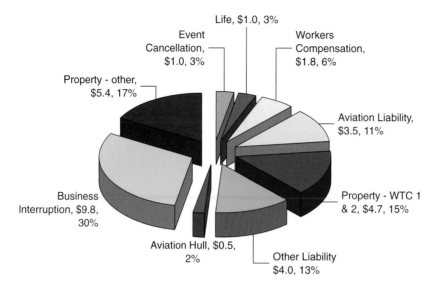

FIGURE 5–12 September 11, 2001, distribution of losses by insurance type ($ in billions). (Source: Insurance Information Institute, 2004)

amended in both 2005 and 2007, extending its current benefits to consumers until 2014. The latest version of the act is governed by the following rules:

- The insurance companies enrolled have to make terrorism insurance available to all commercial customers if demanded. The customers may opt to exclude terrorism if they wish to reduce the premiums of their insurance coverage.

- The definition of an "act of terrorism" is that of the Secretary of Treasury.

- The U.S. government is ensuring assistance to the industry of up to $100 billion a year for terrorism-related insurance claims for which the program trigger criteria have been met.

- For a specific incident to qualify for protection by the U.S. government, the combined losses of the incident should exceed $100 million.

- The insurance companies agree to pay up to 20% of the direct earned premium for each year per claim before federal assistance becomes available. The government agrees to pay 85% of the portion of the claim that exceeds the insurer's deductibles.

With the launch of the Terrorism Risk Insurance Act, in a sense the U.S. government has agreed to act as a re-insurer of insurance companies by guaranteeing to absorb a significant amount of losses after terrorist incidents that qualify to trigger the program. One major difference between the 2002 and 2007 versions of the act is that the 2002 version only provided coverage for "international" terrorist attacks whereas the 2007 version includes acts of "domestic" terrorism (Government Accountability Office, "Terrorism Insurance: Effects of the Terrorism Risk Insurance Act of 2002," 2004; Marsh, 2008).

The "Another Voice" section by Jack Suwanlert provides a comparison of how security is handled differently by public and private entities.

Conclusion

Safety and security are two key concepts in the scope of homeland security. However, they are both difficult to ensure to the levels that most citizens would prefer. The complexity of the systems and infrastructure we depend on today only increases our overall vulnerability and increases the difficulty of mitigating the risks we face. In addition to our personal vulnerabilities, we also face much systematic vulnerability, which will affect the society in case the risk becomes a reality.

The public and private sectors are under constant risk from natural, technological, and terrorist threats.

In dealing with those distinct vulnerabilities, the homeland security approach should be inclusive and interactive rather than top-down and exclusive. Only with the participation of different stakeholders and the public can those systematic vulnerabilities be detected and improved. The interdependencies of systems make it almost impossible to improve safety and security on a subsystem level. In light of this observation, homeland security can only be ensured if it can bring together people from all levels of the public, governmental, and private sectors, as well as academia and nongovernmental organizations.

Key Terms

All-Hazards Planning: The disaster planning and preparedness philosophy that advocates for holistic preparedness and flexible disaster planning to ensure the response can be improvised to deal with the many unknowns of any disaster situation. In one sense it is the opposite of "scenario planning."

Business Continuity Planning (BCP): The process of identification and remediation of commercial and organizational impacts of disasters through planning and strategy. Business continuity planning typically involves strategizing for the continuity and protection of the human resource, critical business processes, information systems, infrastructure, and organizational reputation.

Consequence: The result of a terrorist attack or other hazard that reflects the level, duration, and nature of the loss resulting from the incident. For the purposes of the NIPP, consequences are divided into four main categories: public health and safety, economic, psychological, and governance impacts. (Source: NIPP)

Crisis Management: A proactive management effort to avoid crisis, and the creation of strategy that minimizes adverse impacts of crisis to the organization when it could not be prevented. Effective crisis management requires a solid understanding of the organization, its strategy, liabilities, stakeholders, and legal framework combined with advanced communication, leadership, and decision-making skills to lead the organization through the crisis with minimizing potential loss.

Critical Infrastructure (and Key Resources) Government Coordinating Council (GCC): The GCC brings together diverse federal, state, local, and tribal interests to identify and develop collaborative strategies that advance critical infrastructure protection. GCCs serve as a counterpart to sector coordinating councils for each critical infrastructure and key resource sector. They provide interagency coordination around CI/KR strategies and activities, policy and communication across government, and between government and the sector to support the nation's homeland security mission. Government coordinating councils for each sector are comprised of representatives from DHS, the sector-specific agency, and the appropriate supporting federal departments and agencies. (Source: DHS)

Critical Infrastructure: Assets, systems, and networks, whether physical or virtual, so vital to the United States that the incapacity or destruction of such assets, systems, or networks would have a debilitating impact on security, national economic security, public health or safety, or any combination of those matters. (Source: NIPP)

Cybersecurity: The prevention of damage to, unauthorized use of, or exploitation of, and, if needed, the restoration of electronic information and communications systems and the information contained therein to ensure confidentiality, integrity, and availability. Includes protection and restoration, when needed, of information networks and wireline, wireless, satellite, public safety answering points, and 911 communications systems and control systems. (Source: NIPP)

Director of Central Intelligence (DCI): Director of the Central Intelligence Agency. In the aftermath of the 9/11 intelligence reform, the DCI is reporting to the Director of National Intelligence (DNI) for overall intelligence coordination purposes.

Director of National Intelligence (DNI): The statutory authority created based on the recommendations of the 9/11 Commission and is tasked by the president to coordinate the holistic intelligence of the United States. Directors of member agencies of the intelligence community report to the DNI. DNI is also responsible from establishing budget priorities for the overall U.S. intelligence effort.

Domestic Readiness Group (DRG): The DRG is an interagency body convened on a regular basis to develop and coordinate preparedness, response, and incident management policy. This group evaluates various policy issues of interagency importance regarding domestic preparedness and incident management and makes recommendations to senior levels of the policymaking structure for decision. During an incident, the DRG may be convened by DHS to evaluate relevant interagency policy issues regarding response and develop recommendations as may be required. (Source: NRF)

Environmental Protection Agency (EPA): The U.S. Environmental Protection Agency is an agency of the federal government of the United States responsible for protecting the natural environment (i.e., air, water, and land) and therefore the health of citizens.

Federal Energy Regulatory Commission (FERC): The FERC regulates and oversees energy industries in the economic, environmental, and safety interests of the American public.

Federal On-Scene Coordinators (OSCs): Federal OSCs are the federal officials pre-designated by EPA and the USCG to coordinate response resources during oil spill and HAZMAT responses. The OSC, either directly or through his or her staff, monitors, provides technical assistance, and/or directs federal and potentially responsible party resources.

Government Accountability Office (GAO): The GAO is known as "the investigative arm of Congress" and "the congressional watchdog." GAO supports the Congress in meeting its constitutional responsibilities and helps improve the performance and ensure the accountability of the federal government for the benefit of the public.

Hazardous Material (HAZMAT): Materials, substances, or chemicals that are deemed to have adverse effects on human health and the environment. Typical examples of HAZMAT include but are not limited to biological, chemical, and radiological agents and materials. HAZMAT incidents may be intentional (terrorism) or unintentional (man-made/technological). Oil spills, poisonous gas releases, nuclear waste incidents, and dirty bombs are examples of HAZMAT related incidents.

Incident Management Planning Team (IMPT): Incident command organization made up of the command and general staff members and appropriate functional units of an incident command system organization. (Source: NRF)

Intelligence: Intelligence is secret, state activity to understand or influence foreign entities. (Source: CIA)

Intelligence Community: The collective body of U.S. government agencies that have been tasked with the responsibility of collecting, analyzing, or acting upon intelligence.

Information Sharing and Analysis Center (ISAC): ISACs are sectoral information analysis and sharing centers that bring together representatives and decision makers of a given sector for the purposes of critical infrastructure protection and disaster preparedness.

National Infrastructure Protection Plan (NIPP): U.S. government plan that lays the framework for critical infrastructure and key asset protection activities. The plan is complemented with sector-specific annexes that detail sector-specific planning, response, and coordination bodies for effective disaster preparedness and incident response.

National Response Coordination Center (NRCC): The NRCC is FEMA's primary operations center during disaster response. The center is also the vital for resource coordination between different emergency support functions.

National Response Team (NRT): The U.S. National Response Team is an organization of 16 federal departments and agencies responsible for coordinating emergency preparedness and response to oil and hazardous substance pollution incidents. The Environment Protection Agency (EPA) and the U.S. Coast Guard (USCG) serve as Chair and Vice Chair, respectively.

North American Electric Reliability Corporation (NERC): The North American Electric Reliability Corporation's mission is to ensure the reliability of the bulk power system in North America.

Nuclear Regulatory Commission (NRC): The NRC regulates commercial nuclear power plants and other uses of nuclear materials, such as in nuclear medicine, through licensing, inspection, and enforcement of its requirements.

Sector Coordinating Council: Private sector counterparts to the GCCs, these councils are self-organized, self-run, and self-governed organizations that are representative of a spectrum of key stakeholders within a sector. SCCs serve as the government's principal point of entry into each sector for developing and coordinating a wide range of Critical Infrastructure/Key Resources (CI/KR) protection activities and issues. (Source: NIPP)

Smart Box: Designed to be "tamper evident," the Smart Box couples an internationally approved mechanical seal affixed to an alternate location on the container door with an electronic container security device designed to deter and detect tampering of the container door.

TOPOFF: Abbreviation for "Top Officials." TOPOFF is a congressionally mandated annual disaster preparedness and response exercise designed to improve incident-management/decision-making capability of the nation's "top officials" at every level of the government during an incident of national significance.

Transportation Workers Identity Card (TWIC): TWICs are tamper-resistant biometric credentials that will be issued to workers who require unescorted access to secure areas of ports, vessels, outer-continental-shelf facilities, and all credentialed merchant mariners. (Source: TSA)

Terrorism Risk Insurance Act (TRIA): Signed into law by President George W. Bush on November 26, 2002. The act created a federal "backstop" for insurance claims related to acts of terrorism.

Unmanned Airborne Vehicles (UAVs): UAVs are airborne vehicles controlled from a ground command center that are used in high-risk intelligence collection efforts and zones as well as in relatively safe target areas where the mission does not require the involvement of a human pilot. UAVs are used in intelligence collection efforts in Iraq as well as for border patrolling activities at the southwest border of the United States.

U.S. Computer Emergency Readiness Team (US-CERT): Established in 2003 to protect the nation's Internet infrastructure, US-CERT coordinates defense against and responses to cyber attacks across the nation.

Vulnerability: The vector of physical, social, geographical, and political factors that influence or define the combined susceptibility to a disaster of a given person, place, or other physical entity.

Review Questions

1. What are the key intelligence agencies in the United States? Briefly comment on their roles in terms of homeland security.
2. Describe how intelligence has evolved in the United States.
3. What is the role of the private sector in homeland security? What are your suggestions to improve private-sector participation and coordination with the Department of Homeland Security?

4. What are the different transportation modes in the United States? How does the U.S. government protect each? Discuss what types of criteria should be used for prioritizing budgets for protecting different transportation modes.

5. Name three different forms of critical infrastructure. For each, describe their vulnerabilities to terrorism, and what is being done at the federal level to reduce these vulnerabilities.

6. Name the various coordination bodies established by the private sector, government, and nongovernment sectors for the purposes of critical infrastructure protection and explain the responsibilities for each coordination/cooperation body.

7. What are the available communications channels between the Department of Homeland Security and the general public? Which of those channels are more effective for informing the public? What is the public's role in supporting homeland security activities?

References

American Petroleum Institute. 2005. "Security Guidelines for the Petroleum Industry." http://api.org/policy/otherissues/upload/SecurityGuideEd3.pdf.

American Petroleum Institute. 2008. "Energy Security: Help Reduce the Threat." http://www.api.org/ehs/partnerships/community/energy-security.cfm.

American Society of Civil Engineers/American Water Works Association. 2006. "Guidelines for the Physical Security of Water Utilities." http://www.asce.org/static/1/redirect.cfm?prmType=WISE&prmFile=20061/00_Complete_Document

Association of American Railroads. 2004. "Freight Raill Security Briefing". http://www.aar.org/Rail_Safety/Security.pdf

Association of Metropolitan Sewage Agencies (AMSA). 2004. "Wastewater Sector Security Link Vol. 1, no. 1." http://newsmanager.commpartners.com/amsawssl/issues/2004-06-17.html.

Blumenthal, H. 2003. "Department of Human Services Private Sector Information Sharing: ISAC Program." Government Symposium on Information Sharing and Homeland Security. Pennsylvania.

Central Intelligence Agency. 2007. "Offices of CIA." https://www.cia.gov/offices-of-cia/index.html.

Central Intelligence Agency. 2008. "CIA Organization Chart." https://www.cia.gov/about-cia/leadership/cia-organization-chart.html.

Central Intelligence Agency. 2008. "History of the Intelligence and Analysis Directorate." https://www.cia.gov/offices-of-cia/intelligence-analysis/history.html.

Central Intelligence Agency. 2008. "The CIA Crime and Narcotics Center." https://www.cia.gov/offices-of-cia/intelligence-analysis/organization-1/the-cia-crime-and-narcotics-center.html.

Communications Sector Coordinating Council. 2007. "Communications Sector Specific Infrastructure Protection Plan." http://www.dhs.gov/xlibrary/assets/nipp-ssp-communications.pdf.

Communications Sector Coordinating Council. 2008. "What is the CSCC?" http://www.commscc.org/.

Congressional Research Service. 2004. "Border Security and Unmanned Aerial Vehicles." http://www.fas.org/irp/crs/RS21698.pdf.

Congressional Research Service. 2004. "RL32506 — The Proposed Authorities of a National Intelligence Director: Issues for Congress and Side-by-Side Comparison of S.2845, H.R. 10, and Current Law." http://www.fas.org/irp/crs/RL32506.pdf.

Congressional Research Service. 2004. "RS21948 — The National Intelligence Director and Intelligence Analysis." http://www.fas.org/irp/crs/RS21948.pdf.

Congressional Research Service. 2006. "Border Security: Barriers Along the U.S. International Border." http://fas.org/sgp/crs/homesec/RL33659.pdf.

Congressional Research Service. 2007. "Terrorism and Security Issues Facing the Water Infrastructure Sector." http://www.fas.org/irp/crs/RL32189.pdf.

Congressional Research Service. 2007. "Terrorism and Security Issues Facing the Water Infrastructure Sector." http://www.fas.org/sgp/crs/terror/RL32189.pdf.

Congressional Research Service. 2008. "FY 2009 Appropriations for State and Local Homeland Security." http://www.fas.org/sgp/crs/homesec/RS22805.pdf.

Coppola, D. 2003. "Annotated Organizational Chart for the Department of Homeland Security." Washington, DC: Bullock & Haddow, LLC.

Department of Energy. 2007. "Energy Sector Specific Infrastructure Plan." ftp://ftp.nerc.com/pub/sys/all_updl/cip/Energy_Redacted_All.pdf.

Department of Homeland Security. 2002. "National Strategy for Homeland Security." http://www.dhs.gov/xlibrary/assets/nat_strat_hls.pdf.

Department of Homeland Security. 2003. "National Strategy for the Protection of Physical Infrastructure and Key Assets." http://www.dhs.gov/xlibrary/assets/Physical_Strategy.pdf.

Department of Homeland Security. 2004. "Agency Responsibilities by Functional Areas, Functions and Tasks." NRP Initial Plan Draft, Appendix A, Table 6.2.

Department of Homeland Security. 2004. "Fact Sheet: Arizona Border Control Initiative." http://www.dhs.gov/xnews/releases/press_release_0520.shtm.

Department of Homeland Security. 2004. "The National Plan for Research and Development in Support of Critical Infrastructure Protection." http://www.dhs.gov/xlibrary/assets/ST_2004_NCIP_RD_PlanFINALApr05.pdf.

Department of Homeland Security. 2004. "Fiscal Year 2005 Freight Rail Security Program Application Kit." http://www.ojp.usdoj.gov/odp/docs/FY2005FRSP.pdf.

Department of Homeland Security. 2005. "Fact Sheet: Arizona Border Control Initiative — Phase II." https://www.dhs.gov/xnews/releases/press_release_0646.shtm.

Department of Homeland Security. 2005. "FY 2006 Critical Infrastructure Protection Program." http://www.ojp.usdoj.gov/odp/newsreleases/FY06_IPP_PressKit.pdf.

Department of Homeland Security. 2006. "DHS Releases Cyber Storm Public Exercise Report." http://www.dhs.gov/xnews/releases/pr_1158341221370.shtm.

Department of Homeland Security. 2006. "FY 2007 Critical Infrastructure Protection Program." http://www.dhs.gov/xlibrary/assets/grants-2007-infrastructure-protection.pdf.

Department of Homeland Security. 2007. "Budget in Brief FY 2008." http://www.dhs.gov/xlibrary/assets/budget_bib-fy2008.pdf.

Department of Homeland Security. 2007. "DHS Moves Forward on Border Fencing and Technology Improvements." http://www.dhs.gov/xnews/releases/pr_1197058374853.shtm.

Department of Homeland Security. 2007. "Overview: FY 2007 Infrastructure Protection Program Final Awards." http://www.dhs.gov/xlibrary/assets/grants_ippawardsfy07.pdf.

Department of Homeland Security. 2007. "Strategy to Enhance International Supply Chain Security." http://www.dhs.gov/xlibrary/assets/plcy-internationalsupply-chainsecuritystrategy.pdf.

Department of Homeland Security. 2007. "The National Response Framework ESF#10 Annex." http://www.fema.gov/pdf/emergency/nrf/nrf-annexes-all.pdf.

Department of Homeland Security. 2007. "FY 2008 Critical Infrastructure Protection Program." http://www.fema.gov/government/grant/ipp/index.shtm#tsp.

Department of Homeland Security. 2007. "Overview: FY 2007 Infrastructure Protection Program Awards." http://www.dhs.gov/xlibrary/assets/grants-2007-infrastructure-protection.pdf.

Department of Homeland Security. 2008. "Budget in Brief FY 2009." http://www.dhs.gov/xlibrary/assets/budget_bib-fy2009.pdf.

Department of Homeland Security. 2008. "FY 2008 Port Security Grant Program." http://www.fema.gov/government/grant/psgp/index.shtm.

Department of Homeland Security. 2008. "Cyber Storm: Securing Cyber Space." http://www.dhs.gov/xprepresp/training/gc_1204738275985.shtm.

Department of Homeland Security. 2008. "National Cybersecurity Division." http://www.dhs.gov/xabout/structure/editorial_0839.shtm.

Department of Transportation Maritime Administration. 2002. "U.S. Waterborne Foreign Trade Containerized Cargo Stats." https://www.marad.dot.gov/Marad_Statistics/Con-Pts-02.htm.

Digital National Security Archive. 2003. "Overview of U.S. Intelligence." http://nsarchive.chadwyck.com/esp_essay.htm.

Environmental Protection Agency. 1998. "How Wastewater Treatment Works: The Basics." http://www.epa.gov/npdes/pubs/bastre.pdf.

Environmental Protection Agency. 2002. "FY 2003 Budget in Brief." http://www.epa.gov/ocfo/budget/2003/2003bib.pdf.

Environmental Protection Agency. 2006. "EPA Budget in Brief FY 2007." http://www.epa.gov/budget/2007/2007bib.pdf.

Environmental Protection Agency. 2006. "EPA Water Security Initiative (WaterSentinel)." http://www.epa.gov/safewater/watersecurity/pubs/fs_watersecurity_securityinitiative.pdf.

Environmental Protection Agency. 2007. "EPA Budget in Brief FY 2008." http://www.epa.gov/budget/2007/2008bib.pdf.

Environmental Protection Agency. 2007. "Water Sector Specific Infrastructure Protection Plan." http://www.dhs.gov/xlibrary/assets/Water_SSP_5_21_07.pdf.

Environmental Protection Agency. 2008. "EPA Budget in Brief FY 2009." http://www.epa.gov/budget/2007/2009bib.pdf.

Government Accountability Office. 2004. "GAO-04-1062 Maritime Security." http://www.gao.gov/new.items/d041062.pdf

Government Accountability Office. 2004. "Terrorism Insurance: Effects of the Terrorism Risk Insurance Act of 2002." http://www.gao.gov/new.items/ d04806t.pdf.

Government Accountability Office. 2006. "GAO-07-39 Critical Infrastructure Protection: Progress Coordinating Government and Private Sector Efforts Varies by Sectors' Characteristics." http://www.gao.gov/new.items/d0739.pdf.

Government Accountability Office. 2006. "Securing Wastewater Facilities." http://www.gao.gov/new.items/d06390.pdf.

Government Accountability Office. 2007. "GAO-07-412 Port Risk Management." http://www.gao.gov/new.items/d07412.pdf

Government Accountability Office. 2007. "Passenger Rail Security — Federal Strategy and Enhanced Coordination Needed to Prioritize and Guide Security Efforts." http://www.gao.gov/cgi-bin/getrpt?GAO-07-583T.

Greenberg, W.J. 2003. "September 11, 2001: A CEO's Story." *Harvard Business Review*, vol 10.1225/R0210D pp. 7–8.

Harrald, C., Coppola, D.P., and Yeletaysi, S. 2003. "Assessing the Financial Impacts of the World Trade Center Attacks on Publicly Held Corporations." TIEMS Conference Proceedings. Provence, France.

Kavanaugh, P. 2002. "Current State of Crisis Management as an Industry in Canada." The Health Canada Emergency Preparedness Forum, October 28, 2002.

Lerbinger, O. 1997. "The Crisis Manager." New York: Lawrence Erlbaum Associates.

Marsh & Mclennan Company 2008. "Terrorism Risk Insurance Act (TRIA) Is Extended by Congress." http://global.marsh.com/documents/TRIA_Is_Extended_2nd_Edition.pdf.

McDaniel, G., ed. 1994. "IBM Dictionary of Computing." New York: McGraw-Hill.

Medical News Today. 2006. "Landfills, Chemical Weapon Debris Possibly a Good Match, Computer Model Suggests." http://www.medicalnewstoday.com/articles/46108.php.

MILNET. 2006. "Changes to the U.S. Intelligence Community." http://www.milnet.com/Changes%20to%20Intelligence%20Community.html.

Minuteman Civil Defense Corps. 2008. "Volunteer Saves Illegal Alien from Certain Death." http://bborderops.com/index.php?option=com_content&task=view&id=41&Itemid=2.

National Coordination Center for Telecommunications. 2008. "Program Information." http://www.ncs.gov/ncc/.

Northrop Grumman. 2004. "Press Release: HSDN." http://www.it.northropgrumman.com/pressroom/press/2004/pr151.html.

Office of the Director of National Intelligence. 2005. "Establishment of the National Clandestine Service (NCS)." http://www.odni.gov/press_releases/20051013_release.htm.

Office of the Director of National Intelligence. 2008. "Members of the Intelligence Community." http://www.intelligence.gov/1-members.shtml.

Office of the Director of National Intelligence. 2008. "ODNI Organization." http://www.dni.gov/aboutODNI/organization.htm.

Office of the Director of National Intelligence. 2008. "ODNI Press Releases 2005." http://www.odni.gov/press_releases/press_releases_2005.htm.

Office of the Director of National Intelligence. 2008. "ODNI Press Releases 2006." http://www.odni.gov/press_releases/press_releases_2006.htm.

Office of the Director of National Intelligence. 2008. "ODNI Press Releases 2007–2008." http://www.odni.gov/press_releases/press_releases.htm.

Richelson, J.T. 1999. "The U.S. Intelligence Community," 4th ed. Boulder, CO: Westview Press.

Richelson, J.T., Gefter, J., Waters, M., et al. 2003. "U.S. Espionage and Intelligence, 1947–1996." Digital National Security Archive. Mfiche 2552 GRN–MTXT.

Smith, B.F. 1983. "The Shadow Warriors: OSS, and the Origins of the CIA." New York: Basic Books.

The White House. 2003. "National Strategy to Secure Cyberspace." http://www.whitehouse.gov/pcipb/cyberspace_strategy.pdf.

The White House. 2005. "Border and Transportation Security". http://www.whitehouse.gov/deptofhomeland/sect3.html

Transportation Sector Government Coordinating Council. 2007. "Transportation Systems Specific Infrastructure Protection Plan." http://www.dhs.gov/xlibrary/assets/nipp-ssp-transportation.pdf.

Transportation Security Administration. 2005. "TSA FY 2004 Budget Briefing". http://www.tsa.gov/public/interweb/assetlibrary/TSA_FY2004_budget_briefing_(public).ppt, visited June 2005, available from the author.

Transportation Security Administration. 2006. "TSA Turns Five." http://www.tsa.gov/5th/index.shtm.

Transportation Security Administration. 2007. "DHS Agencies Announce Enrollment Dates for TWIC in 10 Ports." http://www.tsa.gov/press/releases/2008/0304.shtm.

Transportation Security Administration. 2007. "Fact Sheet: FY 2008 Freight Rail Security Grant Program." http://www.tsa.gov/assets/pdf/fy_2008_frsgp_fs.pdf.

Transportation Security Administration. 2007. "FAQ: Transportation Worker Identification Credential (TWIC)." http://www.tsa.gov/what_we_do/layers/twic/twic_faqs.shtm.

Transportation Security Administration. 2007. "FY 2008 Freight Rail Security Grant Program." http://www.tsa.gov/assets/pdf/fy_2008_frsgp.pdf.

Transportation Security Administration. 2007. "FY 2008 Trucking Security Program Fact Sheet." http://www.tsa.gov/assets/pdf/fy_2008_tsp_fs.pdf.

Transportation Security Administration. 2008. "FY 2008 Intercity Bus Security Grant Program." http://www.tsa.gov/assets/pdf/fy_2008_ibsgp_fs.pdf.

U.S. Customs and Border Protection. 2006. "Border Patrol Overview." http://www.cbp.gov/xp/cgov/border_security/border_patrol/border_patrol_ohs/overview.xml.

U.S. Customs and Border Protection. 2006. "SBInet: Securing U.S. Borders." http://www.dhs.gov/xlibrary/assets/sbinetfactsheet.pdf.

U.S. Customs and Border Protection. 2008. "FY 2007 Performance and Accountability Report." http://www.cbp.gov/linkhandler/cgov/toolbox/publications/admin/fiscal_2007.ctt/fiscal_2007.pdf

U.S. Customs and Border Protection. 2008. "Ports in CSI." http://www.cbp.gov/xp/cgov/border_security/international_activities/csi/ports_in_csi.xml.

U.S. Department of Transportation. 2008. "Serious HAZMAT Incidents in the U.S. 1997–2006." http:/hazmat.dot.gov/pubs/inc/data/tenyr_new_serious.pdf.

U.S. Immigration and Customs Enforcement. 2008. "ICE FY 2007 Accomplishments." http://www.ice.gov/doclib/pi/news/factsheets/fy07accmplshmntsweb.pdf.

U.S. Immigration and Customs Enforcement. 2008. "ICE Operations." http://www.ice.gov/about/operations.htm.

U.S. Coast Guard. 2004. "Secure Seas, Open Ports." http://www.piersystem.com/go/doc/586/41841/.

U.S. Coast Guard. 2007. "Coast Guard Announces Record Drug Seizures." http://www.piersystem.com/go/doc/786/184995/.

U.S. Congress. 1983. "Compilation of Intelligence Laws and Related Laws and Executive Orders of Interest to the National Intelligence Community." Washington, DC: U.S. Government Printing Office.

USA Today. 2005. "Border Patrols Growing in Arizona." March 29. http://www.usatoday.com/news/nation/2005-03-29-borders_x.htm.

Water Environment Research Foundation. 2008. "WERF Research Projects Online Database." http://www.werf.org/.

Water ISAC. 2008. "What is Water ISAC?" http://www.waterisac.org/cs/what_is_waterisac

⁝⁝⁝ 6

Mitigation, Prevention, and Preparedness

What You Will Learn

- The definitions of mitigation, preparedness, and prevention
- Overview of mitigation and preparedness programs
- Where does terrorism fit in the classical life cycle of emergency management?
- Preparedness for chemical, biological, and radiological incidents
- Community issues in preparedness
- Private sector involvement in mitigation and preparedness

Introduction

Mitigation and preparedness constitute one-half of the classic emergency management cycle, with response and recovery completing the sequence (Figure 6–1). Mitigation and preparedness generally occur before a disaster ever occurs, although postdisaster mitigation and preparedness, conducted in recognition that similar events are likely in the future, make these two activities somewhat general to the entire emergency management cycle. This is in contrast to response and recovery, which by definition are only possible in the aftermath of a disastrous event.

In its classical meaning, *mitigation* refers to a sustained action taken to reduce or eliminate risk to people and property from hazards and their effects. Mitigation activities address either or both of

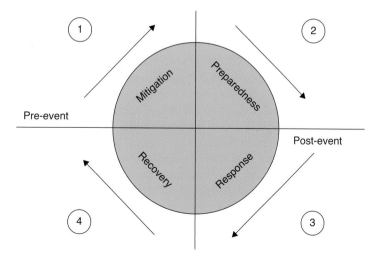

FIGURE 6–1 The four classical phases of disaster management.

the two components of risk, which are probability (likelihood) and consequence. By mitigating either of these components, the risk becomes much less of a threat to the affected population. In the case of natural disasters, the ability of humans to limit the probability of a hazard is highly dependent on the hazard type, with some hazards such as hurricanes or tornadoes impossible to prevent, while avalanches, floods, and wildfires are examples of hazards for which limiting the rate of occurrence is possible. In general, however, mitigation efforts for natural hazards tend to focus on improved consequence management. In terms of man-made disasters, however, there is a much greater range of opportunities to minimize both the probability and the consequences of potential incidents, and both are applied with equal intensity. Mitigation in terms of terrorism, which is a much more complicated process, is discussed later in this chapter.

Preparedness can be defined as a state of readiness to respond to a disaster, crisis, or any other type of emergency situation. In general, preparedness activities can be characterized as the human component of predisaster hazard management. Training and public education are the most common preparedness activities, and, when properly applied, they have great potential to help people survive disasters. While preparedness activities do little to prevent a disaster from occurring, they are very effective at ensuring that people know what to do once the disaster has happened.

The concepts of mitigation and preparedness have been altered since September 11, 2001, when terrorism became viewed as the primary threat facing America. As such, terms like *terrorism prevention* and *terrorism preparedness* have became more popular. One must question, in light of these new terms, whether there is any real difference between the traditional definitions of preparedness and mitigation and what is being conducted in light of the new terrorism hazard.

The National Response Plan (NRP), released in December 2004 to replace the Federal Response Plan as the national framework for disaster management, provided insight into this issue. Although this new plan did not directly define the phases of incident management, it introduced to users the sequential terminology of *prevention*, *preparedness*, *response*, *recovery*, and *mitigation*. The use of this terminology reflects two major changes with respect to the classical incident management approach in the United States. The first change is that mitigation is placed last in this cycle of incident management, which could indicate to readers that the activity (in the context of the plan) is perceived as a postincident one. This is significant mainly because it is altering a set terminology, which has already been widely understood and accepted within the emergency management discipline, feasibly resulting in unnecessary confusion. The second change, which is surely the more radical of the two, is the introduction of the term *prevention*, not only as a concept but also as a distinct phase in the incident management cycle. The plan defined prevention as "actions taken to avoid an incident or to intervene to stop an incident from occurring, which involve actions taken to protect lives and property." The NRP, like the FRP, was a comprehensive plan developed according to the all-hazards approach, but the inclusion of *prevention* as a separate incident phase (especially in light of the preceding definition) gave rise to the question of whether the NRP was focused primarily on terrorism incident management. Prevention, it would seem (in accordance with the definition provided), does not seem applicable to most natural disasters (NRP, 2004, www.dhs.gov).

Since the writing of the Second Edition of this text in 2005, the NRP has been replaced by the National Response Framework, and as such much of the emergency management terminology and functions have changed accordingly. The following section describes several of these changes as they relate to mitigation, prevention, and preparedness.

First, document's title has been changed appropriately to reflect its true nature — namely that it provides guidelines, rules of engagement, and an organizational framework for all stakeholders of a disaster response involving the federal government rather than offering specific steps of action as is typical in an EOP. Second, the NRF does not attempt to redefine the phases of emergency management as occurred in the NRP. In the NRP, prevention was introduced as a distinct phase in the incident management cycle, and in many (but not all) references, as a replacement for mitigation. The NRF makes no direct reference to emergency management cycle, and refers more sensibly to the terms *prevention* and *mitigation. Mitigation* is used comfortably and consistently as part of the all-hazards approach, thereby providing clarity throughout the document. The choice not to push prevention as a distinct emergency management phase is consistent with Secretary Chertoff's vision to establish DHS as managing all-hazards rather than having a distinct focus on terrorism. Ther term *prevention* is most closely associated with terrorism, and therefore finds little applicability in any generalized emergency management approach. The third major difference relates to the adjustments made to general terms that better accommodate the involvement and partnership of nonfederal stakeholders. These entities are better defined in terms of their role with regards to the emergency support functions (ESFs). The final difference is that the framework commits the Federal government to the development of specific emergency response plans based on the 15 incident scenarios identified by the Homeland Security Council. Because incident scenario planning tends to create a rigid response functionality, it is difficult to agree with the approach taken. In such an approach, flexibility is sacrificed and problems may arise when real incidents do not fit the expected parameters. Additionally, this should be seen as a departure from the all-hazards approach as so many of the scores of known hazards are omitted or disregarded, though it is true that these 15 scenarios may be useful as an exercise tool. (For more complete information regarding the NRF and the changes it brings, see DHS, "The National Response Framework," 2007; DHS, "What's New in the NRF," 2007; Public Broadcasting System, "Fixing FEMA," Online News Hour with Secretary M. Chertoff, February 13, 2006.)

Whether we call it prevention or mitigation, proactive incident management is crucial for minimizing the loss of human life, injuries, financial losses, property damage, and interruption of business activities. Specific methods of prevention and mitigation change from hazard to hazard, and incident to incident, but the goals are the same.

Using the all-hazards approach, whether you are mitigating for earthquakes or floods or preparing for a potential terrorist threat, the classic mitigation planning process is an effective guide for the overall process. The traditional mitigation planning process, still conducted by the Federal Emergency Management Agency (FEMA) today under its Department of Homeland Security (DHS) umbrella, consists of four stages: (1) identifying and organizing resources; (2) conducting a risk or threat assessment and estimating losses; (3) identifying mitigation measures that will reduce the effects of the hazards and creating a strategy to deal with the mitigation measures in priority order; and (4) implementing the measures, evaluating the results, and keeping the plan up-to-date. This chapter will expand on these concepts.

Mitigation and preparedness are vital for sustainable emergency management because strategies geared strictly towards post disaster response tend to be costlier than those accounting for predisaster opportunities. However it can be difficult to convince decision makers to invest in mitigation and preparedness activities. (See "Another Voice: Why Is Mitigation and Preparedness the Only Sustainable, Cost-Effective Way of Dealing with Emergencies?")

The next section will focus on mitigation, prevention, and preparedness activities in an effort to identify ongoing programs, as well as new developments as they fit into each subject.

Mitigation Plans, Actions, and Programs

Mitigation activities include many different methods and strategies that have the common goal of reducing the risk associated with potential hazards. To provide a deeper understanding of mitigation, it is important to first understand the nature of natural, man-made, and terrorism risk.

There are many different definitions of risk, each of which may be appropriate within specific circumstances. Stan Kaplan (1997), an acclaimed risk management expert, argues that rather than providing a full definition of risk, one must ask three major questions in considering a specific hazard: (1) What can happen? (2) How likely is it? (3) What are the consequences? This indirect definition provides a much more flexible starting point with which to begin our discussion of risk and how to mitigate it. It also sheds additional light on the complexity of treating risks, which are clearly dynamic in nature. How we consider those risks — and rank them according to our concern — is a factor of the combined answers of those three questions. For instance, although traffic accidents occur on a daily basis, their consequences tend to be relatively minor. Very large meteor strikes, on the other hand, are very rare, but when they do occur, their consequences are globally catastrophic. Each hazard must be considered for its individual characteristics, and it is up to the individual, community, or society that is making the analysis to determine what level of effort will be made to address each according to these individual risk components.

The uncertainty component of risk, contained within the probability of disastrous event occurrence, places the greatest burden on those who are treating a full portfolio of risks that must be compared in relation to each other. Uncertainty forces us to ask ourselves questions that are often difficult and based more on expert judgment than on concrete evidence, such as, "What is the probability that a 7.0-magnitude earthquake will happen in San Francisco Bay within the next 10 years?" or "What is the probability that terrorists will attack and damage a nuclear power plant in the United States?" The probability component of risk is important because it is an equally weighted parameter that helps us to quantify and prioritize mitigation actions when dealing with multiple risks. The determination of probabilities for events is often a difficult and complicated process. While several quantitative methods and tools are available that can be used to determine probabilities, these often tend to be too complex for communities to use. Qualitative methods have been developed to ease this problem, which in turn allows for much easier comparison of risk by communities that attempt treating their risks. The sidebar titled, "Qualitative Representation of Likelihood," illustrates but one example of a system of estimation used to establish qualitative risk likelihood rankings.

Qualitative Representation of Likelihood

This particular qualitative representation system uses words to describe the chance of an event occurring. Each word or phrase has a designated range of possibilities attached to it. For instance, events could be described as follows:

Certain: >99% chance of occurring in a given year (one or more occurrences per year)
Likely: 50%–99% chance of occurring in a given year (one occurrence every 1 to 2 years)
Possible: 5%–49% chance of occurring in a given year (one occurrence every 2 to 20 years)
Unlikely: 2%–5% chance of occurring in a given year (one occurrence every 20 to 50 years)
Rare: 1%–2% chance of occurring in a given year (one occurrence every 50 to 100 years)
Extremely rare: <1% chance of occurring in a given year (one occurrence every 100 or
  more years)

Note that this is just one of a limitless range of qualitative terms and values assigned that can be used to describe the likelihood component of risk. As long as all hazards are compared using the same range of qualitative values, the actual determination of likelihood ranges attached to each term does not necessarily matter.

The second component of risk, hazard consequence, is a detailed examination of the total unwanted impact of the disaster to the community, government, or the interested stakeholders. Consequence is often given an assigned monetary value in order to facilitate comparison with other hazards, but there are many intangible consequences that are very difficult to quantify in such

Table 6–1   Tangible and Intangible Consequences of Disasters

Consequences	Measure	Tangible Losses	Intangible Losses
Deaths	Number of people	Loss of economically active individuals	Social and psychological effects on remaining community
Injuries	Number and injury severity	Medical treatment needs, temporary loss of economic activity by productive individuals	Social and psychological pain and recovery
Physical damage	Inventory of damaged elements by number and damage level	Replacement and repair cost	Cultural losses
Emergency operations	Volume of manpower, person-days employed, equipment and resources expended to relief mobilization cost, investment in preparedness capability	Stress and overwork in relief participants	
Disruption to economy	Number of working days lost, volume of production lost	Value of lost production opportunities, and in competitiveness and reputation	
Social disruption	Number of displaced persons, homeless	Temporary housing, relief, economic production	Psychological, social contacts, cohesion, community morale
Environmental impact	Scale and severity	Cleanup costs, repair costs	Consequences of poorer environment, health risks, risk of future disaster

Source: United Nations Development Programme, *Vulnerability and Risk Assessment*, 2nd ed., Cambridge: Cambridge Architectural Research Limited, 1994.

absolute terms but which have to be considered as well if a comprehensive risk analysis is expected (Table 6–1). Interestingly, the consequences of disasters also have a probabilistic nature. In practice, it is quite hard to assign a single monetary value to the expected damage; probability distributions are used to model the most likely damage estimates. For this reason, qualitative applications of consequence estimation have also been developed. An example is presented in the sidebar, "Qualitative Representation of Consequence."

▪ ▪ ▪ ▬▬▬▬▬▬▬▬▬▬▬▬▬▬▬▬▬▬▬▬▬▬▬▬▬▬▬▬▬▬▬▬

Qualitative Representation of Consequence

As was true with the qualitative representation of likelihood, words or phrases that have associated meanings can be used to describe the effects of a past disaster or the anticipated effects of a future one. These measurements can be assigned to deaths, injuries, or costs (often, the qualitative measurement of fatalities and injuries is combined). The following is one example of a qualitative measurement system for injuries and deaths:

Insignificant: No injuries or fatalities

Minor: Small number of injuries but no fatalities; first-aid treatment required

Moderate: Medical treatment needed but no fatalities; some hospitalization

Major: Extensive injuries, significant hospitalization; fatalities

Catastrophic: Large number of fatalities and severe injuries; extended and large numbers requiring hospitalization

Once both of these factors (probability and consequence) have been determined, it is possible to compare risks against each other, primarily for the purposes of treating the risks through intervention measures. Normally, only limited funds exist for this purpose and, as such, not all risks can be treated. Risk comparison allows for a prioritization of risk, which can help those performing mitigation and preparedness ensure that they are spending their limited funds most wisely. Table 6–2 provides one example of a risk matrix that can be used to compare risks to each other.

Having provided a basic description of the components of risk, it is appropriate to move on to the mitigation of risk. In applying mitigation, risk managers try to minimize probability or consequence or both. In practice, however, it is not always easy, or even possible, to address both. And because each risk is unique, there are different strategies that must be identified, assessed, and applied for successful risk intervention. For example, assume one seeks to minimize the risk of an earthquake. How can one minimize the probability of it happening? In terms of modern science, unfortunately, there is no known way of doing so, and this is true for many natural hazards despite humankind's best efforts. However, one can still mitigate the risk of an earthquake by minimizing its consequences. For the earthquake risk, several known and proven strategies are available to minimize such consequences, such as adopting and enforcing earthquake-resistant building codes, educating the public about earthquakes, and developing robust earthquake response plans.

In dealing with the newly expanded terrorism risk, the mitigation strategy would likely take on a much different approach. In this case, the opportunity to minimize the likelihood of the event's occurrence is very possible, and has been done countless times with great success. Through actionable intelligence collection on terrorist activity, and by infiltration of its social and communication networks, it is possible to stop terrorists before they proceed with their plots. Therefore, theoretically, the probability component of terrorism risk can be reduced through mitigation (or "prevention").

Table 6–2 Example of a Qualitative Risk-Level Analysis Matrix

Likelihood	Consequences				
	Insignificant	Minor	Moderate	Major	Catastrophic
Almost certain	High	High	Extreme	Extreme	Extreme
Likely	Moderate	High	High	Extreme	Extreme
Possible	Low	Moderate	High	Extreme	Extreme
Unlikely	Low	Low	Moderate	High	Extreme
Rare	Low	Low	Moderate	High	High

Source: Emergency Management Australia, "Emergency Risk Management: Application's Guide," Australian Emergency Manual Series, 2000.

Of course, minimizing this likelihood component is a very complex task, requiring governments to allocate significant resources to build and manage necessary systems, establish international partnerships, and build networks to identify and detain terrorists.

The consequence component of terrorism risk can also be mitigated. However, unlike most natural disasters that have a limited range of possible consequences, the options available to terrorists are limited only by their imagination. Terrorists have limitless targets, including facilities, infrastructure, and organizations, so many different strategies must be employed to minimize the impacts of terrorist attacks to each of these potential targets. DHS has developed a manual titled *Reference Manual to Mitigate Potential Terrorist Attacks against Buildings* (the sidebar, "FEMA 426"). This manual discusses the importance of minimizing the impacts of potential terrorist attacks against buildings. Buildings, however, are but one target. Presumably, it may be impossible to mitigate all possible consequences only because to do so would surely exhaust even the richest nation's financial resources. It would seem, then, that the best measures would seek multiple-use solutions, such as building a robust mass-casualty public health system that would not only serve to mitigate the impact of terrorism on humans, but mitigate the consequences of other natural and technological hazards that also may affect the population.

FEMA 426: Reference Manual to Mitigate Potential Terrorist Attacks against Buildings

The Federal Emergency Management Agency (FEMA) developed the *Reference Manual to Mitigate Potential Terrorist Attacks against Buildings* to provide information on how to mitigate the effects of potential terrorist attacks. The intended audience includes the building sciences community of architects and engineers working for private institutions. The manual supports FEMA's mission (to lead America to prepare for, prevent, respond to, and recover from disasters) and the Strategic Plan's Goal 3 (to prepare the nation to address the consequences of terrorism), all of which will be done within the all-hazards framework and the needs of homeland security.

The building science community, as a result of FEMA's efforts, has incorporated extensive building science into designing and constructing buildings against natural hazards (earthquake, fire, flood, and wind). To date, the same level of understanding has not been applied to man-made hazards (terrorism/intentional acts) and technological hazards (accidental events). Since September 11, 2001, terrorism has become a dominant domestic concern. Security can no longer be viewed as a stand-alone capability that can be purchased as an afterthought and put in place. Life, safety, and security issues must become a design goal from the beginning.

The objective of this manual is to reduce physical damage to structural and nonstructural components of buildings and related infrastructure and also to reduce resultant casualties during conventional bomb attacks, as well as attacks using chemical, biological, and radiological agents. Although the process is general in nature and applies to most building uses, this manual is most applicable for six specific types of facilities:

- Commercial office facilities
- Retail commercial facilities
- Light industrial and manufacturing facilities
- Health-care facilities
- Local schools (K–12)
- Higher education (university) facilities

Chapter 1 presents selected methodologies to integrate threat/hazard, asset criticality, and vulnerability assessment information. This information becomes the input for determining relative levels of risk. Higher risk hazards require mitigation measures to reduce risk. The chapter also provides an assessment checklist that compiles many best practices to consider during the design of a new building or renovation of an existing building.

Chapter 2 discusses architectural and engineering design considerations (mitigation measures), starting at the perimeter of the property line, and includes the orientation of the building on the site. Therefore, this chapter covers issues outside the building envelope.

Chapter 3 provides the same considerations for the building — its envelope, systems, and interior layout.

Chapter 4 provides a discussion of blast theory to understand the dynamics of the blast pressure wave, the response of building components and a consistent approach to define levels of protection.

Chapter 5 presents chemical, biological, and radiological measures that can be taken to mitigate vulnerabilities and reduce associated risks for these terrorist tactics or technological hazards.

Appendices A, B, and C contain acronyms, general definitions, and CBR definitions, respectively.

Appendix D describes electronic security systems and design considerations.

Appendices E and F present a comprehensive bibliography of publications and the associations and organizations capturing the building security guidance needed by the building sciences community, respectively.

Source: FEMA 426, June 2003.

The threat of terrorism is not new. Throughout history there have been terrorist organizations and terrorist attacks in all parts of the world, including North America, Europe, and Australia; however, the September 11 attacks resulted in such severe consequences that, not unexpectedly, terrorism became the primary issue on the U.S. government's agenda.

Mitigating the terrorism risk is important in order to minimize potential damage that may result from what is known to be a very real threat, but it is vital to remember that combating terrorism is a complex and long-term task, one that requires both patience and sacrifice. Therefore, all stakeholders — including the government, the public, the private sector, the media, and academia — need to appreciate the benefit of applying mitigation on an all-hazards approach such that all known risks are treated, not only terrorism. Clearly, as has been shown in the years following the September 11 attacks, there are much more likely hazards — hurricanes and floods being the greatest — that have much greater potential to cause harm in terms of both likelihood and consequence. Hurricanes Katrina and Rita are just one of many recent examples.

DHS continues to provide funding for predisaster and postdisaster mitigation projects through FEMA and its other relevant directorates. Details of those initiatives will be provided in the next sections.

FEMA Mitigation Directorate

As a direct consequence of reorganization within the Department of Homeland Security the name of *FEMA Mitigation Division* has been changed to *FEMA Mitigation Directorate* as of April 1, 2007 (FEMA, "Emergency Management Higher Education Project Report," April 16, 2007).

The Mitigation Directorate is still responsible for a vast majority of the U.S. government's hazard mitigation activities, including the National Flood Insurance Program. This directorate performs several organizational activities that serve to promote protection, prevention, and partnerships at the federal, state, local, and individual levels. The overall mission of this directorate is to protect lives and prevent the loss of property from natural and other hazards. The Mitigation Directorate employs the all-hazards approach through a comprehensive risk-based emergency management program.

The Directorate administers the nationwide, risk-reduction programs authorized by the U.S. Congress and is composed of the following divisions:

The *Risk Analysis Division* provides technical expertise and analytical capability in identifying and quantifying risks, hazards, and vulnerabilities. The division runs the following FEMA Mitigation programs:

National Flood Map Modernization Program (NFMM)
National Dam Safety Program
Mitigation Planning Program
National Hurricane Program

The *Risk Reduction Division* is committed to reducing risks and vulnerabilities through proactive intervention measures including but not limited to land use planning, code design, and dissemination of best practices. The division is in charge of the following programs:

National Earthquake Hazards Reduction Program (NEHRP)
Hazard Mitigation Grant Program (HMGP)
Flood Mitigation Assistance Program (FMA)
Pre-Disaster Mitigation Program (PDM)
Severe Repetitive Loss Program (SRL)
Repetitive Flood Claims Program (RFC)
Community Rating System (CRS)

The *Risk Insurance Division*'s prime responsibility is to run the National Flood Insurance Program (NFIP), through which affordable flood insurance is provided to communities vulnerable to flood hazards, and impacts of floods are minimized through enforcement of floodplain management for new and altered buildings and structures (FEMA, "About the Mitigation Directorate," 2007).

FEMA mitigation programs and their funding levels are described in subsequent sections.

National Flood Map Modernization Program

National Flood Map Modernization Program (NFMM) is a multiyear program to improve existing flood maps in the United States and to create new maps based on new technology and standards for those localities that require flood maps for which no previous maps exist. The need for flood map modernization arises because of the dynamic nature of flood hazards that change with geography. Changing information management standards, improvements in information delivery methods such as the Internet, and advances in technologies such as GIS (geographical information systems) are other drivers behind flood map modernization. Conventional flood maps involve paper-based cartographic maps that may be many years old providing limited accuracy in a quickly changing physical environment. To make the updating, sharing, collaboration, and delivery of those maps more efficient, the NFMM is creating electronic maps based on GIS that adhere to newest data management standards (i.e., GIS data models and meta-data).

The resulting maps and data better serve the needs of all parties that use those maps. FEMA Risk Analysis Division takes the lead in this program and acts as the main integrator of data, creator of geographic maps, and the clearinghouse for the dissemination of all flood map products. Community planners, public policymakers, local officials, developers, builders, insurance companies, and individual property owners can all benefit from those map products made available by the program. The improved flood maps provide more reliable information on flood risks and therefore help stakeholders make better informed decisions related to their vulnerability to floods. In the long run, the use if those maps is expected to reduce total costs of flood disasters, as communities and service providers make it a habit to check flooding risks before making land use decisions.

NFMM is a multiyear program that started in 2004 and sustained its funding levels throughout the years that followed. In the fiscal years 2006 and 2007, the program enjoyed a funding level of $198 million, and was funded at $220 million for the fiscal year 2008. The president's budget request for the fiscal year 2009 includes approximately $150 million to fund the activities of the program (FEMA, "Overview of Flood Map Modernization," 2007; DHS, 2008).

National Dam Safety Program

National Dam Safety Program is an initiative of the FEMA Risk Analysis Directorate. The program was created by the Water Resources and Development Act of 1996 and has since been reauthorized twice with new legislation introduced in 2002 and 2006.

The primary goal of the program is to provide funding for states to be used in dam safety–related activities. In that scope, states use program funds to provide dam safety training, increase the frequency of dam safety inspections, create and test emergency response plans, and to promote dam safety awareness through videos and other educative material. Between FY 1998 and FY 2004, the program provided approximately $22 million to states. Other components of the program include dam safety research and dam safety training.

As confirmed by the National Dam Safety Act of 2006 (P.L. 109-460), the program will continue to provide $38.7 million to states as dam safety grants, $9 million for dam safety research, and $3.25 million for dam safety training for the fiscal years 2007 to 2011 (Association of State Dam Safety Officials, 2005; FEMA, "About the National Dam Safety Program," 2007; American Society of Civil Engineers, 2007; Congressional Research Service, "Aging Infrastructure: Dam Safety," 2007).

Mitigation Planning Program

The Mitigation Planning Program administered by FEMA's Risk Analysis Division creates multihazard mitigation planning manuals, "how-to" guidelines, and best-practice documents. Since the program has an all-hazards mitigation scope, it closely works with several partners in different areas of interest and expertise. Some of the program partners include the American Planning Association, Association of State Floodplain Managers, Institute for Business and Home Safety, and National Institute for Building Sciences.

The program also works closely with the (postdisaster) Hazard Mitigation Grant Program and the Pre-disaster Mitigation Programs administered by FEMA's Risk Reduction Division (FEMA, "Hazard Mitigation Planning," 2007).

National Hurricane Program

The National Hurricane Program is a multiagency program designed to lead projects and initiatives that help protect communities and their residents from hurricane hazards. Current partners of the program include (but are not limited to) the National Oceanic and Atmospheric Administration (NOAA), National Weather Service (NWS), U.S. Department of Transportation (USDOT), and U.S. Army Corps of Engineers (USACE).

The primary focus of the program is to support state and community planning and decision making for hurricane evacuations. The program achieves this goal by providing assessment and analysis information of potential hurricane paths, winds, and damage specific to geographies. Advanced modeling and simulation tools are used for such analysis. State and local decision makers use the information to improve their hurricane evacuation plans. (See the sidebars titled "Frequently Asked Questions" and "Digging Deeper: Hurricane Katrina Timeline," for an overview of the program and a summary of the Katrina experience, respectively.)

The program also aids in the creation of material that supports hurricane awareness. Elements of the program get involved in hurricane response and recovery, through its Hurricane Liaison Team composed of hurricane preparedness and response experience. The program also assists in post-storm assessments to ensure validity of previously existing data and assumptions, and to capture best practices and lessons learned. The mitigation component of the program aims to reduce the damage caused by hurricane winds and flooding through improvements in the built environment, including residential and nonresidential buildings and their utility systems.

Annual funding for the program is $5.86 million, of which $2.91 million are spent for FEMA program activities, whereas $2.95 million go to state hurricane mitigation activities through the Emergency Management Performance Grant program (FEMA, "National Hurricane Program," 2008).

Frequently Asked Questions about the National Hurricane Program

Q: What is the National Hurricane Program?
A: Established in 1985, the National Hurricane Program (NHP) conducts assessments and provides tools and technical information to assist State and local agencies in developing hurricane evacuation plans.

Q: How does NHP support development of evacuation plans?
A: State and local governments have primary responsibility for the development and implementation of evacuation plans. Through the NHP, FEMA, with support from Federal agency partners, conducts hurricane evacuation studies that inform these plans. The studies predict probable storm surge and wind effects, analyze the existing transportation system, assess shelter availability and capacity, use behavioral analysis to anticipate public reaction during evacuations, and calculate clearance times — the time required to evacuate the public before the arrival of gale force winds in areas affected by storm surge. The studies also provide recommendations for the extent of evacuation zones. Communities use these technical findings to inform their evacuation policies and procedures and to adjust recommended evacuation zones based on local needs.

Q: Does NHP have the authority to require the States or local communities to follow their evaluation recommendations?
A: No, the NHP does not have any authority over or role in the development and implementation of the State and local evacuation plans. The NHP cannot require State and local communities to follow the evacuation recommendations.

Q: How is NHP responding to the Hurricane Katrina disaster?
A: In response to Hurricane Katrina, FEMA is working with Federal, State, and local officials to conduct a poststorm assessment. FEMA routinely conducts poststorm assessments to determine how well the NHP tools and products have assisted State and local evacuation decision makers. This involves hazard, transportation, and behavioral analyses of evacuations.

FEMA is analyzing the impacted evacuation roadway networks, storm surge basins, and evacuation clearance times that were applied to the response. The findings of this assessment will help uncover necessary improvements for decision assistance models and will lead to tools to ensure the effectiveness of future evacuation orders.

Q: Did FEMA know that a hurricane of this magnitude could strike Louisiana?
A: Yes, FEMA recognized the potential for a massive hurricane to hit Louisiana. The potential for large Category 4 or 5 hurricanes has always existed throughout the Gulf and Atlantic Coastal Region. FEMA has conducted hurricane evacuation studies of Louisiana and provided the results to the State. Various coordination meetings and training sessions also have been held to address the study products with Federal, State, and local officials. Hurricane evacuation studies determine the hurricane surge inundation areas for all category storms. From these

inundation areas, evacuation zones are developed in coordination with State and local emergency management officials. These zones are used to determine where and when the public will be ordered to evacuate.

Q: What steps did NHP take in response to the hurricane threat?
A: A Hurricane Liaison Team was deployed to the National Hurricane Center in Miami, Florida, prior to the landfall of Hurricane Katrina. The team assisted in coordinating advisories from the National Hurricane Center to the Federal, State, and local emergency management agencies. The FEMA Regional Hurricane Program Managers also held periodic calls with State and local officials to coordinate evacuation operations.

Q: What is NHP doing now to prepare for other potential hurricane threats in both the near and distant future — particularly in the Hurricane Katrina-affected areas?
A: The FEMA regional hurricane managers will discuss with the state program managers any changes that must be applied to the existing evacuation plans due to the physical and infrastructure damage from Hurricane Katrina.

Source: FEMA, "NHP FAQ," 2007.

DIGGING DEEPER: HURRICANE KATRINA TIMELINE

Thursday, August 25

Tropical Storm Katrina becomes a hurricane and makes its first landfall in Florida on the morning of August, 25.

Friday, August 26
Louisiana Governor Kathleen Blanco declares state of emergency.
Gulf Coast states request troop assistance from Pentagon.

Saturday, August 27
Mississippi Governor Haley Barbour declares state of emergency.
5 AM CDT — Katrina upgraded to category 3 hurricane.
Governor Blanco asks President Bush to declare federal state of emergency in Louisiana.
Federal emergency declared, DHS and FEMA given full authority to respond to Katrina.

Sunday, August 28
2 AM CDT — Katrina upgraded to category 4 hurricane.
7 AM CDT — Katrina upgraded to category 5 hurricane.
Morning — Louisiana newspaper signals levees may breach.
9:30 AM CDT — New Orleans Mayor Ray Nagin issues mandatory evacuation of the city.
Afternoon — President Bush, FEMA Director Mike Brown, and DHS Secretary Michael
    Chertoff warned of levee failure by National Hurricane Center Director Dr. Max Mayfield.
4 PM CDT — National Weather Service issues special hurricane warning.
Late evening — Reports of water toppling over Lake Pontchartrain levee in New Orleans.
Approximately 30,000 evacuees gather at Superdome with roughly 36 hours worth of food.
Louisiana National Guard requests 700 buses from FEMA for evacuations. FEMA responds to
    the request by saying it can provide 100 buses.

Monday, August 29

7 AM CDT — Katrina makes its second landfall as a category 4 hurricane in Louisiana.

7:30 AM CDT — Bush administration notified of the levee breach.

8 AM CDT — Mayor Nagin reports that water is flowing over levee.

Morning — Brown warns Bush about the potential devastation of Katrina.

Morning — National Hurricane Center Director Max Mayfield warns Bush about the toppling possibility of the levees.

Morning — President Bush calls Secretary Chertoff to discuss immigration.

11 AM CDT — Michael Brown requests that DHS dispatch 1,000 employees to region, and gives them two days to arrive.

Late morning — 17th Street Canal levee in New Orleans breaches.

11 AM CDT — Bush visits Arizona resort to promote Medicare drug benefit.

4:30 PM CDT — Bush travels to California senior center to discuss Medicare drug benefit.

8 PM CDT — Louisiana Governor Blanco again requests assistance from President Bush.

Tuesday, August 30

11 AM CDT — Bush speaks on Iraq at Coronado naval base.

Midday — DHS Secretary Michael Chertoff says he has been notified of the levee failure.

Pentagon claims that there are enough National Guard troops in the region.

Mass looting is reported, and security shortage cited in New Orleans.

2 PM CDT — President Bush plays guitar with country singer Mark Willis.

President Bush returns to Crawford for final night of vacation.

Wednesday, August 31

1:45 AM CDT — FEMA requests ambulances that do not exist.

11:20 AM CDT — FEMA staff warn Brown that people were dying at the Superdome.

National Guard troops arrive in Louisiana, Mississippi, Alabama, and Florida.

Tens of thousands trapped in Superdome as conditions deteriorate.

President Bush organizes task force to coordinate federal response.

Jefferson Parish emergency director says food and water supplies are gone.

Eighty thousand are believed stranded in New Orleans and 3,000 stranded at the convention center without food or water.

Public health emergency declared for the entire Gulf Coast.

President Bush surveys damage from Air Force One.

DHS Secretary Michael Chertoff says he is "extremely pleased with the response" of the government.

Early morning — Blanco again tries to request help from President Bush.

4 PM CDT — President Bush gives first major address on Katrina.

8 PM CDT — FEMA Director Brown claims surprise over size of storm.

Thursday, September 1

7 AM CDT — Bush claims no one expected levees to break.

2 PM CDT — New Orleans Mayor Ray Nagin issues "desperate S.O.S." to federal government.

2 PM CDT — Michael Brown claims not to have heard of reports of violence.

Situation in New Orleans is described as total chaos. Police snipers are placed on roofs to provide protection against looting and other armed criminal activity.

Michael Brown learns of evacuees in convention center.

(Continued)

DIGGING DEEPER: HURRICANE KATRINA TIMELINE –(CONTINUED)

Friday, September 2

Local officials are blamed by White House adviser for inadequate preparedness and response to Katrina.

Government agencies including the National Institutes of Health, Department of Labor, and the Environmental Protection Agency urge DHS to pay attention to worker safety.

Early morning — Bush watches DVD of the week's newscasts created by staff who thought the president "needed to see the horrific reports."

10:35 AM CDT — Bush praises Michael Brown saying that he is "doing a heck of a job."

12 PM CDT — Bush says he is "satisfied with the response but not with all results."

Congress approves $10.5 billion in initial funding for Katrina relief.

Saturday, September 3

Senior Bush administration official claims that Governor Blanco never declared state of emergency.

8:05 PM CDT — FEMA finalizes bus request.

Secretary Chertoff says that Katrina exceeded the foresight of government planners.

The Louisiana Superdome is fully evacuated. Some evacuees transported to Houston Astrodome with buses.

Thursday, September 8

Congress approves an additional $51.8 billion for Katrina relief funding.

Friday, September 9

FEMA Director Brown is removed from his relief duties, and replaced by Vice Admiral Thad Allen, chief of staff of the U.S. Coast Guard.

Monday, September 12

FEMA Director Brown resigns.

Tuesday, September 13

President Bush takes responsibility for flawed response.

Wednesday, September 14

Proposal by Senator Hillary Clinton to form an independent bipartisan investigative panel (like the 9/11 Commission) to investigate flaws in government response to Katrina rejected in the U.S. Senate.

Thursday, September 15

Bush addresses nation, saying that his administration will "learn the lessons" of Katrina.

U.S. House of Representatives establishes independent bipartisan commission to investigate flaws in government response to Katrina.

Sources: ThinkProgress.org, "Katrina Timeline," 2008; Infoplease.com, "Hurricane Katrina Timeline," 2008; CNN, "Katrina Timeline," 2008; Wikipedia, "Hurricane Katrina," 2008, among others.

National Earthquake Hazards Reduction Program

The National Earthquake Hazards Reduction Program (NEHRP) was established by the Earthquake Hazards Reduction Act of 1977 to "reduce the risks of life and property from future earthquakes in the U.S." In 1980, the act was amended to include the National Institutes of Standards and Technology (NIST, then the National Bureau of Standards) and to designate the newly created FEMA as the lead agency. FEMA coordinated NEHRP until 2003, when legislation transferred FEMA's management role in the program to NIST. In this capacity, FEMA planned and managed federal response to earthquakes, funded state and local preparedness exercises, and supported seismic design and construction techniques for new buildings and retrofit guidelines for existing buildings.

As part of this program, the U.S. Geological Survey (USGS) conducts and supports earth science investigations into the origins of earthquakes, predicts earthquake effects, characterizes earthquake hazards, and disseminates earth science information. Additionally, the National Science Foundation (NSF) provides funding to earthquake engineering research, basic earth science research, and earthquake-related social science.

In addition to its lead management role for the program, NIST conducts and supports engineering studies to improve seismic provisions of building codes, standards, and practices for buildings and lifelines (FEMA, "NEHRP," 2007).

Total combined NEHRP funding to the four lead agencies from FY 2005 to FY 2008 rose $127.1 million, to $118.7 million, to $121 million, and finally to $121.5 million. The president's FY 2009 budget request includes $121.5 million for NEHRP (NEHRP, 2007; NEHRP, 2008).

The roles of the four NEHRP agencies were further clarified in the 1990 NEHRP Reauthorization Act, which cast their primary responsibilities as follows:

Federal Emergency Management Agency

Translates research results into technical publications

Supports state and local governments by providing multiple-hazard loss estimation capability for use in planning and response

Prepares technical documents aimed at improving the seismic safety of new and existing buildings

Works with national standards organizations to develop seismic standards for new and existing lifelines

Prepares and disseminates information about building codes and practices

National Institutes of Standards and Technologies

Promotes better building practices among architects and engineers

Works with national standards organizations to develop improved seismic standards for new and existing lifelines

Chairs and provides the secretariat for the Interagency Committee on Seismic Safety in Construction (ICSSC), which recommends practices and policies to reduce earthquake hazards in federally owned, leased, assisted, and regulated facilities

National Science Foundation

Supports research on plate tectonics

Funds engineering research on geotechnical, structural, architectural, and lifeline systems

Supports research on the social and economic aspects of earthquake hazard mitigation

Supports the education of new scientists and engineers in the field

United States Geological Survey

Provides national and regional seismic hazard and risk maps

Conducts engineering seismology studies of the ground-shaking phenomenon

Develops methods and standardized procedures for forecasting earthquakes

Supports an external cooperative grants research program

Operates national seismograph networks

NEHRP is an essential program because of the susceptibility of the entire geography of the United States to earthquake disasters. Relative earthquake risks of U.S. states can be viewed at the following website: http://www.fema.gov/hazard/earthquake/risk.shtm. There are multiple active faults throughout the United States. The San Andreas fault in California and New Madrid fault crossing parts of Illinois, Missouri, Arkansas, Kentucky, and Tennessee are but two examples. These faults are known to have the potential to generate very strong earthquakes. Had the 1906 San Francisco earthquake occurred today, it has been estimated that it would have affected nearly 10 million residents within a 19-county area, and would have caused economic losses ranging from $90 to $120 billion. The earthquake could damage as many as 90,000 buildings and depending on the time of the day, 800 to 3,400 people may lose their lives in collapsed buildings. Many of those consequences are preventable through effective earthquake hazard mitigation, thus the importance of the NEHRP (FEMA, "Plan Ahead for an Earthquake," 2007).

FEMA's Mitigation Grant Programs

FEMA currently has five mitigation grant programs: the Hazards Mitigation Grant Program, Pre-Disaster Mitigation Grant Program, Flood Mitigation Assistance Grant Program, Severe Repetitive Loss Grant Program (SRL), and Repetitive Flood Claims Grant Program (RFC), all of which are administered by the *Risk Reduction Division* of the Mitigation Directorate.

Hazards Mitigation Grant Program

Authorized under Section 404 of the Stafford Act, the Hazard Mitigation Grant Program (HMGP) provides grants to states and local governments to implement long-term hazard-mitigation measures after a major disaster declaration. The purpose of the program is to reduce the loss of life and property due to natural disasters and to enable mitigation measures to be implemented during the immediate recovery from a disaster declaration. Hazard Mitigation Grant Program (HMGP) funding is only available in states following a presidential disaster declaration. Eligible applicants follow:

- State and local governments
- Indian tribes or other tribal organizations
- Certain private nonprofit organizations

Individual homeowners and businesses may not apply directly to the program; however, a community may apply on their behalf. HMGP funds may be used to fund projects that will reduce or eliminate the losses from future disasters. Projects must provide a long-term solution to a problem — for example, elevation of a home to reduce the risk of flood damages as opposed to buying sandbags and pumps to fight the flood. In addition, a project's potential savings must be more than the cost of implementing the project. Funds may be used to protect either public or private property or to purchase property that has been subjected to, or is in danger of, repetitive damage.

The HMGP is directly funded by FEMA's Disaster Relief Fund. The amount of HMGP funds that will be made available depends on the combined funding made available from the Disaster Relief Fund for the Public Assistance program and the Individual Assistance Program. The Public Assistance Program makes funds available to communities in repairing or replacing roads, bridges, and other public infrastructure after a disaster occurs. Individual Assistance Program provides grants for individuals and families in the aftermath of disasters. Funds made available for HMGP can not exceed 7.5% of the total of Public Assistance and Individual Assistance Program grants.

In the aftermath of the severe 2004 hurricane season, which included Hurricanes Frances, Jeanne, Ivan, and Charley, FEMA provided a record $359 million in mitigation funding to the State of Florida through the HMGP. Following Hurricane Katrina, FEMA began accepting applications for Hazard Mitigation Grants, but as the application process continued at the writing of this Third Edition, total funding numbers cannot be provided. However, as of November 26, 2007,

Hurricane Katrina- and Rita-related HMGP grants exceeded $1.1 billion (FEMA, "Frequently Asked Questions Mitigation Grant Programs," 2007; FEMA, "Hazard Mitigation Grant Program," 2007; Government Accountability Office, 2000; FEMA, "FEMA Funds First Hazard Mitigation Project in Orleans Parish," 2007).

Pre-Disaster Mitigation Program

The Pre-Disaster Mitigation (PDM) Program was authorized by Section 203 of the Robert T. Stafford Disaster Assistance and Emergency Relief Act (as amended by Section 102 of the Disaster Mitigation Act of 2000). Funding for the program is provided through the National Pre-Disaster Mitigation Fund to assist state and local governments (including Indian tribal governments) in implementing cost-effective hazard mitigation activities that complement a comprehensive mitigation program. Recipients of this grant must be participating in the National Flood Insurance Program (NFIP) if they have been identified as being at special risk from flood hazards (i.e., have a "Special Flood Hazard Area"), and must have a mitigation plan in effect. The Pre-Disaster Mitigation Program was funded in FY 2006, FY 2007, and FY 2008 at $49.5 million, $100 million, $114 million, respectively. The president's FY 2009 budget request included $75 million for the program (DHS, 2008; FEMA, "Pre-Disaster Mitigation Grant Program," 2007).

Flood Mitigation Assistance Program

The Flood Mitigation Assistance (FMA) Program provides funding to assist states and communities in implementing measures to reduce or eliminate the long-term risk of flood damage to buildings, manufactured homes, and other structures insurable under the National Flood Insurance Program (NFIP). Three types of grants are available under FMA: planning, project, and technical assistance grants. FMA planning grants are available to states and communities to prepare flood mitigation plans. NFIP-participating communities with approved flood mitigation plans can apply for FMA project grants. FMA project grants are available to states and NFIP-participating communities to implement measures to reduce flood losses. Ten percent of the project grant is made available to states as a technical assistance grant. These funds may be used by the state to help administer the program. Communities receiving FMA planning and project grants must be participating in the NFIP. An example of eligible FMA projects includes the elevation, acquisition, and relocation of NFIP-insured structures. FMA program priority for the fiscal years 2007 and 2008 is the funding of mitigation projects that minimize or eliminate the long-term risk of flood damage to properties insured by NFIP. In FY 2007, the program was funded at $31 million inclusive of all types of grants, and in FY 2008 funding included $34 million. However, the president's FY 2009 budget did not request any funding for the FMA program (see Tables 6–3 and 6–4) (FEMA, "FY 2008 Flood Mitigation Assistance (FMA) Program," 2008).

Severe Repetitive Loss Program

The Severe Repetitive Loss Program is a proactive mitigation initiative of the National Flood Insurance Program to reduce or eliminate flood-related damages and insurance claims for the approximately 83,000 residential properties that qualify as structures with severe repetitive flood damage potential. Structures with severe repetitive flood loss potential are defined as structures that meet the following criteria:

- Have four or more NFIP claim payments over $5,000 each, given that at least two such claims have occurred within 10 years of each other, and the total amount paid to the policy holder exceeds $20,000; or
- Have two or more separate claims payments where the total amount paid for the building portion of such claims exceeded the value of the property, given that two such claims have occurred within 10 years of each other.

Table 6–3   FEMA Budget Update, 2004–2006 ($000)

DHS FEMA Budget Review	FY 2004 Enacted	FY 2005 Enacted	FY 2006 President's Budget	FY 2006±FY 2005
Disaster relief fund and disaster loans	1,768,067	2,042,947	2,140,567	97,620
Office of the Under Secretary, PMRR, ARO, public health, radiological, emergency preparedness	476,621	479,465	490,980	11,515
Pre-Disaster Mitigation Fund and National Flood Mitigation Fund	169,115	120,000	178,062	58,062
Emergency food and shelter	152,097	153,000	153,000	—
Flood insurance and flood map modernization	289,292	292,593	295,922	3,329
Cerro Grande	37,837	—	—	—
Rescission of previous year carryover	−3,000	−5,000	—	5,000
Gross discretionary	2,890,029	3,083,005	3,258,531	175,526
Biodefense	884,749	2,507,776	—	−2,507,776
National Flood Insurance Fund Account	1,778,753	1,950,251	2,106,757	156,506
Total	5,553,531	7,541,032	5,365,288	−2,175,744

Source: FEMA, "Budget in Brief 2006 Document," 2005.

The Severe Repetitive Loss Program has been in effect since the Flood Insurance Reform Act of 2004. This program reduces the cost of NFIP claims made by owners of highly vulnerable structures by funding mitigation projects that strengthen those structures against flood damage. Among qualifying projects are flood proofing (historical properties only), relocation, elevation, acquisition, mitigation reconstruction (demolition rebuild), and minor physical localized flood control projects. The program is funded at $40 million per fiscal year from 2005 to 2009 (FEMA, "Severe Repetitive Loss Program," 2008; FEMA, "Guidance for Severe Repetitive Loss Properties," 2008).

Repetitive Flood Claims Program

Another program introduced by the Flood Insurance Reform Act of 2004 is the Repetitive Flood Claims (RFC) Program. The program is conceptually similar to the Severe Repetitive Loss Program but the criteria to qualify for the program is more relaxed. Any state or community which had at least one claim to the National Flood Insurance Program can apply for repetitive flood claim program funding to finance projects to reduce the vulnerability of properties against floods. RFC funds can only be spent to improve structures that are located within a state or community that is ineligible for the Flood Mitigation Assistance (FMA) Program due to cost share or capacity to manage the activities.

In FY 2007, 11 States applied for RFC funding for a total of 24 projects covering 118 properties. A total of $33.7 million in funding was requested. FEMA selected 15 of these projects, covering 41 properties, which were funded by the program's $10 million annual budget. (FEMA, "FY 2007 Repetitive Flood Claims Grant Recipients," 2008; FEMA, "Repetitive Flood Claims (RFC) Program (Fiscal Year 2007)," 2008; FEMA, "Repetitive Flood Claims (RFC) Program (Program Overview)," 2008).

Table 6–4   FEMA Budget Update, 2007–2009

	FY 2007 Revised Enacted	FY 2008 Revised Enacted	FY 2009 President's Budget		FY 2009±FY 2008	
	($000)	($000)	FTE	($000)	FTE	($000)
Operations, planning, and support (OPS)	532,341	724,000	3,458	957,405	994	233,405
Public health	33,885	—	—	—	—	—
Disaster relief fund	1,486,500	1,324,000	2,555	1,900,000	−688	576,000
Disaster readiness and support activities	—	—	—	200,000	—	200,000
Disaster assistance direct loan program	569	875	—	295	−3	−580
Pre-Disaster Mitigation Fund	100,000	114,000	15	75,000	—	−39,000
Emergency food and shelter	151,470	153,000	—	100,000	—	−53,000
National Flood Insurance Fund—discretionary	97,588	111,000	330	156,599	30	45,599
National Flood Mitigation Fund	31,000	34,000	—	—	—	−34,000
Flood Map Modernization Fund	198,980	220,000	43	150,000	—	−70,000
State and local programs	2,724,500	3,367,800	278	1,900,000	—	−1,467,800
Assistance to firefighter grants	662,000	750,000	54	300,000	—	−450,000
Cerro Grande fire claims	—	—	—	−9,000	—	−9,000
Radiological Emergency Preparedness Program (REPP)	−6,477	−997	170	−505	—	492
United States Fire Administration (USFA)	41,349	43,300	—	—	−115	−43,300
Gross discretionary	**6,053,705**	**6,840,978**	**6,903**	**5,729,794**	**218**	**−1,111,184**
National Flood Insurance Fund—mandatory	2,631,396	2,833,000	14	3,037,000	7	204,000
Emergency supplemental	**4,567,000**	**3,030,000**	**—**	**—**	**—**	**−3,030,000**
Rescissions	—	−37,177	—	—	—	37,177
Total budget authority	**13,252,101**	**12,666,801**	**6,917**	**8,766,794**	**225**	**−3,900,007**

Source: DHS, "Budget in Brief 2009 Document, FEMA 2009 Budget Request," 2008.

Other FEMA Mitigation Directorate Programs

National Flood Insurance Program

Congress established the National Flood Insurance Program (NFIP) with the passage of the National Flood Insurance Act of 1968. The NFIP is a federal program enabling property owners in participating communities to purchase insurance as a protection against flood losses in exchange for state and community floodplain management regulations that reduce future flood damages. Flood insurance is designed to provide an alternative to disaster assistance to reduce the escalating costs of repairing damage to buildings and their contents caused by floods. Flood damage is reduced by nearly $1 billion a year through communities implementing sound floodplain management requirements and property owners' purchasing of flood insurance. Additionally, buildings constructed in compliance with NFIP building standards suffer approximately 80% less damage annually than those not built in compliance. And, every $3 paid in flood insurance claims reduces $1 in disaster assistance payments (FEMA, "National Flood Insurance Program," 2005).

The importance of flood insurance was again proven following Hurricanes Katrina, Rita, and Wilma in 2005, when the NFIP paid more than $16 billion in claims. The National Flood Insurance Program paid for more than $16 billion in claims (Figure 6–2). As more communities meet floodplain management eligibility requirements and participate in the program, they will continue to minimize flood risk, while enjoying greater financial protection from inevitable flood damages. As these benefits become more and more apparent to homeowners with each disaster that occurs, participation in the NFIP should continue to increase over time. Figure 6–3 provides an overview of the growth in

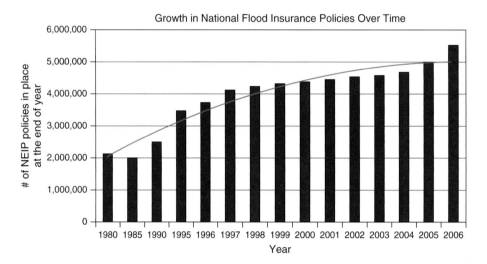

FIGURE 6–2 Losses paid for by the National Flood Insurance Program. (Data source: Insurance Information Institute based on FEMA statistics, 2008, http://www.iii.org)

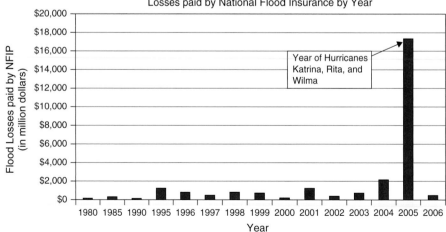

FIGURE 6–3 Growth in National Flood Insurance policies over time. (Data source: Insurance Information Institute based on FEMA statistics, 2008, http://www.iii.org)

the number of flood insurance policies issued by the NFIP. NFIP funding increased from $2.5 billion to $2.8 billion from FY 2006 to FY 2008. The president's FY 2009 budget request included $3.16 billion in mandatory and discretionary funding for the program (NFIP, 2008; Insurance Information Institute, 2008; FEMA, "National Flood Insurance Program," 2008; DHS, 2008).

Prevention Actions and Programs

Prevention refers to actions taken to avoid an incident or to intervene in an effort to stop an incident from occurring in order to protect lives and property. The draft National Incident Management System of August 2007 defines *prevention* as follows:

> *Actions to avoid an incident or to intervene to stop an incident from occurring. Prevention involves actions to protect lives and property. It involves applying intelligence and other information to a range of activities that may include such countermeasures as deterrence operations; heightened inspections; improved surveillance and security operations; investigations to determine the full nature and source of the threat; public health and agricultural surveillance and testing processes; immunizations, isolation, or quarantine; and, as appropriate, specific law enforcement operations aimed at deterring, preempting, interdicting, or disrupting illegal activity and apprehending potential perpetrators and bringing them to justice. (FEMA, "Draft National Incident Management System," August 2007, p. 156)*

According to DHS, the NRP (now called the National Response Framework) may be implemented for threats or potential incidents of national significance to prevent or intervene in order to lessen the impact of an incident. Prevention activities may include heightened inspections; improved surveillance and security operations; public health and agricultural surveillance and testing; immunizations, isolation, or quarantine; and, as appropriate, specific law enforcement operations aimed at deterring, preempting, interdicting, or disrupting illegal activity and apprehending potential perpetrators and bringing them to justice (FEMA, 2005).

As the prevention activities described by DHS imply, most of these activities are related to the prevention of terrorist incidents. Prevention actions related to terrorism threats and incidents include law enforcement activities and protective activities. All federal law enforcement activities are coordinated by the attorney general, generally acting through the FBI. During an incident, initial prevention efforts include, but are not limited to, the following actions:

- Collect, analyze, and apply intelligence and other information.
- Conduct investigations to determine the full nature and source of the threat.
- Implement countermeasures such as surveillance and counterintelligence.
- Conduct security operations, including vulnerability assessments, site security, and infrastructure protection.
- Conduct tactical operations to prevent, interdict, preempt, or disrupt illegal activity.
- Conduct attribution investigations, including an assessment of the potential for future related incidents.
- Conduct activities to prevent terrorists, terrorist weapons, and associated materials from entering or moving within the United States.

As defined within the NRP, any activity that attempts to prevent terrorist attacks can be considered a prevention measure. Several specific DHS prevention programs are discussed in greater detail in Chapter 5.

Several of the recommendations made by the 9/11 Commission, discussed in Chapter 2, also include prevention components. The following examples are provided:

Prevention of proliferation of weapons of mass destruction and their acquisition by terrorist groups: The 9/11 Commission underlines that about two dozen terrorist groups including al-Qaeda have attempted to acquire or develop chemical, biological, radiological, and nuclear weapons. Most of those weapons can be developed relatively inexpensively if the necessary knowledge is available to terrorists. The possible consequences of an attack involving those weapons are very likely to be devastating. Therefore, preventing the proliferation of such weapons or materials that are necessary in their development is a critical task that needs to be performed. The commission recommends that the United States has to work with the international community to get this done. The commission recommends that the United States should sustain its support for the Cooperative Threat Reduction Program, which aims to secure the weapons and highly dangerous materials still scattered in Russia and other countries of the Soviet Union.

Prevention of financial strength and flexibility of terrorist organizations: The United States and its allies made an effort to paralyze the financial networks of terrorists in the recent aftermath of 9/11. This effort aimed to reduce or eliminate the ability of terrorist groups to support their operations and maintain their existence. The experience showed that tracking and blocking of money that is potentially connected to terrorist groups is a very difficult job that demands not only international cooperation, but also the convenience of national laws of international partners. Therefore, other innovative ways of reducing the financial strength and flexibility of terrorist organizations are necessary.

Prevention of terrorist travel: With the advancements in and increased frequency of international travel, terrorist groups were able to gain the mobility to conduct attacks in different parts of the world. This gives an opportunity to governments to identify the terrorist as they enter the transportation system or the country through it border checkpoints. This is a critical task that may prevent some terrorist attacks or at least the penetration of terrorists from one country to another one. But the fact that terrorists also use local resources and people in their activities makes the challenge even tougher.

Prevention of terrorist access to critical infrastructures and key assets: The 9/11 Commission recommends that the improvements being made to protect U.S. borders such as use of terrorist lists, biometric screening, biometric passports, and other threat-related information be shared with and implemented at access points to critical infrastructures and key assets. Such assets may include nuclear power plants, dams, and other infrastructures of national significance and consequences (9/11 Commission, Adapted from the Recommendations of the 9/11 Commission, Chapter 12, "What to Do? A Global Strategy," 2004).

Preparedness Actions and Programs

Preparedness within the field of emergency management can best be defined as a state of readiness to respond to a disaster, crisis, or any other type of emergency situation. It includes those activities, programs, and systems that exist before an emergency that are used to support and enhance response to an emergency or disaster.

Preparedness is important to the overall emergency management cycle because it provides for the readiness and testing of all actions and plans before actual application occurs in response to a real incident or disaster. There is a close connection between mitigation and preparedness. Often, emergency managers argue over whether a specific action should be considered mitigation or preparedness. Oftentimes the lines of distinction become fuzzy, and exact determination impossible. In its most simple terms, preparedness is more about planning for the best response, whereas mitigation includes all the actions that are attempts to prevent the need for a disaster response or to minimize the scope of the needed response.

FIGURE 6–4 Emmitsburg, Maryland, March 10, 2003 — An incident command system course is held at FEMA's National Emergency Training Center, one of dozens of courses offered there each year for first responders, emergency managers, and educators. (Photo by Jocelyn Augustino/FEMA News Photo)

Examples of preparedness for natural hazards are organizing evacuation drills from buildings in case of fires or other threats, providing first-response training to employees so that they can assist each other and their neighbors in small emergencies (Figure 6–4), and preparing a family disaster plan that covers topics such as the designation of a location where family members will meet if they get separated during an event and what personal papers (e.g., prescriptions, insurance records) they might need in the aftermath of an event. More specific examples include the logistical planning for tugboats operating around oil refineries such that they become responsible for responding to fire emergencies in the refinery, or providing training and relocating necessary hazardous materials (HAZMAT) teams to areas where the risk of radiological emergencies is higher, such as nuclear power plants.

In the aftermath of September 11, terrorism preparedness has become a more pressing issue. The risk of terrorists gaining access to and using weapons of mass destruction, such as biological, chemical, and radiological agents, forced the U.S. government to establish an adequate response capability, capacity, and expertise to protect American citizens against a potential attack and respond to it in case these weapons are used. Citizens, who are the most likely targets of these attacks, must be adequately prepared if any response effort is to be successful. DHS has been given the responsibility for this task, although several other federal government agencies, including the Centers for Disease Control and Prevention (CDC) and the Department of Education, for example, provide guidance on a full range of terrorism preparedness activities.

FEMA is responsible for preparing for and responding to natural and technological disasters and terrorism. As such, FEMA produces and publishes several documents that help citizens and businesses to take preparative action against each of these threats, including the new terrorism risk. Unfortunately, the arsenal of weapons available to the growing cadre of international terrorists is expanding — and as new weapons are identified and understood, the public must be educated accordingly. The sidebars "CDC Guidance for Evacuation Preparedness for Chemical Weapons," "FEMA 'Are You Ready' Protective Measures for a Nuclear Blast," and "DHS Ready. Gov Guidance on Explosions," presented in this chapter, and "Preparedness and Response for a Bioterror or Chemical Attack" presented in Chapter 4, provide examples of the guidance provided by DHS, CDC, and FEMA for citizen preparedness against such weapons.

CDC Guidance for Evacuation Preparedness for Chemical Weapons

Some kinds of chemical accidents or attacks may make staying put dangerous. In such cases, it may be safer for you to evacuate or leave the immediate area. You may need to go to an emergency shelter after you leave the immediate area.

How to Know If You Need to Evacuate

You will hear from the local police, emergency coordinators, or government on the radio or television if you need to evacuate. If there is a "code red" or "severe" terror alert, you should pay attention to radio and television broadcasts so that you will know right away if an evacuation order is made for your area.

What to Do

Act quickly and follow the instructions of local emergency coordinators. Every situation can be different, so local coordinators may give you special instructions to follow for a particular situation. Local emergency coordinators may direct people to evacuate homes or offices and go to an emergency shelter. If so, emergency coordinators will tell you how to get to the shelter. If you have children in school, they may be sheltered at the school. You should not try to get to the school if the children are being sheltered there.

The emergency shelter will have most supplies that people need. The emergency coordinators will tell you which supplies to bring with you. Be sure to bring any medications you are taking. If you have time, call a friend or relative in another state to tell him or her where you are going and that you are safe. Local telephone lines may be jammed in an emergency, so you should plan ahead to have an out-of-state contact with whom to leave messages. If you do not have private transportation, make plans in advance of an emergency to identify people who can give you a ride.

Evacuating and sheltering in this way should keep you safer than if you stayed at home or at your workplace. You will most likely not be in the shelter for more than a few hours. Emergency coordinators will let you know when it is safe to leave the shelter.

Source: Centers for Disease Control and Prevention, 2005, www.cdc.gov.

FEMA "Are You Ready" Protective Measures for a Nuclear Blast

Before a Nuclear Blast

To prepare for a nuclear blast, you should do the following:

Find out from officials if any public buildings in your community have been designated as fallout shelters. If none have been designated, make your own list of potential shelters near your home, workplace, and school. These places would include basements or the windowless center area of middle floors in high-rise buildings, as well as subways and tunnels.

If you live in an apartment building or high-rise, talk to the manager about the safest place in the building for sheltering and about providing for building occupants until it is safe to go out.

During periods of increased threat increase your disaster supplies to be adequate for up to two weeks.

Taking shelter during a nuclear blast is absolutely necessary. There are two kinds of shelters: blast and fallout. The following describes the two kinds of shelters:

- Blast shelters are specifically constructed to offer some protection against blast pressure, initial radiation, heat, and fire. But even a blast shelter cannot withstand a direct hit from a nuclear explosion.
- Fallout shelters do not need to be specially constructed for protecting against fallout. They can be any protected space, provided that the walls and roof are thick and dense enough to absorb the radiation given off by fallout particles.

During a Nuclear Blast

The following are guidelines for what to do in the event of a nuclear explosion.

If an attack warning is issued:

Take cover as quickly as you can, below ground if possible, and stay there until instructed to do otherwise.

Listen for official information and follow instructions.

If you are caught outside and unable to get inside immediately:

Do not look at the flash or fireball — it can blind you.

Take cover behind anything that might offer protection.

Lie flat on the ground and cover your head. If the explosion is some distance away, it could take 30 seconds or more for the blast wave to hit.

Take shelter as soon as you can, even if you are many miles from ground zero where the attack occurred — radioactive fallout can be carried by the winds for hundreds of miles. Remember the three protective factors: distance, shielding, and time.

After a Nuclear Blast

Decay rates of the radioactive fallout are the same for any size of nuclear device. However, the amount of fallout will vary based on the size of the device and its proximity to the ground. Therefore, it might be necessary for those in the areas with highest radiation levels to shelter for up to a month. The heaviest fallout would be limited to the area at or downwind from the explosion, and 80% of the fallout would occur during the first 24 hours. People in most of the areas that would be affected could be allowed to come out of shelter within a few days and, if necessary, evacuate to unaffected areas.

Returning to Your Home

Remember the following:

Keep listening to the radio and television for news about what to do, where to go, and places to avoid.

Stay away from damaged areas. Stay away from areas marked "radiation hazard" or "HAZMAT." Remember that radiation cannot be seen, smelled, or otherwise detected by human senses.

Source: Federal Emergency Management Agency, 2005, www.fema.gov.

DHS Ready.Gov Guidance on Explosions

If There Is an Explosion

- Take shelter against your desk or a sturdy table.
- Exit the building ASAP.
- Do not use elevators.
- Check for fire and other hazards.
- Take your emergency supply kit if time allows.

If There Is a Fire

- Exit the building ASAP.
- Crawl low if there is smoke.
- Use a wet cloth, if possible, to cover your nose and mouth.
- Use the back of your hand to feel the upper, lower, and middle parts of closed doors.
- If the door is not hot, brace yourself against it and open slowly.
- If the door is hot, do not open it. Look for another way out.
- Do not use elevators.
- If you catch fire, do not run. Stop-drop-and-roll to put out the fire.
- If you are at home, go to a previously designated meeting place.
- Account for your family members and carefully supervise small children.
- Never go back into a burning building.

If You Are Trapped in Debris

- If possible, use a flashlight to signal your location to rescuers.
- Avoid unnecessary movement so that you don't kick up dust.
- Cover your nose and mouth with anything you have on hand. (Dense-weave cotton material can act as a good filter. Try to breathe through the material.)
- Tap on a pipe or wall so that rescuers can hear where you are.
- If possible, use a whistle to signal rescuers.
- Shout only as a last resort. Shouting can cause a person to inhale dangerous amounts of dust.

Source: Department of Homeland Security, 2005, www.dhs.gov.

Preparedness against Biological and Chemical Attacks and Accidents

Preparedness against biological and chemical attacks and accidents poses a distinct challenge due to the unique consequences that they inflict and the relatively limited experience of emergency management professionals in dealing with them. This unique challenge is being addressed by many local, state, federal, private, and nonprofit agencies throughout the United States. In fact, the majority of preparedness funding under the Department of Homeland Security targets these WMD hazards.

Specific Challenges for Biological/Chemical Terrorism Incident Management

Deliberate biological or chemical incidents will present critical challenges to both the intended targets and those in charge of managing the incident that results. These agents, as with all weapons of mass destruction, present public health threats that are not typically seen in either day-to-day or even major incidents of natural or accidental man-made nature. As such, the methods by which citizens and response officials can prepare for these attacks have only just begun to emerge in the past few years. Chemical incidents do occur with regularity, but it is very rare for them to deliberately target a human population.

Both chemical and biological agents, when used as weapons, have a significant potential to overwhelm the capabilities of the public health infrastructure. There have been several attempts to design a comprehensive framework to prepare for and manage mass casualty medical incidents. The specific response challenges that those defining new preparedness methods must take into account are listed here:

- The existence of a chemical or biological attack may be hard to verify, due to delayed consequences or symptoms.

- The incident may involve multiple jurisdictions, which may make it much more difficult to organize a coordinated response.

- It may be time consuming to identify and isolate the type and source of the chemical or biological agent present on site.

- The incident may have a pinpoint target where a specific crowd is targeted, or may be designed to impact a larger geographic area and even larger crowds, both of which will likely create large crowds of morbidities if not mortalities.

- If large numbers of the public are impacted by the incident, the demand for health care may quickly exceed local, or even regional, medical resources.

- The identification of the involved chemical(s) or biological agent(s) may consume the capacity of local medical laboratories making it mandatory to integrate use of neighboring laboratories.

- Resources of the medical system may be consumed by not only the victims, but also by those who perceive themselves as possible victims who may not be real victims.

- The emergency management officials may have to make extremely difficult public policy decisions very quickly, where lives may have to be sacrificed to save other lives.

- It may be necessary to quarantine the impacted region to insulate the nonimpacted geographies from potential contamination.

- The medical units may have to triage arriving victims if the incoming demand dramatically exceeds the capacity of available resources.

- To decontaminate the impacted geographies and those who were contaminated by the release, necessary decontamination systems, equipment, and human resources may be necessary at multiple locations.

- The medical system may not only have to deal with the physical disease caused by the chemical or biological release, but also with the mental impacts of the "mass paranoia" the incident may have triggered.

These are but a small subset of the potential challenges that must be met. Individual events will present individual response factors that may or may not be known beforehand. To address these issues, physical (equipment, tools, technology), financial, knowledge, and human resources are all necessary. More importantly, a comprehensive system to address these challenges is necessary, and the adequate utilization of such a system demands the provision of training and exercises to those who will be dependent on such a system in a time of crisis. See the sidebar titled "CDC's Strategic Plan for Preparedness and Response to Biological and Chemical Terrorism."

CDC's Strategic Plan for Preparedness and Response to Biological and Chemical Terrorism

The CDC has developed a plan, titled the "Strategic Plan for Preparedness and Response to Biological and Chemical Terrorism," that identifies preparedness and prevention, detection and surveillance, diagnosis and characterization of biological and chemical agents, response, and communication as the five focus areas for comprehensive mass casualty health incident management. Descriptions of each follow.

Preparedness and Prevention

Detection, diagnosis, and mitigation of illness and injury caused by biological and chemical terrorism are complex processes that involve numerous partners and activities. Meeting this challenge requires special emergency preparedness in all cities and states. CDC provides public health guidelines, support, and technical assistance to local and state public health agencies as they develop coordinated preparedness plans and response protocols. CDC also provides self-assessment tools for terrorism preparedness, including performance standards, attack simulations, and other exercises.

Detection and Surveillance

Early detection is essential for ensuring a prompt response to a biological or chemical attack, including the provision of prophylactic medicines, chemical antidotes, or vaccines. CDC is integrating surveillance for illness and injury resulting from biological and chemical terrorism into the U.S. disease surveillance systems, while developing new mechanisms for detecting, evaluating, and reporting suspicious events that might represent covert terrorist acts. As part of this effort, CDC and state and local health agencies form partnerships with front-line medical personnel in hospital emergency departments, hospital care facilities, poison control centers, and other offices to enhance detection and reporting of unexplained injuries and illnesses as part of routine surveillance mechanisms for biological and chemical terrorism.

Diagnosis and Characterization of Biological and Chemical Agents

The CDC and its partners created a multilevel laboratory response network (LRN). The LRN and its partners will maintain an integrated national and international network of laboratories that are fully equipped to respond quickly to acts of chemical or biological terrorism, emerging infectious diseases, and other public health threats and emergencies.

Response

A comprehensive public health response to a biological or chemical terrorist event involves epidemiologic investigation, medical treatment and prophylaxis for affected persons, and the initiation of disease prevention or environmental decontamination measures. CDC assists state and local health agencies in developing resources and expertise for investigating unusual events and unexplained illnesses. If requested by a state health agency, CDC will deploy response teams to investigate unexplained or suspicious illnesses or unusual etiologic agents and provide on-site consultation regarding medical management and disease control. To ensure the availability, procurement, and delivery of medical supplies, devices, and equipment that might be needed to respond to terrorist-caused illness or injury, CDC maintains a national pharmaceutical stockpile.

Communication Systems

U.S. preparedness to mitigate the public health consequences of biological and chemical terrorism depends on the coordinated activities of well-trained health-care and public health personnel throughout the United States who have access to up-to-the minute emergency information. Effective communication with the public through the news media will also be essential to limit terrorists' ability to induce public panic and disrupt daily life.

Source: Centers for Disease Control and Prevention, "Biological and Chemical Terrorism: Strategic Plan for Preparedness and Response," 2005.

Comprehensive Medical and Health Incident Management System

The Medical and Health Incident Management System (MaHIM) designed by Drs. Joseph A. Barbera and Anthony G. Macintyre is one of the most recent and most comprehensive analytical tools designed to help communities develop their own medical mass casualty incident management capacity. The system not only focuses on developing local capacities, but also proposes a framework that can be used to integrate interjurisdictional capacities, should the incident spread beyond local jurisdictional borders.

The goal of the framework is to define as a single system encompassing the medical and public health functions and processes required for adequate management of a mass casualty incident. The system has been designed with an all-hazards approach where special consideration is given to bioterrorism.

The MaHIM system defines the goal of medical consequence management in a mass casualty incident as follows: to maximally limit morbidity (injury or illness) and mortality (deaths) in the population exposed to a major hazard, and to return the community to normalcy as soon as possible. The three primary medical objectives to attain this goal follow:

Reduce hazard exposure: Avoid or minimize the hazard exposure to patients and the population after hazard "release."

Increase hazard resistance: Maximize patient and population resistance to the hazard impact after exposure.

Promote/achieve healing from hazard effects: Maximize the rate and degree of patient and population healing from the hazard impact.

To achieve these goals, the system utilizes principles of effective local and regional organization to provide a detailed description of necessary medical and health emergency operations, and the associated subfunctions and processes. The system underlines the importance of *responsibility* and *authority*. It defines the operational requirements for surge capacity, and provides detailed explanations about support functions critical to system's operation. Figure 6–5 details the MaHIM management process.

MaHIM provides a new vision for the health and emergency medical service communities, and gives them an actionable tool with which they can now structure their preparedness and management efforts in a more systematic fashion. The system describes in detail all functional areas that should be included in a comprehensive, mass casualty health incident management system. The system is currently being implemented in Arlington County, Virginia, as part of a pilot project. The project includes restructuring the county's entire emergency medical system. A more detailed functional description of the system can be downloaded at the following website: www.gwu.edu/~icdrm/publications/MaHIM% 20Model%20Web%20Version%20FEB%2003.pdf (Barbera and Macintyre, 2002; J.A. Barbera and A.G. Macintyre, presentation at the ICDRM/SAIC Monthly Emergency Management Forum, Washington, DC, 2003).

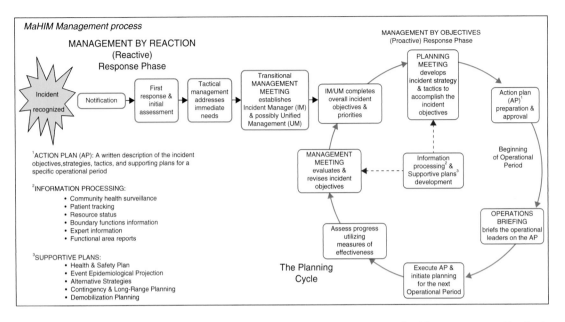

FIGURE 6–5 MaHIM management process. (Adapted from "Planning Cycle," *U.S. Coast Guard Incident Management Handbook*, U.S. Coast Guard COMDTPUB P3120, April 17, 2001)

ANOTHER VOICE: WHY IS MITIGATION AND PREPAREDNESS THE ONLY SUSTAINABLE, COST-EFFECTIVE WAY OF DEALING WITH EMERGENCIES?

Pay Now or Later

Catastrophic disasters are associated with large losses of property and lives, where resources to cope with the disaster overwhelm local governments. Following such disasters, large amounts of capital in the form of disaster aid are necessary in order to put the physical infrastructure back to its original state. Even larger amounts — doubled, tripled, or sometimes quadrupled — are necessary to put the economic and social infrastructure back into a sustainable state. Therefore, local planners and policymakers should be extra careful when allowing settlements and the associated infrastructure systems in precarious zones such as active faults, coastal regions, flood zones, and nuclear power plants. These decisions should not only be based on scientific assessment of potential risks of failure (these are ideally embedded in building codes) but also "life cycle costs" of owning and operating infrastructure systems (LCCs are ideally factored into the "benefit-cost ratio" for capital allocation). LCCs should include allowances for scheduled and emergency maintenance for critical parts of the system, as well as economic allowances for failures.

Case in Point

In the immediate aftermath of Hurricane Katrina, the levees surrounding the city of New Orleans failed, causing the flooding of the entire city and incapacitating local response forces. The failure of the response is attributable, among other things, to the historic ill decision of settling in a very dangerous flood zone and continued expansion despite prior major flooding events, as well as the lack of funding that caused the poor maintenance and near-neglect of critical components of the levee structure which led to their compromise under extreme forces.

By Irmak Renda-Tanali, DSc., MSCE, Assistant Professor; Program Director, Homeland Security Management, Information and Technology Systems Department, Graduate School of Management and Technology, University of Maryland-University College.

Nuclear and Radiological Preparedness

The Nuclear Regulatory Commission (NRC) is the primary federal government agency in charge of regulating the commercial radiological operations within the United States. The NRC's mission is to regulate the nation's civilian use of by-product, source, and special nuclear materials to ensure adequate protection of public health and safety, to promote the common defense and security, and to protect the environment. The NRC's regulatory mission covers three main areas:

> *Reactors:* Commercial reactors for generating electric power and research and test reactors used for research, testing, and training
>
> *Materials:* Uses of nuclear materials in medical, industrial, and academic settings and facilities that produce nuclear fuel
>
> *Waste:* Transportation, storage, and disposal of nuclear materials and waste, and decommissioning of nuclear facilities from service

A key component of the mission of the NRC is to ensure adequate preparedness measures are in place to protect the health and safety of the public. These actions are taken to avoid or reduce radiation dose exposure and are sometimes referred to as *protective measures.*

The overall objective of NRC's Emergency Preparedness (EP) program is to ensure that nuclear power plant operators are capable of implementing adequate measures to protect public health and safety in the event of a radiological emergency. As a condition of their license, operators of these nuclear power plants must develop and maintain EP plans that meet comprehensive NRC EP requirements. Increased confidence in public protection is obtained through the combined inspection of the requirements of emergency preparedness and the evaluation of their implementation.

The NRC maintains oversight of the capability of nuclear power plant operators to protect the public by conducting thorough inspections. The NRC maintains four regional offices (Region I in King of Prussia, Pennsylvania; Region II in Atlanta, Georgia; Region III in Lisle, Illinois; and Region IV in Arlington, Texas) that implement the NRC's inspection program. In addition to these regionally based inspectors, the NRC places "resident inspectors" at each of the nation's operating nuclear plants to carry out the inspection program on a day-to-day basis.

The NRC assesses the capabilities of nuclear power plant operators to protect the public by requiring the performance of a full-scale exercise at least once every two years that includes the participation of government agencies. These exercises are performed in order to maintain the skills of the emergency responders and to identify and correct weaknesses. They are evaluated by NRC regional inspectors and FEMA regional evaluators. Between the times when these two-year exercises are conducted, additional drills are conducted by the nuclear power plant operators that are evaluated by the resident inspectors (Nuclear Regulatory Commission, 2005).

Terrorism Preparedness and Mitigation: Community Issues

The terrorism threat knows no geographic, social, or economic boundaries. Every citizen and every community is potentially at risk. While the DHS focuses on federal and state efforts to prepare for and combat terrorism, local communities are struggling to address the terrorism risk. The following sections will explain several initiatives that have been launched to deal with community issues concerning the terrorist threat.

Corporation for National and Community Service

The mission of the Corporation for National and Community Service (CNCS), an independent federal agency under the White House, is to provide opportunities for Americans of all ages and backgrounds to engage in service that addresses the nation's educational, public safety, environmental, and other human needs to achieve direct and demonstrable results. In doing so, the corporation fosters civic responsibility, strengthens the ties that bind citizens together, and provides educational opportunities for those who make a substantial commitment to service.

CNCS provides opportunities for Americans to serve through three programs: Senior Corps, AmeriCorps, and Learn and Serve America. Members and volunteers serve with national and community nonprofit organizations, faith-based groups, schools, and local agencies to help meet community needs in education, the environment, public safety, homeland security, and other critical areas. The corporation is part of USA Freedom Corps, a White House initiative to foster a culture of citizenship, service, and responsibility and help all Americans answer the president's call to service.

Senior Corps taps the skills, talents, and experience of more than 500,000 Americans aged 55 years and older to meet a wide range of community challenges through three programs: RSVP, Foster Grandparents, and Senior Companions. RSVP volunteers conduct safety patrols for local police departments, participate in environmental projects, provide intensive educational services to children and adults, and respond to natural disasters, among other activities. Foster Grandparents serve one-on-one as tutors and mentors to young people with special needs. Senior Companions help home-bound seniors and other adults maintain independence in their own homes.

Fifty thousand Americans are serving their communities 20 to 40 hours a week through AmeriCorps. Most of AmeriCorps' members are selected by and serve with local and national non-profit organizations such as Habitat for Humanity, the American Red Cross, City Year, Teach for America, and Boys and Girls Clubs of America, as well as with a host of smaller community organizations, both secular and faith based. AmeriCorps operates in a decentralized manner that gives a significant amount of responsibility to states and local nonprofit groups. Roughly three-quarters of all AmeriCorps grant funding goes to governor-appointed state service commissions, which award grants to nonprofit groups in responding to local needs. Most of the remainder of the grant funding is distributed by the corporation directly to multistate and national organizations through a competitive grants process. AmeriCorps*NCCC (National Civilian Community Corps) is a residential program for more than 1,200 members ages 18 to 24. Based on a military model, it sends members in teams of 10 to 14 to help nonprofit groups provide disaster relief, preserve the environment, build homes for low-income families, tutor children, and meet other challenges. Because members are trained in CPR, first aid, and mass care, and can be assigned to new duties on short notice, they are particularly well suited to meet the emerging homeland security needs of the nation.

Learn and Serve America provides grants to schools, colleges, and nonprofit groups to support efforts to engage students in community service linked to academic achievement and the development of civic skills. This type of learning, referred to as *service learning*, improves communities while preparing young people for a lifetime of responsible citizenship. In addition to providing grants, Learn and Serve America serves as a resource on service and service learning to teachers, faculty members, schools, and community groups.

CNCS is an important initiative for homeland security efforts at the local community level because it provides a significant portion of the total federal funding that goes to volunteer organizations and local communities that are trying to improve their homeland security capabilities.

On July 18, 2002, CNCS announced that it had acquired more than $10.3 million in grants. These grants supported 37,000 volunteers for homeland security in public safety, public health, and disaster mitigation and preparedness. The corporation announced on September 10, 2003, the renewal of 17 of the grants from the previous year totaling nearly $4.5 million for homeland security volunteer projects that were developed in the aftermath of the September 11 terrorist attacks.

In January 2004, CNCS announced the availability of $3.2 million in funding for organizations addressing homeland security concerns by engaging students in service learning activities in their schools and communities. The funding was made available through the Corporation's Learn and Serve America program, which provides grants to schools, colleges, and nonprofits to support programs that connect classroom learning with community service. The Homeland Security initiative aimed to engage young people aged 5 to 17 in planning for and responding to health, safety, and security concerns in their schools or communities, including natural disasters, school violence, medical emergencies, or terrorist acts. Examples of activities supported included engaging students in service learning projects to develop school crisis plans, distributing preparedness kits, conducting school safety audits and drills, providing health education, inventory and maintain emergency supplies, or providing language assistance to non–English-speaking populations.

In February 2004, CNCS announced the renewal of 13 AmeriCorps homeland security grants to support 362 AmeriCorps members serving in public safety, public health, and disaster relief and preparedness projects across the country. The grants totaled $3.5 million and supported AmeriCorps projects in 20 states. The grantees included 12 state or local groups and one national organization, the American Red Cross. The grants supported AmeriCorps members' efforts to recruit volunteers, develop disaster response plans, teach disaster preparedness to students, assist firefighting and police operations, train people in first aid and CPR, respond to national and local disasters, and develop partnerships with organizations involved in homeland security such as Citizen Corps councils and Neighborhood Watch Programs. (See sidebar titled, "DHS Secretary Ridge Cites Neighborhood Security as Instrumental to Homeland Security.") Results from the 2003 activities sponsored by the grants included the following:

> AmeriCorps members serving in a program sponsored by the Florida Department of Elder Affairs have recruited over 600 disaster services volunteers who contributed more than 12,000 hours of service, distributed over 200,000 disaster services publications, and reached nearly 2,500 residents with presentations on safety.
>
> Serving with the Green River Area Development District in rural Kentucky, AmeriCorps members have utilized data from a Global Positioning System to map out information about fire stations, emergency shelters, HAZMAT storage facilities, medical facilities, and nursing homes.
>
> Just blocks from the World Trade Center site, Pace University AmeriCorps members have trained 250 people in English, Chinese, and Spanish in emergency preparedness techniques, created a resource list that consolidates all important emergency numbers, and built a "Downtown Needs" website that serves as a volunteer clearinghouse for 2,000 organizations in the downtown area.
>
> AmeriCorps members in the California Safe Corps have taught disaster preparedness classes to more than 1,000 community members, recruited more than 100 new volunteers who have provided over 250 hours of service, and assisted more than 200 victims of disasters.
>
> In Iowa, AmeriCorps members have made presentations on disaster preparedness at 400 schools across the state.
>
> In the summer of 2004, the devastation wrought by Hurricanes Charley and Frances in Florida prompted the CNCS to muster as much assistance as possible to the state. More than 600 national service volunteers have been deployed to provide both direct services and leverage the support of thousands of additional volunteers. The CNCS worked with state and federal disaster officials to deploy even more volunteers as needed.
>
> AmeriCorps members and Senior Corps volunteers specially trained in disaster relief have responded to disasters in more than 30 states. The corporation has a long track record of working with FEMA and other relief agencies in helping run emergency shelters, assisting law enforcement, providing food and shelter, managing donations, and helping families and communities rebuild. Hundreds of national service volunteers have directly assisted victims of the September 11 terrorist attacks by providing family services, organizing blood drives, raising funds, and counseling victims' families (from www.nationalservice.org/news/factsheets/homeland.html and www.nationalservice.org/news/homeland.html).

CNCS volunteers proved to be especially useful and valuable in the aftermath of Hurricane Katrina. CNCS quickly activated its local volunteer base to join the response to the disaster, and also deployed many of its volunteers from other states to take part in the response and recovery operations. Response to Hurricane Katrina constituted the single largest nonmilitary volunteer disaster response in the history of the United States. Close to 600,000 volunteers took part in the response and recovery to Hurricane Katrina of which approximately 35,000 were participants of various CNCS programs. Volunteers with diverse skills and training supported many important activities such as management of evacuee shelter operations, food services, basic health-care services, informing disaster victims on available governmental and nongovernmental benefits, and general postincident counseling services. CNCS volunteers staffed the American Red Cross emergency call center in Fairfax, Virginia.

CNCS did not suspend its efforts in the hurricane-hit region after the response transformed into a long-term recovery operation. The organization worked with established partners including but not limited to FEMA, and the American Red Cross. Volunteers got involved with donation collection, and warehouse management activities. Alabama Emergency Management Agency's emergency phone answering system has been staffed by CNCS volunteers. The corporation funded volunteer pilot operated airlifts to transport patients out of the area, to reunite families, and bring in medical supplies to the region. Trained and equipped members of American Radio Relay League, a CNCS partner have supported emergency radio communications. In the later phases of the recovery effort volunteers collaborating with federal, state, local response units, military units deployed to help with the recovery, and other nonprofit organizations and CNCS volunteers participated in debris removal, helped the elderly and the disabled, repaired damaged roofs, and staffed coordination offices. American Red Cross response vehicles such as mobile kitchens were also staffed by volunteers in many instances. CNCS encouraged the volunteering of college students during their winter and spring breaks, and created opportunities for their direct involvement in the hardest hit areas as volunteers. Those students participated in repair and reconstruction projects, and enjoyed supporting local communities as they helped them recover from the devastation caused by Hurricane Katrina (CNCS, 2006; CNCS, "A Resource Guide for the Strategic Initiatives," 2007; CNCS, "The Power of Help and Hope after Katrina by the Numbers: Volunteers in the Gulf," 2007).

The CNCS Homeland Security Grant Program was discontinued in 2006 after being funded at $10.3 million in FY 2003, at $9.88 million in FY 2004, and at $4.96 million in FY 2005. During that timeframe, 17 grants were funded for a 3-year period and 12 grants were funded for a 2-year period (CNCS, 2005).

■ ■ ■ ▬▬▬▬▬▬▬▬▬▬▬▬▬▬▬▬▬▬▬▬▬▬▬▬▬

DHS Secretary Ridge Cites Neighborhood Security as Instrumental to Homeland Security

In Falcon Heights, Minnesota, a program that trains residents to respond to potential terrorist attacks is becoming a model for other cities and states. Falcon Heights Mayor Sue Gehrz, St. Paul Mayor Randy Kelly, and other officials were joined by Homeland Security Secretary Tom Ridge at a symposium in St. Paul exploring how Americans can protect their food supply, workplaces, and homes. "The potential destruction to life and property from man-made disasters is so large that communities can no longer assume" that agencies in neighboring communities will be available to help, Gehrz said. "That means more individuals need to be trained to assist their families and neighbors until help arrives," she said.

"The only way you can secure the homeland is to make sure the hometowns are secure," Ridge told about 350 people at the symposium. The nation has strengthened security in many ways since the terror attacks of 2001, yet it still needs a greater degree of readiness, he said. "We need to consolidate most of our computer systems and databases in one seamless operation, make it easier for police to communicate with each other, with the rest of federal government, right down to the state and locals," he said.

Since the September 11 attacks, the residents of Falcon Heights have worked together to plan a response to terror attacks, Gehrz said. They have created a community manual on their "intergenerational organizing model" and provided it to more than 70 Minnesota cities and counties. It has been used in Florida, South Carolina, and Washington, DC.

In Falcon Heights, which has a population of 5,600, a total of 65 "neighborhood liaisons" have collected the names, addresses, and phone numbers of people on their blocks, identifying who has medical training or other specialized skills or equipment that might be useful in a disaster, Gehrz said. A neighborhood commission worked with the Red Cross to provide free first-aid training for 62 residents. Police have trained 11 residents how to direct traffic during emergencies. Others will receive 21 hours of training in how to respond to emergencies. "Involving all ages helps reduce fear and protect civil rights," said Gehrz, who is trained as a psychologist. "One of the primary goals of terrorism is to make people feel isolated and vulnerable."

Source: "Falcon Heights Security Efforts Are Becoming a National Model," *Star Tribune*, June 20, 2003, p. 19A.

Citizen Corps

Following the tragic events that occurred on September 11, 2001, state and local government officials have increased opportunities for citizens to become an integral part of protecting the homeland and supporting local first responders. Officials agree that the formula for ensuring a more secure and safer homeland consists of preparedness, training, and citizen involvement in supporting first responders. In January 2002, President George W. Bush launched the USA Freedom Corps to "capture the spirit of service that has emerged throughout our communities following the terrorist attacks."

Citizen Corps, a vital component of USA Freedom Corps, was created to help coordinate volunteer activities that can make communities safer, stronger, and better prepared to respond to emergencies. It provides opportunities for people to participate in a range of measures to make their families, their homes, and their communities safer from the threats of crime, terrorism, and disasters of all kinds.

Citizen Corps is coordinated nationally by FEMA. In this capacity, FEMA works closely with other federal entities, state and local governments, first responders and emergency managers, the volunteer community, and the White House Office of the USA Freedom Corps. One of the initiatives supported by Citizen Corps is the Community Emergency Response Teams (CERT). The program trains citizens to be better prepared to respond to emergency situations in their communities. When emergencies happen, CERT members can give critical support to first responders, provide immediate assistance to victims, and organize spontaneous volunteers at a disaster site. CERT members can also help with non-emergency projects that help improve the safety of the community.

The CERT course is taught in the community by a trained team of first responders who have completed a CERT Train-the-Trainer course conducted by their state training office for emergency management, or FEMA's Emergency Management Institute (EMI), located in Emmitsburg, Maryland. CERT training includes disaster preparedness, disaster fire suppression, basic disaster medical operations, and light search and rescue operations. As of 2008, there were more than 2,800 CERT programs active in many states, counties, and communities nationwide. For more information on CERT, see the CERT website at www.citizencorps.gov/programs/cert.shtm.

Another important Citizen Corps initiative is the Medical Reserve Corps (MRC) program, which coordinates the skills of practicing and retired physicians, nurses, and other health-care professionals, as well as other citizens interested in health issues who are eager to volunteer to address their community's ongoing public health needs and to help their community during large-scale emergency situations.

Local community leaders develop their own Medical Reserve Corps units and identify the duties of the MRC volunteers according to specific community needs. For example, MRC volunteers may deliver necessary public health services during a crisis, assist emergency response teams with patients, and provide care directly to those with less serious injuries and other health-related issues. More information on the MRC program can be found at http://www.medicalreservecorps.gov.

The Neighborhood Watch Program (NWP) and Volunteers in Police Service (VIPS) programs are other Citizen Corps homeland security-related programs.

A relatively new partner program of the Citizen Corps initiative is the Fire Corps program. Launched in 2004, Fire Corps is a partnership between the International Association of Fire Chiefs' Volunteer and Combination Officers Section (IAFC/VCOS), the International Association of Fire Fighters (IAFF), the National Volunteer Fire Council (NVFC), and the U.S. Fire Administration (USFA). Its mission is to help career, volunteer, and combination fire departments supplement existing personnel resources by recruiting citizen advocates. In June 2005, the program signed up its first 250 fire departments in its "citizen advocates" program. The purpose of the program is to help fire departments expand existing programs — or assist in developing new ones — that recruit citizens who donate their time and talents to support the fire service in non-operational roles. Within the first 4 years of its existence Fire Corps has expanded its organization to many states. Currently the organization has a division advocate for all seven divisions across the United states, and 52 state advocates that represent 28 states. More information about Fire Corps can be found at http://firecorps.org (Fire Corps, 2008).

The FY 2004 Homeland Security Appropriations Bill provided $40 million to the Citizen Corps program. In FY 2005, Congress reduced the available funding to $15 million, but raised it to $19.2 million in FY 2006 – despite requests of $50 million both years. Citizen Corps saw its budget fall again in FY 2007 to $14.6 million. The President's FY 2008 budget requested $15 million for the program (DHS, "Overview: FY 2007 Homeland Security Grant Program," 2007; Congressional Research Service, "FY2008 Appropriations for State and Local Homeland Security," 2007).

The SAFE Conference

The first annual conference on "The Community and Homeland Security," in cooperation with the SAFE project, took place in San Francisco on March 27 and 28, 2003. The aim of the conference was to bring together local leaders from several states, leaders responsible for shaping homeland security programs and activities in their communities, with representatives from federal, state, local, nonprofit, private, and international organizations working on homeland security–related issues. The conference allowed all these practitioners, participants, and representatives to voice their concerns and to share their experiences and gave them their first opportunity not only to work together to identify existing problems with homeland security at the local level but to propose possible solutions to these problems (see sidebar titled, "SAFE Conference: The Community and Homeland Security").

Four principal areas of concern on the community level emerged from the discussions in the conference:

Resources: Greater access to resources to fund homeland security programs and projects at the community level

Information: Greater access to practical information about application, eligibility, recruitment, retention, and other concerns

Programming: The need for innovative and effective programming ideas

Customizing: The need to focus on diverse and "special needs" populations

To create more resources and to use available resources more effectively, the following ideas were developed in the conference:

Block grants to communities are an efficient means for providing federal funding for community homeland security efforts.

Communities should partner with the National Governor's Association, the United States Conference of Mayors, the League of Cities, and other professional associations seeking federal funding for community homeland security efforts.

Creative funding ideas practiced in communities around the country need to be identified and
widely disseminated among community homeland security officials.
New partnerships need to be established with the country's business and philanthropic
communities to leverage their resources for community homeland security efforts.

Suggestions for improving access to accurate and timely information regarding homeland security issues included the following:

Establishing an information clearinghouse to catalog homeland security information sources
Establishing a Web-based "chat room" for community officials to exchange ideas and best
practices and to discuss current issues
Establishing a "funding exchange" to share ideas on funding sources and creative funding ideas
Partnering with the Department of Homeland Security and state homeland security operations
to facilitate the flow of information on federal and state programs and funding opportunities
to community officials.

In addition to the homeland security programming currently in place (e.g., CERT training,
Medical RSVP), conference participants identified a need to design and implement programs that fully
leveraged the capabilities of volunteers in the community. Several ideas were considered, including the
following:

The SAFE Project, designed to develop volunteer programs in support of community emergency
management and homeland security operations
The development of Community Emergency Networks (CENs) designed to facilitate communications
between community residents and local homeland security officials before, during, and after a
disaster or terrorism incident

Some of the ideas developed in the conference regarding the "special needs" populations were
as follows:

Reprogramming Community Development Block Grant (CDBG) funding targeted for "special
needs" populations to include homeland security efforts
Establishing "language and culture banks" in communities to facilitate communications
and information flow between public safety and emergency officials and "special needs"
populations
Partnering with national associations and groups that represent the interests of special needs
populations such as the elderly, veterans, minority populations, children, and the disabled
Partnering with foundations and other philanthropic organizations, such as the Annie E. Casey
Foundation, which focuses its efforts and funding in disadvantaged communities
Partnering with local emergency management/homeland security and public health operations
to help these groups identify and serve special needs populations in the community

The existence of voluntary activities for homeland security, such as the SAFE conference, is
important because such activities bring together different stakeholders, provide an opportunity to
share expertise and best practices, and create an environment in which public–private partnerships
can be initiated and brainstorming can occur.

SAFE Conference: The Community and Homeland Security

The National Council on Crime and Delinquency (NCCD) and the SAFE Project (Securing
America's Future for Everyone) hosted the first annual conference on "The Community and

Homeland Security" on March 27 and March 28, 2003, in San Francisco, California. The conference brought over 60 local leaders from around the country, leaders who are responsible for shaping homeland security programs and activities in their communities together with representatives from federal, state, and local government and nonprofit, private, and international organizations working on homeland security–related issues.

The conference allowed participants to voice their concerns and share experiences and gave them their first opportunity not only to work together to identify existing problems with Homeland Security at the local level but also to propose possible solutions. The following excerpts from the conference highlight the myriad needs identified by community leaders relating to preparedness efforts at the community level:

The primary concern of those in attendance was well stated by Carol Lopes (Berkeley, California), who said, "Though there has been a lot of progress, we are willfully unprepared. Community and neighborhood preparedness is the centerpiece of today's work. Our responsibility is to prepare a community before a disaster and assist after a disaster strikes. We must train a cadre of emergency prepared individuals who will interface well with first responders."

Said Chuck Supple (GO SERV): "We must engage citizens to address problems in their own communities to have the greatest possible impact in Community Homeland Security."

Said Valli Wasp (Austin, Texas): "Preparedness must be addressed locally. We need to take this to 'homes' — get rid of the 'land,' get rid of the 'security' — this is about people protecting their homes. If you want people to listen to you, you have to go to where they live."

Said Eileen Garry (U.S. Department of Justice): "Every good idea I have ever heard came from the local level."

One participant expressed concern that "making us fundraisers, in addition to our programmatic [tasks], really stretches municipalities' resources thin. The raw numbers of people required for fundraising exhausts programs." However, such fundraising actions are recognized as vital to any program's success, echoed by Doris Milldyke (Kansas) who said, "Money is the first goal, volunteers are the second." Ann Patton (Tulsa, Oklahoma) stated, "An information clearinghouse would be invaluable," while Doris Milldyke (Kansas) noted that information on VIPS, MRS, and other programs is "notoriously difficult to find," adding, "we need a golden key for information on getting grants."

Chuck Supple (California GO SERV) stated this position well in saying, "We've probably only thought of a 'minutia' of the areas where volunteers would be useful."

Ana-Marie Jones (Oakland, California) warned that "special needs communities are often isolated from services," adding that "[programs] must have a trusted leader who either speaks or has access to the languages of all representative groups — you need more than a 'Spanish press release.'" She suggested that participants "involve special needs communities before the disaster" to be effective.

Source: D. Coppola, G.D. Haddow, and J.A. Bullock, A Report on the First Annual Conference on "The Community and Homeland Security," March 2003, www.nccd-crc.org/new/chs_conference_1.pdf.

The American Red Cross

The American Red Cross (ARC) has always been one of the most important partners of the federal, state, and local governments in disaster preparedness and relief operations. Some of the daily community operations of the Red Cross chapters include senior services, caregivers' support, provision of hospital and nursing home volunteers, lifeline (an electronic personal emergency response service), transportation to medical/doctor's appointments and other essential trips, food pantry and hot lunch programs, homeless shelters and transitional housing services, school clubs and community service learning programs and projects, youth programs (violence and substance abuse prevention, peer education and mentoring, leadership development camps), food and rental assistance, language banks, and community information and referral.

From the first $10.3 million in federal grants provided to involve citizen volunteers in homeland security efforts in 2002, the ARC received $1,778,978, which was distributed by the national headquarters to many individual chapters. The recipient of the greatest portion of these funds was the Greater New York chapter, which received $500,000 of the funds for the recruitment, training, and mobilization of 5,000 new disaster volunteers equipped to respond to another terrorist attack on a local level. These volunteers work with Red Cross service delivery units in New York to train additional volunteers, exponentially increasing the city's force of disaster relief workers.

In 2002, another $371,978 was given to the ARC National Headquarters for a nationwide program aimed at increasing volunteers in communities most vulnerable to terrorist attacks. The grant supported a year-long program with 30 Community Preparedness Corps (CPC) members working in 19 chapters. Corps members worked in chapters to ensure that all community members — totaling some 27 million — have a "family disaster response plan." They tailored plans for those with language barriers and disabilities and for children and the elderly. At the same time, CPC volunteers focused on minimizing intolerance across the country by teaching international humanitarian law and the principles of the International Red Cross Movement (humanity, independence, neutrality, impartiality, voluntary service, unity, and universality).

Corps members also recruited and trained an estimated 400 new volunteers and instructors who made the educational programs available to additional vulnerable communities. Ultimately, corps members working through Red Cross chapters will create a network of hundreds of skilled volunteers across the country.

Additional grants have since been awarded to Red Cross chapters nationwide. In California, funds have been dedicated to the implementation of homeland security measures in Los Angeles, San Francisco, and Sacramento. The Oregon Trail Chapter was awarded a grant funding 400 new volunteers will perform 1,500 hours of service to disaster preparedness. On the East Coast, the Red Cross developed "Disaster Resistant Neighborhood" programs across eight wards of Washington, DC. Through the program these communities created disaster response plans. The southeast Pennsylvania chapter received a grant to create an alliance of more than 100 nonprofits in the Philadelphia area to form the Southeast Pennsylvania Voluntary Organization Active in Disaster (VOAD) to help citizens prevent, prepare for, and respond to disasters.

In 2003, the ARC participated in the TOPOFF 2 national training exercise. The Red Cross used this exercise to practice the screening of emergency shelter residents and supplies for radiation exposure, the logistical support when national stockpiles of medications were mobilized, and keeping the public informed as the national threat level reached the highest "red" alert. In the same year the Red Cross was actively involved with the development of the new National Response Plan. The ARC was the only nongovernmental organization that was invited to the discussions.

Throughout 2004, the Red Cross taught 11 million Americans critical life-saving skills such as first aid, water safety, caregiving, CPR, and the use of automated external defibrillators (AEDs). In addition, the number of people attending presentations or demonstrations for Together We Prepare, community disaster education awareness, and the Masters of Disasters program climbed 6% to 3.9 million. Those programs aim to create safer families and communities.

Another 2004 initiative from the Red Cross involved expanding to diverse audiences with important preparedness and other information. To achieve this goal, the Red Cross expanded and detailed its Spanish-language website and first-aid and preparedness print materials. In cooperation with the CDC the Red Cross initiated a multiyear project to develop and disseminate terrorism preparedness materials to the public.

In 2005, the year of several major hurricanes, some criticism emerged regarding the way the ARC handled its duties during those disasters. In the days leading to the landfall of Hurricane Katrina at the shores of Florida, the ARC was initially praised for its proactive approach in prestaging volunteers and mass care resources, but as the disaster unfolded and showed its destructive face in larger geographies, issues concerning the ARC response to the disaster became more apparent. At the center of the problem were issues between FEMA and the ARC regarding rules of engagement as partners under the new National Response Plan. A Government Accountability Office (GAO) study that looked at the relationship of the two agencies during and after Katrina sheds light on some of the specific issues.

One major issue was the different interpretation of emergency support function 6 (ESF#6) responsibilities and process flow by FEMA and the ARC. The ARC and FEMA are the designated primary agencies for ESF#6 in charge of mass care, housing, and human services. The ARC is directly responsible for mass care. The NRP tasks an ESF#6 coordinator, a FEMA official with the oversight and coordination of all ESF#6 activities including mass care, which according to the ARC is not a perfect model since it designates the oversight of a core ARC competency to a non-ARC official. Therefore, during its response to Katrina, ARC in some instances bypassed the ESF#6 coordinator and tried to work with the FEMA Operations Section Chief. This resulted in tensions between the ARC and FEMA, and in many instances undermined a very much needed partnership between the two agencies.

Another issue that the ARC was criticized for was the frequently changing personnel at facilities that required ongoing working relationships with the staff of other agencies, primarily FEMA. Those short shifts also reduced the exposure of ARC representatives to the operational environment of the ESF#6. The primary explanation for this problem was the ARC's predisposition for involvement in disasters with much shorter life spans, and requiring shorter periods of continuous staffing – neither of which describe the needs of the Hurricane Katrina response where ESF#6 was active for more than three months. Also, since a significant portion of ARC personnel are volunteers, it is more difficult to engage those individuals in longer-term deployments than shorter ones.

In its response to GAO findings, the ARC underlined that it followed the guidance provided in the National Response Plan as it worked with FEMA during Hurricane Katrina. Nevertheless, it is also mentioned that ARC and FEMA are in the process of developing policies and procedures to formalize their agreement on seemingly gray areas of responsibility and ESF#6 operations. Regarding the issues of frequent ARC personnel changes in ESF#6, ARC reports that it has improved the content of its ESF#6 training and hired 14 permanent employees to be trained in ESF#6 procedures and deployed at strategic locations in multiple states to coordinate with state emergency management agencies and officials. (GAO, 2006; PBS, 2005; DHS, 2004).

Two other issues the ARC faced during its response to Hurricane Katrina were the fraudulent money transfers by some ARC subcontractors, and unacceptably long wait times on phone-based services. ARC provides cash payments to disaster victims to help them get through the first few days of a disaster until other means of relief become available. During Hurricane Katrina, ARC established call centers manned by subcontractors to register and provide cash payments to hurricane victims using the money wiring services of a private contractor. The procedure did not have adequate checks and protection against fraudulent money transfers, therefore a group of employees working for the subcontractor staffing the call center found loop holes to transfer money to themselves and their relatives who were not victims of the hurricane. None of those workers were actual ARC employees or volunteers. ARC has also been criticized by people trying to reach the call centers in that wait times were extremely long, and in many instances, hours. Some experts explain those management problems are the result of the unique financial structure of the ARC, which heavily relies on donations; donors generally want their money spent strictly on direct assistance of hurricane victims rather than fixing administrative or managerial problems. This may minimize budgets to fix problems related to functions such as operations, finance, and accounting. (*Washington Post*, 2005).

DIGGING DEEPER: INFLUENZA PANDEMIC MITIGATION AND PREPAREDNESS

An influenza pandemic is regarded as potentially the next large disaster that may threaten the entire globe and require the involvement of many nations and the international community for effective mitigation, prevention, preparedness, and response. *Pandemic* is the global outbreak of an infectious disease. The influenza pandemic is different than the seasonal flu in many ways. Among the differences are:

- Large or global geographic impact as opposed to local impacts of the seasonal flu
- Potential to quickly exhaust available resources of national health systems
- Potential to require medical supply and vaccine availability that is drastically different than what is required to deal with the seasonal flu to deal with a possible mandatory need to vaccinate masses of people within a very short timeframe
- Long-lasting impact on the operations of the government, the general public, and the business sectors caused by drastic intervention measures, difficult to predict human response to those measures (such as risk perception and panic), suspended or delayed economic activity, and diminished confidence

Three influenza pandemics occurred during the 20th century:

- 1918: killed 675,000 in United States and around 50 million worldwide
- 1957: killed at least 70,000 in United States and 1 to 2 million worldwide
- 1968: killed about 34,000 in United States and 700,000 worldwide

The urgency for influenza pandemic mitigation and preparedness has increased in the past few years primarily due to two important medical incidents that at least partially shared the characteristics of an influenza pandemic or carried the potential to evolve into a serious global pandemic. These two incidents are SARS (severe acute respiratory syndrome) and avian influenza (bird-flu). While some characteristics of the two diseases seem to be similar, essentially the root causes and the contagious behavior of those diseases are different. While both are potentially fatal respiratory infections that first initiated in animals and then made the jump to humans with similar flu-like symptoms such as fever and difficulty breathing, there are two major differences. First, avian influenza is caused by a flu virus, whereas SARS has roots similar to the common cold. The second and more important difference is that SARS can be transmitted between humans, whereas in most cases of the avian flu, the transmission has occurred from a bird to a human.

SARS originated in southern China in late 2002. In February 2003, cases were reported in Hong Kong (China). In just a few days, cases were observed in Vietnam, Singapore, Canada, and Germany. Between November 2002 and July 2003, more than 8,000 cases of SARS were reported globally. Those cases caused 774 deaths in 26 countries — most of which were in the Western Pacific.

Avian influenza is bird disease caused by type "A" strains of the influenza virus. While most birds are vulnerable to the virus, many wild bird species carry the viruses with no apparent symptoms. Of all strains of avian influenza "A" viruses, only four are known to have caused human infections: H5N1, H7N3, H7N7, and H9N2. H5N1 causes the most dangerous and fatal infections for humans. From 2003 to 2008, 349 human cases of the avian flu from 14 countries were reported to the World Health Organization, of which 216 were fatal. Indonesia and Vietnam had the highest numbers of human avian influenza deaths, with 94 and 47 lives lost, respectively. While the H5N1 is still primarily a virus that can transmit from an infected bird to a human, cases of human-to-human transmission have been confirmed in at least three incidents in Thailand, Indonesia, and Pakistan. In all of those instances, the transmission occurred through extended close contact (caretaker and infected person). Scientists are not too concerned about this type of transmission, since it is highly preventable, but the possibility of a mutation in the virus genetic code

(Continued)

**DIGGING DEEPER: INFLUENZA PANDEMIC MITIGATION
AND PREPAREDNESS –(CONTINUED)**

that makes the transmission among humans much easier and faster is of real concern to public health officials (see figure).

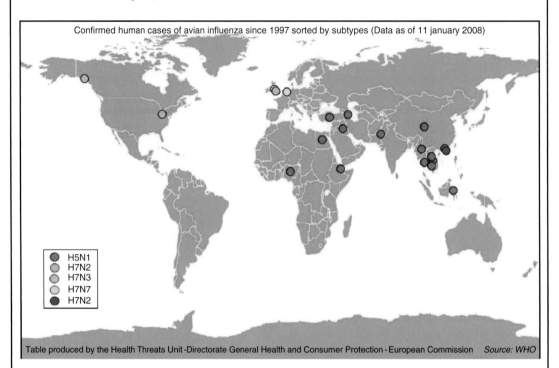

Confirmed human cases of avian influenza since 1997 sorted by subtypes (Data as of 11 january 2008)

H5N1
H7N2
H7N3
H7N7
H7N2

Table produced by the Health Threats Unit -Directorate General Health and Consumer Protection - European Commission *Source: WHO*

Confirmed human cases of avian influenza since 1997 sorted by subtypes. (Data source: World Health Organization, January 11, 2008, http://www.who.org. Map by European Commission Directorate General Health and Consumer Protection, 2008, http://ec.europa.eu/health/ph_threats/com/Influenza/ai_human_en.htm)

Because the entire world is at risk of influenza pandemic, every country is expected to enable resources for preparedness and response in case of a potential outbreak. The World Health Organization supports those efforts by making information, data, knowledge, expertise, research, and guidelines available to the international community. In 2005, the World Health Organization released the "Checklist for Influenza Pandemic Preparedness Planning." The goal of the checklist is to provide national planning authorities a list of required and desired tasks to be completed to achieve a minimum level of preparedness that would increase the chance of success in an actual influenza pandemic response. The checklist is intentionally kept generic to ensure applicability in many nations with varying levels of resources and technical expertise. The checklist includes the following seven items:

1. **Preparing for an emergency:** This step involves the completion of preplanning activities such as the creation of political and public awareness regarding influenza pandemic, the establishment of an overall preparedness strategy, and the appropriation of a budget adequate to sustain preparedness activities and to pay for resources deemed essential in the preparedness strategy.
2. **Surveillance:** Surveillance is one of the most critical steps of pandemic preparedness, as early detection of an outbreak is key to minimize further spread of the disease and initiation of a timely response. Unique and complex predictive procedures may be necessary to detect an outbreak in a timely fashion, which should effectively monitor and analyze multiple

parameters that may be early signals of an upcoming influenza pandemic. For example, constant monitoring of daily cases that report to hospitals with flu-like symptoms may help in the creation of confidence intervals that designate normal conditions and abnormal conditions that may be associated with an uncommon demand for medical care related to a new flu outbreak.

3. **Case investigation and treatment:** This step ensures the creation of capability and resources to complete a first assessment of a virus when it shows signs of a known influenza strain. Adequate laboratory capability is mandatory. Established communication mechanisms with the World Trade Organization and other relevant organizations should occur to disseminate valuable new information in a timely fashion. Guidelines on clinical treatment of the new case should be established along with adequate training for first-response personnel.

4. **Preventing spread of the disease in the community:** Identification and initiation of postincident mitigation and prevention activities are crucial to stop dispersion of the disease to the general public, thus preventing an influenza pandemic outbreak. Some of the activities involved in this step are restrictions to mobility, setup of check points, creation of rules for hospital admissions, creation of a communication system with the general public, and identification of priority rules in case vaccination becomes necessary with a limited supply of vaccine or other preventive medical supplies.

5. **Maintaining essential services:** Government organizations and other vital services should have internal organizational continuity plans to make sure that they can still provide the services the public expects from them even under the extreme operational conditions of an influenza pandemic outbreak. Government agencies in most nations have laws that require them to develop continuity plans, but those plans should be revised and improved based on the unique sets of challenges that may be posed as a direct consequence of the pandemic outbreak.

6. **Research and evaluation:** While countries dealing with an actual influenza pandemic outbreak are very likely to become stretched for resources, an actual outbreak is an important opportunity for research and data collection to improve existing strategies and to test control measures applied for their level of effectiveness. Therefore, nations should make research and evaluation part of their response strategy and establish relationships and partnerships with other nations to ensure that scientific exchange among research communities is not impaired by the circumstances of the ongoing incident.

7. **Implementation, testing, and revision of national plan:** Revision of the national plan for applicability and testing it to improve its use during an actual outbreak are necessary. Make sure to set clear goals and measures of effectiveness that make progress evaluation of the plan easier during actual plan activation.

In the United States, the Department of Health and Human Services (HHS) holds primary responsibility for the coordination of influenza pandemic preparedness, as determined by the Homeland Security Council document, "National Strategy for Pandemic Influenza." The strategy identifies the following three pillars for effective management of a potential influenza pandemic:

Preparedness and communications: Understand roles and responsibilities of different government agencies for the purposes of a potential influenza pandemic outbreak. Establish communications mechanisms and chain of command for effective incident management and decision making.

Surveillance and detection: Ensure continuous "situational awareness" for timely identification outbreaks to limit the spread and to protect the public.

(Continued)

The Role of the Private Sector in Mitigation and Preparedness Activities

The events of September 11 brought to light the importance of private-sector involvement in crisis, emergency, and disaster management. Since that time, an ever-expanding list of private entities has begun focusing on their needs in this area. This section will discuss the essentials of private-sector business continuity planning and disaster management. Most of the components discussed next have been learned as a result of experience with natural disasters or man-made accidents; however, the September 11 attacks have proved that those important components of classical crisis management are also important for terrorism risk management.

Business impact analysis (BIA): The management-level analysis by which an organization assesses the quantitative (financial) and qualitative (nonfinancial) impacts, effects, and loss that might result if the organization were to suffer a business-interrupting event. Performing BIA as a preparedness measure is important because findings from BIA are used to make decisions concerning business continuity management strategy.

Crisis communications planning: Decision making about how crisis communications will be performed during an emergency is important because communication is a critical success factor for effective crisis management. Preventing rumors about your corporation as well as telling your story before someone else does it for you is only possible via a predefined communication policy.

Information technology (IT) and systems infrastructure redundancy planning: There are different techniques and approaches regarding the enforcement of systems redundancy. Each company is unique, with its own IT and system needs and processes; therefore, customized approaches have to be employed to build more reliable systems infrastructure (e.g., backup databases, software, hardware, network redundancy).

Geographic location and backup sites: The selection of the geographic location of headquarters and offices and the distribution of key executives in those buildings are strategically important decisions with regard to minimizing potential losses (both human and physical) during a disaster. The availability of backup sites that allow employees to continue operations in case of physical loss of or damage to a primary facility is a key success factor, but, unfortunately, is usually difficult to justify in terms of cost and benefit.

Transportation planning: The transportation infrastructure is one of the most sensitive infrastructures to emergency and disaster situations. Overloaded transportation infrastructure during crisis is usually a reason for microdisasters in the midst of bigger ones. Therefore, realistic transportation planning is important for a successful response.

Crisis leadership: Research and experience has shown that during crisis situations, people (e.g., employees, staff, customers) need someone to tell them what is going on and explain what is being done about it, even if the information this person communicates is obsolete or redundant. Strong leadership also helps people to regain self-esteem and motivates them to commit to the efforts to overcome the crisis.

Insurance: It is important for companies to have a feasible but protective insurance policy. Realistic risk assessments and modeling are necessary to establish this economic feasibility.

There surely are other components of private-sector risk mitigation and preparedness that are not mentioned in this text; however, these are the most important across the broad range of business types and sizes (Kayyem and Chang, 2002; Smith, 2002). See the sidebar titled "Private-Sector Homeland Security Checklist" for assistance provided by the DHS.

Private-Sector Homeland Security Checklist

The Department of Homeland Security released the following antiterror checklist for the private sector in its May 2003 Homeland Security Information Bulletin:

- Maintain situational awareness of world events and ongoing threats.
- Ensure all levels of personnel are notified via briefings, e-mail, voice mail, and signage of any changes in threat conditions and protective measures.
- Encourage personnel to be alert and immediately report any situation that may constitute a threat or suspicious activity.
- Encourage personnel to avoid routines, vary times and routes, preplan, and keep a low profile, especially during periods of high threat.
- Encourage personnel to take notice and report suspicious packages, devices, unattended briefcases, or other unusual materials immediately; inform them not to handle or attempt to move any such object.
- Encourage personnel to keep their family members and supervisors apprised of their whereabouts.
- Encourage personnel to know emergency exits and stairwells.
- Increase the number of visible security personnel wherever possible.
- Rearrange exterior vehicle barriers, traffic cones, and roadblocks to alter traffic patterns near facilities and cover by alert security forces.
- Institute/increase vehicle, foot, and roving security patrols varying in size, timing, and routes.
- Implement random security guard shift changes.
- Arrange for law enforcement vehicles to be parked randomly near entrances and exits.
- Review current contingency plans and, if not already in place, develop and implement procedures for receiving and acting on threat information; alert notification procedures; terrorist incident response procedures; evacuation procedures; bomb threat procedures; hostage and barricade procedures; chemical, biological, radiological, and nuclear (CBRN) procedures; consequence and crisis management procedures; accountability procedures; and media procedures.
- When the aforementioned plans and procedures have been implemented, conduct internal training exercises and invite local emergency responders (fire, rescue, medical, and bomb squads) to participate in joint exercises.
- Coordinate and establish partnerships with local authorities to develop intelligence and information-sharing relationships.
- Place personnel on standby for contingency planning.
- Limit the number of access points, and strictly enforce access control procedures.

- Approach all illegally parked vehicles in and around facilities, question drivers, and direct them to move immediately; if the owner cannot be identified, have vehicle towed by law enforcement.
- Consider installing telephone caller ID; record phone calls, if necessary.
- Increase perimeter lighting.
- Deploy visible security cameras and motion sensors.
- Remove vegetation in and around perimeters; maintain regularly.
- Institute a robust vehicle inspection program to include checking under the undercarriage of vehicles, under the hood, and in the trunk. Provide vehicle inspection training to security personnel.
- Deploy explosive detection devices and explosive detection canine teams.
- Conduct vulnerability studies focusing on physical security, structural engineering, infrastructure engineering, and power, water, and air infiltration, if feasible.
- Initiate a system to enhance mail and package screening procedures (both announced and unannounced).
- Install special locking devices on manhole covers in and around facilities.
- Implement a countersurveillance detection program.

Source: Continuity Central, May 21, 2003.

Corporate Preparedness and Risk Management in the Sarbanes-Oxley Era

The Sarbanes-Oxley Act of 2002, written by Senator Paul Sarbanes (D-MD) and Representative Paul Oxley (R-OH), was created to protect investors by improving the accuracy and reliability of corporate disclosures. The act is in direct response to financial fraud discovered in the cases of both Enron and WorldCom. However, it was created to cover issues beyond fraud (establishing a public company accounting oversight board, auditor independence, corporate responsibility, and enhanced financial disclosure), and is now a driving force behind corporate business continuity planning. Although the phrase business continuity planning is not once mentioned in the language of the act, continuity professionals claim that Section 404 of the act implies that such measures must be taken for compliance. Section 404 of the act reads as follows:

SEC. 404. MANAGEMENT ASSESSMENT OF INTERNAL CONTROLS.
(a) RULES REQUIRED — The Commission shall prescribe rules requiring each annual report required by section 13(a) or 15(d) of the Securities Exchange Act of 1934 (15 U.S.C. 78m or 78o(d)) to contain an internal control report, which shall
  (1) state the responsibility of management for establishing and maintaining an adequate internal control structure and procedures for financial reporting; and
  (2) contain an assessment, as of the end of the most recent fiscal year of the issuer, of the effectiveness of the internal control structure and procedures of the issuer for financial reporting.
(b) INTERNAL CONTROL EVALUATION AND REPORTING — With respect to the internal control assessment required by subsection (a), each registered public accounting firm that prepares or issues the audit report for the issuer shall attest to, and report on, the assessment made by the management of the issuer. An attestation made under this subsection shall be

made in accordance with standards for attestation engagements issued or adopted by the Board. Any such attestation shall not be the subject of a separate engagement. (Sarbanes Oxley Act of 2002, http://thomas.loc.gov/cgi-bin/query/F?c107:6:./temp/~c107 × 5GHak: e143423.)

Section 404 of Sarbanes-Oxley Act requires companies to include an internal control report that states the responsibility of management for establishing and maintaining an adequate internal controls structure and procedures for financial reporting in their annual report. In addition, it requires management to ensure that the effectiveness of the internal control structure is assessed on an annual basis. The section also requires the external auditing entity to report on management's assessment of the effectiveness of the company's internal controls and procedures with respect to standards defined by the Public Company Accounting Oversight Board. Compliance with the act became effective in April 2005 for most companies.

Even though the section still focuses on financial record management and process control, in order to really ensure those things, it is almost a prerequisite for the company to ensure adequate protection and continuity of its entire core processes. This is where the "business continuity" aspect of the act becomes evident.

To protect the financial processes and records from misconduct or fraud, and to ensure data integrity and resilience, the first step is to identify the risks, threats, and vulnerabilities that may endanger those expectations defined by the act. This is possible through a comprehensive risk and vulnerability assessment followed by a business impact analysis (BIA) to identify the business consequences of possible adverse incidents. The BIA is usually considered as one of the main building blocks of business continuity planning, because its findings usually help the corporations identify and prioritize the risks it has to mitigate, and provide an understanding of recovery goals.

At present, it is too early to comment on whether there is full consensus between what the Sarbanes-Oxley Act demands from corporations and how the corporations interpret those expectations and what they are going to do about it. But it is true that business continuity concepts will adequately address some of the expectations of the act. Business continuity service providers seem to capitalize on this connection and enlarge the market for their services and products. The fact that the Sarbanes-Oxley Act places responsibility for compliance on top management makes it inevitable that these corporations will increase investments aimed at compliance. Business continuity is one of the answers.

Based on recent reports (2007), corporate spending on Sarbanes-Oxley increased until 2005, and stabilized at about $6 billion a year. This includes all the money that corporations spend to comply with the requirements of the 2002 Act (Reuters, "Sarbanes-Oxley Spending Seen at $6 Billion in 2007," February 22, 2007).

A recent BCP-focused journal article has indicated that compliance may require more than basic business continuity planning. The article explained that the act will make senior management involvement in the planning process inevitable, and thus will require them to think about and find solutions beyond their organizations, while paying more attention to service level agreements, continuity of vendors, and suppliers (Benvenuto, 2004; Berman, 2004; Williams, 2005).

DIGGING DEEPER: U.S. GOVERNMENT GUIDANCE ON PANDEMIC PREPAREDNESS PLANNING FOR BUSINESSES WITH OVERSEAS OPERATIONS

Due to the global nature of a potential pandemic influenza outbreak, a panel of representative U.S. agencies (i.e., Department of State, Department of Health and Human Services, Department of Commerce, and Centers for Disease Control and Prevention) have established pandemic planning guidelines for U.S. businesses with overseas operations. A summary of the guidelines follows. The

---

full document can be found at http://www.pandemicflu.gov/plan/workplaceplanning/businesses overseaspdf.pdf.

Plan for Maintaining Business Continuity during and after a Pandemic

- Select a pandemic coordinator at every international facility to oversee local planning, implementation and ensure coordination with organization's overall pandemic coordinator.
- Establish pandemic planning and implementation team(s) at every international facility, including chain of command, with roles, responsibilities, authorities, and lines of communication.
- Understand national and local governments' policies and the potential impact they may have on your business operations and emergency plans.
- Analyze the capability of national and local governments to provide assistance to your company.
- Prepare for the impact of a currency devaluation on your business operations during a pandemic.
- Monitor the status of pandemic as reported through the World Health Organization (WHO) (www.who.int/csr/disease/avian_influenza/en/) and other official sources such as PandemicFlu.gov (www.pandemicflu.gov/).
- Identify circumstances under which business may be forced to close or reduce levels of service.
- Identify essential staff and other critical inputs (e.g., raw materials, suppliers, subcontractor, and logistics) required to maintain critical operations by location and function during a pandemic.
- Identify potential pandemic effects on supply chain and shipments, particularly if the organization uses "just-in-time" delivery.
- Work with suppliers and clients to ensure that all pandemic plans work together to maintain business continuity in the event of transportation or distribution disruptions in accordance with priorities.
- Identify and develop plan to augment the current workforce capability (e.g., engaging temporary workers, cross-train workforce) with special attention to redundant staffing of critical operations.
- Identify business functions that could be outsourced or transferred to other facilities within the organization in the event of high employee absenteeism.
- Review business insurance policies to determine what coverage may be necessary to mitigate the country-specific risks and effects of a pandemic.
- Test plans through regular exercises and revise plans on a periodic basis.

Plan for the Impact of a Pandemic on the Lives and Welfare of Your Employees

- Understand local and national health policies and plans regarding possible quarantines, border closures, airport closures, school closures, and transportation closures.
- Forecast and allow for employee absences during a pandemic due to factors such as personal illness, mental health needs, family member illness, community containment measures and quarantines, school and/or business closures, and public transportation closures.
- Ensure staffing plans have sufficient redundancy to allow for anticipated absenteeism, and cross-train employees to fill essential vacancies that might occur.
- Review and analyze labor laws that determine your obligations to personnel.
- Identify employees with special health or other needs and incorporate the requirements of such persons into your preparedness plan.

- Encourage annual seasonal influenza vaccination for appropriate employees using local public health guidelines.
- Assess availability of medical advice, health care, prescription medications, mental health services, social services, and other support services for employees during a pandemic.
- Review business health insurance policies to determine what coverage may be necessary to mitigate the country-specific risks and effects of a pandemic, and assess changes necessary.
- Assess potential availability of pandemic vaccine in host country, determine its reliability, and plan for its distribution during a pandemic.
- Evaluate need for antiviral medications and plan for access, storage, dispensing by medical personnel, and distribution consistent with local laws and regulations.
- Determine if in-country medical services and/or medications will be available for employees during a pandemic, and consider planning for early evacuation and/or repositioning, if needed.
- Remind employees that normal supply lines may be slowed or inoperable for an extended period of time and to make personal preparations for pandemic for up to 12 weeks.

Establish Policies and Guidelines to Be Implemented during a Pandemic to Avoid Creating Policies "On Demand" in the Midst of a Pandemic

- Establish triggers and set up procedures for activating and terminating company response plan.
- Establish a security plan that includes personnel, asset, and infrastructure protection. Prepare for the possibility of social/security breakdown.
- Align business policies with national and local labor laws.
- Develop and create guidelines for the possible downsizing and evacuation of expatriate employees and families. Guidelines should identify multiple evacuation locations.
- Develop policies for restricting travel (domestic and international) to affected areas and guidance for employees or visitors returning from affected areas.
- Develop options for conducting safer customer contacts in the event of pandemic.
- Develop guidelines to prevent influenza spread at worksite, including facility cleaning and disinfection and social distancing methods to modify frequency and type of contact.
- Develop guidelines to inform and address needs of employees whose jobs will not allow telework (e.g., production or assembly-line workers).
- Establish and clearly communicate policies on sick leave, family leave, and employee compensation. Advise employees who are ill with influenza during a pandemic to stay home.
- Develop or expand guidelines for conducting business online with customers and suppliers, allowing self-service when possible.
- Provide policies and training for employees in the use of personal protective equipment (PPE).
- Determine the need and arrange for appropriate PPE based on WHO and CDC recommendations and provide necessary training.
- Develop culturally and linguistically appropriate guidelines on modes of influenza transmission, symptoms of infection, basic infection control, contingency plans, and travel awareness.
- Establish policies for alternate or flexible worksite (e.g., videoconferencing and telecommuting) and work hours.

Determine Resources Required to Fulfill Actions in Your Pandemic Plan

- Maintain a contact list of current suppliers and develop an alternate list of suppliers for critical supplies and essential resources and services.
- Maintain sufficient and accessible infection control supplies (e.g., hand-hygiene products, tissues, receptacles for their disposal, surgical masks, and thermometers) at all business locations.

(Continued)

DIGGING DEEPER: U.S. GOVERNMENT GUIDANCE ON PANDEMIC PREPAREDNESS PLANNING FOR BUSINESSES WITH OVERSEAS OPERATIONS–(CONTINUED)

- Ensure availability of medical consultations and advice for emergency response.
- Enhance communications and information technology infrastructure as needed to support telecommuting and remote employee and customer access.
- Work with local law enforcement and security firms to develop security plans to protect operations, facilities, and so on.

Create an Emergency Communications System

- Disseminate pandemic plan to all employees and stakeholders in advance of a pandemic, including expected roles/actions for employees and other stakeholders during implementation.
- Maintain current contact information for staff, ancillary personnel, clients, and other stakeholders.
- Anticipate employee fear, anxiety, rumors, and misinformation.
- Ensure that communications are culturally and linguistically appropriate.
- Develop 24/7 means (e.g., hotline, dedicated website) for communicating pandemic status updates/actions to employees and service delivery news to vendors and customers.
- Develop alternate forms of communication (e.g., cell phones, pagers, and other processes, etc.). Consider the lack of modern communication devices in many developing countries.
- Disseminate information for at-home care of ill employees and family members.
- Establish system to account for employee status (e.g., dial-in system).

Work to Coordinate with External Organizations and Your Community

- Familiarize staff with the role of the WHO in pandemic response in your country and region.
- Select point of contact to coordinate with the U.S. embassy or consulate that is nearest to your facility. The embassy may facilitate introductions for business sector to local ministries and officials.
- Coordinate and collaborate with local chambers of commerce or other business associations.
- Collaborate with local and national health officials and emergency responders.
- Share best practices with other businesses to improve community response efforts.

Prepare for Postpandemic Scenarios

- Assess ability and criteria that need to be met to resume normal operations and provide notification of activation of the business resumption plan.
- Assess availability of medical, mental health, and social services for staff after the pandemic.
- Conduct postpandemic review of response and revise plan as needed.
- Prepare for possible follow-on pandemic waves.

Source: U.S. Department of Health and Human Services, "Pandemic Preparedness Planning for US Businesses with Overseas Operations," 2007.

Best Practices

The nature of crisis, emergency, and risk management is very complicated: No matter how much one may discuss the process in the theoretical sense, the complexity of the actual environment in which they must try to implement practical applications cannot be fully appreciated. The two case studies that follow will document private-sector experience with disaster and a multigovernmental approach to preparedness.

The first of the following cases details the experience of Cantor Fitzgerald, a private company devastated by the September 11 attacks. Although the case is mainly concerned with response and recovery, it is included in the mitigation and preparedness chapter because it clearly illustrates the importance that mitigation and preparedness play in the response to a disaster.

CASE STUDY 1: CANTOR FITZGERALD

For Joseph Noviello, September 11 began at 6:30 AM with a phone call confirming that an annual fishing trip with colleagues at the Cantor Fitzgerald bond trading firm was still on, despite some foul weather offshore. Minutes later, the most intense two days of his life would begin as the first plane hijacked by terrorists crashed into Cantor's building.

Watching on TV from his Manhattan apartment, Noviello had no way of knowing what lay in store. Clearly, this was a disaster of a proportion that neither he, nor likely anyone in his position, had dealt with before. Fortunately, he had a plan to follow.

That plan may have saved the company. No firm suffered a worse fate, in terms of lives lost on September 11, than Cantor Fitzgerald and its electronic marketplace unit, eSpeed. More than 700 employees of the two companies died in the destruction of the World Trade Center's north tower, where Cantor and eSpeed shared their headquarters and a vital computer center. Yet eSpeed was up and running when the bond market reopened at 8 AM on September 13, little more than 47 hours after the disaster.

"The difference for us was the planning we had in place," says Noviello, 36, who was promoted to eSpeed's chief information officer after the disaster. eSpeed's systems were built on a dual architecture that replicated all machines, connections, and functionality at the World Trade Center and at a Rochelle Park site, with a third facility in London.

eSpeed, which operates as a freestanding business and also serves as the trading engine for its parent company, lost 180 employees, including about half of its U.S.-based technology staff. But eSpeed had several important assets left. Most of the top technology executives had been out of the office, including Matt Claus, eSpeed's current CTO and Noviello's right-hand man, who had been scheduled to go on the fishing trip.

The response atmosphere was tense, with people unsure as to what had happened to their friends or colleagues. "For days, every time a new face came in the door it was an emotional release," says Noviello. "There was a disaster-recovery contact list, but people were seeking to find each other not for work but to find out who was okay."

Beyond the technical questions were operational details such as advising staff on public transportation options to the suburban site, reestablishing shifts, and making sure there were counselors on duty. Conference calls every two hours kept track of milestones and objectives. "We were talking at 2 AM, at 4 AM," says Noviello. "Who is sleeping during something like this? Work is great therapy."

None of this effort would have succeeded without the duplicate architecture in Rochelle Park. Yet Cantor started moving into the facility only in February. From day one, Rochelle Park was seen as a concurrent system, not a disaster-recovery site.

All that redundancy would be stretched to the limit as eSpeed worked to overcome the technical hurdles before the opening of the bond market Thursday morning. Two of those hurdles were huge: the loss of eSpeed's private network connections and the destruction of the company's ability to handle fulfillment of trades.

The first problem was solved by allowing customers who had overseas offices connected to Cantor's London data center to reroute across their own networks to London. eSpeed worked with

(Continued)

CASE STUDY 1: CANTOR FITZGERALD – (CONTINUED)

customers to reconfigure their servers to point to London and moved or expanded the permissions on customer accounts to connect to that site. For customers without overseas private networks, eSpeed worked to get them access over the Internet until the customers could get their high-speed connections hooked into the Rochelle Park facility.

To solve the second issue, help arrived in the form of one of eSpeed's competitors. ICI/ADP, another electronic trading company, offered to take care of eSpeed's clearing and settling of transactions through its own connection to banks. By Wednesday night, the eSpeed team had mapped its financial back-office system to ADP's system and had successfully sent test transactions to J.P. Morgan Chase & Co. and other banks. The cooperation of other companies, including vendors and fellow financial firms, turned out to be essential to Cantor/eSpeed's quick recovery.

The firm was weakened by the loss of so many people and the related shutdown of its voice-broker business. But it survived as a viable business. Thanks to planning, the company can keep operating, even if something should happen to Rochelle Park. Its data center in London will serve as the mirror site going forward.

And going forward, the company's systems should be even more resilient. "We are learning a lot of lessons as we are restoring the system," says Noviello, including how to automate more aspects of bringing systems back up. "And we are not restoring our bad habits" (Summarized from the original work of Edward Cone and Sean Gallagher, in *Baseline Magazine*, www.baselinemag.com/print_article/0,3668,a17022,00.asp).

The second case provided is adapted from a governmental preparedness activity, a drill that simulated a radiological and biological terrorist attack to the United States called TOPOFF 2 (Figure 6–6).

FIGURE 6–6 Washington, DC, May 13, 2003 — FEMA's Emergency Support Team employees were TOPOFF 2 exercise participants as well as assistants with the response and recovery efforts for the tornadoes that hit the South and Midwest. (Photo by Lauren Hobart/FEMA News Photo)

CASE STUDY 2: TOPOFF 2

On Monday, May 12, 2003, a fake dirty bomb was detonated in downtown Seattle, releasing radioactive material throughout the metropolitan area. At the same time in Chicago, hospitals were inundated with patients complaining of flu-like symptoms associated with pneumonic plague.

Fortunately, the mastermind of both scenarios was not a terrorist group but, rather, the federal government. With a price tag of $16 million, TOPOFF 2 has been the most expensive, comprehensive emergency preparedness exercise ever undertaken.

Designed to test and improve the response capacity of "top officials" in the event of a weapons of mass destruction attack, TOPOFF 2 included more than 8,000 participants from 19 federal agencies, such as the CDC and FEMA, as well as state and local emergency responders, and the ARC, the only nongovernmental agency included in the exercise.

The goals of TOPOFF 2 were to improve the nation's capacity to manage extreme events; create broader frameworks for the operation of expert crisis and consequence management systems; validate authorities, strategies, plans, policies, procedures, and protocols; and build a sustainable, systematic national exercise program to support the national strategy for homeland security.

The fake crisis began around lunchtime on Monday, with the detonation of a radioactive dirty bomb near a coffee roasting plant in Seattle. Two cars were set afire, releasing plumes of smoke. A small explosion was created. Actors playing victims began to moan and cry. A mock television-news crew broke through a police barrier to get at the action. Some of the first emergency workers on the scene ran through the wreckage. Others ambled.

Emergency response staff at all 17 King County hospitals immediately swung into action, directed by Harborview Medical Center's Emergency Services department. Staff members were able to follow the crisis on a virtual TV network set up exclusively for the drill.

A short time later, Harborview employees learned that the explosive device contained radioactive material, although they did not know what kind of radiation was involved. The decontamination team — designated emergency response medical staff, plus engineering and public safety personnel — was called in and began setting up a heated decontamination tent on the road by the hospital's emergency response wing.

Only six people arrived in the first 90 minutes of the crisis, and the rest trickled in later in the afternoon. In the end, Harborview treated about 30 patients, all of whom "survived."

Just 24 hours later and halfway across the country, the scene was quite different as very sick people began turning up in emergency responses in Chicago and across Illinois. Their devastating symptoms were quickly diagnosed as pneumonic plague, unleashed in a biological attack by the same terrorist group.

Thirty-six people "died" among the more than 300 infected. At hospitals across the state, infected patients — volunteers wearing bright yellow T-shirts printed with "Role Player" — mixed in with real patients to test hospitals' ability to meet the crisis amid business as usual. Every once in a while, a volunteer would produce a card indicating that he or she had died.

Even more victims were represented by faxes pouring into the hospital containing a name, a diagnosis, a brief medical history, and a summary of physical findings. These "paper patients" were triaged and treated as live bodies, subject to the same hospital resource allocations.

Richard Fantus, MD, chief of Trauma Services at Advocate Illinois Masonic Medical Center on Chicago's north side, acted as incident commander for his hospital. "We knew early on that something unusual was going on because of what was coming across the mock news network and the communications we received from the public health department," Fantus said.

But he noted that diagnosing all the emergency arrivals was not as straightforward as expected. "Victims came in with various symptoms, many having nothing to do with plague. Some had had heart attacks, some were pregnant, and some had the respiratory symptoms of SARS. Just as in real life, we had to identify who was likely to have been exposed and triage them according

(Continued)

to respiratory symptoms," he says. "Staff was gowned and masked and everyone suspected of exposure immediately went into respiratory isolation."

Vivian Chamberlain was an actor who played a passerby when the false bomb exploded. She had to pretend that her eardrums had burst from the force of the bogus blast.

As the first patient to arrive by ambulance at Bellevue's Overlake Hospital Medical Center, Chamberlain screamed and shook, her ears bleeding, her face marked by soot. But before her injuries could be treated, Chamberlain had to be "decontaminated" of radiation.

Her gurney was wheeled into a $30,000 tent set up in the parking lot and manned by hospital staffers wearing "Level C ensembles," sealed jumpsuits with head masks and respirators costing $950 each.

Chamberlain was put on a back board and her T-shirt and shorts were cut off. Four moon-suited workers scrubbed her body with long-handled brushes and hosed her down with unheated water from a nearby fire hydrant.

"It was awful. It was freezing cold," Chamberlain later said of the "decon" shower as she stood shivering in a hospital gown, a white sheet draped over her shoulders.

All did not go smoothly. One male "victim," who was portraying someone with psychiatric problems, refused to put up a fight as instructed by the paper tag on his hand. Prodding by nurses at first could not persuade the shy young man. Finally getting with the program, he "escaped"from the roped-off area. Then hospital guards refused to capture him, saying their jurisdiction was only inside the perimeter.

"You guys need to get him now!" bellowed Vickie Nostrant, a veteran emergency-room nurse and one of 70 hospital staffers participating. The guards immediately complied. The incident is a small example of glitches that the exercise is designed to reveal, nurses said.

At the same time agencies from around the Puget Sound area responded to the mock crisis in Seattle, and some institutions set up their own simultaneous drills.

At Pacific Lutheran University near Tacoma, students and others acted out a terrorist attack that featured a mock car bomb and a hostage situation.

As part of the overall exercise, events took place in Washington, D.C., and Chicago, where a mock bioterror attack was staged at Midway Airport, and a raid was made on a terrorists' lair. City, county, and federal officials proclaimed the drill a success.

For example, Seattle County Executive Ron Sims said he and others discovered how much work is involved in rerouting the county's transportation system. Because of the mock radiation, numerous bus lines had to be rerouted, a move that affected mass transit in King, Pierce, and Snohomish counties.

After each day's activities, local and federal officials in each city met to discuss how things went. Within a month, a 2-day conference for all participants was planned to review the exercise. By September, a full report was submitted outlining strengths and vulnerabilities (various online reports at www.dhs.gov/dhspublic/display?content735, www.redcross.org/news/ds/terrorism/030512TOPOFF .html, www.aamc.org/newsroom/reporter/august03/bioterrorism.htm, www.emergencypreparednessweek .ca/mr_nr_050202_e.shtml, http://seattletimes.nwsource.com/html/localnews/134726076_topoff13m. html, www.envoyworldwide.com/News/ContinuityInsights.pdf).

Exercises to Foster Preparedness

The Homeland Security Council (HSC), in partnership with DHS, and state and local homeland security agencies, has developed 15 all-hazards planning scenarios for use in national, federal, state, and local homeland security preparedness activities. These scenarios are designed to be the foundational structure for the development of national preparedness standards from which homeland security capabilities can be measured. For the earthquake scenario, see the sidebar titled "HSC Scenario 9."

HSC SCENARIO 9: MAJOR EARTHQUAKE

Executive Summary

Casualties: 1,400 fatalities; 100,000 hospitalizations
Infrastructure Damage: 150,000 buildings destroyed, 1 million buildings damaged
Evacuations/Displaced Persons: 300,000 households
Contamination: From hazardous materials, in some areas
Economic Impact: Hundreds of billions
Potential for Multiple Events: Yes, aftershocks
Recovery Timeline: Months to years

Scenario Overview

General description: Earthquakes occur when the plates that form under the Earth's surface suddenly shift, and most earthquakes occur at the boundaries where the plates meet. A fault is a fracture in the Earth's crust along which two blocks of the crust have slipped with respect to each other. The magnitude of an earthquake, usually expressed by the Richter Scale, is a measure of the amplitude of the seismic waves. The intensity, as expressed by the Modified Mercalli Scale, is a subjective measure that describes how strong a shock was felt at a particular location.

The Richter Scale is logarithmic so that a recording of 7, for example, indicates a disturbance with ground motion 10 times as great as a recording of 6. A quake of magnitude 2 is the smallest quake normally felt by people. Earthquakes with a Richter value of 6 or more are commonly considered major; great earthquakes have magnitude of 8 or more. The Modified Mercalli (MM) Scale expresses the intensity of an earthquake's effects in a given locality in values ranging from I to XII. The most commonly used adaptation covers the range of intensity from the condition of "I — Not felt except by a very few under especially favorable conditions," to "XII — Damage total. Lines of sight and level are distorted. Objects thrown upward into the air."

In this scenario, a 7.2-magnitude earthquake occurs along a fault zone in a major metropolitan area (MMA) of a city. MM Scale VIII or greater intensity ground shaking extends throughout large sections of the metropolitan area, greatly impacting a six-county region with a population of approximately 10 million people. Subsurface faulting occurs along 45 miles of the fault zone, extending along a large portion of highly populated local jurisdictions, creating a large swath of destruction. Soil liquefaction occurs in some areas, creating quicksand-like conditions.

Timeline/event dynamics: While scientists have been predicting a moderate to catastrophic earthquake in the region sometime in the future, there were no specific indications that an earthquake was imminent in the days and weeks prior to this event.

Damage includes a large multistate area of several hundred square miles. Rapid horizontal movements associated with the earthquake shift homes off their foundations and cause some tall buildings to collapse or "pancake" as floors collapse down onto one another. Shaking is exaggerated in areas where the underlying sediment is weak or saturated with water. (Note: In the central and eastern United States, earthquake waves travel more efficiently than in the western United States. An earthquake of a given size in the central and eastern United States may cause damage over a much broader area than the same size earthquake in California.)

Several hours later, an aftershock of magnitude 8.0 occurs. Based on past events, additional aftershocks are possible. Sizable aftershocks (7.0 to 8.0 in magnitude) may occur for months after the original jolt.

Secondary hazards/events: As a result of the earthquake, hazardous contamination impacts of concern include natural gas compression stations and processing plants, oil refineries and major tank farms, and natural gas/crude oil pipelines. In addition, more than 2,000 spot fires occur and widespread debris results. Flooding may occur due to levee failures and breaks in water mains and sewage systems.

Transportation lines and nodes, power generation and distribution, communications lines, fuel storage and distribution, and various structures (ranging from dams to hospitals) may be damaged and will require damage assessment in order to continue operating. Reduced availability of services will be disruptive and costly.

Ground shaking from the earthquake has generated massive amounts of debris (more than 120 million tons) from collapsed structures. In addition, fuel pumps in several gas stations have sustained damage, leaking thousands of gallons of gasoline into the streets. There are numerous reports of toxic chemical fires, plumes with noxious fumes, and spills. Several other local waste treatment facilities have reported wastewater and sewage discharges. A large refining spill has contaminated the port facility and is spilling into the harbor. Significant concern for spilled hazardous materials from storage, overturned railcars, and chemical stockpiles make progress very slowly as triage is conducted.

Key implications: Approximately 1,400 fatalities occur as a direct result of the earthquake. More than 100,000 people are injured and continue to overwhelm area hospitals and medical facilities, most of which have sustained considerable damage. Approximately 18,000 of the injured require hospitalization. As many as 20,000 people are missing and may be trapped under collapsed buildings and underground commuter tunnels.

More than 1 million buildings were at least moderately damaged (40% of the buildings) and more than 150,000 buildings have been completely destroyed.

Service disruptions are numerous to households, businesses, and military facilities. Medical services are overwhelmed and functioning hospitals are limited. Fire and emergency medical services (EMS) stations and trucks were also damaged. Bridges and major highways are down or blocked and damaged runways have caused flight cancellations. There are widespread power outages and ruptures to underground fuel, oil, and natural gas lines. Water mains are broken. Wastewater primary receptors have broken, closing down systems and leaking raw sewage into the streets. As a result, public health is threatened.

More than 300,000 households have been displaced, and many businesses have lost employees and customers. The port has been adversely affected in its capacity to provide export/import and loading/unloading capabilities, and damage to vital parts of the communications infrastructure has resulted in limited communications capabilities.

The disruption to the nation's economy could be severe because the earthquake impacts major supply and transportation centers. Reconstruction, repairs, disposal, and replacement of lost infrastructure will cost billions of dollars. Replacement of lost private property and goods could also cost billions. An overall national economic downturn is probable in the wake of this event.

Mission Areas Activated

Prevention/deterrence/protection: After the earthquake occurs, actions should be taken to protect critical facilities from terrorist attacks and to maintain civil order.

Emergency assessment/diagnosis: Disaster assessments and aerial reconnaissance are necessary. Using real-time seismic data, FEMA runs an earthquake model to provide a preliminary "best guess" at the level of expected damage, subject to confirmation or modification through remote sensing and field assessments. Assessment teams must be deployed and remote sensing initiated.

Emergency management/response: Hazardous material spills must be managed. Emergency medical treatment, shelters, and food must be provided. A joint information center (JIC) is established, and search and rescue teams must be placed on alert, some of which should be activated and deployed. Public utilities and other basic-needs services must be repaired as quickly as possible, and damage assessments should be conducted.

Incident/hazard mitigation: Federal support will be required to coordinate the development of plans to execute mitigation efforts to lessen the effects of future disasters. Mitigation to minimize or avoid future impacts would largely be an issue for recovery and restoration.

Public protection: Structural engineers are inspecting critical building, bridge, freeway, waste facilities, etc., and inspection teams are deployed to inspect hundreds of homes for safe habitability.

Victim care: The massive number of injured and displaced persons requires a warning order for the activation of task forces for the delivery of mass care and health and medical services. Temporary housing strategies must be considered.

Investigation/apprehension: Not applicable.

Recovery/remediation: Hazardous materials will contaminate many areas, and decontamination and site restoration will be a major challenge.

Source: DHS and the Homeland Security Council.

Conclusion

Mitigation, prevention, and preparedness programs are vital to the safety and security of the nation. Since the onset of civilization, people have worked to limit their vulnerability to hazards once they recognized that those hazards existed. Since the attacks of September 11, the focus of mitigation has shifted primarily to mitigation, prevention, and preparedness for terrorist attacks, but the real threat has proven to be the traditional natural and man-made hazards that existed both before and after the attacks began. It is the responsibility of government, which rests most clearly on the Department of Homeland Security, to protect the nation from the consequences of disastrous events. For that reason, it is vital that the all-hazards approach to mitigation, prevention, and preparedness be maintained.

Key Terms

All-Hazards Planning: The disaster planning and preparedness philosophy that advocates for holistic preparedness and flexible disaster planning to ensure the response can be improvised to deal with the many unknowns of any disaster situation. In one sense, it is the opposite of "Scenario Planning."

Avian Influenza: An infection typically seen in birds, although in rare cases human transmission has been observed. Among four strains of the virus known to be infectious for humans, H5N1 is the most dangerous one. Avian influenza is also called "Bird Flu" in daily use.

Bird Flu: Please refer to Avian Influenza.

Business Continuity Planning (BCP): The process of identification and remediation of commercial and organizational impacts of disasters through planning and strategy. Business continuity planning typically involves strategizing for the continuity and protection of the human resource, critical business processes, information systems, infrastructure, and organizational reputation.

Business Impact Analysis (BIA): The management-level analysis by which an organization assesses the quantitative (financial) and qualitative (nonfinancial) impacts, effects, and loss that might result if the organization were to suffer a business-interrupting event. Performing BIA as a preparedness measure is important because findings from BIA are used to make decisions concerning business continuity management strategy.

CERT: Community Emergency Response Team. A community initiative of Citizen Corps to create disaster-resistant communities by training and disaster awareness. CERTs are composed of volunteers trained in basic disaster and medical response. As of 2008, there are more than 2,800 CERT programs all over the United States.

Crisis Management: A proactive management effort to avoid crisis, and the creation of strategy that minimizes adverse impacts of crisis to the organization when it could not be prevented. Effective crisis management requires a solid understanding of the organization, its strategy, liabilities, stakeholders, and legal framework combined with advanced communication, leadership, and decision-making skills to lead the organization through the crisis with minimizing potential loss.

Crisis: A critical turning point with impact to the future state of a given system. Although mostly signaling a deteriorating status of the system, if managed correctly, a crisis can be potentially beneficial. Example: Increased customer confidence to a company that has managed to survive a major crisis in the industry provides competitive advantage.

Disaster Recovery Planning (DRP): The planning effort that primarily deals with the continuity and timely recovery of physical and logical components of information systems infrastructure and applications. The first goal in disaster recovery planning is to ensure a redundant infrastructure that provides for continuity of information technology (IT) systems that support critical business processes. The second goal is to develop a prioritized recovery strategy for systems and applications based on their criticalities for the organization in case of an inevitable system failure or a catastrophic incident.

Epidemic: An infection that affects the public in a larger proportion than day-to-day diseases and infections to the degree that resources of national medical care systems are exhausted or significantly constrained. Epidemics also typically have impacts on the social and economic infrastructures.

ESF (emergency support function): A specific area of expertise deemed critical for a successful disaster operation as identified by the federal disaster response framework. The Federal Response Plan (12 ESFs), the National Response Plan (15 ESFs), and the new National Response Framework (15 ESFs) each identify the various emergency support functions as appendices. The ESFs in the National Response Framework follow: ESF#1 — Transportation, ESF#2 — Communications, ESF#3 — Public Works and Engineering, ESF#4 — Firefighting, ESF#5 — Emergency Management, ESF#6 — Mass Care, Housing, and Human Services, ESF#7 — Resource Support, ESF#8 — Public Health and Medical Services, ESF#9 — Search and Rescue, ESF#10 — Oil and Hazardous Materials Response, ESF#11 — Agriculture and Natural Resources, ESF#12 — Energy, ESF#13 — Public Safety and Security, ESF#14 — Long-Term Community Recovery, and ESF#15 — External Affairs.

FRP: Federal Response Plan.

Hazard: A potential source of danger or unsafe environment.

Influenza: A contagious infection of the respiratory tract. Common symptoms include fever, muscular pain, general tiredness, and chills. Symptoms are typically felt stronger than those caused by the common cold.

Man-Made Disaster: Sometimes also called "technological disaster." Man-made disasters have two common elements: (1) They are not primarily induced by a naturally occurring process. (2) In most instances the cause of the disaster is human error, or failure of systems designed by humans. Examples of man-made disasters include oil spills, radiological incidents, chemical releases, and transportation disasters.

Mitigation: A sustained effort taken to reduce or eliminate risk to people and property from hazards and their effects.

Natural Disaster: A disaster that is primarily induced by the destructive power of nature. Examples of natural disasters include hurricane, earthquake, tsunami, snowstorm, and so on.

NPS (National Planning Scenarios): Fifteen scenarios developed by the Homeland Security Council to aid, develop, and test national disaster response plans.

NRF: National Response Framework.

NRP: National Response Plan.

Pandemic: An epidemic that impacts a large region or has global impacts.

Postdisaster Mitigation: Mitigation activities typically performed in the aftermath of a disaster either to provide a safer environment for the ongoing response or recovery effort or to mitigate potential impacts of the next disaster based on immediate lessons learned from a current one.

Predisaster Mitigation: Mitigation activities engaged prior to the occurrence of the disaster to minimize its impact when it occurs.

Preparedness: A state of readiness to respond to a disaster, crisis, or any other type of emergency situation.

Prevention: Actions taken to avoid an incident or to intervene in an effort to stop an incident from occurring for the purpose of protecting lives and property.

Risk: According to Stan Kaplan, risk is comprised of three components: scenario, probability of scenario, and consequence of scenario.

Tabletop Exercise: A mock disaster game in which participants playing different roles such as decision maker, incident commander, or first responder typically gather around a table and discuss/decide their responses to the incident scenario presented by a moderator. The goal of a tabletop exercise is to simulate a disaster situation for the purposes of exposing the participant to the stressful decision-making conditions of a disaster. Tabletop exercises typically conclude with a debrief session where various parties discuss their respective roles, goals established, priorities, and challenges faced regarding the scenario played.

Terrorism: There are more than 100 definitions of terrorism in the literature. The United Nations defines terrorism as "an anxiety-inspiring method of repeated violent action, employed by (semi-) clandestine individual, group or state actors, for idiosyncratic, criminal or political reasons, whereby — in contrast to assassination — the direct targets of violence are not the main targets."

TOPOFF: Abbreviation for "top officials." TOPOFF is a congressionally mandated annual disaster preparedness and response exercise designed to improve the incident management/decision-making capability of the nation's top officials at every level of the government during an incident of national significance.

Review Questions

1. What are the initiatives that help local communities to mitigate/prepare against potential terrorist attacks? Why is community preparedness an important component of homeland security?

2. What mitigation/preparedness role does the private sector have in terms of homeland security? Do you believe that the private sector learned lessons from the 9/11 terrorist attacks?

3. Try to define *terrorism mitigation* using the common definition of mitigation in terms of the all-hazards approach. (*Hint:* Define risk as a combination of probability and consequence, and list all potential activities that can reduce both components of the potential terrorist event.)

4. What is the importance of international consensus and cooperation for terrorism mitigation/preparedness?

5. Take a quick look at the FEMA document, FEMA 426, *Reference Manual to Mitigate Potential Terrorist Attacks against Buildings* (available at www.fema.gov). What are the two most important factors to minimize damage caused by car bombs to buildings?

References

American Red Cross. 2003. "Largest Terrorism Response Drill in U.S. History Begins." May 12. http://www.redcross.org/news/ds/terrorism/030512TOPOFF.html.

American Red Cross. 2008. "Frequently Asked Questions." http://www.redcross.org/faq/0,1096,0_383_,00.html.

American Society of Civil Engineers. 2007. "Dam Safety Act Signed by President." https://www.aawre.org/pressroom/news/grwk/event_release.cfm?uid=3912.

Association of State Dam Safety Officials. 2005. "What Is the National Dam Safety & Security Program and Why Should It Continue?" http://www.damsafety.org/media/Documents/Legislative%20Handouts/NDSPA%20Handout.pdf.

Barbera, J.A., and Macintyre, A.G. 2002. "Medical and Health Incident Management (MaHIM) System: A Comprehensive Functional System Description for Mass Casualty Medical and Health Incident Management." Washington, DC: Institute for Crisis, Disaster, and Risk Management, The George Washington University.

Benvenuto, N. 2004. "The Relationship between Business Continuity and Sarbanes-Oxley." Protiviti KnowledgeLeader. http://www.protiviti.com/downloads/PRO/pro-us/articles/FeatureArticle_20040312.html.

Berman, A. 2004. "Business Continuity in a Sarbanes-Oxley World." Disaster Recovery Journal, Spring 2004, http://www.drj.com/articles/spr04/1702-01.html.

Citizen Corps. 2003. "Citizen Corps Councils." http://www.citizencorps.gov/councils/.

Citizen Corps. 2003. "Community Emergency Response Team." http://www.citizencorps.gov/programs/cert.shtm.

Citizen Corps. 2003. "Medical Reserve Corps." http://www.citizencorps.gov/programs/medical.shtm.

CNN. 2008. "Katrina Timeline." http://www.cnn.com/SPECIALS/2005/katrina/interactive/timeline.katrina.large/frameset.exclude.html.

Cone, E., and Gallagher, S. 2001. "Cantor Fitzgerald — Forty Seven Hours." www.baselinemag.com/print_article/0,3668,a=17022,00.asp.

Congressional Research Service. 2007. "Aging Infrastructure: Dam Safety." www.fas.org/sgp/crs/homesec/RL33108.pdf.

Congressional Research Service. 2007. "FY2008 Appropriations for State and Local Homeland Security." http://www.fas.org/sgp/crs/homesec/RS22596.pdf.

Coppola, D.P. 2003. "A Report on the First Annual Conference on 'The Community and Homeland Security.'" Washington, DC: Haddow and Bullock, LLC (March).

Coppola, D.P. 2003. "Annotated Organizational Chart for the Department of Homeland Security." Washington, DC: Bullock & Haddow, LLC.

Corporation for National Community Service. 2005. "Congressional Budget Justification for FY 2006." http://www.nationalservice.gov/pdf/2006_budget_justification.pdf.

Corporation for National Community Service. 2006. "National Service Responds: The Power of Hope and Help after Katrina." http://www.nationalservice.gov/pdf/katrina_report.pdf.

Corporation for National Community Service. 2007. "The Power of Help and Hope after Katrina by the Numbers: Volunteers in the Gulf." http://www.nationalservice.gov/pdf/katrina_volunteers_respond.pdf.

Corporation for National Community Service. 2007. "A Resource Guide for the Strategic Initiatives." http://www.nationalservice.org/pdf/07_0913_resourceguide_strategicplan.pdf.

Department of Homeland Security. 2003. "Family Preparedness Guide." Washington, DC.

Department of Homeland Security. 2004. "National Response Plan Appendix ESF#6." Washington, DC.

Department of Homeland Security. 2007. "Budget in Brief 2008." http://www.dhs.gov/xlibrary/assets/budget_bib-fy2008.pdf.

Department of Homeland Security. 2007. "Overview: FY 2007 Homeland Security Grant Program." http://www.dhs.gov/xlibrary/assets/grants-2007-program-overview-010507.pdf.

Department of Homeland Security. 2007. "The National Response Framework." http://www.fema.gov/pdf/emergency/nrf/nrf-base.pdf.

Department of Homeland Security. 2007. "What's New in the NRF." http://www.in.gov/dhs/files/whatsnew.pdf.

Department of Homeland Security. 2008. "Budget in Brief 2009." http://www.dhs.gov/xlibrary/assets/budget_bib-fy2009.pdf.

Emergency Management Australia. 2000. "Emergency Risk Management: Application's Guide." Sydney: Emergency Management Australia.

European Commission. 2008. "Threats to Health — Avian Influenza." http://ec.europa.eu/health/ph_threats/com/Influenza/ai_human_en.htm.

Federal Emergency Management Agency. 2003. "Federal Emergency Management Agency 426: Reference Manual to Mitigate Potential Terrorist Attacks against Buildings." http://www.fema.gov/plan/prevent/rms/rmsp426.

Federal Emergency Management Agency. 2007. "About the Mitigation Directorate." http://www.fema.gov/about/divisions/mitigation.shtm#3.

Federal Emergency Management Agency. 2007. "About the National Dam Safety Program." http://www.fema.gov/plan/prevent/damfailure/ndsp.shtm.

Federal Emergency Management Agency. 2007. "Draft National Incident Management System." http://www.fema.gov/emergency/nims/.

Federal Emergency Management Agency. 2007. "Federal Emergency Management Agency Emergency Management Higher Education Project Report." April 16. http://training.fema.gov/EMIWeb/edu/ARRPT/April%2016,%2007.doc.

Federal Emergency Management Agency. 2007. "Federal Emergency Management Agency Funds First Hazard Mitigation Project in Orleans Parish." November 26. http://www.fema.gov/news/newsrelease.fema?id=41767.

Federal Emergency Management Agency. 2007. "Frequently Asked Questions — Mitigation Grant Programs." http://www.fema.gov/txt/rebuild/grant_faqs.txt.

Federal Emergency Management Agency. 2007. "Hazard Mitigation Grant Program." http://www.fema.gov/government/grant/hmgp/index.shtm.

Federal Emergency Management Agency. 2007. "Hazard Mitigation Planning." http://www.fema.gov/plan/mitplanning/index.shtm#2.

Federal Emergency Management Agency. 2007. "National Hurricane Program Frequently Asked Questions." http://www.fema.gov/library/viewRecord.do?id=2069.

Federal Emergency Management Agency. 2007. "Overview of Flood Map Modernization." http://www.fema.gov/plan/prevent/fhm/mm_main.shtm.

Federal Emergency Management Agency. 2007. "Plan Ahead for an Earthquake." http://www.fema.gov/plan/prevent/earthquake/index.shtm.

Federal Emergency Management Agency. 2007. "Pre-Disaster Mitigation Grant Program." http://www.fema.gov/government/grant/pdm/index.shtm.

Federal Emergency Management Agency. 2008. "FY 2007 Flood Mitigation Assistance (FMA) Program." http://www.fema.gov/government/grant/fma/fma2007.shtm.

Federal Emergency Management Agency. 2008. "FY 2007 Repetitive Flood Claims Grant Recipients." http://www.fema.gov/government/grant/rfc/rfc_fy07_recipients.shtm.

Federal Emergency Management Agency. 2008. "FY 2008 Flood Mitigation Assistance (FMA) Program." http://www.fema.gov/government/grant/fma/fma2008.shtm.

Federal Emergency Management Agency. 2008. "Guidance for Severe Repetitive Loss Properties." www.fema.gov/pdf/nfip/manual200610/20srl.pdf.

Federal Emergency Management Agency. 2008. "National Flood Insurance Program." http://www.fema.gov/plan/prevent/floodplain/index.shtm.

Federal Emergency Management Agency. 2008. "National Hurricane Program." http://www.fema.gov/plan/prevent/nhp/index.shtm.

Federal Emergency Management Agency. 2008. "Repetitive Flood Claims (RFC) Program (Fiscal Year 2007)." http://www.fema.gov/government/grant/rfc/rfc_fy2007.shtm.

Federal Emergency Management Agency. 2008. "Repetitive Flood Claims (RFC) Program (Program Overview)." http://www.fema.gov/government/grant/rfc/index.shtm.

Federal Emergency Management Agency. 2008. "Severe Repetitive Loss Program." http://www.fema.gov/government/grant/srl/index.shtm.

Fire Corps. 2008. "Fire Corps National Advisory Committee Meets." http://firecorps.org/page/630/show_item/172/News.htm.

Frase-Blunt M. 2003. "Operation Topoff 2." http://www.aamc.org/newsroom/reporter/august03/bioterrorism.htm.

Government Accountability Office. 2000. "Federal Emergency Management Agency Disaster Relief Fund." www.gao.gov/cgi-bin/getrpt?GAO/RCED-00-182.

Government Accountability Office. 2006. "Hurricanes Katrina and Rita: Coordination between Federal Emergency Management Agency and the Red Cross Should Be Improved for the 2006 Hurricane Season." http://www.gao.gov/new.items/d06712.pdf.

Infoplease.com. 2008. "Hurricane Katrina Timeline." http://www.infoplease.com/spot/hurricanekatrinatimeline.html.

Insurance Information Institute. 2008. "National Flood Insurance Program." http://www.iii.org/media/facts/statsbyissue/flood/.

Kaplan, S. 1997. "The Words of Risk Analysis." Risk Analysis 17 no. (4), pp. 408–409.

Kayyem, N.J., and Chang, E.P. 2002. "Beyond Business Continuity: The Role of the Private Sector in Preparedness Planning." Cambridge, MA: Belfer Center for Science and International Affairs, John F. Kennedy School of Government, Harvard University. http://bcsia.ksg.harvard.edu/publication.cfm?ctype=paper&item_id=345.

Kulling, P. 1998. "The Terrorist Attack with Sarin in Tokyo." Stockholm: Socialstyresen. http://www.sos.se/SOS/PUBL/REFERENG/9803020E.htm.

National Commission on Terrorist Attacks upon the United States (9/11 Commission). 2004. "What to Do? A Global Strategy." Chapter 12. Washington, DC.

National Earthquake Hazard Reduction Program. 2007. "NEHRP 2007 Annual Report." http://www.nehrp.gov/pdf/2007NEHRPAnnualReport.pdf.

National Earthquake Hazard Reduction Program. 2008. "NEHRP 2009 Program Budget." http://www.nehrp.gov/pdf/ppt_budget_fy09.pdf.

National Flood Insurance Program. 2008. "Flood Statistics." http://www.floodsmart.gov/floodsmart/pages/statistics.jsp.

Nuclear Regulatory Commission. 2005. "Emergency Preparedness and Response." http://www.nrc.gov/about-nrc/emerg-preparedness/faq.html.

Public Broadcasting Service. 2005. "American Red Cross Troubles." December 14. http://www.pbs.org/newshour/bb/health/july-dec05/redcross_12-14.html.

Public Broadcasting Service. 2006. "Fixing Fema" Online News Hour with Secretary M. Chertoff." February 13. http://www.pbs.org/newshour/bb/fedagencies/jan-june06/fema_2-13.html.

Public Safety Canada. 2008. "Is Your Family Prepared?" http://www.emergencypreparednessweek.ca.

Reuters. 2007. "WHO Confirms Human-to-Human Bird-Flu Case." December 27. http://www.reuters.com/article/scienceNews/idUSL2732429220071227.

Reuters. 2007. "Sarbanes-Oxley Spending Seen at $6 Billion in 2007." February 22. http://www.reuters.com/article/fundsFundsNews/idUSN2217546720070222.

Smith, J.D. 2002. "Business Continuity Management: Good Practice Guidelines." United Kingdom: Business Continuity Institute.

ThinkProgress.org. 2008. "Katrina Timeline." http://thinkprogress.org/katrina-timeline.

U.S. Department of Health and Human Services. 2007. "Pandemic Preparedness Planning for US Businesses with Overseas Operations." http://www.pandemicflu.gov/plan/workplaceplanning/businessesoverseaspdf.pdf.

U.S. Department of Health and Human Services. 2008. "General Information on Pandemic and Avian Flu." http://www.pandemicflu.gov/general/index.html.

United Nations Development Programme. 1994. "Vulnerability and Risk Assessment," 2nd ed. Cambridge: Cambridge Architectural Research Limited.

Washington Post. 2005. "Fraud Alleged at Red Cross Call Centers." December 27. http://www.washingtonpost.com/wp-dyn/content/article/2005/12/26/AR2005122600654.html.

White House. 2005. "National Strategy for Pandemic Influenza." http://www.whitehouse.gov/homeland/nspi.pdf.

WikiBirdFlu.org. 2007. "Relationship between Bird Flu and SARS." http://www.wikibirdflu.org/page/Relationship+between+Bird+Flu+and+SARS?t=anon.

Wikipedia. 2008. "Hurricane Katrina." http://en.wikipedia.org/wiki/Hurricane_Katrina.

Williams, B. 2005. "Sarbanes-Oxley: Another Driver for Business Continuity Management." http://www.disaster-resource.com/articles/03p_029.shtml.

World Health Organization. 2003. "SARS." http://www. wpro.who.int/health_topics/sars/.

World Health Organization. 2005. "WHO Checklist for Influenza Pandemic Preparedness Planning." http://www. who.int/entity/csr/resources/publications/influenza/ FluCheck6web.pdf.

World Health Organization. 2008. "Cumulative Number of Confirmed Human Cases of Avian Influenza A/(H5N1)

Reported to WHO." http://www.who.int/csr/disease/ avian_influenza/country/cases_table_2008_01_11/en/ index.html

Yale Center for Public Health Preparedness. 2006. "Preparedness Glossary." http://publichealth.yale.edu/ ycphp/Glossary.html.

7

Response and Recovery

What You Will Learn

- How large-scale emergencies are declared at each level of government, and what kinds of declarations are made
- Legislative actions taken since the September 11 terrorist attacks that affect the nation's response capabilities
- The many Federal homeland security grant programs that are available to states and local communities
- The response roles assumed by each level of government, from local to national (including those of the Department of Homeland Security, as well as other federal agencies and offices), and by private and nonprofit organizations
- What homeland security volunteer programs exist, what each does, and how they are distributed across the country
- How the National Incident Management System and the National Response Framework guide all-hazards emergency response to major incidents in the United States

Introduction

When a natural disaster such as a flood, earthquake, or hurricane occurs, or when a technological incident or terrorist attack happens, local police, fire, and emergency medical personnel are generally the first to respond. Their mission is to rescue and attend to victims, suppress any secondary fires that may have resulted, secure and police the disaster area, and begin the process of restoring order. They are supported in this effort by local emergency management personnel and community government officials.

The adage that "practice makes perfect" comes to mind when considering the unprecedented number of natural and man-made disasters the past decade has presented, which have together tested the capacity of these first responders and the nation's response system as a whole. In the vast majority of cases, the systems in place and the participants responding were both considered efficient and effective. However, the unexpected terrorist attacks of September 11, 2001, the anthrax events that followed shortly thereafter, and the poor response to Hurricane Katrina, each revealed certain weaknesses in this system that clearly needed to be addressed. Although the immediate responses to the World Trade Center attacks were typical of an effective national response system (the most advanced in the world at the time), there still followed an unprecedented loss of lives among both civilians and first responders (Figure 7–1). Several of the primary and support systems in place at the time performed far below expectations, and many established procedures were not followed or were not deemed suitable for the catastrophic scenario that presented. Hurricane Katrina, following just four years later, exposed yet more remaining and several new systemic shortfalls that the terrorism-focused efforts could not have possibly addressed.

The 9/11 attacks were truly a watershed event in emergency management history. In their shadow, agencies at the national, state, and local government levels were prompted to initiate evaluations that

FIGURE 7–1 New York City, New York, September 27, 2001 — An aerial view of the rescue and recovery operations under way in lower Manhattan at the site of the collapsed World Trade Center. (Photo by Bri Rodriguez/FEMA News Photo)

sought to improve existing response procedures and protocols in light of the vast new knowledge and experience that had been attained. The spectacular nature of the attacks, and the apparent threat of subsequent events of equal or greater magnitude, mandated the generation of after-action reports that spurred many changes and improvements in the procedures and protocols that first responders have since applied to their emergency management efforts. Considering the devious and dangerous potential posed by future terrorism events, many of these evaluations focused their attention on what appeared to be a relatively new concept for most of the agencies involved: how best to protect first responders from harm in future attacks.

The federal government responded to this shift in response procedures by updating the Federal Response Plan (FRP). A new prescriptive and functional document, the National Response Plan (NRP), was the product of these efforts. This change was justified under the belief that, because the nature of threats facing the United States had become more complex, and because the effect of future natural, technological, and terrorist events could cause detriment to the American way of life, a "unified national effort" was required to prepare for the response to these events before they occur again. The team members assembled to create this document were charged with making this new national response system as efficient and effective as possible, and to focus on utilizing a unified approach to managing incidents that would result in a significant reduction in the vulnerability of the United States to all hazards.

The NRP, which resulted from these collective efforts, and which was released in January 2005, was billed as an all-discipline, all-hazards plan. The NRP was designed to establish a single, comprehensive framework for the management of domestic incidents, which would likely involve many participants from all government levels. The plan directly addressed the prevention of terrorist attacks, as well as the reduction in vulnerability to all natural and man-made hazards. Finally, it attempted to offer guidance on minimizing the damage and assisting in the recovery from any type of incident that occurred.

Although the plan placed a clear emphasis on retaining the primary responsibility for initial incident response at the local level, with the locally available assets and special capabilities for prevention, it included a more aggressive integration between agencies in charge and sought to establish a workable, unified approach to the management of incidents, especially those involving the criminal element of terrorism.

To carry out the coordinated response approach prescribed in the NRP, the federal government created the National Incident Management System (NIMS). On March 1, 2004, former Department of Homeland Security (DHS) Director Tom Ridge announced the release of NIMS and stated that it was created in order to "provide a consistent nationwide approach for federal, state, and local governments to work effectively and efficiently together to prepare for, respond to, and recover from domestic incidents, regardless of cause, size, or complexity."

Hurricane Katrina (2005) exposed several problems that existed within the new NRP, the most significant reported to be its sheer length. In response, the federal government developed a much more concise National Response Framework (NRF), based heavily upon the systems and organization contained within the original NRP. Upon draft release in early September of 2007, the NRF came under heavy criticism due to the fact that it had been created largely devoid of local or state response agency involvement, and many emergency managers felt that it lacked the detailed operational guidance they had hoped for. After a period of comment and adjustment that was expanded far beyond its initial 30 days, a final NRF was released on January 22, 2008. It remains to be seen what improvements this progression, from FRP, to NRP, to NRF, will have with regard to streamlining the multiagency response that is required during major national-level disasters, including those involving terrorist intent.

Overall, the changing nature of the terrorist threat (e.g., greater population exposure, possible use of weapons of mass destruction) has been the motivator for developing a new approach to response operations. This new approach has sought to initiate a profound transformation on the response community at the state and local levels through implementation of the following four goals:

- To unify crisis and consequence management as a single, integrated function, rather than two separate functions, and integrate all existing federal emergency response plans into a single document (the NRF)

- To provide interoperability and compatibility among federal, state, and local capabilities (through NIMS)

- To enhance response and preparedness capabilities of first responders and state and local governments against all kinds of hazards and threats by providing extensive funding for equipment, training, planning, and exercises

- To integrate the private sector and the business communities at a greater extent into response activities and responsibilities in order to increase resources in hand

It is the purpose of this chapter to describe the functional and operational performance of the U.S. response system, to identify and describe the changes brought about by the creation of the DHS and the actions of DHS and Congress, and to discuss their consequences. Chapter highlights in this regard include legislative and budgetary issues, local and state response capacities, volunteer group response mechanisms, an overview of the Incident Command System and the NIMS, NRP, and the NRF, and the recovery function including various programs available to assist in recovery.

■ ■ Critical Thinking ■

Should the federal emergency management role be crafted by the Department of Homeland Security, by the state and local emergency management organizations that ultimately benefit from the federal assistance provided, or by collaboration among all levels? What benefits and shortcomings would result from each of these three different planning scenarios?

Response Processes

Whenever the national emergency number 911 is called, in any event ranging from a simple traffic accident, to a tornado sighting, or for someone showing signs of a viral disease, the first responders that answer the call are always local officials. But when the size of the incident grows so large that response requirements exceed these local capabilities, and the costs of inflicted damage surpass what the local government can manage, the mayor or county executive must turn to the governor and State government resources for assistance in responding to the event and in helping the community to recover. Each state then calls upon an established system whereby the governor crafts a response that combines various personnel (including the state emergency management agency and the state National Guard), equipment, and funding. And should the disaster exceed the state's abilities to manage, then it is likely that a national disaster has occurred and federal emergency management efforts are required.

The new NRF, like that of its predecessors, dictates the rules by which states initiate an appeal for assistance, and by which that assistance is granted should the president choose to declare a disaster. The new disaster reporting process is similar to that which was stipulated under the original Federal Response Plan, although fundamental changes have certainly occurred. The following gives a brief overview of the declaration process that exists under the NRF, which is described in much greater detail later in this chapter.

Should the governor decide, based on information and damage surveys generated by community and state officials, or predictions of impending disaster or terrorist threat, that the size of the actual or anticipated disaster event has or will exceed the state's capacity to respond, the governor will make a formal request to the president for a presidential major disaster declaration or an emergency declaration. This request is prepared by state officials in cooperation with regional staff from the Federal Emergency Management Agency (FEMA).

At the federal level, the governor's request is analyzed first by FEMA's regional administrator, who evaluates the damage and requirements for federal assistance and makes a recommendation to the FEMA administrator. The FEMA administrator, acting through the secretary of Homeland Security, may then recommend a course of action to the president.

The president considers the FEMA administrator's recommendation, and decides whether or not to declare the disaster a presidential major disaster declaration or an emergency declaration. What constitutes each of these is described in the sidebar titled, "Types of Presidential Declarations."

Types of Presidential Declarations

Presidential Major Disaster Declaration

A Presidential Major Disaster Declaration (Major Declaration) is defined by FEMA to be "any natural catastrophe (including any hurricane, tornado, storm, high water, wind-driven water, tidal wave, tsunami, earthquake, volcanic eruption, landslide, mudslide, snowstorm, or drought), or, regardless of cause, any fire, flood, or explosion, in any part of the United States, which in the determination of the President causes damage of sufficient severity and magnitude to warrant major disaster assistance under [The Stafford] Act to supplement the efforts and available resources of States, local governments, and disaster relief organizations in alleviating the damage, loss, hardship, or suffering caused thereby."

A Presidential major disaster declaration puts into motion long-term Federal recovery programs, some of which are matched by State programs, and designed to help disaster victims, businesses, and public entities.

Emergency Declaration

An Emergency Declaration is defined by FEMA to be "any occasion or instance for which, in the determination of the President, Federal assistance is needed to supplement State and local efforts and capabilities to save lives and to protect property and public health and safety, or to lessen or avert the threat of a catastrophe in any part of the United States."

An emergency declaration is more limited in scope and without the long-term Federal recovery programs of a major disaster declaration. Generally, Federal assistance and funding are provided to meet a specific emergency need or to help prevent a major disaster from occurring.

Sources: Federal Emergency Management Agency (FEMA), "Number of Declarations per Calendar Year Since 1998," Washington, DC: FEMA, 2008; and FEMA, "National Response Framework (DRAFT)," Washington, DC: FEMA, 2007.

Once a presidential declaration has been made, the FEMA administrator, acting on behalf of the Secretary of Homeland Security and/or senior staff designated by the FEMA administrator determines the need to activate components of the NRF to conduct further assessment of the situation, initiate interagency coordination, share information with affected jurisdictions, and/or initiate the deployment of resources. At this time, federal departments and agencies are notified by the DHS National Operations Center (NOC), and may be called on to staff the National Response Coordination Center (NRCC) or the National Infrastructure Coordinating Center (NICC).

If an incident has already occurred, the NRF priority shifts to immediate and short-term response activities. The purpose of these activities is to preserve lives, protect property, and prevent further harm to the environment. The social, economic, and political structures of the affected community or communities are protected as well. Response actions could include the participation of law enforcement officers, fire officials, emergency medical services (mass care, public health, and medical services), officials involved in infrastructure restoration, environmental protection officials, and more.

Either during (if appropriate) or immediately following the response phase, the long-term recovery is initiated (Figure 7–2).

When a major disaster strikes in the United States, or when the threat of disaster is imminent, the aforementioned chronology describes how the most sophisticated and advanced emergency

FIGURE 7–2 Atkins, Arkansas, February 9, 2008 — A FEMA community relations representative searches for residents in a damaged neighborhood in order to provide them with disaster recovery information. (Jocelyn Augustino/FEMA)

management system in the world responds and begins the recovery process. The fundamental pillars on which the system is built are, and continue to be, coordination and cooperation among a significant number of federal, state, and local government agencies; volunteer organizations; and, more recently, the business community.

■ ■ Critical Thinking ■

When the FRP was replaced by the NRP, the president gained the power to initiate a federal response in support of the states, under specific circumstances as outlined in the plan, regardless of a request from a governor. This power was transferred into the new NRF. Do you feel that this takes too much authority away from the states, or that this is a necessary tool?

Legislative Actions

The establishment of the state of homeland security as it exists today involved several bills and laws, essentially determined by homeland and national security presidential directives delivered during the years following the 9/11 attacks. The most significant include the following:

The USA PATRIOT Act of 2001
The Aviation and Transportation Security Act of 2001
The SA 4470 Amendment
The Public Health Security and Bioterrorism Preparedness and Response Act of 2002
The Enhanced Border Security and Visa Entry Reform Act of 2002
The Maritime Transportation Security Act of 2002
The Homeland Security Act of 2002

These laws, among many other goals, attempted to clearly define the mission and organization of emergency management and terrorism preparedness in the United States. The single greatest change that resulted from these laws in the spectrum of emergency management — and also in terms of the changes that have occurred within the federal government itself — was the creation of the DHS. The new department, which integrated 22 existing federal agencies under the direction of a single cabinet-level official for the purpose of streamlining emergency management and counterterrorism activities, was vigorously debated, but finally came into existence in March 2003.

The Federal Emergency Management Agency (FEMA), which was included in this transfer, and which retained its pre-DHS trademark name, was transferred largely intact to form one of five directorates that existed under the original DHS organization, the Directorate of Emergency Preparedness and Response (EP&R). The EP&R mission as defined by the Homeland Security Act of 2002 was similar to that of FEMA prior to its incorporation (to ensure that the nation is prepared for catastrophes — whether natural or technological disasters or terrorist assaults), although there was clearly a new focus that considered more carefully the terrorism hazard. This new directorate supported the original federal government national response and recovery strategy, and dedicated much of its resources to enhancing the abilities of first responders at the local level to carry out that same mission. For several years, however, many of its original (and central) mitigation and preparedness functions were removed from the agency and transferred elsewhere within DHS, only to be returned to FEMA per legislation passed in the aftermath of Hurricane Katrina.

DHS has emphasized through its public relations efforts that it continues to make every effort to support FEMA's original mission of comprehensive emergency management. They assure that FEMA, within DHS, will continue in its efforts to reduce the loss of life and property and to protect the nation's institutions from all types of hazards through risk-based emergency management. In a continuation of FEMA's mitigation role, but using new nomenclature, DHS has asserted it will further the evolution of the emergency management culture from one that reacts to disasters to one that proactively helps communities and citizens avoid becoming victims — with *prevention* being the term of choice to replace *mitigation*.

The Homeland Security Act of 2002 describes the responsibilities of FEMA, within DHS, as follows:

- Helping to ensure the preparedness of emergency response providers for terrorist attacks, major disasters, and other emergencies
- Establishing standards, conducting exercises and training, evaluating performance, and providing funds in relation to the Nuclear Incident Response Team (defined in Section 504 of the bill)
- Providing the federal government's response to terrorist attacks and major disasters
- Aiding the recovery from terrorist attacks and major disasters
- Working with other federal and non-federal agencies to build a comprehensive national incident management system
- Consolidating existing federal government emergency response plans into a single, coordinated national response plan
- Developing comprehensive programs for developing interoperatble communications technology and ensuring that emergency response providers acquire such technology

The responsibility of providing the federal government's response to terrorist attacks and major disasters — item 3 above — is explained in detail in the act, and includes the following:

- Coordinating the overall response to terrorist attacks
- Directing the Domestic Emergency Support Team (DEST), the Strategic National Stockpile (SNS), the National Disaster Medical System (NDMS), and the Nuclear Incident Response Team (each described later in this chapter)
- Overseeing the Metropolitan Medical Response System (MMRS) and coordinating other federal response resources

It is important to note that the new responsibilities of FEMA are not intended to detract from other important functions transferred to DHS, such as those of the U.S. Fire Administration (USFA). In almost all areas, DHS has fully preserved the authority to carry out the original functions of FEMA, including support for community initiatives that promote homeland security.

The following agencies were transferred to DHS, and were integrated into FEMA as a result, through the provisions of the Homeland Security Act of 2002:

- The Integrated Hazard Information System of the National Oceanic and Atmospheric Administration (NOAA), which was renamed "FIRESAT"
- The National Domestic Preparedness Office (NDPO) of the Federal Bureau of Investigation (FBI)
- The Domestic Emergency Support Teams (DEST) of the Department of Justice (DOJ)
- The Office of Emergency Preparedness (OEP), the National Disaster Medical System (NDMS), and the Metropolitan Medical Response System (MMRS) of the Department of Health and Human Services (HHS) (the NDMS was transferred back into HHS in 2007)
- The Strategic National Stockpile (SNS) of HHS

Other legislation that addresses local response issues is presented briefly in Table 7–1.

Budget

The Department of Homeland Security receives one of the largest shares of the federal budget. Each year since its creation, its associated budget requests and funds granted have only increased in size.

Table 7–1 Local Response–Related Legislation

Bill	Title	Homeland Purpose
HR 3153	State Bioterrorism Preparedness Act of 2001	To assist states in preparing for, and responding to, biological or chemical terrorist attacks.
HR 3435	Empowering Local First Responders to Fight Terrorism Act of 2001	To provide for grants to local first-responder agencies to combat terrorism and be a part of homeland defense.
HR 3615	Protecting Our Schools Homeland Defense Act of 2002	To amend the Public Health Service Act to direct the Secretary of Health and Human Services to make grants to train school nurses as "first responders" in the event of a biological or chemical attack.
HR 5169	Wastewater Treatment Works Security Act of 2002	To improve the defense and response of publicly owned water treatment plants against terrorist attacks by assessing risks and locating vulnerabilities.
S 1520	State Bioterrorism Preparedness Act of 2002	To assist states in preparing for, and responding to, biological or chemical attack.
S 1602	Chemical Security Act of 2001	To protect the public against the threat of a chemical terrorist attack.
S 1746	Nuclear Security Act of 2001	To strengthen security at sensitive nuclear facilities.
S 2664	First Responder Terrorism Preparedness Act of 2002	To establish an Office of National Preparedness to coordinate terrorism preparedness and response.
HR 727	Trauma Care Systems Planning and Development Act of 2007	To amend the Public Health Service Act to add requirements regarding trauma care, and for other purposes.
HR 1	Implementing Recommendations of the 9/11 Commission Act of 2007	To provide for implementation of the recommendations of the National Commission on Terrorist Attacks upon the United States.
HR 1674	Tsunami Warning and Education Act	To authorize and strengthen the tsunami detection, forecast, warning, and mitigation program of the National Oceanic and Atmospheric Administration, to be carried out by the National Weather Service, and to establish tsunami warning centers, among other things, to disseminate forecasts and tsunami warning bulletins to federal, state, and local government officials and the public.
HR 5136	National Integrated Drought Information System Act of 2006	Establishes a National Integrated Drought Information System that: (1) provides an effective drought early warning system; (2) coordinates, and integrates as practicable, federal research in support of such a system; and (3) builds on existing forecasting and assessment programs and partnerships.
HR 23	Tornado Shelters Act	To amend the Housing and Community Development Act of 1974 to authorize communities to use community development block grant funds for construction of tornado-safe shelters in manufactured home parks.
HR 5419	Commercial Spectrum Enhancement Act	To amend the National Telecommunications and Information Administration Organization Act to facilitate the reallocation of spectrum from governmental to commercial users; to improve, enhance, and promote the Nation's homeland security, public safety, and citizen-activated emergency response capabilities through the use of enhanced 911 services, to further upgrade Public Safety Answering Point capabilities and related functions in receiving E-911 calls, and to support in the construction and operation of a ubiquitous and reliable citizen-activated system.
S 3678	Pandemic and All-Hazards Preparedness Act	A bill to amend the Public Health Service Act with respect to public health security and all-hazards preparedness and response, and for other purposes.

| S 1152 | Firefighting Research and Coordination Act | A bill to reauthorize the United States Fire Administration, and for other purposes (including: Directs the Administrator to: (1) provide technical assistance and training to state and local fire service officials to establish nationwide and State mutual aid systems for dealing with national emergencies; and (2) develop and make model mutual aid plans for both intrastate and interstate assistance available to state and local fire service officials). |
| S. 2735 | Dam Safety Act of 2006 | A bill to amend the National Dam Safety Program Act to reauthorize the national dam safety program, and for other purposes. |

Sources: Association of Corporate Counsel, 2002, http://www.acca.com/infopaks/homeland/legislativechart .pdf, and http://www.govtrack.us.

In 2004, this amounted to $35.6 billion, rising to $38.5 billion in 2005, to $40.4 billion in 2006, again to $43.0 billion in 2007, and finally to $47.0 billion in 2008. The FY 2009 presidential budget request sought $50.5 billion for DHS. Of this total allocation, approximately $8.77 billion, or 17% (including FEMA grant programs), is targeted for emergency management through FEMA (formerly the EP&R Directorate). Table 7–2 depicts a breakdown of the various components that make up the FEMA budget, including changes from the period FY 2006 through FY 2009 (as proposed).

Local Response

On an operational level, minor disasters occur daily in communities around the United States. Local fire, police, and emergency medical personnel respond to these events in a routine, systematic, and well-planned course of action (Figure 7–3). Firefighters, police officers, and emergency medical technicians respond to the scene and take immediate actions. Their job is to secure the scene and maintain order, rescue and treat those who are injured, contain and suppress fire or hazardous conditions, and retrieve the dead. Some notable facts about first responders that assert their role as the real front line in the nation's defense from disasters of all categories follow:

- There are more than 1 million firefighters in the United States, of which approximately 750,000 are volunteers.

- Local police departments have an estimated 556,000 full-time employees, including about 436,000 sworn enforcement personnel.

- Sheriffs' offices reported about 291,000 full-time employees, including about 186,000 sworn personnel.

- There are more than 155,000 nationally registered emergency medical technicians (EMT). (Department of Homeland Security, www.dhs.gov)

▪▪ Critical Thinking ▪

The nation's system of emergency management relies predominantly upon the efforts of unpaid volunteer first responders. Is this type of system sustainable? Why or why not? What could be done to improve it, and at what cost?

The actions of local first responders are driven by procedures and protocols developed by the responding agencies themselves (e.g., fire, police, and emergency medical). Most communities in the

Table 7–2   FEMA Budget

Budget Component	FY 2006 ($000)	FY 2007 ($000)	FY 2008 ($000)	FY 2009 Requested ($000)
Operations, Planning, and Support	520,045	532,341	724,000	957,405
Public Health	33,660	33,885	0 (transferred to HHS)	0
Disaster Relief Fund	(17,160,500)[a]	1,486,500	1,324,000	1,900,000
Disaster Assistance Direct Loan Program	1,032,861	569	875	295
Pre-Disaster Mitigation Fund	49,500	100,000	114,000	75,000
National Flood Mitigation Fund	28,000	31,000	34,000	0
Emergency Food and Shelter	151,470	151,470	153,000	100,000
National Flood Insurance Fund (Discretionary)	95,854	97,588	111,000	156,599
Flood Map Modernization Fund	198,000	198,980	220,000	150,000
State and Local Programs	0 (Not FEMA)	2,724,500	3,367,800	1,900,000
Assistance to Firefighters Grants	0 (Not FEMA)	662,000	750,000	300,000
Radiological Emergency Preparedness Program	0 (Not FEMA)	(6,477)	(997)	(505)
U.S. Fire Administration	0 (Not FEMA)	41,349	43,300	0
Cerro Grande Fire Claims	0	0	0	9,000
National Flood Insurance Fund (Mandatory)	2,443,836	2,631,396	2,833,000	3,037,000
Total	**($12,607,274)**	**$8,685,101**	**$9,673,978**	**$8,766,794**

[a]FY 2006 Disaster Relief funding includes supplemental funding of $5.962 billion pursuant to P.L. 109-234 to support continuing recovery operations as a result of the 2005 hurricane season; a recision of prior year balances of −$23.4 billion pursuant to P.L. 109-148; a transfer of $752.5 million to the Disaster Assistance Direct Loan Program pursuant to P.L. 109-88 and P.L. 109-148 FY 2006; and a transfer of $712 million to the Small Business Administration to support relief efforts in the Gulf Region. Direct FY 2006 funding for the Disaster Relief Fund, not including the recision of prior year balances, was $6.25 billion.

United States have developed community-wide emergency plans, mandated by the Disaster Mitigation Act of 2000 (DMA 2000), which incorporate these procedures and protocols. In the aftermath of the September 11 terrorist events, many communities have reworked or are reviewing and reworking their community emergency plans to include new and improved methodologies for responding to all forms of terrorist attacks including bioterrorism and other weapons of mass destruction (WMD). These changes are most often driven by available federal and state funds (including grants that require such changes for funds eligibility) and to mirror new programs that have been designed at these two higher levels of government (Table 7–3).

FIGURE 7–3 New York City, New York, October 5, 2001 — Rescue workers continue their efforts at the World Trade Center. (Photo by Andrea Booher/FEMA News Photo)

Table 7–3   Homeland Security Grant Program Funding, FY 2002 – FY 2008

Grant Program	FY 2002 ($000s)	FY 2003 ($000s)	FY 2004 ($000s)	FY 2005 ($000s)	FY 2006 ($000s)	FY 2007 ($000s)	FY 2008 ($000s)	Total ($000s)
UASI	0	596,351	671,017	854,657	710,622	746,900	781,630	**4,361,177**
SHSP	315,700	2,066,295	1,675,059	1,062,285	528,165	509,250	862,925	**7,019,679**
LETPP	0	0	497,050	386,286	384,120	363,750	0	**1,631,206**
MMRS	0	0	46,281	28,221	28,809	32,010	39,832	**175,155**
CCP	0	37,529	34,794	13,486	19,206	14,550	14,573	**134,137**
Totals	**315,700**	**2,700,175**	**2,924,201**	**2,344,935**	**1,670,922**	**1,666,460**	**1,698,959**	**13,321,352**

Sources: DHS, 2007, http://www.dhs.gov/xlibrary/assets/grants_st-local_fy07.pdf; DHS, 2008, http://www .dhs.gov/xnews/releases/pr_1201882312614.shtm.

The federal government has continued to support local level first responders heavily through funding, as described earlier in the discussion of budgets. This funding support has been provided to address four primary areas of focus, including:

- *Planning:* Support of state and local governments in developing comprehensive plans to prepare for and respond to a terrorist attack

- *Equipment:* Assistance for state and local first-responder agencies for the purchase of a wide range of equipment needed to respond effectively to a terrorist attack, including personal protective equipment, chemical and biological detection systems, and interoperable communications gear

- *Training:* Resources to train firefighters, police officers, and emergency medical technicians to respond and operate in response to terrorist attacks, most notably for those that result in a chemically or biologically hazardous environment

- *Exercises:* Support for a coordinated, regular program of exercises that improve response capabilities, practice mutual aid, and assess operational improvements and deficiencies

First-Responder Roles and Responsibilities

The roles and responsibilities of first responders are usually detailed in the community emergency operations plan. Citing the responsibilities of first responders after a terrorist incident provides a useful example of the scope of the changes that these officials are experiencing, as displayed in the following list detailing several of the main objectives for the first responders to a terrorist incident:

- Protect the lives and safety of the citizens and other first responders.
- Isolate, contain, and/or limit the spread of any cyber, nuclear, biological, chemical, incendiary, or explosive devices.
- Identify the type of agent and/or devices used.
- Identify and establish control zones for the suspected agent used.
- Ensure emergency responders properly follow protocol and have appropriate protective gear.
- Identify the most appropriate decontamination and/or treatment for victims.
- Establish victim services.
- Notify emergency personnel, including medical facilities, of dangers and anticipated casualties and proper measures to be followed.
- Notify appropriate state and federal agencies.
- Provide accurate and timely public information.
- Preserve as much evidence as possible to aid in the investigation process.
- Protect critical infrastructure.
- Oversee fatality management.
- Develop and enhance medical EMS.
- Protect property and environment (Source: Bullock & Haddow, LLC, 2003).

Local Emergency Managers

It is primarily the responsibility of the designated local emergency manager to develop and maintain community-level emergency plans. Often, this individual shares a dual responsibility in local government, such as fire or police chief, and serves only part-time as the community's emergency manager. The emergency management profession, and the professional skill and knowledge of the local emergency manager, has progressively matured since the 1980s. Today, there are far more opportunities for individuals to receive formal training in emergency management than ever before, including as recently as five years ago. There are currently more than 140 junior college, undergraduate, and graduate programs that offer courses and degrees in emergency management and related fields. Additionally, FEMA's Emergency Management Institute (EMI) located in Emmitsburg, Maryland, offers emergency management courses on campus and through distance learning programs. EMI has also worked closely with junior colleges, colleges, universities, and graduate schools to develop course work and curriculums in emergency management. Details of EMI's Certified Emergency Manager Program are as follows:

- The International Association of Emergency Managers (IAEM) created the Certified Emergency Manager (CEM) Program to raise and maintain professional standards. It is an internationally recognized program that certifies achievements within the emergency management profession.

- CEM certification is a peer-review process administered through the International Association of Emergency Managers. An individual does not have to be an IAEM member to be certified. Certification is maintained in five-year cycles.

- The CEM program is served by a CEM commission that is composed of emergency management professionals, including representatives from allied fields, education, the military, and private industry.

- Development of the CEM program was supported by FEMA, the National Emergency Management Association (NEMA), and a host of allied organizations (International Association of Emergency Managers, www.iaem.org).

The roles and responsibilities of the county emergency manager are defined by the County Emergency Operations Plan (EOP). The job descriptions of these individuals exhibit the same levels of variance as those in the local first-responder community, primarily on account of the broadening incident threat spectrum that likewise poses a threat at the county level. Although no specific guidelines are given for the new roles of either local or county emergency managers, the essential differences between legacy and more modern emergency operations plans are based on the following requirements:

- Changes in established procedures for handling terrorist incidents

- Changes in necessary response equipment

- Changes in the structure of responding agencies and protocols of operations and interagency cooperation

- Changes in neighboring local, state, and federal emergency operation plans

Funding for First Responders

As of early 2008, the federal government had spent more than $16 billion on funding for first responders since the September 11 terrorist attacks. This funding has come not only in clear recognition of the importance of first responders in managing the new terrorist risk, but also in acknowledgment of their role in protecting citizens from all forms of disaster. Since 2001, this support has come through the provision of several grant programs, which often change from year to year as needs and priorities are evaluated, adjusted, and reevaluated. Several of these programs and their associated funding levels from recent years are discussed below.

The administration authority for the various first-responder and other state homeland security and emergency management grant programs has been transferred time and time again since the establishment of DHS. Before its creation, this funding (which existed at much lower levels) was administered through several different federal agencies — the most significant portion of which was managed by FEMA. After the 2002 establishment of DHS, funding was consolidated under the Emergency Preparedness and Response (EP&R) Directorate. In 2004, the Office of State and Local Government Coordination and Preparedness (SLGCP) was established within DHS to streamline and coordinate all homeland security-based funding to the states and territories — which included first-responder grant programs. Grants were managed by an office within this office appropriately titled the Office for Domestic Preparedness (ODP). One of the greatest accomplishments of ODP was the consolidation of six individual grant programs, including the State Homeland Security Program (SHSP), the Urban Areas Security Initiative (UASI), the Law Enforcement Terrorism Prevention Program (LETPP), the Citizen Corps Program (CCP), the Emergency Management Performance Grants (EMPG), and the Metropolitan Medical Response System Program Grants. All six programs were integrated into the Homeland Security Grant Program (HSGP). Finally, in 2007, when DHS was reorganized yet again according to the post-Katrina Emergency Management Reform Act of 2006, grant administration authority was once again returned to the newly reestablished FEMA.

First-responder grant amounts have varied significantly from year to year. The federal government provided a total of $5.056 billion in grants to state and local governments during FY 2003, but this amount dropped to $4.366 billion during FY 2004. These grants targeted state and local responders, public health agencies, and emergency managers, in their efforts to prepare for disasters. There was considerable dispute between the states during these years, addressed at the congressional level, about how this funding should be disbursed among the states and territories. There existed two schools of opposing thought — one that felt funding should include a minimum amount per state, based on the assumption that nobody can say for sure where the terrorists will strike next, and another that felt funding should be risk based, going to those states with populated urban centers containing obvious terrorist targets. The calculation that determined the amount allocated to each state as a factor of how many people reside in that state — the "per capita funding" — was often used to illustrate how states like Alaska were receiving much more funding per person than states believed to be obvious targets, such as New York or California. In 2005, it was decided by Congress that risk factors would be considered in the determination of funding levels for each state. The amount of funding, however, has wavered since its record high in FY 2003, with funding levels totaling $4.192 billion in FY 2004, $3.985 billion in FY 2005, $3.377 billion in FY 2006, $3.398 billion in FY 2007, and a request of $3.196 billion in FY 2008. The following tables display state-by-state funding levels for several of the grant programs contained within the umbrella of the Homeland Security Grant Program, including UASI, SHSP, LETPP, MMRS, and CCP (each of which is described following the funding tables).

The following programs were funded in FY 2007 under the DHS Appropriations Act of 2007:

State Homeland Security Program (SHSP): This program provides funds to build capabilities at the state and local levels through planning, equipment, training, and exercise activities. SHSP also supports the implementation of state homeland security strategies and various elements of the national emergency management and preparedness systems developed by FEMA and DHS (including the National Preparedness Goal, the NIMS, and the former NRP). All states, U.S. territories, and the District of Columbia were eligible for SHSP funding. Funds were allocated based on risk analysis and the anticipated effectiveness of grant proposals. Each state, the District of Columbia, and Puerto Rico received a minimum allocation of 0.75% of the total funds available ($3,820,000). The four territories received a minimum allocation of 0.25% of the total funds available ($1,270,000) (Table 7–4).

Total SHSP Funding Awarded in FY 2008: $862,900,000.

Urban Areas Security Initiative (UASI): The UASI program focuses on the unique planning, equipment, training, and exercise needs of high-threat, high-density urban areas. Grant recipients use the funding to build a sustainable emergency management capacity with which they are able to prevent, protect, respond, and recover from acts of terrorism. The 45 highest risk urban areas (Table 7–5) were eligible for funding under the FY 2007 UASI program — a number that increased to 60 areas for FY 2008. The six highest risk urban areas, designated Tier I urban areas, competed for $411,000,000 or 55% of available funds. The remaining urban areas, designated Tier II urban areas, competed for $336,000,000 or 45% of available funds. Funds were allocated based on analysis of risk and the anticipated effectiveness of proposed investments by the applicants.

Total UASI Funding Awarded in FY 2008: $781,600,000.

Law Enforcement Terrorism Prevention Program (LETPP): LETPP provides resources to law enforcement and public safety communities to support terrorism prevention activities, such as for establishing or enhancing "fusion centers" and collaborating with non–law enforcement partners, other government agencies and the private sector. LETPP eligibility was the same as the SHSP and CCP programs: All 50 states, the District of Columbia, Puerto Rico, and the U.S. territories were eligible. Funds were allocated based upon risk analysis and the anticipated effectiveness of grant proposals. Each state, the District of Columbia, and Puerto Rico received a minimum allocation of 0.75% of total funds available

Table 7–4 State Homeland Security Program Grant Awards FY 2002–FY 2007

State	FY 2002 ($)	FY 2003 ($)	FY 2004 ($)	FY 2005 ($)	FY 2006 ($)	FY 2007 ($)	Total Award ($)
Alabama	5,317,000	34,506,000	27,972,000	17,688,797	8,300,000	6,010,000	99,793,797
Alaska	2,783,000	18,225,000	14,774,000	9,368,592	4,430,000	3,820,000	53,400,592
American Samoa	828,000	5,408,000	4,384,000	2,779,462	2,115,000	1,270,000	16,784,462
Arizona	5,770,000	38,617,000	31,304,000	20,021,731	8,660,000	9,120,000	113,492,731
Arkansas	4,141,000	26,979,000	21,871,000	13,854,701	4,550,000	3,960,000	75,355,701
California	24,831,000	164,279,000	133,174,000	84,613,815	47,580,000	55,850,000	510,327,815
Colorado	5,220,000	34,591,000	28,041,000	17,796,658	8,080,000	6,430,000	100,158,658
Connecticut	4,626,000	30,158,000	24,448,000	15,491,248	11,160,000	5,840,000	91,723,248
Delaware	2,887,000	18,918,000	15,336,000	9,732,926	6,070,000	3,820,000	56,763,926
District of Columbia	2,747,000	17,916,000	14,524,000	9,184,053	4,270,000	5,960,000	54,601,053
Florida	12,967,000	86,309,000	69,967,000	44,728,449	25,590,000	25,460,000	265,021,449
Georgia	7,797,000	51,767,000	41,964,000	26,726,187	13,360,000	14,240,000	155,854,187
Guam	892,000	5,822,000	4,719,000	2,990,093	1,550,000	1,270,000	17,243,093
Hawaii	3,172,000	20,772,000	16,839,000	10,683,582	4,490,000	3,820,000	59,776,582
Idaho	3,226,000	21,178,000	17,169,000	10,918,426	6,690,000	3,820,000	63,001,426
Illinois	10,604,000	68,884,000	55,841,000	35,298,886	19,080,000	22,300,000	212,007,886
Indiana	6,400,000	41,593,000	33,717,000	21,349,773	10,820,000	8,680,000	122,559,773
Iowa	4,308,000	27,938,500	22,650,000	14,326,334	7,520,000	3,840,000	80,582,834
Kansas	4,151,000	27,004,000	21,891,000	13,849,934	7,850,000	4,470,000	79,215,934
Kentucky	5,048,000	32,839,000	26,621,000	16,861,675	10,510,000	6,420,000	98,299,675
Louisiana	5,331,000	34,488,000	27,959,000	17,679,253	12,020,000	9,460,000	106,937,253
Maine	3,213,000	20,983,000	17,009,000	10,787,521	4,390,000	3,820,000	60,202,521
Maryland	5,881,000	38,622,000	31,310,000	19,866,423	8,120,000	11,800,000	115,599,423
Massachusetts	6,579,000	42,731,000	34,640,000	21,863,377	11,710,000	11,800,000	129,323,377
Michigan	8,958,000	58,080,000	47,083,000	29,739,980	15,650,000	13,670,000	173,180,980
Minnesota	5,631,000	36,766,000	29,804,000	18,895,426	4,790,000	6,580,000	102,466,426
Mississippi	4,255,000	27,665,000	22,426,000	14,190,727	4,650,000	3,820,000	77,006,727
Missouri	6,079,000	39,531,000	32,046,000	20,288,866	17,980,000	7,490,000	123,414,866
Montana	2,967,000	19,350,000	15,687,000	9,949,207	4,490,000	3,820,000	56,263,207
Nebraska	3,502,000	22,822,500	18,502,000	11,724,020	11,200,000	3,820,000	71,570,520
Nevada	3,693,000	24,706,000	20,028,000	12,808,048	8,110,000	5,610,000	74,955,048

(Continued)

Table 7–4 Continued

State	FY 2002 ($)	FY 2003 ($)	FY 2004 ($)	FY 2005 ($)	FY 2006 ($)	FY 2007 ($)	Total Award ($)
New Hampshire	3,187,000	20,899,000	16,942,000	10,748,552	4,320,000	3,820,000	59,916,552
New Jersey	7,948,000	51,893,000	42,067,000	26,626,137	9,170,000	14,100,000	151,804,137
New Mexico	3,574,000	23,357,000	18,934,000	12,016,319	4,530,000	3,820,000	66,231,319
New York	14,953,000	96,664,000	78,362,000	49,417,927	27,460,000	38,810,000	305,666,927
North Carolina	7,706,000	50,748,000	41,140,000	26,126,856	10,780,000	11,170,000	147,670,856
North Dakota	2,794,000	18,183,000	14,741,000	9,336,232	6,270,000	3,820,000	55,144,232
Northern Marian Islands	835,000	5,459,000	4,425,000	2,805,231	1,700,000	1,270,000	16,494,231
Ohio	9,897,000	63,888,000	51,791,000	32,668,546	12,630,000	16,830,000	187,704,546
Oklahoma	4,656,000	30,300,000	24,563,000	15,552,074	8,480,000	5,070,000	88,621,074
Oregon	4,637,000	30,417,000	24,658,000	15,655,892	4,680,000	4,530,000	84,577,892
Pennsylvania	10,512,000	67,759,000	54,929,500	34,676,612	12,810,000	20,230,000	200,917,112
Puerto Rico	4,894,000	31,845,000	25,817,000	16,344,796	4,300,000	3,820,000	87,020,796
Rhode Island	3,063,000	20,029,000	16,237,000	10,291,661	4,460,000	3,820,000	57,900,661
South Carolina	5,028,000	32,899,000	26,670,000	16,925,018	10,040,000	6,130,000	97,692,018
South Dakota	2,868,000	18,722,000	15,177,000	9,618,052	4,380,000	3,820,000	54,585,052
Tennessee	6,140,000	40,058,000	32,475,000	20,585,357	4,780,000	8,250,000	112,288,357
Texas	16,196,000	107,776,000	87,369,000	55,743,279	26,140,000	34,400,000	327,624,279
Utah	3,849,000	25,311,000	20,518,000	13,046,325	4,520,000	3,820,000	71,064,325
Vermont	2,772,000	18,110,000	14,681,000	9,304,415	7,220,000	3,820,000	55,907,415
Virgin Islands	861,000	5,627,000	4,561,000	2,890,316	1,560,000	1,270,000	16,769,316
Virginia	7,062,000	46,399,000	37,614,000	23,921,666	8,720,000	13,650,000	137,366,666
Washington	6,276,000	41,211,000	33,408,000	21,211,105	12,730,000	10,030,000	124,866,105
West Virginia	3,567,000	23,132,000	18,752,000	11,877,517	7,570,000	3,820,000	68,718,517
Wisconsin	5,925,000	38,550,000	31,251,000	19,787,345	8,710,000	7,220,000	111,443,345
Wyoming	2,696,000	17,611,000	14,276,000	9,049,826	4,420,000	3,820,000	51,872,826
Totals	315,700,000	2,066,295,000	1,675,058,500	1,062,285,226	528,165,000	509,250,000	6,156,753,726

Source: DHS, 2007, http://www.dhs.gov/xlibrary/assets/grants_st-local_fy07.pdf.

Table 7–5   Urban Area Security Initiative FY 2007 Grant Awards

State	Urban Areas	FY 2007
	Tier 1 Urban Areas	
California	Bay Area	$34,130,000
	Los Angeles/Long Beach	$72,580,000
District of Columbia	National Capital Region	$61,650,000
Illinois	Chicago	$47,280,000
New Jersey	Jersey City/Newark	$36,070,000
New York	New York City	$134,090,000
Texas	Houston	$25,000,000
	Tier 2 Urban Areas	
Arizona	Phoenix	$11,920,000
	Tucson	$4,900,000
California	Anaheim/Santa Ana	$13,840,000
	Riverside	New in FY08
	San Diego	$15,990,000
	Sacramento	$4,170,000
Colorado	Denver	$7,850,000
Florida	Miami	$11,980,000
	Tampa	$8,610,000
	Orlando	$5,600,000
	Jacksonville	$5,900,000
	Fort Lauderdale	$6,580,000
Georgia	Atlanta	$14,660,000
Hawaii	Honolulu	$5,160,000
Indiana	Indianapolis	$7,710,000
Kentucky	Louisville	New in FY08
Louisiana	New Orleans	$4,380,000
	Baton Rouge	New in FY08
Maryland	Baltimore	$11,910,000
Massachusetts	Boston	$14,210,000
Michigan	Detroit	$14,630,000
Minnesota	Twin Cities	$8,460,000
Missouri	Kansas City	$8,350,000
	St. Louis	$9,260,000
Nevada	Las Vegas	$9,310,000
New York	Buffalo	$5,470,000
	Albany	New in FY08
	Rochester	New in FY08
	Syracuse	New in FY08
North Carolina	Charlotte	$4,970,000
Ohio	Cincinnati	$5,240,000
	Cleveland	$5,520,000
	Toledo	New in FY08
	Columbus	$4,720,000
Oklahoma	Oklahoma City	$4,780,000
Oregon	Portland	$7,790,000
Pennsylvania	Philadelphia	$18,700,000

(Continued)

Table 7–5   Continued

State	Urban Areas	FY 2007
	Pittsburgh	$6,940,000
Rhode Island	Providence	$5,170,000
Tennessee	Memphis	$4,590,000
	Nashville	New in FY08
Texas	Dallas/Fort Worth/Arlington	$20,950,000
	Austin	New in FY08
	San Antonio	$6,750,000
	El Paso	$5,840,000
Virginia	Norfolk	$8,000,000
	Richmond	New in FY08
Washington	Seattle	$10,660,000
Wisconsin	Milwaukee	$4,630,000
Totals		**$746,900,000**

Source: DHS, 2007, http://www.dhs.gov/xlibrary/assets/grants_st-local_fy07.pdf.

Table 7–6   Law Enforcement Terrorism Prevention Program — FY 2004–FY 2007

State	FY 2004	FY 2005	FY 2006	FY 2007	Total Award Amount
Alabama	8,300,000	6,432,289	6,030,000	4,290,000	**25,052,289**
Alaska	4,384,000	3,406,760	3,230,000	2,730,000	**13,750,760**
America Samoa	1,300,000	1,010,713	2,530,000	910,000	**5,751,713**
Arizona	9,289,000	7,280,630	6,290,000	6,520,000	**29,379,630**
Arkansas	6,490,000	5,038,073	3,310,000	2,830,000	**17,668,073**
California	39,517,000	30,768,660	42,370,000	39,880,000	**152,535,660**
Colorado	8,321,000	6,471,512	7,600,000	4,600,000	**26,992,512**
Connecticut	7,255,000	5,633,181	1,850,000	4,170,000	**18,908,181**
Delaware	4,551,000	3,539,246	4,050,000	2,730,000	**14,870,246**
District of Columbia	4,310,000	3,339,656	3,110,000	4,250,000	**15,009,656**
Florida	20,762,000	16,264,891	18,610,000	18,180,000	**73,816,891**
Georgia	12,452,000	9,718,613	11,430,000	10,170,000	**43,770,613**
Guam	1,400,000	1,087,307	1,130,000	910,000	**4,527,307**
Hawaii	4,997,000	3,884,939	3,260,000	2,730,000	**14,871,939**
Idaho	5,095,000	3,970,337	4,870,000	2,730,000	**16,665,337**
Illinois	16,570,000	12,835,959	18,200,000	15,930,000	**63,535,959**
Indiana	10,005,000	7,763,554	5,090,000	6,200,000	**29,058,554**
Iowa	6,721,000	5,209,576	5,470,000	2,750,000	**20,150,576**
Kansas	6,496,000	5,036,340	5,710,000	3,200,000	**20,442,340**
Kentucky	7,899,000	6,131,518	4,320,000	4,590,000	**22,940,518**
Louisiana	8,296,000	6,428,819	8,740,000	6,760,000	**30,224,819**
Maine	5,047,000	3,922,735	3,200,000	2,730,000	**14,899,735**
Maryland	9,291,000	7,224,154	5,910,000	8,430,000	**30,855,154**
Massachusetts	10,279,000	7,950,319	10,240,000	8,430,000	**36,899,319**

Michigan	13,971,000	10,814,538	11,390,000	9,760,000	**45,935,538**
Minnesota	8,844,000	6,871,064	3,490,000	4,690,000	**23,895,064**
Mississippi	6,655,000	5,160,264	3,390,000	2,730,000	**17,935,264**
Missouri	9,509,000	7,377,769	5,610,000	5,350,000	**27,846,769**
Montana	4,655,000	3,617,894	3,260,000	2,730,000	**14,262,894**
Nebraska	5,490,000	4,263,280	1,540,000	2,730,000	**14,023,280**
Nevada	5,943,000	4,657,472	4,180,000	4,000,000	**18,780,472**
New Hampshire	5,027,000	3,908,565	3,140,000	2,730,000	**14,805,565**
New Jersey	12,483,000	9,682,232	7,540,000	10,060,000	**39,765,232**
New Mexico	5,619,000	4,369,571	3,290,000	2,730,000	**16,008,571**
New York	23,253,000	17,970,155	26,010,000	27,710,000	**94,943,155**
North Carolina	12,208,000	9,500,675	9,560,000	7,980,000	**39,248,675**
North Dakota	4,374,000	3,394,993	4,350,000	2,730,000	**14,848,993**
Northern Mariana Islands	1,313,000	1,020,084	970,000	910,000	**4,213,084**
Ohio	15,368,000	11,879,471	9,180,000	12,020,000	**48,447,471**
Oklahoma	7,289,000	5,655,300	6,170,000	3,620,000	**22,734,300**
Oregon	7,317,000	5,693,052	3,400,000	3,240,000	**19,650,052**
Pennsylvania	16,300,000	12,609,677	11,050,000	14,450,000	**54,409,677**
Puerto Rico	7,661,000	5,943,562	3,130,000	2,730,000	**19,464,562**
Rhode Island	4,818,000	3,742,422	2,960,000	2,730,000	**14,250,422**
South Carolina	7,914,000	6,154,552	4,100,000	4,380,000	**22,548,552**
South Dakota	4,504,000	3,497,474	3,180,000	2,730,000	**13,911,474**
Tennessee	9,636,000	7,485,584	3,480,000	5,890,000	**26,491,584**
Texas	25,926,000	20,270,283	24,740,000	24,560,000	**95,496,283**
Utah	6,089,000	4,744,118	3,280,000	2,730,000	**16,843,118**
Vermont	4,356,000	3,383,424	3,520,000	2,730,000	**13,989,424**
Virgin Islands	1,353,000	1,051,024	1,130,000	910,000	**4,444,024**
Virginia	11,161,000	8,698,787	6,340,000	9,750,000	**35,949,787**
Washington	9,913,000	7,713,129	9,260,000	7,170,000	**34,056,129**
West Virginia	5,564,000	4,319,097	5,510,000	2,730,000	**18,123,097**
Wisconsin	9,273,000	7,195,398	6,330,000	5,160,000	**27,958,398**
Wyoming	4,236,000	3,290,846	3,090,000	2,730,000	**13,346,846**
Totals	**497,050,000**	**386,285,537**	**384,120,000**	**363,750,000**	**1,631,205,537**

Source: DHS, 2007, http://www.dhs.gov/xlibrary/assets/grants_st-local_fy07.pdf.

($2,730,000). The four territories each received a minimum allocation of 0.25% of the total funds available ($910,000). In FY 2008, the LETPP program was discontinued, although DHS directed that at least 25% of funds allocated from both SHSP and UASI go toward building state and local law enforcement terrorism prevention capabilities (Table 7–6).
Total LETPP Funding Awarded in FY 2007: $363,750,000.
FY 2008 LETPP Funding Blended into UASI and SHSP funds.
Citizen Corps Program (CCP): Citizen Corps is the department's grassroots initiative to actively involve all citizens in hometown security through personal preparedness, training, and volunteer service. CCP funds were used to support Citizen Corps Councils with efforts to engage citizens in preventing, preparing for, and responding to all hazards, including planning and evaluation, public education and communication, training, participation in exercises, providing proper equipment to citizens with a role in response and management of Citizen Corps volunteer programs and activities. CCP eligibility was the same as the SHSP and LETPP programs: All 50 states, the District of Columbia, Puerto Rico, and the

U.S. territories were eligible for funding. FY 2007 CCP allocations were determined using the USA PATRIOT Act formula. All 50 states, the District of Columbia, and Puerto Rico received a minimum amount of .75% of the total funds available ($109,125). The four territories each received a minimum amount of 0.25% of the total funds available ($36,375). The balance of the CCP funds was distributed on a population share basis.

Total CCP Funding Awarded in FY 2008: $14,500,000

Metropolitan Medical Response System (MMRS) Program: MMRS funds supported MMRS-designated jurisdictions in further enhancement of their integrated, systematic mass casualty incident preparedness to respond to mass casualty events during the first hours of a response, the time crucial to lifesaving and population protection, until significant external assistance can arrive. MMRS funds support local preparedness efforts to respond to all-hazards mass casualty incidents, including CBRNE terrorism, epidemic disease outbreaks, natural disasters, and large-scale hazardous materials incidents. As with previous years, 124 cities were eligible for MMRS funding (see Table 7–7 for a complete list of all eligible jurisdictions). Each of the 124 MMRS jurisdictions received $258,145 to establish and sustain local medical response capabilities.

Total MMRS Funding Awarded in FY 2008: $39,800,000 (DHS, 2007, http://www.dhs.gov/xlibrary/assets/grants_st-local_fy07.pdf).

■ ■ Critical Thinking ■

If you could design any grant program to increase the nation's preparedness to cope with all forms of hazards, what types of items or actions would that grant program support? How would you craft the program regarding eligibility? At what levels would your program need to be funded in order for it to make an actual difference in performance levels nationwide?

State Response

States make up the second tier of emergency response in the United States. State emergency management provides mitigation and preparedness support throughout the year, but comes into play only when called upon by an overwhelmed community, county, or region. Each of the 50 states and six territories that make up the United States maintains a state government Office of Emergency Management. However, where the emergency management office resides within the government structure varies from state to state. In California, the Office of Emergency Services (OES) is located in the Office of the Governor. In Tennessee, the Tennessee Emergency Management Agency (TEMA) reports to the adjutant general. In Florida the emergency management function is located in the Office of Community Affairs. Today, National Guard adjutant generals manage state emergency management offices in less than one-quarter of the states and territories, a number that has fallen from more than 50% only five years ago. Civilian employees lead all other state emergency management offices, a growing trend that recognizes the comprehensive intergovernmental organizational role that is central to the office of emergency management.

Funding for state emergency management offices is provided principally through a combination of DHS support and state budgets. Historically, FEMA has provided up to $175 million annually to the states to fund state and local government emergency management activities. This money is used by state emergency management agencies to hire staff, conduct training and exercises, and purchase equipment. A segment of this funding is targeted for local emergency management operations as designated by the state. State budgets provide funding for emergency management operations, but this funding historically has been inconsistent, especially in those states with minimal annual disaster activity. The principal resource available to governors in responding to a disaster event in their state is the National Guard. The resources of the National Guard that are used for disaster response include

Table 7–7   MMRS Jurisdictions and FY 2007 Funding Levels

State	MMRS Jurisdiction	FY 2007 ($)
Alabama	Birmingham, Huntsville, Mobile, and Montgomery	1,032,581
Alaska	Anchorage and Southeast Alaska	516,290
Arizona	Glendale, Mesa, Phoenix, and Tucson	1,032,581
Arkansas	Little Rock	258,145
California	Los Angeles, San Francisco, San Diego, San Jose, Long Beach, Oakland, Sacramento, Fresno, Santa Ana, Anaheim, Riverside, Glendale, Huntington Beach, Stockton, Bakersfield, Fremont, Modesto, and San Bernardino	4,646,613
Colorado	Aurora, Colorado Springs, and Denver	774,435
Connecticut	Hartford	258,145
Florida	Miami, Jacksonville, Tampa, St. Petersburg, Hialeah, Ft. Lauderdale, and Orlando	1,807,016
Georgia	Atlanta and Columbus	516,290
Hawaii	Honolulu	258,145
Illinois	Chicago	258,145
Indiana	Ft. Wayne and Indianapolis	516,290
Iowa	Des Moines	258,145
Kansas	Kansas City and Wichita	516,290
Kentucky	Lexington/Fayette and Louisville	516,290
Louisiana	Baton Rouge, Jefferson Parish, New Orleans, and Shreveport	1,032,581
Maryland	Baltimore	258,145
Massachusetts	Boston, Springfield, and Worcester	774,435
Michigan	Detroit, Grand Rapids, and Warren	774,435
Minnesota	Minneapolis and St. Paul	516,290
Mississippi	Jackson	258,145
Missouri	Kansas City and St. Louis	516,290
Nebraska	Lincoln and Omaha	516,290
Nevada	Las Vegas	258,145
New Hampshire	Northern New England MMRS	258,145
New Jersey	Jersey City and Newark	516,290
New Mexico	Albuquerque	258,145
New York	Buffalo, New York City, Rochester, Syracuse, and Yonkers	1,290,726
North Carolina	Charlotte, Greensboro, and Raleigh	774,435
Ohio	Akron, Cincinnati, Cleveland, Columbus, Dayton, and Toledo	1,548,871
Oklahoma	Oklahoma City and Tulsa	516,290
Oregon	Portland	258,145
Pennsylvania	Allegheny County and Philadelphia	516,290
Rhode Island	Providence	258,145
South Carolina	Columbia	258,145
Tennessee	Chattanooga, Knoxville, Memphis, and Nashville	1,032,581
Texas	Amarillo, Arlington, Austin, Corpus Christi, Dallas, El Paso, Fort Worth, Garland, Houston, Irving, Lubbock, San Antonio, and Southern Rio Grande	3,355,887
Utah	Salt Lake City	258,145
Virginia	Arlington County, Chesapeake, Newport News, Norfolk, Richmond, and Virginia Beach	1,548,871
Washington	Seattle, Spokane, and Tacoma	774,435
Wisconsin	Madison and Milwaukee	516,290
Total		**$32,010,000**

Source: DHS, 2007, http://www.dhs.gov/xlibrary/assets/grants_st-local_fy07.pdf.

personnel, communications systems and equipment, air and road transport, heavy construction and earth-moving equipment, mass care and feeding, equipment, and emergency supplies such as beds, blankets, and medical supplies.

Not surprisingly, response capabilities and capacities are strongest in those states and territories that experience the highest levels of annual disaster activity. All states and territories, however, being in possession of critical assets and resources, find themselves suddenly striving to reinforce their capabilities against the possibility of a terrorist incident. North Carolina is a state that regularly manages the risk of and response to hurricanes and floods. How the North Carolina Department of Emergency Management describes its response process presents a good example of some of the individual aspects of a mature state response function. The sidebar titled "North Carolina State Emergency Management Response Process" details that function.

North Carolina State Emergency Management Response Process

The [State's] emergency response functions are coordinated in a proactive manner from the State Emergency Operations Center located in Raleigh, North Carolina. Proactive response strategies used by the division include the following:

- Area commands that are strategically located in an affected region to assist with local response efforts using State resources
- Central warehousing operations managed by the State that allow for immediate delivery of bottled water, ready-to-eat meals, blankets, tarps, and the like; field deployment teams manned by division and other State agency personnel that assist severely affected counties; coordinate and prioritize response activity
- Incident action planning that identifies response priorities and resource requirements 12 to 24 hours in advance

The State Emergency Response Team (SERT), which is comprised of top-level management representatives of each State agency involved in response activities, provides the technical expertise and coordinates the delivery of the emergency resources used to support local emergency operations.

When resource needs are beyond the capabilities of State agencies, mutual aid from other unaffected local governments and States may be secured using the Statewide Mutual Aid agreement or Emergency Management Assistance compact. Federal assistance may also be requested through the Federal Emergency Response Team, which collocates with the SERT during major disasters.

Source: North Carolina Department of Emergency Management, www.dem.dcc.state.nc.us.

The changes that continue to occur regarding the role and responsibilities of the state emergency managers are based on the same principles as those occurring at the local level (i.e., changes in procedures to handle terrorist incidents, response equipment, responding agencies and protocols of cooperation, and in local/state/federal operation plans). The sidebar titled, "State, Territorial, or Tribal Emergency Management Responsibilities . . ." summarizes the responsibilities of the various political entities for the public safety and welfare of the residents of each, as stated in the NRF.

State, Territorial, or Tribal Emergency Management Responsibilities as Described in the National Response Framework

States, territories, and tribal nations have the primary responsibility for the public health and welfare of their citizens (under the NRF, the term "State" and discussion of the roles and responsibilities of States typically include those responsibilities that apply to U.S. territories and possessions and tribal nations). State and local governments are closest to those impacted by natural disasters, and have always had the lead in response and recovery. States are sovereign entities, and the Governor has the primary responsibility for the public safety and welfare of residents. U.S. territories and possessions and tribal nations also have sovereign rights and hold special responsibilities.

States have significant resources of their own, including State emergency management and homeland security agencies, State police, health agencies, transportation agencies, and the National Guard. The role of the State government in incident response is to supplement local efforts before, during and after incidents. During incident response, States play a key role coordinating resources and capabilities from across the State and obtaining resources and capabilities from other States. If a State anticipates that its resources may become overwhelmed, each Governor can request assistance from the Federal government or from other States through mutual aid and assistance agreements such as the Emergency Management Assistance Compact.

A primary role of State government in incident management is to supplement and facilitate local efforts before, during, and after incidents. The State provides direct and routine assistance to its local jurisdictions through emergency management program development, coordinating routinely in these efforts with Federal preparedness officials. States must be prepared to maintain or accelerate services and to provide new services to local governments when local capabilities fall short of demands.

States are also responsible for requesting Federal emergency assistance for communities and tribes within their area of responsibility. Thus, States help by coordinating Federal assistance to the local level. In response to an incident, the State helps coordinate and integrate resources and applies them to local needs.

As a State's chief executive, the Governor is responsible for the public safety and welfare of the people of his or her State. The Governor (for the purposes of the NRF, any reference to a State Governor also references the chief executive of U.S. territories):

- Is responsible for coordinating State resources needed to prevent, prepare for, respond to and recover from emergency incidents of all types.
- In accordance with State law, may be able to make, amend or suspend certain orders or regulations in support of the incident response.
- Communicates to the public and helps people, businesses and organizations cope with the consequences of any type of emergency.
- Commands the State military forces (National Guard and State militias).
- Arranges help from other States through interstate mutual aid and assistance compacts, such as the Emergency Management Assistance Compact.
- Requests Federal assistance including, if appropriate, a Stafford Act Presidential declaration of an emergency or disaster, when it becomes clear that State or interstate mutual aid capabilities will be insufficient or have been exceeded.
- Coordinates with impacted tribal nations within the State and initiates requests for a Stafford Act Presidential emergency or disaster declaration on behalf of an impacted tribe when appropriate.

Before being sworn in, each new Governor should:

- Avoid vacancies in key homeland security positions such as the State homeland security director or the State emergency manager. A newly elected Governor should work with his or her transition team to identify these key personnel early to minimize vacancies and encourage overlap with the outgoing administration. As soon as a new Governor selects people for these positions, the department or agency they are about to lead should be informed.

- Ensure that a staff able to manage a disaster response operation is in place on their inauguration day.

- Task their incoming gubernatorial staff, particularly the legal counsel, with reviewing the procedures necessary for them to declare a State emergency and use their emergency powers.

The State Homeland Security Advisor serves as counsel to the Governor on homeland security issues and serves as a liaison between the Governor's office, the State homeland security structure, DHS and other organizations both inside and outside of the State. The advisor often chairs a committee comprised of representatives of relevant State agencies, including public safety, the National Guard, emergency management, public health and others charged with developing preparedness and response strategies.

All States have laws mandating establishment of a State emergency management agency and the emergency operations plan coordinated by that agency. The Director of the State emergency management agency ensures that the State is prepared to deal with large-scale emergencies and is responsible for coordinating the State response in any major emergency or disaster. This includes supporting local governments as needed or requested, and coordinating assistance with the Federal government. If the community's resources are not adequate, local authorities can seek additional assistance from the county or State emergency manager. The State emergency management agency may dispatch personnel to the scene to assist in the response and recovery effort. If a community requires resources beyond those available in the State, local agencies may request certain types of Federal assistance directly. For example, under the Oil Protection Act or the Comprehensive Environmental Response, Compensation, and Liability Act, local and tribal governments can request assistance directly from the Environmental Protection Agency and/or the U.S. Coast Guard without having to go through the State. However, only the Governor can request a Presidential declaration under the Stafford Act.

Heads of other State departments and agencies and their staff develop and train to internal policies and procedures to meet response and recovery needs. They should also participate in interagency training and exercising to develop and maintain the necessary capabilities.

Source: Department of Homeland Security (DHS), "The National Response Framework," Washington, DC: DHS, 2008.

▪▪ Critical Thinking ▪

Should the states take a more active role in emergency management at the local level? Do you feel there is anything that the states could do to improve local capacities without infringing on their jurisdictional rights?

Volunteer Group Response

Volunteer groups are often on the front line of disaster response. National groups such as the American Red Cross and the Salvation Army maintain rosters of local chapters of volunteers who are trained in emergency response. These organizations work collaboratively with local, state, and federal authorities to address the immediate needs of disaster victims. They provide shelter, food, and clothing to disaster victims who have had to evacuate or lost their homes to disasters large and small. Each year, the range of response and recovery functions assumed by volunteer groups in lieu of traditional government response agency efforts only grows.

In addition to the Red Cross and the Salvation Army, there are numerous volunteer groups across the country that provide aid and comfort to disaster victims. The National Volunteer Organizations Against Disasters (NVOAD) is comprised of an association of 49 national member organizations, 54 state and territorial VOADs, and a quickly growing number of county, community, regional, and other local VOADs that are involved in disaster response and recovery operations around the country and abroad. Formed in 1970, NVOAD helps member groups at a disaster location to coordinate and communicate in order to provide the most efficient and effective response. A list of the NVOAD member organizations follows:

- Adventist Community Services
- America's Second Harvest
- American Baptist Men USA
- American Disaster Reserve
- American Radio Relay League
- American Red Cross
- Ananda Marga Universal Relief Team
- Catholic Charities USA
- Christian Disaster Response
- Christian Reformed World Relief Committee
- Church of the Brethren
- Church World Service
- Churches of Scientology Disaster Response
- Convoy of Hope
- Disaster Psychiatry Outreach
- Episcopal Relief and Development
- Feed the Children
- Friends Disaster Service
- HOPE Coalition America
- Humane Society of the United States
- International Aid
- International Critical Incident Stress Foundation
- International Relief and Development
- International Relief Friendship Foundation
- Lutheran Disaster Response
- Medical Teams International

- Mennonite Disaster Services
- Mercy Medical Airlift
- National Association of Jewish Chaplains
- National Emergency Response Team
- National Organization for Victim Assistance
- Nazarene Disaster Response
- Operation Blessing
- Points of Light Foundation and Volunteer Center National Network
- Presbyterian Church
- REACT International
- Samaritan's Purse
- Save the Children
- Society of St. Vincent De Paul
- Southern Baptist Convention
- The Phoenix Society for Burn Survivors
- The Salvation Army
- Tzu Chi Foundation
- United Jewish Communities
- United Methodist Committee on Relief
- United Way of America
- Volunteers of America
- Wider Church Ministries, United Church of Christ
- World Vision (National Volunteer Organizations Against Disasters, 2008)

DHS Volunteer Programs

Volunteerism has been an integral part of life in the United States for decades. After the September 11, 2001, terrorist attacks, this attribute only expanded. What also occurred was that many people who already volunteered in their communities, and many people who had not volunteered but were suddenly drawn to do so, sought out ways in which they could contribute to making their communities more secure. The federal government responded to their outpouring of concern through the creation of USA Freedom Corps, which was created "in an effort to capture those opportunities [to contribute to community security] and to foster a culture of service, citizenship, and responsibility."

Citizen Corps is the arm of USA Freedom Corps that provides opportunities for citizens who want to help make their communities more safe and secure. In the first five years of its existence, following a call by President George W. Bush for two years of volunteer service from every American citizen, almost 24,000 people from all 50 states and U.S. territories volunteered to work with one or more of the Citizen Corps programs. Since then, the numbers have increased. The programs contained within Citizen Corps include:

- Citizen Corps Councils
- Community Emergency Response Teams (CERT)
- Volunteers in Police Service (VIPS)
- Medical Reserve Corps

- Neighborhood Watch
- Fire Corps

While some of these programs are new, others, such as Neighborhood Watch, have been in place for more than a decade. Brief information about the programs and their response component follow, along with the sidebar, "Citizen Corps Facts," which includes various facts about the Corps reported by DHS.

Citizen Corps Facts

- Volunteerism jumped significantly in the United States in the years following the September 11 terrorist attacks, with the greatest single increase coming between 2002 and 2003 when rates rose by about 4 million people. These rates remained high until 2006, when they began falling to levels just above what they were in 2002 (61.2 million people, or 26.7%). (Bureau of Labor Statistics, 2007, http://www.bls.gov/news.release/volun.nr0.htm)
- There are currently more than 125,000 volunteers registered with the Volunteers in Police Service program and over 1,640 registered programs. Volunteers provide well over 1 million hours of service a year.
- Since its inception in 2002, the Medical Reserve Corps has grown to over 147,000 volunteer members. There are 720 communities with federally funded Medical Reserve Corps units.
- There are now 14,791 Neighborhood Watch groups registered on www.usaonwatch.org.
- Fire Corps was started in May 2004. It its first year of existence, almost 300 Fire Corps programs were created. Today there are almost 700 throughout the United States.

Source: Department of Homeland Security, www.dhs.gov.

Citizen Corps Councils

Citizen Corps Councils (CCCs) are established at the state and local levels to promote, organize, and run the various programs that fall under the Citizen Corps umbrella. Funding for these councils is provided by the federal government through grant awards (Table 7–8). As of January 2008, there were Citizen Corps Councils in 55 states and U.S. territories, and 2,292 local communities, all of which serve 76% of the total population of the United States. Figure 7–4 displays the geographic coverage of the CCCs.

Community Emergency Response Teams

The Community Emergency Response Team (CERT) program began as in Los Angeles, California, in 1983. City administrators there recognized that in most emergency situations, average citizens — neighbors, co-workers, and bystanders, for example — were often on the scene during the critical moments before professional help arrived. These officials acted on the belief that, by training average citizens to perform basic search and rescue, first aid, and other critical emergency response skills, they would increase the overall resilience of the community. Additionally, should a large-scale disaster like an earthquake occur, where first-response units would be stretched very thin, these trained citizens would be able to augment official services and provide an important service to the community.

Table 7–8 Citizen Corps Grant Program FY 2003–FY 2007

State	FY 2003	FY 2004	FY 2005	FY 2006	FY 2007	Total
Alabama	638,577	581,000	224,560	318,705	241,443	**2,004,285**
Alaska	390,730	307,000	118,934	169,477	128,392	**1,114,533**
American Samoa	80,067	91,000	35,285	50,210	38,038	**294,600**
Arizona	748,269	650,000	254,176	371,645	281,549	**2,305,639**
Arkansas	446,324	454,000	175,885	250,545	189,807	**1,516,561**
California	3,040,863	2,766,000	1,074,172	1,528,665	1,158,080	**9,567,780**
Colorado	673,142	582,000	225,929	322,819	244,560	**2,048,450**
Connecticut	580,401	508,000	196,661	278,563	211,033	**1,774,658**
Delaware	248,624	319,000	123,559	176,370	133,613	**1,001,166**
District of Columbia	349,645	302,000	116,591	165,142	125,107	**1,058,485**
Florida	1,648,455	1,453,000	567,828	825,770	625,584	**5,120,637**
Georgia	990,886	872,000	339,289	491,715	372,512	**3,066,402**
Guam	106,168	98,000	37,959	53,947	40,869	**336,943**
Hawaii	363,421	350,000	135,628	192,912	146,145	**1,188,106**
Idaho	390,112	357,000	138,610	198,809	150,613	**1,235,144**
Illinois	1,177,228	1,160,000	448,119	633,150	479,659	**3,898,156**
Indiana	796,594	700,000	271,035	384,393	291,207	**2,443,229**
Iowa	348,326	470,000	181,873	257,718	195,241	**1,453,158**
Kansas	429,069	455,000	175,824	249,224	188,806	**1,497,923**
Kentucky	626,504	553,000	214,060	303,974	230,283	**1,927,821**
Louisiana	518,217	581,000	224,438	317,395	240,451	**1,881,501**
Maine	404,492	353,000	136,947	194,686	147,490	**1,236,615**
Maryland	573,772	650,000	252,203	358,657	271,710	**2,106,342**
Massachusetts	801,959	719,500	277,556	389,251	294,887	**2,483,153**
Michigan	1,159,293	978,000	377,549	531,886	402,944	**3,449,672**
Minnesota	699,513	619,000	239,877	340,739	258,136	**2,157,265**
Mississippi	354,489	466,000	180,152	255,984	193,927	**1,450,552**
Missouri	691,778	666,000	257,568	366,319	277,514	**2,259,179**
Montana	391,319	326,000	126,305	179,901	136,289	**1,159,814**
Nebraska	394,442	384,000	148,837	211,443	160,184	**1,298,906**
Nevada	506,839	416,000	162,598	236,583	179,229	**1,501,249**
New Hampshire	420,783	352,000	136,453	194,243	147,154	**1,250,633**
New Jersey	1,026,118	874,000	338,019	478,125	362,216	**3,078,478**
New Mexico	261,816	393,000	152,547	217,943	165,108	**1,190,414**
New York	1,914,389	1,628,000	627,361	881,902	668,107	**5,719,759**
North Carolina	985,617	855,000	331,680	476,796	361,209	**3,010,302**
North Dakota	367,357	306,000	118,524	168,443	127,608	**1,087,932**
Northern Mariana Islands	36,713	92,000	35,613	50,668	38,385	**253,379**
Ohio	1,242,932	1,076,000	414,728	583,359	441,938	**3,758,957**
Oklahoma	613,532	510,000	197,433	280,002	212,124	**1,813,091**
Oregon	580,304	512,000	198,752	283,574	214,829	**1,789,459**
Pennsylvania	1,088,476	1,141,000	440,219	620,360	469,970	**3,760,025**
Puerto Rico	669,610	536,000	207,498	293,959	222,696	**1,929,763**
Rhode Island	241,554	337,000	130,653	185,286	140,368	**1,034,861**
South Carolina	526,468	554,000	214,863	307,104	232,655	**1,835,090**
South Dakota	369,155	315,000	122,101	173,780	131,651	**1,111,687**

Tennessee	730,723	675,000	261,332	372,552	282,236	**2,321,843**
Texas	1,884,037	1,815,000	707,661	1,020,062	772,774	**6,199,534**
Utah	535,072	426,000	165,623	238,682	180,820	**1,546,197**
Vermont	307,953	305,000	118,119	167,921	127,213	**1,026,206**
Virgin Islands	197,788	95,000	36,692	52,177	39,528	**421,185**
Virginia	912,254	781,000	303,686	434,038	328,817	**2,759,795**
Washington	836,784	694,000	269,275	384,998	291,665	**2,476,722**
West Virginia	451,932	389,000	150,785	213,669	161,870	**1,367,256**
Wisconsin	410,063	649,000	251,200	356,198	269,847	**1,936,308**
Wyoming	347,612	297,000	114,886	163,562	123,910	**1,046,970**
Totals	**37,528,557**	**34,793,500**	**13,485,710**	**19,206,000**	**14,550,000**	**119,563,767**

Source: DHS, 2007, http://www.dhs.gov/xlibrary/assets/grants_st-local_fy07.pdf.

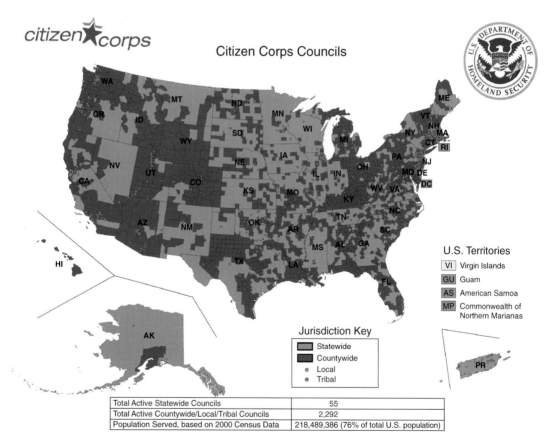

FIGURE 7–4 Map of Citizen Corps Councils in the United States and its territories. (Source: Citizen Corps, 2008)

Beginning in 1993, FEMA began to offer CERT training on a national level, providing funding to cover start-up and tuition costs for programs. As of January 2008, CERT programs had been established in more than 2,846 communities in all 50 states, the District of Columbia, and several U.S. territories. CERT teams remain active in the community before a disaster strikes, sponsoring events such as drills, neighborhood cleanup, and disaster-education fairs. Trainers offer periodic refresher sessions to CERT members to reinforce the basic training and to keep participants involved and practiced in

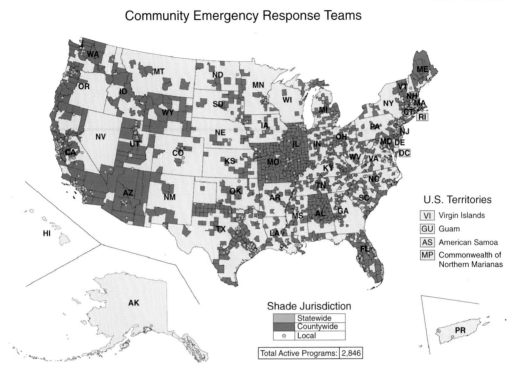

FIGURE 7–5 CERT programs in the United States and its territories. (Source: FEMA, 2008)

their skills. CERT members also offer other nonemergency assistance to the community with the goal of improving the overall safety of the community. Figure 7–5 illustrates the geographic coverage of CERT in the United States.

Volunteers in Police Service Program

Since September 11, 2001, the demands on state and local law enforcement have increased dramatically. Limited resources at the community level have resulted from these increased demands, and regular police work has ultimately suffered. To address these shortfalls, the Volunteers in Police Service (VIPS) program was created. The basis of the program is that civilian volunteers are able to support police officers by doing much of the behind-the-scenes work that does not require formal law enforcement training, thereby allowing officers to spend more of their already strained schedules on the street. Although the concept is not new, federal support for such programs is.

The VIPS draws on the time and recognized talents of civilian volunteers. Volunteer roles may include performing clerical tasks, serving as an extra set of "eyes and ears," assisting with search and rescue activities, and writing citations for accessible parking violations, just to name a few. As of January 2008, there were 1,644 official VIPS programs registered throughout the United States. Figure 7–6 illustrates the geographic coverage of VIPS in the United States.

Medical Reserve Corps Program

The Medical Reserve Corps (MRC) was founded after the 2002 State of the Union Address, to establish teams of local volunteer medical and public health professionals who can contribute their skills

FIGURE 7–6 VIPS programs in the United States and its territories. (Source: FEMA, 2008)

and experience when called on in times of need. The program relies on volunteers who are practicing and retired physicians, nurses, dentists, veterinarians, epidemiologists, and other health professionals, as well as other citizens untrained in public health but who can contribute to the community's normal and disaster public health needs in other ways (which may include interpreters, chaplains, legal advisers, etc.).

Local community leaders develop their own Medical Reserve Corps units and recruit local volunteers who address the specific community needs. For example, MRC volunteers may deliver necessary public health services during a crisis, assist emergency response teams with patients, and provide care directly to those with less serious injuries and other health-related issues. MRC volunteers may also serve a vital role by assisting their communities with ongoing public health needs (e.g., immunizations, screenings, health and nutrition education, and volunteering in community health centers and local hospitals). The MRC unit decides, in concert with local officials (including the local Citizen Corps Council) on when the community Medical Reserve Corps is activated during a local emergency. As of January 2008, there were 719 MRC programs established throughout the United States. Figure 7–7 illustrates the geographic coverage of MRC programs in the United States.

Neighborhood Watch Program

The Neighborhood Watch program has been in existence for more than 30 years in cities and counties throughout the United States. The program is based on the concept that neighbors who join together

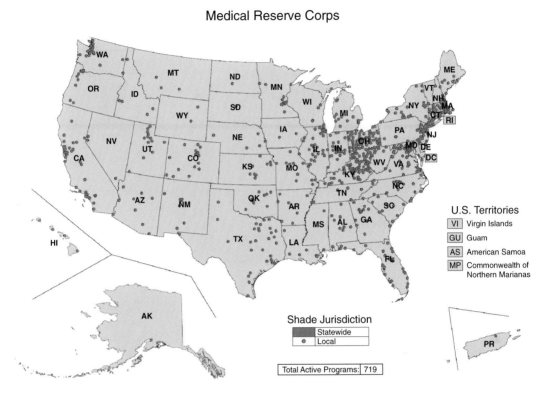

FIGURE 7–7 MRC programs in the United States and its territories. (FEMA, 2008)

to fight crime will be able to increase security in their surrounding areas and, as a result, provide an overall better quality of life for residents. Understandably, after September 11, 2001, when terrorism became a major focus of the U.S. government, the recognized importance of programs like Neighborhood Watch took on much greater significance.

The Neighborhood Watch program is not maintained by the National Sheriff's Association, which founded the program initially. At the local level, the Citizen Corps Councils help neighborhood groups who have banded together to start a program to carry out their mission. Many printed materials and other guidance are available for free to help them carry out their goals.

Neighborhood Watch programs have successfully decreased crime in many of the neighborhoods where they have been implemented. In total, as of January 2008, there were 14,791 programs spread out throughout the United States and the U.S. territories. In addition to serving a crime prevention role, Neighborhood Watch has also been used as the basis for bringing neighborhood residents together to focus on disaster preparedness and terrorism awareness; to focus on evacuation drills and exercises; and even to organize group training, such as the CERT training. Figure 7–8 illustrates the geographic coverage of Neighborhood Watch programs in the United States.

Fire Corps

The Fire Corps was created in 2004 under the umbrella of USA Freedom Corps and Citizen Corps. The purpose of the program, like the VIPS program with the police, was to enhance the ability of fire

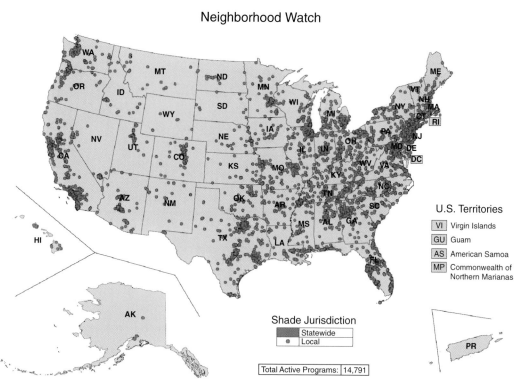

FIGURE 7–8 Neighborhood Watch programs in the United States and its territories. (FEMA, 2008)

departments to utilize citizen advocates and provide individuals with opportunities to support their local fire departments with both time and talent.

Fire Corps was created as a partnership between the International Association of Fire Chiefs' Volunteer Combination Officers Section (VCOS), the International Association of Fire Fighters (IAFF), and the National Volunteer Fire Council (NVFC). By participating in the program, concerned and interested citizens can assist in their local fire department's activities through tasks such as administrative assistance, public education, fund-raising, data entry, accounting, public relations, and equipment and facility maintenance, to name just a few.

Any fire department that allows citizens to volunteer support service is considered a Fire Corps program, but programs can become official through registering with a local, county, or state CCC, if one exists. Official Fire Corps programs will be provided with assistance on how to implement a non-operational citizen advocates program or how to improve existing programs. A Fire Corps National Advisory Committee has been established under the program in order to provide strategic direction and collect feedback from the field. As of January 2008, there were 687 established Fire Corps programs throughout the United States and U.S. territories. Figure 7–9 illustrates the geographic coverage of Fire Corps programs in the United States.

DHS Response Agencies

With the passage of the Homeland Security Act of 2002, several government agencies and offices that managed components of the nation's response framework were consolidated into the Department of

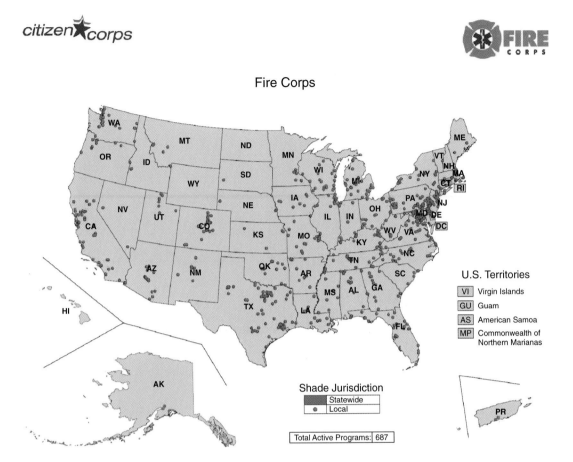

FIGURE 7–9 Fire Corps programs in the United States and its territories.

Homeland Security. Originally, these various components were brought into DHS and merged together to form an Emergency Preparedness and Response (EP&R) Directorate, composed most prominently by the functions of the original FEMA. During the course of the Department of Homeland Security's thus-far brief history, several of these components have moved within the structure of DHS — many falling under the direction of the newly reformed FEMA while others have since been removed from the Department entirely or are facing permanent closure. These agencies and offices, each of which is described in detail below, include:

Federal Emergency Management Agency (FEMA)
Integrated Hazard Information System of the National Oceanic and Atmospheric Administration
National Domestic Preparedness Office of the Federal Bureau of Investigation
Domestic Emergency Support Teams of the Department of Justice
Office of Emergency Preparedness
National Disaster Medical System
Metropolitan Medical Response System
Strategic National Stockpile

Federal Emergency Management Agency

The Federal Emergency Management Agency — a former independent agency that became part of the new DHS in March 2003 — is tasked with responding to, planning for, recovering from, and

FIGURE 7–10 Arlington, VA, March 7, 2002 — A nighttime view of the Pentagon building shows the progress made in the reconstruction of the area damaged by the terrorist attack on the Pentagon on September 11, 2001. (Photo by Jocelyn Augustino/FEMA News Photo)

mitigating against disasters. The FEMA Response Division provides the core operational and logistical disaster response capability of the federal government, which is called upon to save and sustain lives, minimize suffering, and protect property in a timely and effective manner in communities that become overwhelmed by natural disasters, acts of terrorism, or other emergencies. FEMA response program activities encompass the coordination of all federal emergency management response operations, response planning, and logistics programs and integration of federal, state, tribal, and local disaster programs. This coordination is designed to facilitate the delivery of immediate emergency assistance to individuals and communities impacted and overwhelmed by emergency and disaster events.

FEMA's disaster response responsibilities within DHS, which are very similar to those maintained by the agency prior to its incorporation into DHS, include (among others):

- Coordinating with local and state first responders to manage disasters requiring federal assistance and to recover from their effects (as stipulated in the NRF)
- Administering the Disaster Relief Fund
- Maintaining administration of the National Flood Insurance Program
- Administering the training and other responsibilities of the U.S. Fire Administration
- Offering mitigation grant programs, including the Hazards Mitigation Grant Program, the Pre-Disaster Mitigation Program, and the Flood Mitigation Assistance Program
- Administering the Citizen Corps Program

Integrated Hazard Information System

The Integrated Hazard Information System (IHIS) was transferred from the National Oceanic and Atmospheric Administration (NOAA) into the DHS EP&R Directorate. At the time of transfer, its name was changed to "FIRESAT." IHIS, originally named the Hazards Support System (HSS), was a classified information system developed by the Department of Defense (DOD) in 1997 to compile data obtained from various satellites and sensors, such as those used to detect ballistic missiles and others that continuously monitor weather conditions in the United States. In late 2000, after DOD tested the system, HSS was turned over to the U.S. Geological Survey (USGS) in the Department of the Interior and renamed IHIS, where it would be used to detect wildfires and volcanic eruptions around the world. However, Congress directed USGS to cease expenditures on IHIS, apparently because of concerns about unauthorized reprogramming of those funds. Since then, no funding has been authorized for IHIS. The agreement by Congress and the administration to move IHIS to DHS included "the transfer of workstations, software, documentation, and its communications component." However, the president did not request funding for FIRESAT for FY 2004 (Bea, 2003).

National Domestic Preparedness Office

The National Domestic Preparedness Office (NDPO), within the Department of Justice (DOJ), coordinated all federal efforts, including those of the DOD, FEMA, the Department of Health and Human Services (HHS), the Department of Energy (DOE), and the Environmental Protection Agency (EPA), to assist state and local first responders with planning, training, equipment, and exercises necessary to respond to a conventional or nonconventional WMD incident.

NDPO's various functions were transferred into the new DHS and placed under the direction of the FEMA-dominated EP&R Directorate. Among the functions of the NDPO transferred were:

- Serve as a single program and policy office for WMD to ensure that federal efforts are in harmony and represent the most effective and cost-efficient support to the state and local first-responder community
- Coordinate the establishment of training curriculum and standards for first-responder training to ensure consistency based on training objectives and to tailor training opportunities to meet the needs of the responder community
- Facilitate the efforts of the federal government to provide the responder community with detection, protection, analysis, and decontamination equipment necessary to prepare for, and respond to, an incident involving WMD
- Provide state and local governments with the resources and expertise necessary to design, conduct, and evaluate exercise scenarios involving WMD
- Communicate information to the state and local emergency response community

Domestic Emergency Support Team

The Domestic Emergency Support Team (DEST) is designed to be an interagency team of experts, operating on a stand-by basis, which can be quickly mobilized. This team, even within DHS (and directed by FEMA per the Stafford Act), is led by the FBI to provide an on-scene commander (special agent in charge) with advice and guidance in situations involving weapons of mass destruction (WMDs), or other significant domestic threats. The DEST guidance can range from information management and communications support to instructions on how to best respond to the detonation of a chemical, biological, or nuclear weapon, or a radiological dispersal device. As specialized predesignated teams, DEST has no permanent staff at DHS, the FBI, or at any other federal agency.

Office of Emergency Preparedness

The Office of Emergency Preparedness (OEP) was responsible for oversight, coordination, and management of emergency preparedness and response and recovery activities in the Department of Health and Human Services prior to its transfer to DHS. There were two principal programs of OEP that now exist within DHS under separate functional units. They are the National Disaster Medical System (NDMS) and the Metropolitan Medical Response System (MMRS) and are described in further detail later.

Before its move into DHS, OEP served as the lead for Emergency Support Function (ESF) #8 within the Federal Response Plan — Health and Medical. Under the NRF, HHS has maintained this responsibility under the new ESF #8, Public Health and Medical Services. The tasks performed by the NDMS and MMRS, which were fulfilled within ESF #8, are still performed as before but under different direction.

National Disaster Medical System

The National Disaster Medical System (NDMS), which originally resided within the Office of Emergency Preparedness of HHS, was transferred to the DHS EP&R Directorate per the Homeland Security Act of 2002, but now falls back under the direction of HHS as stipulated in the post-Katrina Emergency Management Reform Act of 2006 (including its $33.8 million budget). NDMS is a federally coordinated system that is responsible for supporting federal agencies in the management and coordination of the federal medical response to major emergencies and federally declared disasters. In doing so, it establishes a single, integrated national medical response capability for assisting state and local authorities in dealing with the medical and health effects of major disasters. NDMS also cares for casualties of U.S. military operations overseas who have been airlifted back to the United States.

NDMS consists of more than 8,000 volunteer health professionals and support personnel organized into disaster assistance teams that can be activated and deployed anywhere in the country to assist state and local emergency medical services. Several operational units within NDMS assist in this function:

Disaster Medical Assistance Team (DMAT) — A DMAT is a group of professional and para-professional medical personnel, supported by logistical and administrative staff, designed to provide medical care during a disaster or other event. Each team has a sponsoring organization, such as a major medical center, public health or safety agency, nonprofit, public, or private organization that signs a Memorandum of Agreement (MOA) with DHS. The DMAT sponsor organizes the team and recruits members, arranges training, and coordinates the dispatch of the team.

Disaster Mortuary Operational Response Team (DMORT) — DMORTs, like DMATs, are composed of private citizens, each with a particular field of expertise, who are activated in the event of a disaster. During an emergency response, DMORTs work under the guidance of local authorities by providing technical assistance and personnel to recover, identify, and process deceased victims. Teams are composed of funeral directors, medical examiners, coroners, pathologists, forensic anthropologists, medical records technicians and transcribers, fingerprint specialists, forensic odontologists, dental assistants, x-ray technicians, mental health specialists, computer professionals, administrative support staff, and security and investigative personnel. Their duties include setting up temporary morgue facilities, victim identification, forensic dental pathology, forensic anthropology, and processing, preparation, and disposition of remains.

Veterinary Medical Assistance Team (VMAT) — VMATs are composed of private citizens who are activated in the event of a disaster. During an emergency response, VMATs work under the guidance of local authorities by providing technical assistance and veterinary services. Teams are composed of clinical veterinarians, veterinary pathologists, animal health technicians (veterinary technicians), microbiologist/virologists, epidemiologists, toxicologists, and various scientific and support personnel. Their tasks include assessing the medical needs of animals, medical treatment and stabilization of animals, animal disease surveillance, zoonotic disease surveillance and public health assessments, technical assistance to ensure food and water quality, hazard mitigation, animal decontamination, and biological and chemical terrorism surveillance.

Federal Coordinating Centers (FCCs) — FCCs recruit hospitals and maintain local non-federal hospital participation in the NDMS, coordinate exercise development and emergency plans with participating hospitals and other local authorities in order to develop patient reception,

404 INTRODUCTION TO HOMELAND SECURITY

transportation, and communication plans, and during system activation, coordinate the reception and distribution of patients being evacuated to the area.

National Pharmacy Response Team (NPRT) — NPRTs are located in each of the 10 Department of Homeland Security regions. NPRTs are activated in times of disaster to assist in chemoprophylaxis (preventive medicine) or the vaccination of hundreds of thousands, or even millions of Americans. They may be activated in any scenario that is expected to require the assistance of hundreds of pharmacists, pharmacy technicians, and students of pharmacy.

National Nurse Response Team (NNRT) — NNRTs are specialty DMATs designed for use in scenarios expected to require the activation of hundreds of nurses to assist in chemoprophylaxis, a mass vaccination program, or a scenario that overwhelms the nation's supply of nurses in responding to a WMD event. The NNRTs are directed by the NDMS in conjunction with a regional team leader in each of the 10 standard federal regions. Each NNRT is composed of approximately 200 civilian nurses. National Nurse Response Team members are required to maintain appropriate certifications and licensure within their discipline, stay current in treatment recommendations for diseases compatible with weapons of mass destruction, complete web-based training courses in disaster response, humanitarian relief, bioterrorism, and other relevant training, participate in regular training exercises, and be available to deploy when needed.

Metropolitan Medical Response System

The Metropolitan Medical Response System (MMRS) provides funding to cities that upgrade and improve their own planning and preparedness to respond to mass casualty events. The concept for the program began in 1995 in the Washington, DC, metropolitan area with the creation of the Metropolitan Medical Strike Team (MMST). This first team, which pooled resources from several adjoining jurisdictions, was created primarily for the response to chemical incidents, but was able to provide on-site emergency health and medical services following WMD terrorist incidents.

The MMST concept was expanded to several cities under the guidance and funding of the federal government through the authority of the Defense against Weapons of Mass Destruction Act of 1996 (Nunn-Lugar-Domenici legislation). The program's name was changed to the Metropolitan Medical Response System to highlight its national system-oriented approach.

In 2003, the MMRS was transferred to FEMA under DHS as stipulated by the Homeland Security Act of 2002. Later, in October 2004, the program was moved again into the Office of Domestic Preparedness (ODP), but still within DHS under the Office of State and Local Government Coordination and Preparedness (SLGCP). In 2007, MMRS was returned to FEMA according to the post-Katrina Emergency Management Reform Act. The program has grown from the 25 teams created in 1995 to almost 130 municipalities. However, the president's Fiscal Year 2008 budget proposes to eliminate the $33 million in annual funding that supports the program.

The sidebar titled "MMRS Capabilities and Impacts" provides a detailed description of capabilities and the difference the MMRS makes at the local level.

MMRS Capabilities and Impacts

MMRS Capabilities

- Initial identification of agents
- Ability to perform operations in OSHA levels A, B, and C personal protective equipment, avoiding secondary responder casualties

- Enhanced triage, treatment, and decontamination capabilities at the incident site and definitive care facilities
- Maintenance of local caches sufficient to treat 1,000 patients exposed to chemical agents
- Ability to transport uncontaminated/decontaminated patients to area hospitals for definitive care
- Ability to maintain a viable health system
- Ability to transport patients to participating NDMS hospitals throughout the nation
- Mechanisms to activate mutual aid support from local, state, and federal emergency response agencies
- Ability to integrate additional response assets into the ongoing incident command structure

MMRS Local Level Impacts

- Requires development of response plans unique for each city.
- Creates integrated immediate response structure.
- Creates additional local and regional support networks.
- Integrates with local mass casualty plans.
- Brings together and encourages city planning agencies to interact where they never interacted before.
- Encourages and initiates hospital WMD planning.
- Encourages local health-care providers to develop appropriate medical treatment protocols.

Source: Department of Health and Human Services, www.hhs.gov.

Strategic National Stockpile

The Strategic National Stockpile (SNS) began in 1999, when Congress charged HHS and Centers for Disease Control and Prevention (CDC) with the establishment of the capability to provide a resupply of large quantities of essential medical material to states and communities during an emergency within 12 hours of the federal decision to deploy to that region. The system that was developed was called the National Pharmaceutical Stockpile (NPS).

As stipulated in the Homeland Security Act of 2002, on March 1, 2003, the NPS was transferred from HHS to DHS, and was given the new title Strategic National Stockpile. The program was established so that it could be managed jointly by DHS and HHS, and to be able to work with governmental and nongovernmental partners to continually seek ways to upgrade the nation's public health capacity to respond to national emergencies. With the signing of the BioShield legislation, however, the SNS program was returned to HHS for oversight and guidance.

During a national emergency, state, local, and private stocks of medical material will be depleted quickly. The SNS is designed to help all state and local first responders bolster their response to a national emergency, through the provision of specially designed 12-hour Push Packages, private vendors, or a combination of both, depending on the situation. Like most federal response programs, the SNS is not a first-response tool, but one that supplements the initial local response efforts.

The SNS is a national repository of antibiotics, chemical antidotes, antitoxins, life support medications, IV administration supplies, airway maintenance supplies, and medical/surgical items.

The SNS is designed to supplement and resupply state and local public health agencies in the event of a national emergency anywhere and at anytime within the United States or its territories. The system is also set up to allow for the acquisition of additional pharmaceuticals and/or medical supplies not maintained directly by the SNS through the use of private vendors (which can ship supplies to arrive within 24 to 36 hours of the request). In some areas, the vendors, which are preregistered under the program, can actually provide the first wave of supplies that arrive.

The sidebar "The Strategic National Stockpile" gives an overview of how the SNS functions, and how its components interact with local and state organizations.

The Strategic National Stockpile

The Strategic National Stockpile (SNS) program is committed to have 12-hour Push Packages delivered anywhere in the United States or its territories within 12 hours of a Federal decision to deploy. The 12-hour Push Packages have been configured to be immediately loaded onto either trucks or commercial cargo aircraft for the most rapid transportation. Concurrent to SNS transport, the SNS program will deploy its Technical Advisory Response Unit (TARU). The TARU staff will coordinate with State and local officials so that the SNS assets can be efficiently received and distributed on arrival at the site.

DHS will transfer authority for the SNS materiel to the State and local authorities once it arrives at the designated receiving and storage site. State and local authorities will then begin the breakdown of the 12-hour Push Package for distribution. SNS TARU members will remain on-site in order to assist and advise State and local officials in putting the SNS assets to prompt and effective use.

The decision to deploy SNS assets may be based on evidence showing the overt release of an agent that might adversely affect public health. It is more likely, however, that subtle indicators, such as unusual morbidity and/or mortality identified through the nation's disease outbreak surveillance and epidemiology network, will alert health officials to the possibility (and confirmation) of a biological or chemical incident or a national emergency. To receive SNS assets, the affected State's Governor's office will directly request the deployment of the SNS assets from CDC or DHS. DHS, HHS, CDC, and other Federal officials will evaluate the situation and determine a prompt course of action.

The SNS program is part of a nationwide preparedness training and education program for State and local health-care providers, first responders, and governments (to include Federal officials, Governors' offices, State and local health departments, and emergency management agencies). This training explains the SNS program's mission and operations and also alerts State and local emergency response officials to the important issues they must plan for in order to receive, secure, and distribute SNS assets.

To conduct this outreach and training, CDC and SNS program staff are currently working with DHS, HHS agencies, regional emergency response coordinators at all of the U.S. Public Health Service regional offices, State and local health departments, State emergency management offices, the Metropolitan Medical Response System cities, the Department of Veterans Affairs, and the Department of Defense.

Source: Centers for Disease Control and Prevention, www.cdc.gov.

Urban Search and Rescue

The concept of formally maintained Urban Search and Rescue (US&R or USAR) teams was introduced in the early 1980s. The Fairfax County (Virginia) Fire and Rescue and the Metro-Dade County (Florida) Fire Department each created specialized search and rescue teams trained for rescue operations in collapsed buildings. Urban search and rescue involves the location, rescue (extrication), and initial medical stabilization of victims trapped in confined spaces. Structural collapse is most often the cause of victims being trapped, but victims may also be trapped in transportation accidents, mines, and collapsed trenches. The initial teams created to carry out these tasks were so successful in this specialty that they were often sent abroad on missions, representing the U.S. government relief efforts, through support of the Department of State and the Office of Foreign Disaster Assistance (OFDA) of the U.S. Agency for International Development (USAID). These teams have deployed to Mexico City, the Philippines, and Armenia, providing vital search and rescue support in earthquake-induced disasters in each of these areas.

Beginning in 1991, urban search and rescue became a component of federal response operations under the Federal Response Plan, when the US&R concept was incorporated as an individual emergency support function. From that starting point, the size of the US&R system grew considerably, with FEMA sponsoring the creation of 25 national urban search and rescue task forces. There are now a total of 28 national task forces, staffed and equipped to conduct round-the-clock search and rescue operations following any disaster that requires their specialized talents and equipment. In 2003, when FEMA was transferred into DHS, the US&R system transferred with FEMA, intact. FEMA, under DHS, maintains its primary agency designation under ESF #9, Search and Rescue.

How the teams are structured and operate is discussed in the sidebar titled "Urban Search and Rescue (US&R) Teams."

Urban Search and Rescue (US&R) Teams

- If a disaster event warrants national US&R support, DHS will deploy the three closest task forces within 6 hours of notification and additional teams as necessary. The role of these task forces is to support State and local emergency responders' efforts to locate victims and manage recovery operations.
- Each task force consists of two 31-person teams, four canines, and a comprehensive equipment cache. For every US&R task force, there are 62 positions. To ensure that a full team can respond to an emergency, the task forces have at the ready more than 130 highly trained members.
- A task force is really a partnership between local fire departments, law enforcement agencies, Federal and local governmental agencies, and private companies.
- A task force is totally self-sufficient for the first 72 hours of a deployment.
- The equipment cache used to support a task force weighs nearly 60,000 pounds and is worth about $1.4 million. Add the task force members to the cache, and you can completely fill a military C-141 transport or two C-130s.
- US&R task force members work in four areas of specialization: search, to find victims trapped after a disaster; rescue, which includes safely digging victims out of tons of collapsed concrete and metal; technical, made up of structural specialists who make rescues safe for the rescuers; and medical, which cares for the victims before and after a rescue.
- In addition to search and rescue support, the DHS provides hands-on training in search and rescue techniques and equipment, technical assistance to local communities, and in some cases Federal grants to help communities better prepare for US&R operations.

- The bottom line in US&R: Someday, lives may be saved because of the skills these rescuers gain. These first responders consistently go to the front lines when the nation needs them most.
- Not only are these first responders a national resource that can be deployed to a major disaster or structural collapse anywhere in the country, they are also the local firefighters and paramedics who answer local 911 calls.
- Events such as the 1995 bombing of the Alfred P. Murrah Federal Office Building in Oklahoma City, the Northridge earthquake, the Kansas grain elevator explosion in 1998, and earthquakes in Turkey and Greece in 1999 underscore the need for highly skilled teams to rescue trapped victims.
- What the task force can do: Conduct physical search and rescue in collapsed buildings; provide emergency medical care to trapped victims; deploy search and rescue dogs; assess and control gas, electric service, and hazardous materials; and evaluate and stabilize damaged structures.

Sources: Federal Emergency Management Agency, www.fema.gov; and Department of Homeland Security, www.dhs.gov.

Maritime Search and Rescue

The U.S. Coast Guard (USCG) is one of only two federal agencies (including the U.S. Secret Service) that transferred into the new Department of Homeland Security as an independent entity, thus reporting directly to the Secretary of Homeland Security as opposed to one of the five directorates. The USCG maintains several distinct missions within DHS, but one of those, search and rescue, has resulted in strong cooperation with FEMA and the EP&R Directorate. Specifically, USCG maintains the authority and responsibility for the various tasks related to maritime search and rescue.

Maritime search and rescue (SAR) is one of the Coast Guard's oldest missions. Minimizing the loss of life, injury, property damage, or loss by rendering aid to persons in distress and property in the maritime environment has always been a Coast Guard priority. Coast Guard SAR response involves multiple-mission stations, cutters, aircraft, and boats linked by communications networks. The Coast Guard is the SAR coordinator for U.S. aeronautical and maritime search and rescue regions that are near America's oceans, including Alaska and Hawaii. To meet this responsibility, the Coast Guard maintains SAR facilities on the East, West, and Gulf coasts; in Alaska, Hawaii, Guam, and Puerto Rico; and on the Great Lakes and inland U.S. waterways.

The USCG maintains that, in performing their SAR goal, they are guided by two program objectives:

1. Save at least 93% of those people at risk of death on waters over which the Coast Guard has SAR responsibility.
2. Prevent the loss of at least 80% of the property that is at risk of destruction on the waters over which the Coast Guard has SAR responsibility.

Additionally, the USCG maintains standards of operation by which they plan to fulfill these goals and objectives:

Readiness: Search and rescue unit ready to proceed within 30 minutes of notification of a distress.
Transit: Search and rescue unit on scene, or within the search area, within 90 minutes of getting under way.

VHF-FM Distress Net Standard: 100% VHF-FM continuous coverage to receive a 1-W signal out to 20 nautical miles around the U.S. Atlantic, Pacific, Gulf of Mexico, and Great Lakes coasts. This is the primary distress alerting and SAR communications method for U.S. coastal waters.

406-MHz Emergency Position Indicating Radio Beacon (EPIRB): Maximum use of the 406-MHz EPIRB in the offshore environment. The beacon's superior alerting, position indicating, and signaling capabilities significantly improve system effectiveness and efficiency. Beacon registration provides useful SAR response information and mitigates false alarm response costs. Currently about 70% of U.S. beacons are registered.

Command and Control Standard: Initiate action within 5 minutes of initial notification of a distress incident. Process and evaluate information about the SAR incident and determine appropriate action.

Computer-Assisted Search Planning (CASP) System Standard: Use CASP for planning guidance for all cases involving incidents outside the 30 fathom mark when:

- The duration of an incident has or could have exceeded 24 hours, and

- There is uncertainty concerning the incident time, incident location, or type of search object(s) involved.

Automated Mutual-Assistance Vessel Rescue (AMVER) System Standard: Use AMVER for identification of rescue resources for all cases involving incidents on the high seas. The Coast Guard actively seeks to increase participation in this voluntary reporting system. Each year, more vessels participate in the system and more lives are saved.

SAR Planner Training Standard for SAR Mission Coordinators: 100% attendance and completion of resident SAR planner training at the National SAR School for Area, District, Section, and Group SAR planners.

The Coast Guard currently maintains six separate programs under the SAR, as briefly described in the sidebar, "U.S. Coast Guard Search and Rescue Programs."

U.S. Coast Guard Search and Rescue Programs

Rescue 21

The Coast Guard currently uses the National Distress and Response System to monitor for maritime distress calls and coordinate response operations. The system consists of a network of VHF-FM antenna sites with analog transceivers that are remotely controlled by regional communications centers and rescue boat stations providing coverage out to approximately 20 nautical miles from the shore in most areas.

Salvage Assistance and Technical Support

The Marine Safety Center Salvage Assistance and Response Teams provide on-scene technical support during maritime catastrophes in order to predict events and mitigate their impact.

Operational Command, Control, and Communications

The National Strike Force Coordination Center (NSFCC) provides oversight and strategic direction to the strike teams, ensuring enhanced interoperability through a program of standardized operating procedures for response, equipment, training, and qualifications. The NSFCC conducts at least six major government-led spill response exercises each year under the National Preparedness for

Response Exercise program; maintains a national logistics network, using the Response Resource Inventory; implements the Coast Guard Oil Spill Removal Organization program; and administers the National Maintenance Contract for the Coast Guard's $30 million inventory of prepositioned spill response equipment.

AMVER

AMVER (Automated Mutual-Assistance Vessel Rescue) is a ship-reporting system for search and rescue. It is a global system that enables identification of other ships in the area of a ship in distress, which could then be sent to its assistance. AMVER information is used only for search and rescue, and is made available to any rescue coordination center in the world responding to a search and rescue case. The Coast Guard actively seeks to increase participation in this voluntary reporting system. Each year, more vessels participate in the system and more lives are saved. Currently, ships from more than 143 nations participate.

AMVER represents "free" safety insurance during a voyage by improving the chances for aid in an emergency. By regular reporting, someone knows where a ship is at all times on its voyage in the event of an emergency. AMVER can reduce the time lost for vessels responding to calls for assistance by orchestrating a rescue response, utilizing ships in the best position or with the best capability to avoid unnecessary diversions in response to a Mayday or SOS call.

Pollution Control

The Response Operations Division develops and maintains policies for marine pollution response. They also coordinate activities with the international community, intelligence agencies, and the Federal government in matters concerning threats or acts of terrorism in U.S. ports and territorial waters.

National Strike Force

The National Strike Force (NSF) was established in 1973 as a direct result of the Federal Water Pollution Control Act of 1972. The NSF's mission is to provide highly trained, experienced personnel and specialized equipment to Coast Guard and other Federal agencies to facilitate preparedness and response to oil and hazardous substance pollution incidents in order to protect public health and the environment. The NSF's area of responsibility covers all Coast Guard districts and Federal response regions.

The strike teams provide rapid response support in incident management, site safety, contractor performance monitoring, resource documentation, response strategies, hazard assessment, oil spill dispersant and operational effectiveness monitoring, and high-capacity lightering and offshore-skimming capabilities.

Source: Department of Homeland Security, www.dhs.gov.

Other Response Agencies

Each of the agencies listed in the preceding section operates under the management of the Department of Homeland Security, and in several cases, under the Federal Emergency Management Agency, regardless of whether or not a disaster declaration has occurred. However, there are several other agencies within the Federal government that bring emergency response capabilities to the federal response system, in many cases operating in their respective organizations without any clear

FIGURE 7–11 New York City, New York, September 18, 2001 — FBI members look toward the wreckage at the World Trade Center. (Photo by Andrea Booher/FEMA News Photo)

day-to-day contact with DHS outside of a declared disaster. As stipulated in the NRF, these agencies can all be called upon to provide their services in times of need, under the coordination efforts of FEMA, in response to major disasters that require federal support (namely, presidentially declared disasters and emergencies). These departments and agencies are discussed individually.

Federal Bureau of Investigation

The Federal Bureau of Investigation (FBI), part of the Department of Justice, is the lead federal agency (LFA) for crisis management and investigation of all terrorism-related matters, including incidents involving a WMD. Within the FBI's role as LFA, the FBI federal on-scene commander (OSC) coordinates the overall federal response until the attorney general transfers the LFA role to FEMA (Figure 7–11). The primary response-related units within the FBI include:

- *FBI Domestic Terrorism/Counterterrorism Planning Section (DTCTPS):* The DTCTPS serves as the point of contact (POC) to the FBI field offices and command structure as well as other federal agencies in incidences of terrorism, the use or suspected use of WMD, and/or the evaluation of threat credibility. If the FBI's Strategic Information and Operations Center (SIOC) is operational for exercises or actual incidents, the DTCTPS will provide staff personnel to facilitate the operation of SIOC.

- *FBI Laboratory Division:* Within the FBI's Laboratory Division reside numerous assets, which can deploy to provide assistance in a terrorism/WMD incident. The Hazardous Materials Response Unit (HMRU) personnel are highly trained and knowledgeable and are equipped to direct and assist in the collection of hazardous and/or toxic evidence in a contaminated environment.

- *FBI Critical Incident Response Group (CIRG):* The Crisis Management Unit (CMU), which conducts training and exercises for the FBI and has developed the concept of the Joint Operations Center (JOC), is available to provide on-scene assistance to the incident and integrate the concept of the JOC and the Incident Command System (ICS) to create efficient management of the situation.

Department of Defense

In the event of a terrorist attack or an act of nature on American soil resulting in the release of chemical, biological, radiological, or nuclear material or high-yield explosive (CBRNE) devices, the local law enforcement, fire, and emergency medical personnel who are first to respond may become quickly overwhelmed by the magnitude of the attack. The Department of Defense (DOD) has many unique war-fighting support capabilities, both technical and operational, that could be used in support of state and local authorities, if requested by DHS, as the lead federal agency, to support and manage the consequences of such a domestic event.

When requested, the DOD will provide its unique and extensive resources in accordance with the following principles. First, DOD will ensure an unequivocal chain of responsibility, authority, and accountability for its actions to ensure the American people that the military will follow the basic constructs of lawful action when an emergency occurs. Second, in the event of a catastrophic CBRNE event, DOD will always play a supporting role to the LFA in accordance with all applicable law and plans. Third, DOD support will emphasize its natural role, skills, and structures to mass mobilize and provide logistical support. Fourth, DOD will purchase equipment and provide support in areas that are largely related to its war-fighting mission. Fifth, reserve component forces are DOD's forward-deployed forces for domestic consequence management.

All official requests for DOD support to CBRNE consequence management (CM) incidents are made by the LFA to the executive secretary of the DOD. While the LFA may submit the requests for DOD assistance through other DOD channels, immediately upon receipt, any request that comes to any DOD element shall be forwarded to the executive secretary. In each instance the executive secretary will take the necessary action so that the deputy secretary can determine whether the incident warrants special operational management. In such instances, upon issuance of Secretary of Defense guidance to the chairman of the Joint Chiefs of Staff (CJCS), the Joint Staff will translate the secretary's decisions into military orders for these CBRNE-CM events, under the policy oversight of the ATSD(CS). If the deputy secretary of defense determines that DOD support for a particular CBRNE-CM incident does not require special consequence management procedures, the secretary of the Army will exercise authority as the DOD executive agent through the normal director of Military Support and Military Support to Civil Authorities (MSCA) procedures, with policy oversight by the ATSD(CS).

Additionally, DOD has established 10 Weapons of Mass Destruction Civil Support Teams (WMD-CST), each composed of 22 well-trained and equipped full-time National Guard personnel. Upon Secretary of Defense certification, one WMD-CST will be stationed in each of the 10 FEMA regions around the country, ready to provide support when directed by their respective governors. Their mission is to deploy rapidly, assist local responders in determining the precise nature of an attack, provide expert technical advice, and help pave the way for the identification and arrival of follow-up military assets. By congressional direction, DOD is in the process of establishing and training an additional 17 WMD-CSTs to support the U.S. population. Interstate agreements provide a process for the WMD-CST and other National Guard assets to be used by neighboring states. If national security requirements dictate, these units may be transferred to federal service.

In August 2005, the Department of Defense announced that it had, for the first time, created operational plans of war that included U.S. territory, primarily for use in the response to a major terrorist attack within the nation's borders. The plans are based on 15 possible attack scenarios that assume simultaneous attacks throughout the country. Northern Command, a new military sector created in 2002 whose territory includes the United States, developed these domestic war plans. In the event of military involvement in a domestic disaster, as stipulated in these plans, ground troop responsibilities would range from crowd control to high-end, full-scale disaster management following attacks that utilize WMDs. What is important to note about these plans, which are the first of their kind, is that they maintain in explicit verbiage that military assets utilized in a domestic incident will be provided in support of civilian response units, including police, fire, and EMS officials. They do allow, however, for the military to assume command in mass casualty situations where local response units are clearly overwhelmed and no longer able to adequately perform their duties.

These military plans are based on two separate documents, entitled CONPLAN 2002 and CONPLAN 0500 (CONPLAN is short for "Concept Plan"). CONPLAN 2002 was drafted to centralize missions of domestic basis into a single document, covering land, sea, and air operations. The plan covers the pre- and post-attack timeframes, which enables the military to help prevent terrorist attacks from occurring (either within or outside the United States). CONPLAN 0500, on the other hand, covers the organizational response to the 15 hypothetical scenarios mentioned earlier. These two plans have yet to gain approval of the Secretary of Defense.

These plans represent a great advancement for military involvement in domestic disaster response. Though it was always assumed that the military may have to lend support in response to a large-scale terrorist attack within the United States, no formalized plans had been created to dictate how that would be carried out. Through these plans, the military will be able to formalize both its responsibilities and capabilities, and will likely be able to exercise in this role before its members are required to perform.

Organizations that are concerned with civil liberties have raised alarm about the idea of greater military involvement in homeland security operations. These groups feel that such defined military involvement would run counter to the 1878 Posse Comitatus Act, which prevents military forces from participating in domestic law enforcement in any form (this act was reiterated in the Homeland Security Act of 2002). However, military drafters of the two CONPLANs assert that the military role would fall under Article 2 of the Constitution, which allows the president to use the military to defend the nation as he sees fit, which is allowable under the Posse Comitatus Act (Washington Post, 2005).

Department of Energy

Through its Office of Emergency Response, the Department of Energy (DOE) manages radiological emergency response assets that support both crisis and consequence management response in the event of an incident involving a WMD. DOE is prepared to respond immediately to any type of radiological accident or incident with its radiological emergency response assets.

Through its Office of Nonproliferation and National Security, DOE coordinates activities in nonproliferation, international nuclear safety, and communicated threat assessment. DOE maintains the following capabilities that support domestic terrorism preparedness and response:

- *Aerial Measuring System (AMS):* AMS is an aircraft-operated radiation detection system that uses fixed-wing aircraft and helicopters equipped with state-of-the-art technology instrumentation to track, monitor, and sample airborne radioactive plumes and/or detect and measure radioactive material deposited on the ground.

- *Atmospheric Release Advisory Capability (ARAC):* ARAC is a computer-based atmospheric dispersion and deposition modeling capability operated by Lawrence Livermore National Laboratory (LLNL), and its role in an emergency begins when a nuclear, chemical, or other hazardous material is, or has the potential of being, released into the atmosphere. ARAC's capability consists of meteorologists and other technical staff using three-dimensional computer models and real-time weather data to project the dispersion and deposition of radioactive material in the environment.

- *Accident Response Group (ARG):* ARG is DOE's primary emergency response capability for responding to emergencies involving U.S. nuclear weapons. ARG members will deploy with highly specialized, state-of-the-art equipment for weapons recovery and monitoring operations. ARG advance elements focus on initial assessment and provide preliminary advice to decision makers.

- *Federal Radiological Monitoring and Assessment Center (FRMAC):* For major radiological emergencies affecting the United States, the DOE established an FRMAC. The center is the control point for all federal assets involved in the monitoring and assessment of off-site radiological conditions. FRMAC provides support to the affected states, coordinates federal off-site radiological environmental monitoring and assessment activities, maintains a technical liaison with tribal nations and state and local governments, responds to the assessment needs of the LFA, and meets the statutory responsibilities of the participating federal agency.

- *Nuclear Emergency Search Team (NEST):* NEST is DOE's program for dealing with the technical aspects of nuclear or radiological terrorism. Response teams vary in size from a five-person technical advisory team to a tailored deployment of dozens of searchers and scientists who can locate and then conduct or support technical operations on a suspected nuclear device.

- *Radiological Assistance Program (RAP):* Under RAP, DOE provides, upon request, radiological assistance to DOE program elements, other federal agencies, state, tribal, and local governments, private groups, and individuals. RAP provides resources (trained personnel and equipment) to evaluate, assess, advise, and assist in the mitigation of actual or perceived radiation hazards and risks to workers, the public, and the environment.

- *Radiation Emergency Assistance Center/ Training Site (REAC/TS):* The REAC/TS is managed by DOE's Oak Ridge Institute for Science and Education in Oak Ridge, Tennessee, and it maintains a 24-hour response center staffed with personnel and equipment to support medical aspects of radiological emergencies.

- *Communicated Threat Credibility Assessment:* DOE is the program manager for the Nuclear Assessment Program (NAP) at LLNL. The NAP is a DOE-funded asset specifically designed to provide technical, operational, and behavioral assessments of the credibility of communicated threats directed against the U.S. government and its interests.

- *Nuclear Incident Response:* This program provides expert personnel and specialized equipment to a number of federal emergency response entities that deal with nuclear emergencies, nuclear accidents, and nuclear terrorism. The emergency response personnel are experts in such fields as device assessment, device disablement, intelligence analysis, credibility assessment, and health physics.

Department of Health and Human Services

The Department of Health and Human Services (HHS), as the lead federal agency for Emergency Support Function (ESF) #8 (health and medical services), provides coordinated federal assistance to supplement state and local resources in response to public health and medical care needs following a major disaster or emergency. Additionally, HHS provides support during developing or potential medical situations and has the responsibility for federal support of food, drug, and sanitation issues. Resources are furnished when state and local resources are overwhelmed and public health and/or medical assistance is requested from the federal government.

HHS, in its primary agency role for ESF #8, coordinates the provision of federal health and medical assistance to fulfill the requirements identified by the affected state/local authorities having jurisdiction. Included in ESF #8 is overall public health response; triage, treatment, and transportation of victims of the disaster; and evacuation of patients out of the disaster area, as needed, into a network of military services, veterans affairs, and pre-enrolled non-federal hospitals located in the major metropolitan areas of the United States.

ESF #8 utilizes resources primarily available from:

1. Within HHS
2. ESF #8 support agencies
3. The National Disaster Medical System
4. Specific non-federal sources (major pharmaceutical suppliers, hospital supply vendors, international disaster response organizations, and international health organizations)

Other than the agencies integrated under FEMA, the CDC may also be used in response activities. CDC is the federal agency responsible for protecting the public health of the country through prevention and control of diseases and response to public health emergencies. CDC works with national and international agencies to eradicate or control communicable diseases and other preventable conditions. The CDC's Bioterrorism Preparedness and Response Program oversees the agency's effort to prepare state and local governments to respond to acts of bioterrorism. In addition, CDC has designated emergency response personnel throughout the agency who are responsible for responding to biological, chemical, and radiological terrorism. CDC has epidemiologists trained to investigate and control outbreaks or illnesses, as well as laboratories capable of quantifying an individual's exposure to biological or chemical agents.

Environmental Protection Agency

The Environmental Protection Agency (EPA) is chartered to respond to WMD releases under the National Oil and Hazardous Substances Pollution Contingency Plan (NCP) regardless of the cause of the release. EPA is authorized by the Comprehensive Environmental Response, Compensation, and Liability Act (CERCLA); the Oil Pollution Act; and the Emergency Planning and Community Right-to-Know Act to support federal, state, and local responders in counterterrorism.

EPA will provide support to the FBI during crisis management in response to a terrorist incident. In its crisis management role, the EPA on-scene commander (OSC) may provide the FBI special agent in charge (SAC) with technical advice and recommendations, scientific and technical assessments, and assistance (as needed) to state and local responders. The EPA's OSC will support DHS during consequence management for the incident. EPA carries out its response according to the FRP's ESF #10, Hazardous Materials. The OSC may request an environmental response team that is funded by the EPA if the terrorist incident exceeds available local and regional resources. The EPA chairs the National Response Team (NRT).

Department of Agriculture

It is the policy of the U.S. Department of Agriculture (USDA) to "be prepared to respond swiftly in the event of national security, natural disaster, technological, and other emergencies at the national, regional, state, and county levels to provide support and comfort to the people of the United States." USDA has been charged with ensuring the safety of the nation's food supply. Since September 11, the concern that bioterrorism will impact agriculture in rural America, namely, crops in the field, hoofed animals, and food-safety issues related to food in the food chain between the slaughterhouse and/or processing facilities and the consumer, has only grown. USDA offices that address this concern include:

- *Office of Crisis Planning and Management (OCPM):* This USDA office coordinates the emergency planning, preparedness, and crisis management functions and the suitability for employment investigations of the department.
- *USDA State Emergency Boards (SEBs):* The SEBs have responsibility for coordinating USDA emergency activities at the state level.
- *Farm Service Agency:* This USDA agency develops and administers emergency plans and controls covering food processing, storage, and wholesale distribution; distribution and use of seed; and manufacture, distribution, and use of livestock and poultry feed.
- *The Food and Nutrition Service (FNS):* This USDA agency provides food assistance in officially designated disaster areas on request by the designated state agency. Generally, the food assistance response from FNS includes authorization of Emergency Food Stamp Program benefits and use of USDA-donated foods for emergency mass feeding and household distribution, as necessary. FNS also maintains a current inventory of USDA-donated food held in federal, state, and commercial warehouses and provides leadership to the FRP under ESF #11, Food.

- *Food Safety and Inspection Service:* This USDA agency inspects meat and meat products, poultry and poultry products, and egg products in slaughtering and processing plants; assists the Food and Drug Administration in the inspection of other food products; develops plans and procedures for radiological emergency response in accordance with the Federal Radiological Emergency Response Plan (FRERP); and provides support, as required, to the FRP at the national and regional levels.

- *Natural Resources Conservation Service:* This USDA agency provides technical assistance to individuals, communities, and governments relating to proper use of land for agricultural production; provides ʌssistance in determining the extent of damage to agricultural land and water; and provides support to the FRP under ESF #3, Public Works and Engineering.

- *Agricultural Research Service (ARS):* This USDA agency develops and carries out all necessary research programs related to crop or livestock diseases; provides technical support for emergency programs and activities in the areas of planning, prevention, detection, treatment, and management of consequences; provides technical support for the development of guidance information on the effects of radiation, biological, and chemical agents on agriculture; develops and maintains a current inventory of ARS-controlled laboratories that can be mobilized on short notice for emergency testing of food, feed, and water safety; and provides biological, chemical, and radiological safety support for USDA.

- *Economic Research Service:* This USDA agency, in cooperation with other departmental agencies, analyzes the impacts of the emergency on the U.S. agricultural system, as well as on rural communities, as part of the process of developing strategies to respond to the effects of an emergency.

- *Rural Business-Cooperative Service:* This USDA agency, in cooperation with other government agencies at all levels, promotes economic development in affected rural areas by developing strategies that respond to the conditions created by an emergency.

- *Cooperative State Research, Education, and Extension Service (CSREES):* This USDA agency coordinates use of land-grant and other cooperating state college and university services and other relevant research institutions in carrying out all responsibilities for emergency programs.

- *Rural Housing Service:* This USDA agency will assist the Department of Housing and Urban Development by providing living quarters in unoccupied rural housing in an emergency situation.

- *Rural Utilities Service:* This USDA agency will provide support to the FRP under ESF #12, Energy, at the national level.

- *Office of Inspector General (OIG):* This USDA office is the department's principal law enforcement component and liaison with the FBI. OIG, in concert with appropriate federal, state, and local agencies, is prepared to investigate any terrorist attacks relating to the nation's agriculture sector, to identify subjects, interview witnesses, and secure evidence in preparation for federal prosecution. As necessary, OIG will examine USDA programs regarding counterterrorism-related matters.

- *Forest Service (FS):* This USDA agency will prevent and control fires in rural areas in cooperation with state, local, and tribal governments and appropriate federal departments and agencies. They will determine and report requirements for equipment, personnel, fuels, chemicals, and other materials needed for carrying out assigned duties.

Nuclear Regulatory Commission

The Nuclear Regulatory Commission (NRC) is the lead federal agency (in accordance with the Federal Radiological Emergency Response Plan) for facilities or materials regulated by NRC or by an NRC agreement. NRC's counterterrorism-specific role, at these facilities or material sites, is to exercise the Federal lead for radiological safety while supporting other federal, state, and local agencies in crisis and consequence management. Emergency management assistance that is provided by the NRC includes:

- *Radiological Safety Assessments:* NRC provides facilities (or materials users) with technical advice to ensure on-site measures are taken to mitigate negative "off-site" consequences. NRC serves as the primary federal source of information regarding on-site radiological conditions and off-site radiological effects. The commission supports the technical needs of other federal agencies by providing descriptions of devices or facilities containing radiological materials and assessing the safety impact of terrorist actions and of proposed tactical operations of any responders. Safety assessments are coordinated through an NRC liaison at the Domestic Emergency Support Team (DEST), Strategic Information and Operations Center (SIOC), Command Post (CP), and Joint Operations Center (JOC).

- *Protective Action Recommendations:* NRC contacts state and local authorities and offers them advice and assistance on the technical assessment of radiological hazards and, if requested, provides advice on protective actions for the public. NRC coordinates any recommendations for protective actions through an NRC liaison at the CP or JOC.

- *Responder Radiation Protection:* NRC assesses the potential radiological hazards to any responders and coordinates with the radiation protection staff of an affected facility (or disaster site) to ensure that personnel responding to the scene are observing the appropriate precautions.

- *Information Coordination:* NRC supplies other responders and government officials with timely information concerning the radiological aspects of an event. NRC liaises with the Joint Information Center to coordinate information concerning the federal response.

▨ ▨ Critical Thinking ▨

How does the involvement of the Department of Defense in the nation's emergency management system differ from all other federal agencies? Why is this difference significant? Do you feel that anything should be done to change the way the military supports domestic emergency management?

National Incident Management System (NIMS)

A difficult issue in any response operation is determining who is in charge of the overall response effort at the incident. This concept of control, or leadership, is most commonly referred to in the emergency management community as *incident command*. With the significant shift in legislation brought about by the creation of the Department of Homeland Security, and the new emphasis on terrorism, the issue of incident command was in danger of becoming even more difficult and, likewise, confusing and even conflicting. To address the concerns that many officials at the local, state, and federal levels expressed in light of the changes that were occurring in the emergency management world, President George W. Bush called on the Secretary of Homeland Security, by means of Homeland Security Presidential Directive No. 5, to develop a nationally based incident command system. The purpose of this system, it was assumed, was to provide a consistent nationwide approach for federal, state, tribal, and local governments to work together to prepare for, prevent, respond to, and recover from domestic incidents — regardless of their cause, size, or complexity.

On March 1, 2004, following the collective efforts of state and local government officials, representatives from a wide range of public safety organizations, and the Department of Homeland Security, the product result of HSPD-5 was released. The NIMS, as it is called, incorporated existing knowledge, lessons learned, and best practices into a new comprehensive national approach to domestic incident management and command that appeared to fully account for the many recent changes in federal response requirements that resulted for the reasons mentioned above. This document was

FIGURE 7–12 New York City, New York, September 21, 2001 — Rescue operations continue far into the night at the World Trade Center. (Photo by Andrea Booher/FEMA News Photo)

created such that it addressed all jurisdictional levels and all functional disciplines involved in emergency management.

The NIMS represents a core set of doctrine, principles, terminology, and organizational processes to enable the management of disasters at all government levels. One very important aspect of this new framework is that it recognized the value of an existing system, the Incident Command System (ICS), and stressed the importance of effective incident command as a way of better managing disaster events. The well-known National Commission on Terrorist Attacks Upon the United States (the 9/11 Commission) identified ICS as an answer to many of the coordination problems that arose during the response to the September 11 attacks, and recommended a national adoption of ICS to enhance command, control, and communications capabilities during disaster response (Figure 7–12).

To better understand the processes by which NIMS helps in the management of events requiring multiple levels of government, it is necessary to have a brief understanding of the Incident Command System. The ICS was developed in California in 1970 after a devastating wildfire. During the after-action analysis of the response to the fire, which caused hundreds of millions of dollars in damage, killed 16 people, and left hundreds of families without homes, it was recognized that problems with communications and with coordination between different agencies made operations much less effective than they could have been. Following this analysis, Congress mandated that a system be created to address these coordination issues, and the result was a system called FIRESCOPE ICS, developed by the U.S. Forest Service, the California Department of Forestry and Fire Protection, the Governor's Office of Emergency Services, and several local and county fire departments.

FIRESCOPE ICS effectively standardized the response to wildfires in California. It resulted in a common terminology being used by all responding agencies, which significantly reduced the confusion. It established common procedures to be applied to firefighting, which significantly reduced the amount of time needed to coordinate between two or more agencies that would be working together on attacking a fire. Several "field tests" had shown that the system was effective, and by 1981 it was being applied throughout Southern California. So effective was FIRESCOPE ICS at standardizing coordination to wildfire events, that departments began to apply its methods to other events unrelated to wildfires. It was soon recognized as being effective for the response to floods, hazardous materials (HAZMAT) spills and leaks, earthquakes, and even major transportation accidents.

There are multiple functions in the ICS, including common use of terminology, integrated communications, a unified command structure, resource management, and action planning. A planned set of directives includes assigning one coordinator to manage the infrastructure of the response and assigning personnel, deploying equipment, obtaining resources, and working with the numerous agencies that respond to the disaster scene. In most instances, the local fire chief or fire commissioner is designated the incident commander.

The ICS was designed to remain effective at each of the following three levels of incident escalation:

1. Single jurisdiction and/or single agency
2. Single jurisdiction with multiagency support
3. Multijurisdictional and/or multiagency support

There are five major management systems within the ICS. They include command, operations, planning, logistics, and finance. Each is described here:

Command: The command section includes developing, directing, and maintaining communication and collaboration with the multiple agencies on site, as well as working with local officials, the public, and the media to provide up-to-date information regarding the disaster.

Operations: The operations section handles the tactical operations, coordinates the command objectives, develops tactical operations, and organizes and directs all resources to the disaster site.

Planning: The planning section provides the necessary information to the command center to develop the action plan to accomplish the objectives. This section also collects and evaluates information as it is made available.

Logistics: The logistics section provides personnel, equipment, and support for the command center. This section handles the coordination of all services that are involved in the response from locating rescue equipment to coordinating the response for volunteer organizations such as the Salvation Army and the Red Cross.

Finance: The finance section is responsible for the accounting for funds used during the response and recovery aspect of the disaster. The finance section monitors costs related to the incident and provides accounting procurement time recording cost analyses.

Under the ICS, there is almost always a single incident commander. However, even under this single command figure, the ICS allows for something called a *unified command* (UC). Unified command is often used when there is more than one agency with incident jurisdiction or when incidents cross multiple political jurisdictions. Within this UC framework, agencies are able to work together through the designated members of the UC, often with a senior official from each agency or discipline participating in the UC, to establish a common set of objectives and strategies and a single plan of action. Due to the nature of disasters, multiple government agencies often need to work together to monitor the response and manage the large number of personnel responding to the scene. ICS allows for the integration of the agencies to operate under a single response management.

Although NIMS was built upon this ICS system, the new system extends far beyond the initial scope of ICS. This is to be expected, of course, considering the exponentially greater size of the incidents regularly managed under NIMS (despite that NIMS was designed to be effectively used to manage small, single-jurisdictional events such as house fires or automobile accidents). NIMS establishes standardized incident management processes, protocols, and procedures that all responders, whether they are federal, state, tribal, or local, can use to coordinate and conduct their cooperative response actions. Using these standardized procedures, it is presumed that all responders will be able to share a common understanding, and will be able to work together with very little mismatch. The following are the key components of the new incident management system:

- **Incident Command System (ICS).** NIMS establishes ICS as a standard incident management organization with five functional areas — command, operations, planning, logistics, and finance/administration — for management of all major incidents. To ensure further coordination, and during incidents involving multiple jurisdictions or agencies, the principle of unified command has been universally incorporated into NIMS. This unified command not only coordinates the efforts of many jurisdictions, but provides for and ensures joint decisions on objectives, strategies, plans, priorities, and public communications.

- **Communications and Information Management.** Standardized communications during an incident are essential, and NIMS prescribes interoperable communications systems for both incident and information management. NIMS recognizes that responders and managers across all agencies and jurisdictions must have common access to the full operational picture, thereby allowing for efficient and effective incident response.

- **Preparedness.** Preparedness incorporates a range of measures, actions, and processes accomplished before an incident happens. NIMS preparedness measures include planning, training, exercises, qualification and certification, equipment acquisition and certification, and publication management. NIMS stresses that each of these measures helps to ensure that preincident actions are standardized and consistent with mutually agreed-on doctrine. NIMS further places emphasis on mitigation activities to enhance preparedness. Mitigation includes public education and outreach; structural modifications to reduce the loss of life or destruction of property; code enforcement in support of zoning rules, land management, and building codes; and flood insurance and property buy-out for frequently flooded areas.

- **Joint Information System (JIS).** The Joint Information System provides the public with timely and accurate incident information and unified public messages. This system employs Joint Information Centers (JICs) and brings incident communicators together during an incident to develop, coordinate, and deliver a unified message. This is performed under the assumption that it will ensure federal, state, and local levels of government are releasing the same information during an incident.

- **NIMS Integration Center (NIC).** To ensure that NIMS remains an accurate and effective management tool, a NIMS NIC will be established by the DHS secretary to assess proposed changes to NIMS, capture and evaluate lessons learned, and employ best practices. The NIC will provide strategic direction and oversight, supporting both routine maintenance and continuous refinement of the system and its components over the long term. It will also develop and facilitate national standards for NIMS education and training, first-responder communications and equipment, typing of resources, qualification and credentialing of incident management and responder personnel, and standardization of equipment maintenance and resources. Finally, the NIC will continue to use the collaborative process of federal, state, tribal, local, multidisciplinary, and private authorities to assess prospective changes to NIMS.

Figure 7–13 illustrates how NIMS was developed on the structure originally outlined in the Incident Command System. The NRP, which guides the federal support of state, county, tribal, and local response to disasters, was built on the NIMS framework. Together, these three coordinated concepts have likely helped to further eliminate coordination problems that may have existed before in the absence of such complementary systems.

Federal Response

Almost every facet of the nation's emergency response system has undergone change to some degree as a result of the reaction to the September 11 terrorist attacks on America. While some of the

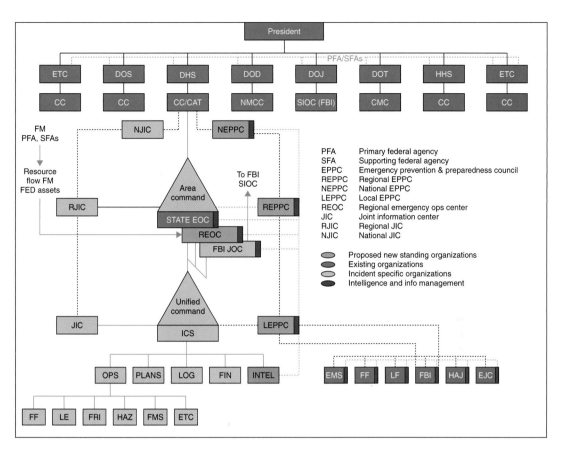

FIGURE 7–13 National structure for NIMS operations.

more significant adjustments have occurred at the federal level — most notably the creation of the Department of Homeland Security — all state and most local agencies have followed this lead. As for the response to major disasters, namely those requiring action by multiple levels of government, these changes have resulted in a shift toward increased federal control and direction. This shift is most notable with regard to events that involve a criminal element such as exists with intentional disasters (e.g., sabotage or civil unrest) and terrorist-driven threats or events. These changes have all been formalized through the transformation of the federal response framework from the old Federal Response Plan (FRP) — which was successfully applied during several terrorist event responses including the Murrah Federal Building bombing and the September 11 attacks — to the NRP (NRP) in the years immediately following the September 11 attacks — to the NRF, released January 2008 in response to criticisms and shortcomings of the NRP.

It has traditionally been the case that a federal response may be initiated in two ways: A governor can request a presidential disaster declaration or the president can declare a presidential emergency upon damage to federal entities (as was the case for the *Discovery* tragedy). Today, however, there is a third mechanism. The president, through FEMA, can predeploy resources (personnel and equipment) to a location where a disaster declaration is imminent due to an impending disaster. These authorities first appeared in the NRP, and remain unchanged under the NRF. It is important to note that, although a formal declaration does not have to be signed by the president for the federal government to begin response, the governor of the affected state must make a formal request for assistance to occur, and must specify in the request the specific needs of the disaster area. Under the new NRF, the president may unilaterally declare a major disaster or emergency if extraordinary circumstances exist. For summaries of procedures on disaster declaration by the president and assistance without the president's declaration, see the sidebars, "Presidential Major Disaster Declaration Process Guidelines" and "Federal Assistance without a Presidential Declaration," respectively.

Presidential Major Disaster Declaration Process Guidelines

- The Stafford Act (§401) requires that: "All requests for a declaration by the President that a major disaster exists shall be made by the Governor of the affected State." A State also includes the District of Columbia, Puerto Rico, the Virgin Islands, Guam, American Samoa, and the Commonwealth of the Northern Mariana Islands. The Marshall Islands and the Federated States of Micronesia are also eligible to request a declaration and receive assistance.
- Contact is made between the Governor of the affected State (including the District of Columbia), or territory, and the FEMA Regional Administrator. This contact may take place prior to or immediately following the disaster.
- State and Federal officials conduct a preliminary damage assessment (PDA) to estimate the extent of the disaster and its impact on individuals and public facilities. This information is included in the Governor's request to show that the disaster is of such severity and magnitude that effective response is beyond the capabilities of the State and the local governments and that Federal assistance is necessary. Normally, the PDA is completed prior to the submission of the Governor's request. However, when an obviously severe or catastrophic event occurs, the Governor's request may be submitted prior to the PDA. Nonetheless, the Governor must still make the request.
- Based on the PDA findings, the Governor submits a request to the president through the FEMA Regional Administrator for either a major disaster or an emergency declaration and identifies the affected counties. As part of the request, the Governor must take appropriate action under State law and direct execution of the State's emergency plan. The Governor has to provide in the request information on the nature and amount of State and local resources that have been or will be committed to alleviating the results of the disaster, provide an estimate of the amount and severity of damage and the impact on the private and public sector, and provide an estimate of the type and amount of assistance needed under the Stafford Act.
- The completed request, addressed to the President, is submitted through the FEMA Regional Administrator, who evaluates the damage and requirements for Federal assistance and makes a recommendation to the FEMA Administrator.
- The FEMA Administrator, acting through the Secretary of Homeland Security, may then recommend a course of action to the President.
- Based on the Governor's request, the president may declare that a major disaster or emergency exists, thereby activating the NRP and setting in motion the full array of available Federal programs to assist in the response and recovery effort. The Governor, appropriate Members of Congress, and Federal departments and agencies are immediately notified of a Presidential declaration.

Source: Federal Emergency Management Agency, "National Response Framework," 2008, http://www.fema.gov/emergency/nrf/.

■ ■ ■

Federal Assistance without a Presidential Declaration

In many cases, assistance may be obtained from the Federal government without a Presidential declaration. For example, FEMA places liaisons in State EOCs and moves commodities near incident sites that may require Federal assistance prior to a Presidential declaration. Additionally, some types of assistance, such as Fire Management Assistance Grants — which provide support to States experiencing severe wildfires — are performed by Federal departments or agencies under their own authorities and do not require Presidential approval. Finally, Federal departments and agencies may provide immediate lifesaving assistance to States under their own statutory authorities without a formal Presidential declaration.

Source: Federal Emergency Management Agency, "National Response Framework," 2008, www.fema.gov.

■ ■ ■

Under the NRF, the president maintains the ultimate discretion in making a disaster declaration. There are no set criteria by which he or she is bound, no government regulations to guide which events are declared disasters and which are not. FEMA has developed a number of factors it considers in making its recommendation to the president, including individual property losses per capita, level of damage to existing community infrastructure, level of insurance coverage, repetitive events, and other subjective factors. But in the end, the decision to make the declaration is the president's alone. One major change in the verbiage of the plan, as changed in the NRP, concerns the prevention of terrorist attacks. In situations where the Homeland Security Operations Center determines that a terrorist threat exists for which federal intervention is required to prevent an incident from occurring, DHS provides support as necessary under the direction of the attorney general, through the FBI.

A presidential disaster declaration can be made in as short a time as a few hours, as was the case in the 1994 Northridge earthquake, the 1995 Oklahoma City bombing, and the September 11 World Trade Center attacks (Figure 7–14). Sometimes it takes weeks for damages to be assessed and the capability of state and local jurisdictions to fund response and recovery efforts to be evaluated. Should the governor's request be turned down by the president, the governor has the right to appeal, an appeal that will be considered, especially if new damage data become available and are included in the appeal.

Presidential declarations are routinely sought for such events as floods, hurricanes, earthquakes, and tornadoes. In recent years, governors have become more inventive and have requested presidential disaster declarations for snow removal, drought, West Nile virus, and economic losses caused by failing industries, such as the Northwest salmon-spawning decline.

Once a disaster declaration has been made, the full range of federal government resources becomes available to assist the affected state or states. The federal assistance is guided through the invocation of the NRP, which is detailed later in this chapter. Through this plan, and under the guidance of the Department of Homeland Security, 32 signatory federal agencies and the American Red Cross provide all forms of assistance as dictated under the 15 emergency support functions (also detailed later in this chapter). A declaration also paves the way for federal funding to pay for response activities at all government levels (including reimbursing the expenses of federal agencies that do respond), and certain recovery costs to individuals, businesses, nonprofit agencies, and public entities.

From January 1953 to December 2007, there were 1,734 presidential disaster declarations, averaging 32 declarations per year (Table 7–9). As an illustration of disaster declaration activity in a single year, in 1999 there were 50 major disaster declarations in 38 states:

18 for hurricanes (13 alone for Hurricane Floyd)
11 for tornadoes

FIGURE 7–14 New York City, New York, September 27, 2001 — Search dogs proved very helpful to the search and rescue teams throughout the cleanup effort at the World Trade Center. (Photo by Bri Rodriguez/FEMA News Photo)

Table 7–9   Total Major Disaster Declarations, 1953–2007

Year	Declarations
1953	13
1954	17
1955	18
1956	16
1957	16
1958	7
1959	7
1960	12
1961	12
1962	22
1963	20
1964	25
1965	25
1966	11
1967	11
1968	19
1969	29
1970	17
1971	17
1972	48
1973	46
1974	46
1975	38
1976	30

1977	22
1978	25
1979	42
1980	23
1981	15
1982	24
1983	21
1984	34
1985	27
1986	28
1987	23
1988	11
1989	31
1990	38
1991	43
1992	45
1993	32
1994	36
1995	32
1996	75
1997	44
1998	65
1999	50
2000	45
2001	45
2002	49
2003	46
2004	68
2005	48
2006	52
2007	63
Total	**1,734**
Average	**32**

Source: FEMA, 2008.

7 for floods
6 for winter storms
6 for severe storms
1 for a flash flood
1 for winter freeze

Before the creation of the NRP, and subsequent NRF, there were several individual response plans that guided the government response to several different kinds of emergencies or disasters. However, HSPD-5 directed DHS to develop the NRP such that all existing federal plans were integrated into that one document or directly linked through formal coordination mechanisms — giving it the distinction of serving as the single guide for federal response. The following list contains the various plans and operation guidelines integrated or linked under the NRP:

- Federal Response Plan (FRP)

- Federal Radiological Emergency Response Plan (FRERP)

- Domestic Terrorism Concept of Operations Plan (CONPLAN)
- Mass Mitigation Emergency Plan (Distant Shore)
- National Oil Spill and Hazardous Substances Pollution Contingency Plan (NCP)

The NRP essentially replaced the Federal Response Plan, and accommodated the needs of events covered under the FRERP, CONPLAN, Distant Shore, and NCP, as well as several newly identified or newly addressed issues through the development of various *incident annexes*. These annexes, which have not yet been developed for the new NRF and are therefore still applicable in their original NRP format, include the following (described in much greater detail later in this chapter):

- Biological incident
- Catastrophic incident
- Cyber incident
- Food and agriculture incident
- Nuclear/radiological incident
- Oil and hazardous materials incident
- Terrorism incident law enforcement and investigation

National Response Framework (NRF)

The NRF was developed to be a single document by which emergency management efforts at all levels of government could be structured. The NRF has been described by FEMA as being "a guide to how the Nation conducts all-hazards response." It is meant to be scalable, flexible, and adaptable in coordinating the key roles and responsibilities of response participants throughout the country, at all levels of government. It describes specific authorities and practices for managing incidents that range from serious local events to large-scale national-level terrorist attacks or catastrophic natural disasters. The NRF was built directly upon the structure of the NIMS, itself developed to provide a consistent template for managing incidents.

The NRF is the latest iteration in a progression of emergency response documents guiding federal emergency management action. The first in this series of documents was the Federal Response Plan, released in 1992, which focused most specifically on the roles and responsibilities of the federal government in assistance to overwhelmed state and local jurisdictions. Following the 9/11 attacks, it was determined that the document guiding national response required a more comprehensive approach in order to define the state, local, and other roles in the greater scheme of major disaster response and recovery. As a result, the National Response Plan (NRP) was released in 2004, thereby replacing the Federal Response Plan. Nine months after Katrina's landfall, however, a notice of change to the NRP was released, incorporating preliminary lessons learned from the 2005 hurricane season. These changes were based upon suggestions of various emergency management stakeholders, many of whom felt that the NRP was overly bureaucratic, repetitive, and national in focus. FEMA officials felt that one of the greatest criticisms came in that users did not consider the NRP to be a "plan" as its name suggested, but rather a framework guiding the types of actions that could be taken in response to the variety of possible incidents that might occur. In response, the Department of Homeland Security developed and released the NRF in September of 2007, and provided a period for comments by local and state stakeholders. Changes were made to the draft framework based upon these comments, and on January 22, 2008, the final NRF was released. The document became official 60 days following its release, thereby superseding the NRP.

The NRF is built upon the template established under the NIMS, which was called for by Homeland Security Presidential Directive (HSPD) 5 in the aftermath of the September 11 terrorist attacks. NIMS enables all levels of government, the private sector, and nongovernmental organizations (NGOs) to work together during an emergency or disaster event. The NRF and NIMS, working together, seek to ensure that all stakeholders are operating under a common set of emergency management principles.

The NRF can either be partially or fully implemented in the lead-up or response to an emergency or disaster threat, thereby allowing for what is considered a "scaled" response that tasks only those agencies and resources that are actually needed.

Organization of NRF

The NRF is comprised of:

- A core document: Describes the principles that guide national response roles and responsibilities, response actions, response organizations, and planning requirements that together work to achieve an effective national response to any incident that occurs
- The Emergency Support Function (ESF) Annexes: Group federal resources and capabilities into functional areas that are most frequently needed in a national response (e.g., transportation, firefighting, mass care)
- The Support Annexes: Describe essential supporting aspects that are common to all incidents (e.g., financial management, volunteer and donations management, private-sector coordination)
- The Incident Annexes: Address the unique aspects of how we respond to seven broad incident categories (e.g., biological, nuclear/radiological, cyber, mass evacuation)
- Partner Guides: Provide ready references describing key roles and actions for local, tribal, state, federal, and private-sector response partners

The NRF describes not only the roles and responsibilities of public-sector agencies, but also includes the private sector, NGOs, and individuals and households. Communities, tribes, states, the federal government, NGOs, and the private sector are each informed of their respective roles and responsibilities, and how their actions complement each other. Each governmental level is tasked with developing capabilities needed to respond to incidents, including the development of plans, conducting assessments and exercises, providing and directing resources and capabilities, and gathering lessons learned.

The scope of the NRF includes domestic incidents of all sizes, regardless of state or federal involvement. The NRF can be partially or fully implemented in response to or anticipation of a natural or technological hazard, or a terrorist threat. By defining what is called "selective implementation," the NRF allows for a scaled response. In this manner, events that start out small but grow larger in scope can be applicable to the plan from the moment they begin. This also allows for what is considered more seamless transition from local, to state, and ultimately to federal involvement as incidents grow in size. One of the greatest changes between the NRF and previous versions of the response document is that no formal declaration is required before the NRF may be invoked. For the NRF doctrine and nature of assistance available, see the sidebars, "National Response Framework Response Doctrine" and "Types of Federal Disaster Assistance Available under the NRF," respectively.

National Response Framework Response Doctrine

The response doctrine of the NRF defines basic roles, responsibilities, and operational concepts for response across all levels of government and with NGOs and the private sector. The overarching objective of response activities contained within the NRF centers upon saving lives and protecting property and the environment.

Five key operations principles define response actions in support of the nation's response mission. Taken together, these five principles constitute the national response doctrine. The response doctrine is rooted in America's federal system and the Constitution's division of responsibilities between federal and state governments. Because this doctrine reflects the history of emergency management and the distilled wisdom of responders and leaders at all levels, it gives elemental form to the NRF. This doctrine evolved in response to changes in the political and strategic landscape, lessons learned from operations, and the introduction of new technologies. The doctrine influences the way in which policy and plans are developed, forces are organized and trained, and equipment is procured. It promotes unity of purpose, guides professional judgment, and enables responders to best fulfill their responsibilities." Response doctrine is comprised of five key principles:

- Engaged partnership
- Tiered response
- Scalable, flexible, and adaptable operational capabilities
- Unity of effort through unified command
- Readiness to act

Source: DHS, National Response Framework, 2008, www.dhs.gov.

Types of Federal Disaster Assistance Available under the NRF

The National Response Framework (NRF) makes available the following types of assistance:

Preincident Services

- Interagency information and intelligence sharing is conducted to enable counterterrorism activities.
- Resources and staff can be prepositioned to ensure effective response in anticipation of a disaster.

Immediate Relief Delivery — Response Actions

- Assets are mobilized and resources are deployed to support the incident.
- Teams with specialized capabilities such as the NDMS, the HHS Secretary's Emergency Response Team, the Epidemic Intelligence Service, HHS behavioral health response teams, the U.S. Public Health Service Commissioned Corps, and Urban Search and Rescue teams are deployed.
- A Joint Field Office (JFO) and other field facilities are established to provide incident management, public health, and other community support.
- Assistance is provided to support immediate law enforcement, fire, ambulance, and emergency medical service actions; emergency flood fighting; evacuations; transportation system detours; emergency public information; actions taken to minimize additional damage; urban search and rescue; the establishment of facilities for mass care; the provision of public health and medical services, food, ice, water, and other emergency

essentials; debris clearance; the emergency restoration of critical infrastructure; control, containment, and removal of environmental contamination; and protection of responder health and safety.

- During the response to a terrorist event, law enforcement actions to collect and preserve evidence and to apprehend perpetrators are conducted.

Assistance to Speed Recovery and Reduce Damage from Future Occurrences

- Loans and grants to repair or replace damaged housing and personal property are provided.
- Grants to repair or replace roads and public buildings, incorporating to the extent practical hazard-reduction structural and nonstructural measures, are provided.
- Technical assistance to identify and implement mitigation opportunities to reduce future losses is provided.
- Other assistance, including crisis counseling, tax relief, legal services, and job placement may also be provided.

Source: Department of Homeland Security (DHS), "The National Response Plan," Washington, DC: DHS, 2005.

Roles and Responsibilities Defined by the NRF

The NRF Core Document provides an overview of the roles and responsibilities of key emergency management stakeholders at the local, tribal, state, and federal levels who are involved in the implementation of the NRF, including the private sector and nongovernmental organizations (NGOs). The following section describes exactly who is involved with the NRF at each jurisdictional level, and what each must do to build and maintain emergency response capabilities.

Local Level

Disaster response almost always begins locally, and remains local in terms of actual incident command and control responsibility. This responsibility rests both with the individual members of the community themselves and the public officials elected by them in the county and city governments. The responsibilities of the following individuals are specifically mentioned in the NRF.

Chief Elected or Appointed Official

A mayor, city manager, or county manager, as a jurisdiction's chief executive officer, is responsible for ensuring the public safety and welfare of the people of that jurisdiction. Specifically, this official provides strategic guidance and resources during preparedness, response, and recovery efforts by:

- Establishing strong working relationships with local jurisdictional leaders and core private-sector organizations, voluntary agencies, and community partners. This official must get to know, coordinate with, and train with local partners in advance of an incident and to develop mutual aid and/or assistance agreements for support in response to an incident.
- Leading and encouraging local leaders to focus on preparedness by participating in planning, training, and exercises.

- Supporting participation in local mitigation efforts within the jurisdiction and, as appropriate, with the private sector.
- Understanding and implementing laws and regulations that support emergency management and response.
- Ensuring that local emergency plans take into account the needs of:

  The jurisdiction, including persons, property, and structures.

  Individuals with special needs, including those with service animals.

  Individuals with household pets.
- Encouraging residents to participate in volunteer organizations and training courses.
- Work closely with members of Congress during incidents and on an ongoing basis regarding local preparedness capabilities and needs.

Emergency Manager

The local emergency manager has the day-to-day authority and responsibility for overseeing emergency management programs and activities. They must work with chief elected and appointed officials to ensure that there are effective emergency plans in place and activities being conducted. Their role includes:

- Coordinating all components of the local emergency management program, to include assessing the availability and readiness of local resources most likely required during an incident and identifying and correcting any shortfalls.
- Coordinating the planning process and working cooperatively with other local agencies and private-sector organizations.
- Developing mutual aid and assistance agreements.
- Coordinating damage assessments during an incident.
- Advising and informing local officials about emergency management activities during an incident.
- Developing and executing public awareness and education programs.
- Conducting exercises to test plans and systems and obtain lessons learned.
- Involving the private sector and NGOs in planning, training, and exercises.

Department and Agency Heads

The local emergency manager is assisted by, and coordinates the efforts of, employees in departments and agencies that perform emergency management functions. The emergency management responsibilities of department and agency heads include:

- Collaborating with the emergency manager during development of local emergency plans and providing key response resources.
- Participating in the planning process to ensure that specific capabilities (e.g., firefighting, law enforcement, emergency medical services, public works, environmental and natural resources agencies) are integrated into a workable plan to safeguard the community.
- Developing, planning, and training to internal policies and procedures to meet response and recovery needs safely.
- Participating in interagency training and exercises to develop and maintain the necessary capabilities.

Individuals and Households

Although not formally a part of emergency management operations, individuals and households are considered as playing an important role in the overall emergency management strategy under the NRF. Specifically, the NRF states that community members can contribute by:

- Reducing hazards in and around their homes.
- Preparing an emergency supply kit and household emergency plan.
- Monitoring emergency communications carefully.
- Volunteering with an established organization.
- Enrolling in emergency response training courses.

Private Sector and NGOs

In almost every large-scale emergency incident, and some small-scale ones, the government must work together with private-sector and NGO groups as partners in emergency management. The roles of private-sector organizations include:

- Providing for the welfare and protection of their employees in the workplace.
- Private-sector components of the nation's critical infrastructure, including water, power, communications, transportation, medical care, security, and numerous other services, must work together with emergency managers to ensure effective response and recovery.
- Planning for the protection of information and the continuity of business operations.
- Planning for, responding to, and recovering from incidents that impact their own infrastructure and facilities.
- Collaborating with emergency management personnel before an incident occurs to ascertain what assistance may be necessary and how they can help.
- Developing and exercising emergency plans before an incident occurs.
- Where appropriate, establishing mutual aid and assistance agreements to provide specific response capabilities.
- Providing assistance (including volunteers) to support local emergency management and public awareness during response and throughout the recovery process.

Participation of the private sector varies based on the nature of the organization and the nature of the incident. The five distinct roles that private-sector organizations play are summarized in Table 7–10.

The NRF states that NGOs play "enormously important roles before, during, and after an incident." NGOs provide sheltering, emergency food supplies, counseling services, and other vital support services to support response and promote the recovery of disaster victims. These groups often provide specialized services that help individuals with special needs, including those with disabilities. NGOs bolster and support government efforts at all levels — for response operations and planning. NGOs impacted by a disaster may also need government assistance. NGOs collaborate with responders, governments at all levels, and other agencies and organizations. Examples of NGO and voluntary organization contributions include:

- Training and managing volunteer resources.
- Identifying shelter locations and needed supplies.
- Providing critical emergency services to those in need, such as cleaning supplies, clothing, food and shelter, or assistance with postemergency cleanup.
- Identifying those whose needs have not been met and helping coordinate the provision of assistance.

Table 7–10 Private-Sector Response Role under NRF

Category	Role in This Category
Impacted Organization or Infrastructure	Private-sector organizations may be impacted by direct or indirect consequences of the incident. These include privately owned critical infrastructure, key resources, and other private-sector entities that are significant to local, regional, and national economic recovery from the incident. Examples of privately owned infrastructure include transportation, telecommunications, private utilities, financial institutions, and hospitals. Critical infrastructure and key resources (CIKR) are grouped into 17 sectors that together provide essential functions and services supporting various aspects of the American government, economy, and society.
Regulated and/or Responsible Party	Owners/operators of certain regulated facilities or hazardous operations may be legally responsible for preparing for and preventing incidents from occurring and responding to an incident once it occurs. For example, federal regulations require owners/operators of nuclear power plants to maintain emergency plans and facilities and to perform assessments, prompt notifications, and training for a response to an incident.
Response Resource	Private-sector entities provide response resources (donated or compensated) during an incident — including specialized teams, essential service providers, equipment, and advanced technologies — through local public-private emergency plans or mutual aid and assistance agreements, or in response to requests from government and nongovernmental-volunteer initiatives.
Partner with State/Local Emergency Organizations	Private-sector entities may serve as partners in local and state emergency preparedness and response organizations and activities.
Components of Nation's Economy	As the key element of the national economy, private-sector resilience and continuity of operations planning, as well as recovery and restoration from an actual incident, represent essential homeland security activities.

States, Territories, and Tribal Governments

The primary emergency management role of state, territorial, and tribal governments is to supplement and facilitate local efforts before, during, and after an emergency incident occurs. These government agencies provide direct and routine assistance to their local jurisdictions through emergency management program development and by routinely coordinating these efforts with federal officials. They must be prepared to maintain or accelerate the provision of commodities and services to local governments when local capabilities fall short of demands. The roles and responsibilities of the following individuals are described in greater detail in the NRF.

Governor

The public safety and welfare of a state's citizens are fundamental responsibilities of the governor. The governor:

- Is responsible for coordinating state resources and providing the strategic guidance needed to prevent, mitigate, prepare for, respond to, and recover from incidents of all types.
- In accordance with state law, may be able to make, amend, or suspend certain orders or regulations associated with response.
- Communicates to the public and helps people, businesses, and organizations cope with the consequences of any type of incident.

- Commands the state military forces (National Guard personnel not in federal service and state militias).

- Coordinates assistance from other states through interstate mutual aid and assistance compacts, such as the Emergency Management Assistance Compact

- Requests federal assistance including, if appropriate, a Stafford Act presidential declaration of an emergency or major disaster, when it becomes clear that state capabilities will be insufficient or have been exceeded.

- Coordinates with impacted tribal governments within the state and initiates requests for a Stafford Act presidential declaration of an emergency or major disaster on behalf of an impacted tribe when appropriate.

State Homeland Security Advisor

The State Homeland Security Advisor serves as counsel to the governor on homeland security issues and may serve as a liaison between the governor's office, the state homeland security structure, DHS, and other organizations both inside and outside of the state. The adviser often chairs a committee comprised of representatives of relevant state agencies, including public safety, the National Guard, emergency management, public health, and others charged with developing prevention, protection, response, and recovery strategies. This also includes preparedness activities associated with these strategies.

Director, State Emergency Management Agency

All states have laws mandating establishment of a state emergency management agency and the emergency plans coordinated by that agency. The state Director of Emergency Management ensures that the state is prepared to deal with large-scale emergencies and is responsible for coordinating the state response in any incident. This includes supporting local governments as needed or requested and coordinating assistance with other states and/or the federal government. If local resources are not adequate, authorities can seek additional assistance from the county emergency manager or the state Director of Emergency Management. The state emergency management agency may dispatch personnel to the scene to assist in the response and recovery effort.

Other State Departments and Agencies

State department and agency heads and their staffs develop, plan, and train to internal policies and procedures to meet response and recovery needs safely. They also participate in interagency training and exercises to develop and maintain the necessary capabilities. They are vital to the state's overall emergency management and homeland security programs, as they bring expertise spanning the NRF's Emergency Support Functions and serve as core members of the state emergency operations center.

Indian Tribes

The U.S. government has a trust relationship with Indian tribes and recognizes their right to self-government. As such, tribal governments are responsible for coordinating resources to address actual or potential incidents. When local resources are not adequate, tribal leaders seek assistance from states or the federal government. For certain types of federal assistance, tribal governments work with the state, but as sovereign entities they can elect to deal directly with the federal government for other types of assistance. In order to obtain federal assistance via the Stafford Act, a state governor must request a presidential declaration on behalf of a tribe. The tribal leader is responsible for the public safety and welfare of the people of that tribe. As authorized by tribal government, the tribal leader:

- Is responsible for coordinating tribal resources needed to prevent, protect against, respond to, and recover from incidents of all types. This also includes preparedness and mitigation activities.

- May have powers to amend or suspend certain tribal laws or ordinances associated with response.

- Communicates with the tribal community, and helps people, businesses, and organizations cope with the consequences of any type of incident.
- Negotiates mutual aid and assistance agreements with other tribes or jurisdictions.
- Can request federal assistance under the Stafford Act through the governor of the state when it becomes clear that the tribe's capabilities will be insufficient or have been exceeded.
- Can elect to deal directly with the federal government. Although a state governor must request a presidential declaration on behalf of a tribe under the Stafford Act, federal departments or agencies can work directly with the tribe within existing authorities and resources.

Federal Government

When an incident occurs that exceeds or is anticipated to exceed local or state resources — or when an incident is managed by federal departments or agencies acting under their own authorities — the federal government uses the NRF to involve all necessary department and agency capabilities, organize the federal response, and ensure coordination with response partners. Under the NRF, the federal government's response structures are adaptable specifically to the nature and scope of a given incident. The principles of unified command are applied at the headquarters, regional, and field levels to enable diverse departments and agencies to work together effectively. Using unified command principles, participants share common goals and synchronize their activities to achieve those goals.

Coordination of Federal Responsibilities

The president leads the federal government response effort to ensure that the necessary coordinating structures, leadership, and resources are applied quickly and efficiently to large-scale and catastrophic incidents. The president's Homeland Security Council and National Security Council, which bring together cabinet officers and other department or agency heads as necessary, provide national strategic and policy advice to the president during large-scale incidents that affect the nation.

Federal assistance can be provided to state, tribal, and local jurisdictions, and to other federal departments and agencies, in a number of different ways through various mechanisms and authorities. Federal assistance does not require coordination by DHS, and can be provided without a presidential major disaster or emergency declaration (as is the case with the National Oil and Hazardous Substances Pollution Contingency Plan, the Mass Migration Emergency Plan, the National Search and Rescue Plan, and the National Maritime Security Plan).

When the overall coordination of federal response activities is required, it is implemented through the Secretary of Homeland Security. Other federal departments and agencies carry out their response authorities and responsibilities within this authority and direction. Several presidential directives outline the following primary lanes of responsibility that guide federal support at national, regional, and field levels.

Incident Management

The Secretary of Homeland Security is the principal federal official for domestic incident management. By presidential directive and statute, the secretary is responsible for coordination of federal resources utilized in the prevention of, preparation for, response to, or recovery from terrorist attacks, major disasters, or other emergencies. The role of the Secretary of Homeland Security is to provide the president with an overall architecture for domestic incident management and to coordinate the federal response, when required, while relying upon the support of other federal partners. Depending on the incident, the secretary also contributes elements of the response consistent with DHS's mission, capabilities, and authorities. The FEMA Administrator, as the principal advisor to the president, the secretary, and the Homeland Security Council on all matters regarding emergency management, helps the secretary in meeting these responsibilities. Federal assistance for incidents that do not require

DHS coordination may be led by other federal departments and agencies consistent with their authorities. The Secretary of Homeland Security may monitor such incidents and may activate specific NRF mechanisms to provide support to departments and agencies without assuming overall leadership for the federal response to the incident. The following four criteria define situations for which DHS shall assume overall federal incident management coordination responsibilities within the NSF and implement the NSF's coordinating mechanisms:

- A federal department or agency acting under its own authority has requested DHS assistance
- The resources of state and local authorities are overwhelmed and federal assistance has been requested
- More than one federal department or agency has become substantially involved in responding to the incident
- The secretary has been directed by the president to assume incident management responsibilities

Law Enforcement

- The attorney general is the chief law enforcement officer of the United States. Generally acting through the FBI, the attorney general has the lead responsibility for criminal investigations of terrorist acts or terrorist threats by individuals or groups inside the United States or directed at U.S. citizens or institutions abroad, as well as for coordinating activities of the other members of the law enforcement community to detect, prevent, and disrupt terrorist attacks against the United States. This includes actions that are based on specific intelligence or law enforcement information. In addition, the attorney general approves requests submitted by state governors pursuant to the Emergency Federal Law Enforcement Assistance Act for personnel and other federal law enforcement support during incidents. The attorney general also enforces federal civil rights laws and will provide expertise to ensure that these laws are appropriately addressed.

National Defense and Defense Support of Civil Authorities

The primary mission of the Department of Defense (DOD) and its components is national defense. Because of this critical role, resources are committed after approval by the secretary of defense or at the direction of the president. Many DOD components and agencies are authorized to respond to save lives, protect property and the environment, and mitigate human suffering under imminently serious conditions, as well as to provide support under their separate established authorities, as appropriate. The provision of defense support is evaluated by its legality, lethality, risk, cost, appropriateness, and impact on readiness. When federal military and civilian personnel and resources are authorized to support civil authorities, command of those forces will remain with the secretary of defense. DOD elements in the incident area of operations and National Guard forces under the command of a governor will coordinate closely with response organizations at all levels.

International Coordination

The secretary of state is responsible for managing international preparedness, response, and recovery activities relating to domestic incidents and the protection of U.S. citizens and U.S. interests overseas.

Intelligence

The Director of National Intelligence leads the intelligence community, serves as the president's principal intelligence advisor, and oversees and directs the implementation of the National Intelligence Program.

Other Federal Departments and Agencies

Under the NSF, various federal departments or agencies may play primary, coordinating, and/or support roles based on their authorities and resources and the nature of the threat or incident. In situations where a federal department or agency has responsibility for directing or managing a major aspect of a response being coordinated by DHS, that organization is part of the national leadership for the incident and is represented in the field at the Joint Field Office in the Unified Coordination Group, and at headquarters through the National Operations Center and the National Response Coordination Center, which is part of the National Operations Center. In addition, several federal departments and agencies have their own authorities to declare disasters or emergencies. For example, the secretary of health and human services can declare a public health emergency. These declarations may be made independently or as part of a coordinated federal response. Where those declarations are part of an incident requiring a coordinated federal response, those federal departments or agencies act within the overall coordination structure of the NSF.

Response Actions under the NRF

The NRF was created to strengthen, organize, and coordinate emergency response actions across all levels of government and with all involved stakeholders. The NRF's reiterates the long-standing notion that incident response should begin and continue at the lowest jurisdictional level capable of handling the required actions. The NRF applies to incidents of all types, including acts of terrorism, major disasters, and other emergencies. The NRF core document describes and outlines key tasks related to the three phases of an effective response capacity, namely: prepare, respond, and recover. An overview of the key tasks associated with response is provided below.

Depending on the size, scope, and magnitude of an incident, communities, states, and, in some cases, the federal government will be called to action. Four key actions typically occur in support of a response:

Gain and Maintain Situational Awareness
Baseline Priorities

Situational awareness requires continuous monitoring of relevant sources of information regarding actual and developing incidents. The scope and type of monitoring vary based on the type of incidents being evaluated and needed reporting thresholds. Critical information is passed through established reporting channels according to established security protocols. Priorities are summarized in the following.

Providing the right information at the right time: For an effective national response, jurisdictions must continuously refine their ability to assess the situation as an incident unfolds and rapidly provide accurate and accessible information to decision makers in a user-friendly manner. It is essential that all levels of government, the private sector (in particular, owners/operators of critical infrastructure and key resources [CIKR]), and NGOs share information to develop a common operating picture and synchronize their response operations and resources.

Improving and integrating national reporting: Situational awareness must start at the incident scene and be effectively communicated to local, tribal, state, and federal governments and the private sector, to include CIKR. Jurisdictions must integrate existing reporting systems to develop an information and knowledge management system that fulfills national information requirements.

Linking operations centers and tapping subject-matter experts: Local governments, tribes, states, and the federal government have a wide range of operations centers that monitor events and provide situational awareness. Based on their roles and responsibilities, operations centers should identify information requirements, establish reporting thresholds, and be familiar with the expectations of decision makers and partners. Situational awareness is greatly improved when experienced technical specialists identify critical elements of information and use them to form a common operating picture.

Local, Tribal, and State Actions

Local, tribal, and state governments can address the inherent challenges in establishing successful information-sharing networks by:

- Creating fusion centers that bring together into one central location law enforcement, intelligence, emergency management, public health, and other agencies, as well as private-sector and nongovernmental organizations when appropriate, and that have the capabilities to evaluate and act appropriately on all available information.

- Implementing the National Information Sharing Guidelines to share intelligence and information and improve the ability of systems to exchange data.

- Establishing information requirements and reporting protocols to enable effective and timely decision making during response to incidents. Terrorist threats and actual incidents with a potential or actual terrorist link should be reported immediately to a local or regional Joint Terrorism Task Force.

Federal Actions

The National Operations Center (NOC) serves as the national fusion center, collecting and synthesizing all source information, including information from state fusion centers, across all-threats and all-hazards information covering the spectrum of homeland security partners. Federal departments and agencies should report information regarding actual or potential incidents requiring a coordinated federal response to the NOC. Such information may include:

- Implementation of a federal department or agency emergency plan.

- Actions to prevent or respond to an incident requiring a coordinated federal response for which a federal department or agency has responsibility under law or directive.

- Submission of requests for coordinated federal assistance to, or receipt of a request from, another federal department or agency.

- Requests for coordinated federal assistance from state, tribal, or local governments, the private sector, and NGOs.

- Suspicious activities or threats, which are closely coordinated among the Department of Justice/Federal Bureau of Investigation (FBI) Strategic Information and Operations Center (SIOC), the NOC, and the National Counterterrorism Center (NCTC).

The primary reporting method for information flow is the Homeland Security Information Network (HSIN). Additionally, there are threat-reporting mechanisms in place through the FBI where information is assessed for credibility and possible criminal investigation. Each federal department and agency must work with DHS to ensure that its response personnel have access to and are trained to use the HSIN common operating picture for incident reporting.

Alerts

When notified of a threat or an incident that potentially requires a coordinated federal response, the NOC evaluates the information and notifies appropriate senior federal officials and Federal operations centers: the National Response Coordination Center (NRCC), the FBI SIOC, the NCTC, and the National Military Command Center. The NOC serves as the primary coordinating center for these and other operations centers. The NOC alerts department and agency leadership to critical information to inform decision making. Based on that information, the Secretary of Homeland Security coordinates with other appropriate departments and agencies to activate plans and applicable coordination structures of the NRF as required. Officials should be prepared to participate, either in person or by secure video teleconference, with departments or agencies involved in responding to the incident. The NOC maintains the common operating picture that provides overall situational awareness for incident information. Each federal department and agency must ensure that its response personnel are trained to utilize these tools.

Operations Centers

Federal operations centers maintain active situational awareness and communications within and among federal department and agency regional, district, and sector offices across the country. These operations centers are often connected with their state, tribal, and local counterparts, and can exchange information and draw and direct resources in the event of an incident.

Activate and Deploy Resources and Capabilities
Baseline Priorities

When an incident or potential incident occurs, responders assess the situation, identify and prioritize requirements, and activate available resources and capabilities to save lives, protect property and the environment, and meet basic human needs. In most cases, this includes development of incident objectives based on incident priorities, development of an incident action plan by the incident command in the field, and development of support plans by the appropriate local, tribal, state, and/or federal government entities. Key activities are summarized in the following.

Activating people, resources, and capabilities: Across all levels, initial actions may include activation of people and teams and establishment of incident management and response structures to organize and coordinate an effective response. The resources and capabilities deployed and the activation of supporting incident management structures should be directly related to the size, scope, nature, and complexity of the incident. All responders should maintain and regularly exercise notification systems and protocols.

Requesting additional resources and capabilities: Responders and capabilities may be requested through mutual aid and assistance agreements, the state, or the federal government. For all incidents, especially large-scale incidents, it is essential to prioritize and clearly communicate incident requirements so that resources can be efficiently matched, typed, and mobilized to support operations.

Identifying needs and pre-positioning resources: When planning for heightened threats or in anticipation of large-scale incidents, local or tribal jurisdictions, states, or the federal government should anticipate resources and capabilities that may be needed. Based on asset availability, resources should be pre-positioned and response teams and other support resources may be placed on alert or deployed to a staging area. As noted above, mobilization and deployment will be most effective when supported by planning that includes prescripted mission assignments, advance readiness contracting, and staged resources.

Local, Tribal, and State Actions

In the event of, or in anticipation of, an incident requiring a coordinated response, local, tribal, and state jurisdictions should:

- Identify staff for deployment to the emergency operations center (EOC), which should have standard procedures and call-down lists to notify department and agency points of contact.

- Work with emergency management officials to take the necessary steps to provide for continuity of operations.

- Activate incident management teams (IMTs) as required. IMTs are incident command organizations made up of the command and general staff members and appropriate functional units of an incident command system organization. The level of training and experience of the IMT members, coupled with the identified formal response requirements and responsibilities of the IMT, are factors in determining the "type," or level, of the IMT.

- Activate specialized response teams as required. Jurisdictions may have specialized teams including search and rescue teams, crime scene investigators, public works teams, hazardous materials response teams, public health specialists, or veterinarians/animal response teams.
- Activate mutual aid and assistance agreements as required.

Federal Actions

In the event of, or in anticipation of, an incident requiring a coordinated federal response, the National Operations Center, in many cases acting through the National Response Coordination Center, notifies other federal departments and agencies of the situation and specifies the level of activation required. After being notified, departments and agencies should:

- Identify and mobilize staff to fulfill their department's or agency's responsibilities, including identifying appropriate subject-matter experts and other staff to support department operations centers.
- Identify staff for deployment to the NOC, the NRCC, FEMA Regional Response Coordination Centers (RRCCs), or other operations centers as needed, such as the FBI's Joint Operations Center. These organizations have standard procedures and call-down lists, and will notify department or agency points of contact if deployment is necessary.
- Identify staff who can be dispatched to the Joint Field Office (JFO), including federal officials representing those departments and agencies with specific authorities, lead personnel for the JFO sections (Operations, Planning, Logistics, and Administration and Finance) and the ESFs.
- Begin activating and staging federal teams and other resources in support of the federal response as requested by DHS or in accordance with department or agency authorities (Figure 7–15).
- Execute prescribed mission assignments and readiness contracts, as directed by DHS.

FIGURE 7–15 New York City, New York, November 7, 2001 — FEMA interpreter Richie Park explains tele-registration procedures and disaster assistance options to business owner Betsy Chun at the Disaster Assistance Service Center in New York City. (Photo by Larry Lerner/FEMA News Photo)

Coordinate Response Actions

Baseline Priorities

Coordination of response activities occurs through response structures based on assigned roles, responsibilities, and reporting protocols. Critical information is provided through established reporting mechanisms. The efficiency and effectiveness of response operations are enhanced by full application of the NIMS with its common principles, structures, and coordinating processes. Specific priorities include the following.

Managing emergency functions: Local, tribal, and state governments are responsible for the management of their emergency functions. Such management includes mobilizing the National Guard, pre-positioning assets, and supporting communities. Local, tribal, and state governments, in conjunction with their voluntary organization partners, are also responsible for implementing plans to ensure the effective management of the flow of volunteers and goods in the affected area.

Coordinating initial actions: Initial actions are coordinated through the on-scene incident command and may include: immediate law enforcement, rescue, firefighting, and emergency medical services; emergency flood fighting; evacuations; transportation detours; and emergency information for the public. As the incident unfolds, the on-scene incident command develops and updates an incident action plan, revising courses of action based on changing circumstances.

Coordinating requests for additional support: If additional resources are required, the on-scene incident command requests the needed support. Additional incident management and response structures and personnel are activated to support the response. It is critical that personnel understand roles, structures, protocols, and concepts to ensure clear, coordinated actions. Resources are activated through established procedures and integrated into a standardized organizational structure at the appropriate levels.

Identifying and integrating resources and capabilities: Resources and capabilities must be deployed, received, staged, and efficiently integrated into ongoing operations. For large, complex incidents, this may include working with a diverse array of organizations, including multiple private-sector entities and NGOs through prearranged agreements and contracts. Large-scale events may also require sophisticated coordination and time-phased deployment of resources through an integrated logistics system. Systems and venues must be established to receive, stage, track, and integrate resources into ongoing operations. Incident command should continually assess operations and scale and adapt existing plans to meet evolving circumstances.

Coordinating information: Effective public information strategies are essential following an incident. Incident command may elect to establish a Joint Information Center (JIC), a physical location where the coordination and dissemination of information for the public and media concerning the incident are managed. JICs may be established locally, regionally, or nationally depending on the size and magnitude of an incident. In the event of incidents requiring a coordinated federal response, JICs are established to coordinate federal, state, tribal, local, and private-sector incident communications with the public. By developing media lists, contact information for relevant stakeholders, and coordinated news releases, the JIC staff facilitates dissemination of accurate, consistent, accessible, and timely public information to numerous audiences.

Local, Tribal, and State Actions

Within communities, NIMS principles are applied to integrate response plans and resources across jurisdictions and departments and with the private sector and NGOs. Neighboring communities play a key role in providing support through a framework of mutual aid and assistance agreements. These agreements are formal documents that identify the resources that communities are willing to share during an incident. Such agreements should include:

- Definitions of key terms used in the agreement
- Roles and responsibilities of individual parties

- Procedures for requesting and providing assistance
- Procedures, authorities, and rules for allocation and reimbursement of costs
- Notification procedures
- Protocols for interoperable communications
- Relationships with other agreements among jurisdictions
- Treatment of workers' compensation, liability, and immunity
- Recognition of qualifications and certifications

States provide the majority of the external assistance to communities. The state is the gateway to several government programs that help communities prepare. When an incident grows beyond the capability of a local jurisdiction, and responders cannot meet the needs with mutual aid and assistance resources, the local emergency manager contacts the state. Upon receiving a request for assistance from a local government, immediate state response activities may include:

- Coordinating warnings and public information through the activation of the state's public communications strategy and the establishment of a JIC
- Distributing supplies stockpiled to meet the emergency
- Providing needed technical assistance and support to meet the response and recovery needs of individuals and households
- The governor suspending existing statutes, rules, ordinances, and orders for the duration of the emergency, to the extent permitted by law, to ensure timely performance of response functions
- Implementing state donations management plans and coordinating with NGOs and the private sector
- Ordering the evacuation of persons from any portions of the state threatened by the incident, giving consideration to the requirements of special needs populations and those with household pets or service animals
- Mobilizing resources to meet the requirements of people with special needs, in accordance with the state's pre-existing plan and in compliance with federal civil rights laws

In addition to these actions, the Governor may activate elements of the National Guard. The National Guard is a crucial state resource, with expertise in communications, logistics, search and rescue, and decontamination. National Guard forces employed under State Active Duty or Title 32 status are under the command and control of the governor of their state and are not part of federal military response efforts. Title 32 Full-Time National Guard Duty refers to federal training or other duty, other than inactive duty, performed by a member of the National Guard. Title 32 is not subject to Posse Comitatus restrictions, and allows the governor, with the approval of the president or the secretary of defense, to order a guard member to duty to:

- Perform training and other operational activities
- Conduct homeland defense activities for the military protection of the territory or domestic population of the United States, or of the infrastructure or other assets of the United States determined by the secretary of defense to be critical to national security, from a threat or aggression against the United States

State-to-State Assistance

If additional resources are required, the state should request assistance from other states by using interstate mutual aid and assistance agreements such as the Emergency Management Assistance Compact (EMAC). Administered by the National Emergency Management Association, EMAC is a congressionally ratified organization that provides form and structure to the interstate mutual aid and assistance process. Through EMAC or other mutual aid or assistance agreements, a state can request and receive assistance from other member states. Such state-to-state assistance may include:

- Invoking and administering a statewide mutual aid agreement, as well as coordinating the allocation of resources under that agreement
- Invoking and administering EMAC and/or other compacts and agreements, and coordinating the allocation of resources that are made available to and from other states

Requesting Federal Assistance

When an incident overwhelms or is anticipated to overwhelm state resources, the governor may request federal assistance. In such cases, the affected local jurisdiction, tribe, state, and the federal government will collaborate to provide the necessary assistance. The federal government may provide assistance in the form of funding, resources, and critical services. Federal departments and agencies respect the sovereignty and responsibilities of local, tribal, and state governments while rendering assistance. The intention of the federal government in these situations is not to command the response, but rather to support the affected local, tribal, and/or state governments.

Robert T. Stafford Disaster Relief and Emergency Assistance Act

When it is clear that state capabilities will be exceeded, the governor can request federal assistance, including assistance under the Robert T. Stafford Disaster Relief and Emergency Assistance Act (Stafford Act). The Stafford Act authorizes the president to provide financial and other assistance to state and local governments, certain private nonprofit organizations, and individuals to support response, recovery, and mitigation efforts following presidential emergency or major disaster declarations. The Stafford Act is triggered by a presidential declaration of a major disaster or emergency, when an event causes damage of sufficient severity and magnitude to warrant federal disaster assistance to supplement the efforts and available resources of states, local governments, and the disaster relief organizations in alleviating the damage, loss, hardship, or suffering.

Proactive Response to Catastrophic Incidents

Prior to and during catastrophic incidents, especially those that occur with little or no notice, the state and federal governments may take proactive measures to mobilize and deploy assets in anticipation of a formal request from the state for federal assistance. Such deployments of significant federal assets would likely occur for catastrophic events involving chemical, biological, radiological, nuclear, or high-yield explosive weapons of mass destruction, large-magnitude earthquakes, or other catastrophic incidents affecting heavily populated areas. The proactive responses are utilized to ensure that resources reach the scene in a timely manner to assist in restoring any disruption of normal function of state or local governments. Proactive notification and deployment of federal resources in anticipation of or in response to catastrophic events will be done in coordination and collaboration with state, tribal, and local governments and private-sector entities when possible.

Federal Assistance Available without a Presidential Declaration

In many cases, assistance may be obtained from the federal government without a presidential declaration. For example, FEMA places liaisons in state EOCs and moves commodities near incident sites that may require federal assistance prior to a presidential declaration. Additionally, some types of assistance, such as Fire Management Assistance Grants — which provide support to states experiencing severe wildfires — are performed by federal departments or agencies under their own authorities and do not require presidential approval. Finally, federal departments and agencies may provide immediate lifesaving assistance to states under their own statutory authorities without a formal presidential declaration.

Other Federal or Federally Facilitated Assistance

The NRF covers the full range of complex and constantly changing requirements in anticipation of, or in response to, threats or actual incidents, including terrorism and major disasters. In addition to Stafford Act support, the NRF may be applied to provide other forms of support to federal partners. Federal departments and agencies must remain flexible and adaptable in order to provide the support that is required for a particular incident.

Federal-to-Federal Support

Federal departments and agencies execute interagency or intra-agency reimbursable agreements, in accordance with the Economy Act or other applicable authorities. The NRF's Financial Management Support Annex contains additional information on this process. Additionally, a federal department or agency responding to an incident under its own jurisdictional authorities may request DHS coordination to obtain additional federal assistance. In such cases, DHS may activate one or more emergency support function to coordinate required support. Federal departments and agencies must plan for federal-to-federal support missions, identify additional issues that may arise when providing assistance to other federal departments and agencies, and address those issues in the planning process. When providing federal-to-federal support, DHS may designate a federal resource coordinator to perform the resource coordination function.

International Assistance

A domestic incident may have international and diplomatic implications that call for coordination and consultations with foreign governments and international organizations. An incident may also require direct bilateral and multilateral actions on foreign affairs issues related to the incident. The Department of State has responsibility for coordinating bilateral and multilateral actions, and for coordinating international assistance. International coordination within the context of a domestic incident requires close cooperative efforts with foreign counterparts, multilateral/international organizations, and the private sector. Federal departments and agencies should consider in advance what resources or other assistance they may require or be asked to accept from foreign sources and address issues that may arise in receiving such resources. Detailed information on coordination with international partners is further defined in the International Coordination Support Annex.

Response Activities

Specific response actions will vary depending on the scope and nature of an incident. Response actions are based on the objectives established by the incident command and Joint Field Office (JFO)'s Unified Coordination Group. Detailed information about the full range of potential response capabilities is contained in the Emergency Support Function Annexes, Incident Annexes, and Support Annexes.

Department and Agency Activities

Federal departments and agencies, upon receiving notification or activation requests, implement their specific emergency plans to activate resources and organize their response actions. Department and agency plans should incorporate procedures for:

- Designation of department or agency representatives for interagency coordination, and identification of state, tribal, and local points of contact.

- Activation of coordination groups managed by the department or agency in accordance with roles and responsibilities.

- Activation, mobilization, deployment, and ongoing status reporting for resource-typed teams with responsibilities for providing capabilities under the NRF.

- Readiness to execute mission assignments in response to requests for assistance (including prescripted mission assignments), and to support all levels of department or agency participation in the response, at both the field and national levels.

- Ensuring that department or agency resources (e.g., personnel, teams, or equipment) fit into the interagency structures and processes set out in the framework.

Regional Response Activities

The FEMA regional administrator deploys a liaison to the state EOC to provide technical assistance and also activates the Regional Response Coordination Center (RRCC). Federal department and agency personnel, including ESF primary and support agency personnel, staff the RRCC as required. The RRCCs:

- Coordinate initial regional and field activities.

- In coordination with state, tribal, and local officials, deploy regional teams to assess the impact of the event, gauge immediate state needs, and make preliminary arrangements to set up operational field facilities.

- Coordinate federal support until a JFO is established.

- Establish a JIC to provide a central point for coordinating emergency public information activities.

Incident Management Assistance Team

In coordination with the RRCC and the state, FEMA may deploy an Incident Management Assistance Team (IMAT). IMATs are interagency teams composed of subject-matter experts and incident management professionals. IMAT personnel may be drawn from national or regional federal department and agency staff according to established protocols. IMAT teams make preliminary arrangements to set up federal field facilities and initiate establishment of the JFO.

Emergency Support Functions

The NRCC or RRCC may also activate specific ESFs by directing appropriate departments and agencies to initiate the initial actions delineated in the ESF Annexes.

Demobilize

Demobilization is the orderly, safe, and efficient return of a resource to its original location and status. Demobilization should begin as soon as possible to facilitate accountability of the resources and be fully coordinated with other incident management and response structures.

Local, Tribal, and State Actions

At the local, tribal, and state levels, demobilization planning and activities should include:

- Provisions to address and validate the safe return of resources to their original locations.

- Processes for tracking resources and ensuring applicable reimbursement.

- Accountability for compliance with mutual aid and assistance provisions.

Federal Actions

The Unified Coordination Group oversees the development of an exit strategy and demobilization plan. As the need for full-time interagency response coordination at the JFO wanes, the Unified Coordination Group plans for selective release of federal resources, demobilization, transfer of responsibilities, and closeout. The JFO, however, continues to operate as needed into the recovery phase to coordinate those resources that are still active. ESF representatives assist in demobilizing resources and organizing their orderly return to regular operations, warehouses, or other locations.

Key NRF Concepts

The key concepts, systems, and components upon which the NRF was built were drawn directly from the NIMS. This close association has resulted in a core set of common concepts, principles, terminology, and technologies that exist throughout both documents. These key concepts, systems, and components include.

Incident Command System

The NIMS concept is modeled upon the Incident Command System (ICS), which was developed by the federal, state, and local wildland fire agencies during the 1970s. ICS is structured to facilitate activities in five major functional areas: command, operations, planning, logistics, and finance/administration. In some circumstances, intelligence and investigations may be added as a sixth functional area.

Multiagency Coordination System

The Multiagency Coordination System (MACS) is designed to help coordinate activities that occur above the field level, and to prioritize demands for critical or competing resources. Examples of multiagency coordination include a state or county emergency operations center, a state intelligence fusion center, the National Operations Center, the FEMA National Response Coordination Center, the Department of Justice/FBI Strategic Information and Operations Center, the FBI Joint Operations Center, and the National Counterterrorism Center.

Unified Command

Unified command allows for more efficient multijurisdictional or multiagency management of emergency events. It enables agencies with different legal, geographic, and functional responsibilities to coordinate, plan, and interact with each other in an effective manner. Unified command allows all agencies with jurisdictional authority or functional responsibility for the incident to jointly provide management direction to an incident through a common set of incident objectives and strategies and a single Incident Action Plan. Under unified command, each participating agency maintains its authority, responsibility, and accountability.

Field Level Incident Command

Under the NRF, local responders use ICS to manage response operations. ICS is designed to enable effective incident management by integrating a combination of facilities, equipment, personnel, procedures and communications operating within a common organizational structure. A basic strength of ICS is that it is already widely adopted and used in incidents of any size. Typically, the incident command is structured to facilitate activities in five major functional areas: command, operations, planning, logistics, and finance/administration. ICS defines certain key roles for managing an ICS incident, as follows.

The incident commander is the individual responsible for all response activities, including the development of strategies and tactics and the ordering and release of resources. The incident commander has overall authority and responsibility for conducting incident operations and is responsible for the management of all incident operations at the incident site.

When multiple command authorities are involved, the incident may be led by a unified command comprised of officials who have jurisdictional authority or functional responsibility for the incident under an appropriate law, ordinance, or agreement. The unified command provides direct, on-scene control of tactical operations.

The command staff consists of a public information officer, safety officer, liaison officer, and other positions. The command staff reports directly to the incident commander.

The general staff normally consists of an operations section chief, planning section chief, logistics section chief, and finance/administration section chief. An intelligence/investigations section may be established, if required, to meet response needs.

At the tactical level, on-scene incident command and management organization are located at an incident command post, which is typically comprised of local and mutual aid responders.

Field Level Area Command

If necessary, an area command may be established to assist the executive official that is responsible for providing management oversight for multiple incidents being handled by separate incident command posts or to oversee management of a complex incident dispersed over a larger area. The area command does not have operational responsibilities and is activated only if necessary, depending on the complexity of the incident and incident management span-of-control considerations. The area command or incident command post provides information to, and may request assistance from, the local emergency operations center.

Local Emergency Operations Center

Local EOCs are the physical locations where multiagency coordination occurs. EOCs are used to establish an operational "picture" of the incident, provide external coordination for on-scene commanders, and secure additional resources as needed. The core functions of an EOC include coordination, communications, resource allocation and tracking, and information collection, analysis, and dissemination. EOCs may be permanent organizations and facilities staffed 24 hours a day, 7 days a week, or they may be established only as required. Standing EOCs are typically directed by a full-time emergency manager. EOCs may be organized by major discipline (fire, law enforcement, medical services, etc.), by jurisdiction (city, county, region, etc.), by ESF (communications, public works, engineering, transportation, resource support, etc.), or, more likely, by some combination thereof. The chief elected or appointed official provides policy direction and supports the incident commander and emergency manager, as needed.

State Emergency Operations Center

State EOCs are the physical location where state agency emergency management coordination efforts occur. Every state maintains an EOC that can expand as necessary to manage events requiring state-level assistance. The local incident command structure directs on-scene emergency management activities and maintains command and control of on-scene incident operations, while state EOCs are activated only in support of local EOCs. The key function of state EOC personnel is to ensure that state agency personnel who are located at the scene have the necessary response resources.

Joint Information Center

In order to coordinate the release of emergency information and other public affairs functions, a JIC may be established. The JIC serves as a focal point for coordinated and timely release of incident-related information to the public and the media. Information about where to receive assistance is communicated directly to victims and their families in an accessible format and in appropriate languages.

Joint Field Office

Federal incident support to the state is generally coordinated through a JFO. The JFO provides the means to integrate diverse federal resources and engage directly with the state. Within the JFO, there is one key operational group, and two key officials, including.

Unified Coordination Group

The Unified Coordination Group is comprised of senior officials from the state and key federal departments and agencies, and is established at the JFO. Using unified command principles, this group provides national support to achieve shared emergency response and recovery objectives.

State Coordinating Officer

The SCO plays a critical role in managing the state response and recovery operations following presidential disaster declarations. The governor of the affected state appoints the SCO, and lines of authority flow from the governor to the SCO, following the state's policies and laws. For events in which a declaration has not yet occurred but is expected (such as with an approaching hurricane), the Secretary of Homeland Security or the FEMA administrator may pre-designate one or more federal officials to coordinate with the SCO to determine resources and actions that will likely be required and begin deployment of assets. The specific roles and responsibilities of the SCO include:

- Serving as the primary representative of the governor for the affected state or locality with the Regional Response Coordination Center (RRCC — see above) or within the JFO once it is established.

- Working with the federal coordinating officer to formulate state requirements, including those that are beyond state capability, and to set priorities for employment of federal resources provided to the state.

- Ensuring coordination of resources provided to the state via mutual aid and assistance compacts.

- Providing a linkage to local government.

- Serving in the Unified Coordination Group in the JFO.

Governor's Authorized Representative

As the complexity of the response dictates, the NRF recognizes that the governor may empower a governor's authorized representative to:

- Execute all necessary documents for disaster assistance on behalf of the state, including certification of applications for public assistance.

- Represent the governor of the impacted state in the Unified Coordination Group, when required.

- Coordinate and supervise the state disaster assistance program to include serving as its grant administrator.

- Identify, in coordination with the SCO, the state's critical information needs for incorporation into a list of essential elements of information (critical items of specific information required to plan and execute an operation).

Homeland Security Council and National Security Council

The Homeland Security Council (HSC) and National Security Council (NSC) advise the president on national strategic policy during large-scale incidents. These councils ensure coordination for all homeland and national security-related activities among executive departments and agencies and promote effective development and implementation of related policy. The HSC and NSC ensure unified leadership across the federal government. The Assistant to the President for Homeland Security and Counterterrorism and the Assistant to the President for National Security Affairs coordinate interagency policy for domestic and international incident management, respectively, and convene interagency meetings to coordinate policy issues. Both councils use well-established policy development structures to identify issues that require interagency coordination. To support domestic interagency policy coordination on a routine basis, HSC and NSC deputies and principals convene to resolve significant policy issues. They are supported by the following two policy coordination committees at the assistant secretary level.

Domestic Readiness Group

The Domestic Readiness Group (DRG) is an interagency body convened on a regular basis to develop and coordinate preparedness, response, and incident management policy. This group evaluates various policy issues of interagency importance regarding domestic preparedness and incident management and makes recommendations to senior levels of the policymaking structure for decision. During an incident, the DRG may be convened by DHS to evaluate relevant interagency policy issues regarding response and develop recommendations as may be required.

Counterterrorism Security Group

The Counterterrorism Security Group (CSG) is an interagency body convened on a regular basis to develop terrorism prevention policy and to coordinate threat response and law enforcement investigations associated with terrorism. This group evaluates various policy issues of interagency importance regarding counterterrorism and makes recommendations to senior levels of the policymaking structure for decision.

National Operations Center

The National Operations Center (NOC) is the primary national hub for situational awareness and operations coordination across the federal government for incident management. It provides the Secretary of Homeland Security and other key officials with information necessary to make critical national-level incident management decisions. The NOC is a permanent, nonstop multiagency operations center. NOC staff monitor threat and hazard information from across the United States and abroad, supported by a 24/7 watch officer contingent, including:

- NOC managers
- Selected federal interagency, state, and local law enforcement representatives
- Intelligence community liaison officers provided by the DHS Chief Intelligence Officer
- Analysts from the Operations Division's interagency planning element; and
- Watch standers representing dozens of organizations and disciplines from the federal government and others from the private sector.

The NOC facilitates information sharing and operations coordination with other federal, state, tribal, local, and nongovernmental partners. During emergency response, the NOC develops and distributes spot reports, situation reports, and other information-sharing tools. The following operational components of the NOC provide integrated mission support.

National Response Coordination Center

The National Response Coordination Center (NRCC) is FEMA's primary emergency management operations and resource coordination center. The NRCC constantly monitors potential or developing incidents and supports the efforts of regional and field components as needs arise. The NRCC can increase staffing in anticipation of or in response to an emergency by activating ESFs and other personnel in order to provide resources and policy guidance to a JFO or other local incident management structure. The NRCC conducts operational planning, deploys national-level entities, and collects and disseminates incident information as it is analyzed.

National Infrastructure Coordinating Center

The NICC monitors the nation's critical infrastructure and key resources on an ongoing basis. During an incident, the NICC allows the sharing of information across the various components of critical infrastructure and key sectors through entities such as information sharing and analysis centers and sector coordinating councils.

National Military Command Center

The National Military Command Center (NMCC) is the nation's focal point for continuous monitoring and coordination of worldwide military operations. It directly supports key military officials, including the chairman of the Joint Chiefs of Staff, the secretary of defense, and the president. The center participates in a wide variety of activities, ranging from missile warning and attack assessment to management of peacetime contingencies such as Defense Support of Civil Authorities (DSCA) activities. In conjunction with monitoring the current worldwide situation, the center alerts the Joint Staff and other national agencies to developing crises and will initially coordinate any military response required.

National Counterterrorism Center

The National Counterterrorism Center (NCTC) integrates and analyzes all intelligence pertaining to terrorism and counterterrorism for the federal government, and conducts strategic operational planning using this information.

Strategic Information and Operations Center

The FBI SIOC is the focal point and operational control center for all federal intelligence, law enforcement, and investigative law enforcement activities related to domestic terrorist incidents or threats. The SIOC maintains direct communication with the NOC and serves as an information clearinghouse to help collect, process, vet, and disseminate information relevant to law enforcement and criminal investigation efforts.

Other DHS Operations Centers

Depending on the type of incident, the operations centers of other DHS operating components may serve as the primary operations management center in support of the secretary. These include the U.S. Coast Guard, Transportation Security Administration, U.S. Secret Service, and U.S. Customs and Border Protection operations centers.

NRF Emergency Support Functions

Through the NRF, FEMA coordinates response support from across the federal government and certain NGOs by calling up, as needed, one or more of the 15 ESFs. The ESFs are coordinated by FEMA through its National Response Coordination Center (NRCC). ESFs are used to coordinate specific functional capabilities and resources provided by federal departments and agencies and with certain private-sector and nongovernmental organizations when applicable. ESF functions are coordinated by a single agency but may rely on several agencies to provide resources specific to each functional area. The mission of the ESFs is to provide the greatest possible access to capabilities of the federal government regardless of which agency has those capabilities.

For each ESF there is an ESF coordinator, a primary agency, and several support agencies (based upon authorities, resources, and capabilities). The categories of resources provided under the ESFs are consistent with those identified in the NIMS. ESFs may be selectively activated for both presidentially declared and nondeclared incidents as circumstances require, although not all incidents requiring federal support result in the activation of ESFs. FEMA has the ability to deploy assets and emergency management capabilities through the ESFs into an area in anticipation of an approaching storm or event that is expected to cause severe negative consequences.

A list of the 15 ESFs and a description of the scope of each is found in Table 7–11.

Once ESFs are activated, they may have a headquarters, regional, and field presence. At FEMA headquarters, the ESFs support decision making and coordination of field operations within the NRCC. The ESFs deliver regional-level technical support and other services in the Regional Response Coordination Centers, and in the joint field office and incident command posts. At all levels, FEMA issues mission assignments to obtain resources and capabilities from across the ESFs in support of the affected states. At the headquarters, regional, and field levels, ESFs provide staff to support the incident command sections for operations, planning, logistics, and finance/administration, as requested, which enables the ESFs to work collaboratively. Similar structures organize response at the field, regional, and headquarters levels.

Table 7–11   NRF Emergency Support Functions and Primary Responsibilities

ESF #1 — Transportation
ESF Coordinator: Department of Transportation
Aviation/airspace management and control
Transportation safety
Restoration and recovery of transportation infrastructure
Movement restrictions
Damage and impact assessment

ESF #2 — Communications
ESF Coordinator: DHS (National Communications System)
Coordination with telecommunications and information technology industries
Restoration and repair of telecommunications infrastructure
Protection, restoration, and sustainment of national cyber and information technology resources
Oversight of communications within the federal incident management and response structures

ESF #3 — Public Works and Engineering
ESF Coordinator: Department of Defense (U.S. Army Corps of Engineers)
Infrastructure protection and emergency repair
Infrastructure restoration
Engineering services and construction management
Emergency contracting support for life-saving and life-sustaining services

ESF #4 — Firefighting
ESF Coordinator: Department of Agriculture (U.S. Forest Service)
Coordination of federal firefighting activities
Support to wildland, rural, and urban firefighting operations

ESF #5 — Emergency Management
ESF Coordinator: DHS (FEMA)
Coordination of incident management and response efforts
Issuance of mission assignments
Resource and human capital
Incident action planning
Financial management

ESF #6 — Mass Care, Emergency Assistance, Housing, and Human Services
ESF Coordinator: DHS (FEMA)
Mass care
Emergency assistance
Disaster housing
Human services

ESF #7 — Logistics Management and Resource Support
ESF Coordinator: General Services Administration and DHS (FEMA)
Comprehensive, national incident logistics planning, management, and sustainment capability
Resource support (facility space, office equipment and supplies, contracting services, etc.)

ESF #8 — Public Health and Medical Services
ESF Coordinator: Department of Health and Human Services
Public health
Medical
Mental health services
Mass fatality management

ESF #9 — Search and Rescue
ESF Coordinator: DHS (FEMA)

Life-saving assistance

Search and rescue operations

ESF #10 — Oil and Hazardous Materials Response
ESF Coordinator: Environmental Protection Agency

Oil and hazardous materials (chemical, biological, radiological, etc.) response

Environmental short- and long-term cleanup

ESF #11 — Agriculture and Natural Resources
ESF Coordinator: Department of Agriculture

Nutrition assistance

Animal and plant disease and pest response

Food safety and security

Natural and cultural resources and historic properties protection

Safety and well-being of household pets

ESF #12 — Energy
ESF Coordinator: Department of Energy

Energy infrastructure assessment, repair, and restoration

Energy industry utilities coordination

Energy forecast

ESF #13 — Public Safety and Security
ESF Coordinator: Department of Justice

Facility and resource security

Security planning and technical resource assistance

Public safety and security support

Support to access, traffic, and crowd control

ESF #14 — Long-Term Community Recovery
ESF Coordinator: DHS (FEMA)

Social and economic community impact assessment

Long-term community recovery assistance to states, tribes, local governments, and the private sector

Analysis and review of mitigation program implementation

ESF #15 — External Affairs
ESF Coordinator: DHS

Emergency public information and protective action guidance

Media and community relations

Congressional and international affairs

Tribal and insular affairs

The emergency support functions of the NRF are, in order:

- ESF #1, Transportation (Coordinator: Department of Transportation)

Supports DHS by assisting federal, state, tribal, and local governmental entities, voluntary organizations, nongovernmental organizations, and the private sector in the management of transportation systems and infrastructure during domestic threats or in response to incidents. ESF #1 also participates in prevention, preparedness, response, recovery, and mitigation activities. ESF #1 carries out the Department of Transportation (DOT)'s statutory responsibilities, including regulation of transportation, management of the nation's airspace, and ensuring the safety and security of the national transportation system.

- ESF #2, Communications (Coordinators: DHS/National Protection and Programs/Cybersecurity and Communication/National Communications System)

Supports the restoration of the communications infrastructure, facilitates the recovery of systems and applications from cyber attacks, and coordinates federal communications support to response efforts during incidents requiring a coordinated federal response. ESF #2 implements the provisions of the Office of Science and Technology Policy (OSTP) National Plan for Telecommunications Support in Non-Wartime Emergencies (NPTS). ESF #2 also provides communications support to federal, state, tribal, and local governments and first responders when their systems have been impacted, and provides communications and information technology (IT) support to the joint field office (JFO) and JFO field teams. The National Communications System (NCS) and the National Cybersecurity Division (NCSD) work closely to coordinate the ESF #2 response to cyber incidents.

- ESF #3, Public Works and Engineering (Coordinator: U.S. Army Corps of Engineers)

Assists DHS by coordinating and organizing the capabilities and resources of the Federal government to facilitate the delivery of services, technical assistance, engineering expertise, construction management, and other support to prepare for, respond to, and/or recover from a disaster or an incident requiring a coordinated Federal response. Activities within the scope of this function include conducting preincident and postincident assessments of public works and infrastructure; executing emergency contract support for life-saving and life-sustaining services; providing technical assistance to include engineering expertise, construction management, and contracting and real estate services; providing emergency repair of damaged public infrastructure and critical facilities; and implementing and managing the DHS/Federal Emergency Management Agency (FEMA) Public Assistance Program and other recovery programs.

- ESF #4, Firefighting (Coordinator: U.S. Forest Service)

Provides federal support for the detection and suppression of wildland, rural, and urban fires resulting from, or occurring coincidentally with, an incident requiring a coordinated federal response for assistance.

- ESF #5, Emergency Management (Coordinator: FEMA)

Supports overall activities of the federal government for domestic incident management. ESF #5 serves as the coordination ESF for all federal departments and agencies across the spectrum of domestic incident management from hazard mitigation and preparedness to response and recovery. ESF #5 identifies resources for alert, activation, and subsequent deployment for quick and effective response. During the postincident response phase, ESF #5 is responsible for the support and planning functions. ESF #5 activities include those functions that are critical to support and facilitate multi-agency planning and coordination for operations involving incidents requiring federal coordination. This includes alert and notification; staffing and deployment of DHS and FEMA response teams, as well as response teams from other federal departments and agencies; incident action planning; coordination of operations; logistics management; direction and control; information collection, analysis, and management; facilitation of requests for federal assistance; resource acquisition and management; federal worker safety and health; facilities management; financial management; and other support as required.

- ESF #6, Mass Care, Emergency Assistance, Housing, and Human Services (Coordinator: FEMA)

Coordinates the delivery of federal mass care, emergency assistance, housing, and human services when local, tribal, and state response and recovery needs exceed their capabilities. When directed by the president, ESF #6 services and programs are implemented to assist individuals and households impacted by potential or actual disaster incidents. ESF #6 is organized into four primary functions:

Mass Care: Includes sheltering, feeding operations, emergency first aid, bulk distribution of emergency items, and collecting and providing information on victims to family members.

Emergency Assistance: Assistance required by individuals, families, and their communities to ensure that immediate needs beyond the scope of the traditional "mass care" services provided at the local level are addressed. These services include support to evacuations (including registration and tracking of evacuees); reunification of families; provision of aid and services to special needs populations; evacuation, sheltering, and other emergency services for household pets and services animals; support to specialized shelters; support to medical shelters; nonconventional shelter management; coordination of donated goods and services; and coordination of voluntary agency assistance.

Housing: Includes housing options such as rental assistance, repair, loan assistance, replacement, factory-built housing, semipermanent and permanent construction, referrals, identification and provision of accessible housing, and access to other sources of housing assistance. This assistance is guided by the National Disaster Housing Strategy.

Human Services: Includes the implementation of disaster assistance programs to help disaster victims recover their nonhousing losses, including programs to replace destroyed personal property, and help to obtain disaster loans, food stamps, crisis counseling, disaster unemployment, disaster legal services, support and services for special needs populations, and other federal and state benefits.

- ESF #7, Logistics Management and Resource Support (Coordinators: General Services Administration, FEMA)

Assists DHS by:

(FEMA) Providing a national disaster logistics planning, management, and sustainment capability that harnesses the resources of federal logistics partners, key public and private stakeholders, and NGOs to meet the needs of disaster victims and responders; and

(GSA) Supporting federal agencies and state, tribal, and local governments that need resource support prior to, during, and/or after incidents requiring a coordinated federal response.

- ESF #8, Public Health and Medical Services (Coordinator: Department of Health and Human Services)

Provides the mechanism for coordinated federal assistance to supplement state, tribal, and local resources in response to a public health and medical disaster, potential or actual incidents requiring a coordinated federal response, and/or during a developing potential health and medical emergency. Public Health and Medical Services include responding to medical needs associated with mental health, behavioral health, and substance abuse considerations of incident victims and response workers. Services also cover the medical needs of members of the "at risk" or "special needs" population. Public Health and Medical Services include behavioral health needs consisting of both mental health and substance abuse considerations for incident victims and response workers and, as appropriate, medical needs groups defined in the core document as individuals in need of additional medical response assistance, and veterinary and/or animal health issues. ESF #8 provides supplemental assistance to state, tribal, and local governments in the following core functional areas:

Assessment of public health/medical needs
Health surveillance
Medical care personnel

Health/medical/veterinary equipment and supplies
Patient evacuation
Patient care
Safety and security of drugs, biologics, and medical devices
Blood and blood products
Food safety and security
Agriculture safety and security
All-hazard public health and medical consultation, technical assistance, and support
Behavioral health care
Public health and medical information
Vector control
Potable water/wastewater and solid waste disposal
Mass fatality management, victim identification, and decontaminating remains
Veterinary medical support

- ESF #9, Search and Rescue (SAR) (Coordinator: FEMA)

Rapidly deploys components of the federal SAR response system to provide specialized lifesaving assistance to state, tribal, and local authorities when activated for incidents or potential incidents requiring a coordinated federal response. The federal SAR response system is composed of the primary agencies that provide specialized SAR operations during incidents or potential incidents requiring a coordinated federal response. This includes:

Structural Collapse (Urban) Search and Rescue (US&R)
Waterborne Search and Rescue
Inland/Wilderness Search and Rescue
Aeronautical Search and Rescue

- ESF #10, Oil and Hazardous Materials Response (Coordinator: Environmental Protection Agency)

Provides federal support in response to an actual or potential discharge and/or uncontrolled release of oil or hazardous materials when activated. Response to oil and hazardous materials incidents is generally carried out in accordance with the National Oil and Hazardous Substances Pollution Contingency Plan (NCP). Appropriate general actions under this ESF can include, but are not limited to: actions to prevent, minimize, or mitigate a release; efforts to detect and assess the extent of contamination (including sampling and analysis and environmental monitoring); actions to stabilize the release and prevent the spread of contamination; analysis of options for environmental cleanup and waste disposition; implementation of environmental cleanup; and storage, treatment, and disposal of oil and hazardous materials. In addition, ESF #10 may be used under appropriate authorities to respond to actual or threatened releases of materials not typically responded to under the NCP but that pose a threat to public health or welfare or to the environment.

- ESF #11, Agriculture and Natural Resources (Coordinator: Department of Agriculture)

Supports state, tribal, and local authorities and other federal agency efforts to provide nutrition assistance; control and eradicate, as appropriate, any outbreak of a highly contagious or economically devastating animal or zoonotic disease, or any outbreak of an economically devastating plant pest or disease; ensure the safety and security of the commercial food supply; protect natural and cultural resources and historic properties (NCH); and provide for the safety and well-being of household pets during an emergency response or evacuation situation.

- ESF #12, Energy (Coordinator: Department of Energy)

Facilitates the restoration of damaged energy systems and components when activated for incidents requiring a coordinated federal response. ESF #12 is an integral part of the larger Department of Energy (DOE) responsibility of maintaining continuous and reliable energy supplies for the United States through preventive measures and restoration and recovery actions. ESF #12 collects, evaluates, and shares information on energy system damage and estimations on the impact of energy system outages within affected areas. Additionally, ESF #12 provides information concerning the energy restoration process such as projected schedules, percent completion of restoration, and geographic information on the restoration. ESF #12 facilitates the restoration of energy systems through legal authorities and waivers. ESF #12 also provides technical expertise to the utilities, conducts field assessments, and assists government and private-sector stakeholders to overcome challenges in restoring the energy system.

- ESF #13, Public Safety and Security (Coordinator: Department of Justice)

Provides a mechanism for coordinating and providing federal-to-federal support; federal support to state, tribal, and local authorities; and/or support to other ESFs, consisting of law enforcement, public safety, and security capabilities and resources during potential or actual incidents requiring a coordinated federal response.

- ESF #14, Long-Term Community Recovery (Coordinator: FEMA)

Provides a mechanism for coordinating federal support to state, tribal, regional, and local governments, nongovernmental organizations (NGOs), and the private sector to enable community recovery from the long-term consequences of extraordinary disasters. ESF #14 accomplishes this by identifying and facilitating availability and use of sources of recovery funding, and providing technical assistance for community recovery and recovery planning support. ESF #14 support will vary depending on the magnitude and type of incident.

- ESF #15, External Affairs (Coordinator: DHS)

Ensures that sufficient assets are deployed to provide accurate, coordinated, timely, and accessible information to the various groups affected by the disaster. ESF #15 provides the resource support and mechanisms to implement the NRF Incident Communications Emergency Policy and Procedures (ICEPP) described in the Public Affairs Support Annex. ESF #15 coordinates federal actions to provide the required external affairs support to federal, state, tribal, and local incident management elements to coordinate communications to their audiences. The Joint Information Center (JIC) ensures the coordinated release of information under ESF #15. The planning and products component of External Affairs develops all external and internal communications strategies and products for the ESF #15 organization. And finally, ESF #15 provides the resources and structure for the implementation of the ICEPP.

Table 7–12 lists the various roles assumed by the different federal agencies with regard to the 15 ESFs.

NRF Support Annexes

The NRF Support Annexes describe how federal departments and agencies; state, tribal, and local entities; the private sector; volunteer organizations; and nongovernmental organizations (NGOs) coordinate and execute the functional processes and administrative requirements necessary for the management of emergency and disaster incidents. The actions described in these annexes are applicable to nearly every type of incident that may occur, whether natural, technological, or intentional in origin. The annexes, which may be fully or partially implemented, may each support several emergency support functions (ESFs), as needed.

As was true with the ESFs, there are roles and responsibilities assumed by federal departments and agencies, NGOs, and the private sector for each support annex. The overarching nature

Table 7–12 Roles Assumed by the Different Federal Agencies with Regard to the 15 ESFs

Emergency Support Functions

Agency	#1 - Transportation	#2 - Communications	#3 - Public Works and Engineering	#4 - Firefighting	#5 - Emergency Management	#6 - Mass Care, Emergency Assistance, Housing, and Human Services	#7 - Logistics Management and Resource Support	#8 - Public Health and Medical Services	#9 - Search and Rescue	#10 - Oil and Hazardous Materials Response	#11 - Agriculture and Natural Resources	#12 - Energy	#13 - Public Safety and Security	#14 - Long-term Community Recovery	#15 - External Affairs
USDA			S		S	S	S	S		S	C/P/S	S		P	S
USDA/FS	S	S	S	C/P		S	S	S	S	S			S		
DOC	S	S	S	S	S		S	S	S	S	S	S	S	S	S
DOD	S	S	S	S	S		S	S	P	S	S	S	S	S	S
DOD/USACE	S		C/P	S		S	S	S	S	S	S	S	S	S	
ED					S										S
DOE	S		S		S		S	S		S	S	C/P	S	S	S
HHS			S		S	S	S	C/P	S	S	S			S	S
DHS	S	S	S		S		S			S	S	S	S		C
DHS/FEMA	S	P	P	S	C/P	C/P/S	C/P	S	C/P	S	S			C/P	P
DHS/NCS		C/P					S					S			
DHS/USCG	S		S	S				S	P	P			S		
HUD					S	S								P	S
DOI	S	S	S	S	S	S	S	S	P	S	P/S	S	S	S	S
DOJ	S				S	S		S	S	S	S		C/P		S
DOL			S		S	S	S	S	S	S	S	S		S	S
DOS	S		S	S	S			S		S	S	S			S

C = ESF coordinator   P = Primary agency   S = Support agency

Emergency Support Functions

Agency	#1 - Transportation	#2 - Communications	#3 - Public Works and Engineering	#4 - Firefighting	#5 - Emergency Management	#6 - Mass Care, Emergency Assistance, Housing, and Human Services	#7 - Logistics Management and Resource Support	#8 - Public Health and Medical Services	#9 - Search and Rescue	#10 - Oil and Hazardous Materials Response	#11 - Agriculture and Natural Resources	#12 - Energy	#13 - Public Safety and Security	#14 - Long-Term Community Recovery	#15 - External Affairs
DOT	C/P		S		S	S	S	S		S	S	S		S	S
TREAS					S	S							S	S	S
VA			S		S	S	S	S					S		S
EPA			S	S	S			S		C/P	S	S	S	S	S
FCC		S			S										S
GSA	S	S	S		S	S	C/P	S		S	S				S
NASA					S			S		S			S		S
NRC		S			S					S		S			S
OPM					S		S								S
SBA					S	S								P	S
SSA						S							S		S
TVA			S		S							S			S
USAID								S	S						S
USPS	S				S	S		S			S		S		S
ACHP											S				
ARC			S		S	S		S			S			S	
CNCS			S			S								S	
DRA														S	
HENTF											S				
NARA											S				
NVOAD						S								S	

C = ESF coordinator   P = Primary agency   S = Support agency of functions covered by the annexes frequently involves either the support to, or the cooperation of, all departments and agencies involved in incident management efforts to ensure seamless transitions between preparedness, response, and recovery activities. Each annex is managed by one or more coordinating agencies and is supported by various cooperating agencies. The responsibilities of coordinating and cooperating agencies are identified below.

Coordinating Agency

Coordinating agencies are responsible for implementing the processes detailed in the annexes. These federal agencies support DHS incident management efforts by providing the leadership, expertise, and authority to implement critical and specific aspects of the response. When the functions of a particular support annex are required, the agency serving as the coordinator is responsible for:

- Orchestrating a coordinated delivery of those functions and procedures identified in the annex
- Providing staff for operations functions at fixed and field facilities
- Notifying and subtasking cooperating agencies
- Managing tasks with cooperating agencies, as well as appropriate state, tribal, or local agencies
- Working with appropriate private-sector organizations to maximize use of available resources
- Supporting and keeping ESFs and other organizational elements informed of annex activities
- Planning for short- and long-term support to incident management and recovery operations
- Conducting preparedness activities such as training and exercises to maintain personnel who can provide appropriate support

Cooperating Agencies

Cooperating agencies have specific expertise and capabilities that allow them to assist the coordinating agency in executing incident-related tasks or processes. When the procedures within a support annex are needed to support elements of an incident, the coordinating agency will notify cooperating agencies of the circumstances. Cooperating agencies are responsible for:

- Conducting operations, when requested by DHS or the coordinating agency, consistent with their own authority and resources
- Participating in planning for short- and long-term incident management and recovery operations and the development of supporting operational plans, standard operating procedures, checklists, or other job aids, in concert with existing first-responder standards
- Furnishing available personnel, equipment, or other resource support as requested by DHS or the support annex coordinator
- Participating in training and exercises aimed at continuous improvement of response and recovery capabilities

When requested, and upon approval of the secretary of defense, the Department of Defense (DOD) provides defense support of civil authorities during domestic incidents. Accordingly, DOD is considered a cooperating agency for the majority of support annexes.

The support annexes of the NRF are summarized next.

- Critical Infrastructure and Key Resources (Coordinator: DHS)

Describes policies, roles, and responsibilities, and the concept of operations for assessing, prioritizing, protecting, and restoring critical infrastructure and key resources (CIKR) during actual or potential domestic incidents. Specifically, this annex does the following:

Describes roles and responsibilities for CIKR preparedness, protection, response, recovery, restoration, and continuity of operations

Establishes a concept of operations for incident-related CIKR preparedness, protection, response, recovery, and restoration

Outlines incident-related actions to expedite information sharing and analysis of actual or potential impacts to CIKR and facilitate requests for assistance and information from public- and private-sector partners

- Financial Management (Coordinator: FEMA and others)

Provides basic financial management guidance for all NRF departments and agencies providing assistance for incidents requiring a coordinated federal response. The financial management function is a component of ESF #5 (Emergency Management). The processes and procedures described ensure that funds are provided expeditiously and that financial operations are conducted in accordance with established federal law, policies, regulations, and standards.

- International Coordination (Coordinator: Department of State)

Provides guidance on carrying out responsibilities for international coordination in support of the federal government's response to a domestic incident with an international component. The NRF role of the Department of State is to fully support federal, state, tribal, and local authorities in effective incident management and preparedness planning. A domestic incident will have international and diplomatic impacts and implications that call for coordination and consultations with foreign governments and international organizations. An incident may also require direct bilateral and multilateral actions on foreign affairs issues related to the incident, for which DOS has independent and sole responsibility.

- Private-Sector Coordination (Coordinator: DHS)

Describes the policies, responsibilities, and concept of operations for incident management activities involving the private sector during emergencies and disasters. The annex describes the activities necessary to ensure effective coordination and integration with the private sector, both for-profit and not-for-profit, including the nation's critical infrastructure, key resources, other business and industry components, and NGOs engaged in response and recovery. This annex applies incidents that involve the private sector in any of the following ways:

Impacted organization or infrastructure
Response resource
Regulated and/or responsible party
Member of the state emergency management organization

- Public Affairs (Coordinator: DHS)

Describes the policies and procedures used to mobilize federal assets to prepare and deliver risk and emergency communications messages to the public. The annex is applicable to all federal departments and agencies responding under the NRF.

- Tribal Relations (Coordinator: DHS)

Describes the policies, responsibilities, and concept of operations for coordination and interaction of federal incident management activities with those of tribal governments and communities during incidents requiring a coordinated federal response. Because tribal governments are fully integrated into the NRF, this annex addresses only those factors in the relationship between federal departments and agencies and the federally recognized tribes.

- Volunteer and Donations Management (Coordinator: FEMA)

Describes the coordination processes used to support the state in ensuring the most efficient and effective use of unaffiliated volunteers, unaffiliated organizations, and unsolicited donated goods to support all ESFs, including offers of unaffiliated volunteer services and unsolicited donations to the federal government.

- Worker Safety and Health (Coordinator: Department of Labor/Occupational Safety and Health Administration)

Provides federal support to response and recovery organizations in assuring response and recovery worker safety and health during emergency incidents. This annex describes the technical assistance resources, capabilities, and other support to ensure that response and recovery worker safety and health risks are anticipated, recognized, evaluated, communicated, and consistently controlled.

NRF Incident Annexes

The incident annexes address contingency or hazard situations requiring specialized application of the NRF. These annexes, which were not reengineered when the NRF was released and are therefore a carryover from the legacy NRP, describe the following components for each of the specialized incident types:

Policies: Each annex explains unique authorities pertinent to that incident, the special actions or declarations that may result, and any special policies that may apply.

Situation: Each annex describes the incident situation as well as the planning assumptions, and outlines the approach that will be used if key assumptions do not hold (for example, how authorities will operate if they lose communication with senior decision makers).

Concept of Operations: Each annex describes the concept of operations appropriate to the incident, integration of operations with NRF elements, unique aspects of the organizational approach, notification and activation processes, and specialized incident-related actions. Each annex also details the coordination structures and positions of authority that are unique to the type of incident, the specialized response teams or unique resources needed, and other special considerations.

Responsibilities: Each incident annex identifies the coordinating and cooperating agencies involved in an incident-specific response; in some cases this responsibility is held jointly by two or more departments.

As is true with the Support annexes described above, there are coordinating and cooperating agencies that have been identified for each incident annex. The responsibilities of these agencies in the incident annexes are identical to those detailed in the support annexes.

Each of the incident annexes is described below.

- Biological Incident Annex (Coordinator: Department of Health and Human Services)

Outlines the actions, roles, and responsibilities associated with response to a disease outbreak of known or unknown origin requiring federal assistance, including threat assessment notification procedures, laboratory testing, joint investigative/response procedures, and activities related to recovery. The broad objectives of the federal government's response to a biological terrorism event, pandemic influenza, emerging infectious disease, or novel pathogen outbreak are to:

Detect the event through disease surveillance and environmental monitoring
Identify and protect the population(s) at risk
Determine the source of the outbreak
Quickly frame the public health and law enforcement implications
Control and contain any possible epidemic (including providing guidance to State and local public health authorities)
Augment and surge public health and medical services

Track and defeat any potential resurgence or additional outbreaks
Assess the extent of residual biological contamination and decontaminate as necessary

- Catastrophic Incident Annex (Coordinator: DHS)

Establishes the context and overarching strategy for implementing and coordinating an accelerated, proactive national response to a catastrophic incident (a more detailed NRF Catastrophic Incident Supplement (NRF-CIS), designated "For Official Use Only," has not been released for public view). A catastrophic incident is any natural or man-made incident resulting in extraordinary levels of mass casualties, damage, or disruption severely affecting the population, infrastructure, environment, economy, national morale, and/or government functions. Recognizing that federal and/or national resources are required to augment overwhelmed state, local, and tribal response efforts, the NRF-CIA establishes protocols to pre-identify and rapidly deploy key essential resources (e.g., medical teams, urban search and rescue teams, transportable shelters, and medical and equipment caches) that are expected to be urgently needed/required to save lives and contain incidents. Accordingly, upon designation by the Secretary of Homeland Security of a catastrophic incident, federal resources — organized into incident-specific "packages" — deploy in accordance with the NRF-CIS and in coordination with the affected state and incident command structure. An important factor associated with NRF-CIA designated disasters is that federal assets unilaterally deployed in accordance with the NRF-CIS do not require a state cost-share. Departments and agencies assigned primary responsibility for one or more functional response areas under the NRF-CIS appendixes include:

Mass Care: American Red Cross
Search and Rescue: Department of Homeland Security
Decontamination: Department of Homeland Security, Environmental Protection Agency, and
    Department of Health and Human Services
Public Health and Medical Support: Department of Health and Human Services
Medical Equipment and Supplies: Department of Health and Human Services
Patient Movement: Department of Health and Human Services and Department of Defense
Mass Fatality: Department of Health and Human Services
Housing: Department of Homeland Security
Public and Incident Communications: Department of Homeland Security
Transportation: Department of Transportation
Private-Sector Support: Department of Homeland Security
Logistics: Department of Homeland Security

- Cyber Incident Annex (Coordinators: DHS, Department of Defense, Department of Justice)

Discusses policies, organization, actions, and responsibilities for a coordinated approach to prepare for, respond to, and recover from cyber-related emergency incidents impacting critical national processes and the national economy. A cyber-related emergency may take many forms: an organized cyber attack, an uncontrolled exploit such as a virus or worm, a natural disaster with significant cyber consequences, or other incidents capable of causing extensive damage to critical infrastructure or key assets. Federal government responsibilities include:

Providing indications and warning of potential threats, incidents, and attacks
Information sharing both inside and outside the government, including best practices,
    investigative information, coordination of incident response, and incident mitigation
Analyzing cyber vulnerabilities, exploits, and attack methodologies
Providing technical assistance
Conducting investigations, forensics analysis, and prosecution
Attributing the source of cyber attacks

Defending against the attack

Leading national-level recovery efforts

- Food a nd Agriculture Incident Annex (Coordinators: Department of Agriculture, Department of Health and Human Services)

Describes how the various involved agencies will respond to emergency incidents involving the nation's agriculture and food systems. A food and agriculture incident may threaten public health, animal nutrition, food production, aquaculture, livestock production, wildlife, soils, rangelands, and agricultural water supplies. Responding to the unique attributes of this type of incident requires separate planning considerations that are tailored to specific health and agriculture concerns and effects of the disease (e.g., deliberate contamination versus natural outbreaks; plant and animal versus processed food, etc.). The objectives of a coordinated federal response to an incident impacting food and agriculture are to:

Detect the event through the reporting of illness, disease/pest surveillance, routine testing, consumer complaints, and/or environmental monitoring

Establish the primary coordinating agency

Determine the source of the incident or outbreak

Control and contain the distribution of the affected source

Identify and protect the population at risk

Assess the public health, food, agriculture, and law enforcement implications

Assess the extent of residual biological, chemical, or radiological contamination and decontaminate and dispose as necessary

Support effective and coordinated communication between federal, state, and local responders to a potential or actual incident that require a coordinated federal response impacting food and agriculture

Minimize public health and economic impacts of a food and agriculture-related incident

Specify roles and responsibilities of coordinating federal agencies and departments

Provide transition from response to rapid recovery following a food and agriculture-related incident

- Nuclear/Radiological Incident Annex (Coordinators: DHS, Department of Defense, Department of Energy, Environmental Protection Agency, National Aeronautics and Space Administration, Nuclear Regulatory Commission)

Facilitates an organized and coordinated response by federal agencies to terrorist incidents involving nuclear or radioactive materials, and accidents or incidents involving such material. These nuclear/radiological incidents, which include sabotage and terrorist incidents, involve the release or potential release of radioactive material that poses an actual or perceived hazard to public health, safety, national security, and/or the environment (including the terrorist use of radiological dispersal devices (RDDs, or "dirty bombs") or improvised nuclear devices (INDs), reactor plant accidents (commercial or weapons production facilities), lost radioactive material sources, transportation accidents involving nuclear/radioactive material, and foreign accidents involving nuclear or radioactive material.) This annex:

Provides planning guidance and outlines operational concepts for the federal response to any nuclear/radiological incident, including a terrorist incident, that has actual, potential, or perceived radiological consequences within the United States or its territories, possessions, or territorial waters, and that requires a response by the federal government.

Describes federal policies and planning considerations on which this annex and federal agency-specific nuclear/radiological response plans are based.

Specifies the roles and responsibilities of federal agencies for preventing, preparing for, responding to, and recovering from nuclear/radiological incidents.

Includes guidelines for notification, coordination, and leadership of federal activities, and coordination of public information, congressional relations, and international activities.

Provides protocols for coordinating federal government capabilities to respond to radiological incidents. These capabilities include, but are not limited to:

The Interagency Modeling and Atmospheric Assessment Center (IMAAC), which is responsible for production, coordination, and dissemination of consequence predictions for an airborne hazardous material release

The Federal Radiological Monitoring and Assessment Center (FRMAC), established at or near the scene of an incident to coordinate radiological assessment and monitoring

The Advisory Team for Environment, Food, and Health (known as "the Advisory Team"), which provides expert recommendations on protective action guidance.

- Oil and Hazardous Materials Incident Annex (Coordinators: Environmental Protection Agency, U.S. Coast Guard)

Describes the roles, responsibilities, and coordinating mechanisms for managing major oil and hazardous materials pollution incidents. This annex addresses those oil and hazardous materials incidents that are managed through concurrent implementation of the NRF and the National Oil and Hazardous Substances Pollution Contingency Plan (NCP), but are not ESF #10 (Oil and Hazardous Materials Response) activations. The NCP provides the organizational structure and procedures for federal response to releases of oil and hazardous materials, and addresses incident prevention, planning, response, and recovery. The hazardous materials addressed under the NCP include certain substances considered weapons of mass destruction (i.e., chemical agents, biological agents, and radiological/nuclear material). The NCP establishes structures at the national, regional, and local levels that are used to respond to thousands of incidents annually. When an NRF incident does occur, these NCP structures remain in place to provide hazard-specific expertise and support. This annex describes how the NCP structures work with NRF coordinating structures during major emergency or disaster incidents.

- Terrorism Incident Law Enforcement and Investigation Annex (Coordinator: Federal Bureau of Investigation)

Facilitates a federal law enforcement and investigative response to all threats or acts of terrorism within the United States, regardless of whether they are deemed credible and/or whether they are major or minor in scope. This annex provides planning guidance and outlines operational concepts for the federal law enforcement and investigative response to a threatened or actual terrorist incident, and acknowledges and outlines the unique nature of each threat or incident, the capabilities and responsibilities of the local jurisdictions, and the law enforcement and investigative activities necessary to prevent or mitigate a specific threat or incident. The law enforcement and investigative response to a terrorist threat or incident within the United States is a highly coordinated, multiagency state, local, tribal, and federal responsibility. The attorney general holds the lead responsibility for criminal investigations of terrorist acts or terrorist threats by individuals or groups inside the United States, or directed at U.S. citizens or institutions abroad, under Homeland Security Presidential Directive (HSPD) No. 5. Acting through the FBI, the attorney general, in cooperation with other federal departments and agencies engaged in activities to protect national security, also coordinates the activities of the other members of the law enforcement community to detect, prevent, preempt, and disrupt terrorist attacks. Although not formally designated under this annex, other federal departments and agencies may have authorities, resources, capabilities, or expertise required to support terrorism-related law enforcement and investigation operations. Agencies may be requested to participate in federal planning and response operations, and may be requested to designate liaison officers and provide other support as required.

Partner Guides

Response Partner Guides were developed in conjunction with the NRF in order to provide local, tribal, state, federal, and private-sector response stakeholders with a reference of their key roles and actions in coordinated response. The Partner Guides include:

- Local Government Response Partner Guide
- State Response Partner Guide
- Private-Sector and Nongovernmental Response Partner Guide
- Federal Response Partner Guide

See sidebar titled, "NRF Federal Level Operations Coordination," for a summary of overall coordination.

NRF Federal Level Operations Coordination

- The secretary of Homeland Security is the principal federal official responsible for domestic incident management.
- All Federal departments and agencies may play significant roles in incident management and response activities, depending on the nature and size of an event. The policies, operational structures, and capabilities to support an integrated federal response are defined in the Emergency Support Functions (see below), and are coordinated through prescripted mission assignments, and formalized in interagency agreements.
- The FEMA administrator is the principal advisor to the president, the secretary of Homeland Security, and the Homeland Security Council regarding emergency management. The FEMA administrator's duties include operation of the National Response Coordination Center, the effective support of all emergency support functions, and, more generally, preparation for, protection against, response to, and recovery from all-hazards incidents. Reporting to the secretary of Homeland Security, the administrator also is responsible for management of the core DHS grant programs supporting homeland security.
- Other DHS agency heads have a lead response role or an otherwise significant role, depending on the type and severity of the event. For example, the U.S. Coast Guard commandant has statutory lead authority for certain mass migration management scenarios and significant oil/hazardous substance spill incidents in the maritime environment.
- The DHS director of operations coordination is the secretary's principal advisor for the overall departmental level of integration of incident management operations and oversees the National Operations Center.

Source: FEMA, "National Response Framework," Washington, DC, 2008.

▨ ▨ Critical Thinking ▨

The NRF is a comprehensive document, but it cannot possibly cover every possible need that may arise in every emergency incident. In light of the wide array of emergencies and disasters that could occur in your community, are there any specific community-level needs that might fall outside the spectrum of the NRF that are not explicitly detailed (e.g., the needs of children in emergencies)?

Recovery

The recovery function is not easy to classify; it often begins in the initial hours and days following a disaster event and can continue for months and in some cases years, depending on the severity of the event (Figure 7–16). Unlike the response function, where all efforts have a singular focus, the recovery function or process is characterized by a complex set of issues and decisions that must be made by individuals and communities. These issues include the following:

- Rebuilding homes
- Replacing property
- Resuming employment
- Restoring businesses
- Permanently repairing and rebuilding infrastructure

Since the establishment of DHS, the recovery function has remained relatively unchanged, although minor changes affecting the nomenclature and classification of the available assistance, as well as some relief programs and grants, have occurred. Because the recovery function has such long-lasting impacts and usually high costs, the participants in the process are numerous. They include all levels of government, the business community, political leadership, community activists, and individuals. The major players and programs will be listed here and changes, if any, will be described.

Given that the federal government plays the largest role in providing the technical and financial support for recovery, this section will focus on the federal role. It will discuss the structure and the

FIGURE 7–16 New York City, New York, 2001 and 2008 — Aerial photographs of "ground zero." (Source: www.noaa.gov [2001] and Google Earth [2008])

various programs available to assist individuals and communities in the postdisaster environment and will briefly reference the various national voluntary organizations that provide some assistance for recovery. See the sidebar "Quick Facts on Recovery" a brief historical summary.

Quick Facts on Recovery

In the period from 1990 to 1999, FEMA spent more than $25.4 billion for declared disasters and emergencies compared to $3.9 billion in current dollars for 1980–1989.

For the 1990–1999 period, more than $6.3 billion was provided in grants for temporary housing, home repairs, and other disaster-related needs for individuals and families. An additional $14.8 billion went to States and local governments for cleanup and restoration projects, including more than $1.37 billion for mission-assigned work undertaken by other Federal agencies.

In the 1990s, a total of 88 declarations were issued for hurricanes and typhoons, for which FEMA obligated more than $7.78 billion for disaster costs. The most costly to FEMA was Hurricane George in 1998, followed closely by Hurricane Andrew in 1992.

The most frequently declared disaster type was flooding resulting from severe storms, with more than $7.3 billion committed by FEMA for response and recovery costs. The most costly were the Midwest floods in 1993 and the Red River Valley floods in 1997.

By November 2002, FEMA had given a total of $306,102,000 in disaster recovery funding for the victims of September 11 attacks. The distribution among programs follows:

- Temporary housing: mortgage and rental assistance ($76,275,000), minimal home repair ($1,450,000), transient accommodations ($1,225,000), rental assistance ($26,150,000)
- Individual family grants ($25,400,000)
- Crisis counseling assistance and training program ($162,400,000)
- Unemployment assistance ($13,200,000)
- Legal services ($2,000)

Source: Federal Emergency Management Agency, www.fema.gov.

Disaster Recovery Operations in the National Response Framework

The NRF addresses the need for structured principles and procedures by which individuals, communities, and the nation recover from the consequences of emergencies and disasters. Recovery operations may require significant contributions from all sectors of society, each of which is addressed. There are two phases of recovery identified in the NRF, including:

Short-term recovery: This is the period when recovery actions that begin immediately upon occurrence of the disaster, which overlap with response actions, are taken. This phase includes actions such as providing essential public health and safety services, restoring interrupted utility and other essential services, reestablishing transportation routes, and providing food and shelter for those displaced by the incident. Although called "short term," some short-term recovery activities may last for weeks. Short-term recovery actions are addressed in several functional areas of the NRF.

Long-term recovery: This is the period that involves the restoration of lives and livelihoods beyond the emergency phase of the disaster, once lifelines and critical societal components have been restored or replaced. This phase falls squarely within the direction of Emergency Support Function #14, "Long-Term Community Recovery," and often continues for several months or years after the disaster has ended.

Recovery can include the development, coordination, and execution of service- and site-restoration plans; reconstitution of government operations and services; programs to provide housing and promote restoration; long-term care and treatment of affected persons; and additional measures for social, political, environmental, and economic restoration. Under the NRF, recovery operations and programs:

- Identify needs and resources
- Provide accessible housing and promote restoration
- Address care and treatment of affected persons
- Provide recovering victims with appropriate recovery information
- Facilitate community restoration
- Incorporate mitigation measures and techniques, as feasible

Recovery Coordination

As in the response phase, the Joint Field Office (JFO) serves as the central coordination point among local, tribal, state, and federal governments, as well as private-sector and nongovernmental entities that are providing recovery assistance. The NRF outlines several recovery actions that may take place under this structure, including:

Coordinating assistance programs to help individuals, households, and businesses meet basic needs and return to self-sufficiency. Such programs include housing assistance, other needs assistance, crisis counseling services, disaster legal services, and unemployment or reemployment programs. Other activities include coordinating with local and tribal governments the need for and locations of disaster recovery centers.

Establishing disaster recovery centers. Federal, state, tribal, local, voluntary, and nongovernmental organizations determine the need for and location of disaster recovery centers. Disaster recovery center staff provide recovery and mitigation program information, advice, counseling, and related technical assistance.

Coordinating with private-sector and nongovernmental organizations involved in donations management and other recovery activities. Donations and volunteer management in the past have been chaotic and disorganized, often leading to what is called "the second disaster." The NRF addresses these issues by tasking various federal agencies and offices with the management of these two functions.

Coordinating public assistance grant programs authorized by the Stafford Act. These programs aid local, tribal, and state governments and eligible private nonprofit organizations with the cost of emergency protective services, debris removal, and the repair or replacement of disaster-damaged public facilities and associated environmental restoration.

Coordinating with the private sector on restoration and recovery of CIKR. Activities to restore and facilitate the recovery of critical infrastructure and key resources is primarily the responsibility of the private sector, who owns the majority of these components. The restoration and repair of these facilities is integral to the recovery of the community, and therefore almost always requires the assistance of the federal and state governments. The NRF guides the emergency management stakeholders in working with the owners and operators of these facilities to ensure that critical services return (which include, for example, water, power, natural gas and petroleum, emergency communications, and health care).

Coordinating mitigation grant programs to help communities reduce the potential impacts of future disasters. The NRF addresses the most important concept behind recovery, which is to ensure that new disaster information is applied such that pre-existing hazard vulnerabilities are effectively reduced.

At a certain point in the recovery operation it will be determined that operations no longer require the services of a full JFO, and that office will be closed. At this point, ongoing activities are led by the individual agencies that hold recovery responsibilities under the NRF. Federal partners then work directly with their regional or headquarters offices to administer and monitor recovery programs, support, and technical services.

Each of the primary and support agencies of ESF #14 have distinct programs aimed at facilitating recovery, based on their individual agency-specific expertise. The following subsections describe each agency's recovery function.

Department of Agriculture

Provides emergency loans and grants for the agricultural sector; economic and technical assistance for recovery of rural community facilities, businesses, utilities, and housing; technical assistance for agricultural market recovery, community planning, and community development; and resource conservation assistance.

Department of Homeland Security

Federal Emergency Management Agency

Provides technical assistance in community, tribal, and state planning; recovery and mitigation grant and insurance programs; outreach, public education, and community involvement in recovery planning; building science expertise; and natural hazard vulnerability/risk assessment expertise.

Office for Civil Rights and Civil Liberties

Provides expertise in issues related to special needs populations to ensure that they are an integral part of the recovery process.

Office of Infrastructure Protection

Provides technical expertise in protective measures for critical infrastructure.

Office of the Private Sector

Provides expertise in private-sector capabilities and services; provides coordination with private-sector organizations.

Transportation Security Administration

Coordinates security of the nation's transportation system in times of national emergency.

Department of Housing and Urban Development

Provides building technology technical assistance, and assistance for housing; community redevelopment and economic recovery; public services; infrastructure; mortgage financing; and public housing repair and reconstruction.

Small Business Administration

Provides long-term loan assistance to homeowners, renters, businesses of all sizes, and nonprofit organizations for repair, replacement, mitigation, relocation, or code required upgrades of incident-damaged property. Loan assistance is provided to small businesses to address adverse economic impacts due to the incident.

Department of Commerce

Economic and Statistics Administration
Performs economic impact assessment.

Economic Development Administration
Provides economic recovery and growth assistance, technical assistance in community planning, and economic assessment expertise.

National Institute of Standards and Technology
Provides building science expertise.

National Oceanic and Atmospheric Administration
Provides natural hazard vulnerability analysis, provides assistance on coastal zone management and building community resilience, supplies geospatial technology assistance and coastal inundation information, performs ecosystem and damage assessments, and provides technical assistance in recovering fisheries, restoring habitat, and rebuilding coastal communities.

Department of Defense: U.S. Army Corps of Engineers

Provides technical assistance in community planning and civil engineering, and natural hazard risk assessment expertise, and supports the development of national strategies and plans related to permanent and accessible housing, debris management, and the restoration of public facilities and infrastructure.

Department of Energy

Assists in the economic assessment of an incident based on degradation to energy infrastructure, provides the appropriate support and resources to assist in energy infrastructure restoration, provides technical advice in radioactive debris management, and provides technical support for energy efficiency and sustainability practices and technology.

Department of Health and Human Services

Collaborates with state, tribal, and local officials on prioritizing restoration of the public health and private medical and health-care service delivery infrastructures to accelerate overall community recovery, provides the expertise necessary to meet the long-term physical and behavioral health needs of affected populations, coordinates HHS benefit programs with affected populations, and provides technical assistance (in the form of impact analyses and recovery planning support of public health and private medical and other health-care service delivery infrastructure).

Department of the Interior

Provides technical assistance in community planning, and natural and cultural resources and historic properties expertise and assistance; community liaison for federally owned lands and facilities; and natural hazard vulnerability analysis expertise.

Department of Labor

Conducts incident unemployment programs, and provides job training and retraining assistance and expertise in economic assessment.

Department of Transportation

Provides technical assistance in transportation planning and engineering and transportation assistance programs.

Department of the Treasury

Ensures economic and financial resilience and vitality, including reliability of public and private payment systems and financial flows, and removal of impediments to economic activity.

Environmental Protection Agency

Provides technical assistance in contaminated debris management, environmental remediation, and watershed protection, planning, management, and restoration; provides technical assistance in developing appropriate drinking water and wastewater infrastructure projects and in identifying financial assistance options; and provides technical assistance on using environmentally sound and sustainable approaches in rebuilding businesses and communities.

Corporation for National and Community Service

Provides trained National Service Participants (including AmeriCorps members, Learn and Serve America volunteers, and Retired and Senior Volunteer Program volunteers) as human resource support for long-term community recovery to include:

- Support for development and operation of long-term recovery committees and to help meet individual (especially for special needs residents) and community unmet needs as they are identified.
- Support for reestablishment and renewal of the community-level private voluntary sector (civic, nonprofit, and voluntary organizations).
- Canvassing, information distribution, and registration support.
- Case management assistance.

Delta Regional Authority

Serves as regional planner and provider of technical assistance through the local development districts; facilitates and coordinates federal investment in the Delta Regional Authority region; reduces fragmentation and duplication; and provides local/state matching funds.

American Red Cross

Provides long-term individual and family services, case management, assistance with unmet needs, and health and human services both directly and through other agencies.

National Voluntary Organizations Active in Disasters

- Provide canvassing, needs assessment, and information distribution support to local, tribal, state, and federal operations.
- Provide assistance with locating housing resources and short-term lodging assistance, as well as assistance for repairing and rebuilding homes.
- Provide assistance with unmet needs related to obtaining/completing permanent housing.
- Provide debris clearance in concert with homeowners and local government.
- Develop, train, and operate community long-term recovery committees to help meet individual and community needs as identified.
- Provide long-term individual and family services, case management, assistance with unmet needs for individuals and families, and health and human services.
- Provide financial assistance to affected individuals and families for unmet needs.

Coordination of Disaster Recovery

The practical work of implementing the recovery process occurs at the Joint Field Office. Two organizational structures, or branches, divide the recovery assistance functions. These branches assess state and local recovery needs at the outset of the disaster and relevant time frames for program delivery. The human services branch coordinates assistance programs to help individuals, families, and businesses meet basic needs and return to self-sufficiency. It is responsible for the donations management function. The infrastructure support branch coordinates assistance programs to aid state and local governments and eligible private nonprofit organizations to repair or replace damaged public facilities. The two branches assist in identifying appropriate agency assistance programs to meet applicant needs, synchronizing assistance delivery and encouraging incorporation of mitigation measures where possible. In addition to the work of the disaster recovery centers (DRCs), applicant briefings are conducted for local government officials and certain private nonprofit organizations to inform them of available recovery assistance and how to apply.

Federal disaster assistance available under a major disaster falls into three general categories: individual assistance, public assistance, and hazard mitigation assistance. Individual assistance is aid to individuals, families, and business owners. Public assistance is aid to public and certain private nonprofit entities for emergency services and the repair or replacement of disaster-damaged public facilities. Hazard mitigation assistance is funding available for measures designed to reduce future losses to public and private property. A detailed description of the first two types of assistance follows.

FEMA'S Individual Assistance Recovery Programs

Individual assistance programs are oriented to individuals, families, and small businesses, and the programs include the Individuals and Households Program, SBA loans, disaster unemployment assistance, legal services, special tax considerations, and crisis counseling. The disaster victim must first register for assistance and establish eligibility before receiving this assistance. These programs are described next.

Individuals and Households Program

The Individuals and Households Program (IHP) is a program coordinated jointly by FEMA and the affected states. When a major disaster is declared, the IHP provides both money and services to people in the declared areas whose property has been damaged or destroyed and whose losses are not covered by insurance. To receive assistance under this program, disaster victims must register for assistance and first have their eligibility established.

IHP has two separate programs that address the needs of individuals and households. The housing assistance program works to ensure that people whose homes are damaged by a disaster have a safe place to live while it is repaired or replaced. The other needs assistance (ONA) program provides financial assistance to individuals and households who have disaster-related expenses or serious needs, but who do not qualify for Small Business Administration (SBA) loans (see next subsection). These two programs are designed to provide funds for expenses that are not covered by insurance. They are available only to U.S. citizen homeowners and renters, noncitizen nationals, or qualified aliens. The following is a list of the types of assistance available through this program and what each provides:

Temporary Housing — Funding that covers the cost of renting an alternate house or apartment when a victim's residence is uninhabitable due to disaster damage.

Repair — Funding that covers the cost of repair to damage that was caused by the disaster, but which was not covered by insurance. These repairs must be geared toward making the home "safe and sanitary" to qualify.

Replacement — Funding to cover the cost of replacing a home destroyed by a disaster.

Permanent Housing Construction — Funding for the construction of a new home. This type of assistance occurs only in very unusual situations, in remote locations where no other type of housing is possible.

Other Needs Assistance (ONA) — Funding for necessary and serious needs caused by the disaster. This includes medical, dental, funeral, personal property, transportation, moving and storage, and other expenses that FEMA approves. To receive ONA, the victim may first need to apply for an SBA loan.

Small Business Administration Disaster Loans

Following federally declared disasters, the U.S. Small Business Administration (SBA) normally provides federally subsidized loans to repair or replace homes, personal property, or businesses that sustained damages not covered by insurance. For many individuals the SBA disaster loan program is the primary form of disaster assistance. The SBA can provide three types of disaster loans to qualified homeowners and businesses:

- Home disaster loans to homeowners and renters to repair or replace disaster-related damage to home or personal property

- Business physical disaster loans to business owners to repair or replace disaster-damaged property, including inventory and supplies

- Economic injury disaster loans, which provide capital to small businesses and to small agricultural cooperatives to assist them through the disaster recovery period

Disaster Unemployment Assistance

The Disaster Unemployment Assistance (DUA) program provides unemployment benefits and re-employment services to individuals who have lost their jobs as a result of the disaster. Benefits begin with the date the job was lost, and can be continued for up to 26 weeks after the presidential declaration date. The DUA program is available to people who are not covered by other unemployment insurance programs or who cannot qualify for other unemployment compensation.

Legal Services

Following a disaster, the Young Lawyers Division of the American Bar Association may be contracted by FEMA to provide free legal assistance to disaster victims. These services are provided to low-income individuals who, prior to or because of the disaster, are unable to afford adequate legal services to meet their postdisaster-related needs. Legal advice under this program is limited to cases that will not result in any attorney or other fees. The assistance that participating lawyers provide typically includes the following:

- Assistance with insurance claims (life, medical, property, etc.)

- Counseling on landlord/tenant problems

- Assisting in consumer protection matters, remedies, and procedures

- Replacement of wills and other important legal documents destroyed in a major disaster

Special Tax Considerations

Taxpayers who have sustained a casualty loss from a declared disaster may deduct that loss on the federal income tax return for the year in which the casualty actually occurred, or elect to deduct the loss on the tax return for the preceding tax year. To qualify, victims' losses must be greater than 10% of the adjusted gross income for the tax year by at least $100. Additionally, the Internal Revenue Service (IRS) can expedite refunds due to taxpayers in a federally declared disaster area. This service is available to any taxpayer in a federally declared disaster area.

Crisis Counseling

The Crisis Counseling Assistance and Training Program (CCP) is designed to provide supplemental funding to states for short-term crisis counseling services. Two separate portions of the CCP can be funded: immediate services and regular services. A state may request either or both types of funding. The immediate services program is intended to enable the state or local agency to respond to the immediate mental health needs with screening, diagnostic, and counseling techniques, as well as outreach services such as public information and community networking. The regular services program is designed to provide up to 9 months of crisis counseling, community outreach, and consultation and education services to people affected by the disaster. To be eligible for crisis counseling services funded by this program, the person must be a resident of the designated area or must have been located in the area at the time the disaster occurred. The person must also have a mental health problem that was caused by or aggravated by the disaster or its aftermath, or he or she must benefit from services provided by the program.

Public Assistance Programs

Public assistance, oriented to public entities, is designed to facilitate the repair, restoration, reconstruction, or replacement of public facilities or infrastructure damaged or destroyed by a federally declared disaster. Eligible applicants include state governments, local governments, and any other political subdivision of a state, Native American tribes, and Alaska Native villages. Certain private nonprofit (PNP) organizations may also receive assistance, including educational, utility, irrigation, emergency, medical, rehabilitation, and temporary or permanent custodial care facilities, and other PNP facilities that provide essential services of a governmental nature to the general public.

As soon as is possible and practical following a disaster declaration, the state, assisted by FEMA, briefs state, local, and PNP officials to inform them of the assistance available and how to apply for it (Figures 7–17 and 7–18). To receive this assistance, a Request for Public Assistance must be filed with the state within 30 days of the time the area is designated as eligible. Following the briefing, a "Kickoff Meeting" is conducted where damages are discussed, needs assessed, and a plan of action put in place. A team made up of federal, state, and local representatives initiates the project, including documenting the eligible facilities, the eligible work, and the eligible cost for fixing the damages to every public or PNP facility identified by state or local representatives. The team prepares a project worksheet (PW) for each project. Projects are grouped into the following categories:

> Category A: Debris removal
> Category B: Emergency protective measures
> Category C: Road systems and bridges
> Category D: Water control facilities
> Category E: Public buildings and contents
> Category F: Public utilities
> Category G: Parks, recreational, and other

FEMA reviews and approves the PWs and obligates the federal share of the costs (75% or more) to the state. The state then disburses funds to local applicants.

Other Federal Agency Disaster Recovery Funding

Other federal agencies have programs that contribute to social and economic recovery. Most of these additional programs are triggered by a presidential declaration of a major disaster or emergency

FIGURE 7–17 New York City, New York, October 30, 2001 — FEMA/New York State Disaster field office personnel meet to coordinate federal, state, and local disaster assistance programs. (Photo by Andrea Booher/FEMA News Photo)

FIGURE 7–18 New York City, New York, October 20, 2001 — Disaster field office staff continue to work with other agencies operating near "ground zero" to provide information about disaster assistance programs. (Photo by Andrea Booher/FEMA News Photo)

under the Stafford Act. However, the secretary of the Department of Agriculture and the administrator of the Small Business Administration have specific authority relevant to their constituencies to declare a disaster and provide disaster recovery assistance. All of the agencies are part of the structure of the NRF.

Conclusion

The motives behind the establishment of the DHS are almost as numerous as the number of agencies it involves, and include politics, power, public relations, or a real need to improve the federal response and recovery systems because of the new spectrum of threats made apparent by the September 11 attacks. For whatever reason or combination of reasons, a system that had demonstrated its operational capabilities in both natural disasters and terrorism events in Oklahoma City, New York, and the Pentagon became subject to significant and ongoing change. As a result of the integration of different agencies and the need for new procedural systems to operate together, the NRP was developed with the NIMS. NIMS and the National Response Framework (that has since replaced the NRP) together serve as references and guidelines to determine how the nation's first responders and agencies involved in response operate.

The effort to include citizens and the private sector as active partners is commendable. Programs developed under the Citizen Corps Councils provide the opportunity to build strong communities. However, they have been poorly supported by the political leadership and are underfunded. Further collaboration with the business sector will allow for enhanced preparedness and protection of the critical infrastructure and provide a better understanding of its vulnerabilities and how to respond if it is attacked.

As a final point, it is essential to bear in mind that the massive integration of many agencies into one has its drawbacks: Independence is compromised and the overall redundancy of the system decreases. The NRF and NIMS define how different agencies operate together but it should not jeopardize or change the agencies' own integrity and mission. Although redundancy is an attribute that all organizations try to get rid of, it is also what often saves the day during a crisis situation. "Too efficient" systems with minimal backup, no duplication of function, and low flexibility/adaptability have been shown to be more vulnerable to unexpected situations, to fail in a worse manner, and to be less agile when responding to and dealing with an emergency. Thus, an excessive integration to reduce redundancy can cause the involved agencies to depend on each other rather than empower each other — and this might lead the way for a catastrophic chain reaction of failure to occur in certain conditions.

CASE STUDY 1: THE SPACE SHUTTLE *COLUMBIA* DISASTER

The Event

On February 1, 2003, the Space Shuttle *Columbia,* flying mission STS-107, reentered Earth's atmosphere following its 28th successful space flight that began on January 16 of that year. It was carrying seven astronauts, including Commander Rick D. Husband, Pilot William C. McCool, Payload Commander Michael P. Anderson, Mission Specialists David M. Brown, Kalpana Chawla, and Laurel Blair Salton Clark, and Payload Specialist Ilan Ramon. The flight had been delayed a total of 13 times since its originally scheduled lift-off date of January 11, 2001.

On January 16, 2003, when the shuttle finally lifted off, a piece of insulation on one of the shuttle's fuel tanks broke off about 82 seconds into the flight. The event was considered inconsequential by mission specialists. However, because of the speed the shuttle was traveling at the time

(1,650 mph), and the delicate nature of the shuttle's protective thermal skin, the insulation caused a small breach that did not pose any problems until the "burn" period experienced upon reentry.

During the reentry burn period (which began at 8:44 AM), several stages of shuttle positioning and speed, according to normal procedural systems, caused the shuttle to slow down considerably from its 17,500-mph speed. The friction caused by the shuttle entering the Earth's atmosphere at over 20 times the speed of sound, which results in an incredible release of energy, caused the leading edge of the wings to rise to as much as 3,000 degrees Fahrenheit.

Ground control crews began to notice failures in many of the instruments in the left wing. Progressively, more problems arose, but the control teams were having trouble determining the root of the problems and communicating with the crew to gain more insight into what was happening. The last transmission from the crew came at 8:59 AM, which was cut off after just one word. At 9:05 AM, a loud explosion was heard over Texas, and evidence that the shuttle had begun to disintegrate was clear to the naked eye.

The destruction of the shuttle showered debris across an area of hundreds of square miles in East Texas and Western Louisiana (a very small amount of material was also found in Arkansas). In total, over 2,000 individual debris fields were noted by recovery crews. As had been true with the Space Shuttle *Challenger*, the event was witnessed by the entire nation via breaking news reports. NASA immediately issued a warning to the public that all debris should be considered hazardous material, with the potential to cause injuries or death, and that any information on the location of debris should be immediately reported to local authorities (Wikipedia, 2005).

The Response

The response to the shuttle disaster has been called the largest deployment of civilian government agencies in history.

Due to the large area in which the debris had fallen, scores of police and fire departments were immediately called to action by reports from citizens. As true first responders, these officials began, albeit without any real organization, to collect and document the shuttle debris. It was almost guaranteed that, beyond the initial seven astronauts and the space shuttle, there would be no additional fatalities, injuries, or destruction caused by the disaster. However, the work hours and resources required for such a large operation were assuredly going to be excessive — and likewise a strain on the state and local agencies involved.

President Bush immediately assessed the situation with FEMA and DHS officials, and issued emergency declarations for the states of Texas and Louisiana. It is important to note that these declarations were made in the absence of any formal request for assistance from the governors of either of those states. It was later declared by the administration that this action was considered appropriate because the space shuttle *Columbia* itself was considered federal property, and therefore the authority to make such declarations existed.

The disaster declaration, as per the Stafford Act, authorized the Federal Emergency Management Agency (FEMA) under Emergency Support Function (ESF) #5 to coordinate federal aid and the management of resources used by all responders in the response and recovery to the disaster. FEMA announced that Michael Brown, FEMA Deputy Director and Acting Undersecretary of the newly created Department of Homeland Security, would lead FEMA's efforts in what was considered a "search, find, and secure" operation.

From the onset, the agencies' priorities were threefold: ensure public safety, retrieve evidence-pieces of the shuttle that could ultimately determine the cause of the tragedy, and reimburse expenses of state and local governments and private citizens who may have sustained property

(Continued)

damage as a result of the accident and search. NASA quickly identified potential hazardous materials, such as tanks containing toxic substances or unexploded pyrotechnic devices, and once found, the Environmental Protection Agency (EPA) secured the material. The EPA also worked with state and local authorities to clear school campuses and public access areas, and tested air and water samples taken along the flight path for shuttle contaminates. Using the resources of the Emergency Response and Removal Service (ERRS) contractors and the U.S. Coast Guard (USCG) Gulf Strike Team, EPA found no evidence of hazardous material in the atmosphere or drinking water supplies. Early in the recovery effort, teams from NASA, the FBI, the National Guard, Urban Search and Rescue (US&R) organizations, the Department of Public Safety, and others conducted a successful search in East Texas to recover and bring home the bodies of *Columbia*'s crew.

On February 2, FEMA announced that its principal mission was to assist the state and local response agencies in mapping the debris fields and collecting any debris reported or found. The agency reported that they had coordinated the following activities:

- Established an Interagency Initial Operating Facility (IOF) at Barksdale Air Force Base in Louisiana. Representatives from NASA, FEMA, the FBI, the EPA, and the Department of Defense were to be assembled there to coordinate response activities.

- Assigned liaisons from the FBI, the EPA, the Department of Transportation, the General Services Administration, and the Department of Defense to FEMA's Regional Operations Center in Denton, Texas. FEMA assigned state liaisons to the Texas State Emergency Operations Center and the State Command Post in Lufkin, Texas.

- Began the process of establishing two disaster field offices (DFOs) in Lufkin, Texas, and at the Barksdale Air Force Base in Louisiana. The Lufkin DFO would serve as the primary operational DFO for all operations, including staging assets and deploying field teams for search, find, and secure operations. Barksdale Air Force Base in Louisiana would serve as the investigative center and storage location. A third (satellite) DFO was set up the next day at the Fort Worth Naval Air Station.

- Deployed special Mobile Emergency Response Systems (MERS) communications equipment to Lufkin, Texas.

- Announced that the EPA had deployed HAZMAT teams to collect debris, mobilized Airborne Spectral Photo-Imaging of Environmental Contaminants Technology (ASPECT) aircraft to help locate debris using infrared sensors to detect hazardous chemicals, and deployed the Trace Atmospheric Gas Analyzer Unit to provide mobile analytical support.

- Announced that the U.S. Coast Guard (now part of DHS) had deployed members of its Gulf Strike Team, based in Mobile, Alabama, to Lufkin to assist with debris recovery operations there. One of three located throughout the country, Gulf Strike Team personnel are specially trained and equipped to respond to incidents involving oil or hazardous chemical spills (FEMA, 2003c).

These teams had been deployed within hours to the disaster area to assist local fire, law enforcement, and emergency management authorities already on site. More than 60 agencies, including public and private groups, responded with personnel, supplies, and equipment. The Lufkin DFO was the regional center of all search-related operations. This was the first major response performed by the newly created Department of Homeland Security.

By the next day, February 3, FEMA had established a Joint Information Center (JIC) at the Lufkin Civic Center in Lufkin, Texas, to serve as the distribution point for information disseminated to the public, and to which the public could go to retrieve information. The JIC was comprised of representatives from FEMA, the EPA, NASA, the American Red Cross (ARC), the U.S. Forest Service, the U.S. Coast Guard, the Department of Health and Human Services (HHS), and several other agencies involved in the response at the federal and state levels. FEMA also announced that additional U.S. Coast Guard strike teams and the Texas and Louisiana National Guard were participating in the search, that water quality was being tested in both states, and that hazardous spills were being addressed.

On February 5, four days after the shuttle disaster, FEMA released a fact sheet describing the procedures by which materials were to be collected by state and local response agencies. The following are the guidelines from that fact sheet:

The following guidelines are designed to assist public service personnel to determine when and how to collect and document space shuttle material. If the material is less than 18 inches in length and does not appear to be hazardous, then it may be collected under the following guidelines:

PRIVATE CITIZENS ARE NOT AUTHORIZED TO COLLECT MATERIAL

The following trained personnel are authorized to collect nonhazardous materials:

Local, State or Federal Law Enforcement Personnel

Fire, Medical, or Emergency Services Personnel

U.S. Forest Service or Texas Forest Service

Federal Emergency Management Agency (FEMA)

Environmental Protection Agency (EPA)

National Aeronautics and Space Administration (NASA)

*Only nonhazardous material may be collected under these guidelines. If the material includes any of the following, officials should contact **936-699-1032** or **936-699-1034** to report what they have found so that specially trained personnel can be deployed:*

Stored Energy: *High-pressure tanks and cylinders. Landing gear and tires.*

Monomethyl Hydrazine: *Clear liquid stored in tanks, strong fishy odor.*

Nitrogen Tetroxide: *Greenish liquid or brownish vapor, stored in tanks, bleach-like odor.*

Ammonia: *Clear liquid, stored in tanks, very strong ammonia smell.*

Pyrotechnic Devices: *Landing gear, window frames, crew seats, hatches, and antennae.*

Biological Material: *Any biological material, including human or animal remains.*

The following procedure should be followed by authorized, trained personnel if the identified material is nonhazardous:

Photograph items before they are moved.

Carefully document the location of the items (to include GPS data if available).

Attach a tag to the item with the location the item was found and the name and phone number of the individual collecting the item. Include any information you think may be relevant to the investigation. Documentation for large items may be recorded with permanent marker directly on the hardware.

Wear gloves (preferably not cloth) when handling items and do not open, adjust or move any switches, components or boxes.

If possible, seal the item in a plastic bag.

Transport the item to your local command post.

(Continued)

CASE STUDY 1: THE SPACE SHUTTLE *COLUMBIA* DISASTER – (CONTINUED)

*If an item is marked SECRET, CONFIDENTIAL, or SSOR do not leave this item unattended before handover to NASA personnel. With any questions or for more information, please contact DPS at the Lufkin Emergency Operation Center, **936-699-1077** (FEMA, 2003e).*

On February 6, the President amended the original disaster declaration to include any state within which shuttle debris was found. Additionally, the declaration was amended such that FEMA was authorized to reimburse a full 100% of the costs incurred by local and state agencies in their efforts to retrieve shuttle materials (FEMA, 2003f). By this point, 115 pieces of shuttle material had been found by 174 officials searching in Louisiana. Texas was using 800 National Guard troops, 353 Department of Public Safety personnel, and 140 Forest Service employees in the search. Additionally, the EPA had collected over 1,100 bags of hazardous materials through the efforts of 370 employees working in 60 teams (FEMA, 2003g).

March 1 marked 1 month of operations in the response and recovery of the shuttle disaster. By this point there were over 5,200 federal and state officials working on the response, and four collection centers had been established to accept the debris that had been located (FEMA, 2003h). On March 27, a Bell 407 helicopter, involved in the search for shuttle debris, crashed in poor weather. Two members of the crew, Texas Forest Service employee Charles Krenek and pilot Jules F. Mier, Jr., died, and three other crew members were injured. This event brought the death toll of the disaster to nine. Air operations in the search were suspended until April 10, until it was determined that flights could resume under the safest possible conditions (FEMA, 2003i).

On April 17, FEMA announced that it would be handing over operational control of the recovery mission to NASA on April 30, nearly 3 months following the disaster. Also announced were the following updates on the progress of the search:

- Ground crews had searched over 83% of the 704,000 assigned acres.

- Air operations had searched 577 (92%) of the assigned 629 grid (2-by-2 mile) areas.

- Water operations had concluded.

- More than 79,900 pounds of shuttle material had been shipped to Kennedy Space Center in Florida, representing approximately 37% of the weight of the craft.

- All reported debris in Louisiana had been picked up.

- Under the FEMA Public Assistance Program, Texas had been obligated $2.6 million and Louisiana had been obligated $395,000 for approved county/parish shuttle debris recovery related activities (FEMA, 2003j).

FEMA turned over control of the recovery operation to NASA on April 30. The same day, NASA opened the Columbia Recovery Operation (CRO) office at the Johnson Space Center in Houston. FEMA closed the disaster field office in Lufkin, Texas, on May 10. On May 5, FEMA released a recap of the search for the Space Shuttle *Columbia* debris material. This announcement included the following final statistics about the disaster recovery:

- After 3 months, search personnel recovered more than 82,500 pieces of shuttle debris equaling a total weight of 84,800 pounds, or almost 40% of the total dry weight of the shuttle.

- Ground, water, and air searches combined covered more than 2.28 million acres.

- Water operations successfully identified more than 3,100 targets and covered 23 square miles.

- More than 16,500 ground search personnel and their support personnel searched an unprecedented 680,748 acres.

- Total person-hours used in the recovery effort amounted to approximately 1.5 million.

- Under the FEMA Public Assistance program, $10 million was the amount projected for Texas to reimburse eligible costs associated with the recovery effort. As of May 1, $3.98 million had been obligated. For Louisiana, projected reimbursable payments were $500,000, while $396,000 had been obligated.

- Outside Texas and Louisiana, searches had been concluded in New Mexico and California. Searches continued in Nevada and Utah.

- No debris was found west of Littlefield, Texas, or east of Fort Polk, Louisiana.

- More than 130 federal, state, and local agencies participated in the recovery effort.

- Approximately 25,000 personnel took part in the recovery operation.

- The operation was supported by more than 270 organizations including businesses and volunteer groups (FEMA, 2003j).

EPA Involvement

FEMA tasked the Environmental Protection Agency with the management of all hazardous materials found in the search area. This disaster marked new territory for many of the agencies involved, including EPA and NASA, which had never before worked together on a project. Additionally, as NASA had warned repetitively that all shuttle debris should be considered hazardous, this was to be one of the EPA's greatest operational challenges to date. More than 1,900 employees from the agency were deployed.

The EPA's response was based out of Region 6, headquartered in Dallas, Texas. The EPA's primary mission in the response effort was to protect public health and the environment, and their first task was to remove shuttle material from school property — a task completed by February 4, only 3 days following the disaster. The search teams were set up so that an EPA team accompanied each 20-person search crew in order to handle any debris found within the search grids. In addition, EPA personnel responded to any other reports of potential debris sites that were called in to FEMA DFOs. Finally, the EPA was charged with staffing the four local debris collection centers that were established to process the tens of thousands of pieces of shuttle material that were collected over the course of the recovery operation.

To handle such a large operation, the EPA had national teams suspend regular operations and deploy to Region 6, where the disaster had occurred, to help staff the 24-hour-per-day demands of the shuttle response. On the day of the disaster, the EPA initiated flights of their Airborne Spectral-Imagery of Environmental Contaminants Technology (ASPECT) aircraft, which was able to locate shuttle parts containing potentially hazardous materials. Based on these flights, EPA experts were able to determine that there were no major concentrations of hazardous materials present in the debris fields that could pose a major health hazard to the human populations in the surrounding areas. The EPA also mobilized its Trace Atmospheric Gas Analyzer vehicle, which has the ability to collect real-time outdoor air quality samples while in motion.

On average, each EPA team processed between 10 and 15 sites per day, with the goal of processing a county every 3 to 5 days (per team). EPA dive teams conducted searches of small ponds and lakes, while side-scan sonar was utilized in larger bodies of water to locate debris.

(*Continued*)

Finally, the EPA was tasked with the data management of collected shuttle debris. The location, description, and other information about each piece was collected in the field in handheld computers, and uploaded each night onto a central computer database, in order to assist NASA in determining the cause of the crash and other investigative goals (EPA, 2003).

All Agency Involvement
The following federal agencies, among others, participated:

> Defense Coordinating Element
> Defense Criminal Investigation Service
> Department of Defense
> Department of Health and Human Services
> Department of the Interior
> Department of Transportation
> Environmental Protection Agency
> Federal Bureau of Investigation
> Federal Emergency Management Agency
> General Services Administration
> National Aeronautics and Space Administration
> National Imagery and Mapping Agency
> National Park Service
> National Transportation Safety Board
> National Weather Service
> Naval Research Laboratory
> Office of Personnel Management
> U.S. Air Force
> U.S. Army
> U.S. Army Corp of Engineers
> U.S. Attorney's Office
> U.S. Coast Guard
> U.S. Fire Service
> U.S. Fish and Wildlife
> U.S. Forest Service
> U.S. Marshal Service
> U.S. Navy
> Urban Search and Rescue

Participating state agencies and other entities included, among others, the following:

Arkansas National Guard
Colorado Forest Service
Florida Division of Forestry
Louisiana Department of Wildlife and Fisheries
Louisiana National Guard
Louisiana Office of Emergency Preparedness
Louisiana State Police
Maryland Task Force 1
New Mexico National Guard
North Carolina Forest Service

Oklahoma National Guard
Stephen F. Austin University
Texas Army National Guard
Texas Commission on Environmental Quality
Texas Department of Criminal Justice
Texas Department of Mental Health Mental Retardation
Texas Department of Public Safety
Texas Department of Transportation
Texas Division of Emergency Management
Texas Engineering Extension Service
Texas Fish & Wildlife Department
Texas Forest Service
Texas National Resources Information System Service
Texas Task Force 1
Texas Water Development Board
University of Texas Center for Space Research
Virginia Department of Forestry

Participating local agencies and other entities included, among others, the following:

Angelina County Economic Development Partnership
Angelina County Sheriff's Office
Arlington Police Department
Broward County Sheriff
City of Lufkin
City of San Diego Fire Department
City of Dallas Fire Department
City of Ft. Worth Fire Department
Ft. Worth Independent School District
Galveston County Sheriff
Houston Police Department
Jasper County Sheriff
Kern County Fire Department
San Augustine County Sheriff

Participating volunteer agencies, among others, include following:

Alpine Rescue Team
American Red Cross
Civil Air Patrol
The Salvation Army
The Texas Baptist Men

In support of EPA, the U.S. Navy was assigned to coordinate water search operations. An operations base was set up at Toledo Bend Reservoir. There were eight dive teams working the reservoir: three U.S. Navy, two EPA, and one each from the city of Galveston, city of Houston, and the Texas Department of Public Safety. In addition, six boats equipped with side and multibeam scanning sonar looked for dive targets, including four on the reservoir and two on Lake Nacogdoches. The Navy also deployed various handheld sonar units and an autonomous unit that were programmed to search underwater areas independently. About 130 personnel worked the water search operation.

(Continued)

CASE STUDY 1: THE SPACE SHUTTLE *COLUMBIA* DISASTER–(CONTINUED)

Following a tremendous initial search effort by local governments and volunteers, four base camps were established to house interagency crews at the request of the Texas Forest Service. These crews relieved the search burden on state and local resources by bringing in firefighting crews from other parts of the nation. Crews from 39 states joined the effort. In total, about 4,500 personnel arrived and about 155 crews of 20 people each daily combed through NASA-assigned search areas in a corridor 240 by 10 miles wide from Ellis County in the west to Toledo Bend Reservoir in the east. Four crew base camps were set up: Nacogdoches (1,100 personnel), Palestine (about 1,000), Hemphill (about 1,000), and Corsicana (about 1,350). A mobilization unit was established at Longview Airport to assist crew arrival, travel to and from base camps, and departure. Since February 14, these out-of-state crews had expended nearly 132,000 person-hours on the search.

Extensive air searches were used in the search. Operating out of two facilities, one in the Lufkin area and one in the Palestine area, 33 helicopters and nine fixed-wing aircraft flew search grids over the 240-by-10 mile corridor seeking possible debris sites. Possible sites were relayed to ground crews for inspection.

The State of Texas rushed to assist local communities in the initial search, and continued to support the federal agencies responding to the event. The Texas Department of Public Safety's Division of Emergency Management coordinated the state response. Among state agency personnel committed were the following: 353 state troopers, about 800 National Guard, four aircraft, 17 helicopters, 140 Texas Forest Service personnel, 35 horse-mounted search teams, 20 Texas Department of Transportation personnel, 27 Texas Commission of Environmental Quality personnel, and various other units such as dogs and handlers, mapping support personnel, and game wardens.

Conclusion

As a test of response capabilities, many have argued that the Department of Homeland Security was given an easy assignment — there were only seven initial fatalities, no injuries, and very little destruction. However, from a coordination standpoint, the event was colossal. As previously mentioned, it was the single greatest mobilization of civil service employees in the history of the nation, and with very few exceptions, the operation was carried off without a hitch. All local and state costs were reimbursed by the federal government, and many working relationships were created in the response and recovery phases when counterparts were able to work face to face in a relatively low-stress environment. The event proved that FEMA had retained its agency status within DHS, and was able to continue functioning as it had before the Homeland Security Act was signed just 4 months earlier.

References

Bullock & Haddow, LLC. 2003. North Carolina: "Madison County Terrorism Annex to Basic Emergency Response Plan."

Environmental Protection Agency. (2003). "Response to the Columbia Space Shuttle Incident." www.epa.gov/columbia.

Federal Emergency Management Agency. 2003a. "President Declares Emergency in Texas and Louisiana in Response to Space Shuttle Tragedy." FEMA Press

Release, February 1. www.fema.gov/news/newsrelease.fema?id=2406.

Federal Emergency Management Agency. 2003b. "FEMA to Lead Search, Find, and Secure Mission Following Space Shuttle Tragedy." FEMA Press Release, February 1. www.fema.gov/news/newsrelease.fema?id=2405.

Federal Emergency Management Agency. 2003c. "FEMA Puts Federal Resources into Action to Assist State and

Local Authorities in Search, Find, and Secure Mission for *Columbia* Debris." FEMA Press Release, February 2. www.fema.gov/news/newsrelease.fema?id=2407.

Federal Emergency Management Agency. 2003d. "FEMA Establishes Joint Information Center for *Columbia* Debris Search, Find, and Secure Mission at Lufkin Civic Center." FEMA Press Release, February 3. www.fema.gov/news/newsrelease.fema?id=2409.

Federal Emergency Management Agency. 2003e. "*Columbia* Material Collection Guidelines: Fact Sheet." FEMA Press Release, February 5. www.fema.gov/news/newsrelease.fema?id=2414.

Federal Emergency Management Agency. 2003f. "President Amends *Columbia* Emergency Declaration to Include All States." FEMA Press Release, February 6. www.fema.gov/news/newsrelease.fema?id=2416.

Federal Emergency Management Agency. 2003g. "FEMA Updates Search, Find, and Secure Activities for Columbia Emergency." FEMA Press Release, February 6. www.fema.gov/news/newsrelease.fema?id=2415.

Federal Emergency Management Agency, 2003h. "Good Progress Made in One Month of Shuttle Recovery." FEMA Press Release, March 1. www.fema.gov/news/newsrelease.fema?id=2458.

Federal Emergency Management Agency 2003i. "FEMA Will Hand On-Going Recovery Operations to NASA April 30." FEMA Press Release, April 17. www.fema.gov/news/newsrelease.fema?id=2534.

Federal Emergency Management Agency. 2003j. "Recap of the Search for *Columbia* Shuttle Material." FEMA Press Release, May 5. www.fema.gov/news/newsrelease.fema?id=2808.

Wikipedia. 2005. "Space Shuttle *Columbia* Disaster." http://en.wikipedia.org/wiki/Space_Shuttle_Columbia_disaster.

CASE STUDY 2: THE LONDON TERROR ATTACKS, JULY 7, 2005

On Thursday, July 7, 2005, just before 9 AM, four suicide bombers blew themselves up — three on London subway trains and one on a bus. The explosions resulted in the deaths of 56 people, including the bombers, and injured more than 700 others. The entire London subway system was closed for the remainder of the day, and cellular telephone systems were jammed, leading to commuter chaos. The following timeline illustrates the attacks and the step-by-step response by British authorities.

8:50 AM — Three explosions occur almost simultaneously on three London underground trains: between Aldgate and Liverpool Street stations on the Circle Line, between Russell Square and King's Cross stations on the Piccadilly Line, and at Edgware Road station on the Circle Line.

At first, police are only aware of the Aldgate/Liverpool Street train attack. The Russell Square/King's Cross blast was not reported until 8:56, and the Edgware blast at 9:17. A review of technical data and witness accounts showed that the three bombs actually went off within about 50 seconds.

9:47 — The No. 30 bus on Upper Woburn Place near Tavistock Square is destroyed by a fourth explosion. Pictures show the roof of the double-decker bus ripped off and witnesses report seeing body parts in the road, Reuters reports.

10:02 — Scotland Yard says it is dealing with a "major incident."

10:20 — Metropolitan Police post a message on their website reporting that a major transportation incident has happened in London and that it is responding to six metro stations and one confirmed explosion in a public bus. Cause, severity, and impact of the explosions are not known at this point.

(Continued)

10:47 — Home Secretary Charles Clarke says multiple London blasts have caused "terrible injuries."

11:15 — European Union commissioner for justice and security affairs Franco Frattini tells reporters in Rome that the blasts in London are terrorist attacks.

11:35 — London police chief tells Reuters news agency there are "indications of explosives" at one of the blast sites.

12:00 PM — British Prime Minister Tony Blair says the "barbaric" London blasts are terrorist attacks and were designed to coincide with the G8 summit in Scotland. He will return to London.

12:15 — A group calling itself the Group of al-Qaeda of Jihad Organization in Europe lays claim to the blasts, posting a statement on an Islamist website. The claim cannot be independently verified.

12:27 — Police and hospital officials tell Reuters that a total of 185 people are wounded across London, 10 of them seriously and 7 critically.

12:30 — Metropolitan Police confirmed explosions in three metro stations and one public bus and continues its presence on the incident sites. At the time the police do not provide numbers of casualties but underline that there are many.

12:51 — Emergency services personnel tell CNN writer William Chamberlain that all survivors had been evacuated from King's Cross station, leaving the dead below ground "in the double digits."

12:53 — Britain's Home Secretary Charles Clarke tells the House of Commons there were four explosions in central London and the underground system will be closed all day. They would decide later in day whether to resume bus services. Earlier six attacks were reported.

2:38 — U.S. law enforcement sources cite the British government as saying that at least 40 people have been killed. London hospitals report at least 300 wounded, the Associated Press reports.

3:26 — London deputy police chief Brian Paddick says police had no warning of the attacks and have not received any claims of responsibility. He says police are keeping an open mind over who carried out the attacks and that it is unclear whether a claim of responsibility by al-Qaeda is genuine or whether suicide bombers were involved. No arrests have been made in connection with the attacks.

3:41 — Assistant chief ambulance officer Russell Smith says the service has treated 45 patients with serious or critical injuries. A further 300 patients have been treated for minor injuries.

4:30 — London Police announce that the Metropolitan Police Service Casualty Bureau has been opened and ask the public to call the hotline if they are concerned about their loved ones who may have been affected by the incidents. The police announced the number of the confirmed fatalities as 33 for the first time and mentioned that the incidents were caused by terrorists.

4:32 — Transport authorities say Docklands Light Railway services in east London and mainline rail services have resumed, except out of King's Cross and Victoria stations. Buses in central London are also returning to service. All underground services remain suspended.

5:43 — Prime Minister Tony Blair says that Britain will not be intimidated by terrorism and promises intense police and security services action to bring those behind the bombings to justice. "I would also pay tribute to the stoicism and resilience of the people of London who have responded in a way typical of them," says Blair.

5:49 — The United Nations Security Council passes a resolution condemning the London attacks and expressing "outrage and indignation at today's appalling terrorist attacks against the people of the United Kingdom that cost human life and caused injuries and immense human suffering."

7:15 — Metropolitan police updates the number of confirmed fatalities as 37 and confirms that the incidents involved four explosive devices.

This timeline is based on multiple sources including CNN, and the London Metropolitan Police media releases: www.cnn.com/2005/WORLD/europe/07/07/london.timeline/index.html, www.met.police.uk/news/op_theseus/response1.htm, www.met.police.uk/news/op_theseus/response2 .htm, www.met.police.uk/news/op_theseus/response3.htm, and www.met.police.uk/news/op_theseus/ response4.htm.

Observations and Comments on Incident

London Metropolitan Police: London Metropolitan Police immediately responded to all potential incident scenes and fulfilled their first-response responsibility. The unique aspect of the incident management by the Metropolitan Police was consistent and persistent behavior in terms of releasing information to the media and the public. The department did not speculate on the incidents and their outcomes and public impacts at any time. The Metropolitan Police chose to release factual information only when the validity of the information was confirmed by credible sources, in many cases its investigators or cooperating government officials. The first casualty numbers were announced about 4:30 PM by the department. Until then various sources in the media were reporting a range of casualty numbers (between 2 and 90) (based on Multiple London Metropolitan Police Press Releases and media coverage on July 7, 2005).

London Fire Brigade: Around 200 firefighters were called to explosions at Aldgate, Edgware Road, and King's Cross London underground stations and an explosion on a bus at Tavistock Square on Thursday, July 7. Twelve fire appliances with 60 firefighters attended the incident at Edgware Road, 12 fire appliances with 60 firefighters attended the incident at King's Cross, 10 fire appliances with 50 firefighters attended the Aldgate incident, and 4 fire appliances with 20 firefighters were called to Tavistock Square. Throughout the morning, several new specialist fire rescue units were deployed to work with the other emergency services to evacuate casualties and make the incident locales safe (London Fire Brigade, www.london-fire.gov.uk/news/ statement.asp).

London Emergency Medical Services: The response of the emergency medical service units to the bomb attacks in London has generally been assessed as "adequate" by experts. The incident claimed more than 50 lives, left more than 700 hurt, and kept about 100 overnight in hospital, 22 of whom were in critical condition as of July 8. Hospitals responding to the crisis included St. Mary's hospital in Paddington, the Royal Free hospital in Hampstead, St. Thomas's hospital, and Great Ormond Street children's hospital, which does not have an emergency department but took in 22 patients. Hospitals in London were put on major incident alert within minutes of the first explosion, which occurred at 0851 BST in the third carriage of an underground train traveling in a tunnel 100 meters from Liverpool Street station. Less than a mile away, at the Royal London hospital in Whitechapel, medical staff implemented a well-rehearsed strategy to cope with the first of 208 patients. The shock waves from the blast were the cause of the most frequently seen injuries on that day, which are particularly traumatic for air-filled parts of the body. The waves can cause perforated eardrums, collapsed lungs, and perforated bowels. But the force can also devastate soft tissue — the blast was responsible for many of the limbs lost during the attacks. Smoke inhalation resulting in lung damage, burns, and ripped skin caused by debris such as glass shards were also

(Continued)

CASE STUDY 2: THE LONDON TERROR ATTACKS, JULY 7, 2005–(CONTINUED)

common injuries ("Medical Teams Praised for Reaction to Bombings," www.newscientist.com/article.ns?id=dn7649).

Leadership and Crisis Communications

U.K. Prime Minister Tony Blair was participating in the G8 summit in Gleneagles, Scotland, when he learned about the terror attacks. At 12 PM that day, Blair appeared before the media in Gleneagles and gave a three-and-a-half-minute-long speech about the day's terrorist incidents.

Mr. Blair's style of communication on that day has demonstrated his leadership skills and expertise in crisis communications. An analytical piece about the way he delivered his speech marks the following nuances in his speech as critical to conveying the right message in the right way:

He demonstrated his passion for his people and did not choose to hide his emotions.

He shared his emotions (grief), but also presented a strong image that communicated he and his government were there and ready to deal with the problem.

He improvised his speech instead of reading it, which proved that it was not "business as usual" for him.

He used many long pauses to communicate the gravity of the situation.

He avoided speculations and focused on stating the limited number of facts he was informed about.

He sincerely communicated his condolences to the families who lost loved ones in the attacks.

He used strong and direct vocabulary to describe the events ("barbaric").

The analysis above is based on analysis by T.J. Walker ("Crisis Communications with Class," www.mediatrainingworldwide.com). For the video of the complete speech, see http://relay.westminsterdigital.co.uk/demand.php?c=number10/statements&m=statementFull2005-07-07.wmv&.wvx. For a transcript of the speech, see www.number-10.gov.uk/output/Page7853.asp.

Key Terms

Demobilization: The orderly, safe, and efficient return of a resource or resources to their original location and status.

Disaster Declaration: The process by which the chief executive official of a jurisdiction (e.g., the mayor, governor, or president) identifies a situation as being beyond the capacity of that particular jurisdiction to responsed. Under established statutory authorities at the state and federal levels, disaster declaration frees up various resources in support of the affected governments.

Emergency Declaration: Any occasion or instance for which, in the determination of the president, federal assistance is needed to supplement state and local efforts and capabilities to save lives and to protect property and public health and safety, or to lessen or avert the threat of a catastrophe in any part of the United States. An emergency declaration is more limited in scope and without the long-term federal recovery programs of a major disaster declaration. Generally, federal assistance and funding are provided to meet a specific emergency need or to help prevent a major disaster from occurring.

Emergency Support Function (ESF): Used by the federal government and many state governments as the primary mechanism at the operational level to organize and provide assistance. ESFs align categories of resources and provide strategic objectives for their use. ESFs exist within the NRF, and in most state and local emergency operations plans. ESFs utilize standardized resource management concepts such as typing, inventorying, and tracking to facilitate the dispatch, deployment, and recovery of resources before, during, and after an incident.

Federal Response Plan: A plan guiding the overall delivery of federal assistance in Stafford Act (presidentially declared) disasters that was replaced by the National Response Plan in 2004.

Incident Command System (ICS): A system by which emergency incidents of all sizes are managed, developed by the federal, state, and local wildland fire agencies during the 1970s. ICS is structured to facilitate activities in five major functional areas: command, operations, planning, logistics, and finance/administration. In some circumstances, intelligence and investigations may be added as a sixth functional area.

Individual Assistance: Individual assistance programs are oriented to individuals, families, and small businesses, and the programs include the Individuals and Households Program, Small Business Administration loans, disaster unemployment assistance, legal services, special tax considerations, and crisis counseling. The disaster victim must first register for assistance and establish eligibility before receiving this assistance.

Joint Field Office: The JFO coordinates federal incident support to the state, allowing the integration of diverse federal resources. Within the JFO, there is one key operational group, and two key officials, including the Unified Coordination Group and the State Coordinating Officer.

Joint Information Center (JIC): A JIC may be established in emergency situations in order to coordinate the release of emergency information and other public affairs functions. The JIC serves as a focal point for coordinated and timely release of incident-related information to the public and the media. Information about where to receive assistance is communicated directly to victims and their families in an accessible format and in appropriate languages.

Long-Term Recovery: This is the period that involves the restoration of lives and livelihoods beyond the emergency phase of the disaster, once lifelines and critical societal components have been restored or replaced. This phase falls squarely within the direction of Emergency Support Function #14, "Long-Term Community Recovery," and often continues for several months or years after the disaster has ended.

Multiagency Coordination System (MACS): A system designed to help coordinate activities that occur above the field level, and to prioritize demands for critical or competing resources. Examples of multiagency coordination include a state or county emergency operations center, a state intelligence fusion center, the National Operations Center, the FEMA National Response Coordination Center, the Department of Justice/FBI Strategic Information and Operations Center, the FBI Joint Operations Center, and the National Counterterrorism Center.

National Incident Management System (NIMS): A system that provides a proactive approach guiding government agencies at all levels, the private sector, and nongovernmental organizations to work seamlessly to prepare for, prevent, respond to, recover from, and mitigate the effects of incidents, regardless of cause, size, location, or complexity, in order to reduce the loss of life or property and harm to the environment.

National Response Framework (NRF): A document released in 2008 to replace the National Response Plan that guides how the nation conducts all-hazards response. The framework documents the key response principles, roles, and structures that organize national response. It describes how communities, states, the federal government, and private-sector and nongovernmental partners apply these principles for national response. It also describes special circumstances where the federal government must exercise a larger role, including incidents where federal interests are involved and catastrophic incidents where a state would require significant support. It was designed to allow all response stakeholders to provide a unified national response.

National Response Plan: A plan released in 2004 to replace the Federal Response Plan that guided the response actions of local, state, and federal resources to major "incidents of national significance." This plan was replaced in 2008 by the NRF.

NRF Cooperating Agency: Cooperating agencies have specific expertise and capabilities that allow them to assist the coordinating agency in executing incident-related tasks or processes. When the procedures within a support annex are needed to support elements of an incident, the coordinating agency will notify cooperating agencies of the circumstances.

NRF Coordinating Agency: Coordinating agencies are responsible for implementing the processes detailed in NRF annexes. These federal agencies support DHS incident management efforts by providing the leadership, expertise, and authorities to implement critical and specific aspects of the response. When the functions of a particular support annex are required, the agency serving as the coordinator must carry out various responsibilities as stipulated in the NRF.

Posse Comitatus Act: A law passed in 1878 that restricts the use of the armed forces to perform domestic law enforcement.

Presidential Major Disaster Declaration: Any natural catastrophe (including any hurricane, tornado, storm, high water, wind driven water, tidal wave, tsunami, earthquake, volcanic eruption, landslide, mudslide, snowstorm, or drought), or, regardless of cause, any fire, flood, or explosion, in any part of the United States that in the determination of the president causes damage of sufficient severity and magnitude to warrant major disaster assistance under the Stafford Act to supplement the efforts and available resources of states, local governments, and disaster relief organizations in alleviating the damage, loss, hardship, or suffering caused thereby.

Public Assistance: Public assistance, oriented to public entities, is designed to facilitate the repair, restoration, reconstruction, or replacement of public facilities or infrastructure damaged or destroyed by a federally declared disaster. Eligible applicants include state governments, local governments and any other political subdivision of a state, Native American tribes, and Alaska Native villages. Certain private nonprofit (PNP) organizations may also receive assistance, including educational, utility, irrigation, emergency, medical, rehabilitation, and temporary or permanent custodial care facilities, and other PNP facilities that provide essential services of a governmental nature to the general public.

Short-Term Recovery: This is the period when recovery actions that begin immediately upon occurrence of the disaster, which overlap with response actions, are taken. This phase includes actions such as providing essential public health and safety services, restoring interrupted utility and other essential services, reestablishing transportation routes, and providing food and shelter for those displaced by the incident. Although called "short term," some short-term recovery activities may last for weeks. Short-term recovery actions are addressed in several functional areas of the NRF.

State Coordinating Officer (SCO): The SCO plays a critical role in managing the state response and recovery operations following presidential disaster declarations. The governor of the affected state appoints the SCO, and lines of authority flow from the governor to the SCO, following the state's policies and laws. For events in which a declaration has not yet occurred but is expected (such as with an approaching hurricane), the secretary of Homeland Security or the FEMA administrator may predesignate one or more federal officials to coordinate with the SCO to determine resources and actions that will likely be required, and begin deployment of assets.

Strategic National Stockpile: CDC's Strategic National Stockpile (SNS) consists of strategically placed repositories of medicine and medical supplies that can be called on to protect the public in the event of a public health emergency severe enough to deplete local supplies. Once federal and local authorities agree that the SNS is needed, medicines will be delivered to any state in the United States within 12 hours. Each state has plans to receive and distribute SNS medicine and medical supplies to local communities as quickly as possible.

Unified Command: A system that allows for more efficient multijurisdictional or multiagency management of emergency events by enabling agencies with different legal, geographic, and functional responsibilities to coordinate, plan, and interact with each other in an effective manner. Unified command allows all agencies with jurisdictional authority or functional responsibility for the incident to jointly provide management direction to an incident through a common set of incident objectives and strategies and a single incident action plan. Under unified command, each participating agency maintains its authority, responsibility, and accountability.

Unified Coordination Group: The Unified Coordination Group is comprised of senior officials from the states and key federal departments and agencies, and is established at the JFO. Using unified command principles, this group provides national support to achieve shared emergency response and recovery objectives.

Urban Search and Rescue: Urban search and rescue (US&R) involves the location, rescue (extrication), and initial medical stabilization of victims trapped in confined spaces. While structural collapse is the most common origin of trapped victims, transportation accidents, mines, and collapsed trenches may also cause such to occur. US&R is considered a "multihazard" discipline, as it may be needed for a variety of emergencies or disasters, including earthquakes, hurricanes, typhoons, storms and tornadoes, floods, dam failures, technological accidents, terrorist activities, and hazardous materials releases.

Zoonotic: A disease that can be spread between animals and people.

Review Questions

1. In your opinion, what are the most important differences between the NRF, the NRP, and the FRP?

2. Do you feel that the creation of the Department of Homeland Security has improved emergency response in the United States? Why or why not?

3. If you were an appointed local emergency manager, would you be satisfied with the actions of the federal government in terms of preparedness for large-scale emergency events? What would be the greatest benefits and problems for you under this new structure (the NRF) from a response perspective? Answer the same question from a regional emergency manager officer and a FEMA high-level officer point of view.

4. What was the basis of the decision to create the National Incident Management System (NIMS)? Why wasn't the ICS used instead? What benefits are gained by having a NRF that is based on the NIMS?

5. The establishment of the Department of Homeland Security, and the many subsequent changes to the national emergency management framework, are seen by many local emergency managers as inhibiting their efforts to establish an effective all-hazards emergency response capacity. What are your opinions on this stance? Explain your answer.

References

American Corporate Council Association (ACCA). 2002. "107th Congress Homeland Security Legislation." http://www.acc.com/infopaks/homeland/legislativechart.pdf.

Bea, Keath, W. Krouse, D. Morgan, W. Morrissey, and C. Redhead. 2003. Emergency Preparedness and Response Directorate of the Department of Homeland Security. Congressional Research Service. http://fas.org/sgp/crs/RS21367.pdf

Bullock & Haddow, LLC. 2003. Personal interviews with the Chief of Staff and Deputy Chief of Staff of the Federal Emergency Management Agency.

Department of Homeland Security. 2007. "FY 2007 Homeland Security Grant Program." http://www.dhs .gov/xlibrary/assets/grants_st-local_fy07.pdf.

Environmental Protection Agency. 2008. "National Oil and Hazardous Substances Pollution Contingency Plan." http://www.epa.gov/OEM/content/lawsregs/ ncpover.htm.

Federal Bureau of Investigation. 2001. "Domestic Terrorism Concept of Operations Plan." http://www .fbi.gov/publications/conplan/conplan.pdf.

Federal Emergency Management Agency. 1992. "Federal Response Plan." http://library.findlaw .com/1992/Apr/1/127810.html.

Federal Emergency Management Agency. 2001. "Federal Radiological Emergency Response Plan."

http://www.fas.org/nuke/guide/usa/doctrine/national/ frerp.htm.

Federal Emergency Management Agency. 2004. "National Response Plan." http://www.dhs.gov/xlibrary/ assets/NRPbaseplan.pdf.

Federal Emergency Management Agency. 2008. "National Response Framework." http://www.fema .gov/emergency/nrf/.

Federal Emergency Management Agency. 2008. "Number of Declarations per Calendar Year Since 1998." Washington, DC. http://www.fema.gov/government/grant/pa/stat1.shtm.

Washington Post. 2005. "War Plans Drafted to Counter Terror Attacks in U.S." *The Washington Post*, August 8, p. A1. http://www.washingtonpost.com/wp-dyn/content/ article/2005/08/07/AR2005080700843_pf.html.

8

Communications

What You Will Learn

- How risk communication efforts inform the public about what hazard risks they face and what they can do to prepare for or mitigate them
- How the federal government performs risk communication through the Ready.Gov website and other efforts
- What role the news media has in informing the public about hazard risks
- How the federal government warns the public of terrorist risk through the Homeland Security Advisory System
- How the Federal Emergency Management Agency manages crisis communications

Introduction

Communicating messages to the general public is a critical yet underdeveloped aspect of effective emergency management. Such messages fall under three basic categories: risk communication, warning, and crisis communication. Risk communication involves alerting and educating the public to the risks they face and how they can best prepare for and mitigate these risks in order to reduce the impacts of future disaster events. Warning involves delivering notice of an actual impending threat with sufficient time to allow recipient individuals and communities to take shelter, evacuate, or take other mitigative action in advance of a disaster event. Crisis communication involves the provision of timely, useful, and accurate information to the public during the response and recovery phases of a disaster event.

The emergency management community as a whole has vast experience in practicing risk and warning communications. Preparedness programs have been an active part of emergency management in this country for decades, and public education programs conducted by the Federal Emergency Management Agency (FEMA), the American Red Cross, the Salvation Army, local fire departments, and other public- and private-sector agencies have disseminated millions of brochures and checklists describing the risks of future disaster events and the steps that individuals and communities can take to reduce and prepare for them. In recent years, these programs have embraced new technologies to disseminate this information, including video and, most significantly, the Internet. There is a wealth of knowledge supported by scientific research concerning effective means to communicate hazard risk messages for natural disaster and selected technological disaster risks.

The design and implementation of warning systems has similarly advanced in the past decades. From the Civil Defense sirens to the Emergency Broadcast Network to weather radios, warning systems alerting the public to sudden or impending disaster events have become more sophisticated and widely used. Broadcasting timely information that allows individuals to make appropriate shelter and evacuation decisions is at the core of the warning systems designed for natural hazards such as tornadoes and tsunamis. Watch and warning notices for floods and hurricanes provide individuals and community leaders with valuable information on the path and potential destructiveness of severe storms that could result in flooding events. The public media — television, radio, and most recently the Internet — are the mechanisms most often used by emergency officials to issue watch and warning notices.

The importance of communicating with the public during the response and recovery phases of a natural or technological disaster event has only recently been fully embraced by emergency officials. Too often in the past, little value was placed on communicating with the public during and after a disaster event, and emergency officials had little training and interest in this area. This changed in the 1990s as FEMA, under the direction of James Lee Witt, made a commitment and marshaled the resources to develop and implement an aggressive public affairs program designed to deliver timely and accurate messages to the public in a time of crisis. The messages focused on what measures government and private-sector officials were taking to help a community in responding to and recovering from a disaster event and the methods by which individuals and communities could apply for and receive federal, state, and local disaster relief. FEMA established a working partnership with the media to deliver these messages through press conferences, individual interviews, satellite feeds, radio actualities, and the Internet. One of their greatest accomplishments in this regard was the publication of *Recovery Times*, a newspaper supplement developed and maintained by FEMA to be distributed by local newspaper outlets in disaster-affected areas. Over time, this public affairs model created by FEMA has gained wider acceptance by state and local emergency officials.

The threat of terrorism has altered the playing field for emergency managers by introducing new hazards that are not fully understood, creating an altered risk perception among members of the public (who are concerned about terrorism victimization), and presenting new response and recovery (mostly cleanup) procedures and practices, new information uncertainties, new restrictions on the release of information to the public, and new demands for public information. Do the communications models developed in the past for communicating risk, warning, and crisis messages concerning natural and technological hazards apply to terrorism-related communications? Will the traditional delivery systems — television, Internet, radio, and print — adequately disseminate terrorism-related information? Will emergency and government officials find a balance between the need to provide timely and accurate information to the public and the need to conduct criminal investigations?

These are the types of questions that are addressed in this chapter, which includes sections on risk communication, warning, and crisis communication. A case study of the October 2002 sniper attacks in Washington, DC, is also included in the chapter.

Risk Communication

The federal government, through the Department of Homeland Security (DHS), has initiated several programs to achieve a goal of community and individual resilience to the effects of terrorism and other disasters. One of the primary methods employed to achieve such preparedness is public education.

Public education has long been recognized as an effective method for decreasing the damaging potential of hazards and risks, and the media are often central in such projects (Mullis, 1998). Furthermore, the role of the media in previous risk-related public education endeavors dealing with natural and technological hazards and public health issues has been well documented. From teaching citizens to build tornado-resistant safe rooms to minimizing tsunami drowning and preventing teen pregnancy, public and private agencies have partnered with, cooperated with, or utilized the various players collectively referred to as the mass media to achieve the goal of reducing public risk.

While the news media's reporting on risks has often been blamed for inciting a "culture of fear" (Glassner, 1999) in which people are afraid of a multitude of risks that have only a minute chance of ever occurring, the news media have also been integral in helping to create what could be considered the most risk-free era in recorded history (Walsh, 1996). However, no studies have been conducted to measure the efficacy of the media in informing and educating the public about terrorism and other "intentional" hazards.

The new focus on terrorism within the borders of the United States has brought to question the degree of risk faced by individual Americans. Although the topic has become a daily concern of all media outlets, the effect that this new attention has had on decreasing the vulnerability of the average citizen to that particular hazard is questionable. Citizens have indicated through polls that the threat of terrorist attacks on American soil is one of their primary concerns, and they have looked to their leaders for guidance on personal preparedness for such a threat. The federal government has recognized this concern and has sought to confront the preparedness issue through actions taken by DHS to address national vulnerabilities. DHS has also embarked on a public education campaign the likes of which has not been seen since the Civil Defense drills of the 1950s taught citizens to "duck and cover" during air raids (Waugh, 2000). The media have been involved in this effort from the beginning, and regardless of their goals, intentions, or the level to which they have actually partnered with the federal government in their actions, it is likely that the news media have never before played such a central role in risk communication.

With such a great quantity of headlines, stories, editorials, investigative reports, and briefings related to terrorism, it would seem that all citizens should be able to decode from the barrage of messages relayed by DHS the information they need to protect themselves. However, considering that never before have the media and government risk communicators focused on any one subject so intensely, established risk perception and communication models are largely ineffective. DHS and the emergency management community in general must ask the following questions now and before planning future activities:

How can risk communicators best make contact with the general public?
Can the news media serve as effective risk communicators for terrorism in the United States?
Do the established risk communications models apply to terrorism and other intentional hazards?

▦ ▦ Critical Thinking ▦

Why are the news media considered such an important asset to emergency preparedness public education efforts? Are other sources more effective? Why or why not? Give examples to support your answer.

Emergency Management and Risk Communication in the United States

The most widely practiced form of emergency management in the United States, and the only form practiced by FEMA, is comprehensive emergency management (CEM). This four-phase cyclical system groups actions into the general categories of mitigation, preparedness, response, and recovery. For a given hazard there are generally pre-event actions (mitigation and preparedness) and post-event actions (response and recovery) performed. The response phase includes the immediate period of reaction after a disaster occurs (when critical emergency resources are required). Recovery includes the long-term rebuilding that begins after the emergency functions related to disaster response are no longer required. Mitigation is defined as any activity that prevents or reduces the impact of a disaster, and preparedness involves predisaster planning and training addressing the possibility of future disasters (Waugh, 2000). Like response, disaster preparedness is also always managed at the local level and is considered to be more of a local government responsibility than any of the other phases of CEM.

Preparedness generally consists of training the local first responders and educating the public about ways to prepare for specific hazards within specific communities. A hazard is an event or physical condition that has the potential to cause fatalities, injuries, property damage, infrastructure damage, agricultural loss, damage to the environment, interruption of business, or other types of harm or loss (FEMA, 1997). The risk associated with a hazard is identified as the probability (likelihood) of the hazard occurring, multiplied by the consequence of the hazard should it occur. For many hazard risks, public education is seen as the most effective means to reduce both the likelihood and consequence components significantly. Emergency management public education efforts utilize numerous resources, including in-school education, distribution of pamphlets and fact sheets, and inserts in phone books and utility mailings, among many others. However, it is the use of the various forms of the news media that has often been seen as the most effective means of public education.

The federal government took a more active role in community preparedness during the Clinton administration while FEMA was under the direction of James Lee Witt (a move taken by several governments throughout the world during the same period). Director Witt espoused the idea that the emergency response community must shed the view that the media were adversaries and work to form media partnerships in order to be more effective in public disaster preparedness education. Witt worked to institutionalize such tasks as creating media education materials and public service announcements, ensuring availability of "approved" hazard experts, providing training in emergency management terminology and actions for reporters and anchor people, and promoting more responsible reporting by the media. The success of these changes was measured through the increased resilience of communities to hazards in which such changes in individual behavior were known to be the primary means of reducing vulnerability (such as during tsunamis and tornadoes).

In the wake of the September 11, 2001, terrorist attacks and the anthrax mail attacks shortly thereafter, the "all-hazards" approach of the federal government focused its efforts on preparedness and mitigation (prevention) of future terrorist attacks (Figure 8–1). Although terrorism had been considered a high-risk hazard by the federal government for some time, it was not necessarily on the minds of the American public. After these events, however, terrorism became an obvious primary concern of both the government and its citizens. Terrorism was no longer seen as something that affected isolated locations known to be at high risk and was instead regarded as a hazard that could affect anyone at any place and any time, a hazard that could result in a mass casualty event (one that overwhelms the capacity of local health officials to respond). Additionally, the possibility of terrorists employing weapons of mass destruction (WMD) — chemical, biological, radiological, explosive, or nuclear — became a reality.

On November 25, 2002, President Bush signed into law the Homeland Security Act of 2002, investing in the new DHS the mission of protecting the United States from further terrorist attacks, reducing the nation's vulnerability to terrorism, and minimizing the damage from potential terrorist attacks and natural disasters. DHS began working to organize the federal response to the consequences

FIGURE 8–1 New York City, New York, September 27, 2001 — FEMA workers needed to stay current with the news in regard to the terrorist attacks on the World Trade Center and the Pentagon. (Photo by Bri Rodriguez/FEMA News Photo)

of disasters but concentrated its efforts on preparedness and response capabilities to combat terrorism (as is evident by changes in federal funding trends). DHS officials were still operating under the same constraints of the previous administration in terms of what they could do to increase preparedness at the community level. DHS repeatedly acknowledged that, even in the event that a terrorist attack be declared a national disaster, local communities would need to be prepared to be self-sufficient for a minimum of 48 hours. However, public demand for more federal action and information required DHS to address these public education needs.

The Ready.gov campaign is DHS's primary effort to increase individual citizen preparedness at the community level. It is essentially a website, designed by the Ad Council, that offers citizens, businesses, and children with explicit directions detailing what they can do to prepare themselves and their families for all hazards, including terrorism. Other efforts at informing the public, which are equal components in the larger public education effort, include the five-color–coded Homeland Security Alert System and more specific public announcements and alerts, such as the well-known "duct tape and plastic" incident (in which DHS Director Tom Ridge made a general appeal to people in the United States to buy those particular items to protect themselves from the effects of a possible WMD terrorist attack).

Personal preparedness from disasters, as described by the Ready.gov website, includes three major components. Specifically, they are "get a kit" (one that contains materials to ensure potable water, food, clean air, first aid, and special needs items), "make a plan" (in which individuals or families determine actions to be taken in the event of specific disasters), and "be informed" (generally by obtaining information about hazards and their associated personal mitigation and preparedness measures). To measure the effectiveness of a citizen's degree of terrorism-hazard preparedness, these three components must be used as performance measures. For the specific case of terrorism, "vigilance" (or actively looking for and reporting suspicious behavior that could be linked to terrorism) is included as a performance measure for personal terrorism preparedness (DHS, 2003).

Since late 2004, DHS has added two components to their Ready.gov site to expand on the specific groups that may benefit from the preparedness information they provide. The first group is the business community. The website instructs business owners and administrators on how to (1) plan to stay in business, (2) talk to your people, and (3) protect your investment. The second group is children.

Past Research Focusing on Risk Communication: The Power of the News Media

According to acclaimed risk communication experts Baruch Fischhoff, M. Granger Morgan, Ann Bostrom, and Cynthia Atman, risk communication is "communication intended to supply laypeople with the information they need to make informed, independent judgments about risks to health, safety, and the environment" (Morgan *et al.*, 2002). Creating messages that satisfy these high ideals requires extensive time, experience, and planning, and is therefore more often successful in educating the public about old risks that are well understood than new risks such as terrorism. Although it would seem from a purist's point of view that anything short of the aforementioned definition would not suffice, some authors have defined risk communication to be the mere action of reporting on any existing or proposed hazard regardless of the story's ability to result in any increase in public awareness, knowledge, or preparedness (Willis, 1997).

The news media play a significant role in disaster and emergency management both before and after disasters occur. The media are well recognized for the invaluable service they have consistently performed during the initial critical moments of a disaster, when the emergency response efforts are mobilized. In these events, the media serve to transmit warning messages and alerts and give instructions on where to evacuate, where to seek medical care and shelter, and where to go for more specific information (Mileti, 1999). Jim Willis (1997) writes, "[T]here may be no other area of journalism [than risk communication] where the Fourth Estate has such an awesome responsibility." Furman (2002) contends that the media's ability to educate people during these times is, in many cases, more likely to save lives than many other components of emergency response, adding that "people will die if they don't get good information." The emergency response community has embraced the media for their capability in response, recognizing that they will be the primary, if not the only, means of informing large masses of potential victims (McCormick Tribune Foundation, 2002).

With regard to the preparedness phase of emergency management, the primary risk communication tasks that have been assumed by the media include raising citizen awareness to the presence of an existing or future hazard and providing information to those citizens regarding prevention or protection (Burkhart, 1991). The effectiveness of the media as a conduit of educational information has been studied extensively, most notably in the area of public health. A great number of these studies have shown a positive correlation between the use of the media and an increase in the promoted knowledge or behavior. Piotrow (1990) and a team of researchers working in Nigeria found that the promotion of family planning and clinic sites on local television played a significant role in the number of people utilizing those services. Westoff and Rodriguez (1995) found that there was a strong correlation between patients who reported that they had been exposed to family planning messages in the media and the use of contraceptives by those same patients.

Witzer (1997) writes that "exposure to electronic and print media is associated with later marriage and with greater knowledge and use of family planning among men and women in Sub-Saharan Africa." Jones, Beniger, and Westoff (1980) found that there was a strong correlation between mass media coverage of the adverse affects of the birth-control pill and discontinuation rates among users. Similar results were found relating to sex education among young adults (Brown and Keller, 2000) and early initiation of breast-feeding (McDivitt *et al.*, 1993). Nelken (1987) found in one study that more than 60% of Americans learn about cancer prevention from the media, whereas less than 20% do so from physicians.

With natural and technological hazards, the behavioral modifications and preparatory measures taken by recipients as a result of media risk communication also look promising. Mitigation specialists at FEMA claim that the media's role in community and citizen preparedness is critical if such efforts are to succeed (FEMA, 1998). Dennis Mileti (1999) found that personal preparedness was most likely to be undertaken by those people who are most attentive to the news media, but that other attributes are often necessary in conjunction with that attention. Media risk communication has been widely credited as an important supplemental component to official communication in public preparedness to hazards (Burkhart, 1991). Singer and Endreny (1993) contend that there are many factors determining how people view hazards (including personal experience and contact with other people), but with hazards that are extreme in consequence and rare in occurrence (such as terrorism) the media are the most influential source of information. Walsh (1996) found that several studies indicate that people use the media for obtaining information on hazards more than any other source.

The primary source of the news media's ability to effectively communicate and educate most likely lies in the institutionalized methods of attracting viewers and providing timely information that has been developed and refined over centuries. Burkhart (1991) writes, "[I]n the preparedness phase, the mass media are positioned between the actors who evaluate a threat and decide upon a message, and the media audience." Burkhart adds that it is the media's ability to influence perceived risk and the credibility of the source of information that gives them such power over public behavior. McCombs and Shaw's (1972) research, which found that audiences not only are alerted to important issues by the media but that they learn "how much importance to attach to an issue or topic from the emphasis the media place on it" supports Burkhart's convictions.

This positive view of the media as a successful risk communicator comes not without contention. There are many social scientists who feel that the media, for various reasons, are ineffective at informing the public about the risks they face. Winston (1985) feels that it is the "built-in, organizational, competitive, and institutional biases" that prevent the media from informing citizens about hazards. These biases are coupled with procedural standards that can also make effective communication of risk difficult. For instance, Singer and Endreny (1993) report that the media inform about "events rather than issues, about immediate consequences rather than long-term considerations, about harms rather than risks," and Wenham (1994) describes how the media "tell how bad things are, while [emergency management agencies] make things better." Burkhart (1991) feels that it is a deficiency of knowledge about hazards and disaster management among journalists that makes them unable to effectively communicate due to both a lack of understanding of the most basic concepts and their inability to act as a "surrogate for the layman, to absorb and transform technical information to a public that is often even less well-prepared to grasp technical information and concepts." Such criticisms are repeated by Singer and Endreny (1993). There are other, similar reasons identified by research efforts that sought to explain the media's risk communication deficiencies, including restrictions of time and space that prevent adequate knowledge transfer (Willis, 1997) and the media's insistence on taking control of the selection and presentation of message format that leads to a decrease in message effectiveness (Burkhart, 1991).

There is another subgroup of studies that find the news media to be largely ineffective as a risk communicator but assign less blame to them for such problems. Raphael (1986) turns the focus of the blame onto the public, stating that "citizens often display a magical belief in goodness and protection and a sense of generalized risk, which may explain why people pay less attention to preparedness information provided by the media outside of the context of an emergency." Jerry Hauer from the New York City Office of Emergency Management feels that it is the tendency of the emergency management community to exclude the media from training and drills due to the fear that the media will leak operational plans to terrorists and the fear that the media will cause mass public panic that has prevented them from being able to effectively inform the public (McCormick Tribune Foundation, 2002). This position is supported by Burkhart (1991), who states, "Media are often limited by the nature of the information they receive," and Bremer and Bremer (2002), who state, "Terrorism presents a major dilemma to political leaders in terms of how to get enough attention without bringing too much attention to the problem." Furman (2002) adds, "It is difficult to educate the American people because there's very little we can tell them to do. . . . You're faced with the problem of just how much you want to tell the American people, because, in the end, there's very little we can give them."

There is a third type of research that claims that while the news media are, in fact, ineffective at educating the public, they still play a vital role in risk communication. McCallum, Hammond, and Morris (1990) state that "regardless of reservations about their ability to play the role effectively, the media do carry considerable information about certain hazards and risks to most people." This view of the media as informer is fairly widespread. Willis (1997) states that while the media too often avoid contributing to the solution to the problems, they are effective at raising attention to issues and communicating degrees of urgency. Mullis (1998) further promotes this argument, stating that the media are effective at initiating preparedness activities. Burkhart (1991) found that while media warnings were too imprecise to be effective, they "were able to get people talking to other people about the danger mentioned in media warnings." Cohen (1963) succinctly characterized this phenomenon as follows: "The press may not be successful much of the time in telling its readers what to think, but it is stunningly successful in telling them what to think about."

▪ ▪ Critical Thinking ▪

Do you feel that the media are effective risk communicators? Why or why not? If you do not believe that the media are effective risk communicators, then to which of the three schools of research regarding the effectiveness of news media risk communication listed above do you subscribe? (1) The news media are ineffective at informing the public of the risks they face because of media bias. (2) The news media are largely ineffective as risk communicators but the focus of blame falls on the public. (3) The media are ineffective at educating the public but still play a vital role in risk communication. Explain your answer.

Accuracy of Information

A second area that must be examined when considering the ability of the media to communicate risk is their capacity to do so in a way that imparts to the public an accurate perception of their personal risk of victimization. In what is probably one of the earliest descriptions of the media's power to influence public risk perception and, likewise, preparedness and mitigative behavior, Walter Lippmann (1922) writes in his acclaimed *Public Opinion* that

> *We shall assume that what each man does is based not on direct and certain knowledge, but on pictures made by himself or given to him. If his atlas tells him that the world is flat, he will not sail near what he believes to be the edge of our planet for fear of falling off.*

Willis (1997) writes that because the media's depiction of public health and safety-related issues has either an indirect or a direct effect on public behavior, the media's responsibility to be as accurate as possible in their presentation of such hazards is vital. In the case of terrorism, DHS has established a five-color–coded Homeland Security Alert System that is intended to inform the public about the current risk of a terrorist attack within the United States. At certain times, the risk is raised in specific locations, such as a city, a landmark, or a building. While the media often refer to this system when it goes up or down in severity, they also provide exhaustive unrelated information that heavily influences public perception. It is this perception that people must use in judging their own risk and, likewise, preparing themselves appropriately. It is important for the media not to understate risks because people will otherwise not expend the time and money needed to adequately prepare themselves, but exaggerating the risk of a hazard can have drastic consequences, including stress-related health problems and financial and economic effects including business and tourism losses.

Thus far, research has found that the media tend to overstate the risk of the hazards on which they focus (which also tend to be those that are the least likely to occur), while they understate commonly occurring hazards (Singer and Endreny, 1993). Altheide (2002) found that almost 80% of Americans feel that they are subject to more risk than their parents were 20 years ago, when in fact evidence has shown that we have a "competitive advantage in terms of disease, accidents, nutrition, medical care, and life expectancy" and that the media's portrayal of risk is mainly to blame. One reason this occurs is that the media do not have the time or resources to ensure the accuracy of their reports beyond reasonable doubt. Willis (1997) found that while scientists use elaborate methods of ensuring the validity of their findings, journalists depend on secondary or tertiary sources that confirm or refute their primary source, all of whom may be incorrect in their assumptions. Warner (1989) feels the problem lies in the media's tendency to use vivid imagery in reporting risk, such as comparing the number of people who die as a result of smoking as equivalent to three fully seated jumbo jets crashing every day. Singer and Endreny (1993) claim that daily reporting of rare hazards, which tend to be more "newsworthy," make these events subject to the availability heuristic. Walsh (1996) notes that over 2 million Americans canceled travel plans to Europe in 1986 because of fears of terrorism, when their actual risk would have been reduced significantly more if they had lost 10 pounds and traveled to Europe as planned.

Related to this concern that the media do not give the public accurate perceptions of risks is the fear that the public will become emotionally afraid of risks rather than becoming aware of their dangers. This distinction is important because it determines the types of preparedness measures citizens take in response to the messages they receive and the rationality with which those actions are made. When people are presented with a risk, they are more likely to take preventive and preparatory measures if they are led to believe that the risk is a danger that can be managed rather than one that they should fear. Past research has found that increasing the levels of public fear can actually cause a decrease in public preparedness behavior (Mullis, 1998). Unfortunately, it may be that the nature of media culture promotes and even amplifies fear by attempting to draw viewers through entertainment and "framing." Walsh (1996) contends that the media pay attention only to issues and situations that frighten viewers, "filling coverage with opinions rather than facts or logical perspective." Furedi (1997) takes a slightly different but related alternative stance on the subject in stating that "the media's preoccupation with risk is a symptom of the problem and not its cause," as the media can only amplify fear that already exists.

Essential Components of Effective Risk Communication

Numerous components of effective risk communication have been identified as vital to the success of an effective campaign. Morgan and his colleagues (2002) conclude that effective risk communication requires authoritative and trustworthy sources. They add that if the acting communicators are perceived by the public as having a vested personal interest in the result of such preparedness, they may be skeptical about the communicators' intentions. Dennis Mileti (1999) contends that several characteristics must be considered in creating the messages, including the following: amount of material, speed of presentation, number of arguments, repetition, style, clarity, ordering, forcefulness, specificity, consistency, accuracy, and extremity of the position advocated. These characteristics are adjusted depending on whether the communicators intend to attract attention or enhance the acceptance of their message (Mileti, 1999). Singer and Endreny (1993) claim that in order for a message to be considered comprehensive, it should contain an annual mortality associated with the hazard (if known), the "spatial extent" of the hazard, the time frame associated with the hazard, and the alternatives for mitigating the hazard.

Communicators must also ensure that their messages are understood by those whom they are trying to reach, which undoubtedly changes from community to community depending on the demographic makeup of each. Mileti (1999) writes, "Most hazard-awareness and education programs have assumed a homogeneous 'public,' and have done little to tailor information materials to different groups." He adds that hazard-awareness programs are more effective if they rely on multiple sources transmitting multiple messages through multiple outlets and that radio and television are best at maintaining hazard awareness, whereas printed materials tend to provide more specific instructions on what should be done.

These are obviously high standards when considering the strict time, length, and content guidelines within which journalists must work. Highlighting the difficulty of both creating and analyzing such endeavors and the need for such a study as this, Morgan and his colleagues (2002) write, "As practiced today, risk communication is often very earnest but also surprisingly ad hoc. Typically, one can find neither a clear analysis of what needs to be communicated nor solid evidence that messages have achieved their impact. Nor can one find tested procedures for ensuring the credibility of information."

Future Research to Improve News Media Risk Communication

The objectives of future research projects should be (1) to determine how effective the news media have been as a conduit of information to citizens as part of a larger terrorism-related public education campaign being conducted by DHS, and (2) to develop a risk communications model by which media-provided public education pertaining to terrorism and other intentional hazards can be most effectively applied. Media reports in print, television, and radio formats should be examined for their content to (1) see if they meet the minimum information requirements established by risk communication experts, (2) determine if responsibility for preparedness is focused on the individual or the government, and (3) determine if an accurate portrayal of risk has been made. Surveys should be conducted with a random representative sample of American citizens to determine (1) the levels to which they have prepared for terrorism, (2) by what information they were motivated to do so, and (3) if their perception of risk reflects the level of risk portrayed by DHS and other federal sources. All collected and analyzed data should be used to determine which forms of risk communication are the most effective at creating a more informed, prepared citizenry and to generate a list of risk communications' "fundamental requirements" relating to the task of terrorism that builds on established risk communications models. From these models, strategic recommendations can be targeted to the various agencies and industries that regularly perform risk communication.

Existing Government Public Awareness Campaigns

Ready.gov, with its partners in the public, private, and volunteer sectors, is the government's official risk communication website, providing information to three primary groups (Figure 8–2): Americans

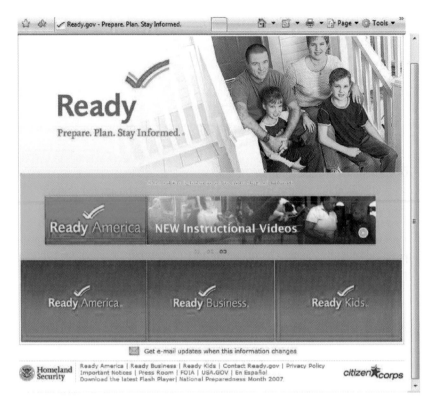

FIGURE 8–2 Department of Homeland Security Ready.gov website.

(adult citizens), businesses, and kids. Ready America, the original focus of the website, instructs the American public to perform three preparedness activities, namely:

Get a Kit (see "Ready America Emergency Kit Recommended Contents" sidebar)
Make a Plan (see Figure 8–3)
Be Informed (see "'Be Informed' Ready.gov Fact Sheets" sidebar)
This site also provides more specific emergency preparedness information for three special populations:
Older Americans
People with disabilities
Pet owners

Ready Business was the second component developed in the DHS public education effort. Ready Business focuses on business continuity and crisis management concepts to help businesses prepare for and respond to disasters. Through this online instructional guide, businesses are instructed to take action in three primary subject areas.

Plan to Stay in Business includes the following actions:

Be informed (knowing what kinds of emergencies might affect the company)
Continuity planning (how to carefully assess how the company functions, both internally and externally)
Emergency planning (how to protect employees)
Emergency supplies (survival basics, including fresh water, food, clean air, and warmth)
Deciding to stay or go (basics for sheltering in place or evacuating)
Fire safety (fire is the most common source of business disasters)

Ready
Prepare. Plan. Stay Informed.

Family Emergency Plan

Make sure your family has a plan in case of an emergency. Before an emergency happens, sit down together and decide how you will get in contact with each other, where you will go and what you will do in an emergency. Keep a copy of this plan in your emergency supply kit or another safe place where you can access it in the event of a disaster.

Out-of-Town Contact Name: _____   Telephone Number: _____

Email: _____

Neighborhood Meeting Place: _____   Telephone Number: _____

Regional Meeting Place: _____   Telephone Number: _____

Evacuation Location: _____   Telephone Number: _____

Fill out the following information for each family member and keep it up to date.

Name: _____   Social Security Number: _____
Date of Birth: _____   Important Medical Information: _____

Name: _____   Social Security Number: _____
Date of Birth: _____   Important Medical Information: _____

Name: _____   Social Security Number: _____
Date of Birth: _____   Important Medical Information: _____

Name: _____   Social Security Number: _____
Date of Birth: _____   Important Medical Information: _____

Name: _____   Social Security Number: _____
Date of Birth: _____   Important Medical Information: _____

Name: _____   Social Security Number: _____
Date of Birth: _____   Important Medical Information: _____

Write down where your family spends the most time: work, school and other places you frequent. Schools, daycare providers, workplaces and apartment buildings should all have site-specific emergency plans that you and your family need to know about.

Work Location One   School Location One
Address: _____   Address: _____
Phone Number: _____   Phone Number: _____
Evacuation Location: _____   Evacuation Location: _____

Work Location Two   School Location Two
Address: _____   Address: _____
Phone Number: _____   Phone Number: _____
Evacuation Location: _____   Evacuation Location: _____

Work Location Three   School Location Three
Address: _____   Address: _____
Phone Number: _____   Phone Number: _____
Evacuation Location: _____   Evacuation Location: _____

Other place you frequent   Other place you frequent
Address: _____   Address: _____
Phone Number: _____   Phone Number: _____
Evacuation Location: _____   Evacuation Location: _____

Important Information	Name	Telephone Number	Policy Number
Doctor(s):			
Other:			
Pharmacist:			
Medical Insurance:			
Homeowners/Rental Insurance:			
Veterinarian/Kennel (for pets):			

FIGURE 8–3 Ready America Family Plan cover page. (Source: Department of Homeland Security, "Ready America," 2008, http://www.ready.gov/america/_downloads/familyemergencyplan.pdf)

Medical emergencies (information about first aid and CPR)
Influenza pandemic (basic information about how to get more information on pandemic planning)

Talk to Your People includes general advice on informing and educating employees in emergency management basics and response principles:

Involve co-workers (including all staff in the emergency planning process)
Practice the plan (planning and conducting emergency drills and exercises)
Promoting preparedness (encouraging employees to follow the Ready America advice)

Crisis communications plan (company planning on how to stay in contact with employees and customers in a disaster situation)

Employee health (addressing the special health needs of employees that arise in disasters)

Protect Your Investment instructs businesses in ways to ensure the safety of physical assets, including:

Insurance coverage
Planning for utility disruption
Securing facilities, buildings, and plants
Securing equipment
Protecting heating, ventilation, and air conditioning systems
Ensuring cyber security

The third and final component of the Ready.Gov website is Ready Kids. This web page is designed to help parents and teachers educate children in grades 4 and 5 about emergency preparedness, emergency response, and how to help their family to prepare for disasters. The site contains simple and illustrated step-by-step instructions about the kinds of things families can do to be better prepared, and the role that children can play in this effort (Figure 8–4). The website was developed in consultation with several established children- and emergency-focused organizations, including:

American Psychological Association
American Red Cross
National Association of Elementary School Principals
National Association of School Psychologists
National Center for Child Traumatic Stress
National PTA
U.S. Department of Education
U.S. Department of Health and Human Services

DEAR FAMILY,

Family Reproducible Worksheet

To prepare for emergencies, families can collect items that might be useful and put them in an emergency supply kit. Go to www.ready.gov and click on *Ready Kids* to find out how your family can prepare for unexpected situations. Then complete this crossword puzzle to give you an idea of what kinds of things should be part of your family's emergency supply kit.

CLUES

ACROSS:

2. _ _ _ _ _ light: A handy tool to have if the lights go out!

4. Every person needs one gallon of this per day!

6. This comfortable piece of furniture should not be part of a family's supply kit.

8. Furry family members that should be part of your preparedness plan.

9. Some people have a _ _ _ _ _ between meals if they are hungry.

10. You might find water, a flashlight, or a whistle in an emergency supply _ _ _.

11. Fun items that families can play together.

DOWN:

1. Families can create a communication _ _ _ _ so that they know where to meet and who to call during an emergency.

3. _ _ _ _ _ _ _ _ bag: Great for napping or keeping warm.

5. Every family member should carry a contact list with at least _ _ _ different phone numbers that will allow you to keep in touch during an emergency.

7. It's important to get the _ _ _ _ _ about different kinds of emergencies, so that you know what to expect.

9. Keep an extra pair of these in your supply kit to keep your feet dry!

FIGURE 8–4 Crossword puzzle from the Ready.Gov *Ready Kids* website. (Source: Ready.Gov, 2008)

Ready America Emergency Kit Recommended Contents

    Water (1 gallon of water per person per day for at least 3 days, for drinking and sanitation)

    Food (at least a 3-day supply of nonperishable food)

    Battery-powered or hand-crank radio and a NOAA Weather Radio with tone alert and extra batteries for both

    Flashlight and extra batteries

    First aid kit

    Whistle to signal for help

    Dust mask to help filter contaminated air and plastic sheeting and duct tape to shelter-in-place

    Moist towelettes, garbage bags, and plastic ties for personal sanitation

    Wrench or pliers to turn off utilities

    Can opener for food (if kit contains canned food)

    Local maps

Other items listed for consideration include:

    Prescription medications and glasses

    Infant formula and diapers

    Pet food and extra water for your pet

    Important family documents such as copies of insurance policies, identification, and bank account records in a waterproof, portable container

    Cash or traveler's checks and change

    Emergency reference material such as a first aid book or information from www.ready.gov

    Sleeping bag or warm blanket for each person. Consider additional bedding if you live in a cold-weather climate.

    Complete change of clothing including a long-sleeved shirt, long pants, and sturdy shoes. Consider additional clothing if you live in a cold-weather climate.

    Household chlorine bleach and medicine dropper — When diluted nine parts water to one part bleach, bleach can be used as a disinfectant. Or in an emergency, you can use it to treat water by using 16 drops of regular household liquid bleach per gallon of water. Do not use scented, color-safe bleaches, or bleaches with added cleaners.

    Fire extinguisher

    Matches in a waterproof container

    Feminine supplies and personal hygiene items

    Mess kits, paper cups, plates and plastic utensils, and paper towels

    Paper and pencil

    Books, games, puzzles or other activities for children

Source: DHS, "Ready America," 2008, http://www.ready.gov/america/getakit/index.html.

"Be Informed" Ready.gov Fact Sheets (Examples)

The Ready America website contains preparedness and response information for citizens in the following areas:

Biological threat
Blackouts
Chemical threat
Earthquakes
Explosions
Extreme heat
Fires
Floods
Hurricanes
Influenza pandemic
Landslide and debris flow (mudslide)
Nuclear threat
Radiation threat
Thunderstorms
Tornadoes
Tsunamis
Volcanoes
Wildfires
Winter storms and extreme cold

Several of these resources are presented here.

Be Informed — Biological Threat

A biological attack is the deliberate release of germs or other biological substances that can make you sick. Many agents must be inhaled, enter through a cut in the skin, or be eaten to make you sick. Some biological agents, such as anthrax, do not cause contagious diseases. Others, like the smallpox virus, can result in diseases you can catch from other people.

If There Is a Biological Threat

Unlike an explosion, a biological attack may or may not be immediately obvious. While it is possible that you will see signs of a biological attack, as was sometimes the case with the anthrax mailings, it is perhaps more likely that local health-care workers will report a pattern of unusual illness or there will be a wave of sick people seeking emergency medical attention. You will probably learn of the danger through an emergency radio or TV broadcast or some other signal used in your community. You might get a telephone call or emergency response workers may come to your door.

In the event of a biological attack, public health officials may not immediately be able to provide information on what you should do. It will take time to determine exactly what the illness is, how it should be treated, and who is in danger. However, you should watch TV, listen to the radio, or check the Internet for official news, including the following:

- Are you in the group or area authorities consider in danger?
- What are the signs and symptoms of the disease?
- Are medications or vaccines being distributed?
- Where?
- Who should get them?
- Where should you seek emergency medical care if you become sick?

During a Biological Emergency

If a family member becomes sick, it is important to be suspicious.

Do not assume, however, that you should go to a hospital emergency room or that any illness is the result of the biological attack. Symptoms of many common illnesses may overlap.

Use common sense, practice good hygiene and cleanliness to avoid spreading germs, *and* seek medical advice.

Consider if you are in the group or area authorities believe to be in danger.

If your symptoms match those described (on the Ready.Gov website) and you are in the group considered at risk, immediately seek emergency medical attention.

If You Are Potentially Exposed

Follow instructions of doctors and other public health officials.

If the disease is contagious, expect to receive medical evaluation and treatment. You may be advised to stay away from others or even deliberately quarantined.

For noncontagious diseases, expect to receive medical evaluation and treatment.

If You Become Aware of an Unusual and Suspicious Substance Nearby

Quickly get away.

Protect yourself. Cover your mouth and nose with layers of fabric that can filter the air but still allow breathing. Examples include two to three layers of cotton such as a T-shirt, handkerchief, or towel. Otherwise, several layers of tissue or paper towels may help.

Wash with soap and water.

Contact authorities.

Watch TV, listen to the radio, or check the Internet for official news and information including what the signs and symptoms of the disease are, if medications or vaccinations are being distributed, and where you should seek medical attention if you become sick.

If you become sick, seek emergency medical attention.

Be Informed — Chemical Threat

A chemical attack is the deliberate release of a toxic gas, liquid, or solid that can poison people and the environment.

Possible Signs of Chemical Threat

Many people suffering from watery eyes, twitching, choking, having trouble breathing or losing coordination

Many sick or dead birds, fish or small animals

If You See Signs of Chemical Attack

Quickly try to define the impacted area or where the chemical is coming from, if possible.

Take immediate action to get away.

If the chemical is inside a building where you are, get out of the building without passing through the contaminated area, if possible.

If you can't get out of the building or find clean air without passing through the area where you see signs of a chemical attack, it may be better to move as far away as possible and "shelter in place."

If you are outside, quickly decide what is the fastest escape from the chemical threat. Consider if you can get out of the area, or if you should follow plans to shelter in place.

If You Think You Have Been Exposed to a Chemical

If your eyes are watering, your skin is stinging, and you are having trouble breathing, you may have been exposed to a chemical.

If you think you may have been exposed to a chemical, strip immediately and wash.

Look for a hose, fountain, or any source of water, and wash with soap if possible, being sure
not to scrub the chemical into your skin.

Seek emergency medical attention.

Be Informed — If There Is an Explosion

Take shelter against your desk or a sturdy table.

Exit the building ASAP.

Do not use elevators.

Check for fire and other hazards.

Take your emergency supply kit if time allows.

If There Is a Fire

Exit the building ASAP.

Crawl low if there is smoke.

Use a wet cloth, if possible, to cover your nose and mouth.

Use the back of your hand to feel the upper, lower, and middle parts of closed doors.

If the door is not hot, brace yourself against it, and open slowly.

If the door is hot, do not open it. Look for another way out.

Do not use elevators.

If you catch fire, do not run. Stop-drop-and-roll to put out the fire.

If you are at home, go to a previously designated meeting place.

Account for your family members, and carefully supervise small children.

Never go back into a burning building.

If You Are Trapped in Debris

If possible, use a flashlight to signal your location to rescuers.

Avoid unnecessary movement so that you don't kick up dust.

Cover your nose and mouth with anything you have on hand. (Dense-weave cotton material
can act as a good filter. Try to breathe through the material.)

Tap on a pipe or wall so that rescuers can hear where you are.

If possible, use a whistle to signal rescuers.

Shout only as a last resort. Shouting can cause a person to inhale dangerous amounts of
dust.

Be Informed — Nuclear Threat

A nuclear blast is an explosion with intense light and heat, a damaging pressure wave, and widespread radioactive material that can contaminate the air, water, and ground surfaces for miles
around. During a nuclear incident, it is important to avoid radioactive material, if possible.
While experts may predict at this time that a nuclear attack is less likely than other types, terrorism by its nature is unpredictable.

If There Is Advance Warning of an Attack

Take cover immediately, as far below ground as possible, although any shield or shelter will
help protect you from the immediate effects of the blast and the pressure wave.

If There Is No Warning

Quickly assess the situation.

Consider if you can get out of the area or if it would be better to go inside a building to limit
the amount of radioactive material you are exposed to.

If you take shelter, go as far below ground as possible, close windows and doors, and turn
off air conditioners, heaters, or other ventilation systems. Stay where you are, watch TV,
listen to the radio, or check the Internet for official news as it becomes available.

To limit the amount of radiation you are exposed to, think about shielding, distance, and time.

- Shielding: If you have a thick shield between yourself and the radioactive materials, more of the radiation will be absorbed, and you will be exposed to less.
- Distance: The farther away you are away from the blast and the fallout, the lower your exposure.
- Time: Minimizing time spent exposed will also reduce your risk.

Use available information to assess the situation. If there is a significant radiation threat, health-care authorities may or may not advise you to take potassium iodide. Potassium iodide is the same stuff added to your table salt to make it iodized. It may or may not protect your thyroid gland, which is particularly vulnerable, from radioactive iodine exposure. Plan to speak with your health-care provider in advance about what makes sense for your family.

Be Informed — Radiation

A radiation threat, commonly referred to as a "dirty bomb" or "radiological dispersion device" (RDD), is the use of common explosives to spread radioactive materials over a targeted area. It is not a nuclear blast. The force of the explosion and radioactive contamination will be more localized. While the blast will be immediately obvious, the presence of radiation will not be clearly defined until trained personnel with specialized equipment are on the scene. As with any radiation, you want to try to limit exposure. It is important to avoid breathing radiological dust that may be released in the air.

If There Is a Radiation Threat or "Dirty Bomb"

If you are outside and there is an explosion or authorities warn of a radiation release nearby, cover your nose and mouth and quickly go inside a building that has not been damaged. If you are already inside, check to see if your building has been damaged. If your building is stable, stay where you are. Close windows and doors; turn off air conditioners, heaters, or other ventilation systems.

If you are inside and there is an explosion near where you are or you are warned of a radiation release inside, cover nose and mouth and go outside immediately. Look for a building or other shelter that has not been damaged and quickly get inside. Once you are inside, close windows and doors; turn off air conditioners, heaters, or other ventilation systems.

If you think you have been exposed to radiation, take off your clothes and wash as soon as possible.

Stay where you are, watch TV, listen to the radio, or check the Internet for official news as it becomes available.

Remember: To limit the amount of radiation you are exposed to, think about time, distance, and shielding.

- Time: Minimizing time spent exposed will also reduce your risk.
- Distance: The farther away you are away from the blast and the fallout the lower your exposure.
- Shielding: If you have a thick shield between yourself and the radioactive materials more of the radiation will be absorbed, and you will be exposed to less.

As with any emergency, local authorities may not be able to immediately provide information on what is happening and what you should do. However, you should watch TV, listen to the radio, or check the Internet often for official news and information as it becomes available. Source: Department of Homeland Security, www.ready.gov.

The Ready.Gov campaign is an ongoing multiyear project funded through the DHS budget, designed and administered by the Advertising Council (www.adcouncil.org), an organization with over 60 years of experience in developing public service announcements. The website itself is just one (albeit, the primary) component of a much larger preparedness campaign that includes television, radio, print, outdoor, and Internet advertisements that inform recipients on the importance of emergency preparedness and guide them to the website as a repository of information.

The Ready.Gov website came under considerable criticism in 2006 by the Federation of American Scientists (FAS) for containing information that was reputed to be inaccurate and incomplete. FAS released an analysis of Ready.Gov identifying shortcomings and offering suggestions for improvement. FAS maintains that the Ready.Gov website, which has been accessed by over 23 million individuals, contains numerous problems despite being updated in July 2006. The FAS posted a website, Really Ready (www.reallyready.org), that mirrors the government website — even containing identical illustrations, colors, and fonts — which offers risk information to the public on the same topics addressed by the Ready.Gov website.

▧ ▧ Critical Thinking ▧

Do you believe that the Ready.Gov website offers useful information to the public? If so, do you believe that average Americans will access this information and use it to their benefit? Why or why not? Can you think of a more effective way to communicate risk to the general public?

Warning

In March 2002, the White House Office of Homeland Security unveiled a new terrorist warning system called the Homeland Security Advisory System (HSAS). The system was color coded with accompanying written descriptions that identified the threat level for a possible terrorist attack at any given time (Figure 8–5). Currently DHS provides a detailed explanation of how the HSAS works (see sidebar titled "Understanding the Homeland Security Advisory System").

Since its inception, concerns have been raised about the level of information provided through the HSAS. These concerns are shared by both the general public and members of the first-responder community (e.g., police, fire, and emergency medical technicians), as well as local officials responsible for ensuring public safety. Several organizations have expanded on the information provided by DHS by developing additional guidance on actions that individuals, families, neighborhoods, schools, and businesses should take. Recommendations developed by the American Red Cross and released in August 2003 are presented in the online appendices. A copy of "California State Agency Guidance: Homeland Security Advisory System," developed by the Governor's Office for Emergency Services in California, is available online at http://www.oes.ca.gov/Operational/OESHome.nsf/PDF/HomelandSecGuide/$file/HomelandSecGuide.pdf.

The Partnership for Public Warning (PPW) was formed in January 2002 as a partnership among the private sector, academia, and government entities at the local, state, and federal levels for the purpose of better coordinating disaster warning programs. PPW is a nonprofit entity with its stated mission to "[p]romote and enhance efficient, effective, and integrated dissemination of public warnings and related information so as to save lives, reduce disaster losses and speed recovery" (PPW, 2008). In May 2003, PPW published "A National Strategy for Integrated Public Warning Policy and Capability," which examined the current status of public warning systems, practices, and issues across the United States. The report stated, "Working together in partnership, the stakeholders should assess current warning capability, carry out appropriate research and develop the following:

A common terminology for natural and man-made disasters
A standard message protocol

FIGURE 8–5 Homeland Security Advisory System.

National metrics and standards
National backbone systems for securely collecting and disseminating warnings from all official sources
Pilot projects to test concepts and approaches
Training and event-simulation programs
A national multimedia education and outreach program (Partnership for Public Warning, 2003).

Understanding the Homeland Security Advisory System

The world has changed since September 11, 2001. We remain a nation at risk to terrorist attacks and will remain at risk for the foreseeable future. At all threat conditions, we must remain vigilant, prepared, and ready to deter terrorist attacks. The following threat conditions each represent an increasing risk of terrorist attack. Listed under each threat condition are some suggested protective measures, recognizing that the heads of federal departments and agencies are responsible for developing and implementing appropriate agency-specific protective measures.

Low Condition (Green)
This condition is declared when there is a low risk of terrorist attacks. Federal departments and agencies should consider the following general measures in addition to the agency-specific protective measures that they develop and implement:

Refining and exercising as appropriate preplanned protective measures
Ensuring that personnel receive proper training on the Homeland Security Advisory System and specific preplanned department or agency protective measures

Institutionalizing a process to ensure that all facilities and regulated sectors are regularly assessed for vulnerabilities to terrorist attacks and all reasonable measures are taken to mitigate these vulnerabilities

Guarded Condition (Blue): This condition is declared when there is a general risk of terrorist attacks. In addition to the protective measures taken in the previous threat condition, federal departments and agencies should consider the following general measures in addition to the agency-specific protective measures that they will develop and implement:

Checking communications with designated emergency response or command locations

Reviewing and updating emergency response procedures

Providing the public with any information that would strengthen their ability to act appropriately

Elevated Condition (Yellow): An Elevated Condition is declared when there is a significant risk of terrorist attacks. In addition to the protective measures taken in the previous threat conditions, federal departments and agencies should consider the following general measures in addition to the protective measures that they will develop and implement:

Increasing surveillance of critical locations

Coordinating emergency plans as appropriate with nearby jurisdictions

Assessing whether the precise characteristics of the threat require the further refinement of preplanned protective measures

Implementing, as appropriate, contingency and emergency response plans

High Condition (Orange): A High Condition is declared when there is a high risk of terrorist attacks. In addition to the protective measures taken in the previous threat conditions, federal departments and agencies should consider the following general measures in addition to the agency-specific protective measures that they will develop and implement:

Coordinating necessary security efforts with federal, state, and local law enforcement agencies or any National Guard or other appropriate armed forces organizations

Taking additional precautions at public events and possibly considering alternative venues or even cancellation

Preparing to execute contingency procedures, such as moving to an alternate site or dispersing their workforce

Restricting threatened facility access to essential personnel only

Severe Condition (Red): A Severe Condition reflects a severe risk of terrorist attacks. Under most circumstances, the protective measures for a Severe Condition are not intended to be sustained for lengthy time periods. In addition to the protective measures in the previous threat conditions, federal departments and agencies also should consider the following general measures in addition to the agency-specific Protective Measures that they will develop and implement:

Increasing or redirecting personnel to address critical emergency needs

Assigning emergency response personnel and pre-positioning and mobilizing specially trained teams or resources

Monitoring, redirecting, or constraining transportation systems

Closing public and government facilities

Source: Department of Homeland Security, www.dhs.gov.

Terror Alerts Become More Specific

Critics of the Homeland Security Advisory System have complained since its inception that the warnings it provides are much too vague, or are geographically much too broad to be useful for local or even state emergency management agencies. The nation consists of about 700,000 law enforcement officers, and a population of 300 million, all of whom were affected by these vague terror alerts by being asked to increase vigilance. This problem was so serious that, in 2003, the nation's governors called the lack of effective communications their number one concern in the war on terror.

Later that year, then–DHS Secretary Tom Ridge met with the governors at their annual conference, giving a public address aimed at soothing their concerns. He assured them that the flow of information would increase, but that it would probably never increase to the amount that the governors were asking. At this meeting, Ridge told the governors that they would be asked to select five staff members who would be given high-level security clearances. In conjunction with the governors, they would be given access to a secure website that would provide details about specific alerts, but they would not be allowed to pass the information on to lower ranks. Ridge also promised the governors flexibility to determine their state's security priorities in heightened alerts, after 150 key locations designated by the federal government had been locked down.

As Ridge promised, the terror alerts did become more location specific, as was seen in late 2004 and in 2005 and 2006 (see sidebar titled "Chronology of Changes to the Homeland Security Advisory System"). On August 1, 2004, the HSAS was raised to Orange for the financial sector in New York City, Washington, DC, and northern New Jersey. This was the first time a specific geographic threat was issued. The warning was given after intelligence analysis and reports pointed to a possible attack on those sectors after al-Qaeda surveillance was detected. That advisory was retracted on November 10 of that same year, more than 3 months later, after permanent protective measures were put in place. Then, after the July 7, 2005, terror attacks on the subway and bus systems in London, the HSAS terror alert level was raised to Orange for the mass transit portion of the transportation sector (including regional and intercity passenger rail, subways, and bus systems). While this was not done because of any specific intelligence indicating that an attack was due to occur in the United States, it allowed for further protective measures to be put into place in case a previously undetected attack was to occur. These measures included the following:

- Additional law enforcement
- Bomb-detecting K-9 teams
- Increased video surveillance
- Spot testing in certain areas
- Additional perimeter barriers
- Extra intrusion detection equipment
- Increased inspections of trash receptacles and other storage areas

---

Chronology of Changes to the Homeland Security Advisory System

March 12, 2002 — Introduction of Homeland Security Advisory System at Yellow

September 10, 2002 — Raised from Yellow to Orange

The U.S. intelligence community received information, based on debriefings of a senior al-Qaeda operative, of possible terrorists attacks timed to coincide with the anniversary of the September 11 attacks on the United States. Information indicated that al-Qaeda cells had been established in several South Asian countries in order to conduct car-bomb and other attacks on U.S. facilities.

September 24, 2002 — Lowered from Orange to Yellow

Based on a review of intelligence and an assessment of threats by the intelligence community, as well as the passing of the anniversary of the September 11 terrorist attacks and the disruption of potential terrorist operations in the United States and abroad, the Attorney General in consultation with the Homeland Security Council returned the threat level to elevated or "Yellow."

February 7, 2003 — Raised from Yellow to Orange

Intelligence reports suggested that al-Qaeda leaders had emphasized planning for attacks on apartment buildings, hotels, and other soft or lightly secured targets in the United States.

February 27, 2003 — Lowered from Orange to Yellow

The decision to lower the threat level was based on a review of how intelligence had evolved and progressed over the preceding three-week period, as well as counterterrorism actions taken to address specific aspects of the threat situation. Among the factors considered was the passing of the time period in or around the end of the Muslim Hajj that ended mid-February 2003.

March 17, 2003 — Raised from Yellow to Orange

The intelligence community believed that terrorists would attempt multiple attacks against U.S. and Coalition targets worldwide in the event of a U.S.-led military campaign against Saddam Hussein. Reporting indicated that al-Qaeda would attempt to launch terrorist attacks against U.S. interests claiming that they were defending Muslims or the Iraqi people rather than Saddam Hussein's regime.

April 16, 2003 — Lowered from Orange to Yellow

Following a review of intelligence and an assessment of threats by the intelligence community, the Department of Homeland Security, in consultation with the Homeland Security Council, made the decision to lower the threat advisory level.

May 20, 2003 — Raised from Yellow to Orange

In the wake of terrorist bombings in Saudi Arabia and Morocco, intelligence reports indicated that terrorist might attempt attacks against targets in the United States.

May 30, 2003 — Lowered from Orange to Yellow

The decision was based on a number of factors including a review of the intelligence and an assessment of the threats by the intelligence community. The U.S. intelligence community concluded that the number of indications and warnings that led to raising the level had decreased along with the heightened vulnerability associated with the Memorial Day holiday.

December 21, 2003 — Raised from Yellow to Orange

The U.S. intelligence community had received a substantial increase in the volume of threat-related intelligence reports. These sources suggested the possibility of attacks against the nation around the holiday season and beyond.

January 9, 2004 — Lowered from Orange to Yellow

The threat level was lowered based on a careful review of available intelligence and with the passing of the holidays and many large gatherings that occurred during that time.

August 1, 2004 — Raised from Yellow to Orange, specifically for the financial services sectors in New York City, northern New Jersey, and Washington, DC

Unusually specific threat information about where al-Qaeda would like to attack is received.

November 10, 2004 — Lowered from Orange to Yellow, for the financial services sectors in New York City, northern New Jersey, and Washington, DC

After the threat level was raised, state and local leaders and the private sector worked to strengthen security in and around specific buildings and locations as well as throughout the financial services sector, leading to the change.

July 7, 2005 — Raised from Yellow to Orange for mass transit

The threat level is raised from Yellow to Orange in light of the terror attacks in London; targeted only the mass transit portion of the transportation sector. This included regional and inner city passenger rail, subways, and metropolitan bus systems. No credible threat information indicated an attack was imminent in the United States.

August 12, 2005 — Lowered from Orange to Yellow for mass transit

After working closely with federal, state, and local partners to develop and implement sustainable mass transit security measures tailored to the unique design of each region's transit system, DHS decides to lower the national threat level for the mass transit portion of the transportation sector from Orange to Yellow.

August 10, 2006 — Raised from Yellow to Red for flights originating in the United Kingdom bound for the United States; raised to Orange for all commercial aviation operating in or destined for the United States.

The U.S. government raised the threat level to its highest level of alert — Severe, or Red — for commercial flights originating in the United Kingdom and bound for the United States. This action is taken to coordinate the alert level with that which was in place in Britain at the time, and as a precaution against any remaining threats (especially those of "copycats").

August 13, 2006 — Lowered from Red to Orange for flights originating in the United Kingdom bound for the United States; remains at Orange for all domestic and international flights. DHS lowered the aviation threat level from Red to Orange for flights from the United Kingdom to the United States. A ban on liquids and gels in carry-on baggage remains in full effect.

Source: DHS, DHS.Gov, 2008, http://www.dhs.gov/xabout/history/editorial_0844.shtm.

Crisis Communications

Communications has become an increasingly critical function in emergency management. The dissemination of timely and accurate information to the general public, elected and community officials, and the media plays a major role in the effective management of disaster response and recovery activities. Communicating policies, goals, and priorities to staff, partners, and participants enhances support and promotes a more efficient disaster management operation.

During the 1990s, FEMA established a strong communications capability that worked very effectively in numerous natural disasters and during the response to the bombing at the Murrah Federal Office Building in Oklahoma City. There are many similarities between communicating public messages during a terrorist crisis and communicating public messages during a crisis caused by a natural hazard. Former New York Mayor Rudy Giuliani successfully implemented a communications strategy in the aftermath of the World Trade Center attacks that was very similar to the FEMA model.

However, there are significant differences between natural and terrorist events and communications, especially in the area of information collection and dissemination to the public. The anthrax incidents and the sniper attacks in the Washington, DC, metropolitan area clearly highlighted one of the most significant differences: the need to share timely information with the public during an ongoing crisis versus the needs of the criminal investigators to protect and hold close information as they seek to identify and detain the parties responsible for the incident. This very delicate balancing act will likely be repeated time and again in the years to come; how officials, the public, and the media will come to terms with this issue is not especially clear at this time.

In this section, we will examine the underlying concepts of the FEMA model and examine some of the research conducted to date on crisis communications during a terrorist crisis.

The FEMA Model

The mission of an effective disaster communications strategy is to provide timely and accurate information to the public. The foundation of an effective disaster communications strategy is built on the four critical assumptions:

- Customer focus
- Leadership commitment
- Inclusion of communications in planning and operations
- Media partnership

Customer Focus

An essential element of any effective emergency management system is a focus on customers and customer service. This philosophy should guide any communications with the public and with all partners in emergency management. A customer service approach includes placing the needs and interests of individuals and communities first, being responsive and informative, and managing expectations. The FEMA emergency information field guide illustrates the agency's focus on customer service and its strategy of getting messages out to the public as directly as possible. The introduction to the guide states the following:

> As members of the Emergency Information and Media Affairs team, you are part of the frontline for the agency in times of disaster. We count on you to be ready and able to respond and perform effectively on short notice. Disaster victims need to know their government is working. They need to know where and how to get help. They need to know what to expect and what not to expect. Getting these messages out quickly is your responsibility as members of the Emergency Information and Media Affairs team (FEMA, 1998).

The guide's mission statement reinforces this point further:

> To contribute to the well-being of the community following a disaster by ensuring the dissemination of information that:

> Is timely, accurate, consistent, and easy to understand
> Explains what people can expect from their government
> Demonstrates clearly that FEMA and other federal, state, local, and voluntary agencies are working together to provide the services needed to rebuild communities and restore lives (FEMA, 1998)

The customers for emergency management are diverse. They include internal customers, such as staff, other federal agencies, states, and other disaster partners. External customers include the general public, elected officials at all levels of government, community and business leaders, and the media. Each of these customers has special needs, and a good communications strategy considers and reflects their requirements.

Leadership Commitment

Good communications starts with a commitment by the leadership of the emergency management organization to sharing and disseminating information both internally and externally. The director of any emergency management organization must endorse and promote open lines of communications among the organization's staff, partners, and public in order to effectively communicate (Figure 8–6). This leader must model this behavior in order to clearly illustrate that communications is a valued function of the organization.

In the 1990s, FEMA Director James Lee Witt embodied FEMA's commitment to communicating with the FEMA staff and partners, the public, and the media. Witt was a very strong advocate for keeping FEMA staff informed of agency plans, priorities, and operations. He characterized a proactive approach in communicating with FEMA's constituents, and his accessibility to the media was a significant departure from that of previous FEMA leaders. Director Witt exhibited his commitment to effective communications in many ways:

> During a disaster response, he held media briefings daily, and sometimes two or three times a day. He would hold special meetings with victims and their families.
>
> He led the daily briefings among FEMA partners during a disaster response.
>
> He devoted considerable time to communicating with members of Congress, governors, mayors, and other elected officials, during times of disaster and nondisaster.
>
> He met four or five times a year with the state emergency management directors, FEMA's principal emergency management partners.

FIGURE 8–6 Oklahoma City, Oklahoma, December 12, 2007 — Oklahoma Governor Brad Henry speaks with reporters before touring a neighborhood severely impacted by an ice storm. (Earl Armstrong/FEMA)

He gave speeches all over this country and around the world to promote better understanding of emergency management and disaster mitigation.

Through Witt's leadership and commitment to communications, FEMA became an agency with a positive image and reputation. Communications led to increased success in molding public opinion and garnering support for the agency's initiatives in disaster mitigation.

Inclusion of Communications in Planning and Operations

The most important part of leadership's commitment to communications is inclusion of communications in all planning and operations. This means that a communications specialist is included in the senior management team of the emergency management organization. It means that communications issues are considered in the decision-making processes and that a communications element is included in all organizational activities, plans, and operations.

In the past, communicating with external audiences, or customers, and in many cases internal customers, was neither valued nor considered critical to a successful emergency management operation. Technology has changed the equation. In today's world of 24-hour television and radio news and the Internet, the demand for information is never-ending, especially in an emergency response situation. Emergency managers must be able to communicate critical information in a timely manner to their staff, partners, the public, and the media.

To do so, the information needs of the various customers and the best methods by which to communicate with these customers must be considered at the same time that planning and operational decisions are being made. For example, a decision process on how to remove debris from a disaster area must include discussion of how to communicate information on the debris removal operation to community officials, the public, and the media.

During the many major disasters that occurred in the 1990s, Director Witt assembled a small group of his senior managers who traveled with him to the sites of disasters and worked closely with him in managing FEMA's efforts. This group always included FEMA's director of public affairs. Similarly, when planning FEMA's preparedness and mitigation initiatives, Witt always included staff from Public Affairs in the planning and implementation phases. Every FEMA policy, initiative, or operation undertaken during this time included consideration of the information needs of the identified customers, and a communications strategy to address these needs was developed.

Media Partnership

The media plays a primary role in communicating with the public. No government emergency management organization could ever hope to develop a communications network comparable to those networks already established and maintained by television, radio, and newspaper outlets across the country. To effectively provide timely disaster information to the public, emergency managers must establish a partnership with their local media outlets.

The goal of a media partnership is to provide accurate and timely information to the public in both disaster and nondisaster situations. The partnership requires a commitment by both the emergency manager and the media to work together; it also requires a certain degree of trust between both parties.

Traditionally, the relationship between emergency managers and the media has been tenuous. Conflicts have arisen as a result of the emergency manager's need to respond quickly and the media's need to obtain information on the response so that it can report it just as quickly. These conflicts sometimes resulted in inaccurate reporting and tension between the emergency manager and the media. The loser in such conflicts is always the public, which relies on the media for its information.

It is important for emergency managers to understand the needs of the media and the value they bring to facilitating response operations. An effective media partnership provides the emergency manager with a communications network to reach the public with vital information. Such a partnership provides the media with access to the disaster site, access to emergency managers and their staff, and access to critical information that informs and ensures the accuracy of the reports before they reach the public.

An effective media partnership helps define the roles of the emergency management organizations, manage public expectations, and boost the morale of the relief workers and the disaster victims. All of these factors can speed the recovery of a community from a disaster event and promote preparedness and mitigation efforts designed to reduce the loss of life and property from the next disaster event.

Communications Infrastructure

FEMA built a substantial communications infrastructure to support its communications objectives. Resources were devoted to hiring and training staff with experience in working with the media and community and providing these employees with the tools they needed to be successful. FEMA built and maintained a television studio with satellite capabilities and an audio studio with radio broadcast capabilities. The agency also established an interactive website where radio actualities and print information could be posted instantaneously. FEMA hired still and video photographers who were dispatched to the field, filing their photos electronically each night. These photos were then made available to media outlets around the country via the Internet.

Local emergency managers developed similar capabilities on a smaller scale in communities around the country. A research project conducted by graduate students at George Washington University found that many jurisdictions in the Washington, DC, metro area have built varying degrees of communications infrastructure such as communications plans, Web and fax communication capabilities, and trained staff who served them well during recent natural and man-made events. A copy of the research project is presented in the sidebar "Communicating during Emergencies."

■ ■ ■ ▬▬▬▬▬▬▬▬▬▬▬▬▬▬▬▬▬▬▬▬▬▬▬▬▬▬

Communicating during Emergencies

By Jane A. Bullock, George D. Haddow and Richard Bell

(Note: Research support for this paper was provided by Lauren Block, Tracy R. Bolo, Amina Chaudary, Brain D. Cogert, David DeCicco, Aspasia Papadopoulos, Robert Paxton, and Michael Stinziano.)

Introduction

Communicating with the public is one of the critical tasks facing emergency management agencies (EMAs). Reaching the widest possible audience with the most up-to-date, credible information can save lives and property, reduce public fears and anxiety, and maintain the public's trust in the integrity of government officials.

We recently conducted a survey of how EMA communicators had fared during a number of national disasters and terrorist attacks. Our concern about the adequacy of EMA communications planning has been heightened by a striking change in the intensity of media coverage. In describing their work with the press, our respondents used imagery very much like that which they applied to the emergency event itself. They found themselves swamped by a veritable "tidal wave" of reporters almost literally beating down their doors.

In this article, we review the findings of our survey and interviews and lay out the principal suggestions we received from a cross-section of EMAs on putting the personnel and infrastructure in place to execute robust, flexible communications plans.

Methodology

This article is based on responses to a questionnaire that we received from communicators involved in the following recent natural disasters or terrorist attack, including interviews in most cases with the principal spokesperson involved:

Tropical Storm Allison, Harris County Texas, Office of Emergency Management, Mayor's Office, June 5–10, 2001

The Hayman forest fire, Colorado, Public Affairs, U.S. Forest Service, Rocky Mountain Region, Summer 2000

Attack on the Pentagon, northern Virginia, Office of the Assistant Secretary of Public Affairs and Media Relations, U.S. Department of Defense, September 11, 2001

Attack on the Pentagon, northern Virginia, Capitol Police, September 11, 2001

Sniper attacks, Washington, DC, metro area, Media Services, Montgomery County Police Department, Fall 2002

Anthrax attack on Hart Senate Office Building, Washington, DC, October 2001

Anthrax attacks, Office of Communications, Division of Media Relations, Centers for Disease Control and Prevention, Fall 2001

F4 level tornado, La Plata, Maryland, Maryland Emergency Management Agency, April 28, 2002

Planning

Creating a communications plan on the fly during a crisis is an extremely daunting task. The absence of a plan virtually guarantees that communicators will not be able to reach the public as effectively as they would if they had a plan in place.

Producing a workable written plan is inherently an agency-by-agency process, contingent on available personnel, budget limitations, and so on. By soliciting critical review of the plan from all the affected participants — the public, the press, other government agencies — EMAs have the opportunity to produce the best possible plan under the circumstances.

Some of the EMAs with whom we talked had highly elaborate communications plans. But regardless of length, they all agreed that their plans made them more effective during emergencies. And the EMAs who had been through a trial by fire without a written communications plan were equally adamant about putting such a plan in place as soon as possible.

People

The most well-written communications plan is not worth much without a strong commitment from elected officials and department managers to put the infrastructure in place to carry out the plan.

The spokesperson's credibility is a key to his/her effectiveness at representing the government, reassuring the public, and keeping the media happy. In some jurisdictions, the highest ranking elected official or the head of the department managing the crisis will be the lead communicator, giving them a kind of automatic credibility at the onset of an event (like New York Mayor Rudy Giuliani after 9/11).

Given the increasing intensity of media coverage, the media spokesperson plays an increasingly important role in ensuring the overall effectiveness of an EMA. In order to maintain the spokesperson's credibility as a source with the media, the spokesperson needs to be "at the table" for all senior management decisions. If reporters believe that a spokesperson is not fully integrated into the decision-making process, they will inevitably be more suspicious of the information they do receive.

By participating in decision making, the spokesperson can also play a vital internal role by making sure that decision makers have fully considered how their decisions may play out in the media, giving them a better chance of avoiding public relations blunders.

After the terrorist attack on the Pentagon on September 11, 2001, Arlington County officials significantly upgraded its top public communications official. The change was more than just a title change (from Assistant County Manager for Public Information to Director of Communications and Public Affairs). The county also raised the position's salary and provided that the new director would report directly to the county manager. The job description for this new position includes the development of "a comprehensive communications program that will provide a cohesive image, identity, and brand message both externally and internally by optimizing the use of existing electronic resources (Internet, intranet, and cable television) and non-electronic sources (print media) as well as developing new communications venues."

If possible, one person should be the principal spokesperson (the single voice/single face model). Nothing is likely to be more confusing to the media or the public than dealing with a constantly changing array of talking heads. (There's a reason almost all the daily White House press briefings are handled by one person!)

Media Training

Learning to be a media spokesperson in the middle of a crisis is risky. There is no substitute for practical media training before a crisis arrives. In Harris County, Texas, the three authorized spokespeople had all been through a FEMA-approved 32-hour public information officer (PIO) course offered through the Texas Department of Public Safety's Office of Emergency Management. The Forest Service spokesperson during the 2002 Hayman forest fire had roughly 50 hours of formal media training. In addition, the agency's public affairs staff worked with him on "war game" crises, creating what he called "murder boards" to put him through the kind of tough questioning he would encounter in a real crisis. And the Capitol Police officer who handled the anthrax attack on the Senate Hart Building was a media trainer himself with over 160 hours of training.

Infrastructure

Building an Emergency Operations Center

Just as some jurisdictions had no written EM plan, some did not have an emergency operations center (EOC), although there was broad agreement that having a well-equipped EOC was the physical foundation for an effective communications effort.

For planning purposes, the EOC should have redundant communications capabilities, both internally and with the outside. No communications technology works every time. Land lines can fail; during the attack on the Pentagon, there were frequent problems with cell phones.

Without a well-equipped EOC, crisis managers face difficult hurdles staying on top of what is happening. After the September 11 attack on the Pentagon, local officials found that their EOC was ill equipped for the emergency management team to communicate with first responders or to receive accurate information from the scene. Phone lines were down, and the room was not equipped with radios or televisions. They were forced to delay press briefings until they could verify facts with first responders and people on-site.

EOCs should be designed with the media in mind. The Harris County, Texas, EOC has an on-site press room with telephone and computer access. EOCs can make life easier for television reporters by preparing video footage (called "B-roll") of scenes that reporters could use, like the interior of the emergency operations center. EOCs can also prepare fact sheets and other printed background materials on the major threats that the agency has identified.

Communicators can also provide the press with special support if necessary. During the Hayman forest fire, the Forest Service gave out personal protective equipment to reporters (hard hats, fire clothes, etc.).

Carving through the Jurisdictional Jungle

The communications plan provides a framework for mapping and, where possible, negotiating communications procedures about how to handle one of the most common problems of the EMA universe, overlapping jurisdictions. Such overlaps are inherent in the nature of almost every large-scale emergency event. A comprehensive plan must include not only local, state, and federal law enforcement and emergency management agencies but also the spectrum of veterinary and public health agencies (in light of the threat of the use of biological, chemical, or radiological weapons by terrorists).

In the aftermath of the anthrax attacks, the Centers for Disease Control and Prevention has published a useful analysis of the similarities and differences in public health and law enforcement investigations and the steep learning curves for both sets of agencies in their collaborations. ("Collaboration between Public Health and Law Enforcement: New Paradigms and Partnerships for Bioterrorism Planning and Response," by Jay C. Butler et al., http://www.cdc .gov/ncidod/EID/vol8no10/020400.htm). The authors emphasize the importance of pre-existing relationships between law enforcement and public health agencies and the need for practice exercises, and call for adding liaisons who are cross-trained in the public health aspects of communicable diseases and in law enforcement and criminal investigations.

Even without a written communications plan, an informal prior agreement can be helpful in reducing confusion. In the case of the anthrax attack on the Hart Senate Office Building, there was no written plan. But the Capitol Police Board and the House and Senate leadership had previously determined that the Capitol Police would be the designated agency to handle media inquiries after any terrorist or criminal incidents within the Capitol complex. Members of Congress — a group not known for being media-shy — conferred with the police spokesperson before holding their own press conferences, and the spokesperson attended these events, off camera, to provide guidance as needed.

In our study, several communicators highlighted the importance of maintaining clear channels of communications with all of the government agencies involved, regardless of which agency had been designated the lead communications agency. This cross-agency communications is essential for keeping everyone "on the same page" so that reporters do not get confusing or conflicting information from their contacts at other agencies. Up-to-date e-mail and fax lists are a relatively cheap way to distribute breaking information to other agencies in a timely way.

The Office of Emergency Management in Harris County used an Internet e-mail and pager software they developed to reach more than 140 media outlets in the region, 125 law-enforcement agencies, 54 fire departments, 29 cities, and selected individuals throughout the surrounding 41 counties. After tropical storm Allison, the office expanded the list of individuals requesting real-time information, adding more elected federal, state, and local officials and media outlets. (Copies of the Harris County plans can be downloaded from http://www.hcoem.org.)

Working with the Media

Building Prior Relationships

The media play an integral part in EMA outreach efforts to keep the public informed and up-to-date. But without pre-existing relationships with reporters, it's not uncommon or unexpected that in the heat of the moment, EMAs might come to look upon the press in a crisis as adversaries engaged in a "feeding frenzy" for new facts.

Planning is essential to building relationships with the media, so that EMAs and the media understand each other's needs and operating styles and how to work together as much as possible as allies. Both EMAs and the press share a deep concern about protecting the health and welfare of the public. Far from being adversaries, reporters can be valuable allies, particularly in devising an effective communications plan in the first place.

Harris County's Office of Emergency Management had a policy of inviting reporters in twice a year to talk about how the agency could better meet the needs of the press. Such conversations are no guarantee, of course, against future disagreements. But such meetings do allow for EMAs and reporters to share each others' perspectives in a nonstressful environment, reducing the possibility of misunderstandings later on during crises. And such exchanges also allow EMAs to plan to meet the media's needs where possible. Another useful technique for improving media relations is to schedule meetings with the editorial boards of local media outlets.

Conserving Credibility with the Media

Credibility is a dynamic asset in a crisis; a spokesperson can lose credibility quickly if the media and the public come to believe they're being misinformed or underinformed. Every effort should be made to ensure that whatever information is released to the public is accurate and up-to-date. As one PIO told us, his goal was to be "the first and best source of information, especially if it's bad news."

Misinformation only compounds one of the other common communications problems during crisis, the rapid spread of unfounded rumors, the rebutting of which can take up valuable time. During the Capitol Hill anthrax attack, many Capitol Hill reporters — who were used to covering policy debates, not terrorist attacks — were anxious about their own medical conditions, having been in the "hot zone" at some point. Congressional staffers, their usual sources of information, were also anxious about their own health and provided information often based on rumor, outside their areas of legislative expertise. Reporters, frustrated with what seemed to them to be the slow release of information, would go with these rumor sources and end up being forced to backtrack later. Many of the communications managers in our survey said that combating such rumors was one of the most difficult tasks they faced during a crisis.

Limiting the amount of information that reaches the public poses a different kind of challenge. It is not uncommon for government or corporate managers to use the control of the release of information as a way of gaining or preserving bureaucratic power. But in a crisis, this withholding tendency can aggravate the public's anxieties. In Arlington County, Virginia, after the September 11 attack on the Pentagon, officials found that although they might not have any new, more specific information about what might happen next, citizens still wanted frequent updates and reassurances from their county government.

In a crisis management setting, withholding information may very well result in a loss of power and control. Our respondents agreed that one should lean in the direction of making more, rather than less, information available, consistent with law enforcement and public safety considerations.

In a full-blown media circus, even a vigorous attempt at openness may not be enough to halt a media feeding frenzy. One of the more striking examples of this press intensity came from the Montgomery County, Maryland, police during the Washington, DC, area sniper attacks in fall 2002. The department was already providing frequent media releases, one-on-one interviews, Web updates, and as many as four press briefings a day.

But reporters wanted more. Some went so far as to peer through a half-inch opening in the window shades at the operations center, stealing a look at text on a dry erase board. Within seconds, they were questioning Montgomery County police chief Charles Moss about the information they had gleaned, showing little concern about whether their questions might endanger public safety.

Keeping Alternative Media Channels Open

In addition to the traditional media (TV, radio, newspapers), EMAs have access to newer media like e-mail, websites, and local cable TV, which can be used to reach the public directly. Because these tools also do not reach as wide an audience as traditional mass media, they should be seen as adjuncts, not substitutes.

These unmediated channels can be very effective tools for providing the public with a great deal of information without tying up large numbers of EMA staff. However, if an EMA is using a website, it is essential that staff update the site on a frequent basis; stale information drives users away.

The agencies we surveyed reported a wide range of satisfaction in using new media tools. In some cases, results were disappointing because too few people were aware of the local cable TV channel or did not know the agency had a website. On the other hand, one agency reported over 1.6 million contacts on its website from press, first responders, and the public and regarded the website as a valuable component of its overall communications strategy.

Conclusion

Communicating during emergencies is necessarily fraught with uncertainty: The unexpected is most likely to happen. No emergency communications plan can fully encompass all of the scenarios that may arise. But the findings from our survey show that EMAs can take steps to create a robust communications plans, train spokespeople, and build the infrastructure that will allow EMAs to roll with the punches and maximize their effectiveness at getting their messages to the press, the public, and other government agencies.

Terrorism Application

As noted earlier, Mayor Giuliani was an effective communicator in the aftermath of the World Trade Center attacks. He quickly assumed the role of principal government spokesperson, providing information, solace, and comfort to victims and their families, fellow New Yorkers, the nation, and the world through a series of planned and unplanned media events and interviews over the course of the days and months after September 11. Giuliani has been praised for his candor, his sensitivity, and his availability during these efforts. He has set a standard by which public officials will be judged in future tragedies.

In Washington, DC, a different communications scenario surfaced in the days and weeks after the first anthrax-contaminated letter was discovered in the office of then U.S. Senate Majority Leader Tom Daschle in October 2001. A series of public officials and scientists issued often-conflicting information to the public as both the officials and the public struggled to understand the nature and the reach of the anthrax threat. The failure to communicate accurate and timely information reduced public confidence in the government response and increased the confusion and misinformation surrounding the events.

What factors made Mayor Giuliani's efforts successful and caused the situation in Washington to worsen? What type of information and infrastructure support did Giuliani have that may or may not have been available to the public officials in Washington? Was the commitment to inform the public different in New York City than it was in Washington, DC?

A study of the anthrax attacks, funded by the Century Foundation, concluded that "the timely flow of information from experts to the public via the mass media will be the nation's best protection against panic and potential disaster" (Thomas, 2003). To reach this goal, the media and public officials will need to change the way they work together and possibly establish new protocols for determining the methods by which sensitive information is collected and disseminated to the public. These issues must ultimately be balanced against the public's right to know. As the study found, the public is often smarter and better informed than both the media and public officials believe (Thomas, 2003).

A report entitled "What Should We Know? Whom Do We Tell? Leveraging Communications and Information to Counter Terrorism and Its Consequences" found that the dissemination of information before a terrorist incident is as critical, if not more so, as delivering timely and accurate information during and after a crisis (Chemical and Biological Arms Control Institute, 2002). Preincident planning and coordination and public education and awareness campaigns are critical elements in establishing clear lines of communications among responding agencies, significantly improving the opportunities to collect accurate information and make it available to the public through the mass media. Again, changes in current practices and relationships among responders and with the media must occur to meet the information needs before, during, and after future terrorist attacks (Chemical and Biological Arms Control Institute, 2002).

The Washington, DC, sniper attacks provide valuable insight into the difficulties in communicating with the public during an ongoing crisis. The tension between the need to provide timely and complete information when such information was lacking and the need to avoid compromising an ongoing criminal investigation was clearly evident during this nearly month-long crisis. A case study of this event and its media coverage is presented at the end of this chapter.

9/11 Commission Findings on First-Responder Communications

The National Commission on Terrorist Attacks Against the United States, also known as the 9/11 Commission, found that inadequate communications contributed greatly to hindering the ability of responding agencies to respond to the events that unfolded, and directly led to the high number of police and fire department employees who were killed when the towers collapsed. It was discovered during the after-action review that many of these first responders were unable to communicate either with each other or with their commanders, and many of the open channels were quickly overcome by the heavy traffic. The following excerpt from the commission report describes these troubles:

> *The attacks of September 11, 2001, overwhelmed the response capacity of most of the local jurisdictions where the hijacked airliners crashed. . . . The inability to communicate was a critical element at the World Trade Center, Pentagon, and Somerset County, Pennsylvania, crash sites, where multiple agencies and multiple jurisdictions responded. The occurrence of this problem at three very different sites is strong evidence that compatible and adequate communications among public safety organizations at the local, state, and federal levels remains an important problem.*

The commission recommended that more funding and research be set aside to ensure that first-responder interoperable communication is improved to prevent these issues in the future. The First Response Coalition (FRC), an association of citizens, individual first responders, and advocacy groups concerned about first-responder issues (formed in 2004), developed a white paper, "It's Time to Talk: Achieving Interoperable Communications for America's First Responders." This report addressed the scope of the communications interoperability problem, examined the reasons public safety departments cannot communicate, and the importance of interoperability to first responders and the communities they protect. It also explored the barriers to interoperability, including cost, lack of coordinated planning, and scarcity of spectrum resources. The report, which can be found on the FRC website (www.firstresponsecoalition.org), concluded with the First Response Coalition's plan to make public safety communications interoperability a national priority and created a funding mechanism that would allow first responders to obtain the communications equipment and infrastructure they desperately need.

Funding for interoperable communications has increased since these two findings were released. The Department of Commerce and DHS together established the Public Safety Interoperable Communications (PSIC) Grant Program. Under this program, $968.4 million was made available to the states, territories, and the District of Columbia. Additionally, the DHS Office of Grants and Training administers the Interoperable Communications Technical Assistance Program (ICTAP), which is closely associated with the DHS Urban Areas Security Initiative (UASI). This program seeks to help local public safety agencies in designated urban areas communicate with each other in the event of a WMD attack.

In March of 2008, an interesting development in the drive for interoperable communications occurred when Jay Cohen, DHS Undersecretary for Science and Technology, told a House panel that despite the fact that agency had made significant progress toward providing first responders with interoperable radio technology, first responders were not always enthusiastic about sharing communications. The undersecretary stated that, "technology is not the problem with interoperability . . . it's the culture" (Government Executive Magazine, 2008).

Conclusion

The experience of emergency managers with natural disasters provides at minimum a guide to the development of effective terrorism-related communications strategies. However, there is much work to be done to adapt existing risk, warning, and crisis communications models to the new hazards, the new partners, and the new dynamic between response and recovery and criminal activity associated with the new terrorist threat. One thing will remain constant: Communication with the public about the terrorist threat must receive the same attention and resources that are now going to new technologies, new training programs, and new organizations. It has never been more important that public officials talk to the public, and it has never been more difficult than it is now. If this problem is not addressed properly, it can only compound in the worst way the terrible consequences of any terrorist incident.

CASE STUDY 1: WASHINGTON, DC, SNIPER ATTACKS

Introduction

In America's post-9/11 era of terror awareness, the extreme actions of groups like al-Qaeda are no longer necessary to spark detrimental anxiety-based social reactions. The two "snipers" who placed the nation's capital under a state of siege for 3 weeks with one rifle and a box of bullets confirmed this fact. Washington, DC's latest duct-tape and plastic "panic buying" spree, set off by the Department of Homeland Security's momentary "Terrorism Threat Index" increase, illustrates that the mere hint of a future event can now induce "irrational" behavior. Clearly, the emergency management community can no longer simply blame the media for such strong public sentiments.

Controlling public fear is a public safety task that falls squarely on the shoulders of local government, but like other terrorism preparedness and response functions, fear management must be supported by the federal government to be effective. There exists a rapidly growing need for agencies to adopt formal fear management capabilities staffed by appropriately trained, dedicated officials. In many cases of terrorism, fear is the greatest emergency that must be managed, and irresponsible or inadequate attempts to do so can actually increase the public's risk. Using the recent sniper crisis as an example, this case study will examine the roots of public fear and the often-distorted reality of risk and will propose methods by which emergency management agencies can successfully manage fear should a terror-based event occur within their jurisdiction.

Background

The residents of the Washington, DC, metropolitan area[1] were confronted with a dramatically heightened sense of personal vulnerability in the 12 1/2 months leading up to the sniper crisis. On September 11, 2001, during the worst terrorist attack to take place on American soil, the city became the target of two hijacked airplanes.[2] Less than 1 month later, several letters containing anthrax were mailed to federal government offices, resulting in the closing of several buildings,[3] a mass prophylaxis with the antibiotic Cipro, and the death of several Washington, DC, postal workers. Ever-increasing security measures became impossible to avoid, with numerous streets surrounding federal buildings closed to the public, military vehicles with mounted machine guns positioned around the Pentagon, and all the while the media reporting that the emergency response capabilities of the Washington, DC, government would be severely deficient should a mass casualty event occur in the near future (Ward, 2001).

It was easy to surmise that, to international and "homegrown" terrorists alike, Washington, DC, was a likely target. Reported levels of stress among area residents were much higher than those observed throughout the rest of the country, as indicated by several polls (Diaz and O'Rourke, 2002). By the time the sniper announced his presence on the morning of October 3, 2002, by killing four people, Washingtonians had already been pushed to the limits of their psychological stress tolerance.

Reactions and Actions

To study this case, we must first examine the reactions and actions of the authorities (the police department and other government officials), the media, and the public. These three groups were intimately linked by the virtual dearth of information that was available. The links can be simplified through the understanding that the authorities gathered and analyzed the information, the media broadcast the information, and the public received the information and acted upon it. The information flow diagram shown in Figure 8–7 depicts these links.

The following pages provide a broader understanding of each of these groups' actions in order to offer insight into why each may have acted as they did.

The Authorities

The individuals considered the "authorities" include the local, state, and federal government officials who were involved with the various aspects related to the response to the sniper crisis. Because this was primarily a law enforcement response to an event that involved only conventional weapons, the local police departments were the lead agencies involved.[4] These authorities were the sole source of credible information during the crisis.

The Montgomery County Police Department (MCPD) was the first to become involved in the crisis on the morning of October 3, primarily because the majority of killings had taken place in Montgomery County, Maryland. Having authority in the affected jurisdiction, the MCPD put forth Chief Charles Moose as the official spokesperson for the media.[5] Although Chief Moose could provide only basic information concerning the characteristics of the victims and the locations of the shootings, he was immediately recognized as the leader in the crisis.[6] For the remainder of the crisis, the media (and likewise, the public) continued to look to Chief Moose for information and guidance. In fact, even though FBI agents ultimately arrested the suspects outside of Chief Moose's jurisdiction, it was Chief Moose who officially announced the arrest.

Chief Moose proclaimed that this was one of the greatest challenges he had ever faced (Stockwell, Ruane, and White, 2002). He had never been required to fulfill such an important public relations role. The crisis quickly escalated to an international scale, and Chief Moose became the one man the world turned to for information so desperately sought. Chief Moose faced a major

(Continued)

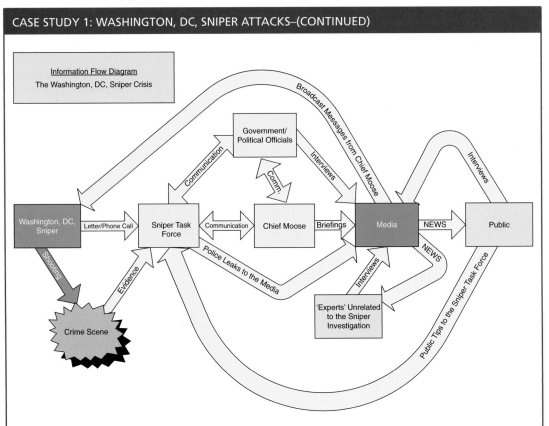

FIGURE 8–7 Information flow diagram during the Washington, DC, sniper crisis.

problem in that he often did not have very much information to give, and when he did, he felt that giving anything specific would jeopardize the investigation.

Chief Moose provided very little information detailing the actual risk people faced. He would regularly assure the public that police were doing their best to keep people safe and that the bulk of police resources were focused on solving the case, but he could not tell people how concerned they should be about personal safety. On at least one occasion he even stated that "we've not been able to assure anyone their safety in regards to this situation" (Ruane and Stockwell, 2002).

The Washington, DC, Metropolitan Police Department (MPD) publicly issued a list of "Tips for Staying Safe." This list told residents to keep moving when outside, to walk in a rapid zigzag pattern, and to avoid brightly lit open spaces. It also stated, "Remember that a sniper with the right equipment can shoot accurately from about 500 yards, the equivalent of five football fields" (Hurdle, 2002). These tips did not give any indication to residents of what their actual risk from the sniper might be. Some residents followed the advice they were given in these messages, but it is arguable that the lack of Chief Moose's endorsement of the tips prevented them from being widely observed.

School administrators became major players in the response to the sniper threat. Several schools were closed in the Richmond, Virginia, area after a sniper letter proclaiming that children were not safe was found at a shooting scene. Schools in other areas of Virginia and Maryland were closed as well, though no specific threats were given to the administrators of those schools as in Richmond. These closings were said to have been the result of a fear of liability among school administrators (*Economist*, 2002) and were not based on solid evidence. While they claimed that "there was no other way to guarantee students' safety" (Gettleman, 2002), the fact remained that they did not want to be held responsible for making a decision to let school stay in session and then have a child shot in their "jurisdiction" during such a high-profile crisis. In fact, none of the schools shut down during the sniper crisis were shut down after the September 11 terrorists attacks or after any other unsolved murders in the area (Reel, 2002). A further explanation could be heard in the words of Henrico County Public School Superintendent Mark Edwards, who stated, "The decision was not based on any specific threats, but on 'the volume of concern'" (Gettleman, 2002). Such statements strengthened arguments that these actions were based on a reaction to fear, not the risk itself. Of course, it is undeniable that there existed a genuine concern for the safety of the children in the motivation of these decisions, echoed by Montgomery County Superintendent Jerry West, who said, "We have always taken very seriously every day the level of threat to our children. We have always consistently done everything we can do to keep our children safe" (Schulte, 2002). The closing of schools became a focus of media attention and undoubtedly affected public opinion about personal safety.[7]

Politicians also become involved in the public reaction to the crisis, and in several cases used the events to further their own agendas. Kathleen Kennedy Townsend, in her gubernatorial campaign in Maryland, began attacking her opponent's opposition to a federal ban on assault weapons, stating that the gun control would be an answer to the voters' fears (Fineman, 2002). Connie Morella, campaigning for the House of Representatives, said, "I'm still knocking on doors, and when I do that, I think I'm a comfort to the people at home. I mean, if I'm out there doing that, people say, 'Hey, it must be all right'" (Barker, 2002).

There is finally the issue of unnamed authorities passing unreleased information to the media. It is important to stress both the detriment and opportunities presented by these insider "leaks." In numerous instances, the press learned of confidential information that was either never to be shared or not to be released immediately, and they broadcast that information, to the obvious dismay of Chief Moose. While on many occasions these leaks increased the tensions observed between the Sniper Task Force officials and the media, it cannot be overlooked that leaks were directly attributed to the capture of the two suspects.

The Media

The media was virtually the only bridge of information between the authorities and the public (Figure 8–7 earlier). Media agencies gleaned information from a myriad of sources, but the only information broadcast that could be deemed "factual" or "credible" almost always came directly from Chief Moose. In addition, that which was leaked was usually confirmed or denied by Chief Moose. Media coverage, regarding air time, was almost total when the crisis began and immediately after each successive victim. Regular news shows became dominated by the case, and there were constant "special reports" with additional information that was considered "related" to the case.

Coverage of the sniper crisis spanned the globe, and early on there were as many international news agencies as national ones camped outside the Montgomery County Police Department. The number of articles seen in the national and international press surged with each successive shooting, peaking immediately after the capture of Muhammad and Malvo. The actual daily number of articles, taken from major national and international newspapers, is displayed in Figure 8–8.

The media had a particularly strong influence in this crisis. Because the events were statistically so rare, and there were so few victims overall, there were startlingly few people outside of the immediate families and close friends of those victims who had any personal experience with "sniping" events.[9] In light of this fact, it is safe to say that members of the public received more than 99% of their information concerning the crisis from the media.[10] To put this statistic in

(Continued)

CASE STUDY 1: WASHINGTON, DC, SNIPER ATTACKS–(CONTINUED)

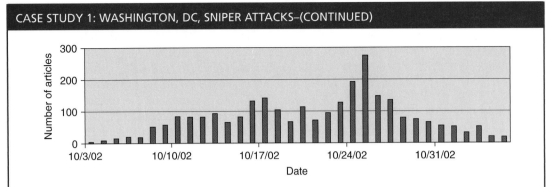

FIGURE 8–8 Number of articles related to the sniper crisis[8] appearing in 47 major international newspapers.

perspective, it can be compared to the findings of an *L.A. Times* poll in which respondents claimed their "feelings about crime" were based 65% on what they read and saw in the media, and 21% on experience[11] (Walsh, 1996, p. 9).

The media agencies often looked to alternate sources of information to achieve a competitive edge over one another. It was not uncommon to see "serial killings" experts speaking on news talk shows or to see "geographic profiling" experts doing the same (most notably after Chief Moose announced that geographic profilers were being used in the case). None of these alternate sources could provide any factual information outside of what was already known by the public, as they were not directly connected to the investigation (see Figure 8–7).

As stated earlier, there existed an explicit tension between the media and Chief Moose. This rift was most visible on October 9, when Chief Moose lashed out at the press for publishing information pertaining to a message written on a tarot card found at the school where a 13-year-old boy was shot. In another instance that angered Chief Moose, CNN reported, hours before the information was officially released, that the 13th shooting victim had died (Shales, 2002). Chief Moose's public scolding of the media (the result of a combination of sustained high levels of stress and inexperience with such high-profile events), however, was limited after the initial statements made in relation to the tarot card.

A fact that must be noted for its uniqueness is that the media was obviously used by the police as a direct mode of communication with the sniper. Chief Moose would "speak" to the sniper using cryptic messages at regularly scheduled press conferences without giving the media any prior indication that he would be doing this. Chief Moose did acknowledge his recognition of this important role the media played, one they were more than willing to fulfill.

The Public

The general public includes, for the sake of this case study, the people of the Washington, DC, and Richmond, Virginia, metropolitan areas. These people were the vulnerable group involved in the crisis — the sniper's targets. They were also the target of the media's and the authorities' information. The public was not only a target of these other players (including the sniper) but also a major source of information and action. The public demand for information fueled the media frenzy that occurred. Their fear of the sniper was the driving force in many of the decisions, rational or irrational, that were made by the authorities. Finally, the public was an integral component in the hunt for the sniper, and it was tips received from several members of the public that eventually led the police to Malvo and Muhammad.

Public action and reaction became the subject of many stories. This exhibited behavior became the focus of countless articles, detailing "newsworthy" actions that were performed in the name of safety.

Examples of such actions, followed by percentages of the affected population who admitted to performing them derived from a *Washington Post* poll (if available), include the following:

Used different gas stations than one normally used (Morin and Deane, 2002) — 36%
Avoided stores/shopping centers close to highways (Morin and Deane, 2002) — 32%
Crouched down while pumping gas (Ropeik, 2002a)
Ran or weaved through parking lots (Walker, 2002)
Avoided outdoor activities (Irvin and Mattingly, 2002) — 44%
Kept constant movement in public places (Eccleston, 2002)
Stayed at home except when absolutely necessary (Johnson and Finer, 2002) — 13%
Drove when one would normally have taken Metro (*Washington Post*, 2002b) — 11%
Watched or listened to the news more than usual (*Washington Post*, 2002b) — 71%

Gas station attendants were witness to much of this fear because so many people believed that the stations were a preferred target location of the sniper. One attendant reported that "some people, when they get out of their cars, they are so scared that their hands shake, and they can't get their [credit] cards into the [gas pumps]" (Nakamura and Davis, 2002).

The public was a responsible recipient of this flood of information, and generally followed any behavioral advice they were given by the authorities. They learned the meaning of terms like "Code Blue" and "Code Red,"[12] how to identify .223-firing assault rifles, the meaning of ballistics tests and what government agency conducts them, and how to identify box trucks, Chevy Astro Vans, and ladder racks. The public was told to call in their tips to the FBI tip line, and by the time the sniper was caught, over 90,000 calls had been placed (Whitlock, 2002).

What the public did not do, however, was panic. As much as the media wrote stories detailing the "paralyzing fear" experienced by the average person, life did go on with civility. There were no events where people were pushing each other over to get inside the "safety" of a store, for example. The public was fearful but intelligent, receptive to advice, and obviously able to process information well enough to locate the sniper within 24 hours once they learned the car and license plate information.

So Why Was Everyone So Afraid?

In their article "Rating the Risks," Slovic, Fischhoff, and Lichtenstein (1979) begin as follows: "People respond to the hazards they perceive." The exhibited responses to the sniper at personal, local, regional, and even federal levels would indicate that sources influencing risk perception during the crisis existed at extreme levels. In this section, the sniper crisis will be compared to models developed in recent and historical research in order to better explain the peculiar public risk behavior observed. This examination will be structured according to the four "Risk Perception Fallibility" conclusions of Slovic, Fischhoff, and Lichtenstein found in their 1979 article "Rating the Risks."

Risk Perception Fallibility Conclusion 1: "Cognitive limitations, coupled with the anxieties generated by facing life as a gamble, cause uncertainty to be denied, risks to be distorted, and statements of fact to be believed with unwarranted confidence."

People tend to fear a risk less as they become better informed, with more specific details of the risk. However, the amount a person can discover about a risk will almost never be complete, as the actual likelihood or consequence most risks pose cannot be quantified in a way that addresses the specific threat faced by individuals (even well-known risks such as cancer or heart disease) (Ropeik, 2002c). The more uncertainty a risk poses, or, as Slovic, Fischhoff, and Lichtenstein state, "the more of a gamble something is," the more people will fear it. The sniper, who could strike anyone, anywhere, at any time, presented citizens in the Washington, DC, metropolitan area with the ultimate in uncertainty.

(*Continued*)

In the face of uncertainty, people will consciously or subconsciously make personal judgments based on very imperfect information in order to establish some individual concept of the risk they face (Slovic, Fischhoff, and Lichtenstein, 1979). These judgments based on uncertainties and imperfect information often cause people to wrongly perceive their own risk, more often in a way that overstates reality. There could scarcely have been more uncertainty in regard to the public's knowledge of useful information in the sniper crisis. Members of the public were constantly told by the media that the police had very little to work with, because the sniper was leaving few clues at crime scenes (Patrick, 2002). People had no idea how great of a threat the sniper was in comparison to other public safety threats the police handled during routine action because these statistics were never released. Considering the amount of resources police dedicated, it would appear that the threat to public safety was greater than anything people in the area had ever faced, and considering the ineffectiveness of the actions of the police in catching the sniper (such as the systems of roadblocks),[13] the public could assume only that the police were powerless to combat this "enormous" threat. Many other factors external to the investigation gave an impression of dire seriousness and great uncertainty as well. Every time a media "expert" would attempt to define the sniper's actions, stating that he would likely not strike in place X or at time Y, the sniper would strike in that place or at that time. The great number of white vans in circulation gave the impression that the sniper was everywhere.[14] The fact that schools were being closed, outdoor activities were regularly canceled, the government was talking of bringing in the national guard, and the New York–based Guardian Angels were in the area pumping gas only strengthened the public's view that the risk was greater than it actually was. Frequent talk that the crisis may be the result of terrorism propagated the idea that the sniper might be just the first in a series of snipers that could become a regular part of life in America.[15] In a survey that asked citizens of the Washington, DC, metropolitan area how concerned they were that they might personally become a victim of the sniper, 19% said a great deal and 31% said somewhat scared — a total of 50% (Washington Post, 2002b).

Risk Perception Fallibility Conclusion 2: "Perceived risk is influenced (and sometimes biased) by the imaginability and memorability of the hazard. People may, therefore, not have valid perceptions even for familiar risks."

People are more afraid of those things that they can imagine or that they can remember. These easily available risks, as they are called, tend to be overestimated regarding their likelihood of occurrence. Generally, people tend to fear what they hear about repetitively or constantly. This phenomenon is referred to as the *availability heuristic*, which states that people perceive an event to be likely or frequent if instances of the event are easy to imagine or recall. This is a perception bias that can be correct when considering events that are, in fact, frequently observed, such as in the case of those who believe that automobile accidents are common because almost everyone they know has been involved in one. However, when a risk that is spectacular but not necessarily common receives constant media attention, such as high-school shootings did in the 1990s (particularly the Columbine attack),[16] people often wrongly assume that similar events are very likely to occur. In the case of the sniper, where coverage in newspapers and on television, radio, and the Internet was constant, receiving front-page placement every day from October 4 until the suspects were captured on October 24,[17] it would follow that people would likely assume their personal risk was greater than it actually was. Again, the omnipresence of white vans and white box trucks, both intimately associated with the sniper crisis through the police and the media, gave people a constant reminder of the sniper. Many of the decisions by government officials to close schools, restrict the movement of students, and cancel outdoor activities altered people's daily lives in such a way that they were made constantly aware of the crisis around them. In addition, seeing sniper victims on TV who were similar to themselves, doing things they regularly did, made it easy for people to imagine succumbing to the same fate.

In an October 13 *Washington Post* poll that asked participants if they felt most threatened by the sniper shootings, the anthrax letters, or the September 11 attacks, 44% responded the sniper shootings, 29% responded the September 11 attacks, and 13% responded the anthrax letters (*Washington Post*, 2002b). Slovic and his colleagues (1979) described how events that are "out of sight [are] effectively out of mind." It would follow that the opposite was true of the sniper: that which is always in sight is always on people's minds.

Risk Perception Fallibility Conclusion 3: "[Risk management] experts' risk perceptions correspond closely to statistical frequencies of death. Laypeople's risk perceptions [are] based in part on frequencies of death, but there [are] some striking discrepancies. It appears that for laypeople, the concept of risk includes qualitative aspects such as dread and the likelihood of a mishap being fatal. Laypeople's risk perceptions were also affected by catastrophic potential."

It can be difficult for people to completely understand the statistics they are given, and even more difficult for them to conceptualize how those statistics apply to them personally. Furthermore, these statistics tend to do little to affect the way people perceive the risks that are calculated. This is not to say that the average person lacks sufficient intelligence to process numbers; it is just that the numbers are not the sole source of influence on public risk perception. In ranking their risks, people tend to rely more on qualitative factors than on the quantitative likelihood of a hazard resulting in personal consequence (Slovic, Fischhoff, and Lichtenstein, 1979). People are generally more concerned with the consequences than the likelihoods of risks.

In consideration of the statistics provided to the public by the media, it is important to examine their quality and usefulness to the recipients. While it is clear that everyone knew the number of people killed by the sniper, few knew the actual number of people living in the affected area or the actual murder rate in "normal" years within that same area. Without complete information, the given statistics were meaningless and likely misleading. In fact, in the absence of complete information, people assumed that their chances of becoming a sniper victim were much greater than they really were. Economists have classified this tendency of people to overestimate unknown or unclear risks as "risk-ambiguity aversion" (*Economist*, 2002). However, even if the statistics were straightforward, it is difficult for people to understand how those numbers affect them as individuals, even if they are risk "experts" (Jardine and Hrudey, 1997).

Slovic, Fischhoff, and Lichtenstein (1980), in their article "Facts and Fears: Understanding Perceived Risk," proposed that there are 18 risk characteristics that influence public risk perception. These qualitative measures have helped to explain what attributes of a risk cause public fear. According to their measures, the risk of being killed by the sniper ranks among the most feared risks, as it is dreaded, has consequences that are fatal, "affects me," is new, is not easily reduced, and is uncontrollable, among other reasons. The sniper risk, not surprisingly, falls close to terrorism and crime on the authors' ranking of risks' ability to elicit fear.

Risk Perception Fallibility Conclusion 4: "Disagreements about risk should not be expected to evaporate in the presence of 'evidence.' Definitive evidence, particularly about rare hazards, is difficult to obtain. Weaker information is likely to be interpreted in a way that reinforces existing beliefs."

The sniper announced his presence with a true mass-murder event.[18] The initial news reports described an ensuing crisis that left open the possibility that the murders may continue at an equally high rate of incidence (five killings in 16 hours). By the end of October 3, police had little to work with, and there was little hope that the sniper would be quickly captured. The public had been told from the very beginning that they were dealing with a killer who was a grave threat to public safety. Due to psychological factors described in the previous three risk perception fallibility conclusions, people were made to believe they were at high risk. This became the frame of reference in which the public was to define the sniper risk, and one that would now be very difficult to alter.

The crisis continued for 3 weeks. Many (often heavily editorialized) articles did try to enlighten people about their actual personal risk, some even giving detailed statistics that illustrated to the public that their vulnerability to the sniper was extremely low. Unfortunately, not

(*Continued*)

only did these articles rarely (if ever) get front-page coverage but they were greatly outnumbered by articles telling people that their lives were in grave danger from the sniper. In the end, it was not the "long-shot" statistics nor the articles that told people to remain calm that were believed but the fear-mongering and sensational articles given priority coverage by newspapers and news networks. This is not surprising, considering the findings of Slovic, Fischhoff, and Lichtenstein's research. They state that "people's beliefs change slowly and are extraordinarily persistent in the face of contrary evidence. New evidence appears reliable and informative if it is consistent with one's initial belief; contrary evidence is dismissed as unreliable, erroneous, or unrepresentative." They add that "convincing people that the catastrophe they fear is extremely unlikely is difficult under the best conditions. Any mishap could be seen as proof of high risk, whereas demonstrating safety would require a massive amount of evidence" (Slovic, Fischhoff, and Lichtenstein, 1979), evidence that is sometimes impossible to obtain in an accurate or timely manner.

This stoicism is compounded by the fact that once people make their initial judgments, they believe with overwhelming confidence that their beliefs are correct. This phenomenon, called the *overconfidence heuristic*, suggests that people often are unaware of how little they know about a risk and how much more information they need to make an informed decision. More often than not, people believe that they know much more about risks than they actually do. With regard to the sniper, having overconfidence in incorrect information was inevitable considering the nature of the media coverage. For instance, with "expert" profilers giving descriptions of the killer's "most likely" demographics as a lone young, white male, it is no surprise that everyone was caught off guard when the pair turned out to be two black males (Fears and Thomas-Lester, 2002). However, with no confirmed information provided about the suspects prior to their arrest, there logically should have been no surprise no matter what race/ethnicity or age he, she, or they were.

This phenomenon has been linked to media coverage of other spectacular events in the past, specifically in regard to the way in which people's rating of risks depends on the amount of media coverage a risk receives. For example, one study showed that the percentage of crimes covered by the media that involve perpetrators and victims of different races is of a greater proportion than occurs in reality. In other words, one is more likely to see a news story describing a white victim of a black attacker than a story depicting a black victim of a black attacker, even though the latter is more common. This inconsistency in coverage is seen as the main reason that Caucasians overestimate their likelihood of being a victim of interracial crime by a factor of 3 (Twomey, 2001). Paul Slovic wrote in his 1986 article "Informing and Educating the Public about Risk" that "strong beliefs are hard to modify" and "naïve views are easily manipulated by presentation format."

Often, it is only time that can change people's opinions about the risks they personally face. One major reason people are more scared of a new risk than an old risk is that they have not been able to gather enough information to alter their initial impression. After time has passed, and they realize that their expectations for victimization have not been realized for themselves or anybody that they know, they begin to question the validity of their views. Had the sniper not been caught, the general public would have gained a more accurate appreciation of how small their chance of becoming a victim was, much in the manner that people are no longer as concerned about the child abductions that seemed to plague the United States during 2001.[19] Fortunately, the sniper was caught before this hypothesis could be tested.

Reality — Statistics of the Crisis

"Of all the grim facts surrounding [the] Oklahoma City [bombing], perhaps the grimmest is the one nobody talks about: against the backdrop of everyday American tragedy, 167 deaths is not many. . . . In a typical year, guns kill 38,000 Americans and about that many die on our roads. These numbers routinely go up or down 2% or 3% — half a dozen Oklahoma bombings — without making the front page" (political commentator Robert Wright, *Time*, May 1995; cited in Walsh, 1996, p. 18).

In the 3 weeks during which the sniper terrorized more than 5 million people in the Washington, DC, metropolitan area, shooting 13 people and killing 10, "routine" crime took place virtually unnoticed. In the District of Columbia alone, there were 239 assaults with a deadly weapon, 32 people shot, and 22 people murdered (Barger, 2002). This accounts for just 10% of the total area where the sniper operated, so it can be assumed that there were far more of these "routine" murders than 22. However, not one of these crimes merited front-page coverage in the newspapers.

In the previous section it was necessary to put aside statistics in order to understand public risk perception, but now the statistics alone must be analyzed to determine how the real risk people faced during those 3 fearful weeks from the sniper compared to the other risks they face in their daily lives without second thought. Richard Wilson of Harvard University writes in his article, "Analyzing the Daily Risks of Life," that "to compare risks we must calculate them" (1979, p. 57). To calculate the statistical risk that the citizens of the Washington, DC, metropolitan area faced, it is necessary to ascertain the population of the area where the sniper operated. These statistics will not be perfect by any means, as they cannot account for the ever-increasing zone in which the sniper operated (*Economist*, 2002). Additionally, although the sniper operated within a large geographic area, there was not an equal distribution of murders across the total area (Montgomery County was the location of seven of these murders, for example). However, these statistics will be more accurate in terms of personal risk (see description in notes 24 and 25), because the virtually random selection of victims who were performing a wide range of activities brings the population and personal risk almost to equality.

To achieve this rough estimate of personal risk, it would be possible to consider the number of victims, divided into the total population of the affected area, spread out over the period in which the sniper was operating. This would not be accurate in projecting future risk, however, because the operating environment changed for the sniper in the early morning of October 3. When the police were not aware of his presence, it was possible for the sniper to repeatedly attack within a short period of time. Shortly after initiation of the crisis, when the sniper's presence was officially recognized, his attacks required more time[20] (presumably for more detailed planning). It is therefore necessary to estimate how the murders would have progressed over the course of a year in the context of a postawareness scenario. In operating under this assumption, it can be said that the four murders that took place on the morning of October 3 would have likely been only one murder had the police been on alert for the sniper. In that case, the statistics to work with are as follows:

- Number of people shot (adjusted for postawareness): 10
- Number of people killed (adjusted for postawareness): 7
- Population, Washington, DC, metropolitan area:[21] 4,922,152 (83.16% of total sniper-area population)
- Population, Richmond-Petersburg metropolitan area:[22] 996,512 (16.84% of total sniper-area population)
- Population, total affected area: 5,919,152
- Number of days the sniper operated (10/2/02–10/24/02):[23] 23
- Multiplier (for 365 day average): 15.870
- National murder rate: 5.5/100,000
- Washington, DC, metropolitan area murder rate: 7.4/100,000
- Richmond-Petersburg metropolitan area murder rate: 11.1/100,000

(*Continued*)

CASE STUDY 1: WASHINGTON, DC, SNIPER ATTACKS–(CONTINUED)

Using these numbers, we may derive the following population risk factors for the people living in the area where the sniper operated:

- Chance of being shot by the sniper in the next 12 months:[24] 2.7/100,000 or 1/37,297

- Chance of being killed by the sniper in the next 12 months:[25] 1.9/100,000 or 1/53,325

Comparing these figures against the risks that people face in their daily lives with little or no concern will put the real risk from the sniper into statistical perspective. Table 8–1 lists the likelihood of death from various causes, listed in order of decreasing risk. According to these figures, a person was more likely to be accidentally poisoned or to die in a car accident than to be shot and possibly killed by the sniper. As previously noted, the other risks have higher variance between individual and population risk, as more can be done on the personal level to mitigate them (such as wearing a seatbelt or a life preserver), but the fact remains that for the average of all people these statistics are accurate.

Lessons Learned and Future Implications

Now that the sniper crisis has been compared to risk perception models and the population risk statistics have been calculated, we can ask the question, "Should the public have been so deeply fearful during the sniper crisis?" The answer, according to these established models, is yes, they definitely should have been, considering the information they received. However, according to the statistical data and risk comparison, they did not need to be so afraid, and there are ways in which the media,

Table 8–1 Likelihood of Death from Various Causes

Hazard	Annual risk	Lifetime risk
2000 murder rate, sniper area (weighted)[a]	1/12,870	1/167
2000 murder rate, national	1/18,182	1/236
Car accident[b]	1/18,752	1/244
Accidental fall	1/20,728	1/270
Accidental poisoning	1/22,388	1/292
Murdered with a gun	1/25,196	1/328
Shot by sniper	1/37,297	1/484
Hit by car while walking	1/45,117	1/588
Killed by sniper	1/53,325	1/693
Drowning (accidental)	1/77,308	1/1,008
Fire/smoke inhalation	1/81,487	1/1,062
Lightning	1/4,262,813	1/55,578

[a] The Washington, DC, metropolitan area (WMA)/Richmond-Petersburg metropolitan area (RPMA) combined crime rate was found by taking the crime rate of the WMA (7.1/100,000) and multiplying it by the WMA percentage of total population area (83.16%), and then taking the RPMA crime rate (11.1/100,000) and multiplying it by the RPMA percentage of total population (16.84%), to give a combined crime rate of 7.77/100,000. The WMA and RPMA 2000 murder rate data are taken from *Crime in the United States, 2000* (FBI, 2001).
[b] See Memmott (2002b). All figures other than those associated with the sniper are attributed to this source.

emergency responders, and other federal, state, and local government officials can limit this type of fear in the future.

1.   Respond Separately to the Event and to the Fear

The authorities, namely the police and the government officials, dedicated a vast amount of resources to the sniper investigation because of the high level of public fear and concern, not because of some recognized disproportionate threat to public safety.[26] Conversely, they did little, if anything, to treat the fear itself. When emergency management agencies respond in this way, they can actually amplify the level of anxiety by signaling to the public that their crippling fears are justified,[27] and move emergency management and police resources away from routine but necessary public safety work. These actions increase people's susceptibility to other health-related risks by preventing them from exercising and through the damaging physiological effects of fear-induced stress.[28] Variations of the statement, "People will never feel safe again until the sniper is caught," repeated in every newspaper, echoed the primary motivation behind this large-scale response.

In the future, police and government officials should treat the event and the fear of the event as two separate problems that need to be addressed separately. This is a need that has already been recognized in past crime and terrorism crises (Warr, 2000). There should be a separate function of emergency management — a "fear management team" consisting of members with backgrounds in sociology, psychology, emergency management, public education, and public relations, among others. This team would have several subfunctions, described below.

Measure levels of public fear: There are established ways in which fear can be measured in real-time status, including by conducting surveys, recognizing behavioral indicators (what people are doing to avoid what they fear — changes in routine, for example), and establishing recognition-triggers for "transient public episodes of fear" (how a population is acting as a whole in response to fear — drops in the number of public transportation users, for example) (Warr, 2000). Emergency management can only respond to a high level of fear if they know it exists. Not all events will be as obvious as the sniper crisis.

Develop an informed, educational public relations message: As a part of regular emergency management operations, a trusted leader with decision-making power must be identified and put forth to communicate with the public through the media. The members of the fear management team would process information culled from their monitoring of public fear to create communications through the trusted official in a manner that adequately and accurately addresses public fear. They would develop mental models that give emergency responders a clear understanding of what exactly the public does and does not understand about the risk and what they believe emergency responders are doing and/or are able to do to ensure their security. They would work directly with the emergency response team to inform them about the exact information the public needs to correct or adjust their belief in order to more closely match reality. They would work with government officials as well, helping them to inform the public through reinforcement of the messages given by the emergency response spokesperson.

Address public fear directly: The fear management team would coordinate the services of mental health specialists in an effort to further reduce public fear to more "healthy" levels. These public health officials would address the public directly, through media outlets, or through community groups.[29] Because they would have information directly related to the crisis, they would be able to make accurate and informed communications through the media (unlike the uninformed "experts" that were prevalent during the sniper crisis who did not have access to secure information). The information would not be compromised by this team, because it would not be necessary to share the specifics — however, the public would recognize that the team members, as trusted public health officials, were making informed decisions and would more likely invest more faith in these opinions in adjusting their perceptions.

Assist local government/community authorities in decision making: Both local government and community groups must respond to crises, and their actions often directly affect the public. School superintendents need to know when it is appropriate to cancel school, and community groups need to know when public events must be postponed. Without direction from emergency response (the most "informed" source of information), they will not act with consistency and will likely send a mixed message to the public. In addition, the overreaction by one influential government or community leader can lead to secondary responses from other less organized or less informed groups.[30] This fear management team would serve as an advisory board for government and community groups, ensuring that their leaders are able to make decisions based on the most complete and current information, and allowing the groups to work in consensus rather than as separate entities.

2. *Increase Responsible Reporting by the Media*

The media have a responsibility to ensure that during crisis events, public safety information reaches a wide audience in a timely and accurate manner, a duty they are recognizing and embracing more each year (Moore, 2002). However, most newspaper and television news employees have never received crisis communications training, and therefore have no idea how to fulfill this role. The media operate as a business and are motivated primarily by ratings and viewer and reader numbers, which ensure steady income generation; the media cannot be expected to cease provisions of blanket coverage during extreme events such as the sniper crisis. The industry functions within a time-compressed environment in which editors often must develop stories using incorrect or incomplete information. Journalists will continue to proactively seek information on crises using their own means, and there will always be leaks made to the media by emergency management and public officials.

The media are adroit at using scare tactics and fear-mongering to harness public attention and often do little to calm nerves once that attention is obtained. These agencies must learn as an industry that they can contribute to public safety by providing accurate, responsible, and useful information while still maintaining these traditional "shock" methods to attract viewers, and thereby preserve a competitive edge without sacrificing integrity. For the media to participate in a crisis response constructively, they need to add to the glut of sensationalism a balance of rationality — a reality check for the public to process information and judge individual risk. If they broadcast a message that says, "Four of the victims were shot while pumping gas at local gas stations," for example, they need to qualify this statement by adding, "however, there have been approximately 10.5 million gas transactions made at over 1,000 gas stations in the affected area during the crisis so far" (Memmott, 2000b) in order to give adequate perspective to the original statement. Emergency management must recognize the media as willing participants in the process and provide them with this information that may not be readily available otherwise.

The media should recognize and act upon the public's tendency to anchor and adjust[31] in forming perceptions on risk. This cannot be denied. If a story informs citizens that "this is the greatest number of law enforcement officers ever dedicated to a criminal investigation in county history,"[32] readers may incorrectly infer that their lives are at greater risk than ever before,[33] and all future information will be processed within this context. If they are later told in an article that is given proportional emphasis,[34] for instance, that, "although 10 people have been killed by the sniper in the past 3 weeks, there are an average of 38 people killed in traffic accidents alone during the same time period in the Washington, DC, metropolitan area" (Memmott, 2002b), they will be able to rank their personal risk more appropriately.

Media agencies must also avoid irresponsible reporting aimed at "creating" stories. Martha Moore of *USA Today* cites as an example of this phenomenon the many cases in which local news stations will make announcements, before a coming storm, for example, that "people should prepare by stocking up on batteries and water before the stores run out of these items." Following this statement, the news agency will post teams at local stores to report that people are crowding these local stores in order to get their hands on the few remaining batteries and bottles of water that remain, causing successive waves of panic buying[35] (Moore, 2002). Similar situations occurred during the sniper crisis. The media would report that "gas stations are the preferred location of the sniper," and then run stories showing how people were not going to gas stations, which had the snowball effect of making consumers progressively more afraid to visit gas stations.

The media agencies are not villains. Quite to the contrary, they are a vital component to emergency management without which risk communication would be nearly impossible. Also, not all of today's media reporting is misinformed or irresponsible. There are many news agencies that employ reporters who are trained or knowledgeable in crisis communications and risk perception and who regularly practice the suggestions made above. For example, in a *USA Today* article titled, "How to Cope? Keep Guard and Spirits Up," the author suggested that residents of the DC area "take a lesson from people in other nations who confront such fears every day: Get on with life — but be more alert than ever to dangers and more kind than ever to others" (Memmott, 2002a). The knowledge and experience of reporters like this must be shared across the industry. The journalist's goal is to provide the public with timely information; the extent to which that information is both accurate and effective depends largely on the level of cooperation provided by emergency management.

3.   *Establish Public Risk Perception and Risk Communication Training Standards for Emergency Management, Government Officials, and the Media*

The federal government requires both emergency responders and public officials to complete training and prove competencies in performing many of the tasks associated with their job duties. While many first responders who communicate directly with the public are trained in public relations and communications, they are often not trained in crisis communications, risk perception, or risk communication. Their support teams, who provide the information on which their public response is based, are just as likely to lack adequate training in these areas. A statement from an ATF agent who described the extensive damage a .223 bullet fired from a rifle does to the human body or the MPD safety tip that reminded residents that a sniper could hit victims from 500 yards are examples of statements that neither provided useful information to the public nor controlled fear. If emergency responders and government officials are to effectively treat the fear associated with a crisis, they must be trained in methods that have proven successful in the past and develop a clear understanding of what drives human fear. Training in these studies will not become institutional unless the need is recognized throughout the emergency management sector. These training opportunities must also be made available to the media in order to ensure a comprehensive approach to fear management. If this training is conducted through a partnership between media and emergency management, interpersonal relationships will likely be created, thus further enhancing fear management.

If training in risk perception and risk communication became a requirement for emergency management public relations — related tasks, fear management would become a routine organizational function. The existence of a fear management team, as proposed above, would be better understood and utilized across all functions of emergency management agencies if management-level employees had a more comprehensive understanding of its purpose. Industry observance of this requirement would be more accepted if the federal or state government covered the costs for this training as they do for many other law enforcement and public safety programs.

Chief Moose did an outstanding job as a crisis manager and leader, but he did little to combat fear directly. Considering the lack of experience among emergency response officials with terrorism in the United States, it is unlikely that many of them would be prepared to take on such a difficult task as fear management. However, if the threat of terrorism is growing, as the FBI and the Department of Homeland Security claim it is, then the need for such training is obvious.

4.   *Seize the Opportunity during Periods of Increased Public Attention for Risk Education*

Almost every person in the Washington, DC, metropolitan area and likely the entire United States can say with confidence that they know what a .223 caliber bullet is and what it looks like, can identify Bushmaster as a brand of rifle, can tell approximately how far (in meters) a sniper can hit a target, can describe a box truck, and knows what a ladder rack on a Chevy Astro Van looks like. When people are afraid, they pay attention and they learn. It cannot be overlooked that despite the number of police looking for the sniper, it was a truck driver who located the sniper after learning the make, model, and license plate number of the sniper's vehicle on the news.

People will listen to emergency response and government suggestions if the source of information is trusted and holds decision-making authority.[36] These rare mass-education opportunities must not be wasted. Emergency managers have a moral obligation under such circumstances to inform people of the real risks they face and tell them what it is they need to do to protect themselves from those risks. Telling people to weave while going through a parking lot during the sniper crisis is likely to make people think twice about going to the store, but it is unlikely that the information will save more than a few, if any, lives. Telling people that if they feel the need to drive long distances to purchase gas in order to feel safe, then they must also be sure to wear their seat belt because car accidents are a much more likely killer than the sniper, instantly contributes to a decrease in risk of thousands of people.

Modified Information Flow Diagram — The Road Ahead

On March 1, the emergency management functions of the federal government were officially transferred into the Department of Homeland Security. Secretary Tom Ridge has been given exactly one year to reorganize and improve the functions of 22 absorbed agencies in a way that more effectively prevents, prepares for, responds to, and recovers from future terrorist attacks (and natural and technological disasters). Concurrently, the states have been spending billions of their own dollars to prevent and prepare for terrorist attacks, primarily following the direction of the federal government. This opportunity to improve current emergency management systems must not pass by without a full examination of the vital importance of managing public fear.

The information flow diagram shown in Figure 8–9 is provided as a possible solution to managing fear at the local level. The diagram depicts how a fear management team would operate within the overall flow of crisis information and within the range of emergency management activities.

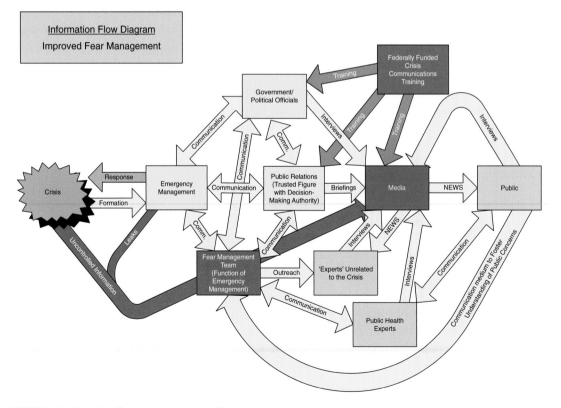

FIGURE 8–9 Information flow diagram: improved fear management.

Federally funded crisis communications training is displayed in order to indicate the likely recipients of this training. Although this design is simplified, it can be easily adapted to suit the needs of almost any local emergency response to a crisis that captures extensive public attention. Figure 8–9 does not directly address where the additional resources provided in federally declared disasters would apply or how the command structure would accommodate these resources, as it remains to be seen how the DHS reorganization will alter existing response systems.

Conclusion

Fear is irrational only if people have enough information about a hazard to perform a personal risk analysis, find that the likelihood of the hazard affecting them is smaller than or equal to risks they face on a daily basis with little or no thought, and are still afraid. When there are little or no means for people to gather information to make informed personal risk analyses, they tend to overestimate personal vulnerability because of incomplete and often incorrect information. Only information can combat fear, and only the government (in partnership with the media) can provide for that need.

On November 7, 2002, two people in New York City were hospitalized and confirmed to be infected with bubonic plague — the first cases in that city in more than 100 years. Bubonic plague is a disease that is historically one of the greatest killers of humankind, decimating over a third of the population of Europe during the Middle Ages. To the people of New York City, this disease was dreaded, new, fatal, globally catastrophic, involuntary, and notoriously hard to control. Why did fear not reign in New York when this information hit the newsstands? The answer lies in the way the information was first reported by Dr. Thomas Frieden, the health commissioner of New York City (a city that has in recent years experienced two major health crises — the first U.S. outbreak of West Nile virus and the anthrax letters in 2001). After announcing the two cases of the disease, Dr. Frieden made the following statement:

> *Bubonic plague does not spread from person to person. There is no risk to New Yorkers from the two individuals who are being evaluated for plague. Those patients became ill within 48 hours of arriving in New York City. Therefore, we are confident that their exposure occurred in New Mexico. More than half of the plague cases in the United States are in New Mexico. A wood rat and fleas from the rodent that were found on the couple's property in Santa Fe, New Mexico, tested positive in July for plague. Bubonic plague is a bacterial disease in rodents transmitted to humans through the bites of infected fleas (CNN, 2002).*

The story barely lasted a week.

Notes

1. Includes the District of Columbia, Northern Virginia, and several counties in Maryland. The population of this region, according to the 2000 census, is 4,922,640 (FAIR, 2002b).

2. While only one plane crashed into a building in the Washington, DC, metropolitan area (the Pentagon), it is believed that the plane that crashed into a Pennsylvania field was heading for either the White House or the U.S. Capitol (Lochhead, 2002).

3. As of late November 2002, the Brentwood Postal Facility, where the three postal workers who contracted anthrax worked, remained closed, with no planned reopening in the near future (Fernandez, 2002).

4. Presidential Decision Directive-39 (PDD39), signed by President Clinton in 1995, gives the Department of Justice, through the Federal Bureau of Investigation (FBI), lead agency authority in incidents where weapons of mass destruction are used or if the event is considered

terrorism (Watson, 2000). The sniper crisis was never officially classified as such, so Chief Moose remained in command.

5. Initially, MCPD spokeswoman Captain Nancy Demme was issuing statements to the media, but Chief Moose assumed the public relations role upon further consideration of the severity of the crisis.

6. Chief Moose, who holds a PhD in urban studies, was seen not only as a trustworthy leader but also as the lead decision maker. It was important that he addressed the media, considering all information passed through his hands — something a spokesperson of a lower rank could not claim. Moose was credited for his on-camera compassion, shedding tears on occasion, and uttering comments throughout the crisis that showed his "human" side. At one point, for instance, he urged parents to spend more time with their children (Sun and Ly, 2002).

7. In a *Washington Post* poll, 82% of respondents said that they approved of the way their local schools were handling the situation (*Washington Post*, 2002b).

8. Numbers attained by searching for the keyword "sniper," using the Lexis/Nexis "general news search" of 47 major newspapers from throughout the world.

9. Many people were affected by the secondary effects of the sniper, such as long traffic jams caused by roadblocks or school closings. However, as the direct consequence of the sniper was death or injury caused by shooting, only a very small group was *directly* affected.

10. Fear of crime, often cited as being overestimated by the public, is also mainly established through media coverage. In the 1990s, when the murder rate in the United States dropped by 20%, the murder coverage on network newscasts increased by 600%. As a result, 62% of Americans "believed crime was soaring, and described our society as 'truly desperate' about crime" (Jacobson, 2001).

11. The findings of this poll have been reinforced by other studies on the subject. When Esther Madriz, a professor at Hunter College in New York City, interviewed women in New York City about their fears of crime they frequently responded with the phrase "I saw it in the news." The interviewees identified the news media as both the source of their fears and the reason they believed those fears were valid. Asked in a national poll why they believe the country has a serious crime problem, 76% of people cited stories they had seen in the media. Only 22% cited personal experience (Glassner, 1999, p. xxi).

12. School security codes — Code Blue signifies that all outdoor activities are canceled and positive ID is required to enter the building, and Code Red signifies that students are locked in their classroom in case a threat actually exists within the building (Lambert, 2002).

13. In one of the most comprehensive roadblock systems set up after the October 22 shooting (which occurred during the morning rush-hour traffic), one person was quoted in the *Washington Post* as saying that, after getting off the highway and onto the back roads, "I didn't see a single police car on the way in [to his job in College Park, Maryland]. If you're trying to stop someone, you'd have to have a tighter net, and that simply wasn't there. I was a novice trying to make my way through, and it was fairly easy" (Layton and Shaver, 2002).

14. Mark Warr, a sociology professor at the University of Texas, Austin, writes, "People may experience fear merely in anticipation of possible threats or in reaction to environmental clues (e.g., darkness, graffiti) that imply danger" (Warr, 2000). To many people, the sight of ever-present white vans was a constant reminder that the sniper was still at large. To some, the sight of a white van was influential enough to elicit a physical response. A Connecticut business traveler, working in the area in a white Chevy van, stated, "I pull into a gas station, and people jump down. Little kids point and say, 'Look, the sniper'" (Snyder, 2002).

15. During the sniper crisis, it was reported in several newspapers that an al-Qaeda suspect in Belgium had admitted during interrogations that members of al-Qaeda had been trained in the

terrorist training camps to shoot targets from 50 to 250 meters. The suspect added that al-Qaeda planned to use snipers to kill U.S. senators while they were golfing (Reid, 2002).

16. In 1999, two students of Columbine High School in Littleton, Colorado, shot and killed 13 of their classmates. The extensive media coverage led to the public perception that school shootings were on the rise, when in fact, the incidence of school shootings was actually falling that year (Kisken, 2001).

17. As of November 15, the sniper case was still receiving daily front-page coverage in the *Washington Post*.

18. The sniper was by definition, both a serial killer and a mass murderer. Serial killers are defined as people who kill several people over a period of days, weeks, or years, killing in cycles, shifting between active and "cooling off" periods, while mass murderers kill several people at one time, usually in one location, over a couple of hours without a "cooling off" period (Macalester College, 2002).

19. After a media frenzy followed a series of high-profile child abductions during the early summer of 2001, there was great apprehension reported among parents who began to fear for the safety of their children. Later reports showed that the majority of child abductions were due to child custody disputes and not performed by strangers. The frenzy quickly died down once public knowledge about these facts became more common (STATS, 2002).

20. In addition, the sniper attacks waned in frequency over time, but this factor will not be considered because the sampling period was too short to derive a long-term frequency (*Economist*, 2002).

21. 2000 census information (FAIR, 2002a).

22. 2000 census information (FAIR, 2002b).

23. The murders that took place before this date were committed for the purposes of robbery or passion and are therefore not included in the analysis of population risk.

24. The number of people in the affected area (5,919,152) divided by the number of people shot during the sniper crisis (10, adjusted), times the year-adjustment multiplier (15.870).

25. The number of people in the affected area (5,919,152) divided by the number of people killed during the sniper crisis (7, adjusted), times the year-adjustment multiplier (15.870).

26. This is not an uncommon action for authorities to take. For instance, the Environmental Protection Agency's Science Advisory Board discovered that "agency resources tend to be directed to problems 'perceived' to be the most serious rather than those that actually pose the greatest threat" (Walsh, 1996).

27. Barry Glassner writes in *The Culture of Fear* that "the turnabout in [American] domestic public spending over the past quarter century, from child welfare and antipoverty programs to incarceration, did not . . . produce reductions in *fear* of crime. Increasing the number of cops and jails arguably has the opposite effect: It suggests that the crime problem is all the more out of control" (Glassner, 1999).

28. James Walsh (1996), author of *True Odds: How Risk Affects Your Everyday Life*, writes, "When European terrorism reared up in 1986, 2 million Americans changed their travel plans. The reality, of course, was that most of these people could have done a lot more to enhance their life expectancies by losing 10 pounds and going to Europe as planned."

29. In Loudoun County, Maryland, a community group formed after 9/11 to help people cope with the stress gave free public seminars to help people cope with the sniper stress (Helderman and Goldenbach, 2002).

30. Barry Glassner, author of *The Culture of Fear*, wrote, "Since the first sniper shooting October 2, a sort of domino effect has spurred decision-makers: School systems have decided, in conference calls with local law enforcement arranged through the Washington Council of Governments, to suspend all outdoor activities. Then day-care centers and youth soccer

leagues have followed the lead of their public school systems, and the smaller community groups have fallen into line" (Reel, 2002).

31. The anchoring and adjustment heuristic states that people use a natural starting point as a first approximation in analyzing how a risk affects them. The initial anchoring point is then adjusted as more information is received (Slovic, Fischhoff, and Lichtenstein, 1979). (Anchors are generally set according to the first information a person receives about a risk.)

32. In a CNN article titled "Sniper Probe 'Unprecedented' for Region," it was reported that "a conservative estimate would put at 1,000 the number of officers and experts from various federal, state, and local law enforcement officers assigned to the case, and the size of the investigation grows with each new development — and shooting — in the case" (Loughlin, 2002).

33. Irresponsible reporting has not only caused undue stress on numerous occasions, but has hurt local economies as well. In the 1990s the media widely reported on a crime wave against tourists in Florida, which resulted in 10 murders. Barry Glassner (1999), author of *The Culture of Fear*, writes that the event was labeled a crime wave only because the media chose to label it as such. "Objectively speaking, 10 murders out of 41 million visitors did not even constitute a ripple, much less a wave, especially considering that at least 97% of all victims of crime in Florida are Floridians. Although the Miami area had the highest crime rate in the nation during this period, it was not tourists who had most cause for worry. One study showed that British, German, and Canadian tourists who flock to Florida each year to avoid winter weather were more than 70 times more likely to be victimized at home." This type of reporting made many tourists think twice before traveling to Florida, and the tourism industry suffered as result.

34. Often, articles that proclaim bad news are given front-page coverage and are in great quantity while those reporting good news are given secondary status and appear less frequently (Johnson, 2002).

35. The phenomenon observed when people irrationally stock up on certain "survival" groceries they believe will be needed but unavailable after a disaster occurs.

36. People tend to heed government suggestions, so they should be rational and helpful, and most importantly, carefully thought out. During the anthrax crisis, when public fear was at epidemic levels, 36% of Americans were washing their hands after opening mail as the U.S. Postal Service had instructed them to do. In areas where people had actually contracted anthrax-related sicknesses, hand-washing incidence was higher — 45% in Washington, DC, and 57% in Trenton, New Jersey — this from an attack that killed only 5 of over 400 million people. People were not acting irrationally, but listening to the advice they had been told by their government (Pelton, 2001). The government warned the public not to hoard the antibiotic Cipro, but the media reported they were stockpiling the drug to such an extreme as to cause pharmacy shortages. Surveys showed that only 4% of Americans had bought the antibiotic against the advice of the government.

Key Terms

Risk Communication: Any communication intended to supply laypeople with the information they need to make informed, independent judgments about risks to health, safety, and the environment (Morgan *et al.*, 2002).

Crisis Communication: The provision of timely, useful, and accurate information to the public during the response and recovery phases of a disaster event.

Warning: The delivery of notice of an actual impending threat with sufficient time to allow recipient individuals and communities to take shelter, evacuate, or take other mitigative action in advance of a disaster event.

Mass Media: Channels of communication for popular consumption, which could include books, magazines, advertisements, newspapers, newsletters, radio, television, the Internet, cinema, theater, and videos, among many others.

News Media: A subcomponent of the mass media focused on presenting current news to the public.

Ready.Gov: A government-sponsored website developed by the Advertising Council to educate the public, businesses, and children about hazard risks in the United States.

Homeland Security Advisory System (HSAS): A color-coded chart used by the Department of Homeland Security to communicate the current terrorism threat to the American public, businesses, local and state governments, and other stakeholders.

Comprehensive Emergency Management: An emergency management philosophy that seeks to reduce risk and prevent injuries, damages, and fatalities, by treating hazards before, during, and after an event has occurred. There are generally four accepted functions performed in comprehensive emergency management: mitigation, preparedness, response, and recovery.

Review Questions

1. Identify and discuss the four critical assumptions underlying the crisis communications efforts of the Federal Emergency Management Agency (FEMA) in the 1990s.
2. Discuss the role of the mass media in risk and crisis communications.
3. Review the content and communication delivery mechanisms used in the Department of Homeland Security's Ready.gov campaign. Do you feel this is useful information that could effectively prepare the public for a disaster?
4. How would you reengineer the Homeland Security Advisory System (HSAS)? How many alert levels would you include, what colors and titles would you associate with each alert level, and what preparedness messages designed for individuals and communities would you associate with each alert level?
5. In reviewing the case study of the Washington, DC, sniper attacks, it is clear that Montgomery County Police Chief Charles Moose was the principal government spokesperson and appeared in front of the media daily. In many of his media appearances, Chief Moose had little information to share with the media and the public principally because of the sensitive nature of the ongoing criminal investigation to identify and comprehend the snipers. These media appearances were a unique opportunity for Chief Moose to deliver preparedness messages to the community. Identify those preparedness messages that Chief Moose did deliver to the community over the course of the sniper crisis and provide suggestions of additional preparedness messages he could have delivered.

References

Airline Industry Information (AII). 2002. "BALPA Issues Advice to Concerned Crew Traveling to Washington, DC." October 18.

Altheide, D.L. 2002. "Creating Fear: News and the Construction of Crisis." New York: Aldine de Gruyter.

Anderson, P. 2002. "Sniper Suspect Linked to Tacoma Shootings." *Seattlepi.com*, October 28. http://seattlepi.nwsource.com/local/93210_tacoma28ww.shtml.

Ansell, J., and Wharton, F. 1992. "Risk: Analysis, Assessment, and Management." Chichester, England: John Wiley & Sons.

Atwater, B.F., Marco, C.V., Bourgeois, J., Dudley, W.C., Hendley, J.W., II, and Stauffer, P.H. 1999. "Surviving a Tsunami — Lessons Learned from Chile, Hawaii, and Japan." Washington, DC: USGS Information Services.

The Australian. 2002. "Sniper Search Goes Airborne." *The Australian*, October 17, p. 8.

Barger, B. 2002. "At the Intersection of Bravado and Fear." *The Washington Post*, November(3), p. B2.

Barker, J. 2002. "Montgomery Seeks to Ensure Safety of Voters." *The Baltimore Sun*, October(22), p. 1B.

Bremer, A.L., and Bremer, P. 2002. "The Terrorist Threat." In *Terrorism: Informing the Public*, edited by N. Ethiel. Chicago: McCormick Tribune Foundation, pp. 14–39.

Brown, J.D., and Keller, S.N. 2000. "Can the Mass Media Be Healthy Sex Educators?" *Family Planning Perspectives*, 32(no. 5), pp. 255–256.

Bullock, J. 2003. Several interviews over a 2-month period with the former FEMA chief of staff. Washington, DC.

Burkhart, F.N. 1991. "Media, Emergency Warnings, and Citizen Response." Boulder, CO: Westview Press.

CBS News. 2002. "A Deadly Journey? Crimes and Clues." www.cbsnews.com/htdocs/maryland_murders/frame-source.html,540,400.

Centers for Disease Control and Prevention. 2002. "Suicide in the United States." National Center for Injury Prevention and Control. www.cdc.gov/ncipc/factsheets/suifacts.htm.

Chemical and Biological Arms Control Institute. 2002. "What Should We Know? Whom Should We Tell? Leveraging Communication and Information to Counter Terrorism and Its Consequences." Michael J. Powers, Project Director. Washington, DC, December.

Clines, F. 2002a. "Widening Fears, Few Clues as Sixth Death Is Tied to Sniper." *New York Times*, October 5, p. A1.

Clines, F. 2002b. "The Hunt for a Sniper." *New York Times*, October 15, p. A1.

CNN. 2002. "Bubonic Plague Suspected in NYC Visitors." CNN.com, November 7. www.cnn.com/2002/health/11/07/ny.plague/index.html.

Cohen, B.C. 1963. "The Press and Foreign Policy." Princeton, NJ: Princeton University Press.

Connor, T., and H. Kennedy. 2002. "Cops Flood Site of VA Shooting." *Daily News (New York)*, October 20, p. 3.

Coppola, C. P., MD. Series of interviews. Dr. Coppola operated on the 13-year-old boy who was shot at the middle school in Bowie, Maryland, on October 7, 2002.

Coppola, D. 2002. Research on public risk perception in Mexico City, Mexico.

De Morales, L. 2002. "Did on-the-Spot Coverage Put Lawmen on the Spot?" *The Washington Post*, October(24), p. C1.

Department of Homeland Security (DHS). 2003. Ready.gov website. Washington, DC: DHS. www.ready.gov.

Diaz, K., and Rourke, L.O. 2002. ""D.C. Area Breathes Easier, But Not Deeply." *Star Tribune (Minneapolis)*, October(25), p. 20A.

Disaster Management Center. 1995. "Disaster Preparedness." The University of Wisconsin. http://dmc.engr.wisc.edu/courses/preparedness/BB04-intro.html.

Dishneau, D. 2002. "Virginia Shooting Linked to Sniper Spree." *The Toronto Star*, October(6), p. A9.

Ebner, J., and L. Herring. 2002. "In Disasters, Panic Is Rare; Altruism Dominates." American Sociological Association, August 7. www.asanet.org/media/panic.html.

Eccleston, R. 2002. "Killings Have Washington Terrorized." *The Australian*, October(14), p. 12.

Economist. 2002. "The Logic of Irrational Fear." *The Economist*, October, p. 19.

Enders, J. 2001. "Measuring Community Awareness and Preparedness for Emergencies." *Australian Journal of Emergency Management*, Spring, pp. 52–59.

Federation for American Immigration Reform. 2002a. DC"PMSA." Washington, DC. www.fairus.org/html/msas/042dcwdc.htm.

Federation for American Immigration Reform. 2002b. "Richmond-Petersburg Metropolitan Area." www.fairus.org/html/msas/042varip.htm.

Fears, D., and Thomas-Lester, A. 2002. "Blacks Express Shock at Suspects' Identity." *The Washington Post*, October(26), p. A17.

Federal Bureau of Investigation. 2001. "Crime in the United States, 2000." *The Federal Bureau of Investigation (FBI) Uniform Crime Reports*. Washington, DC: FBI, October 22.

Federal Emergency Management Agency (FEMA). 1998. "Making Your Community Disaster Resistant: Project Impact Media Partnership Guide." Washington, DC: FEMA.

Federal Emergency Management Agency (FEMA). 1997. "Multi Hazard: Identification and Assessment." Washington, DC: FEMA.

Fernandez, M. 2002. "Brentwood Postal Plant Fumigation Postponed." *The Washington Post*, November(13), p. B3.

Fineman, H. 2002. "The 'Anxiety Election'." *National Affairs*, October(21), p. 32.

Furedi, F. 1997. "Culture of Fear: Risk-Taking and the Morality of Low Expectation." London: Cassell.

Furman, M. 2002. "Good Information Saves Lives." In *Terrorism: Informing the Public*, edited by N. Ethiel. Chicago: McCormick Tribune Foundation, pp. 54–57.

Gettleman, J. 2002. "The Hunt for a Sniper: The Scene." *New York Times*, October(21), p. A14.

Glassner, B. 1999. "The Culture of Fear." New York: Basic Books.

Government Executive Magazine. 2008. "DHS Says Responders Resistant to Communications Sharing." GovExec.Com. April 2. http://www.govexec.com/story_page.cfm?articleid=39677&sid=60.

Government Printing Office. 2002. U.S. Code Title 28, Part II, Chapter 33, Section 540B. www.access.gpo.gov/uscode/uscmain.html.

Haddow, G. 2003. Several interviews over a 2-month period with the former FEMA deputy chief of staff. Washington, DC.

Helderman, R., and Goldenbach, A. 2002. "Autumn's Diversions Disrupted." *The Washington Post*, October(20), p. T3.

Higham, S., and Kovaleski, S. 2002. "Encounters with Sniper Suspects." *The Washington Post*, November(3), p. A1.

Houston Chronicle. 2002. "Sniper's Score: 5 Shots, 5 Dead." *Houston Chronicle*, October(4), p. A1.

Hurdle, J. 2002. "Holidaying in the Line of Fire." *The Daily Telegraph (London)*, October(19), p. 4.

Instituto Ciudadano de Estudios Sobre la Inseguridad A.C. 2002. "Primera Encuesta Nacional sobre Inseguridad Publica en las Entidades Federativas." Mexico City. May.

Irvin, C.W., and Mattingly, D. 2002. "Anxiety Becomes Part of Daily Routine." *The Washington Post*, October(17), p. T3.

Jacobson, L. 2001. "Media — The Perception of Panic." *McGill Tribune via U-Wire*, November, p. 14.

Jardine, C.G., and Hrudey, S.E. 1997. "Mixed Messages in Risk Communication." *Risk Analysis*, 17(no. 4), pp. 489–498.

Johnson, D., and Finer, J. 2002. "Sniper Casts Shadow of Fear over Weekend." *The Washington Post*, October(13), p. C1.

Johnson, P. 2002. "Out in TV Land, 'Local News Is in Bad Shape'." *USA Today Online*, November, p. 11.

Johnson, P., and Moore, M. 2002. "Media Reports Touch Raw Nerves in Washington." *USA Today*, October(10), p. 2A.

Jones, E.F., Beniger, J.R., and Westoff, C.F. 1980. "Pill and IUD Discontinuation in the United States, 1970–1975: The Influence of the Media." *Family Planning Perspectives*, 12(no. 6), pp. 293–300.

Kennedy, H., Mbugua, M., and Pienciak, R. 2002. "Cops Hunt Two Targets." *The Daily News (New York)*, October(24), p. 2.

Kisken, T. 2001. "Climate of Fear Overblown, Sociologist Says." *Ventura County Star*, November(6), p. B1.

Kornblut, A. 2002. "Elusive Sniper Joins DC's Nightmares." *The Boston Globe*, October(20), p. A1.

Kovaleski, S., and Ruane, M. 2002a. "Hundreds of Leads to a Gunman." *The Washington Post*, October(7), p. A1.

Kovaleski, S., and Ruane, M. 2002b. "Boy, 13, Shot by Sniper at School." *The Washington Post*, October(8), p. A1.

Kovaleski, S., and Williams, M. 2002. "Experts Suggest Motive Is Tied to Crafts Store." *The Washington Post*, October(16), p. A13.

Kurtz, H. 2002. "The Leak that Sank the Suspects." *The Washington Post*, October(25), p. C1.

Lambert, R. 2002. "The Washington Sniper Is Not the Only Fear Stalking the United States Right Now." *The Times (London)*, October, p. 18.

Layton, L., and Shaver, K. 2002. "Experts, Travelers Question Efficacy of Massive Dragnets." *The Washington Post*, October(23), p. A17.

Lichtblau, E., and van Natta, D. 2002. "The Hunt for a Sniper." *New York Times*, October(25), p. A1.

Lippmann, W. 1922. "Public Opinion." New York: Free Press.

Lochhead, C. 2002. "One Year Later." *San Francisco Chronicle*, September(12), p. A17.

Loughlin, S. 2002. "Sniper Probe 'Unprecedented' for Region." CNN Washington Bureau, October, 24.

Macalester College. 2002. "Serial Killers." www
.macalester.edu/~psych/whathap/UBNRP/serialkillers/
serialkillers.html.

McCallum, D.B., Hammond, S.L., and Morris, L.
1990. "Public Knowledge of Chemical Risks in Six
Communities." Washington, DC: Georgetown University
Medical Center, Institute for Health Policy Analysis.

McCombs, M., and Shaw, D. 1972. "The Agenda-Setting
Function of Mass Media." *Public Opinion Quarterly*, 36,
pp. 176–187.

McCormick Tribune Foundation. 2002. "Terrorism:
Informing the Public." In *Cantigny Conference Series*,
edited by N. Ethiel. Chicago: McCormick Tribune
Foundation, pp. 173–193.

McDivitt, J.A., Zimicki, S., Hornik, R., and Abulaban,
A. 1993. "The Impact of the Healthcom Mass Media
Campaign on Timely Initiation of Breastfeeding in
Jordan." *Studies in Family Planning*, 24(no. 5), pp.
295–309.

Memmott, M. 2002a. "How to Cope? Keep Guard and
Spirits Up." *USA Today*, October(18), p. 6A.

Memmott, M. 2002b. "Fear May Be Overwhelming, But
So Are the Odds." *USA Today*, October(18), p. 6A.

METRO. 1998. "Washington Metropolitan Area Transit
Authority." National Transit Database. www.ntdprogram
.com/NTD/Profiles.nsf/1998+30+Largest+Agencies/
3030/$File/P3030.PDF.

Miga, A. 2002a. "Sniper 'Witness' Arrested." *The Boston
Herald*, October(19), p. 3.

Miga, A. 2002b. "Death Penalty Sought for Sniper." *The
Boston Herald*, October(26), p. 1.

Miga, A., and Rothstein, K. 2002. "Zeroing In." *The
Boston Herald*, October(24), p. 1.

Mileti, D.S. 1999. "Disasters by Design." Washington,
DC: Joseph Henry Press.

Miller, J. 2002. "Who? How? When? What? Where?"
In *Terrorism: Informing the Public*, edited by N. Ethiel.
Chicago: McCormick Tribune Foundation, pp. 50–54.

Moore, M.T. 2002. "Presentation at the NAS Natural
Disasters Roundtable." Washington, DC: National
Academy of Sciences, October 31.

Morello, C., Davenport, C., and Harris, H. 2002. "Pair
Seized in Sniper Attacks." *The Washington Post*,
October(25), p. A1.

Morello, C., and Stockwell, J. 2002. "No Attacks, No
Arrests, No Shortage of Anxiety." *The Washington Post*,
October(14), p. A1.

Morello, C., and White, J. 2002. "Eighth Killing Linked to
Sniper." *The Washington Post*, October(12), p. A1.

Morgan, M.G., Fischoff, B., Bostrom, A., and Atman,
C.J. 2002. "Risk Communication: A Mental Models
Approach." Cambridge: Cambridge University Press.

Morin, R., and Deane, C. 2002. "Half of Area Residents in
Fear, Post Poll Finds." *The Washington Post*, October(24),
p. A1.

Mullis, J.-P. 1998. "Persuasive Communication Issues in
Disaster Management." *Australian Journal of Emergency
Management*, Autumn, pp. 51–58.

Nakamura, D., and Davis, P. 2002. "Suddenly, D.C.
Gas Looks Cheap Enough." *The Washington Post*,
October(15), p. A7.

Naudet, J., and G. Naudet. 2001. September 11
Documentary. CBS. Two-hour film shot during the
September 11 World Trade Center attack response.

Nelken, D. 1987. "Selling Science: How the Press
Covers Science and Technology." New York: W.H.
Freeman.

Nielsen, S., and Lidstone, J. 1998. "Public Education and
Disaster Management: Is There Any Guiding Theory?"
Australian Journal of Emergency Management, Spring,
pp. 14–19.

Ottawa Citizen. 2002. "Canadians Told to Avoid
Washington." *The Ottawa Citizen*, October(13),
p. A8.

Partnership for Public Warning (PPW). 2003. "A National
Strategy for Integrated Dissemination of Public Policy and
Capability." http://www.partnershipforpublicwarning
.org/ppw/docs/nationalstrategy.pdf.

Partnership for Public Warning (PPW). 2008. "PPW
Mission." http://www.partnershipforpublicwarning
.org/ppw/about.html#mission.

Patrick, A. 2002. "Eight Dead, But Still No Real Clues."
Sunday Age (Melbourne), October(13), p. 1.

Pelton, T. 2001. "36% of Americans Wash Up After
Handling Mail." *The Baltimore Sun*, December(18),
p. 8A.

Perspectives.org. 2002. "Friend's Apparent Accidental
Shot Lodges Near Brain." www.perspectivescs.org/guns/
example2.htm.

Phillips, C. 2002. "Malvo Spent Childhood Looking for Father Figure." *The Seattle Times*, November(21), p. A1.

Pienciak, R., and Kennedy, H. 2002. "Sniper's Ransom." *The Daily News (New York)*, October(22), p. 3.

Piotrow, P.T., Rimon, J.G., Winnard, K., Kincaid, D.L., Huntington, D., and Convisser, J. 1990. "Mass Media Family Planning Promotion in Three Nigerian Cities." *Studies in Family Planning*, 21(no. 5), pp. 265–274.

Raphael, B. 1986. "When Disaster Strikes: How Individuals and Communities Cope with Catastrophes." New York: Basic Books.

Rashbaum, W., and Flynn, K. 2002. "Sniper Hits a Teacher at Stuyvesant Town." *New York Times*, October(3), p. B1.

Reel, M. 2002. "A Region Running Scared?" *The Washington Post*, October(19), p. A1.

Reid, T. 2002. "Al Qaeda Trained Snipers for U.S. Attacks." *The Times (London)*, October(19), p. 21.

Rennie, D. 2002. "Sniper Stretches City's Nerves to Breaking Point." *The Daily Telegraph (London)*, October(22), p. 10.

Ropeik, D. 2002a. "Fear Factors in an Age of Terrorism." *MSNBC Online*, October, p. 15.

Ropeik, D. 2002b. "We Should Fear Too Much Fear." *Milwaukee Journal Sentinel*, October(23), p. 23A.

Ropeik, D. 2002c. "Presentation on Risk Perception." The National Academy of Sciences Roundtable on Natural Disasters, October, p. 31.

Ruane, M., and Stockwell, J. 2002. "Montgomery Bus Driver Fatally Shot." *The Washington Post*, October(23), p. A1.

Schulte, B. 2002. "Schools Shaken by Threat But Won't Shut Down." *The Washington Post*, October(23), p. A1.

Self Knowledge. 2002. "Definition of Fear." www.selfknowledge.com/35217.htm.

Shales, T. 2002. "TV News Feels Its Way in Dark Times." *The Washington Post*, October(23), p. C1.

Shrader-Frechette, K.S. 1991. "Risk and Rationality." Berkeley: University of California Press.

Singer, E., and Endreny, P.M. 1993. "Reporting on Risk: How the Mass Media Portray Accidents, Diseases, Disasters, and Other Hazards." New York: Russell Sage Foundation.

Slovic, P. 1986. "Informing and Educating the Public about Risk." *Risk Analysis*, 6(no. 4), pp. 403–415.

Slovic, P., Fischhoff, B., and Lichtenstein, S. 1996. "Cognitive Processes and Societal Risk Taking." In *Cognition and Social Behavior 165–184*, edited by J.S. Carroll and J.W. Payne. Potomac, MD: Lawrence Erlbaum Associates.

Slovic, P., Fischhoff, B., and Lichtenstein, S. 1980. "Facts and Fears: Understanding Perceived Risk." In *Societal Risk Assessment: How Safe Is Safe Enough?*, edited by R. Schwing, and W.A. Albers Jr. *181–214* New York: Plenum.

Slovic, P., Fischhoff, B., and Lichtenstein, S. 1979. "Rating the Risks." *Environment*, 21(no. 3), pp. 14–20, 36–39.

Snyder, D. 2002. "Fear Is Traveling the Lanes of I-95." *The Washington Post*, October(21), p. A14.

STATS. 2002. "Abducting the Headlines." www.stats.org/newsletters/0208/abduction.htm.

Stephen, A. 2002. "America — Andrew Stephen Reports on Panic in Washington." *New Statesman*, Ltd, October, p. 22.

Stockwell, J., Ruane, M., and White, J. 2002. "Man Shot to Death at Pr. William Gas Station." *The Washington Post*, October(10), p. A1.

Sun, L.H., and Ly, P. 2002. "Story 'Not About Me,' Reserved Moose Says." *The Washington Post*, October(28), p. A10.

Thomas, P. 2003. "The Anthrax Attacks." New York: The Century Foundation, June 1.

Timberg, C., and Shear, M. 2002. "Dragnet Comes Up Empty Again." *The Washington Post*, October(21), p. A1.

Tresniowski, A., Podesta, J.S., Morehouse, M., and Billups, A. 2002. "Stalked by Fear." *People Magazine*, October(28), p. 58.

Twomey, J. 2001. "Media Fuels Fear about Youth Crime." *The Baltimore Sun*, May(13), p. 1C.

Vulliami, E. 2002. "America Stays Indoors as Sniper Roams Free." *The Observer*, October(13), p. 1.

Walker, W. 2002. "Terror Grips D.C. Region." *Toronto Star*, October(23), p. A20.

Wallace, C. 2002. "A New Kind of Killer?" ABC News, October, p. 15.

Walsh, J. 1996. "True Odds: How Risk Affects Your Everyday Life." Santa Monica, CA: Merritt Publishing.

Ward, B. 2001. "History's Lessons Lost in the Turmoil." *The Ottawa Citizen*, September(18), p. A10.

Warner, K.E. 1989. "The Epidemiology of Coffin Nails." In *Health Risks and the Press: Coverage on Media Coverage of Risk Assessment and Health* 73–88, edited by M. Moore. Washington, DC: The Media Institute.

Warr, M. 2000. "Fear of Crime in the United States: Avenues for Research and Policy." In *Measurement and Analysis of Crime and Justice 451–489*, edited by D. Duffee. Rockville, MD: National Institute of Justice.

Washington Post. 2002a. "Crime and Justice." *The Washington Post*, October(3), p. B2.

Washington Post. 2002b. "Washington Area Sniper Poll." *The Washington Post*, October, 24.

Watson, D. 2000. Statement of Mr. Dale Watson, Asst. Director, FBI Counterterrorism Division, before the Subcommittee on National Security. U.S. House of Representatives, March 22.

Watson, R. 2002. "Suburbs in Terror of the Beltway Sniper after Boy Is Shot." *The Times (London)*, October, p. 8.

Waugh, W.L., Jr 2000. "Living with Hazards, Dealing with Disasters: An Introduction to Emergency Management." New York: M.E. Sharpe.

Wenham, B. 1994. "The Media and Disasters: Building a Better Understanding." In *International Disaster Communications: Harnessing the Power of Communications to Avert Disasters and Save Lives*, edited by Fred H. Cate. Washington, DC: The Annenberg Washington Program. http://www.annenberg.northwestern.edu/pubs/disas/disas6.htm.

Westoff, C.F., and Rodriguez, G. 1995. "The Mass Media and Family Planning in Kenya." *International Family Planning Perspectives*, 21(no. 1), pp. 26–31, 36.

Whitlock, C. 2002. "The Sniper Case: Out of 90,000 Calls, Just 3 Broke It Open." *Post Gazette (Pittsburgh)*, October 25. www.post-gazette.com/nation/20021025probenat2p2.asp.

Wiggins, C. 2002. "Warm Waters Attract People and Sharks." *The Standard (Baker County)*, March, p. 27.

Willis, J. 1997. "Reporting on Risks: The Practice and Ethics of Health and Safety Communication." Westport, CT: Praeger.

Wilson, R. 1979. "Analyzing the Daily Risks of Life." *Technology Review*, 81(no. 4), pp. 41–46.

Winston, J.A. 1985. "Science and the Media: The Boundaries of Truth." *Health Affairs*, 6, pp. 5–23.

Witzer, M. 1997. "In Sub-Saharan Africa, Levels of Knowledge and Use of Contraceptives Are Linked to Media Exposure." *International Family Planning Perspectives*, 23(no. 4), pp. 183–184.

9

Technology

What You Will Learn

- How homeland security research and development funding is distributed among various federal government agencies
- What research and development efforts are performed by the Department of Homeland Security, and by what offices that work is done
- Where in the federal government structure research and development are performed in the areas of weapons of mass destruction and information and infrastructure
- The names and functions of the various government research facilities
- The source and function of maritime homeland security research
- Where homeland security research and development efforts are occurring outside the Department of Homeland Security

Introduction

While addressing the Piedmont Triad Partnership (a North Carolina business association) in 2003, Department of Homeland Security (DHS) Undersecretary Charles McQueary stated that, "If I were asked to describe the Department of Homeland Security, I would say it's a story about science and technology." This quotation clearly asserted the emphasis that DHS had and continues to place on homeland security technologies. The astounding funding levels dedicated to technology research and development (R&D) only serve as further testimony in support of McQueary's statements. Technology is the fastest developing field in the homeland security effort, and it continually changes and improves as it proceeds. Technology has revolutionized not only the field of emergency management, but has drastically affected government operations, national defense, the efforts and progress of the national laboratory, research and development facilities, and the work at the nation's universities. Technology is likely to transform the way all scientific work is conducted in the future.

DHS announced at the time of its establishment that it "is committed to using cutting-edge technologies and scientific talent" to create a safer country. In this vein, the Directorate of Science and Technology (S&T) was formed, which still exists today despite the many iterations of DHS organizational change. The S&T Directorate was tasked under the original development plans with assuming the research needs of the new department, and for organizing the scientific, engineering, and technological resources of the country in order to adapt their use to the newly recognized needs under the counterterrorism drive created by the September 11, 2001, terrorist attacks. Universities, the private sector, and federal laboratories have all become important DHS partners in this endeavor.

Tens of billions of dollars have already been spent by DHS and other agencies with related missions on developing and exploiting technologies for use in the fight against terrorism and, on occasion, for emergency management in general. As is true in all areas of research, not all of the technology developed has been successful, although many innovative and useful systems have resulted. These efforts come not without critics, and many people have expressed sentiments that the push toward increased use of technological solutions does not necessarily decrease vulnerabilities, but rather increases reliance on technologies that could fail. For this reason, there remains significant dissent over the actual overall value of technology as a homeland security tool.

Despite these controversies, it is undeniable that the way of life in the United States has changed as the result of a great investment in technology by the federal government. This chapter will examine that investment and offer different views on its value.

Overview of Involved Agencies and Budgets

Although the Department of Homeland Security has the most prominent stake in homeland security–related research efforts, there are many other agencies that are involved in homeland security R&D efforts dispersed throughout the federal government. As DHS was gaining center-stage prominence in the homeland security effort and was emerging as a leading agency for these issues, many research and scientific programs were under way under the other agencies' management that preceded the Department's creation. The efforts of these organizations were almost immediately given new direction and resources to use in the fight against a more prominent terrorist hazard — a "shot in the arm," so to speak. Table 9–1 lists the agencies involved in the homeland security R&D field and their recent budgets. Overall, the total federal investment in homeland security R&D in FY 2008 totaled about $4.902 billion, up almost 4.5% from the FY 2007 budget ($4.691 billion). Figures 9–1 and 9–2 show funding distribution by agencies and years.

Department of Homeland Security

Before the establishment of DHS, most R&D efforts dealing with issues relevant to homeland security were dispersed among a wide variety of agencies, and this situation remains. However, the clear trend since 2003 has been to make DHS a focus for such R&D, and as of 2008 over one-fifth of all R&D funding is managed by DHS (placing it second only after HHS). Inside DHS, the S&T Directorate has been established in order to coordinate and manage R&D efforts. For the first three years of the directorate's existence, R&D efforts were dispersed throughout the various directorates and independent agencies (e.g., the Coast Guard). However, as early as FY 2006, all R&D efforts were consolidated under S&T. A more detailed description of S&T and the research this directorate conducts follows.

Table 9–1 Federal Homeland Security R&D Appropriations ($ millions)

Agency	FY 2002	FY 2003	FY 2004	FY 2005	FY 2006	FY 2007	FY 2008
Agriculture	175	155	40	161	105	45	129
Commerce	20	16	23	73	62	59	68
DOD	259	212	267	1079	1270	1175	1278
Energy	50	48	47	67	68	68	71
DHS	266	737	1,028	1,240	1,300	1,005	996
EPA	95	70	52	33	40	41	53
HHS	177	1,653	1,724	1,795	1,827	1,829	1,815
NASA	73	73	88	89	93	97	94
NSF	229	271	321	326	329	329	357
DOT	106	7	3	2	3	1	2
All Others	0	0	32	42	41	42	40
Total	**1,451**	**3,243**	**3,626**	**4,893**	**5,138**	**4,691**	**4,902**

Source: Office of Management and Budget, "Budget of the U.S. Government FY 2008," 2008, http://www.whitehouse.gov/omb/budget/fy2008/.

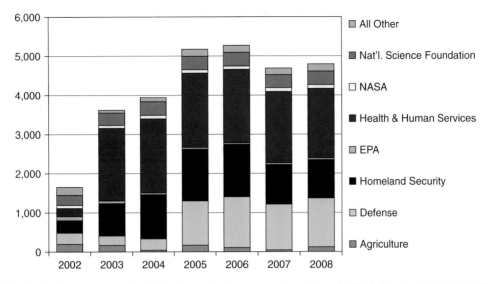

FIGURE 9–1 Federal homeland security R&D budget authority by agency (in millions of dollars). (Source: American Association for the Advancement of Science, based on Office of Management and Budget data, March 2007)

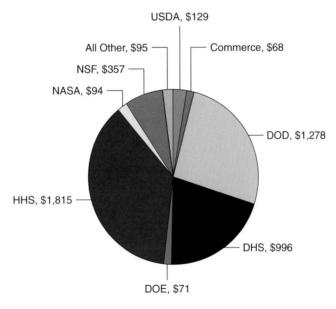

FIGURE 9–2 Distribution of the FY 2006 federal funds between agencies (in millions of dollars). (Source: American Association for the Advancement of Science, based on Office of Management and Budget data, March 2007)

DHS Directorate of Science and Technology

The Science and Technology Directorate (S&T), led by an undersecretary of homeland security, is the primary R&D office within the Department of Homeland Security. Since August 10, 2006, S&T has been led by Jay M. Cohen. The S&T Directorate underwent a major reorganization in late 2006 as stipulated by Secretary Chertoff's six-point plan (Figure 9–3). This realignment led to the creation of six major divisions and four offices, each of which is described in the following sections.

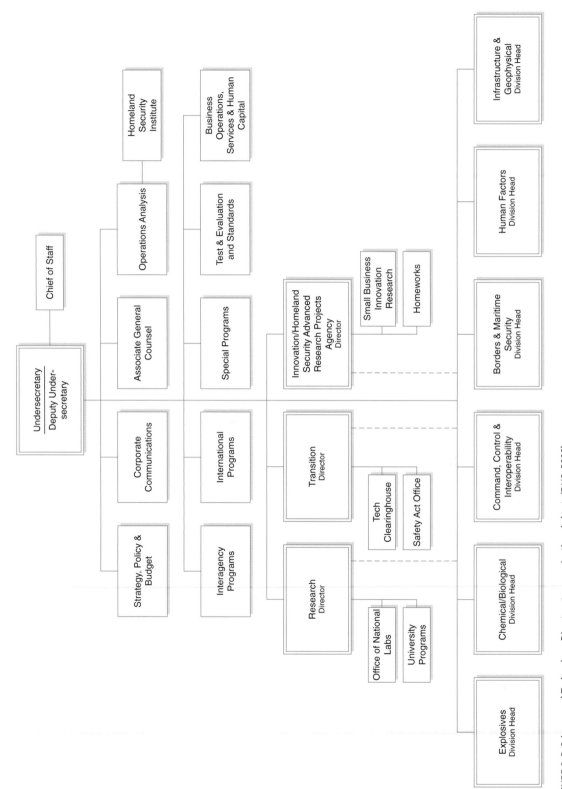

FIGURE 9–3 Science and Technology Directorate organizational chart. (DHS, 2008)

S&T Divisions

Borders and Maritime Security Division — Develops tools and technologies that improve the security of borders and waterways.

Chemical and Biological Division — Works to increase preparedness against chemical and biological threats through improved threat awareness, advanced surveillance and detection, and protective countermeasures.

Command, Control, and Interoperability Division — Develops interoperable communication standards and protocols for emergency responders, cybersecurity tools for maintaining Internet integrity, and automated capabilities to recognize and analyze potential threats.

Explosives Division — Develops the technical capabilities to detect, interdict, and reduce the impacts of non-nuclear explosives used in terrorist attacks against mass transit, civil aviation, and critical infrastructure.

Human Factors Division — Applies the social and behavioral sciences to improve detection, analysis, and understanding and response to homeland security threats.

Infrastructure and Geophysical Division — Focuses on identifying and mitigating the vulnerabilities of critical infrastructure and key assets that are integral to social and economic stability.

S&T Programs

Homeland Security Centers of Excellence — Bring together leading experts and researchers to conduct multidisciplinary homeland security research and education. The centers are authorized by Congress and chosen by S&T through a competitive selection process. Each center is led by a university in collaboration with partners in other institutions, agencies, laboratories, think tanks, and the private sector. The Centers are listed in the sidebar, "Homeland Security Centers of Excellence."

Homeland Security Institute — The Department's first government "think tank" or federally funded research and development center. This program regularly publishes journals, newsletters, and reports detailing the latest trends and advancements in homeland security, including the *Journal of Homeland Security* (http://www.homelandsecurity.org/newjournal/), and the *Homeland Security Weekly Newsletter* (http://www.homelandsecurity.org/Newsletter Archives.aspx).

Innovation — Oversees the Homeland Security Advanced Research Projects Agency (HSARPA), focusing on homeland security R&D that could lead to significant technology breakthroughs and greatly enhance departmental operations.

Laboratory Facilities — Programs are executed through the Office of National Laboratories (ONL). ONL provides a "coordinated, enduring core of productive science, technology, and engineering laboratories, organizations, and institutions, which can provide the knowledge and technology required to secure the Nation" (DHS, 2008, www.dhs.gov).

SAFECOM — The federal umbrella program designed to foster first-responder interoperability R&D. This program is supported by the DHS Office of Emergency Communications.

SAFETY Act — Provides liability protections for sellers of qualified antiterrorism technologies. The Support Anti-Terrorism by Fostering Effective Technologies Act of 2002 provides the statutory authority for such an endeavor. The SAFETY Act provides incentives for the development and deployment of antiterrorism technologies by creating a system of "risk management" and a system of "litigation management." The purpose of the Act is to ensure that the threat of liability does not deter potential manufacturers or sellers of antiterrorism technologies from developing and commercializing technologies that could feasibly save lives. The Act creates certain liability limitations for "claims arising out of, relating to, or resulting from an act of terrorism," where qualified antiterrorism technologies have been deployed.

TechSolutions — Provides information, resources, and technology solutions that address mission capability gaps identified by the emergency response community. The program's goal is to field technologies that meet 80% of their operational requirement in a 12- to 15-month timeframe, and at a cost commensurate with the proposal but less than $1 million per project. Goals are accomplished through rapid prototyping or the identification of existing technologies that satisfy identified requirements. First responders are able to submit technology gaps that they identify to the program in order to help guide the direction of technologies that are developed.

Test and Evaluation and Standards — Provides technical support and coordination to assist the nation's emergency responders in the acquisition of equipment, procedures, and mitigation processes that are safe, reliable, and effective

University Programs — Engages the academic community to create learning and research environments in areas critical to homeland security. One of the key initiatives of this program is the DHS Scholarship and Fellowship Program, which provides tuition and other financing for students pursuing degrees in fields associated with homeland security.

Homeland Security Centers of Excellence

Center for Risk and Economic Analysis of Terrorism Events (CREATE), led by the University of Southern California, evaluates the risks, costs, and consequences of terrorism, and guides economically viable investments in countermeasures that make the nation safer and more secure.

National Center for Food Protection and Defense (NCFPD), led by the University of Minnesota, defends the safety of the food system from pre-farm inputs through consumption by establishing best practices, developing new tools, and attracting new researchers to prevent, manage, and respond to food contamination events.

National Center for Foreign Animal and Zoonotic Disease Defense (FAZD), led by Texas A&M University, protects against the introduction of high-consequence foreign animal and zoonotic diseases into the United States, with an emphasis on prevention, surveillance, intervention, and recovery.

National Consortium for the Study of Terrorism and Responses to Terrorism (START), led by the University of Maryland, informs decisions on how to disrupt terrorists and terrorist groups, while strengthening the resilience of U.S. citizens to terrorist attacks.

National Center for the Study of Preparedness and Catastrophic Event Response (PACER), led by Johns Hopkins University, optimizes our nation's preparedness in the event of a high-consequence natural or man-made disaster, as well as develops guidelines to best alleviate the effects of such an event.

Center for Advancing Microbial Risk Assessment (CAMRA), led by Michigan State University and established jointly with the U.S. Environmental Protection Agency (EPA), fills critical gaps in risk assessments for decontaminating microbiological threats — such as plague and anthrax — answering the question, "How clean is safe?"

University Affiliate Centers to the Institute for Discrete Sciences (IDS-UACs) are led by Rutgers University, the University of Southern California, the University of Illinois at Urbana-Champaign, and the University of Pittsburgh. They collaborate with IDS, based at Lawrence Livermore National Laboratory, to conduct research on advanced methods for information analysis and the development of computational technologies to protect the nation.

Regional Visualization and Analytics Centers (RVACs) are led by Penn State University, Purdue University, Stanford University, the University of North Carolina at Charlotte, and the University of Washington. They collaborate with the National Visualization and Analytics Center, based at Pacific Northwest National Laboratory, to conduct research on visually-based analytic techniques that help people gain insight from complex, conflicting, and changing information.

In February 2008, the DHS announced a new round of grants that will help to create five new Centers of Excellence, each co-chaired by two or three universities. These new centers include:

- **Center of Excellence for Border Security and Immigration** is led by the University of Arizona at Tucson and the University of Texas at El Paso. The new center will conduct research and develop technologies, tools, and advanced methods to balance immigration and commerce with border security. Their focus will be to assess threats and vulnerabilities, improve surveillance and screening, analyze immigration trends, and help to enhance policy and law enforcement efforts.
- **Center of Excellence for Explosives Detection, Mitigation, and Response** is led by Northeastern University in Boston, MA, and the University of Rhode Island in Kingston. The new center will conduct research to evaluate the risks, costs, and consequences of terrorism, and develop new methods to protect the nation. Their primary focus will be to detect improvised explosive devices, enhance aviation cargo security, provide next-generation baggage screening, detect liquid explosives, and enhance suspicious passenger identification.
- **Center of Excellence for Maritime, Island, and Port Security** is led by the University of Hawaii in Honolulu and Stevens Institute of Technology in Hoboken, NJ. The new center will conduct research and develop new ways to strengthen maritime security and safeguard populations and properties unique to U.S. islands and other remote and extreme environments. Examples include protecting the Alaskan Pipeline and other infrastructure and enhancing response and recovery plans for natural disaster threats like earthquakes and tsunamis.
- **Center of Excellence for Natural Disasters, Coast Infrastructure, and Emergency Management** will be led by the University of North Carolina at Chapel Hill and Jackson State University in Jackson, MS. The new center will conduct research on safeguarding populations, properties, and economies as it relates to the consequences of catastrophic natural disasters.
- **The Center of Excellence for Transportation Security** will be led by Texas Southern University in Houston, Tougaloo College in Tougaloo, MS, and the University of Connecticut. The new center will conduct research and develop new technologies, tools, and advanced methods to defend, protect, and increase the resilience of transportation infrastructure.

Source: DHS, 2008, www.DHS.gov

S&T Budget

The amount of funding under the overall DHS budget dedicated to science and technology has steadily risen each year since the department's creation. This growth signifies the steadily increasing role that technology is taking on in modern emergency management, especially in the area of terrorism prevention and response. It is important to remember that these funds are only in addition to similar project funds being supplied by many other federal agencies, which together comprise a much

Table 9–2   Department of Homeland Security R&D (S&T Directorate) Budget
($ millions)

FY 2004	FY 2005	FY 2006	FY 2007	FY 2008	FY 2009
$912,751	$1,115,450	$1,467,075	$846,916	$830,118	$868,837 (requested)

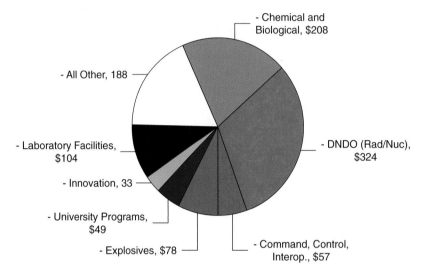

FIGURE 9–4 S&T budget allocations within DHS (in millions of dollars). (Source: American Association for the Advancement of Science, December 2007)

larger homeland security–related R&D budget. Table 9–2 and Figure 9–4 illustrate the DHS-specific S&T budget allocation.

The S&T Directorate is responsible for setting the national agenda and giving direction and setting priorities for R&D efforts in other departments and agencies, regardless of the funding source. S&T is unique among federal R&D agencies in that it has responsibility for the entire cycle of science and technology (i.e., from product research to bringing the product to the market and deploying it).

The S&T Directorate has established the Homeland Security Advanced Research Project Agency (HSARPA). This agency, based on the existing model of the Defense Advanced Research Project Agency (DARPA) in the Department of Defense, distributes resources within the directorate, awards money for the extramural grants, develops and tests potential technologies, and accelerates or prototypes development of technologies for deployment. The directorate has also created a Homeland Security Advisory Committee consisting of 20 members appointed by the undersecretary representing first responders, citizen groups, researchers, engineers, and businesses to provide science and technology advice to the undersecretary. DHS has also created a new federally funded R&D center (FFRDC), the Homeland Security Institute, to act as a think tank for risk analyses, simulations of threat scenarios, analyses of possible countermeasures, and strategic plans for counterterrorism technology development. The various federal agencies involved in homeland security R&D are listed in the sidebar titled, "Federal Agencies Involved in Homeland Security R&D." Various successes identified by DHS are listed in the sidebar "Science and Technology Directorate Accomplishments."

Federal Agencies Involved in Homeland Security R&D

Department of Homeland Security — DHS R&D was decreased in both FY 2007 (from $1.3 billion to $1.005 billion) and FY 2008 (to $996 million), primarily because of congressional frustration with DHS R&D operations, and the feeling that it grew too rapidly in the aftermath of September 11 and needed to be cut back. Research on radiological and nuclear countermeasures has continued to increase, in FY 2008 over 17% to $320 million in the recently separated Domestic Nuclear Detection Office (DNDO). Science and Technology (S&T) Directorate funding, however, fell for a second year in a row, cutting funding in most R&D areas. The Innovation program created under the reorganization of the Directorate led to an increase in funding for the development of "revolutionary technological breakthroughs" from $38 million to $60 million. Funding for University and Fellowship Programs, a key R&D component, fell for a third year in a row to $39 million.

Department of Health and Human Services — In FY 2008, $1.7 billion of the $1.815 billion in Department of Health and Human Services (HHS) homeland security R&D funding is going to biodefense research, a decrease from the previous two years. The amount dedicated to actual research increased, however, as previous research budgets included construction costs of new laboratories. The vast majority of these research activities is performed through the National Institutes of Health (NIH) and the Centers for Disease Control and Prevention (CDC). The counterterrorism portfolio now includes not only the traditional biodefense research portfolio but also chemical threats and nuclear/radiological threats (including the development of medical countermeasures against each).

Department of Defense — The Department of Defense (DOD) increased its homeland security R&D by 1% in FY 2008, up to $765 million from the previous year to a total of $79 billion. Weapons development is a major part of both the increase of 5.5% or $3.5 billion) and the total DOD research budget of $68.1 billion, including $2.9 billion in development funds requested as part of a 2008 war supplemental funding bill. Science and Technology, however, experienced a 20.1% loss in funding levels ($2.8 billion cut, resulting in $10.9 billion total), which erased seven years of gains. Even the notorious Defense Advanced Research Projects Agency (DARPA) saw its budget fall 1% to $3.1 billion. Of this entire budget allocation, only $1.278 billion is reserved for homeland security activities.

Department of Agriculture — The U.S. Department of Agriculture (USDA) saw a large (189.7%) increase in homeland security R&D funding in 2008 to a total of $129 million. Of this amount, the greatest percentage is dedicated to finding security solutions for the nation's food and agriculture. Of the total, $58 million are earmarked to strengthen research in areas such as improving vaccines and identifying genes affecting disease resistance, automated diagnostic methods to rapid detection and identification of pathogens and chemical contaminants, rapid response systems to bioterror agents, and conducting genomic analyses of priority pathogens of livestock and wildlife species to advance vaccine discovery. In recognition of the pandemic influenza threat, $4.5 million has been earmarked for avian influenza research.

Environmental Protection Agency — Funding for homeland security R&D within the EPA was at its highest in 2002, just after the September 11 attacks, when it totaled $95 million. It has fallen since, with $53 million budgeted in FY 2008. A good portion of this funding is devoted to protecting drinking water supplies against terrorist attack through vulnerability assessments and a laboratory network for surveillance. The EPA homeland security R&D budget funds the agency's National Homeland Security Research Center

(NHSRC), which conducts R&D on a wide variety of terrorist threats that may have an impact on the natural environment, such as radiation, drinking water contamination, and the environmental impacts of clean-up technologies after a terrorist attack.

National Institutes of Standards and Technology — The R&D efforts of the National Institute of Standards and Technology (NIST), under the Department of Commerce, is funded at its highest levels ever in FY 2008 ($68 million). This funding is dedicated to cryptography and computer security and providing other scientific and technical support to DHS in these and other areas.

National Science Foundation — The National Science Foundation (NSF) funds research to combat bioterrorism in the areas of infectious diseases and microbial genome sequencing. These programs increased 8.5% to $357 million in FY 2008.

Department of Energy — The focus of the Department of Energy (DOE) homeland security R&D budget (which amounts to $71 billion in FY2008, a 3.8% increase over the previous year) involves countering terrorist threats to energy facilities, most notably those that house radiological or nuclear materials.

Source: American Association for the Advancement of Science, 2007, www.aaas.org.

Science and Technology Directorate Accomplishments

Launched Air Cargo Explosives Detection Pilot Program — The S&T Directorate launched this program at San Francisco International Airport and at Seattle-Tacoma International Airport, to capture vital information associated with enhanced air cargo screening and inspection, and will provide critical knowledge to help the Transportation Security Administration (TSA) make future decisions and assist in technological R&D planning for the national air cargo security infrastructure.

Released National Interoperability Baseline Survey Results — The Office for Interoperability and Compatibility's SAFECOM program released the final results of its National Interoperability Baseline Survey, fielded earlier this year to measure the capacity for interoperable communications among emergency response agencies nationwide. By identifying the nation's interoperability capacities, survey findings will help policymakers and emergency response leaders make informed decisions about strategies for improving interoperability and target resources. The landmark analysis surveyed 22,400 law enforcement, fire, and emergency medical service agencies nationwide and had a response rate of approximately 30%.

Conducted TSA Rail Security Explosives Detection Pilot Programs — Rail Security Explosives Detection Pilot Programs were conducted in Baltimore, MD, and Jersey City, NJ, to test and evaluate security equipment and operative procedures as part of DHS's broader efforts to protect citizens and critical infrastructure from possible terrorist attacks.

Held Groundbreaking for National Biodefense Analysis and Countermeasures Center — The S&T Directorate started construction on a new facility to house research activities that directly support S&T Directorate biological and agricultural terrorism countermeasures programs. Activities are presently conducted through two centers at interim facilities, the Biological Threat Characterization Center and the National Bioforensics Analysis Center (NBFAC). The new NBACC will be roughly 160,000 square feet and house a staff of approximately 120.

Initiated Development of Cargo Security Prototypes — The S&T Directorate started developing prototypes of a technology that will significantly heighten the security of cargo containers. Known as the Advanced Container Security Device (ACSD), the technology is an in-container sensor capable of detecting and warning of intrusion on any side of a container, its door openings, or the presence of people hiding within a container.

Flight Tested Counter-MANPADS Technologies — The S&T Directorate completed Phase II of a multiphase program to migrate military countermeasures technology to commercial aircraft to protect against shoulder-fired, anti-aircraft missiles known as man-portable air defense systems (MANPADS). During Phase II, prototype counter-MANPADS systems were integrated onto aircraft and the Federal Aviation Administration (FAA) certified their safety and airworthiness. Additionally, the S&T Directorate initiated Phase III of the program, selecting three firms to receive $7.4 million in combined contract awards to assess alternative methods to counter the MANPADS threat.

Demonstrated a Wireless Border Security Communications Network — The S&T Directorate installed and tested an initial Border Network (BorderNet) prototype, enabling border patrol officers to remotely access databases, sensor alerts, and geo-spatial information via vehicle-mounted computers and handheld devices. BorderNet is a wireless communication network that, when fully established, will connect law enforcement officers in the field to real-time information from law enforcement databases and geographic information systems.

Tested System That Increased Boarding Team Communications Capability by 50% — The S&T Directorate tested a repeater-based communications system that permits communication among boarding team members, no matter where they are in the ship. Repeaters are small transmission devices that are deployed like breadcrumbs as officers enter and search a ship. With small breadcrumb repeaters widely distributed throughout the ship, 100% connectivity between boarding team members was maintained in areas that provided less than 50% connectivity without repeaters.

Enhanced BioWatch Capabilities — While operating the baseline BioWatch monitoring system in approximately 30 cities, the S&T Directorate continued to develop Biowatch enhancements (Generation 2) to provide better spatial coverage and indoor detection capabilities for the nation's top 10 threat cities. In addition, the Biological Warning and Incident Characterization (BWIC) system was piloted in two BioWatch cities. BWIC interprets warning signals from BioWatch, public health surveillance data, and incident characterization tools (plume and epidemiologic models) to quickly determine the impacts a release may have.

Improved Resources for Chemical Threat Response — A first sourcebook of data for nontraditional chemical agents (NTAs) was completed and the S&T Directorate developed methods to collect conventional forensic information (e.g., fingerprints) in highly toxic environments, useful to enable safe investigation of a chemical warfare attack, for example.

Delivered Violent Intent Prediction Model — The S&T Directorate delivered an initial version of a group violent incident model, an analytical framework to test scenarios that can help assess the likelihood of radicalization and identify group intent to engage in violence. The model applies social and behavioral science research and theory to understand terrorist motivation, intent, and behavior, including terrorist recruitment and the intent to engage in violence.

Developed Technology Integration Template — The result of four regional technology integration (RTI) pilots provided a model template for cost-effective technology integration that can be replicated at similar venues nationwide. Key capabilities being tested at the pilot locations include: atmospheric monitoring and detection systems for chemical and biological toxins, monitoring and detection systems that are integrated with existing emergency response and traffic management infrastructures (like video surveillance systems); planning and exercise tools to evaluate multijurisdictional performance for state and local decision makers; and technologies credentialing emergency responders and verifying victims' identities during an incident.

Source: Department of Homeland Security, *Budget in Brief*, 2008.

■ ■ Critical Thinking ■

In your opinion, is federal funding better spent on all-hazards first-responder preparedness, or on R&D efforts to find new emergency management solutions for terrorist hazards? Based on the FY 2008 funding levels for both of these activities (listed throughout this text), would the American public be better served by transferring funding from R&D to first-responder preparedness, or vice versa? Explain your answer.

R&D Efforts Focused on Weapons of Mass Destruction

The DHS website states, "The S&T Directorate will tap into scientific and technological capabilities to provide the means to detect and deter attacks using weapons of mass destruction. S&T will guide and organize research efforts to meet emerging and predicted needs and will work closely with universities, the private sector, and national and Federal laboratories." This effort can be subdivided into two fields: chemical and biological, and radiological and nuclear. In both fields, the Directorate's aim is to carry research to develop sensors to detect such weapons from production to employment. The different organizations within the federal sector that will support and serve the R&D efforts of S&T are detailed in the following section.

Chemical and Biological Defense Information and Analysis Center

The Chemical and Biological Defense Information and Analysis Center (CBIAC, www.cbiac.apgea .army.mil) is a DOD Information Analysis Center (IAC), administratively managed by the Defense Technical Information Center (DTIC). The center serves as the DOD focal point for information related to chemical and biological defense technology. Its function is to generate, acquire, process, analyze, and disseminate chemical and biological science and technology information in support of military resources; the chemical and biological defense research, development, and acquisition community; and other federal, state, and local government agencies. The CBIAC accomplishes its mission by the following means:

- Identifying and acquiring relevant data and information from all available sources and in all media
- Processing data and acquisitions into suitable storage and retrieval systems
- Identifying, developing, and applying available analytical tools and techniques for the interpretation and application of stored data and acquisitions
- Disseminating focused information, data sets, and technical analyses to managers, planners, scientists, engineers, and military field personnel for the performance of mission-related tasks
- Anticipating requirements for chemical and biological science and technology information
- Identifying and reaching out to emerging chemical and biological defense organizations

Defense Threat Reduction Agency

The Defense Threat Reduction Agency (DTRA, www.dtra.mil) safeguards national interests from weapons of mass destruction (chemical, biological, radiological, nuclear, and high explosives) by controlling and reducing the threat and providing quality tools and services for the war fighter. DTRA performs four essential functions to reach its mission: combat support, technology development, threat control, and threat reduction. Moreover, the agency's work covers a broad spectrum of activities:

- Shaping the international environment to prevent the spread of weapons of mass destruction
- Responding to requirements to deter the use and reduce the impact of such weapons
- Preparing for the future as WMD threats emerge and evolve

The activities concerning homeland security are as follows:

- DTRA draws on the disparate chemical and biological weapons defense expertise within the DOD to increase response capabilities.
- The Advanced Systems and Concepts Office (ASCO) stimulates, identifies, and executes high-impact seed projects to encourage new thinking, address technology gaps, and improve the operational capabilities of DTRA.

Department of State

The Department of State (www.state.gov) contributes to the counterterror effort related to weapons of mass destruction through diplomatic and intelligence gathering efforts. The Department of State provides information and assessments of potential chemical and biological weapons sources throughout the world and analyzes what different countries and groups are doing to increase, decrease, or support WMD development and stockpiling.

Centers for Disease Control and Prevention

The Centers for Disease Control and Prevention (CDC, www.cdc.gov) is recognized as the lead federal agency for protecting the health and safety of people by providing credible information to enhance health decisions and promoting health through strong partnerships. CDC serves as the national focus for developing and applying disease prevention and control, environmental health, and health promotion and education activities designed to improve the health of the people of the United States, with the mission to promote health and quality of life by preventing and controlling disease, injury, and disability. CDC provides information about the effects and treatment for exposure to chem-bio weapons and has valuable expertise in its 12 centers, institutes, and offices. The most prominent and relevant of the 12 follow:

- The National Center for Chronic Disease Prevention and Health Promotion prevents premature death and disability from chronic diseases and promotes healthy personal behaviors.
- The National Center for Health Statistics provides statistical information that will guide actions and policies to improve the health of the American people.
- The National Center for HIV, STD, and TB Prevention provides national leadership in preventing and controlling human immunodeficiency virus infection, sexually transmitted diseases, and tuberculosis.
- The National Center for Infectious Diseases prevents illness, disability, and death caused by infectious diseases in the United States and around the world.
- The National Immunization Program prevents disease, disability, and death from vaccine-preventable diseases in children and adults.

- The Epidemiology Program Office strengthens the public health system by coordinating public health surveillance; providing support in scientific communications, statistics, and epidemiology; and training in surveillance, epidemiology, and prevention effectiveness.

- The Public Health Practice Program Office strengthens community practice of public health by creating an effective workforce, building information networks, conducting practice research, and ensuring laboratory quality.

Lawrence Livermore National Laboratory

The Lawrence Livermore National Laboratory (LLNL, www.llnl.gov) provides information about nuclear and radiological weapons. Its activities are explained more broadly in the R&D section.

U.S. Nuclear Regulatory Commission

The U.S. Nuclear Regulatory Commission (NRC, www.nrc.gov) is an independent agency established to regulate civilian use of nuclear materials. The NRC's mission is to regulate the nation's civilian use of by-product, source, and special nuclear materials to ensure adequate protection of public health and safety, to promote the common defense and security, and to protect the environment. The NRC's regulatory mission covers three main areas:

Reactors: Commercial reactors for generating electric power and nonpower reactors used for research, testing, and training

Materials: Uses of nuclear materials in medical, industrial, and academic settings and facilities that produce nuclear fuel

Waste: Transportation, storage, and disposal of nuclear materials and waste, and decommissioning of nuclear facilities from service

The NRC carries out its mission by conducting several activities, but most of them are not directly related to the homeland security purpose. The commission performs them as part of its mission to regulate the normal use of radiological material, but many of its capabilities and resources can be used during a radiological or nuclear incident. The major contribution fields are commission direction setting and policymaking, radiation protection, establishment of a regulatory program, nuclear security and safeguards information on how to promote the common defense and security, public affairs, congressional affairs, state and tribal programs, and international programs.

Efforts Aimed at Information and Infrastructure

DHS has been given the primary responsibility for detecting and deterring attacks on the national information systems and critical infrastructures, and the S&T Directorate is developing a national R&D enterprise to support this mission. The three main issues concerning information and infrastructure are as follows: Internet security, telecommunication, and the security systems. The directorate coordinates and integrates several organizations to accomplish its mission, as discussed in the next sections.

National Infrastructure Protection Center (Former)

When DHS was first established in 2002, the National Infrastructure Protection Center (NIPC) operated directly under DHS to provide information about current efforts and possible threats coming from cyberspace. After reorganization in 2004, this center was fully integrated into the Information Analysis and Infrastructure Protection Directorate. These tasks were again moved in 2007 under the Post-Katrina Emergency Management Reform Act, when they were placed in the new National Protection and Programs Directorate's Office of Infrastructure Protection. The original center's mission, which was transferred in its entirety (and is now performed by two separate DHS endeavors — the

U.S. Computer Emergency Response Team [U.S. CERT] and the National Operations Center [NOC]), was to produce infrastructure warnings under the titles of assessments, advisories, alerts, and information bulletins (InfoBulletins), which are developed and distributed in a manner that is consistent with DHS's advisory and information-sharing system. These threat warning products are based on material that is significant, credible, and timely, and that address cyber and/or infrastructure dimensions with possibly significant impact. These products will often be based on classified material and include dissemination restrictions, but the center will then seek to develop a sensitive "tear-line" version for distribution to critical sector coordinators, general law enforcement authorities, state and local authorities, and others as appropriate. Details about each product follow:

- Assessments address broad, general incident, or issue awareness information and analysis that is both significant and current, but they do not necessarily suggest immediate action.

- Advisories address significant threat or incident information that suggests a change in readiness posture, protective options, and/or response.

- Alerts address major threat or incident information addressing imminent or in-progress attacks targeting specific national networks or critical infrastructures.

Federal Computer Incident Response Center (Former)

The Federal Computer Incident Response Center (FedCIRC — formerly the Federal Computer Intrusion Response Capability), the federal civilian government focal point for computer security incident reporting and providing assistance with incident prevention and response, was moved intact in 2002 into the Information Analysis and Infrastructure Protection (IAIP) Directorate. It remained there until 2007 when it was absorbed into DHS National Cyber Security Division per the Post-Katrina Emergency Management Reform Act. The Center focused on four major activities, each of which is now managed by the Cyber Security Division:

Incident Prevention: The center provides a patch authentication and dissemination capability that can assist organizations in identifying and patching known vulnerabilities specific to their systems. The center provides informational notices and advisories about current threats and vulnerabilities.

Incident Reporting: The center receives incident reports from federal agencies/departments that allow it to identify deliberate targeting efforts and other trends. By sharing sanitized incident information in return, all civilian agencies/departments can withstand or quickly recover from attacks against U.S. information resources.

Incident Analysis: The center has a partnership with CERT/CC and offers Incident and Vulnerability Notes to illustrate the range of adverse events affecting federal agencies/ departments as reported.

Incident Response: The center provides personnel, appropriate remediation, and recovery activities for the aftermath.

SANS Institute

The SANS (Systems Administration, Audit, Network, Security) Institute (www.sans.org) is active in the fields of information security research, certification, and education, and provides a platform for professionals to share lessons learned, conduct research, and teach the information security community. Besides the various training programs and resources aimed at informing its members and the community, the centers described in the following are part of SANS.

Internet Storm Center: This center was created to detect rising Internet threats. It uses advanced data correlation and visualization techniques to analyze data from a large number of firewalls and intrusion detection systems in over 60 countries. Experienced analysts constantly monitor the Storm Center data feeds, and search for trends and anomalies in order to identify potential threats. When a potential threat is detected, the team immediately begins an intensive investigation to gauge the threat's severity and impact. The Storm Center may request correlating data from an extensive network of security experts from across the globe, and possesses the in-house expertise to analyze captured attack tools quickly and thoroughly. Critical information is then disseminated to the public in the form of alerts and postings.

Center for Internet Security (CIS) and SCORE: CIS formalizes the best practice recommendations once consensus between the SANS Institute and SCORE is reached and the practices are validated. The latter become minimum standards benchmarks for general use by the industry. Both organizations rely on and have very broad contact with the field experts.

CERT Coordination Center

The CERT Coordination Center (CERT/CC, www.cert.org) is located at the Software Engineering Institute (SEI), a federally funded R&D center at Carnegie Mellon University in Pittsburgh, PA. SEI was charged by DARPA in 1988 to set up a center to coordinate communication among experts during security emergencies and to help prevent future incidents.

The CERT/CC is part of the larger SEI Networked Systems Survivability Program, whose primary goals are to ensure that appropriate technology and systems management practices are used to resist attacks on networked systems and to limit damage and ensure continuity of critical services in spite of successful attacks, accidents, or failures. The center's research areas are summarized in the following.

Vulnerability Analysis and Incident Handling: Analyze the state of Internet security and convey that information to the system administrators, network managers, and others in the Internet community. In these vulnerability and incident-handling activities, a higher priority is assigned to attacks and vulnerabilities that directly affect the Internet infrastructure (e.g., network service providers, Internet service providers, domain name servers, and routers).

Survivable Enterprise Management: Help organizations protect and defend themselves. To this end, risk assessments that help enterprises identify and characterize critical information assets and then identify risks to those assets have been developed, and the enterprise can use the results of the assessment to develop or refine their overall strategy for securing their networked systems.

Education and Training: The center offers training courses to educate technical staff and managers of computer security–incident response teams as well as system administrators and other technical personnel within organizations to improve the security and survivability of each system. The center's staff also take part in developing curricula in information security and has compiled a guide, *The CERT® Guide to System and Network Security Practices*, published by Addison-Wesley.

Survivable Network Technology: The center focuses on the technical basis for identifying and preventing security flaws and for preserving essential services if a system is penetrated and compromised. The center does research for new approaches to secure systems and analysis of how susceptible systems are to sophisticated attacks and finding ways to improve the design of systems. Another focus is on modeling and simulation. The center has developed "Easel," a tool that is being used to study network responses to attacks and attack mitigation strategies. And finally, the center is also developing techniques that will enable the assessment and prediction of current and potential threats to the Internet. These techniques involve examining large sets of network data to identify unauthorized and potentially malicious activity.

National Communications System

Through the National Communications System (NCS, www.ncs.gov), DHS supports the telecommunications critical infrastructure and R&D of tools and technology to prevent disruption or compromise of these services. The NCS was established in 1963 as a "single unified communications system to serve the president, Department of Defense, diplomatic and intelligence activities and civilian leaders." The NCS mandate included linking, improving, and extending the communications facilities and components of various federal agencies, focusing on interconnectivity and survivability. The NCS's national security and emergency preparedness (NS/EP) capabilities were broadened in 1984 when it began coordinating and planning NS/EP telecommunications to support crises and disasters.

With the U.S. Information Agency being absorbed into the U.S. State Department in October 2000, the NCS membership currently stands at 24 members. The NCS also participates in joint industry–government planning through its work with the President's National Security Telecommunications Advisory Committee (NSTAC), with the NSC's National Coordinating Center for Telecommunications (NCC), and the NCC's subordinate Information Sharing and Analysis Center (NCC-ISAC).

The NCS comprises numerous programs and committees that represent the majority of the national efforts in the field of communication for national emergencies and crises. The President's National Security Telecommunications Advisory Committee (NSTAC) and the Office of the Manager NCS (OMNCS) have been given the tasks of providing access control, priority treatment, user authentication, and other survivability features supporting NS/EP telecommunications to the Advanced Intelligent Network (AIN). The OMNCS has established an AIN Program to address the emerging technology and an associated AIN Program Office to plan, coordinate, and oversee the effort. Two very important examples of initiatives follow:

- The Alerting and Coordination Network (ACN) provides a stable emergency voice communications network connecting telecommunications service providers' Emergency Operations Centers (EOCs) and Network Operations Centers (NOCs) to support NS/EP telecommunications network restoration coordination, transmission of telecommunications requirements and priorities, and incident reporting when the Public Switched Telephone Network (PSTN) is inoperable, stressed, or congested. The ACN is operational 24 hours a day, 7 days a week, to support the National Coordinating Center (NCC) during normal and emergency operations.

- The Emergency Notification Service (ENS) is a full-time service established to notify critical government personnel during emergencies using multiple communication channels, including telephone, short message service (SMS), pager, and e-mail. Within minutes of receiving an activation order from an authorized representative of an organization, an automated process makes multiple attempts to reach intended recipients until they confirm delivery or until a predetermined number of attempts have been made. After 30 minutes, a report detailing confirmation of delivery is returned to the originator of the notification. Messages can be recorded in advance or when the notification is initiated and can be sent as a general notification or a sensitive notification.

To initiate, coordinate, restore, and reconstitute NS/EP telecommunications services or facilities, the NCS continues to develop new capabilities and reevaluate or upgrade older ones. The NCS's current capabilities are given in the sidebar titled, "Service Programs of the National Communications System." The current initiatives going on under the NCS's National Coordination Center for Telecommunications can be summarized as follows:

- In January 2000, the national coordinator for Security, Infrastructure Protection, and Counterterrorism designated the NCC-ISAC as the Information Sharing and Analysis Center for telecommunications. The NCC-ISAC will facilitate voluntary collaboration and information sharing among its participants, gathering information on vulnerabilities, threats, intrusions, and anomalies from telecommunications industry, government, and other sources. The NCC-ISAC will analyze the data with the goal of averting or mitigating impact on the telecommunications infrastructure.

Service Programs of the National Communications System

CRIS: The Communications Resource Information Sharing initiative provides a directory of readily available Federal telecommunications assets, services, and capabilities that may be shared with other government agencies to support national security/emergency preparedness (NS/EP) needs. Participation is voluntary and limited to NCS members and their affiliates, and assets are only available if their use does not interfere with departmental or agency missions or operations.

GETS: The Government Emergency Telecommunications Service is a nationwide NS/EP switched voice and voice band data communications service that provides authorized local, State, and Federal government users with communications during disasters by using surviving PSTN resources. GETS provides access authorization, enhanced routing, and priority treatment in local and long-distance telephone networks and is accessible through a dialing plan and personal identification number (PIN). GETS uses three major types of networks: the major long-distance networks provided by interexchange carriers (AT&T, MCI WorldCom, and Sprint); the local networks provided by local exchange carriers (Bell operating companies and independent companies, cellular carriers, and personal communication services); and government-leased networks (including the Federal Telecommunications System and the Defense Information System Network).

NTCN: The National Technology Coordination Network connects participating government and industry organizations via a multimodal conferencing bridge. The bridge links disparate communications systems and allows for voice communications including dedicated line, high-frequency radio, satellite telephone, and switched wireline telephone. Telecommunications industry participants are connected to the bridge through the National Telecommunications Alliance's Alerting and Coordination Network (ACN). The ACN is a nonpublic network system developed to provide communications and coordination capabilities to industry members during Public Network (PN) outages.

SHARES: The Shared Resources High-Frequency (HF) Radio Program provides a single interagency emergency message handling system to transmit NS/EP information during disasters by consolidating HF radio resources belonging to 91 Federal and Federally affiliated organizations. SHARES stations are in every State and at 20 overseas locations. The network consists of 1,101 HF radio stations located in the United States and abroad, 335 emergency planning and response personnel, and over 250 HF frequencies. It also provides the Federal community a forum for addressing issues affecting HF radio operability. The manager of NCC is responsible for day-to-day operations of SHARES, while the manager of NCS is responsible for the overall SHARES program.

TSP: The Federal Communications Commission (FCC) established the Telecommunications Service Priority program in 1988 to provide priority provisioning and restoration of NS/EP telecommunication services. Under the TSP program, service vendors are authorized and required to provision and restore services with TSP assignments before services without such assignments. As a result, a telecommunications service with a TSP assignment will receive full attention by the service vendor before any non-TSP service. Non-Federal government users who request TSP restoration or provisioning must be sponsored by a Federal organization.

Source: National Communications System, 2008, www.ncs.gov.

- The NCC-ISAC uses an Information Sharing and Analysis System (ISAS) to analyze the information provided by the NCC-ISAC participants. The ISAS incorporates capabilities for automated correlation of inputs with other inputs and all-source information. The ISAS provides advanced automation, analysis, modeling, data fusion, and correlation processes to support the near real-time exchange of critical information, assessments, and warning information involving vulnerabilities, threats, and affecting the telecommunications infrastructure.

The last issue for emergency communication is wireless communication. Wireless network congestion was widespread on September 11, 2001, and with wireless traffic demand estimated at up to 10 times the normal amount in the affected areas and double nationwide, the need for wireless priority service became critical and urgent. Since the early 1990s, OMNCS has worked to develop and implement a nationwide cellular priority access capability in support of NS/EP telecommunications. As a result of a petition filed by the NCS in October 1995, the FCC set the wireless Priority Access Service (PAS) as voluntary. For example, the Wireless Priority Service (WPS), the NCS program implementation of the FCC PAS, is the wireless complement to the landline Government Emergency Telecommunications Service (GETS). GETS utilizes the PSTN to provide enhanced landline priority service to qualified NS/EP personnel.

As a result of the events of September 11, 2001, the National Security Council issued the following guidance to the Office of the Manager, National Communications System (OMNCS):

> NCS *has to move forward on implementing an immediate solution using channel reservation capability from one vendor for the Washington, DC, area; based on lessons learned in DC, the NCS will make a recommendation on whether to expand the immediate solution to other metro areas. In parallel, the NCS will proceed with deploying a priority access queuing system for wireless nationwide.*

The two proposed solutions and related matters are discussed in more detail in the sidebars, "National Coordinating Center for Telecommunications Wireless Priorities" and "Wireless Priority Service Priority Areas."

National Coordinating Center for Telecommunications Wireless Priorities

In the early 1990s, the OMNCS initiated efforts to develop and implement a nationwide cellular priority-access capability in support of national security and emergency preparedness (NS/EP) telecommunications, and pursued a number of activities to improve cellular call completion during times of network congestion. Subsequently, as a result of a petition filed by the NCS in October 1995, the FCC released a Second Report and Order (R&O) on wireless Priority Access Service (PAS). The R&O offers Federal liability relief for NS/EP wireless carriers if the service is implemented in accordance with uniform operating procedures. The FCC made PAS voluntary, found it to be in the public interest, and defined five priority levels for NS/EP wireless calls (see sidebar titled, "Wireless Priority Service Priority Areas").

Wireless Priority Service (WPS), the National Communications System (NCS) program implementation of the FCC PAS, is the wireless complement to the landline Government Emergency Telecommunications Service (GETS). GETS utilizes the Public Switched Telephone Network (PSTN) to provide enhanced landline priority service to qualified NS/EP personnel. WPS users are authorized and encouraged to use GETS to better their probability of completing their NS/EP call during periods of wireless and landline network congestion. Wireless network congestion was widespread on September 11, 2001. With wireless traffic demand estimated at up to 10 times normal in the affected areas and double nationwide, the need for wireless priority service became a critical and urgent national requirement.

Reacting to the events of September 11, 2001, the National Security Council issued guidance to the National Communications System (NCS) that stated the following:

> *With the White House guidance in October 2001, the NCS began immediate acquisition of service for the Washington, D.C., metropolitan area and recommended and proceeded with services for New York City as well. The February 2002 Olympics in Salt Lake City also warranted immediate service. The NCS entered into subcontracts with the Immediate WPS service providers, T-Mobile (previously VoiceStream) and Globalstar. T-Mobile's implementation of the Immediate Solution became operational during May 2002 in Washington and New York. By November 2002, T-Mobile supported 2,084 WPS users in Washington and 725 in New York, for a total of 2,809 WPS cellular users. Globalstar also supported 1,506 customers as well.*
>
> *Due to the requirement for nationwide WPS coverage, multiple carriers and multiple access technologies are needed. WPS is based on the two digital access technologies most widely available in the United States, GSM (i.e., Cingular, Nextel, and T-Mobile) and Code Division Multiple Access (CDMA) (i.e., Sprint PCS and Verizon Wireless). Nationwide WPS is provided in two major phases, Initial Operating Capability (IOC) and Full Operating Capability (FOC). IOC is a GSM-based solution only, consisting of priority radio channel access at call origination. IOC began December 31, 2002, and it satisfied the requirements of the FCC Second R&O for invocation of the service on a call-by-call basis by dialing the WPS prefix (*272) at the start of each NS/EP WPS call. FOC provides a full, end-to-end capability, beginning with the NS/EP wireless caller, through the wireless networks, through the interexchange carrier (IXC) and/or local exchange carrier (LEC) wireline networks, and to the wireless or wireline called party. T-Mobile began deploying WPS FOC in December 2003. Cingular (and formerly AT&T Wireless) began deploying WPS FOC in July 2004. Nextel also deployed WPS in July 2004, and [began to] upgrade to FOC in April 2005. As of May 2005, there were over 11,500 WPS users. It is the objective of NCS to provide the WPS capability to an estimated NS/EP wireless user population of 200,000 GSM users and 150,000 CDMA users.*

Source: National Communications System, www.ncs.gov.

Wireless Priority Service Priority Areas

Executive Leadership and Policy Makers (Priority 1): Includes those holding high-level government positions. Examples include the President of the United States, the President's Cabinet, select military leaders, Governors, mayors, and county commissioner offices — as well as a minimum number of support staff for each of these officials.

Disaster Response/Military Command and Control (Priority 2): Includes those in charge of security and emergency response from the local to the Federal level. Personnel selected for this priority should be responsible for ensuring the viability or reconstruction of the basic infrastructure in an emergency area. In addition, personnel essential to continuity of government and national security functions (such as the conduct of international affairs and intelligence activities) are also included in this priority. Examples include Federal and State emergency teams and emergency managers.

Public Health, Safety, and Law Enforcement Command (Priority 3): Includes those in charge of protecting life and property, and who maintain law and order after an event. Examples include local and State police officers, local fire departments, and emergency medical technicians.

Public Services/Utilities and Public Welfare (Priority 4): Includes those who manage public works, assess damage to utilities, manage their repairs and coordinate transportation for emergency response. Examples include Army Corps of Engineers, power, water, sewer, transportation, and telecommunications departments.

Disaster Recovery (Priority 5): Includes those in charge of recovery after initial response to a disaster. Examples include medical, damage assessment, and disaster shelter coordination and management.

Source: NCC Wireless Priority Service, 2008.

Laboratories and Research Facilities

The R&D function is the most important aspect of the S&T Directorate. It will rely on several existing agency programs to accomplish this task, including Department of Defense (DOD), Department of Energy (DOE), and Department of Agriculture (USDA) programs, among others. A significant portion of the funding attached to these programs comes from DOD's newly created National Bioweapons Defense Analysis Center, responsible for nearly the entire biological countermeasures portfolio.

DHS intends to establish an Office for National Laboratories that will coordinate DHS interactions with DOE national laboratories with expertise in homeland security. The office has the authority to establish a semi-independent DHS headquarters laboratory within existing federal laboratories, national laboratories, or FFRDC to supply scientific and technical knowledge to DHS; the most recent indications are that DHS plans to do so with at least five national labs. In addition to Livermore, DHS has initial plans to establish four other labs-within-labs at the Los Alamos, Sandia, Pacific Northwest, and Oak Ridge National Laboratories. DHS will also establish one or more university-based centers for homeland security.

The national and federal laboratory system possesses significant expertise in the area of weapons of mass destruction in addition to massive computing power. These labs include the following:

DOE National Nuclear Security Administration Labs: Lawrence Livermore Laboratory, Los Alamos National Laboratory, Sandia National Laboratory.

DOE Office of Science Labs: Argonne National Laboratory, Brookhaven National Laboratory, Oak Ridge National Laboratory, Pacific Northwest National Laboratory, other DOE laboratories.

Department of Homeland Security Labs: Environmental Measurements Laboratory, Plum Island Animal Disease Center.

Department of Health and Human Services Labs: HHS operates several laboratories focused on wide-ranging health and disease prevention issues.

U.S. Customs Laboratory and Scientific Services: The U.S. Customs Laboratory and Scientific Services perform testing to determine the origin of agricultural and manufactured products.

This section starts with an overview of the facilities cited above and relevant programs and then discusses other R&D activities, such as the university-based center approach, and partnerships between DHS and other agencies.

Lawrence Livermore National Laboratory

The Homeland Security Organization at Lawrence Livermore National Laboratory (LLNL, www .llnl.gov) provides comprehensive solutions integrating threat, vulnerability, and trade-off analyses, advanced technologies, field-demonstrated prototypes, and operational capabilities to assist federal, state, local, and private entities in defending against catastrophic terrorism. The center is also dedicated to pursuing partnerships with universities and the private sector to fulfill its mission.

Los Alamos National Laboratory

Los Alamos National Laboratory (LANL, www.lanl.gov) is a Department of Energy (DOE) laboratory, managed by the University of California, and is one of the largest multidisciplinary institutions in the world. The Center for Homeland Security (CHS) was established in September 2002 to engage the laboratory's broad capabilities in the areas of counterterrorism and homeland security. It provides a single point of contact for all external organizations.

The organization's emphasis is in the key areas of nuclear and radiological science and technology, critical infrastructure protection, and chemical and biological science and technology. Current LANL projects with a key role in homeland security include the following:

- BASIS (the Biological Aerosol Sentry and Information System), a biological early warning system that was tested and installed at the 2002 Salt Lake City Winter Olympics.
- A novel nuclear detector, the Palm CZT Spectrometer, is also in development and deployment, providing real-time gamma and neutron detection and isotope identification in a handheld device.
- LANL has also been active in the anthrax bacterial DNA analysis and the computerized feature identification tool known as GENIE, for Genetic Image Exploitation.

Sandia National Laboratory

The Sandia National Laboratory (www.sandia.gov) have been active since 1949 in the development of science-based technologies that support national security. Through science and technology, people, infrastructure, and partnerships, Sandia's mission is to meet national needs in six key areas, including:

- Nuclear weapons
- Nonproliferation
- Defense systems and assessments
- Homeland security
- Science, technology, and engineering
- Energy and infrastructure assurance

Argonne National Laboratory

Argonne National Laboratory (www.anl.gov) is one of the Department of Energy's largest research centers. It is also the nation's first national laboratory, chartered in 1946. Argonne's research falls into four broad categories:

Basic science: This program seeks solutions to a wide variety of scientific challenges. This includes experimental and theoretical work in materials science, physics, chemistry, biology, high-energy physics, and mathematics and computer science, including high-performance computing.

National security: This program has increased in significance in recent years. This program uses Argonne capabilities developed over previous years for other purposes that help counter the terrorist threat. These capabilities include expertise in the nuclear fuel cycle, biology, chemistry, and systems analysis and modeling. This research is helping develop highly sensitive instruments and technologies to detecting chemical, biological, and radioactive threats and identify their sources. Other research is helping to detect and deter possible weapons proliferation or actual attacks.

Energy resources: This program helps to insure that a reliable supply of efficient and clean energy exists in the future. The laboratory's scientists and engineers are working to develop advanced batteries and fuel cells, as well as advanced electric power generation and storage systems.

Environmental management: This program includes work on managing and solving environmental problems and promoting environmental stewardship. Research includes alternative energy systems, environmental risk and economic impact assessments, hazardous waste site analysis and remediation planning, treatment to prepare spent nuclear fuel for disposal, and new technologies for decontaminating and decommissioning aging nuclear reactors.

Industrial technology development is an important activity in moving benefits of Argonne's publicly funded research to industry to help strengthen the nation's technology base.

Brookhaven National Laboratory

Established in 1947 on Long Island, New York, Brookhaven National Laboratory (BNL, www .bnl.gov) is a multiprogram national laboratory operated by Brookhaven Science Associates for the Department of Energy (DOE). Six Nobel Prizes have been awarded for discoveries made at BNL. Brookhaven has a staff of approximately 3,000 scientists, engineers, technicians, and support people, and hosts more than 4,000 guest researchers annually. Brookhaven National Laboratory's role for the DOE is to produce excellent science and advanced technology with the cooperation, support, and appropriate involvement of our scientific and local communities. The fundamental elements of BNL's role in support of the four DOE strategic missions follow:

- To conceive, design, construct, and operate complex, leading edge, user-oriented facilities in response to the needs of the DOE and the international community of users
- To carry out basic and applied research in long-term, high-risk programs at the frontier of science
- To develop advanced technologies that address national needs and to transfer them to other organizations and to the commercial sector
- To disseminate technical knowledge, educate new generations of scientists and engineers, maintain technical capabilities in the nation's workforce, and encourage scientific awareness in the general public

Major programs that are managed at the laboratory include the following:

- Nuclear and high-energy physics
- Physics and chemistry of materials
- Environmental and energy research
- Nonproliferation
- Neurosciences and medical imaging
- Structural biology

Oak Ridge National Laboratory

The Oak Ridge National Laboratory (ORNL, www.ornl.gov) is a multiprogramming science and technology laboratory managed for the Department of Energy (DOE) by UT-Battelle, LLC. Scientists and engineers at ORNL conduct basic and applied R&D to create scientific knowledge and technological solutions that strengthen the nation's leadership in key areas of science; increase the availability of clean, abundant energy; restore and protect the environment; and contribute to national security. In their national security mission, ORNL provides federal, state, and local government agencies and departments with technology and expertise to support their national and homeland security needs. This technology and expertise is also shared with the private sector.

Pacific Northwest National Laboratory

The Pacific Northwest National Laboratory (PNNL, www.pnl.gov) is a DOE laboratory that delivers breakthrough science and technology to meet selected environmental, energy, health, and national security objectives; strengthen the economy; and support the education of future scientists and engineers.

PNNL's mission in national security supports the U.S. government's objectives against the proliferation of nuclear, chemical, and biological weapons of mass destruction and associated delivery systems. About one-third of PNNL's $600 million annual R&D budget reflects work in national security programs for the Departments of Energy, Defense, and most other federal agencies. The focus is on issues that concern the Air Force, Army, Defense Advanced Research Projects Agency, Defense Threat Reduction Agency, Navy, and nuclear nonproliferation.

Scientists and engineers at PNNL are finding ways to diagnose the life of the Army's Abrams tank, developing technologies that verify compliance with the Comprehensive Nuclear Test Ban Treaty, helping North Korea secure spent nuclear fuel in proper storage canisters, and training border enforcement officials from the United States and foreign countries.

Other Department of Energy Laboratories and Objectives

The Department of Energy (www.energy.gov) also has other affiliated organizations in addition to the ones cited above that focus on various homeland security issues. The topics addressed in these facilities include:

  Cybersecurity protection — These programs are aimed at protecting the information and systems that the DOE depends on, which only increases in scope as it grows in dependence on newer technologies.

  Managing operations security — This program seeks to manage security operations for DOE facilities in the national capital area, and to develop policies designed to protect national security and other critical assets entrusted to DOE.

  Preventing the spread of weapons of mass destruction — DOE plays an integral part in nuclear nonproliferation, countering terrorism, and responding to incidents involving weapons of mass destruction. The department does this by providing technology, analysis, and expertise developed through this program.

Environmental Measurements Laboratory

The Environmental Measurements Laboratory (EML, www.eml.st.dhs.gov), a government-owned, government-operated laboratory, is directly part of the Science and Technology (S&T) Directorate. The laboratory advances and applies the science and technology required for preventing, protecting against, and responding to radiological and nuclear events in the service of homeland and national security.

EML's current programs focus on issues associated with environmental radiation and radioactivity. Specifically, EML provides DHS with environmental radiation and radioactivity measurements in the laboratory or field, technology development and evaluation, personnel training, instrument calibration, performance testing, data management, and data quality assurance.

The two unique facilities of the lab follow:

Environmental Chamber: A 25-cubic-meter facility, the only one in the United States that can generate atmospheres with controlled aerosols and gases for calibration and testing of new instruments

Gamma Spectrometry Laboratory: A fully equipped laboratory with high-efficiency, high-resolution gamma sensors

Plum Island Animal Disease Center

The Plum Island Animal Disease Center (PIADC, www.ars.usda.gov/plum/) became part of DHS on June 1, 2003. While the center remains an important national asset in which scientists conduct basic and applied research and diagnostic activities to protect the health of livestock on farms across the nation from foreign disease agents, it was also tasked with a new mission to help DHS to protect the country from terrorist threats, including those directed against agriculture.

The U.S. Department of Agriculture (USDA) is responsible for research and diagnosis to protect the nation's animal industries and exports from catastrophic economic losses caused by foreign animal disease (FAD) agents accidentally or deliberately introduced into the United States. While continuing its mission, it works closely with DHS personnel to fight agroterrorism.

On September 11, 2005, the Department of Homeland Security announced that the Plum Island Animal Disease Center would be replaced by a new federal facility, the National Bio and Agro-Defense Facility (NBAF). The NBAF will research high-consequence biological threats involving zoonotic (i.e., transmitted from animals to humans) and foreign animal diseases. It will allow basic research; diagnostic development, testing, and validation; advanced countermeasure development; and training for high-consequence livestock diseases. The new facility is being designed to:

- Integrate those aspects of public and animal health research that have been determined to be central to national security

- Assess and research evolving bioterrorism threats over the next 5 decades

- Enable the Departments of Homeland Security and Agriculture (USDA) to fulfill their related homeland defense research, development, testing, and evaluation (RDT&E) responsibilities.

Department of Health and Human Services Labs

The Department of Health and Human Services (www.hhs.gov) operates several laboratories focused on various health and disease prevention issues. The laboratories have extensive programs, and more details can be found later in this chapter.

U.S. Customs Laboratory and Scientific Services

DHS Customs and Border Protection Laboratories and Scientific Services (www.cbp.gov/xp/cgov/import/operations_support/labs_scientific_svcs/) coordinates technical and scientific support to all CBP trade and border protection activities. The mission of the program is to provide rapid, quality scientific, forensic, and weapons of mass destruction services to the CBP officials and other counterparts. One of the principal responsibilities of the CBP science officers is to manage the Customs Gauger/Laboratory Accreditation program. The program calls for the accreditation of commercial gaugers and laboratories so that their measurements and analytical results can be used by customs for entry and admissibility purposes. The staff edits and publishes the Customs Laboratory Bulletin, which, as a customs-scientific journal, is circulated internationally and provides a useful forum for technical exchange on subjects of general customs interest. U.S. Customs and Border Protection maintains the following laboratory facilities:

Springfield (VA) Laboratory: The Springfield Laboratory is a centralized facility that provides scientific support to CBP headquarters and the laboratories listed below. This facility provides analytical services to CBP legal and regulatory functions and to CBP offices that require scientific support, and develops new analytical methods and evaluates new instrumentation. The activities of this facility vary in supporting CBP commercial and enforcement mission. The laboratory maintains the analytical uniformity among all CBP laboratories, and maintains technical and scientific exchange with other federal enforcement agencies, technological branches of foreign customs agencies, and the military.

New York (NY) Laboratory: The New York CBP services the greater New York City area including the New York Seaport, JFK Airport, the Port of Newark, and Perth Amboy. The laboratory provides scientific, forensic, and WMD services to CBP customers, including radiation detection, chemical WMD detection and identification, participation in the Laboratories and Scientific Services (LSS) national WMD strike team, and membership in the Food Emergency Response Network (FERN). This laboratory also trains DHS personnel on field radiation equipment

Chicago (IL) Laboratory: The Chicago Laboratory services all of the New England states, Illinois, Iowa, Nebraska, Wisconsin, Michigan, Kansas, Missouri, Indiana, part of Minnesota, and New York except the New York City Metro area. This facility provides technical advice and analytical services to CBP officers, U.S. Immigration and Customs Enforcement (ICE) agents, border patrol officers, and other entities on a wide range of issues. These services assist CBP officers in collecting revenue based on import duties and enforcing the law. The services provided to ICE agents and border patrol officers pertain primarily to law enforcement and forensics-related issues. The laboratory also provides training to its customers on interdiction, identification, and determination of weapons of mass destruction (WMD).

Savannah (GA) Laboratory: The Savannah Customs Laboratory serves ports from Philadelphia, PA, to Key West, FL. The facility conducts chemical and physical testing of all types of commodities, narcotics, and other controlled substances. The Savannah Laboratory operates two state-of-the art, custom-built mobile laboratories to meet the on-site testing needs of Southeastern U.S. ports used for the detection of materials for WMD.

Southwest Regional Science Center (Houston, TX): The Southwest Regional Science Center provides technical and scientific services to all of the ports of entry and Border Patrol sectors in the following eight States: Alabama, Tennessee, Mississippi, Louisiana, Arkansas, Oklahoma, Texas, and New Mexico. This geographic area contains 80% of the border between the United States and Mexico. This facility provides technical and scientific services to manage, secure, and control the nation's border and to prevent terrorists and terrorist weapons from entering the United States. Services provided include forensic crime scene investigation, WMD interdiction, and trade enforcement. Forensic scientists provide support to law enforcement investigations with the analysis of latent prints, controlled substances, pharmaceuticals, audio and video enhancements, accident investigation, and expert witness testimony.

Los Angeles (CA) Laboratory: The Los Angeles Laboratory services all of southern California, and southern Nevada, including Las Vegas, Arizona, and the California–Mexico border in these areas. The staff of chemists, textile analysts, and physical scientists is trained to assist in meeting the CBP mission in areas of trade, forensics, and WMD. Among the laboratory's functions are forensic support such as evidence collection and analysis of trace, controlled substances and pharmaceuticals; technical support for chemical, biological, explosives, and radiation WMD issues; and latent print processing at the crime scene or in the laboratory. The laboratory has mobile vans equipped with field instrumentation to analyze and identify certain unknown chemicals, textile construction and applications on textiles, controlled substances, explosives, and WMD chemical agents and radiation. The Los Angeles laboratory has vehicle-mounted and handheld detectors for rapid scan and identification of radiation sources from cargo containers.

San Francisco (CA) Laboratory: The laboratory serves the northern two-thirds of California, as well as the states of Oregon, Washington, North Dakota, South Dakota, Minnesota, Alaska, Hawaii, Colorado, Utah, Nevada, Montana, and Idaho. Major ports located in this service area include San Francisco, Portland, Seattle, Blaine, Anchorage, Honolulu, and Denver. This facility provides technical advice, forensic, and other scientific services to the CBP officials and other agencies on a wide range of imported and exported commodities. The laboratory also provides supports in weapons of mass destruction (WMD), explosives, hazardous materials, and crime scene investigation. Several staff members are qualified radiation isotope identification device (RIID) trainers, and continuously provide RIID operation trainings, and provide CBP Radiation Detection Program and Response Protocol at the Pacific Northwest National Laboratory Radiation Academy (RADACAD) in Richland, Washington. The laboratory operates a small mobile unit that provides on-site examination and analyses of commercial shipments and training for local CBP officers, and crime scene investigation (fingerprint collection), and examination and analysis on any suspicious illicit radioactive materials entering this country.

San Juan (PR) Laboratory: The San Juan Laboratory serves the ports of Puerto Rico and the U.S. Virgin Isands. This facility conducts chemical and physical testing of a wide variety of importations and forensic samples. Most of the facility's specialization has been in the area of controlled substances and other forensic samples. The San Juan Laboratory provides vital technical support and training to local and foreign law enforcement officials in areas such as WMB, radioactive material detection, crime scene management, and narcotics field test kits. The San Juan Laboratory mobile operations encompass active participation in WMD activities, forensic analysis, and crime scene management through all ports of Puerto Rico and the U.S. Virgin Islands.

Academic Research Institutions

Universities, their research centers, institutes, and qualified staff represent a very important portion of the scientific research in the United States. These facilities account for an estimated one-third of the total federal budget available for R&D activities. The S&T Directorate has already started to show its recognition of the importance of these institutions in the overall homeland security R&D effort through both awarding them R&D grants and by funding Homeland Security Centers of Excellence on their campuses.

Homeland Security Centers of Excellence

The Science and Technology Directorate, through its Office of University Programs, is further-ing the homeland security mission by engaging the academic community to create learning and research environments in areas critical to homeland security. Through the Homeland Security Centers of Excellence program, DHS has invested in university-based partnerships to develop cen-ters of multidisciplinary research where important fields of inquiry can be analyzed and best prac-tices developed, debated, and shared. The department's Homeland Security Centers of Excellence (HS-Centers) bring together the nation's best experts and focus its most talented researchers on a variety of threats that include agricultural, chemical, biological, nuclear/radiological, explo-sive, and cyberterrorism as well as the behavioral aspects of terrorism. The current HS-Centers were previously listed in this chapter in the "Homeland Security Centers of Excellence" sidebar. In FY 2008, only $49 million in funding will be available for university programs — an amount equal to FY 2007 but down from previous years. If the president's FY 2009 budget request passes as writ-ten, funding for university programs will fall by over 10% to $43.8 million.

Maritime Research

The scope of the S&T Directorate encompasses the pursuit of a full range of research into the use, preservation, and exploitation of the national waterways and oceans. The U.S. Coast Guard Research and Development Center is in charge of conducting research to support defense of this resource and of the homeland.

U.S. Coast Guard

The Research and Development (R&D) Center is the Coast Guard's (www.uscg.mil) sole facility performing research, development, test, and evaluation (RDT&E) in support of the Coast Guard's major missions of maritime mobility, maritime safety, maritime security, national defense, and protection of natural resources. The center has as its mission "to be the Coast Guard's pathfinder, anticipating and meeting future technological challenges, while partnering with others to shepherd the best ideas into implementable solutions."

The Coast Guard RDT&E program produces two types of products: the development of hardware, procedures, and systems that directly contribute to increasing the quality and productivity of the operations and the expansion of knowledge related to technical support of operating and regulatory programs.

R&D Efforts External to the Department of Homeland Security

The majority of homeland security R&D funding is provided to federal agencies other than the Department of Homeland Security.

Department of Health and Human Services

National Institutes of Health

The National Institutes of Health's (NIH, www.nih.gov) most relevant effort in homeland security R&D is in bioterrorism-related research. It has conducted work in the field for much longer than the existence of the Department of Homeland Security, but it emerged as a high-priority R&D agency after the 2001 anthrax mail situation. Budget allocations, which tend to be a reliable predictor of federal priorities, have clearly indicated that this dedication to bioterrorism detection and countermeasures remains. In the FY 2008 budget, NIH saw a decrease in homeland security research funding of $14 million from the previous year, down to $1.815 billion. NIH is clearly the leader within the federal government for homeland security R&D efforts for its biodefense research portfolio. Most of this amount is funded by the National Institute of Allergy and Infectious Disease (NIAID). The biodefense priorities of NIAID include, in addition to biodefense research, the development of medical countermeasures against radiological and nuclear threats, and medical countermeasures against chemical threats.

Centers for Disease Control and Prevention

The Centers for Disease Control and Prevention (CDC, www.cdc.gov) is another component of HHS that traditionally performed WMD terrorism R&D. However, with the opening of the Biodefence Advanced Research and Development Agency, CDC homeland security R&D funds have diminished. In fact, the majority of CDC terrorism activities, which are not R&D in nature, include the management of the Strategic National Stockpile (SNS) and funding for state and local responders to upgrade their abilities to prepare for and manage WMD events.

Biodefense Advanced Research and Development Agency

As part of its expanding effort to fund anthrax research and other R&D related to defenses against terrorist threats, the Office of the Secretary of Health and Human Services funded biodefense R&D

in the newly created Biodefense Advanced Research and Development Authority (BARDA, www.hhs
.gov/aspr/barda/index.html) in FY 2008. BARDA funds advanced R&D of new biodefense countermeasures as part of an HHS-wide effort to secure an adequate supply of such countermeasures for the
Strategic National Stockpile.

Department of Defense

The Department of Defense (DOD) has had a fluctuating budget for homeland security R&D since
2001. In FY 2008, DOD enjoyed an increase in R&D funding of 8.7%, to a total allocation of $1.278
billion. The vast majority of DOD R&D funding is provided through the Defense Advanced Research
Projects Agency (DARPA), which works mainly on applications that serve the needs of the military
(e.g., biological warfare defense and the Chemical and Biological Defense Program). The outcome of
this research, however, often has applications that can be applied by civilian first responders despite
the military origin of the projects that generated them. The DOD Chemical and Biological Defense
Program (CBDP) is another research-oriented agency that performs homeland security research activities, devoting a third of its $1 billion appropriation to research.

Department of Agriculture

Even more so than DOD, the USDA has witnessed widely fluctuating R&D budgets since
the September 11 terrorist attacks. Actual fiscal year funding amounts have varied from less than
$50 million to over $170 million. Since 9/11, USDA has invested a considerable amount of research
effort toward developing security mechanisms to protect dangerous pathogens, which could be used
as terror weapons and are located in many laboratories dispersed throughout the United States.
Increases in funding in FY 2006 and 2007 were dedicated to renovating facilities that performed
animal research and diagnosis at the National Centers for Animal Health in Ames, Iowa. These
efforts are aimed at protecting the U.S. food supply from acts of sabotage and terrorism — both
of which could have potentially devastating effects on the U.S. economy. The FY 2008 funding
for USDA homeland security R&D efforts is $129 million, an increase of almost 190% over the pre-
vious year.

Environmental Protection Agency

The Environmental Protection Agency (EPA) has seen steady but small federal allocations of homeland security R&D funding since September 11. Since that year EPA research related to homeland
security has been focused primary on drinking water security research (which would involve EPA
efforts to develop better surveillance and laboratory networks for drinking water supplies to counter
potential terrorist threats) and decontamination research (to develop better technologies and methods
for decontaminating terrorist attack sites). EPA also conducts threat and consequence assessments and
tests potential biodefense and other decontamination technologies. Much of this work is conducted at
EPA's National Homeland Security Research Center (NHSRC) in Cincinnati. NHSRC develops expertise and products that are used to prevent, prepare for, and recover from public health and environmental emergencies arising from terrorist threats and incidents. Research and development efforts
focus on the following five primary areas:

> **Threat and Consequence Assessment:** Investigates human exposure to chemical, biological, and
> radiological contaminants to define dangerous levels of these contaminants and establish
> protective cleanup goals.
>
> **Decontamination and Consequence Management:** Focuses on decontamination of buildings and
> outdoor environments, as well as the safe disposal of contaminated materials.
>
> **Water Infrastructure Protection:** Protects the nation's drinking water sources and distribution
> systems and ensures the safety of wastewater collection, treatment, and disposal procedures.

Response Capability Enhancement: Works directly with emergency responders and local governments to provide tools and information needed to make informed decisions in the event of an attack.

Technology Testing and Evaluation: Evaluates technologies that show potential for use in homeland security applications. These evaluations are used by water utility operators, building owners, emergency responders, and others to make informed decisions when purchasing security technology.

National Institute of Standards and Technology

The Department of Commerce (DOC) is home to the National Institute of Standards and Technology (NIST), which funds R&D in cryptography and computer security, and which provides scientific and technical support to DHS in these areas.

National Science Foundation

The National Science Foundation (NSF) funds research to combat bioterrorism in the areas of infectious diseases and microbial genome sequencing. These programs increased to $357 million in FY 2008.

Conclusion

Homeland security represents an entirely new spectrum of issues of R&D and technology and an opportunity to revitalize old issues under the homeland security umbrella. Establishing DHS and the S&T Directorate brought a new, major player into the federally supported R&D efforts. There was much discussion and disgruntlement within the research community concerning the lack of involvement of the NSF in the development of the homeland security R&D agenda. In fact, several people questioned the need for the S&T as opposed to just increasing the NSF or NIST's portfolios.

With a spectrum of activity varying from research to development to deployment, and a span of subjects from bioterrorism to personal protective equipment, from communication tools to nonproliferation, and from detection devices to mass production of vaccines, the S&T Directorate has been given a monumental task. The directorate not only coordinates the R&D facilities of many organizations but also has the authority to set priorities in others. The university-based HS-Centers provide a level of new funding that has not been available for some time and provide one of the best funded opportunities for specific R&D to benefit emergency management.

Although the context of change leaves little room for conclusions, the extraordinary budget given to the S&T Directorate either in existing programs or in new ones will provide the emergency-management and first-responder communities new capabilities never before imagined. It is to be hoped that these technological "toys" do not give a false sense of confidence and overshadow the real requirements of building an improved capacity to mitigate, prepare for, respond to, and recover from the risks of terrorism (Figure 9–5).

The changes that can be implied with the establishment of the university-based centers should be watched closely. These centers comprise the most concrete platform for the partnership, or "integration," of academia, the private sector, and the federal government in support of homeland security. The establishment and progress of these centers must be followed carefully in order to discover the answer to two fundamental questions:

- How ready are these sectors to work together? That is, can the most basic goal of survival and safety of the homeland be a motivation strong enough to overcome the sectors' administrative and functional differences?

FIGURE 9–5 New York City, New York, September 29, 2001—Lobby of hotel near the World Trade Center site. (Photo by Andrea Booher/FEMA News Photo)

- Will real integration occur? The R&D field may be the place that shows whether integration at the large scale as proposed by the DHS is really possible or not. This field is probably the most appropriate one because research, development, and deployment are very close functions. But this task may be more difficult than it seems because it involves many different organizations, whose cooperation, successes, or failures can put the success of the entire organization at risk.

Key Terms

BioWatch: A program aimed at detecting the release of pathogens into the air, thereby providing warning to the government and public health community of a potential bioterror event. This is performed through the use of aerosol samplers mounted on pre-existing EPA air quality monitoring stations that collect air, passing it through filters. These filters are manually collected at regular, reportedly 24-hour, intervals and are analyzed for potential biological weapon pathogens using polymerase chain reaction (PCR) techniques. While filters from the BioWatch program were initially shipped to and tested at a federal laboratory in California, state and local public health laboratories now perform the analyses.

MANPADS: A man-portable air defense system is a missile firing device, used to destroy aircraft, that is easily carried or transported by a person.

SAFECOM: A communications program of the DHS Office for Interoperability and Compatibility that, with its federal partners, provides research, development, testing and evaluation, guidance, tools, and templates on communications-related issues to local, tribal, state, and federal emergency response agencies.

Review Questions

1. Identify the six divisions of research in the DHS Science and Technology Directorate and explain what each does to contribute to counterterrorism efforts.

2. Define in your own words why HSARPA was established, and explain its scope and objectives.

3. What are the Homeland Security Centers of Excellence, and what are the research and development goals of each?

4. What government laboratories are working to develop WMD countermeasures? What specific areas of research is each focused on?

5. What government laboratories are working to protect critical information and infrastructure from terrorist attack? What specific areas of research is each focused on?

References

Department of Homeland Security. 2003. "Medical Treatment of Radiological Casualties." www .appc1.va.gov/emshg/docs/Radiologic_Medical_ Countermeasures_051403.pdf.

National Emergency Management Association. 2003. "National Response Plan." www.nemaweb.org/docs/ national_response_plan.pdf

Office of Homeland Security. 2002. "National Strategy for Homeland Security." www.whitehouse.gov/ homeland/book.

Telecommunications Service Priority. 2003. "Welcome to the TSP Website, National Coordination Center for Telecommunications (NCC)," December 4. http: //tsp.ncs.gov/.

10

The Future of Homeland Security

Introduction

This chapter is provided to identify and briefly explain several of the most pressing issues confronting the role of emergency management and disaster assistance programs in homeland security, both in general and specific to the Department of Homeland Security (DHS). Just as the Federal Emergency Management Agency (FEMA) has been the federal government leader in the national emergency management system since its 1979 inception, DHS has assumed a similar leadership role in the creation and management of a national system to ensure the security of the nation.

Even now, seven years after the September 11 attacks, a measure of how effectively DHS can perform in this leadership position, and exactly what role emergency management and disaster assistance functions will ultimately play within DHS and the national homeland security system, have not been adequately developed. The massive failure of the federal government's response to Hurricane Katrina in August 2005 and the ongoing failure of the recovery efforts three years later indicate very clearly that this single critical issue has yet to be resolved.

We believe that FEMA's history offers two important lessons for DHS as it progresses in its difficult mission. First, it is critical for DHS to take all of the necessary steps to ensure that the nation's emergency management and disaster assistance capabilities, especially those at the federal government level, are not marginalized. Additionally, these emergency management agencies must be given the tools that enable them to effectively manage the new terrorist threat with which they have been confronted. Second, terrorism, in all of its forms, must not become the singular risk driving DHS policy. In the absence of an all-hazards approach coupled with the growing risk caused by global warming, the scene will surely be set for a repeat of the Hurricane Katrina fiasco.

The FEMA History Lesson

Prior to 1979, federal emergency management and disaster preparedness, response, and recovery programs and capabilities were scattered among numerous federal government agencies, including the White House. There was little if any coordination among these disparate parts. Communicating with the federal government during a disaster had become such a problem that the National Governor's Association petitioned then-President Jimmy Carter, to consolidate all federal programs into a single agency.

On April 1, 1979, President Carter signed the executive order that established the Federal Emergency Management Agency, moving federal disaster programs, agencies, and offices from across the federal government into a single executive branch agency. The director of FEMA was charged with integrating these diverse programs into one cohesive operation capable of delivering federal resources and assistance through a new concept called the *integrated emergency management system*. This system was centered on an all-hazards approach.

With the election of President Ronald Reagan in 1980, the focus of FEMA's policies and programs shifted dramatically from an all-hazards approach to a single focus on nuclear attack planning through its Office of National Preparedness. At the same time, agency leadership and personnel struggled to integrate its many diverse programs. This focus on a single low-probability/high-impact event and the inability of the agency's many parts to function effectively as one led to the disastrous responses to Hurricane Hugo, the Loma Prieta earthquake, and Hurricane Andrew. There were numerous calls for the abolition of FEMA, including from several members of Congress.

President Bill Clinton, elected in 1992, appointed the first FEMA director who was an experienced emergency manager. Under James Lee Witt's leadership, FEMA once again adopted an all-hazards approach, became a customer-focused organization that worked closely with its state and local emergency management partners, and effectively responded to an unprecedented series of major disasters across the country. These included major natural disasters but also terrorist events such as the first World Trade Center bombing and the Oklahoma City bombing.

The new FEMA successfully launched a national community-based disaster mitigation initiative, Project Impact, and for the first time reached out to the nation's business community to partner in emergency management at the national and community levels.

By the time of the election of President George W. Bush in 2000, FEMA had gained the trust of the public, the media, its partners, and elected officials in all levels of government. FEMA functioned as a single agency as envisioned when it was created in 1979 and possessed one of the most favorable brand names in government.

Upon taking office in 2001, the Bush administration began to deconstruct FEMA. It was assumed that a program like Project Impact, which focused on individual and private-sector responsibility, would thrive under a Republican administration. Instead it was eliminated (based on an argument that it was not effective), and funding for other natural disaster mitigation programs was dramatically reduced. However, the effect of Project Impact was given national media attention after an earthquake struck Seattle and the mayor of Seattle credited his city's participation in the Project Impact program for the minimal losses the city experienced as a result of that quake.

The emphasis on the national security functions of FEMA was highlighted when new FEMA Director Joe Allbaugh reinstated the Office of National Preparedness and all indications were that FEMA would once again focus on national security issues.

This process was accelerated after the September 11, 2001, terrorist attacks. FEMA became part of the new Department of Homeland Security (DHS) and the all-hazards approach, while acknowledged in speeches, was replaced by a single focus on terrorism. More importantly, the director of FEMA no longer reported directly to the president and was replaced in the president's cabinet by the DHS secretary. In the first major reorganization of DHS that began in July of 2005, the FEMA of the 1990s was disassembled and its parts spread throughout the department.

In August 2005, Hurricane Katrina stuck the Gulf Coast and history repeated itself. DHS/FEMA was unable to provide the support needed by state and local officials for adequate response and hundreds of Americans died as a result. DHS/FEMA continues to this day to fail in the recovery phase as well. As this chapter is written in March 2008, FEMA's reputation is as sullied as it was in August 1992 after the botched response to Hurricane Andrew.

Despite DHS's current organizational restructuring, serious questions remain concerning FEMA's and the federal government's capabilities in responding to a catastrophic disaster whether it be a hurricane, earthquake, flood, or another terrorist attack. The nation's emergency management system remains broken. How it will be repaired and returned to its former capability remains to be seen.

Lessons for Homeland Security from the FEMA Experience

The writer George Santayana once famously said, "Those who ignore history are doomed to repeat it." There are two critical lessons to be learned from the FEMA experience that provide some perspective on how the Department of Homeland Security may function in the future.

First and foremost, it will take time for DHS to become a functioning organization. DHS was cobbled together in much the same way that FEMA was, bringing together an estimated 178,000 federal workers from 22 agencies and programs in a very short time period. It took FEMA nearly 15 years and several reorganizations to effectively coordinate and deliver the full resources of the federal government to support state and local governments in responding to major disasters. DHS is less than six years old and it is already undertaking its second major reorganization. If FEMA's experience is any kind of indicator, it will be at least another decade before DHS will achieve full functionality.

Second, the single focus on a low-probability/high-impact event (i.e., a major terrorist attack similar to September 11) will undermine DHS's capabilities in responding to high-probability/low-impact events. A FEMA staffer once said that you don't plan for the maximum event probable; you plan for the maximum event possible. This is especially critical for FEMA's response and recovery and preparedness and mitigation programs. In terms of natural and traditional man-made disasters (hurricanes, earthquakes, hazardous materials incidents, etc.), these programs' capabilities have been marginalized. The 2004 hurricanes in Florida and the resulting congressional and media investigations of fraud and incompetence that characterized the federal response and the miserable performance in Hurricane Katrina are clear evidence of the negative impact this single focus can have in an all-hazards world.

Clearly, DHS has repeated the mistakes made by FEMA in the past and at this time, seems intent on continuing on this path in the future. These mistakes will impact all of the department's functions but none more so that the traditional emergency management functions: mitigation, preparedness, response, and recovery.

DHS's primary mission is to prevent a terrorist attack on American soil. The emergency management and disaster assistance functions centered in FEMA contribute little to this mission. However, should another terrorist event occur in the future, as everyone including President Bush and Vice President Cheney concede that it will, these emergency management and disaster assistance functions will be critical to preparing our people, reducing the impact, and mounting an effective response and recovery that gets Americans back on their feet quickly. Marginalizing these capabilities as it pursues its primary mission is a mistake that FEMA made in the past and one that DHS cannot afford to repeat now and in the future.

The Future of Emergency Management in Homeland Security

Rebuilding the nation's emergency management system, especially the role of the federal government in this system, does not conflict with the primary mission of DHS. In fact, it is a critical element in the overall homeland security strategy. However, we feel several steps must be taken to rebuild and enhance the nation's emergency management system and to return the federal government to a leadership role in this area.

Reestablish FEMA as an Executive Branch Agency

In March 2004, former FEMA Director James Lee Witt in testimony before a joint hearing of two House Government Reform subcommittees strongly recommended that FEMA be removed from the Department of Homeland Security and be reestablished as an executive branch agency that reports directly to the president. Witt stated, "FEMA, having lost its status as an independent agency, is being buried beneath a massive bureaucracy whose main and seemingly only focus is fighting terrorism while an all-hazards mission is getting lost in the shuffle" (Peckenpaugh, 2004).

Moving FEMA out of DHS and consolidating its traditional mitigation, preparedness, response, and recovery programs will ensure that the all-hazards approach will be reinstated and that FEMA and its state and local partners will once again focus on dealing with all manner of disaster events including terrorist attacks. Emergency management professionals will once again be in charge of preparing the public, reducing future impacts through hazard mitigation, and managing the resources of the federal government in support of state and local governments in responding to major disasters and fostering a speedy and effective recovery from these events.

This system worked very well in the 1990s when the United States had the most sophisticated and efficient emergency management system in the world. This system effectively responded to hundreds of major natural disasters across the country and successfully managed the federal response to the Oklahoma City bombing and the September 11 attacks in New York City and at the Pentagon. This system also produced comprehensive preparedness and training programs and the first national community-based hazard mitigation initiative.

The post-Katrina reorganization of DHS and FEMA has returned the preparedness, mitigation, response, and recovery programs to FEMA. But this reorganization did not provide the FEMA administrator direct access to the president of the United States. Only the president can vest the authority in the FEMA administrator that is needed for a successful federal response.

Reestablishing FEMA outside of DHS will not conflict with DHS's primary mission to prevent terrorist attacks on American soil and will enhance those critical elements in the homeland security system that will be called on when the next event occurs.

Re-Create the Federal Response Plan

The Federal Response Plan (FRP) successfully guided the federal government's response to over 350 presidentially declared disasters from Hurricane Andrew through the September 11 attacks. The FRP was an agreement signed by department and agency heads from 32 federal departments and agencies and the American Red Cross.

The FRP had three critical elements:

1. The president designated and empowered the director of FEMA to direct the actions of the 32 signatories to the plan.
2. Each signatory to the plan agreed to make specific resources available during a major disaster event.
3. Each signatory to the plan would be reimbursed for any resources expended at the direction and authorization of FEMA.

The bottom line is that when the president declared a major disaster event, the FRP ensured that the full resources of the federal government would be brought to bear in support of state and local government and directed by FEMA. No single agency was expected to carry the full federal responsibility and everyone knew that the director of FEMA was in charge.

The FRP was replaced first by the National Response Plan in 2004, and most recently by the National Response Framework in 2008. The FRP was developed through extensive planning and negotiations among emergency management specialists at FEMA and the other federal agencies over a five-year period. The National Response Plan was developed by DHS in less than a year with limited involvement from outside of DHS. The National Response Framework was developed by the DHS deputy secretary's office after an aborted attempt by the emergency management community to reform the National Response Plan.

The National Response Plan attempted to build on the FRP, but instead managed to confuse the roles of the individual departments and agencies and to marginalize the authority and the role of the FEMA Director in directing the federal response. The National Response Framework is just what its title indicates, a framework for how the nation as a whole will prepare for and respond to a major disaster. It is not a plan for managing the federal response to a major disaster and similar to the National Response Plan fails to designate what agency will direct the federal response.

A major step in rebuilding the nation's emergency management system and rebuilding the trust of the state and local emergency managers and the public must be re-creating the Federal Response Plan with FEMA returned to the role of directing the plan. The FRP is a proven method for delivering federal resources in support of state and local efforts in a timely and cost-efficient manner.

Encourage Community-Based Homeland Security

Since September 11, 2001, the federal government has taken the lead in homeland security and the vast majority of policy and program initiatives have focused on federal capabilities and responsibilities. With the exception of the Citizen Corps program and Web-based awareness campaigns such as Ready.gov, very little has been done to effectively involve the American public in homeland security activities.

The "Redefining Readiness" study conducted by the New York Academy of Medicine identified numerous problems with the assumptions of homeland security planners in developing smallpox and dirty bomb plans without input from the public. Involving the public in developing community-based homeland security plans is critical to the successful implementation of these plans.

This study and others have discovered that a large segment of the public is ready and willing to participate in these planning efforts and to be part of a community-based effort to deal with the new homeland security threats. Mechanisms for involving the public in this process are needed.

A good model for such a mechanism is Project Impact, the former FEMA initiative to develop disaster-resistant communities. At its height, more than 225 Project Impact communities were functioning across the country with support from FEMA. Each community had created a community partnership that involved all stakeholders in the community, including the business sector, in identifying community risks, identifying what could be done to mitigate these risks, and developing and implementing a plan to take action to reduce the impacts of future disaster events in their community.

The Project Impact model is based on an all-hazards approach, and including the new risks from terrorism into this model would be simple. The city of Tulsa, Oklahoma, has done just that, successfully incorporating homeland security efforts into its Project Impact programs that were originally developed to address flood and tornado risks.

The bottom line is that the general public must be involved in the development and implementation of community homeland security plans, and DHS and its partners in state and local government should invest more resources in developing the planning processes needed to involve the public in the nation's homeland security system.

Improve Communications

Communicating with the public is another area that needs to be improved if the nation is going to have a truly effective homeland security system. To date, DHS has shown little interest in communicating with the public, and when it has the results have not always been positive—the "duct tape and plastic" fiasco serves as a classic example. FEMA's failed communications in Hurricane Katrina is another. DHS and its state and local partners need to address three factors to improve its communications with the American people.

First, there must be a commitment from the leadership, not only at DHS and its state and local partners, but at all levels of government including the executive level to communicate timely and accurate information to the public. This is especially important in the response and recovery phases to a terrorist incident.

In a disaster scenario, the conventional wisdom that states information is power, and that hoarding information helps to retain such power, is almost categorically reversed. Withholding information during disaster events generally has an overall negative effect on the well-being of the public, and on the impression the public forms about involved authorities. In practice, sharing of information is what generates authority and power, when that information is useful and relates to the hazard at hand. Two shining examples of this fact are the actions of former FEMA Director James Lee Witt and former New York City Mayor Rudy Giuliani. Both leaders went to great lengths to get accurate and timely information to the public in a time of crisis, and their efforts both inspired the public and greatly enhanced the effectiveness of the response and recovery efforts they guided.

To date, DHS leadership and the political leadership have been reluctant to make this commitment to share information with the public. This is something that must change if they expect the American people to fully comprehend the homeland security threat and to become actively engaged in homeland security efforts. Few citizens have any idea of what actual terrorism risks they face, and fewer can actually relate those risks in any comparable fashion to the risks they face every day without notice.

Second, homeland security officials at all levels must resolve the conflict between sharing information with the public in advance and in the aftermath of a terrorist incident that has value for intelligence or criminal prosecution purposes. This is directly linked to the commitment issue discussed in the previous paragraphs and has been repeatedly cited by homeland security officials as reasons for not sharing more specific information with the public.

This is a very difficult issue that, in the past, DHS has tried to ignore. However, the continued frustration among the public and state and local officials with the Homeland Security Advisory System (HSAS) is just one sign that this issue will not solve itself or just go away.

Also at issue is the question of when to release relevant information to the public without compromising intelligence sources and/or ongoing criminal investigations. This is an issue that rarely if ever confronts emergency management officials dealing with natural and unintentional man-made disasters. Therefore, there is little precedent or experience for current homeland security officials to work with in crafting a communications strategy that balances the competing need for the public to have timely and accurate information with the need to protect intelligence sources and ongoing criminal investigations. To date, the needs of the intelligence and justice communities have clearly been judged to outweigh those of the public.

Members of Congress and DHS Secretary Michael Chertoff have spoken often about reworking the HSAS. This would be a critical first step in reestablishing trust with the public for the warning system. From this starting point, if the commitment is there among the homeland security leadership, additional communications mechanisms can be developed to ensure that the public gets timely and accurate information both in advance of any terrorist incident and during the response and recovery phases in the aftermath of the next terrorist attack.

Third, more effort must be invested by federal departments and agencies to better understand the principal terrorist threats that our nation faces (i.e., biological, chemical, radiological, nuclear, and explosives), and to develop communications strategies that educate and inform the public about these threats with more useful information. The 2001 Washington, DC, anthrax incident is a perfect example of uninformed or misinformed public officials sharing what is often conflicting and, in too many instances, wrong information with the public.

The nation's public officials must become better informed about these principal risks and be ready and capable of explaining complicated information to the public. As the anthrax incident made clear, this is not a luxury, but a necessity if the response to similar incidents in the future is to be successful.

Decades of research and a new generation of technologies now inform emergency managers as they provide information about hurricanes, tornadoes, earthquakes, and hazardous materials incidents to the public. A similar research effort must be undertaken for these five new terrorist risks and communications strategies that will ensure that homeland security officials at all levels are capable of clearly explaining to the public the hazards posed by these threats.

These communications strategies must consider how to communicate to the public when incomplete information is all that is available to homeland security officials. In the vast majority of cases, this partiality of information is probable. A public health crisis will not wait for all the data to be collected and analyzed, nor will the public. Homeland security officials must develop strategies for informing the public effectively, as the crisis develops, by forming effective messages that are able to explain to the public how what is being said is the most accurate information available based on the information that, likewise, is available—despite its incomplete nature. Clearly, this is not an easy task, but it is not impossible. The public will increasingly expect such communications efforts, so the sooner such a system is in place, the better the next incident will be managed.

Partner with the Business Sector

The DHS and numerous business groups, such as the Business Roundtable, acknowledge that an effective partnership between government and business must be established as part of the nation's homeland security efforts. This is only logical considering that almost 85% of the nation's infrastructure is privately held.

However, in the seven years since the attacks of September 11, 2001, no such partnership has been established. There has been some progress and cooperation, but there is no overall strategy in place to incorporate the business sector into the government's emergency management planning for homeland security.

This issue was clearly illustrated in the response to Hurricane Katrina. There are countless examples of efforts by members of the business community to provide resources and assistance to the victims of the hurricane only to be frustrated by uncooperative federal officials.

Numerous issues must be resolved before such a strategy can be designed and implemented. A significant issue that must be addressed is how the government will protect and use confidential information that it is asking or requiring the business community to provide. The business community, which has vast institutional knowledge about this privacy issue as well as countless other issues that have been presented in the homeland security approach, must be included in the planning process not only for terrorism response planning but also for natural disaster management.

One possible avenue for establishing and nurturing an effective partnership with the business sector is to start at the community level. Issues such as what the government will do with confidential information are likely to be less critical at the community level, allowing for lessons to be learned in progressive steps. Additionally, there is an established history of public–private partnerships in emergency management at the community level, many of which started with FEMA's Project Impact program. To illustrate this point, the following message received by our team of authors from Kathleen Criss, emergency management coordinator for the University of Pittsburgh Medical Center, is provided:

> *I want to share with you the PA Region 13 program, which has been acknowledged as one of the first and is considered a national best practice for regional mutual aid by FEMA and several other organizations. Robert Full, Chief of Allegheny County Emergency Services and the nominated Chair of the PA Region 13 Counter Terrorism Task Force, has been actively working with the business community since 1999. A public/private partnership was established during the Year 2000 planning and continues today to address "all hazards" and homeland security concerns.*
>
> *There is a formal plan in place to activate the Business Liaison role in the Allegheny County Emergency Operations Center during a crisis; this plan has been tested several times through actual disaster events and drills. We are currently working on IT solutions to improve emergency communications, alerting capabilities, and resource sharing at times of disaster. Members of the business community were also invited to attend hazard mitigation training courses with first responders, participate in workshops to improve security in chemical and other "critical infrastructure" organizations, and planning meetings to document the County's hazard mitigation plan for submission to the Commonwealth of*

Pennsylvania. We also participate regularly in annual disaster drills—from planning to the final after-action report and follow-up to correct deficiencies (Criss, 2005).

Criss indicated in her message that she has been working closely with officials at DHS to promote their efforts as a best practice to other areas of the country, and that

DHS does understand this problem and is trying to the best of its ability to work with these existing groups to improve its own programs, where possible. It is not a quick or easy process to implement. It takes trust and dedication from the public and private sectors to begin this relationship to allow the two sides to work together for the betterment of the community its serves.

There are other examples of public–private partnerships working in homeland security that are built on the attributes noted by Criss. We believe that this bottom-up approach to developing public–private partnerships may be the best avenue for homeland security officials at all levels to pursue.

ANOTHER VOICE: FOUR OPPORTUNITIES FOR FUTURE HOMELAND SECURITY LEADERS, BY BRIDGER MCGAW

The following four opportunities offer future homeland security leaders the ability to improve the effectiveness of homeland security policies and programs:

Opportunity #1: Evolve Emergency Management for the Cyber-Age

Whether it's the operation of interoperable radios, 911 networks, emergency operations centers, evacuation coordination, or power plants, cyber and information technology infrastructure are essential to the effective efforts of the emergency management and homeland security enterprise. The interdependencies between critical infrastructure and cyberspace only continue to increase, requiring more attention from public and private sector leaders. If emergency managers are to be effective in the cyber-age, they must rapidly acknowledge this new paradigm in deterring, preparing for, responding to, or recovering from a future crisis or terrorist event.

While cybersecurity rhetorically is included within the "all-hazards" framework, homeland security advisors, emergency managers, chief information officers, and chief information security officers will have to work and train more closely and aggressively to make it a reality. Decision makers should integrate cybersecurity measures into business continuity plans and incident response and recovery plans, and clearly lay out how their respective organizations will work together to respond to events during a cyber incident.

State and local governments and critical infrastructure owners and operators must evaluate their preparations for addressing the cyber threat. As more and more essential government processes or services are dispersed or managed online, the security of this information and resiliency of networks must be improved. One challenge that should become clear for homeland security decision makers will be establishing stronger security standards, or if necessary, requirements for information technology (IT) and cyber networks to improve their security and resiliency. Waiting for a "cyber 9/11" to occur is not a rational or effective way to mitigate this real and present danger to our homeland. Action is needed now.

Opportunity #2: Support Information Sharing and Intelligence Fusion Centers

The 9/11 Commission made it clear that removing barriers to information sharing would improve counterterrorism actions by government agencies. Leaders in the national security community must make this effort a long-lasting reality. Success of the information-sharing effort cannot be under-valued.

A new tool that Federal, State, and local homeland security entities are embracing is the State and Major Urban Area Fusion Center.[1] The National Strategy for Information Sharing describes how the Fusion Center concept has rapidly evolved to "foster a culture that recognizes the importance of fusing 'all crimes' with national security implications and 'all hazards' information (e.g., criminal investigations, terrorism, public health and safety, and emergency response) which often involves identifying criminal activity and other information that might be a precursor to a terrorist plot."[2] As each Fusion Center grows and matures, homeland security leaders must coordinate collaboration among the fusion centers as well as use them to promote cross-culture interaction between law enforcement and other critical public health and safety communities to improve preparedness and protect individual rights.

Opportunity #3: Integrate Journalists as "First Amendment Responders"

Effective emergency response always cites the use of the media for providing the public with assurance and direction in a crisis. After-action reports in numerous exercises have stated how improved response plan implementation requires public communications plans and established, trusted, and working relationships with the media. Journalists can no longer play a reactive role in homeland security and need to be embraced as true partners in the homeland security enterprise. Trying to control the media is no longer viable because Web 2.0 technologies and mobile devices have allowed everyone to potentially be a citizen journalist. Enabling journalists to more knowledgeably perform their First Amendment responsibilities in crises will improve delivery of trusted, accurate, and timely information on what the public needs to know in order to protect their communities and families, as well as support government response operations. More engagement with the press will only improve efforts to create the much discussed "culture of preparedness" that we need.

Opportunity #4: Invest in the Next Generation of Homeland Security Professionals

Ensuring the quality and effectiveness of the future homeland security workforce should be a national priority. Trained and knowledgeable experts are in high demand across the spectrum of critical homeland security capabilities in both the public and private sectors. Defining the capabilities and knowledge that future homeland security professionals should possess must be undertaken while the subject matter and Department are still evolving.

Some activities are under way. In March 2007, Congress introduced a bill to create a U.S. Public Service Academy as a civilian equivalent of the military academies. In May 2007, President Bush signed Executive Order 13434 for "National Security Professional Development" aiming "to promote the education, training, and experience of current and future professionals in national security positions in executive departments and agencies."[3] In December 2007, DHS unveiled an internal Homeland Security University System to help improve professional development within its own employee ranks, including a Homeland Security Academy built on a partnership with the Navy Postgraduate School Center for Homeland Defense and Security. There are also DHS Centers of Excellence and a "Scholarship for Service" Program that recruits students for vital

---

[1] For more information, see "Federal Efforts Are Helping to Alleviate Some Challenges Encountered by State and Local Fusion Centers," Government Accountability Office, October 2007, http://www.gao.gov/new.items/d0835.pdf.
[2] "The National Strategy for Information Sharing," October 2007, http://www.whitehouse.gov/nsc/infosharing/index.html. Appendix 1.
[3] For details of the Executive Order, see press release, May 2007, http://www.whitehouse.gov/news/releas es/2007/05/20070517-6.html. Bridger McGaw, a homeland security policy and strategic communications consultant, is a graduate of Harvard College and the John F. Kennedy School of Government. He has held several positions as policy adviser, public affairs officer, and press secretary to senior leaders in the Department of Defense, White House, Capitol Hill, and state and local governments. McGaw served on the Century Foundation's 2006 Task Force on homeland security.

(*Continued*)

ANOTHER VOICE: FOUR OPPORTUNITIES FOR FUTURE HOMELAND SECURITY LEADERS, BY BRIDGER MCGAW–(CONTINUED)

---

cybersecurity jobs in Federal departments and agencies as repayment for the government's funding of their education.

We must align these policy initiatives with academic programs and existing scholarships and grants. This will help create a stronger process for educating, recruiting, training, and retaining the qualified public service personnel necessary to implement homeland security programs in the long term. A clearer public service career path will help the "best and brightest" once again see opportunity in government service, improving the likelihood that not only a smaller government, but a more effective one is built.

These four opportunities offer a place to start where real progress can be achieved with long-lasting positive impact on improving the security of our nation.

Conclusion

We believe that the FEMA experience from 1979 to the present may be a harbinger of the Department of Homeland Security's fate as it struggles in the coming decade to establish an integrated and effective national homeland security system. At a minimum, FEMA's experiences should serve as a cautionary tale for homeland security officials at the federal, state, and local levels of government.

The Hurricane Katrina experience should also serve as a warning to DHS that a coordinated federal response is critical during a major catastrophic event and that marginalizing the strong national emergency management system built on a partnership of federal, state and local emergency operations in the 1990s was a terrible mistake.

Reestablishing FEMA as the leader of the nation's emergency management system, re-creating the Federal Response Plan, supporting community-based homeland security efforts involving the general public, communicating timely and accurate information to the public, and establishing a strong and vital partnership with the business sector could ease DHS's growing pains and pave the way for the establishment of a comprehensive homeland security system in this country.

One final note on the FEMA experience. At the core of FEMA's success in the 1990s was its focus on the needs of its customers, the American people. FEMA policies and programs from that period were driven by the needs of disaster victims and by the needs of community residents who wanted to reduce the terrible impacts of future events. Since its inception in 2002, the Department of Homeland Security and its partners in the federal government have been focused almost exclusively on their own needs. Policies and programs have been designed and implemented that meet the needs of these governmental departments and agencies and that were not informed by the needs of the public, their supposed customers.

If the officials at DHS that work in homeland security at the state and local levels change one thing in the future, it is critical that they shift their focus from themselves to the public, and that they plan and implement policies and programs with the full involvement of the public and their partners. It worked very well for FEMA, so there is no reason why it should not do the same for DHS.

References

Criss, Kathleen. 2005. E-mail message to George Haddow, July 14.

Peckenpaugh, Jason. 2004. "Regional Homeland Security Offices Will Be Small." GovExec.Com, March 24.

www.govexec.com/story_page.cfm?articleid=28072&printerfriendlyVers=1&.

Index